The Simpsons, Satire, and American Culture

D1188427

The *Simpsons*, Satire, and American Culture

Matthew A. Henry

THE SIMPSONS, SATIRE, AND AMERICAN CULTURE
Copyright © Matthew A. Henry, 2012.

All rights reserved.

First published in hardcover in 2012 by PALGRAVE MACMILLAN® in the United States—a division of St. Martin's Press LLC, 175 Fifth Avenue, New York, NY 10010.

Where this book is distributed in the UK, Europe and the rest of the world, this is by Palgrave Macmillan, a division of Macmillan Publishers Limited, registered in England, company number 785998, of Houndmills, Basingstoke, Hampshire RG21 6XS.

Palgrave Macmillan is the global academic imprint of the above companies and has companies and representatives throughout the world.

Palgrave® and Macmillan® are registered trademarks in the United States, the United Kingdom, Europe and other countries.

ISBN: 978–1–137–47178–9

The Library of Congress has cataloged the hardcover edition as follows:

Henry, Matthew A., 1965–
    The Simpsons, satire, and American culture / Matthew A. Henry.
        p. cm.
    Includes bibliographical references.
    ISBN 978–1–137–02778–8 (alk. paper)
    1. Simpsons (Television program) I. Title.

PN1992.77.S58H46 2012
791.45′72—dc23   2012011553

A catalogue record of the book is available from the British Library.

Design by Newgen Knowledge Works (P) Ltd., Chennai, India.

First PALGRAVE MACMILLAN paperback edition: November 2014

10 9 8 7 6 5 4 3 2 1

For Kathy, who set me on the path

Contents

Acknowledgments

This book has been a work in progress for many years. Its origins are in a paper I wrote (20 years ago!) for a graduate seminar on postmodern culture while a student at SUNY Brockport. At that point, *The Simpsons* was still a new phenomenon, and virtually no critical work had been done on the show. I am deeply grateful to Mark Anderson for encouraging me to explore uncharted territory. The end product, an essay entitled "The Triumph of Popular Culture: Situation Comedy, Postmodernism, and *The Simpsons*," received great interest when I presented it at the Popular Culture Association conference, and it was quickly accepted for publication in *Studies in Popular Culture*. I would not have had the courage to present this piece at a conference—much less circulate it for publication—if it were not for Mark's faith in my abilities and the confidence he instilled in me as a student and a scholar.

I owe a great debt as well to Earl Ingersoll, my other mentor at SUNY Brockport. Although Earl did not have a direct involvement with my work on *The Simpsons*, he was instrumental in shaping who I am as an academic, as a teacher, and as a human being. Earl believed in me much more than I believed in myself, and without his persistence I would not be where I am today. For his optimism, his encouragement, and his friendship, I am deeply grateful.

This book is the culmination of work that progressed in stages of graduate study at Syracuse University, between 1994 and 1997, and at the University of Texas at Dallas (UTD), between 2002 and 2008. My exposure to queer theory during my time at Syracuse University led to an interest in the depiction of gay identity on *The Simpsons*; parts of chapter 4 were written at that time for a presentation on the topic, then simply entitled "Gay Life on *The Simpsons*." I began to research other aspects of the show while pursuing my doctorate at UTD. I would like to thank Susan Branson for her support of my interests in analyses of contemporary popular culture. Much of the material in chapter 3 was researched as part of a final project for her seminar on women and US popular culture. I also want to thank Susan for suggesting that I make *The Simpsons* the subject of my doctoral dissertation. I wish to thank Dean Terry for allowing me to continue my research on *The Simpsons* as a final project for his course, Critical Media Studies. Most of the information on the history of Fox Television in chapter 1 was gathered as part of that project. My sincerest gratitude goes to my dissertation adviser, Erin Smith, for her guidance and advice at many points over the years. Much of the material in chapter 2 was written as a final project for Erin's Ethnic American Literature course. I am grateful to Erin for her many contributions to various drafts of this project as it moved toward being a completed dissertation—her insights and suggestions have been invaluable. I also wish to thank the following faculty members at UTD for their help along the way: Adrienne McLean, Daniel Wickberg, Thomas Lambert, and Sean Cotter.

I am grateful to John Alberti for his support and for allowing me to use portions of an unpublished work, which he first presented at the Cultural Studies Association conference in Tucson, Arizona, in April 2005. Excerpts from his manuscript appear in chapter 2. A note of thanks is also due to Karma Waltonen for helping to generate ideas about how class is dealt with on *The Simpsons*, particularly the depiction of white trash identity. Karma has an astounding and encyclopedic knowledge of *The Simpsons*, and I appreciate her allowing me to pick her brain for examples. Chapter 5 would be a very different, and I suspect much weaker, chapter without Karma's assistance.

My colleagues Jane Peterson and Rachel Barber Wolf deserve special recognition for their thoughtful commentary and helpful editorial suggestions on various drafts of this project. I greatly appreciate their willingness to patiently read, thoughtfully comment upon, and meticulously proofread the many drafts of the chapters contained in this book. I am very grateful for their contribution to my work.

I also want to acknowledge the support and encouragement I have received along the way from many good friends. For the intellectually stimulating conversations, intensive brainstorming sessions, thoughtful feedback, compassionate concern, drunken revelry, and some truly good laughs, my sincerest thanks go out to Dean Klingler, Carl Silvio, Christina Parish, Steve Fellner, Zia Isola, Anne Kurdock, Lesley Bogad, Josh Stenger, Gerald Butters, Paula Massood, Kevin Beard, Lori Stephens, Kevin McClendon, Jane Peterson, Rachel Barber Wolf, Kay MacIntyre, Dave and Lindy Cockburn, Rachel Robinson, Michael Barlion, Sobia Khan, Matt Hinckley, and Kyle Barron.

I want to thank the administration at Richland College for their ongoing support of my academic work. I would like to extend my thanks as well to the many students I have had over the years, particularly those who enrolled in my cultural studies course, *The Simpsons* and American Culture. The conversations that took place in those classes have had a great influence on my thinking and have shaped many of the ideas presented in this book.

Lastly, I wish to thank Samantha Hasey at Palgrave Macmillan for her initial enthusiasm for this project and her diligent work in getting a proposal read. I want to thank Robyn Curtis, Leila Campoli, Desiree Browne, and Ciara Vincent, also at Palgrave Macmillan, for helping the book through the various stages of production. I also wish to thank the editors and staff at Newgen Imaging Systems for their assistance in ushering the book into its final form.

Portions of this book have appeared elsewhere in print and are used here with permission from the publishers.

Select passages from "The Triumph of Popular Culture: Situation Comedy, Postmodernism, and *The Simpsons*," first published in *Studies in Popular Culture* 17, no. 1 (1994): 85–99, appear throughout the text.

Portions of chapter 3 were published as "Don't Ask Me, I'm Just a Girl": Feminism, Female Identity, and *The Simpsons*" in *Journal of Popular Culture* 40, no. 2 (2007): 272–303.

Portions of chapter 4 were published under the title "'The Whole World's Gone Gay!': Smithers' Sexuality, Homer's Phobia, and Gay Life on *The Simpsons*" in *Popular Culture Review* 13, no. 1 (2002): 19–33. A modified version of this, entitled "Looking for Amanda Hugginkiss: Gay Life on *The Simpsons*," was included in the collection

Leaving Springfield: "The Simpsons" and the Possibility of Oppositional Culture, ed. John Alberti (Detroit: Wayne State University Press, 2004), 321–43.

Portions of chapter 6 were published as "'Gabbin' about God': Religion, Secularity, and Satire on *The Simpsons*" in *Homer Simpson Marches on Washington: Dissent through American Popular Culture*, ed. Joseph J. Foy and Timothy M. Dale (Lexington: University of Kentucky Press, 2010), 141–66.

Introduction

The *Simpsons*, Satire, and American Culture

> The publicly voiced opinion of many thinking adults still holds that entertainment TV in general is usually at best a waste of time and at worst a toxic influence.
>
> —*Robert J. Thompson*[1]

In February 2012, Fox Television aired the five hundredth episode of *The Simpsons*, marking yet another unprecedented milestone in the history of animation and situation comedy. Such longevity is assuredly a testament to the commercial success of a show often dismissed as a mere "cartoon," but it is also a reminder of how incredibly popular *The Simpsons* has been and continues to be with audiences, both in the United States and around the world. Since its premiere in 1989, *The Simpsons* has captivated viewers, earning both popularity and notoriety as well as both high praise and fierce criticism. The inaugural episode, "Simpsons Roasting on an Open Fire" (also known as "*The Simpsons* Christmas Special"), aired on December 17, 1989, and earned the fledgling Fox network an impressive 26.7 million viewers—a remarkable fact considering that Fox then reached only approximately 85 percent of American households.[2] *The Simpsons* was officially launched as a television series on January 14, 1990, with the airing of "Bart the Genius," which earned Fox an equally respectable 24.5 million viewers.[3] Less than a year after its premiere, *The Simpsons* was, as Harry Waters aptly described it, "a breakaway ratings hit, industry trendsetter, cultural template, and a viewing experience verging on the religious for its most fanatical followers."[4] During its heyday in the early 1990s, *The Simpsons* repeatedly ranked in the Nielsen top ten for prime-time television shows—from January 1990 until the start of the second season in October that year, *The Simpsons* was among the top three shows ten times—and throughout the decade, it periodically ranked within the top 25.[5] As the popularity of *The Simpsons* grew, aided in large part by the many controversies surrounding the show in the early 1990s, so did its iconic stature in American culture. The show has now set records as the longest-running prime-time animated show (surpassing *The Flintstones*, which ran for 6 seasons), the longest-running prime-time situation comedy (surpassing *The Adventures of Ozzie and Harriet*, which ran for 14 seasons), and the longest-running scripted television series in primetime (surpassing *Gunsmoke*, which was on for 20 years).[6] *The Simpsons* is currently aired in more than 70 countries and seen by an estimated

70 million people worldwide.[7] *The Simpsons* has also become a monumental merchandising entity, encompassing everything from "official" Simpsons products, such as music CDs and comic books, and product endorsements (e.g., for Butterfinger and Burger King) to a vast array of licensing deals for items such as T-shirts, stickers, dolls, posters, lamps, lunch boxes, toothbrushes, PEZ dispensers, and video games. According to *License! Global* magazine, *The Simpsons* worldwide franchise is now worth an estimated $5 billion.[8] Additionally, the long-awaited big-screen incarnation of the show, *The Simpsons Movie* (1997), opened to critical acclaim and great box office success, both in the United States and abroad.[9] Quite simply, *The Simpsons* is one of the most recognizable and celebrated icons of American popular culture and a bona fide cultural phenomenon.

Such facts beg the question: Why is *The Simpsons* so popular? Although this is an interesting question, it will only be addressed tangentially here. The purpose of this book is not to explain the widespread popularity of *The Simpsons* but to examine the ways in which the show participates in a series of debates taking place in American culture since the early 1980s over a variety of social and political issues. These debates, collectively branded the "culture wars" by James D. Hunter in *Culture Wars: The Struggle to Define America* (1991), have circulated primarily around issues related to race and ethnicity, nationality, social and economic class, gender, sexuality, and religion.[10] At the time of its publication, the analysis of contending "orthodox" and "progressive" forces put forth in *Culture Wars* seemed to many an accurate description of American politics in the Reagan-Bush era. Subsequent research by social scientists, however, cast doubt on Hunter's vision of a nation marked by contentious battles between rivaling worldviews. Two of the most well-known and influential critiques of the culture war thesis are Alan Wolfe's *One Nation, After All* (1998), which is based on a series of in-depth interviews with two hundred middle-class suburbanites, and Morris P. Fiorina's *Culture War? The Myth of a Polarized America* (2004), which draws upon a wide array of surveys and public opinion polls for data.[11] In each case, the authors aim to demonstrate that the American public is less divided, even on controversial issues such as abortion and homosexuality, than the culture war metaphor would indicate. Whereas Wolfe relies upon the self-proclaimed "tolerance" of his interviewees, whom he quotes at length, to refute the culture war thesis, Fiorina primarily does so by distinguishing between a polarized political class (and the political parties each class represents) and the populace at large, which he claims is "largely centrist." Although Fiorina concedes that the political class is indeed more polarized today than in generations past, he forcefully argues that the majority of the population is not; for him, "*partisan* polarization does not reflect *popular* polarization."[12] According to Fiorina, the data indicate that we are a nation of people "closely" but not "deeply" divided. As he succinctly states, "Normal Americans are busy earning their livings and raising their families. They are not very well informed about politics and public affairs, do not care a great deal about politics, do not hold many of their views very strongly, and are not ideological."[13] Irene Taviss Thompson expresses a very similar view in *Culture Wars and Enduring American Dilemmas* (2010), arguing that the "orthodox" versus "progressive" battle sketched by Hunter is overstated and not supported by data. According to Thompson, the proponents of the "culture war thesis" are concerned not with what people think but with "the meaning and understandings enunciated by elites who seek to frame how we think" and the ways that "the competing moral visions of these elites inexorably pull all arguments in to one or the other of the contending camps, effectively eclipsing the middle ground."[14] Like both Wolfe and Fiorina, Thompson believes that the culture war battles are essentially taking place only among political "partisans" and cultural "elites" and that the majority of US citizens have either centrist or moderate political views.

Although I generally admire the work of Wolfe, Fiorina, and Thompson, I have some serious reservations about the arguments each scholar advances. In my view, Fiorina undermines the credibility of his study in stating that it is "more accurate to say that most voters are ambivalent or indifferent" rather than divided in a partisan fashion.[15] Perhaps this is the kind of observation expected from an "objective" social scientist, but it is a surprisingly apathetic position to take. Whereas Fiorina is quite direct about voter apathy and indifference, Thompson only implies it in her discussions of the rhetorical "frames" created by political elites and "culture war partisans."[16] Nonetheless, a strong parallel exists between the analyses of Fiorina and Thompson. Voters assuredly are easily misled and swayed by the empty rhetoric and disinformation that often comprise the "frames" set by elites, although I think this has as much to do with the incredibly low levels of media literacy among the populace—a sad comment on our current educational system—as it does with apathy or the adoption of "centrist" positions. The so-called "elites" Thompson speaks of (i.e., those who are deeply divided culturally, politically, and ideologically) do indeed direct the debate. The problem is that since they control the halls of power and, in large part, the media entities that convey information about what happens there, we *all* become engaged in the "war," whether we like it or not. The reality is that the populace is stuck with a two-party system that forces them either to vote along partisan lines, and thus become aligned with the political class, or to be excluded from the conversation. Moreover, I would argue that the populace is not so much uninterested as uninformed; this is due to numerous factors, including but not limited to a bottom-line corporatism that promotes "soft" news, the relaxing of FCC regulations on media ownership, the shuttering of newspapers and their investigative journalism departments, and the rise of quasi-propagandistic information sources such as the Fox News channel. These realities are precisely what has led to the "crisis of democracy" being discussed today by a host of journalists, educators, and political scientists—and even by some politicians in Congress. As James Q. Wilson notes, to accept the positions of Wolfe, Fiorina, or Thompson is to embrace the idea that politicians, the media, and various interest groups "operate in an ideological vacuum."[17] They don't, of course, nor do the effects of their activities. For Wilson, polarization is not only real and has increased, "but it has also spread to rank-and-file voters through elite influence."[18] Sadly, under the current system, the partisan politicking continues, and it shapes important public policy on domestic issues such as work and family (e.g., equal pay, workplace discrimination, maternity/paternity leave, health care, marriage laws, etc.), which in turn has a profound impact on the lives of the so-called "normal Americans" Fiorina champions.

Clearly, the degree to which ordinary Americans have polarized into hardened camps remains a point of scholarly debate.[19] My own views align more with the culture war thesis proposed by James Hunter, and this is the framework adopted for the analyses of *The Simpsons* presented throughout this book. Although the emphases of the culture war debates have shifted over time, the debates themselves have continued well into the new millennium. *The Simpsons* regularly incorporates many of the culture war issues and debates into its comedic frame, via both parody and satire, and thus provides a rich text for the analysis of television and American culture. As numerous scholars have demonstrated, mainstream media such as film, television, and advertising work largely to reproduce the dominant norms, values, and practices of contemporary American society. Of course, mass media can also work in distinctly oppositional ways, questioning, contesting, and even rejecting dominant discourses. To understand how and perhaps why certain ideologies are perpetuated or disputed within mass media, it is useful to examine those media texts that have the broadest reach and greatest popularity within the culture. Despite the incursions of new media, television remains the predominant form of mass media in American homes and the situation comedy, until very recently, its most popular genre. As Darrell Hamamoto notes, the television situation comedy can be read to reveal "the mores, ideals, prejudices, and ideologies shared—by fiat or default—by the majority of the American public."[20] Hamamoto's claim, which rests upon the notion that mass media function both to reflect and to shape prevailing beliefs, is applicable to many television shows but none more so than *The Simpsons*, which in its lengthy run has engaged more politically charged issues than any other situation comedy in television history. As the growing body of scholarship on *The Simpsons* attests, the show does more than simply mirror (albeit in a distorted fashion) modern American life; it also makes regular interventions into the heated debates surrounding many of the contentious issues that have been gathered under the umbrella of the "culture wars." Much of the scholarship on *The Simpsons* offers insightful commentary, but it does so mainly with a narrow concentration (e.g., genre studies or pedagogical practices) or with a singular focus on a particular topic (e.g., citizenship, postmodernity, commodity culture, religion, etc.). None of this work offers a comprehensive treatment of *The Simpsons* as a satire or a fully developed discussion of how the show satirically engages with important social, political, and cultural issues related to race, class, gender, sexuality, nationality, and religion. The aim of this book is to work toward a more comprehensive understanding of *The Simpsons* by examining how the show engages key cultural issues within a satiric framework. The level of engagement with these concerns is dependent upon numerous factors, including what particular issue is being addressed, how often it is dealt with in the series, how thoroughly it is interrogated within specific episodes, and how viewers receive and interpret the messages.[21] In short, my intention is to explore *The Simpsons'* satirical engagement with a series of highly politicized social and cultural issues, to examine the tensions inherent in the show's status as a commercial and artistic object and the impact this has on openly dealing with such issues, and to explicate the ways in which *The Simpsons* participates in some of the more ideologically loaded debates taking place in American culture.

The Simpsons as Satire

As is well known, *The Simpsons* quickly established itself as a sophisticated satire on contemporary American society and culture. This satirical quality was remarked upon from the start in some of the earliest assessments of *The Simpsons* in the mainstream media. In April 1990, for example, at the end of the first full season of *The Simpsons*, Harry Waters (writing for *Newsweek*) noted that

The Simpsons appealed to adult viewers because of its "sophisticated satire and cultural asides only adults would dig."[22] The following month, Joe Rhodes, writing for Entertainment Weekly, made the astute observation that The Simpsons is "a wicked satire masquerading as a prime-time cartoon."[23] And later that same year, Tom Shales, writing for The Washington Post, praised The Simpsons as a "bull's-eye political satire."[24] As the show gained notoriety in the early 1990s, similar comments were made in mainstream magazines such as Time, Newsweek, Rolling Stone, and Entertainment Weekly and in newspapers such as USA Today, The New York Times, and The Boston Globe.[25] In 1996, The Simpsons even won a prestigious Peabody Award "for providing exceptional animation and stinging social satire, both commodities which are in extremely short supply in television today."[26] What all of these commentators seemed to readily recognize was The Simpsons' engagement with what Paul Simpson calls "the discourse of satire"— that is, the complex interplay between the social and political functions of satire, the rhetorical and discursive methods of the satirist, and the reception and interpretation of satirical texts by audiences.[27]

The Simpsons is foremost a satire upon the idealized images of family life depicted in the traditional nuclear-family sitcoms of the 1950s and 1960s. Such comedies were a familiar genre on television, having been introduced in shows such as The Stu Erwin Show (1950–55) and The Adventures of Ozzie and Harriet (1952–66), but they came to fruition in the late 1950s, centered on the three most prominent and popular examples of the genre: Father Knows Best (1954–58), Leave It to Beaver (1957–63) and The Donna Reed Show (1958–66). These sitcoms primarily offered visions of intact nuclear families headed by a genial patriarch, who was portrayed as knowing, correct, and superior to his wife and children—a structure that worked well to reinforce the prevalent sexual stereotypes of the age—and inhabiting a fictional world in which "the political issues polarizing both communities and families were almost completely avoided."[28] Such images of family life were replicated, although in slightly less idyllic ways, in the popular animated family comedies of the era. The Flintstones (1960–66) and The Jetsons (1962–63) each offered a vision of the traditional nuclear family in its own version of a suburban environment (respectively, the Stone Age and the Space Age), and through this each provided oblique commentary on modern life.[29] Aside from their disparate time frames, the two shows were virtually identical: George Jetson was Fred Flintstone's space-age twin. As commentaries on contemporary American society and the family, the shows were also very similar: The Flintstones, firmly rooted in the past, emphasized how little family life had changed over time; The Jetsons, projected into the future, underscored how little family life was likely to change regardless of technological advancements. Although the success of The Simpsons is in part due to the popularity of both The Flintstones and The Jetsons, it differs significantly from each: whereas the commentary of its predecessors was oblique and mild, the commentary of The Simpsons is overt and often scathing. The Simpsons often self-consciously reminds us of its television predecessors, knowing that its own place within television history shapes how the show is received and understood (and perhaps enjoyed) by audiences today. More important, and more relevant to my purpose here, is The Simpsons' overt appropriation of the nuclear-family sitcom and its reinscription of the animated family comedy, which allow the writers of the show to provide a much sharper satire on American culture and a more cogent critique of contemporary (nuclear) family life.[30] Indeed,

The Simpsons has almost single-handedly ushered in a renaissance in satire on television. As the editors of *Satire TV: Politics and Comedy in the Post-Network Era* (2009) rightly note, "No single program is as important in creating the televisual space for the satire TV boom as *The Simpsons*."[31] *The Simpsons* also set a tone (essentially an ironic one) that is now commonplace in animated shows on television today, most strongly perhaps in *South Park* (1997–), and it provided a template for a new generation of animated family sitcoms, such as *King of the Hill* (1997–2010), *Family Guy* (1999–2002; 2005–), and *American Dad!* (2005–).

Although the nuclear-family sitcom fell out of favor in the 1970s, replaced largely by urban sitcoms and workplace sitcoms, it returned full force in the 1980s in accord with the conservative zeitgeist of the Reagan years. A number of popular sitcoms of that decade carried on the traditions of the postwar era: *Family Ties* (1982–89), *Growing Pains* (1985–92), and the wildly successful *The Cosby Show* (1984–92) each offered a return to the secure ground of middle-class suburbia and the stable nuclear family. However, these shows did incorporate some "updates" that made them more appealing to an audience somewhat cynical of the sitcom tradition, particularly its overt sexism. In deference to the women's movement, for example, *Family Ties*, *Growing Pains*, and *The Cosby Show* (as well as other programs of the era) offered some degree of gender equality within the home: the mother and father in these shows were both college graduates and both wage-earners, thus equals intellectually and economically, which was a quality not to be found in the family sitcoms that defined the genre. The 1990s, however, saw a surge of shows featuring not the middle class but the working class: both critically and economically, the most popular sitcoms of this decade were *Roseanne* (1988–97), *Married . . . with Children* (1987–97), and *The Simpsons* (1989–). Unlike their predecessors, these sitcoms incorporated real-world problems into their stories, thereby problematizing the traditionally hermetic nature of family sitcoms. Moreover, these shows were a revolt against the idealized images of domestic life portrayed by sitcoms such as *Leave It to Beaver* and *Father Knows Best* or, more contemporaneously, *Family Ties* and *The Cosby Show*. Shows such as *Roseanne, Married . . . with Children*, and *The Simpsons* each revived the domestic sitcom, using the traditional nuclear family construct (mom, dad, kids, dog, and a house in the suburbs) in order to skewer its conventions and critique, to varying degrees, the universality and normativity of so-called "traditional family values."

The already heated debate over "family values" in the early 1990s was intensified in 1992 by a comment made by then-president George H. W. Bush. In a speech given at the annual convention of the National Religious Broadcasters in January, Bush infamously stated, "We need a nation closer to *The Waltons* than *The Simpsons*."[32] Not to be outdone, the creators of *The Simpsons* managed to speak back to President Bush's criticism within a matter of days. The episode that aired on January 30 (a rerun of "Stark Raving Dad") began with a brief segment showing the Simpson family watching live footage of Bush's speech on their television. What followed was a sharp critique of the Bush administration and the legacy of Reagan-era economic policies; Bart simply turned to the camera and said, "Hey, we're just like the Waltons; we're praying for an end to the depression too." Clearly, Bush's comment was a lament for the loss of a supposedly better and more stable past and concept of family, perhaps best epitomized by the nuclear family of the 1950s and the paintings of Norman Rockwell. What Bush failed to see is that these were only *idealized* images of family and community, only media-constructed realities. Though the Simpson family is far from the media-constructed norm offered by television sitcoms of the 1950s or the 1980s, it is perhaps closer to the actual norm. *The Simpsons* is quite simply more attuned to the realities of contemporary life—this was true in 1992, and it is still true today. The debate over "family values," a concept that has had increasingly strong cultural purchase over the last two decades, is ongoing. Not surprisingly, the conservative attitude expressed by George Bush Sr. returned full force in the 1996 presidential election, with Bush's sentiments strongly echoed by Bob Dole, and then again in the 2000 presidential "selection," reiterated this time in the words of George Bush Jr. The consistent theme of the conservative political rallying cry was for a return to "traditional family values"—meaning, it seemed, to bourgeois values, compulsory heterosexuality, male dominance, and female submission—and for an increased presence of such values in mainstream popular art forms such as film and television.

Of course, *The Simpsons* is not only a satire upon the idealized images of family life; it is also a knowing and sharp satire upon the complex, excessive, hypocritical, and often idiotic state of contemporary American culture. Among other things, *The Simpsons* exposes the hypocrisy and ineptitude of pop psychology, the shallowness of public education, the venality of corporate greed, ongoing environmental degradation, commercialism, consumerism, and the absurdities of modern child-rearing. More relevant to my analysis, *The Simpsons* can be seen to embody a progressive politics, and it most commonly offers its satire from a leftist political position; from this vantage point, the show works to expose the potential dangers of ideologies such as sexism, racism, homophobia, xenophobia, and religious fundamentalism. The show regularly satirizes America's exclusionary practices, and it repeatedly critiques the treatment of various so-called minorities in American culture, notably those whose status is based on age, race, sex, sexuality, and religion. However, given that it is a part of the commercial television system, there are a number of limitations to the overt political agenda seemingly advanced by the satire on *The Simpsons*. Therefore, the show's satire prompts us to ask questions as well about the viability of subversive or oppositional content on American network television. As Jessamyn Neuhaus has astutely observed, the success of *The Simpsons* "begs one of the fundamental questions in cultural studies: can pop culture ever provide a site of individual or collective resistance or must it always ultimately function in the interests of the capitalist dominant ideology?"[33] Considering that the show's satire is so often aimed at consumer culture, capitalism, television, and even Rupert Murdoch and the Fox Television network, it is necessary to examine not only what *The Simpsons* satirizes but also *how* the show employs its satire.

I begin by situating *The Simpsons* within a tradition of political satire, although not in its classical Greek or Roman forms (i.e., as Horatian or Juvenalian satire); instead, I read *The Simpsons* within the uniquely American tradition of satire, which extends from the eighteenth century to the present and proliferates in a wide variety of art forms, including literature, theater, editorial cartoons, film, and television.[34] There is a diverse body of voices, materials, and political persuasions within this satirical tradition: to name but a few, the literature of Benjamin Franklin, Mark Twain, and Kurt Vonnegut; political cartoons from Thomas Nast, Gary Trudeau, and Aaron McGruder; the films of Stanley Kubrick, Michael Moore, and Spike Lee; and television programs such as Tom and Dick Smothers's *The Smothers Brothers Comedy Hour*, Lorne Michaels's *Saturday Night Live*, and Keenan Ivory Wayans's

In Living Color. As Dustin Griffin points out, contemporary understandings of satire developed out of a consensus achieved in the middle part of the twentieth century in a number of important works, among them Northrop Frye's *Anatomy of Criticism* (1957), Robert Elliott's *The Power of Satire: Magic, Ritual, Art* (1960), Gilbert Highet's *The Anatomy of Satire* (1962), Alvin Kernan's *The Plot of Satire* (1965), and Ronald Paulson's *The Fictions of Satire* (1967).[35] What these works collectively demonstrate is that, in its most general form, satire has remained remarkably consistent over the years in its efforts to expose, censure, and reform. However, significant changes in critical theory during the latter part of the twentieth century have impacted how we now understand satire. For example, New Critical assumptions about the "author," authorial intent, formal unity, and coherence—ideas still in place and largely unchallenged in the late 1950s and early 1960s—have since undergone rigorous interrogation. One would be hard-pressed today to aver, as Alvin Kernan does, that the satirist "sees the world as a battlefield between a definite, clearly understood good, which he represents, and an equally clear-cut evil" or to claim, as does Northrop Frye, that satire can safely assume standards of decency and that its moral norms are "relatively clear."[36] Indeed, these days it is that very kind of certainty—and that Manichaean notion of good and evil—that is often the target of satiric ridicule. New Historicism, ideology critique, and interdisciplinary cultural studies, among other things, have forced us to reconsider how satire functions in society and to think carefully about the ways in which satire sustains or subverts the dominant social and political order. In an "age of irony," as our era has come to be known, things are a bit more complicated, and often we are uncertain what the satiric target might be, what the moral norm is, what the author's perspective is, or if we even have satire at all rather than just parody or irony. This is not to say, however, that we have descended into an abyss of relativism. Simplistic answers cannot always be found, and we grossly misrepresent satire if we assume it always has a preconceived endpoint or "moral" to which the audience must be persuaded. Thus, the still-prevalent view of satire as a simple "rhetoric of persuasion" needs to be modified. Dustin Griffin offers a useful way to think about this; he says,

> We need to supplant the old rhetoric of persuasion with a rhetoric of inquiry and provocation . . . [which] assumes that satirists—though they may not have answers to all their questions—exercise an overall control over the process of exploration, leading us to raise questions we must then ponder.[37]

Griffin acknowledges here a basic function of satire: to provoke thought and raise questions about serious social ills. Such satire is evident today in a wide variety of cultural forms—for example, the stand-up routines of Chris Rock, the essays and books of Al Franken, the films of Michael Moore, the comic strips of Aaron McGruder, the "fake news" segments of Comedy Central's *The Daily Show with Jon Stewart*, and the faux punditry of Stephen Colbert's *The Colbert Report*—all of which use satirical humor to challenge dominant ideologies and to hold accountable those in positions of political power.[38] *The Simpsons*, which preceded many of these examples, was designed with the same aims: to raise awareness about serious issues and to (potentially) effect change. This, of course, coincides very well with creator Matt Groening's own views about the show's purpose, which he expressed in a 1999 interview with *Mother Jones* magazine. Groening says,

> For me, it's not enough to be aware that most television is bad and stupid and perni-
> cious. I think, "What can I do about it?" [. . .] what I want to do is point out the way TV
> is unconsciously structured to keep us all distracted [. . . and] what I'm trying to do—in
> the guise of light entertainment, if that's possible—is nudge people, jostle them a little,
> wake them up to some of the ways in which we're being manipulated and exploited.[39]

In other words, Groening wants to simultaneously evoke laughter and provoke
thought, which is, in its most general sense, the aim of satire.

Before proceeding with the analysis of *The Simpsons*, I want to reflect on the terms
parody and *satire* and underscore the distinctions between them, as they are too often
conflated and confused with one another. Parody, quite simply, is a playful imitation
or a humorous reworking of another text for comic effect, and it is usually designed
to either pay tribute to the original or poke fun at it. In her book *A Theory of Parody*,
one of the most authoritative texts on the subject, Linda Hutcheon flatly states that
parody is "repetition with a critical distance, which marks difference rather than
similarity."[40] Although there is overlap between them, parody and satire must be
understood as distinct modes. In drawing this distinction, I follow Hutcheon's claim
that parody is characterized foremost by "ironic inversion" and is best understood
as "an integrated structural modeling process of revision, replaying, inverting, and
'trans-contextualizing' previous works of art."[41] As Hutcheon notes, "Even the best
works on parody tend to confuse it with satire, which, unlike parody, is both moral
and social in its focus and ameliorative in its intention."[42] Up to this point, I concur
with Hutcheon's views. Hutcheon concludes, however, by arguing that ironic parody
has a variety of effects—what she refers to as a "pragmatic ethos"—which can range
from playful to critical, "from scornful ridicule to reverential homage."[43] And it is
here that I part ways with Hutcheon. If irony is a key dimension of parody and a critical distance is inherent, designed to foster difference rather than similarity, then a
certain degree of critique is inevitable. But the range Hutcheon refers to seems more
accurately to be from what I would call "playful mockery" to reverential homage. The
distinction is one that can be seen by comparing a comedy show such as *Saturday
Night Live* with *The Daily Show with Jon Stewart*, for instance. Whereas the former
might provide a simple parody of a political figure—picture Chevy Chase as a bumbling Gerald Ford or, more recently, Will Ferrell as a befuddled George W. Bush—the
latter would present a sharp criticism of the ideas promoted or policies enacted by
that political figure—picture here Tina Fey's impersonation of Sarah Palin. Both
parody and satire can be humorous, but only in the satire is something of greater significance and social consequence at stake. To be fair, Hutcheon does make clear that
she sees a difference between parody and satire, and throughout her book she does
repeatedly associate satire with ridicule (or, as she puts it, "the transgression of social
norms") and with an overall "ameliorative aim."[44]

The Simpsons is certainly rife with parody—indeed, in many ways it is a much
more parodic than satiric text—and many people have commented on the parodic aspect of the show and the appeal this has for viewers.[45] This is particularly
true of commentary in the mainstream press, but it is also evident in some of the
academic writing on the show (e.g., Dalton et al., Knight, Matheson, and Mittell).
However, the most sustained treatment of the subject of parody is found in Jonathan
Gray's *Watching with "The Simpsons": Television, Parody, and Intertextuality*. In
his introduction, Gray, like others before him, notes that *The Simpsons* is "deeply

parodic, relying on our knowledge of other genres and texts" for its humor; however, to support this view, he cites examples from the show that he claims variously "scorn," "ridicule," "mock," "toy with," and "playfully highlight" aspects of genres such as advertisements, Hollywood film, and television sitcoms.[46] This is problematic, as it too readily conflates terms closely associated with satire (*scorn* and *ridicule*) with those more commonly used to describe the aims of parody. Although both parody and satire are designed to be humorous, satire is a rhetorical and moral art with a very specific purpose: it is designed to *censure* human failings and follies. As Hugh Holman succinctly states, satire's object is to "evoke laughter for a corrective purpose. It always has a target—such as pretense, falsity, deception, arrogance— which is held up to ridicule by the satirist's unmasking of it."[47] Parody, on the other hand, is less moralistic and more focused on the humorous allusions to and playful imitations of other works of art. Gray additionally claims that *The Simpsons* contains "bite-sized instances of parody and satire," as if parody and satire were synonymous terms or interchangeable concepts. Clearly, there is an irony in such casual use of terminology, as Gray's aim is not to demonstrate the social or political dimensions of *The Simpsons*—that is, to illuminate how the show employs satire—but to demonstrate that "parody has great power and potential to write back to and even write over other texts and genres, to contextualize and recontextualize other media offerings, and thus to teach and engender a media literacy of sorts."[48] Gray states that his study is focused on what he calls a "critical intertextuality," which he defines as "those moments when [parody] moves beyond mere postmodern play so as to criticize."[49] Gray also notes that "*The Simpsons* relentlessly ridicules and mocks the aesthetics, structure, and logic of the traditional American family sitcom, ads and promotional culture, and the news." At first glance, this seems to imply that Gray is reading the show as satire; however, what Gray emphasizes here are primarily the codes and tropes of well-known genres and not the social, political, or ideological implications of those art forms.[50] Though interesting, I find Gray's focus on "parodic critique" misleading, as it is only about "genre (re)construction" and intertextuality. More troubling, however, is his casual claim that "parody can be satiric."[51] It is more accurate to say that satire can be parodic, as satire often employs parody as one of its strategies. Indeed, this is something Gray acknowledges in the invaluable collection *Satire TV: Politics and Comedy in the Post-Network Era* (2009), which he edited with Jeffrey P. Jones and Ethan Thompson. In the introduction, he and his coeditors clearly state that "parody is a handy tool in the satirist's collection, and in various ways, contemporary television satire often uses parody for considerable effect."[52] Perhaps it was a matter of casting the net too widely in *Watching with "The Simpsons"* or of using the concept of "text" too loosely, so that everything textual is rendered part of some genre. Whatever the case, Gray unfortunately conflates parody and satire and thus often misreads the satirical aims of *The Simpsons*. Curiously, Gray also quotes Matt Groening's famous statement, which I cited earlier, about the show's purposes and his desire wake people up to the ways in which they are being manipulated and exploited. For Gray, however, Groening's comments show only that "*The Simpsons* has parodically attacked seemingly all major televisual and cinematic genres, from cop shows to talk shows, kids' television to art house," as if Groening's concern were only with aesthetics and not politics, with the conventions of form rather than the very serious problems of manipulation and exploitation.[53] Granted, there is a fine line between mocking parody and satire, and valuable critiques can be found within such parodies, but one should not ignore the real target, which for Groening is clearly a society in need of improvement.

Interpreting *The Simpsons*

As Horace Newcomb notes, television studies as an academic enterprise arose from the "cultural turn" in literary studies toward popular forms of entertainment.[54] Analyzing forms of popular entertainment for the meanings they generated was the aim of two very influential books from the early days of television studies: Raymond Williams's *Television: Technology and Cultural Form* (1974) and John Fiske and John Hartley's *Reading Television* (1978). Williams importantly offered the idea that the defining feature of broadcasting is "planned flow" and thus allowed for moving beyond the determinist and functionalist views that had previously dominated the study of television. As Charlotte Brunsdon explains, Williams's attempt to describe what is specific to the act of watching television has been "internationally generative, particularly in combination with some of the more recent empirical studies of how people do (or don't) watch television."[55] Fiske and Hartley also reject the functionalism of earlier sociological scholarship, and they encourage scholars to move "beyond the strictly objective and quantitative methods of content analysis and into the newer and less well explored discipline of semiotics."[56] In short, Fiske and Hartley demonstrate the now-common idea that signs are not just representational but carry cultural meaning. Drawing upon the work of Stuart Hall, they also bring greater attention to research on "active" audiences and how people use and understand television texts. They highlight that there is neither a single "authorial" identity for television programming nor a single "audience": the audience is not a homogeneous mass but is composed of a wide variety of groups who "actively read" television in ways that connect with their own social backgrounds and cultural experiences. A better understanding of audience practices was the impetus behind other pioneering works, such as David Morley's *The Nationwide Audience* (1980) and Ien Ang's *Watching Dallas* (1985), each of which inspired the first wave of significant television reception studies in the early 1990s.[57] Since that time, qualitative research on audience reception has come to be of critical importance in media studies and the foundation for a body of scholarship that has grown increasingly large as it has turned its attention to other forms of new media (such as video games) and to the problems of media globalization.

   Not surprisingly, a few scholars have begun to conduct ethnographic research on *The Simpsons* (e.g., Alters, Beard, Brook, and Gray). Although recent and limited in scope, these studies offer interesting insights into how various audiences—marked by race, class, gender, nationality, and education level—actively read and respond to *The Simpsons*. Where useful and relevant, I will draw upon the existing ethnographic research to help support my claims, but I will not delve fully into the question of reception. A comprehensive treatment of the reception of *The Simpsons*, which would have to consider both its domestic and international consumption, is tangential to my aims here and simply beyond the scope of this project. My analysis of *The Simpsons* concentrates on the texts produced and distributed as episodes of *The Simpsons* and upon the meanings of these in relation to specific historical and cultural contexts and to the art and aims of satire. After first framing *The Simpsons* within the tradition of satire, I discuss the show thematically, concentrating on issues of race, ethnicity, nationality, class, gender, sexuality, and religion. I provide close textual readings of individual episodes of *The Simpsons*, but I also situate these in the historical, social, and political contexts in which they appear in order to explain how the show engages with relevant cultural events and ideological trends in American culture.

Although I will not concentrate heavily on audiences and the reception of *The Simpsons* in the chapters that follow, I want to turn briefly to a discussion of the ethnographic research Jonathan Gray conducted for *Watching with "The Simpsons,"* as this information has a direct bearing on my analysis of *The Simpsons* as satire. In 2001, Gray solicited the participation of 35 students at Goodenough College in London, a residential college that caters to postgraduates from overseas, and conducted interviews of approximately 45 minutes each with those who had volunteered to take part. Gray discusses the results in a chapter on "interpretive communities," in which he acknowledges that his sample is small and "makes no claim to representativeness," and yet he does draw many conclusions from these interviews.[58] He is careful to stress that the advertisement he placed was not just for fans but for people with "'ANY level of involvement with the show.'"[59] His participants, 15 men and 20 women, ranged in age from 22 to 38. Though a "predominantly white group," there was a mix of nationalities. As he admits, it was a "well-degreed group" (12 with or working toward a PhD, 18 with or working toward a master's degree, and 5 with a bachelor's degree), and "all were middle-class."[60] All interviewees were asked the following questions:

- Why do you watch the show? What do you like about it? (or, why don't you like it?)
- Has your viewing relationship changed to it over time? If so, how? Do you find the same things funny?
- Some say the show is getting worse: do you agree? Why or why not?
- What is wrong with the program? What would "ruin" the show? At what point would you stop watching?
- Does it have a politics at all? If so, what are they?
- Do you think the show's humor has any particular "targets"? If so, what are they?
- Does its humor stick with you, or is it fleeting?
- Do you like the animation? What effects does it have on the program?
- Why do you think the show is so popular?
- What, if any, other shows are like it? How?
- How would you compare it to other shows?
- Rupert Murdoch has said it is the most important show on television. How would you respond?
- Has this interview asked you to talk about *The Simpsons* in a way you wouldn't normally?

Considering my own study of *The Simpsons*, I was interested in those questions that circulated around the idea of the show's politics. What intrigued me most in the responses was the ability of Gray's participants to discuss *The Simpsons* in remarkably sophisticated ways. In a section called "Simpsons-speak," which focuses on the idea of an interpretive community surrounding the show, Gray's interviewees speak of *The Simpsons* as "a helpful litmus test for someone's personality" in social gatherings; of the show being a "generational touchstone"; and of the show fostering inclusiveness "among a certain age and education group . . . [that is] conversant and literate in *The Simpsons* as a cultural artifact and language."[61] More tellingly, in the section called "Watching (for) Parody," Gray reports on how his interviewees take pleasure in the text of *The Simpsons*, exploring their responses to why they watched and what they liked about it. The show was called "smart," "clever," and "sophisticated," and a number of students claimed that it appealed on at least two levels: "There was a consensus," Gray tells us, "that the text has a 'simple,' 'visual,' or 'elementary' level of Homer's stupidity, Bart's wisecracks and slapstick; and a 'deeper' level of smart, parodic-satiric commentary." As Gray himself explains, "What this 'deeper' second level consisted of was relevant and topical parody and political satire."[62] It is worth quoting here at length some of the very insightful commentary by his interview subjects:

> Cleo characterized *The Simpsons* as conducting "a weekly political critique of some kind"; and, to Al, "it's smart because it finds ways of using irony to make political statements." Irony and satire were much-invoked terms, with Janet reflecting what many others told me when she said "I think the satire is why I find it so funny. And that's why it keeps being so funny. If it was just Homer being dumb, it would probably get pretty boring." Not only, therefore, were irony and satire being invoked, but they were elided with *The Simpsons*. To Al, for instance, "satire is really their umm, umm . . . I think it's their principal credo," while to Alyson, "obviously they didn't create irony, but they kind of honed it."[63]

Gray's interviewees also offer a variety of insightful responses to his question regarding the show's "targets." Though posed as a question about parody, it was received by many of the respondents as being about satire; their responses quickly dovetailed into commentary on why they watched *The Simpsons*, which led, as Gray himself notes, into "discussions of who and what was being comically attacked." Among the many topics students named were consumerism, capitalism, American suburbia, the family, television and the media, Fox and/or Rupert Murdoch, politics and politicians, big business, sitcoms, schools, and religion.[64] There is an irony, of course, in Gray's subjects interpreting the show as a satire when Gray himself says almost nothing of satire in his book, choosing instead to explore the idea of intertextual parody.

Having taught for many years a course entitled *The Simpsons* and American Culture, I decided to replicate Gray's survey and assess the differences in the results. I slightly modified a few of Gray's questions and added a few of my own. I also added a few elements to the preliminary portions of the survey form in order to gather other information about the students' backgrounds and identities: specifically, students were provided places to identify their sex, age, and race/ethnicity and to state how many semesters of college-level work they had completed. My interviewees were asked the following questions:

- Have you ever seen a complete episode of *The Simpsons*? YES or NO.
- Do you now watch the show? YES or NO.
- If YES, are you a regular or occasional viewer?
- If YES, why do you watch the show? What do you like about it?
- If NO, why not? What do you dislike about it?

- Has your viewing relationship to the show changed over time? If so, how?
- Some say the show is getting worse: do you agree? Why or why not?
- Does the show have a politics at all? If so, what are they?
- Do you think the show's humor has any particular "targets"? If so, what are they?
- Does the show's humor stick with you, or is it fleeting?
- Why do you think the show is so popular?
- What, if any, other shows are like it? How so? And are those better or worse than *The Simpsons*? Why do you think so?
- Some have claimed that it is the most important show on television. How do you respond to this claim?
- What for you defines "American Culture"?
- What do you expect a course called "*The Simpsons* and American Culture" to be about? And what do you expect to learn from it?

I administered my survey to four different sections of students enrolled in my course between the fall of 2008 and the fall of 2009. Although this was not voluntary, the circumstances of viewership were largely the same—some students were active fans, some casual viewers, and some had never even seen the show. I had a total of 89 participants, more than double Gray's sample. Students in my sample ranged from age 17 to 49, so this covered similar ground. My students were also a very diverse group, but less in terms of nationality than in racial and ethnic group affiliation: 43 students identified as white or Caucasian; 14 as black or African American; 9 as Hispanic; 5 as Asian; and 2 as Native American.[65] The most significant difference between my survey samples and Gray's is education level, which was abundantly clear in the results.

Although many of the responses intrigue me, I'll focus here only on those that speak to the very different kinds of interpretive communities Gray and I are working with. In response to the questions "Does the show have a politics at all? If so, what are they?" 31 students responded with a definite "Yes" and 6 with a definite "No." The majority of responses were somewhere in a murky middle: 20 students offered a "Yes, but" answer, stating they could not explain the politics or did not know of any examples, and another 3 simply stated "Probably" with no further comment. Thirteen students answered "Don't know" or "Not sure," and 16 students left the question blank. In short, 51 students seemed to believe that the show has (or likely has) a politics, whereas only 13 were either unsure or believed it does not. This would seem to replicate to some degree Gray's findings. However, most of my students could not explain those politics. Indeed, among the 31 who said yes, 19 interpreted "politics" in its traditional sense, as associated with governance, offering examples such as "politicians," "Democrats and Republicans," "elections," "the president," "courthouse," "various leaders," and "government issues." Some did appear to have a slightly different idea in mind, perhaps thinking in terms of "targets," as the next question puts it, and offered examples such as "pollution," "war," "global warming," "education," "banning alcohol," "religion," and "corruption." Since the student body is heavily skewed toward the young, I found it useful to divide my group by age into three brackets: 17–19, 20–29, and 30+. My sample contained 36 teenagers, 43 people in their 20s, and 10 people aged 30 or more. What is most interesting is the teens and 20-somethings were the ones who seemed to understand best the politics of the show.

Some 89% of my survey group is under age 30, and all of the "Yes" responses came from individuals in this age bracket. Curiously, all of the students over age 30 were among those who answered "No" or "Don't know" or left the question blank.

The ethnographic studies that Gray and I conducted are small-scale, but they do underscore the validity of Stuart Hall's claim that meaning is always negotiated and that there truly is no telling just how an individual might interpret a given text. Based on the results just presented, it would be fair to say that education level is an important factor in one's ability to understand satire and to parse what Simone Knox calls the "complex double-codedness" of *The Simpsons*—that is, the show's remarkable combination of low-brow comedy and high-brow wit.[66] From the start, fans and critics have commented on *The Simpsons'* ability to skillfully combine slapstick humor with political satire, making it appealing to children and adults alike. The double-coded nature of the show can also be seen when looking at it in an international context. At first glance, the enormous success and popularity of *The Simpsons* outside the United States is peculiar. As Chris Turner points out, comedy is "a legendarily poor traveler, particularly when it comes to social satire," which relies heavily on social context, specific cultural references, and linguistic wordplay.[67] Much of the show's appeal abroad does indeed stem from its satirical elements; equally important, however, if not more so, is the show's use of physical humor and sight gags, its reliance upon archetypes as well as stereotypes, and its focus on the family and emotional relationships.[68]

In the chapters that follow, I offer a reading of *The Simpsons* as a satirical commentary on American culture. I am aware that this view is not uniformly shared, and although I claim *The Simpsons* to be satire, there is no guarantee that it will be read as such by all audiences. Truthfully, I think it more likely that it would not be, since the majority of people are not familiar with the concept of satire; most people do not invest a lot of time in critically reflecting on mass media, and many would simply dismiss *The Simpsons* as "just a cartoon" or as mere entertainment. I also realize that some of my interpretations of episodes of *The Simpsons* run counter to those of other commentators, which I discuss in some detail at various points throughout the chapters. I do not intend to extract singular or definitive meanings from the episodes discussed here, nor do I claim to offer any. Instead, in each of the following chapters, I explore the ways that *The Simpsons* participates in the cultural conversation about a number of contentious "culture war" issues in order to elucidate some of the satirical aims of the show. In doing so, I strive to remain conscious of the dangers of speaking too strictly of satirical intent or purpose, to be wary of the idea that the "meaning" of a text has been deliberately placed there and is simply waiting to be discovered, and to avoid the supposition that "the sociopolitical orientation of a satirist can be read directly off a satirical work."[69] Such ideas would be hardly applicable to a text such as *The Simpsons* anyhow, since individual episodes are the product of many different "authors," including writers, producers, directors, illustrators, and voice actors. As the work of the many scholars cited in this introduction illustrates, meaning is multifaceted and generated in the complex interactions among cultural texts, social contexts, and audiences.

Chapter Overview

Chapter 1 briefly outlines the history of Fox Television and the satirical tradition in American culture, of which *The Simpsons* is an inheritor. I frame the show within these histories to examine and better understand the relationship that has existed between the broadcaster and its flagship show. Since its inception in 1986, Fox has grown into a giant media conglomerate—in large part as a consequence of the success of *The Simpsons*. When *The Simpsons* began in 1989, Fox was a newcomer to the network game and needed to carve out a niche, which it did by offering "edgy" and provocative fare. Though much of this was in the "reality" television mode, a great deal of it was also very satirical, as evidenced in early Fox offerings such as *The Tracy Ullman Show*, *Married . . . with Children*, *The Ben Stiller Show*, and *In Living Color*. As is well known, Fox Television is an outgrowth of News Corporation, headed by Rupert Murdoch, who is best known as a corporate raider and whose newspapers (although ever-ready to exploit sensational stories) have repeatedly expressed notoriously conservative views and have openly supported conservative political candidates in both England and the United States. I thus have to ask: To what degree has Fox's growth and status changed the quality and/or content of *The Simpsons*? Has *The Simpsons* become more "user friendly"? Has *The Simpsons* become less reliant upon satire and more likely to offer parody and slapstick comedy? To answer these questions, I will examine the role of Fox executives in the production of *The Simpsons* and the struggle for creative control among the show's producers and writers. I will also compare and contrast episodes from the early years of the show and more recent years to demonstrate the shifts in sensibilities and goals.

Chapter 2 deals with questions of race and ethnicity and their relation to national identity. Drawing from a large body of scholarship on film and television representations, primarily those concerned with "whiteness," "blackness," and the racial "Other," I examine how *The Simpsons* constructs "American" identity—an identity that has long been coded as white, middle class, suburban, and Protestant (i.e., traditionally WASP). Consideration is first given to the problem of "whiteness" on the show, as it is articulated in both normative and nonnormative ways. The members of the Simpson family embody the "norm" of television situation comedy as racially unmarked whites and so represent a continuation of the tradition of the so-called "WASP sitcoms" of the 1950s and 1960s.[70] However, whiteness itself is problematized on *The Simpsons* through the characters of Krusty the Clown (who is Jewish) and Cletus Delroy, who is positioned as "poor white trash." To address such problems, I provide a critique of the WASP concept and provide an alternative (what I will call McWASP) that more accurately describes the ideological norm of American identity. I then discuss earlier periods of immigration and the integration of certain ethnic groups into "whiteness," as well as the presentation of the contemporary immigrant experience, embodied in Apu Nahasapeemapetilon, proprietor of the local Kwik-E-Mart. Finally, I explore the more recent struggles over defining "Americanness" in the post-9/11 era, examining episodes that deal with patriotism and dissent and the lives of Muslim Americans.

In chapter 3, I take up questions about gender relations, female identity, and feminism. Here I draw upon key works in gender theory and feminist scholarship, particularly those that focus on representations of women in media. This section will specifically explore the representation of women on *The Simpsons* and examine how the show engages the politics of feminist movements within its satire. Of course, *The Simpsons*' engagement with feminism is not simple, since the show both reflects and reflects upon the ideological preoccupations of the culture, which are invariably complex. Understandings of feminism in popular culture are imbued with a great deal of confusion and contradiction. Given *The Simpsons'* regular engagement with contemporary issues and its reflection of American cultural values, it is not surprising that much of the ambivalence and ambiguity that currently surround female identity is often reflected in characterizations and story lines on the show. What *The Simpsons* offers is a complex combination of progressive and traditional attitudes toward female identity and feminist movements. Of course, such conflicting ideologies and representations are in keeping with the times in which *The Simpsons* appeared, for the 1990s itself was an era of renewed ambiguity about women's lives and widespread confusion over gender norms. I will thus examine select episodes of *The Simpsons* (those that feature some of the female characters) in close relation to their historical context and to events taking place in American culture that were reshaping ideas about women's experiences and lives in order to explore how fully the show articulates a feminist sensibility.

Chapter 4 explores the politics of sexuality and queer identity on *The Simpsons*. Drawing upon key works in gender theory, queer theory, and feminist scholarship, I explore the ways in which *The Simpsons* establishes a "queer sensibility," and I examine the ideological implications of its portrayals of queer identity. *The Simpsons* enacts a queer sensibility in many ways but primarily through its abundant allusions to gay life and sexual orientation, its constant toying with the fluid nature of sexuality, its incorporation of regular gay characters (especially Waylon Smithers), and, most recently, its engagement with the highly politicized issue of same-sex marriage. The aim here is to examine the degree to which portrayals of queer identities and lives on *The Simpsons* serve to challenge normative ideologies of gender and sexuality and the degree to which these images might simply reinforce the heterosexual bias of American culture. Heteronormativity is still predominant in American culture today, despite the recent "gay vogue"—that is, the commercialization of queer identity within both media and consumer culture over the past 10 to 15 years—and this normalizing impulse is evident even in ostensibly "gay-friendly" television shows such as *Will & Grace* and *Queer Eye for the Straight Guy*. By contrast, *The Simpsons* appears to promote a progressive political agenda via its regular critique of the oppression of sexual "minorities" in American culture. However, the ways in which issues about sexuality have been addressed and dealt with on the show raise questions once again about the tensions between political satire and commercial interests and about how satirical messages are received by audiences. Therefore, I want to examine more closely how *The Simpsons* employs queer identity in service of its satire. Again, I read select episodes of the show against the social and political changes taking place in the United States, charting the shifts in representation from the early years to more recent ones, shifts that coincide with the increased commodification of queer culture and the intensification of debates over gay and lesbian civil rights in the new millennium.

Chapter 5 addresses the topic of socioeconomic class on *The Simpsons*. I begin with a brief discussion of the ways socioeconomic class is currently conceptualized in the United States, with particular attention to the common perceptions of both the middle class, which is often seen as an ideological "norm," and the working class, which is regularly denigrated. Given that white identity and suburban life on television are most commonly yoked to middle-class status, many presume that the Simpsons are middle-class. However, as I will demonstrate, the Simpsons are very much within the working class, as is evident from both their social behaviors and their economic status. The working-class status of the Simpsons is made quite clear at the start of the series; this is reflected in numerous episodes, many of which focus explicitly on the family's financial struggles, and it remains a consistent image during the first few seasons of the show. However, as *The Simpsons* grew in popularity, the family's working-class identity was subtly modified and made to seem more middle class. One of the means by which this is achieved is through the inclusion of the "white trash" characters Cletus and Brandine Delroy, who first appear in seasons five and six, respectively. This raises questions once again about the problematic nature of creating and "reading" satire and about the ostensibly oppositional status of *The Simpsons*. I argue that "white trash" identity is employed on *The Simpsons* not for satirical purposes but to provide an affirmation of middle-class status for the Simpsons and to reestablish middle-class identity as normative American identity. To support this claim, I provide close readings of select episodes of the show, charting shifts in the representations of working-class and middle-class identity, both on the show and in American culture at large.

Lastly, chapter 6 discusses religion and spirituality on *The Simpsons* and in American culture. In this chapter, I situate *The Simpsons* within the ongoing "culture war" over religion in American culture and read select episodes of the show in relation to this debate. In general, institutional religion (particularly mainstream Christianity) is a target of the show's satire and has been from the start. This does not mean, however, that *The Simpsons* is void of faith or spirituality—indeed, the show demonstrates more of these qualities than any other television comedy, past or present, as analyses from both the religious right and the secular left have noted (e.g., Cantor, Dalton et al., Pinsky, Turner). Ironically, the show was seen initially as amoral and viewed as a corruptive influence upon society by those on the political and religious right; yet after the publication of Mark Pinsky's *The Gospel According to "The Simpsons": The Spiritual Life of the World's Most Animated Family* (2001), there was a reconsideration of the show and a powerful reclamation of it for the faithful, largely under the guise of "family values." No topic on *The Simpsons* has garnered more commentary than religion; not surprisingly, the issues of religion, faith, and spirituality have led to some of the most diverse interpretations of the show among fans and scholars alike. This raises some important questions about how *The Simpsons* engages the ongoing tensions between religious and secular forces in the United States. Some of the questions to be considered in this chapter are: Does *The Simpsons* operate from a theological or a philosophical position? Does it promote a religious worldview or a secular one? Does it aim to satirize only religious fundamentalism or extremist belief of any type? How is the "spiritual" defined by the show, and how does this affect the representations of institutional religion and scientific rationality? To answer these questions, I examine episodes of *The Simpsons* in relation to a number of important historical contexts, including the rise of the religious right in the 1980s, the increasing influence of religiosity during the 1990s, the recent debates over the roles of science and religion in the United States, and the intensification of religious fundamentalism in the post-9/11 environment.

I

"Entertain and Subvert": Fox Television, Satirical Comedy, and *The Simpsons*

Satire is a lesson, parody is a game.

—*Vladimir Nabokov*[1]

In a segment of *The Simpsons* episode "Mr. Spritz Goes to Washington" (March 2003), we see the Simpson family gathered around the television watching Krusty the Clown, who is running for a seat in Congress, engage in a televised debate with his opponent on the Fox News channel. The Fox News anchor begins the segment by saying, "Welcome to Fox News, your voice for evil." This rather shocking announcement is then followed by a satirical attack on the bias in mainstream news media and, more specifically, on the so-called "fair and balanced" reporting that Fox purports to offer. Krusty (the Republican candidate) is introduced as "beloved children's entertainer Krusty the Clown" and is shown standing before an American flag with a halo superimposed above his head; his opponent (the Democratic candidate) is introduced only as "this guy" and shown with a Soviet flag in the background and little red devil horns drawn atop his head. The anchor also refers to Krusty as "Congressman," although, as his opponent exclaims, "He hasn't won yet!" To this the anchor replies, "You make a very adulterous point." This "debate" then concludes with a Krusty campaign commercial, an overtly propagandistic series of cliché images (apple pie, baseball, farmland, etc.) and sounds designed to invoke patriotic sentiment and to make Krusty appear "all-American." We are additionally given a parody of the Fox News channel's infamous "news crawl" at the bottom of the television screen; as the debate unfolds, viewers (of the debate and of *The Simpsons* itself) read the following messages:

> Pointless News Crawls Up 37 Percent...Do Democrats Cause Cancer? Find Out at Foxnews.com...Rupert Murdoch: Terrific Dancer...Dow Down 5000 Points...Study: 92 Percent of Democrats are Gay...JFK Posthumously Joins Republican Party...Oil Slicks Found to Keep Seals Young, Supple...Dan Quayle, Awesome...

This is certainly a witty parody and a fine example of the self-conscious humor so common on *The Simpsons*; more importantly, it is also an excellent example of the pointed satire on *The Simpsons* and a telling reminder of the show's political sensibilities. There is no mistaking this scene for anything but what it is: a satirical attack on the Fox News channel's right-wing political bias and its manipulative strategies. An equally audacious critique was offered at the end of "Mr. Spritz Goes to Washington," along with the end credits; here, viewers saw the following "news" crawl:

> Ashcroft Declares Breast of Chicken Sandwich "Obscene"...Hillary Clinton Embarrasses Self, Nation...Bible Says Jesus Favored Capital Gains Cut...Stay Tuned for Hannity and Idiot...Only Dorks Watch CNN...Jimmy Carter: Old, Wrinkly...

Not surprisingly, executives at Fox News were not pleased about such a sharp critique of their practices; their response to it, however, was surprising: soon after the "Mr. Spritz" episode appeared, lawyers for Fox News threatened legal action against Fox Entertainment, which broadcasts *The Simpsons*, for parodying the news crawl and for using the Fox News logo. News of this move came on the heels of Fox News initiating a lawsuit against comedian Al Franken and his publisher, Penguin Group, for copyright infringement for use of the term "fair and balanced" in the title of Franken's book *Lies and the Lying Liars Who Tell Them: A Fair and Balanced Look at the Right* (2003).[2] In a speech before a crowd in Minneapolis a few days after the suit was filed, Franken quite appropriately exclaimed, "Satire is protected speech. Even if the object of the satire doesn't get it." On August 23, 2003, the federal judge Denny Chin agreed and denied Fox News its request for an injunction to block publication of the book, declaring that "this case is wholly without merit, both factually and legally," and affirming Franken's right to parody the network's slogan as protected by the First Amendment.[3] Such moves by Fox News seemed both unnecessary and trivial to many observers; in the case of *The Simpsons*, it seemed almost absurd, since both Fox News and *The Simpsons* are owned by Rupert Murdoch's News Corporation. In an interview later that fall with Terry Gross on National Public Radio's *Fresh Air*, *Simpsons* creator Matt Groening summed up the situation as follows:

> We called their bluff because we didn't think Rupert Murdoch would pay for Fox to sue itself. So, we got away with it. But now Fox has a new rule that we can't do those little fake news crawls on the bottom of the screen—in a cartoon—because it might confuse the viewers into thinking it's real news.[4]

The Fox spokesman Robert Zimmerman later claimed that the situation was blown out of proportion and that Fox News never threatened legal action. However, Fox did effectively put a ban on the parody of its news show, as Groening made clear during a July 2007 appearance on *The Daily Show with Jon Stewart* to promote *The Simpsons Movie*. In the interview with Stewart, Groening reiterated that he and his staff had been forbidden from parodying Fox News. In discussing the place of *The Simpsons* within the News Corporation empire, Groening stated that he and his writers "love biting the hand that feeds us [and] we love attacking Fox." He then alluded to the previous incident, first stating that he and his team had once "gotten in trouble for attacking Fox news" and then rather sarcastically adding that they were now "forbidden to do that again because the Fox viewer might confuse our cartoon with actual news."[5]

Although the creators of *The Simpsons* were "forbidden" from parodying the Fox News crawl, they have not stopped aiming satirical barbs at Fox Television in general and Fox News in particular. If anything, it has become an almost expected trope in the show. The most recent examples involve some less than subtle jabs at the presumed demographic of Fox News viewers and the ideologies with which they operate. The opening sequence of the episode entitled "The Fool Monty" (November 2010) features a Fox News helicopter flying toward the Statue of Liberty over the skyline of Manhattan. Emblazoned on the side of the copter is the Fox corporate logo and beneath it the statement, "Not Racist, But #1 With Racists." Such a bold declaration might seem hyperbolic—and perhaps would have been if made in an earlier period—but it should be noted that it comes in the wake of the significant change (both symbolic and tangible) ushered in by the election of President Barack Obama, change that Fox News pundits and many of their viewers adamantly opposed and now lament. It's not a far stretch to see this dig at Fox as part of a larger critique of the open support of the conservative Tea Party movement, the backing of various anti-immigration policies, and the frequent attacks on President Obama by Fox channel pundits and some of their audience. Not surprisingly, the joke was not funny to the Fox News anchor Bill O'Reilly, who showed the clip from "The Fool Monty" on his show later that week and then said of the creators of The Simpsons, "Pinheads? I believe so."[6] One week later, the episode "How Munched Is That Birdie in the Window" opened with a similar sequence, only this time the caption beneath the Fox logo read "Unsuitable for Viewers Under 75." Oddly, when this episode was later posted on the Internet via Fox and Hulu, the satirical jab at Fox was gone, replaced by a joke about Homer Simpson and King Kong, prompting some fans to wonder if the show had pushed the envelope too far and was now being censored. As Dave Itzkoff reports, however, this was not the case. Executive producer Al Jean explained to Itzkoff that the producers of The Simpsons—in particular, Matt Groening—were pleased with how the first Fox News joke had provoked Bill O'Reilly and wanted to respond quickly to his comment, so the creative team rushed their second Fox News joke into the following episode. This was so late in the production process that it could be inserted only into the master version shown in the United States and Canada and not into versions shown in foreign markets or on the Internet.[7] Two weeks later, with appropriate timing, the writers offered one more swipe at Fox: in the opening to "Donnie Fatso" (December 2010), the sign on the Fox News helicopter read "Merry Christmas From Fox News...But No Other Holidays," clearly offering an attack on the network's relentless prattle each holiday season about the "War on Christmas."

The satire presented in these and many other Fox News segments on The Simpsons certainly raises awareness of partisan politics and media bias, but it also provokes larger questions about the relationship between the Fox Television network and the television show that has long been credited with building that network. When The Simpsons began in 1989, Fox was a newcomer to the network game and needed to carve out a niche, which it did by offering "edgy" and controversial fare—most provocatively with the show Married... with Children (1987–97). But Fox Television is also an outgrowth of News Corporation, the worldwide media conglomerate headed by Rupert Murdoch, a man whom many see as a ruthless corporate raider and an exemplar of social and economic conservatism. Such facts lead one to wonder how political perspectives that appear to stand in stark contrast to one another can coexist inside Fox Television and on The Simpsons. Since its inception in 1986, both Fox Television and News Corporation have grown significantly and have become powerful cultural forces. One thus has to ask: In what ways has this growth had an impact on the quality and/or content of *The Simpsons*? How much influence do News Corporation executives exert on Fox Television, and does this filter down to the content of *The Simpsons*? How have shifting political tides over the past two decades affected the satirical element of the show? Has *The Simpsons* become more "user friendly" over time? Has it become less satiric and more parodic, or even farcical?

Such questions lead to even larger ones about the possibilities for subversive or oppositional content on television. Considering that the satire on *The Simpsons* is so often aimed at consumer culture, greed, capitalism, television, and, of course, Rupert Murdoch and the Fox Television network, it might seem surprising that *The Simpsons* has remained on the air for so long. Of course, its appeal also lies in its status as a cartoon, its slapstick humor, and its wide-ranging parody, as noted previously. The aim of this chapter is to explore the subversive potential of *The Simpsons* by examining how the show engages with ideological and political debates within American culture. The show has been accused by many of being more "liberal" and less critical of the political Left than the political Right; however, the show has also been embraced and praised by many conservative commentators and viewers. Before interrogating how *The Simpsons* manages this feat, it is important to discuss first the origins of the Fox Television network. Placing *The Simpsons* within the context of the television system helps illuminate the potential for oppositional content and the limitations to that imposed by the show's position as part of a global media empire as well as a merchandising phenomenon. Since satire is the means by which *The Simpsons* most commonly offers oppositional views, it is also important to have a better understanding of this comedic mode; therefore, I will first provide an overview of the tradition in American satire, elaborating here upon ideas briefly presented in the previous chapter. I then discuss the divergent ways in which the satire of *The Simpsons* has been read and assessed by television critics and academic scholars, primarily to provide a frame for analyzing, in the chapters that follow, how *The Simpsons* intervenes in the conversations and debates over issues that have been central to the American "culture wars."

Fox Television, the "Coat-Hanger Network"

To fully understand *The Simpsons*, it is important to know how it first came to be and why it found a comfortable home on the newly formed Fox network, which appeared as a challenger to the Big Three networks (ABC, NBC, and CBS) in the mid-1980s. As Amanda Lotz points out, during the decade from approximately 1985 to 1995, the television industry in the United States experienced a host of dramatic shifts. She says,

> [A] variety of factors—including the success of cable and satellite transmission, the appearance of new broadcast networks, increased ownership conglomeration, decreased regulation, and the emergence of new technologies—combined to usher in a new era of industry competition, forcing adjustments by traditional broadcast networks...[and creating] a rupture commonly identified as the transition to a postnetwork or neo-network era.[8]

Prior to this transition out of the network era, the prospects of a fourth over-the-air broadcast network seemed dim. A new network had not been successfully established since the end of the short-lived DuMont network in 1955, and as the Big Three network oligopoly continued to strengthen during the 1960s and 1970s, the barriers to a fourth network seemed almost insurmountable. Even the Federal Communication Commission (FCC) concluded, in a 1980 special report on the television industry and its practices, that without significant structural changes to the existing system there was little chance for a new network to develop.[9] Of course, one of the prominent obstacles was the FCC's own station allotment plan, put forth in its 1952 *Sixth Report and Order*, which effectively limited the number of VHF channels available in major markets and intermixed VHF and UHF bands.[10] According to Thomas and Litman, this created a structural barrier that "essentially assured the dominance of the network triopoly" for more than two decades.[11] By the early 1980s, however, the potential for establishing a fourth network was much greater, primarily owing to three factors: a significant rise in advertising revenues; the increased number of commercial television stations; and the rapid penetration of pay cable television. Between 1979 and 1986, some 305 new UHF and 20 new VHF stations were established; additionally, as Sterling and Kittross note, cable service rose from just over 18 percent of households in 1979 to nearly 40 percent in 1984.[12]

Because of such changes in the industry, the timing was ideal for Rupert Murdoch to pursue his plan to create a new broadcast network in the United States, expanding the media empire he had established with newspaper holdings in both Australia and England. Creating a new television network was not initially part of Rupert Murdoch's scheme, but after realizing that the fields of entertainment and electronic media would be vital to expansion and financial growth in the United States, Murdoch sought to purchase Twentieth Century Fox in 1983, when the studio was displaying signs of financial difficulty. Although that attempt was blocked by the Warner chairman Steve Ross, Murdoch succeeded in purchasing a half interest in the studio from Marvin Davis, who in 1985 was in desperate need of financial assistance. Murdoch paid $250 million for the half interest in Fox, a figure most analysts agreed was a premium but that Murdoch saw as a wise investment: by this time he had begun planning for a fourth network in the United States, and he understood that owning the film library of the Twentieth Century Fox studio would provide a cost-effective source of programming.[13] Somewhat serendipitously, John Kluge was then looking to sell his company, Metromedia, which owned independent television stations in some of the largest markets in the country (New York, Boston, Chicago, Washington, DC, Dallas, Houston, and Los Angeles).[14] Murdoch purchased Metromedia in 1985 for $2 billion. Many believed the price to be outrageous at the time, but for Murdoch it was money well spent, considering that all of Metromedia's stations were using the VHF band and were located in prime markets. Once the foundation of Metromedia was secured, Murdoch set about acquiring newly available UHF stations as well and seeking out affiliates to broaden the potential reach of his planned new network. Part of the pitch Fox used to gain new affiliates was the changing media environment—that is, the shift to cable television and the increased segmentation of audiences. When the Fox Broadcasting Company, as it was initially called, finally made its debut in October 1986, it premiered on 99 television stations, giving it a coverage of approximately 80% of television households in the United States.[15]

Murdoch has worked hard since the mid-1980s to bring a vast number of media enterprises under the umbrella of News Corporation, which in the United States alone currently owns the Twentieth Century Fox film studio, the Fox Television network, the HarperCollins publishing house, satellite provider DirectTV, the Internet sites MySpace and Photobucket, *The Weekly Standard* magazine, and newspapers such as the *New York Post* and *The Wall Street Journal* (which it acquired along with its parent company, Dow Jones, in 2007). For many, the concentration of so many media entities in the hands of one man is cause for alarm, in part because of the belief that this inevitably leads to the narrowing of viewpoints and the promotion of just one political perspective. To be fair, Murdoch's personal politics are rather difficult to discern, as they have changed significantly over time; one can safely aver, however, that they generally skew rightward. In a 2005 feature on Rupert Murdoch for *New York* magazine, Jonathan Mahler—clearly not a fan of Murdoch, whom he refers to as "New York's preeminent right-wing robber baron"—argues that Murdoch's political position was firmly in place as early as 1976, when he acquired the *New York Post.* According to Mahler, it was while at the *Post* that Murdoch "perfected the mix of hard conservative politics and unapologetic tabloid values with which his name would become synonymous."[16] John Cassidy more recently noted that Murdoch, who has been a US citizen since 1985, is not a member of either of the two dominant political parties and thus not necessarily partisan; nonetheless, Cassidy says, "his political instincts are staunchly conservative—he dislikes taxes and government programs; he's for a strong defense policy; [and] he's suspicious of trade unions and regulators."[17] David McKnight offers a more nuanced view of Murdoch's politics, tracing its development from a "youthful leftism" through an Australian nationalism to a social and economic libertarianism, which he concludes "has been the defining political philosophy for this very political proprietor."[18] This perspective is more accurate, I think, as libertarianism melds better with Murdoch's well-established neoliberal economic views. As many have noted, Murdoch is driven less by a particular ideology than a concern for the bottom line, which means his priority is to use his media outlets and his wealth to promote policies that will benefit News Corporation—a goal that has been accomplished primarily by editorializing in favor of politicians who tout free-market capitalism and by making generous donations to the parties behind those candidates. As Reed Hundt, the chairman of the FCC from 1993 to 1997, accurately stated, "Rupert has amply demonstrated that he's quite willing and able to work with any political party or politician that he thinks is going to be influencing policy."[19] Of course, in most cases this has meant that Murdoch has backed the more conservative political party, as was the case with Margaret Thatcher and the Conservative Party in England and with Ronald Reagan, George Bush Sr., and George Bush Jr. and the Republican Party in the United States.[20] The real essence of Murdoch's position was succinctly and insightfully summed up by Andrew Neil, the former editor of London's *Sunday Times* (which has been owned by Murdoch since 1981), in his book *Full Disclosure.* Neil says,

> Rupert expects his papers to stand broadly for what he believes: a combination of right-wing Republicanism from America mixed with undiluted Thatcherism from Britain. The resulting potage is a radical-right dose of free-market economics, the social agenda of the Christian Moral Majority, and hardline conservative views on subjects like drugs, abortion, law and order, and defence.[21]

Most indicative of Murdoch's politics is his financial support of the neoconservative magazine *Commentary,* when it was still under the editorship of Norman Podhoretz, and his purchase (in 1995) and ongoing funding of the neoconservative magazine *The Weekly Standard*, founded by William Kristol (son of Irving Kristol, the editor of *Commentary* from 1947 to 1952), John Podhoretz (son of Norman Podhoretz and now a columnist for the *New York Post*), and Fred Barnes. Neil Chenoweth reports that Murdoch gave William Kristol a $3 million budget to launch *The Weekly Standard*, which was intended to be a conservative counterpart to *The New Republic*, and he has supported it financially ever since, at a loss of roughly $1 million per year.[22] Although it has a circulation of only about 60,000, *The Weekly Standard* is one of the most widely read insider magazines in Washington, and it exerts an enormous influence on politicians and policy making. As Eric Alterman puts it, "Reader for reader, it may be the most influential publication in America. The magazine speaks directly to and for power. Anybody who wants to know what the [Bush] administration is thinking and what they plan to do has to read this magazine."[23]

Rupert Murdoch, of course, is not the only player here. A less visible but very influential and quite formidable presence within News Corporation is Roger Ailes, who proudly boasts of his disdain for the Left and liberals in general. Among other things, Ailes was a former Republican Party strategist, helping to package and sell Richard Nixon in 1968, Ronald Reagan in 1984, and George H. W. Bush in 1988. Ailes had a hand in developing "tabloid TV" as well, aiding the launch of *The Maury Povich Show* in 1991 and working as a consultant on Fox's *A Current Affair* (1986–96), which was hosted by Povich; he was also the executive producer of *The Rush Limbaugh Show* (1992–96), a short-lived television version of Limbaugh's popular radio program. Ailes became the chief of programming at Fox News in 1996 and, most significantly, was responsible for the creation of Fox's enormously successful *The O'Reilly Factor* (1996–), which put conservative blowhard Bill O'Reilly on the cultural map.[24] Although Rupert Murdoch is the one who generally receives the most attention from the mainstream press, the changes in the media landscape resulting from the efforts of Roger Ailes should not be underestimated. As Jeffrey P. Jones notes, Ailes unleashed "a full-frontal attack on the long-running understanding that television news should center on the reporting of information, doing so in a fair, unbiased, and non-partisan manner. Instead, Fox News showed just how ruthlessly it would pursue audiences and broader conservative ideological dominance by playing on audience fears," especially in the wake of the terrorist attacks of September 11, 2001.[25]

Long before Ailes appeared at Fox, the person most responsible for the development of what was then called the Fox Broadcasting Company (FBC) was Barry Diller, who functioned as chairman and CEO of Fox, Inc. from October 1984 until April 1992. From the start, Diller wanted to approach the task of starting a new network by using people outside the television industry who would not be bound by the traditions of ABC, NBC, and CBS.[26] Diller first sought out Jamie Kellner, who had been president of Orion Pictures, and named him president of Fox television programming in February 1986. Together, Diller and Kellner essentially created and launched FBC. To many of the executives at the Big Three networks, the idea of a fourth network was an absurdity, not only because they had held dominance for so long but also because the Fox affiliate lineup was mainly comprised of low-powered UHF stations rather than those using VHF. Speaking before a group of advertisers in 1986, Brandon Tartikoff, then president of NBC, infamously dismissed the idea that Fox could succeed. As Kellner recalls, after Tartikoff had finished and introduced

Kellner as the next speaker, he needled him about Fox's UHF affiliates: "He took a coat hanger out and bent it in half and said, 'If anybody's having trouble getting Fox, just bring one of these home and attach it to your television set.'"[27]

Diller and Kellner first hired Chiat Day, the Los Angeles ad agency best known for their creative marketing of Apple computers and Nike shoes, to help market the Fox Broadcasting Company. Chiat Day's executives first suggested that Fox drop the acronym FBC—which made the network look and sound too much like the competition—and emphasize the name Fox, which could already be associated with a tradition of quality entertainment via the Twentieth Century Fox film studio. In a grandiose gesture, Chiat Day arranged to have the famous HOLLYWOOD sign transformed into the word *FOX* for the week of the network's later prime-time launch, in 1987. After negotiations with the City of Los Angeles, the Hollywood Chamber of Commerce, the LAPD, and a $25,000 payment, Fox won approval for the alteration, which Alex Ben Block calls "a brilliant publicity stunt."[28] Diller and Kellner also arranged to woo two programming executives, Garth Ancier and Kevin Wendle, away from NBC and over to Fox. At that time, Ancier was the head of comedy programming and Wendle the director of drama development at NBC, which had made itself into the must-see network of the 1980s with a string of hit shows, including *Cheers* (1982–93), *Family Ties* (1982–89), *The Cosby Show* (1984–92), *Night Court* (1984–92), and *The Golden Girls* (1985–92). Although Ancier and Wendle were junior executives at NBC, at Fox they were suddenly in charge of millions of dollars to develop programming for the new network, which was to be bold and experimental: in short, the intent was to provide "smart, irreverent, wiseass shows."[29] To get a sense of the type of programming that might appeal to younger viewers, Andrew Fessell (who had previously worked for Nielsen Media Research and was now vice president of research for Fox) organized a series of focus groups in the spring of 1986, but the results of these were not very helpful. Barry Diller's concept of a Fox show was, according to Mark Morrison, "an alternative to something. Not just another or better version of something that is already there. A little edge to it, but not necessarily edgy."[30] What Diller seemed to be seeking was something with the impudence of parody but not the sting of satire.

The Simpsons turned out to be just the kind of "edgy" show that the network needed to make a name for itself, but no one initially proposed a prime-time cartoon to launch the network. Instead, executives tried to be "edgy" within well-established genres, including the late-night talk show and the action-adventure serial—respectively, *The Late Show Starring Joan Rivers* (1986–87) and *Werewolf* (1987–88), which both aired on Saturday evenings. *The Late Show Starring Joan Rivers* was plagued by problems; Rivers had to constantly fight for control, despite initial promises for full creative control from Fox executives, and she repeatedly found herself in heated arguments over program content with Kevin Wendle, who was the executive in charge of *The Late Show*.[31] *Werewolf*, on the other hand, simply failed to generate much interest. In short, neither show worked very well as a form of "counterprogramming," and each failed to appeal to those specific demographic groups that both Murdoch and Diller believed were being ignored by the major networks: urban youth and ethnic minorities. Determined to prove that Fox was more than just an arm of the Twentieth Century Fox film studio, Diller decided to counterprogram against the Big Three on Sunday nights, which was when the networks often ran movies and reruns, knowing that this time slot would be crucial to the success of the new network.

The two shows developed for the Sunday night lineup—*Married...with Children* and *The Tracey Ullman Show*, which both premiered in April 1987—proved to be much more successful, and they cemented Fox's reputation for "edgy" and risqué programming. *Married...with Children*, a somewhat satiric spin on the nuclear family sitcom, and *The Tracey Ullman Show*, the comedy-variety show that introduced *The Simpsons* to America, helped set Fox apart from the other three networks and garner new viewers from the coveted demographic. It helped, of course, that *Married...with Children* also sparked some controversy, not because it was necessarily satirical but because it was pushing the boundaries of taste. *Married...with Children* came to be Fox's most controversial show and (much to Diller's later dismay) the program most closely associated with the new network in the public mind. Not surprisingly, *Married...with Children* became another source of battles over content. One of the early struggles came in 1989, when Garth Ancier told the producers of *Married...with Children* that a line was being cut from a third-season episode entitled "The Period Piece," in which all three of the show's female main characters simultaneously experience premenstrual syndrome. The controversy centered on a line uttered by Al Bundy during a scene in which he complains to his neighbor and friend Steve Rhodes about the women in his life and the effects of living with PMS: "I think PMS really stands for Pommel Men's Scrotums." Apparently the network felt it was too strong a description and had the line cut; the episode was delayed for a month, and when it finally aired it was retitled "The Camping Episode."[32] The decision to edit lines from the show was both surprising and ironic, considering that Fox executives had again offered full creative control to Ron Leavitt and Michael Moye, the producers of *Married...with Children*, and that the Fox network still boasted that it had no standards and practices department. Although some minor changes were made to this and other episodes of *Married...with Children*, there was still plenty of provocative content to air—enough to inspire Terry Rakolta, a mother from the suburbs of Detroit, Michigan, to initiate a viewer and advertiser boycott of the show, which she believed to be offensive and demoralizing. As she stated in an interview on *Nightline* in March 1989,

> I picked on *Married...With Children* because they are so consistently offensive. They exploit women, they stereotype poor people, they're anti-family. And every week that I've watched them, they're worse and worse. I think this is really outrageous. It's sending the wrong messages to the American family.[33]

Ironically, the boycott, receiving national press coverage, was successful only at raising awareness about Fox, which was still largely unknown to many viewers, and at prompting the public to seek out local Fox affiliates to see this controversial show.[34] The success of *Married...with Children* earned Fox a reputation for "shock-value" programming and sensationalism, and this helped pave the way for *The Simpsons*, which would eventually offer its own unique provocations, create different kinds of controversies, and initiate new battles over "appropriate" content on the Fox network.

The Simpsons came into existence largely because the fundamental programming strategy in Fox's earliest days was to target the same pool of creative talent being used by ABC, NBC, and CBS. One of the first established talents sought for new programming was James L. Brooks, the creator of such television milestones as *The Mary Tyler*

Moore Show (1970–77), *Rhoda* (1977–78), *Lou Grant* (1977–82), and *Taxi* (1978–83). To attract the producers who were in constant demand, and thereby to effectively compete with the Big Three, "Fox made an implicit promise of greater creative freedom, a chance to be more daring in language and content and, for the most part, little network interference in the day-to-day production process."[35] In 1984, James Brooks had left television and followed Barry Diller from Paramount to Twentieth Century Fox in order to make films. Brooks had great success with his first feature for Fox, *Broadcast News* (1987), which he both wrote and directed and which was produced by Gracie Films, the independent film and television production company that Brooks established in 1984. After being guaranteed creative license by Barry Diller, Brooks was willing to step again into television production and agreed to sign on with Fox. As Brooks recalls it, "Diller told me that I could do anything I wanted, that there'd be no censorship."[36] Fox then created a generous series development fund to allow Brooks to experiment and make pilots—and without any pressure to present the developed materials unless he was completely satisfied with them. "I loved the idea of a fourth network," says Brooks. "Barry said it would be lean—no bureaucratic layers, no censorship. It was raw, fledgling."[37] Brooks was allowed to choose either a half-hour or hour-long format, and he was given a guarantee that the network would buy 26 episodes, sight unseen. The result was *The Tracey Ullman Show*, for which Brooks proposed creating a series of "bumpers"—that is, 15- to 20-second shorts—to be used as exit points between skits and around commercial breaks on the show. Brooks contacted the cartoonist Matt Groening, whose work Brooks admired, about doing animated segments of his *Life in Hell* comic strip; instead, Groening created a set of new characters: *The Simpsons*. A total of 49 bumpers were made using *The Simpsons*; these were subsequently so popular that Fox commissioned a pilot production and 13 original episodes for airing in a prime-time slot.[38] Brooks then teamed up with the sitcom writer Sam Simon and Matt Groening to create rough cuts of the new series. Barry Diller initially felt it was a "huge risk" and suggested that they instead air four more specials to test the waters, but upon seeing the rough cuts, he immediately changed his mind about playing it safe.[39] With *The Simpsons*, Fox executives discovered a niche to compete with the other networks and soon found themselves in possession of a hit series. By the summer of 1990, after *The Simpsons'* first season was completed, Richard Zoglin could safely aver in *Time* magazine that "the most telling sign of Fox's success is the degree to which its once scornful rivals are taking notice. Gone are the days when NBC Entertainment chief Brandon Tartikoff could dismiss the fledgling program service as a 'coat-hanger network.'"[40]

Satirical Comedy and the Mass Media

To appreciate how *The Simpsons* functions as satire and why this type of humor found a comfortable home on the Fox network, it is important to have an understanding of the satirical tradition in American culture, particularly its use in the visual arts and mass media, especially television. Satire is a complex art form, one that relies upon an awareness of contemporary issues, a high level of literacy, and a healthy sense of irony to be truly understood. As one might expect, satire is widely misunderstood or misinterpreted today—if it is even recognized at all. This is partly because many people in the United States are, as the filmmaker Michael Moore once put it, "ironically illiterate." Of course, as William Savage rightly notes, the danger of misinterpreta-tion "inheres in any utterance complicated enough to be worth discussing," and this should not disqualify *The Simpsons* (or any other satirical text, for that matter) from being examined as "potential sources of cultural critique."[41] Another difficulty is that satire continues to be viewed primarily as a literary art form, yet we now live in a world defined not by the word but by the image. Literary satire certainly has a very long and distinguished tradition, which is why most discussions of satire today still tend to refer to the Greek, Roman, and English traditions and to standard-bearers such as Horace, Juvenal, Alexander Pope, and Jonathan Swift. In an American con-text, the name most often cited is Mark Twain, but recent studies of literary satire have also included the work of early twentieth-century American writers such as Nathanial West and, more commonly, some of the post–World War II writers associ-ated with "postmodernism"—for example, Kurt Vonnegut, Robert Coover, Donald Barthelme, Joseph Heller, Thomas Pynchon, Don DeLillo, and Ishmael Reed.[42] These writers, however, are just one part of a much longer tradition of satire in American culture, one that has informed a great variety of creative output in the visual arts. Satire has long been associated with the editorial cartoon, the newspaper comic strip, the comic book, and the graphic novel. As Chris Lamb explains in *Drawn to Extremes: The Use and Abuse of Editorial Cartoons* (2004), "[C]artoonists have con-tributed to the political and social fabric of America since the founding of the repub-lic, when Benjamin Franklin's crude drawing 'Join, or Die' called for a united front against England in 1754."[43] Although antecedents can be traced to the Revolutionary War period, the editorial cartoon did not actually flourish as an art until the mid-nineteenth century. Donald Dewey notes in *The Art of Ill Will: The Story of American Political Cartoons* (2007) that with the advent of lithography (ca. 1819), the replication of images was much easier; thus cartoons in print media such as newspapers became more common.[44] The editorial cartoon—which is most closely associated with the art of nineteenth-century satirists such as Thomas Nast, Joseph Keppler, and Bernhard Gillam—constitutes what Richard E. Marschall calls "a journalistic form" because of its ability to convey ideas and political perspectives in ways prose could not.[45] As Lamb, Dewey, and Marschall all make clear, satire was a common strategy of many artists whose editorial cartoons regularly served to criticize governmental politics and politicians. The creators of *The Simpsons* are well aware of this artis-tic legacy, and they have creatively incorporated it into their own satirical cartoon. The influence of Thomas Nast, for example, can be seen in the third-season episode "Mr. Lisa Goes to Washington" (September 1991), which is about Lisa's attempt to expose governmental corruption and which features a series of Nast-like drawings of corrupt Washington politicians depicted as "fat-cats" scratching one another's backs and "pigs" eating from troughs full of taxpayers' money.

The tradition of political cartooning continues to this day, of course, but as Donald Dewey explains, a satirical critique is now as likely to be found in the mul-tipanel comic strip as in the single-panel editorial cartoon.[46] At the end of the nine-teenth century, the nation saw the advent of "the funnies" and the multipanel comic strip, which were designed to attract new readers to the publications of newspaper magnates such as William Randolph Hearst.[47] Satire arrived a short time later, in the form of Al Capp's *L'il Abner* (1934–77) and Walt Kelly's *Pogo* (1943–75), both widely read in syndicated newspapers around the nation. Each offered broad social and political commentary, which "helped raise the status of comic books and strips among intellectuals," and they effectively set the template for today's satirical comic-strip artists.[48] A more broadly cultural form of comic satire was introduced by Harvey Kurtzman's *MAD* magazine, which first appeared as a four-color comic in 1952 and then changed to a magazine format in 1955.[49] *MAD* specialized in parody, offering humorous takes on elements of pop culture, such as advertising slogans, corporate logos, television shows, Hollywood film genres, and media personalities. However, as Stephen Kercher explains in *Revel with a Cause: Liberal Satire in Postwar America* (2006), from its start *MAD* magazine was also invested in satire as a means of critiquing American culture, exposing "all the cloying clichés and the smothering, sanctimonious ideals with which the American public was being bombarded" and attacking "the commercial practices, social conventions, and cultural institutions that underwrote postwar consensus ideology."[50]

The traditions established by Kelly, Capp, and especially Kurtzman have directly influenced an entire generation of cartoonists and satirists, including Matt Groening, creator of *The Simpsons*, who began his career with the underground comic *Life in Hell*. Like other artists of his generation—for example, Gary Trudeau (*Doonesbury*), Berkeley Breathed (*Bloom County, Outland*), Aaron McGruder (*The Boondocks*), and Tom Tomorrow (*This Modern World*)—Matt Groening has used satire in his art, although he was initially less overtly political than some of his peers. Gary Trudeau, for example, the elder statesman of this group, has been notoriously direct in his criticisms of politicians in *Doonesbury*, providing withering critiques of figures such as Ronald Reagan, George Bush Sr., Dan Quayle, Newt Gingrich, Bill Clinton, Janet Reno, and George Bush Jr., among others.[51] Breathed's *Bloom County*, on the other hand, while obviously influenced by *Doonesbury* and certainly politicized, was less direct in its approach; it limited the ridicule of individual real-world figures, yet it still offered potent critiques of media culture and of American domestic and foreign policy. Groening's *Life in Hell* was also less political, at least in its earliest years, and more focused on personal angst; however, after George Bush Sr. won the presidency in 1988, Groening—a committed Democrat who was already angry over the direction that the Reagan administration had taken the nation—vowed to make his comic strip more political, and he soon did so with direct assaults on Bush Sr. and Dan Quayle. The most prolific artist over the past ten years has been Aaron McGruder, whose comic *The Boondocks* "has made more waves more often than any nationally syndicated comic strip since Garry Trudeau's *Doonesbury*."[52] As might be expected, because of the political nature of their work, Trudeau, Breathed, McGruder, Groening, and others like them have been very vocally criticized, and their comic strips have, at one time or another, been censored and/or banned from leading national publications.[53]

As a "postmodern" text that draws upon multiple forms of popular culture, *The Simpsons* is situated within a tradition of satirical art that goes well beyond cartooning. The creators of the show also draw inspiration from the work of many film-makers who have made impressive use of satire in politically engaged comedic films, and homages to these satirical texts appear repeatedly in episodes of *The Simpsons*. Although examples of satiric film can be found in the early part of the twentieth century—for example, Charlie Chaplin's *The Great Dictator* (1940)—the use of satire in film, as in literature, appears to be more commonplace in the postwar environment, most famously, perhaps, in Stanley Kubrick's *Dr. Strangelove: Or, How I Learned to Stop Worrying and Love the Bomb* (1964). Over the past half century, satire has been employed by numerous writers and filmmakers to address a wide range of important contemporary issues, including war-mongering, commercialized violence, poverty, abortion, racism, and political corruption. Fine examples of this can be found in films such as Robert Altman's *MASH* (1970), Sidney Lumet's *Network* (1976), Terry Gilliam's *Brazil* (1985), Michael Moore's *Roger & Me* (1989), Alexander Payne's *Citizen Ruth* (1996), Tim Robbins's *Bob Roberts* (1992), Warren Beatty's *Bulworth* (1998), Spike Lee's *Bamboozled* (2000), Larry Charles's *Borat: Cultural Learnings of America for Make Benefit Glorious Nation of Kazakhstan* (2006), and Joshua Seftel's *War, Inc.* (2008). It is worth noting that most of these films were made outside of the Hollywood studio system; some were produced early in the filmmaker's career, and others were financed largely from independent sources, which allowed for a fair degree of autonomy and risk taking.[54]

Of course, most relevant to my examination of *The Simpsons* is the history of satire on television.[55] As Stephan Kercher notes, social and political satire was "indisputably a rare commodity on network television during the 1950s."[56] This was largely a consequence of the stifling influences of McCarthyism, Cold War jingoism, and the Red Scare, all of which encouraged passivity and conformity among citizens and led to what Carol Stabile and Mark Harrison refer to as "the ideological homogenization of the culture industries."[57] Nonetheless, nonconformist perspectives were occasionally expressed on network television, as in the social satire that peppered Sid Caesar's *Your Show of Shows* (1950–54) or in the routines of such outspoken comics as Mort Sahl and Dick Gregory, who appeared, in the latter part of the decade, as guests on variety and late-night talk shows, including *The Steve Allen Show* (1956–61) and *The Tonight Show* with Jack Paar (1957–62).[58] Satire also had a brief, though uneven, run in the early 1960s via NBC's attempt to create an American version of the BBC comedy *That Was the Week That Was* (1963–65). But the show that was truly groundbreaking and that has had the most lasting influence on those that followed is *The Smothers Brothers Comedy Hour* (1967–69), a CBS comedy/variety show featuring former stand-up comics Tom and Dick Smothers. *The Smothers Brothers Comedy Hour* was developed with the intention of wooing young audiences to the network, but in a very short time, *The Smothers Brothers Comedy Hour* transcended its humble beginnings and became the most controversial television program of the 1960s, notable not only for bringing political satire to network television but also for initiating a showdown with CBS executives over issues of free speech and censorship. After two years of very public wrangling over the content of sketches and controversial guests such as Pete Seeger, the CBS network president Robert D. Wood canceled *The Smothers Brothers Comedy Hour* in April 1969, ostensibly over the brothers' failure to meet a contractual deadline.[59]

The Simpsons owes much to the satirical comedy established by *The Smothers Brothers* and carried on in variety shows such as *Rowan and Martin's Laugh-In* (1968–73), *Saturday Night Live* (1975–), *In Living Color* (1990–94), and *Mad TV* (1995–2009). *In Living Color*, which appeared simultaneously with *The Simpsons* in 1990, was particularly important for its provocative and overtly political satire, helping to reaffirm the "edginess" of the Fox network early on and thereby to draw younger, urban viewers away from the Big Three.[60] Shows such as *In Living Color*, *Saturday Night Live*, and *Mad TV* have succeeded in large part because sketch comedy lends itself quite well to both parody and satire. The sitcom format, in contrast, was (and essentially still is) much less conducive to satire: as studies by David Marc, Gerard Jones, Darrell Hamamoto, and others attest, traditional and conservative ideologies were established as the "norm" for commercial television in the post–World War II years. Jones, for example, notes that the 1950s and 1960s television sitcoms were often didactic, functioning as a form of "pop-culture pedagogy" and quite consciously designed "to teach moral lessons in a mass cultural setting."[61] Moral lessons thus became normalized, accepted, and expected in television sitcoms; consequently, "satire and absurdity became harder to put on the air [and] the sitcom became mainstream America's candy-coated teacher."[62] In the 1970s, however, the template for the situation comedy changed dramatically, beginning with Norman Lear's *All in the Family* (1971–79), which CBS premiered only a year and a half after canceling *The Smothers Brothers Comedy Hour*. At first glance, this seems surprising, as it was clear from the pilot episode that Lear's new sitcom would be provocative if not controversial—indeed, Lear even provided a "warning" to the audience before the pilot began. In a voice-over, Lear read the following text, which viewers also saw on the television screen:

> The program you are about to see is *All in the Family*. It seeks to throw a humorous spotlight on our frailties, prejudices and concerns. By making them a source of laughter, we hope to show—in a mature fashion—just how absurd they are.[63]

CBS was willing to take the risk on *All in the Family* because of a simple reality: the television market was changing rapidly, as was American culture, and if CBS wanted to remain a competitive force, it needed to replace outdated Westerns and variety shows with new urban and "hip" forms of programming; this it did with *The Mary Tyler Moore Show* and *All in the Family*. These two shows, along with *MASH* (1972–83), which also aired on CBS, are examples of what David Marc calls the "literate" sitcom. In discussing the heyday of these three sitcoms, Marc argues that a shift in sensibility had clearly taken place, both on television and in American culture, and that the idea of the "moral lesson" in the television sitcom had not gone away, it had simply swung left—lessons were still being offered, but now rather than supporting the status quo, they were challenging it.[64] Arnold Hano, writing for *The New York Times*, captured this well in his assessment of *All in the Family* after its first season. He said,

> Fifty million Americans are being told, week after week, it does you no good to be a bigot. You end up where you began, plagued by fears and doubts, confused by a world you refuse to accept, clinging to a world that no longer exists. And it is done with laughter…It is to America's credit that satire is succeeding on that unlikeliest of media, TV.[65]

In *Nervous Laughter: Television Situation Comedy and Liberal Democratic Ideology* (1989), Darrell Hamamoto similarly notes a changed perspective in sitcoms, beginning in the 1970s and continuing into the 1980s, and claims that the lessons being offered by television were becoming "progressively more liberating."[66] This was evident in spinoffs from *All in the Family*, such as *Maude* (1972–78) and *The Jeffersons* (1975–85); in shows focused on the black working class, such as *Sanford and Son* (1972–77) and *Good Times* (1974–78); and in shows following in the tradition of *Mary Tyler Moore*, featuring women as struggling singles, single mothers, and/or members of the paid workforce, such as *Rhoda* (1974–78), *One Day at a Time* (1975–84), *Alice* (1976–85), *Roseanne* (1988–1997), and *Murphy Brown* (1988–98). By the early

1990s, Michael Tueth argues, "viewers had come to expect, even in the familiar format of the situation comedy, some presentation of alternative viewpoints and more-or-less direct challenges to the prevailing values and social norms."[67] Tueth's claim is a bit hyperbolic, although it does underscore the idea that a trend was in place, and this trend set the stage for the provocative fare soon to be offered by the upstart Fox Television network.

The Simpsons and the Satirical Tradition

The Simpsons fits very well into the trend toward more "literate" and progressive situation comedies outlined by Marc, Jones, and Hamamoto and into the trajectory of "liberal satire" more broadly traced by Kercher. The aforementioned "Mr. Spritz Goes to Washington" and "The Fool Monty" episodes, with their overt display of disdain for Fox News—and by extension, of the right-wing political views the channel often spotlights—are fine examples of the generally leftist politics of the show. The critiques offered in these and similar episodes are also a confirmation of what many fans and television critics have claimed all along: that *The Simpsons* is one of the most sophisticated shows on network television. Clearly, much of the success of *The Simpsons* stems from its "double-codedness" (i.e., its remarkable combination of low-brow comedy and high-brow wit). As Rebecca Farley reminds us, "double-coding" is a concept used to refer to texts that are composed of two "layers" of meaning that can be decoded by audiences: one layer, the more simplistic, relies upon relatively unsophisticated visuals for its humor, while the other layer, the more complex, relies upon sophisticated verbal jokes.[68] Many have commented on *The Simpsons'* ability to skillfully combine slapstick humor with political satire, making it appealing to children and adults alike. As discussed in the introductory chapter, part of the (primarily visual) appeal of *The Simpsons* is its widespread use of parody as a means of providing both humor and identification for audiences. My interests, however, are in the more complex layer that Farley speaks of, where one finds not only witty "verbal jokes" but sophisticated social satire. The distinction I am drawing here between parody and satire is the same one that underlies Vladimir Nabokov's oft-quoted comment used as an epigraph at the start of this chapter. My emphasis, however, is quite different, and astute readers will recognize that I am ironically invoking Nabokov. Nabokov's pithy statement stands alone quite well as a maxim, but its meaning remains elusive without proper context. As Nabokov repeatedly pointed out, he preferred parody to satire; he was much more interested in "the game" than "the lesson." For Nabokov, satire was simply too didactic. As a writer, Nabokov was more intrigued by the play parody afforded, as can be seen in such seminal works as *Lolita* and *Pale Fire* (both of which, ironically enough, are often viewed as satirical texts by literary critics). In *The Annotated Lolita*, Alfred Appel points out that Nabokov regularly called attention to parody in his work and also "repeatedly denied the relevance of satire," eschewing the "overtly moralist stance of the satirist."[69] As Nabokov himself stated in an interview with Alvin Toffler, published in *Playboy* magazine, "I have neither the intent nor the temperament of a moral or social satirist."[70] Later in this same interview, Nabokov dismisses what might today be called socially conscious or political art. He says,

A work of art has no importance whatever to society. It is only important to the individual, and only the individual reader is important to me. I don't give a damn for the group, the community, the masses, and so forth. Although I do not care for the slogan "art for art's sake"—because unfortunately such promoters of it as, for instance, Oscar Wilde and various dainty poets, were in reality rank moralists and didacticists—there can be no question that what makes a work of fiction safe from larvae and rust is not its social importance but its art, only its art.[71]

Nabokov speaks of art in a rather purist and highly individualist sense here. I too do not care for the slogan "art for art's sake," but I find Nabokov's comments—his protest notwithstanding—a strong echo of that very viewpoint. Nevertheless, I believe that Nabokov's claim about parody and satire is quite insightful. I elect to read against the grain, however, and reverse the focus. Since I am one of those who reads *Lolita*, for example, as a satirical critique of American culture, I am inclined toward art that has what Nabokov calls "social importance," and satire strikes me as more important in that sense than parody. In this and the remaining chapters, satire will be viewed as an elevated, serious, and ultimately more important art form; parody, for my purposes, will be thus subordinated to a position as a strategy of satire, akin to irony, sarcasm, juxtaposition, incongruity, and exaggeration.

As noted previously, many of the early assessments of *The Simpsons* commented on its satirical qualities. This has continued to be a constant refrain in commentary on the show in the mainstream press; indeed, the majority of journalists who have written critiques of *The Simpsons* have tended to highlight the satire. For example, in a very insightful 1997 article examining the role of satire on network and cable television, Joanne Ostrow, the television critic for *The Denver Post*, argues that *The Simpsons* "takes aim at America's blind devotion to consumerism and junk culture, and skewers reactionary thinking in all forms, making sophisticated political points in the context of a cartoon."[72] Similarly, in an article for *The Boston Globe* in 2003, the television critic Matthew Gilbert calls *The Simpsons* "a ruthless satire of America… [filled with] biting social criticism."[73] An emphasis on the satirical element of *The Simpsons* has been common in academic writing about the show as well. For example, Paul Cantor, one of the early defenders of the show in the academic community, claims that *The Simpsons* "offers some of the most sophisticated comedy and satire ever to appear on American television."[74] In their contribution to the collection *"The Simpsons" and Philosophy* (2000), authors William Irwin and J. R. Lombardo note that the show is "rife with satire, sarcasm, irony, and caricature."[75] And in his introduction to the essay collection *Leaving Springfield: "The Simpsons" and the Possibilities of Oppositional Television*, John Alberti boldly states that *The Simpsons* "represents some of the most daring cultural and political satire in television history, beyond even the groundbreaking *Saturday Night Live*."[76]

The acclaim given *The Simpsons* for its intelligence, humor, and sophisticated satire is substantial, but there was a period of time when the show was not well received and met with some rather harsh criticism for not living up to the high standards established in the earliest seasons. Writing for *Salon* in 2000, for example, Jamie Weinman noted that the quality of *The Simpsons* appeared to be in continual decline, despite the praise of some television critics.[77] Although such critique is an inevitable part of the consumption of mass-marketed commodities, it was surprising to find this coming even from longtime fans of the show. Many fans, myself included, noted a significant change after the "peak" years (roughly, the first eight seasons) and a loss of the satirical edge that made the show so unique. By the end of the tenth season, there was a strong consensus that the show had run out of steam—or was at least low on energy—and it was regularly criticized for becoming farcical and pointless. The harsh criticism of *The Simpsons* was abundant in the commentary posted in chat rooms on the Internet, whereas, with the exception of Weinman's essay, it was still minimal in the mainstream media. In the mid-1990s, when the Internet was still in its infancy, tech-savvy fans of *The Simpsons* were posting commentary about individual episodes on the alt.tv.simpsons newsgroup. As Weinman notes,

> [I]f you turn to alt.tv.simpsons, the show's Internet discussion group, it's as if a different show is being talked about. New episodes are routinely panned and held up as evidence that *The Simpsons* has been vulgarized and cheapened. For example, the reviews for this season's opening episode (the one with Mel Gibson) include phrases like "a weak offering of recycled themes," "not many laughs" and, best of all, "I think Homer was hired as a script consultant for this episode."[78]

Some of the contributors to the discussion group provide insightful articulations of why they believe the show has declined in quality. In the words of one fan, Ondre Lombard, *The Simpsons* has "turned into a cold, cynical, anything-for-a-joke series with one-dimensional characters."[79] And the alt.tv.simpsons regular Ben Collins wrote, "The staff believes its own hype. When *TV Guide* says *The Simpsons* is better than ever...the producers run with it, and drag the show through the same rut it's been in for two seasons."[80] By 1995, some fans were becoming more critical (even hostile) and the phrase "worst episode ever" began to appear frequently. The writers, who often reviewed the newsgroup, spoke back to these criticisms in the 1997 episode "The Itchy & Scratchy & Poochie Show." In his review of a new episode of the retooled cartoon show, the Comic Book Guy writes, "Last night's 'Itchy & Scratchy' was, without a doubt, the worst episode ever. Rest assured that I was on the Internet within minutes, registering my disgust throughout the world." Subsequently, the harshest critics in the online discussion groups regularly opened their missives with the tagline "Worst episode ever," an allusion to the small-scale tiff between a few of the writers and some the show's fans.[81] By 2002, the criticisms of the show's quality had become more widespread. In October that year, in an essay for MSNBC quite bluntly titled "*The Simpsons* Has Lost Its Cool," Jon Bonné claims that *The Simpsons*, "once an honest, irreverent portrait of the American family," had "become tired." Bonné continues:

> After more than a decade of revolutionary television, *The Simpsons*—a show that has redefined television for a generation of viewers and is arguably as influential as *I Love Lucy* or *Star Trek*—seems to be gathering momentum on a downhill roll toward mediocrity. When the mighty fall, they fall mightily.[82]

Al Jean, one of the producers who has been with the show from its start, even admits to some problems with quality over the long term. In a 2003 interview on NPR's *Talk of the Nation*, Jean points out the difficulties of being on the air for more than 300 episodes:

> [W]e find it harder and harder not to repeat ourselves. So whereas before we could do simple stories, like Bart is menaced by a bully or Marge considers having an affair, now we have shorter ideas that may not fill a full episode, you know, but that are different

from ones we've done. So I think it's gotten a little faster paced and maybe a little more schizophrenic because of that.[83]

Jean's comments are an accurate description of many episodes of the post-peak seasons—and they seem to confirm that the show experienced a creative lull period. However, in more recent years, there has been a resurgence of energy, partly because of an influx of new writers and partly because of social and political changes in the country after September 11, 2001. Only one year after lamenting the mediocrity of *The Simpsons*, Jon Bonné was back on MSNBC claiming that *The Simpsons*, in its fifteenth season, was back on track and "back to its satirical roots," featuring episodes with "more social satire and less Jerkass Homer."[84] Bonné's reassessment of *The Simpsons* echoed the views of critics such as Matthew Gilbert of *The Boston Globe*, cited previously, and David Carr of *The New York Times*, who earlier that year noted that *The Simpsons* (and other cartoons like it) are "able to get away with a surprising amount of trenchant social critique."[85]

In her engaging article on the "rebirth" of satire on television (primarily on HBO), Joanne Ostrow rightly points out that, "[S]atire always has had an uneasy relationship with TV," and she notes one of the key ironies of even discussing satire and the medium of television in the same breath: "[S]elling the commercial networks on a sort of comedy that aims to be not merely entertaining but subversive is a tough job. Putting satire on TV means walking a fine line between exposing the folly of our consumer society while hoping to keep millions of potential consumers in their seats."[86] A more pessimistic view is offered by John Matoian, a veteran of both Fox and CBS, who claims that satire simply cannot thrive on the commercial networks, whose owners fear, he says, that "the audiences may not be in on the joke, or the advertising community may not be in on the joke. There are so many more restraints in commercial television."[87] Despite Matoian's claims, satire has managed to succeed, if not thrive, in many ways over a long period of time on commercial television, as is evident from the body of scholarship referenced in this chapter. As Douglas Kellner notes in his essay "TV, Ideology, and Emancipatory Popular Culture," "[C]omedy and satire have often been effective means of social criticism and enlightenment, and television has been rife with both."[88] This is not to say, however, that satirists have been free to criticize and ridicule indiscriminately or that their satire has not been tempered or modified in some way by commercial interests. One good example of this is in the experience of the filmmaker Michael Moore in creating programming for both network and cable television. Moore's first foray into television satire was *TV Nation*, which began life on NBC, as a summer replacement, in 1994 and then moved to Fox for its second season. Though the show won an Emmy for "Outstanding Informational Series" for its 1994 season, it failed to gather a large audience and was soon canceled. Moore's next attempt was with *The Awful Truth*, which aired on the Bravo Channel. It only lasted two seasons (a total of 24 episodes), airing from April 1999 to June 2000. Of course, for Moore, the difficulty in getting such shows to succeed is not only about the obstacles posed by advertisers and nervous television executives; it is also about the audience, especially in the United States. In a 1999 discussion of *The Awful Truth* with Scott Simon on NPR's *Weekend Edition*, Moore bluntly states,

> I live in a country where satire, for some reason, has been forgotten and where many of our citizens are ironically illiterate. This show is in part produced by a British network

called Channel 4. The Brits, the Irish, the Canadians, they completely understand and appreciate satire.[89]

To a degree, Moore's comment is disingenuous, for a certain amount of responsibility rests with the artist as well, whose job as a satirist is to walk that fine line between passionate politics and didacticism. Presenting satire on television—or in any format, for that matter—is a tricky balancing act. As Ostrow succinctly states,

> Satire is difficult because it can so easily fall flat or go over the top. Only a gifted writer can successfully lift the material above the already wacky headlines, to deliver something that's ironic but not mean-spirited, a work that ridicules without being ridiculous, something fanciful enough to be fun but with a message delicately woven between the lines.[90]

Matt Groening—who has repeatedly stated that he intends *The Simpsons* to be political, satirical, and subversive—is clearly aware of the difficulties of getting satire to work on television, especially in formats noted for being apolitical and mindless: the situation comedy and the animated cartoon. Stabile and Harrison point out that the little attention devoted to the scholarly study of television animation

> attests to its double devalued status: as the offspring of a conventionally devalued medium (television) whose cultural products have only recently been considered worthy of scholarly scrutiny, and as the odd recombinant form of two similarly degraded genres—the situation comedy or sitcom and the cartoon.[91]

Of course, the devalued position of these art forms ironically makes the animated television show the perfect vehicle for subversive and oppositional content. In an early interview in *Rolling Stone* magazine, Groening stated, "The secret thing I'm trying to do, behind the entertainment, is to subvert. And if I can make myself and my friends laugh and can annoy the hell out of a political conservative, I feel like I've done my job."[92] Not surprisingly, Groening's inspiration for politically engaged cartooning comes primarily from Jay Ward, the creator of *The Bullwinkle Show*, "a short-lived series with a legendary afterlife because of its subversive wit."[93] Groening explains that on the heels of his success with the *Life in Hell* comics, he was called by many Hollywood producers, but he says, "[W]hen they asked what I wanted to do, I said Jay Ward, and they showed me the door." Jim Brooks was different, Groening explains: "He had *Life in Hell* on his wall in his office, and he gave me a call. He didn't show me the door."[94] Groening, who is a lifelong Democrat, considers America to be "a peculiar combination of libertarian self-indulgence and right-wing authoritarianism" and thus deserving, if not in need of, the satirist's scorn.[95] Still, Groening is also quite conscious of how one has to convey "subversive" content in the modern mass media:

> [W]e want people to question, to read. There's a subtext going on with the show that it's OK to be smart, that if you read more books then you get more jokes. But you know what? TV is a barrage of urgent imagery and alarms interspersed with urgent imagery trying to sell you something. So, to operate in that arena, you have to be garish, bold, and physical. You have to hit people over the head with physical gags. No matter how clever you are, you've got to have Homer slam into a brick wall at some point.[96]

For the media scholar Douglas Rushkoff, this subterfuge is key to the success of *The Simpsons* and what makes it an effective "media virus," which is his term for those texts that are able to "infect" the mainstream media with "subversive messages" and "countercultural missiles."[97] Rushkoff elaborates on this idea in his book *Media Virus*, in which he discusses what he calls "media controllers" and "media activists." The media controllers are those who, in the immortal words of Noam Chomsky, "manufacture consent"; the media activists are the "rebels" who subvert the ideological consensus and norms. According to Rushkoff, media activists use viruses to get the mainstream media to "unwittingly promote countercultural agendas that can empower the individuals who are exposed to them."[98] Although the term "virus" is imbued with negative and harmful connotations, and thus seems something of a misnomer here, Rushkoff intends for us to see media viruses as having a positive effect. For Rushkoff, media viruses lead to "evolution." In other words, a media virus is indeed harmful and destructive, but only of traditional and outdated thoughts and beliefs; if it works well, it is consequently constructive of more progressive (and implicitly liberal) ideologies. Rushkoff sees *The Simpsons* as a powerful media virus and argues that the creators of *The Simpsons* consciously choose from the vast array of topics and images available to them and arrange these in a certain way for certain effects, which constitutes an ideological agenda. Though intriguing, Rushkoff's ideas are not without problems. Overall, Rushkoff provides a rather tenuous argument: he is often vague about effects—as in his phrase "some sort of evolution"—and he does not take careful consideration of the ways in which media viruses could have negative consequences. Nonetheless, I do believe his idea is helpful in considering a show such as *The Simpsons*, which is known to have a great many Left-leaning writers and producers on staff and, as satire, is ideologically invested. With an eye toward satire, Rushkoff states, "[T]he media images they [the creators] choose to dissemble are the ones they perceive need to be exposed and criticized."[99] For Rushkoff, animated television programming serves as the perfect vehicle for media viruses because it has "a sufficiently innocuous appearance to permit its irreverence." In short, Rushkoff subscribes to the double-coding theory of television. Of *The Simpsons* he says, "The audience interested in its subversive attitudes is not large enough to keep the show in business, but the millions of kids who tune in every week to watch Bart are. A popular animated children's show is the perfect virus."[100] Other commentators have clearly found Rushkoff's ideas to be useful. David Arnold, for example, follows Rushkoff's lead in claiming that "virus-like, [*The Simpsons*] lulls us into lowering our intellectual defenses, then infects us with satiric, subversive ideas."[101]

Such claims invariably raise questions about what exactly is being satirized and subverted by *The Simpsons*. As noted in the introduction, I believe the show has many specific targets, such as racism, sexism, consumerism, religious fundamentalism, and homophobia. To better understand why these are targets of the show's satire, it is important to have some historical context. As scholars of satire and satirical art have pointed out, satire often derives from frustration with the status quo, indignation over current affairs, and resentment of social wrongs. In a 1999 interview for *Mother Jones* magazine, Brian Doherty asked Matt Groening about his inspiration and the sources of his indignation. Groening's reply is illuminating and worth quoting in its entirety:

> For me, it's not enough to be aware that most television is bad and stupid and pernicious. I think, "What can I do about it?" Is it the nature of the medium, the structure of the networks these days, or some failure of the creators that keeps television so lousy?

I feel a bit like a fish trying to analyse its own aquarium water, but what I want to do is point out the way TV is unconsciously structured to keep us all distracted. With *The Simpsons* and *Futurama*, what I'm trying to do is nudge people, jostle them a little, wake them up to some of the ways in which we're being manipulated and exploited. And in my amusing little way, I try to hit on some of the unspoken rules of our culture. *The Simpsons'* message over and over again is that your moral authorities don't always have your best interests in mind.[102]

In another interview, Groening derides the political climate of the United States as "one of bland consumption and conservatism" and says he makes no apologies for the political content and subversive intent of *The Simpsons*: "Entertain and subvert," he says, "that's my motto."[103]

Of course, the view of *The Simpsons* as satirical and subversive is neither uniform nor unproblematic. The executive producer James Brooks, for example, seems hard-pressed to label the show as subversive. In a 1990 interview with Tom Shales, Brooks concedes that the humor on the show can be wicked and sly, but he rejects the term "subversive," which some in the mainstream press had used to describe *The Simpsons*. Brooks says, "We don't sit down to be subversive. One man's subversive is another man's brash. I don't think of it that way."[104] The producer Mike Reiss similarly claims that the show's creators have no particular agenda to promote. However, in an interview with Douglas Rushkoff, he does admit that the show can have an influence. Reiss says,

> *The Simpsons* is the ultimate of what you call a media virus. It sounds a little insidious because I have kids of my own, and the reason we're a hit is because so many kids watch us and make us a huge enterprise. But we're feeding them a lot of ideas and notions that they didn't sign on for.[105]

Even Matt Groening himself has made comments that appear to partially contradict others he has made that profess to an overt politics, such as those quoted earlier. In a 1998 interview in the *Christian Science Monitor*, for example, Groening says, "For me, it's hard to approach satire directly. I don't think we sit down and say 'How do we satirize this subject?' We are trying to make a solid half-hour of entertainment."[106]

More significantly, certain academics have viewed *The Simpsons* as unsuccessful, seeing the promise of its satirical critiques unfulfilled in a variety of ways. One of the more dismissive readings of *The Simpsons* comes from James M. Wallace, who approaches the show from a Marxist perspective in his essay "A (Karl, Not Groucho) Marxist in Springfield." Early on, Wallace does concede that *The Simpsons* is full of "thoughtful laughter," that it uses incongruity to encourage us "to at least think about how we normally see the world," and that it at times "distances us momentarily from the prevailing ideology of capitalist America."[107] However, he ultimately believes that the show fails as a satire, largely because it offers no image of "what the ideal world is supposed to look like" or has "no vision of what the world should be."[108] Lacking this, he says, "*The Simpsons* does little more than string together isolated and transitory comical moments that in the aggregate add up to no discernible, consistent political point of view, let alone a subversive one."[109] Wallace later concludes that *The Simpsons* is

> the worst kind of bourgeois satire since it not only fails to suggest the possibility of a better world, but teases us away from serious reflection on or criticism of prevailing

practices, and, finally, encourages us to believe that the current system, flawed and comical as it sometimes is, is the best one possible.[110]

From a rigidly Marxist perspective, Wallace has a fair claim: neither of the two episodes he analyzes—"Scenes from the Class Struggle in Springfield" and "Last Exit to Springfield"—offers the kind of indictment of classism or capitalism that would satisfy a Marxist. As I intend to discuss both of these episodes in much greater detail in chapter 5, I will just briefly note here that I do not share Wallace's interpretation of these episodes, nor do I subscribe to his overall view of *The Simpsons*, for two particular reasons. The first is that Wallace conveniently ignores elements of the narrative of each episode that do not support his thesis. The second, and more important, is Wallace's (mis)understanding of satire, evident in his expectation that the satirist provide a "solution" or utopian vision. Though this has been an element of some satirical literature, it is not the primary objective of satire. As Brian Connery and Kirk Combe note in *Theorizing Satire*, "[S]atire tends toward openness and irresolution."[111] In *Satire: A Critical Reintroduction,* Dustin Griffin similarly claims that satire is "an 'open' [rather] than a 'closed' form, both in its formal features (particularly in its reluctance to conclude) and in its more general rhetorical and moral features, in its frequent preference for inquiry, provocation, or playfulness rather than assertion and conclusiveness."[112] Steven Weisenburger makes an even more emphatic assertion along these lines in *Fables of Subversion* by distinguishing between "generative" and "degenerative" satire. Reading contemporary satire within the context of postmodernist thought, Weisenburger argues that degenerative satire aims to "delegitimize"; he says, "[L]oosely in concord with deconstructionist thought, it functions to subvert hierarchies of value and to reflect suspiciously on all ways of making meaning, including its own."[113] I do not want to engage here in defining the postmodern or debating the status of *The Simpsons* as a postmodern text, but I believe it is safe to say that the show operates in what many have called a postmodern society—that is, a culture and an era defined by information exchange, by "spectacle" and spectatorship (following Debord), by the "ecstasy of communication" (following Baudrillard), and by the fast-moving images of advertising and other forms of mass media. The satire present on *The Simpsons* functions within this context; it is designed to raise awareness about what is wrong, harmful, or oppressive in the culture and to provoke thought about how it might be improved, but it does not necessarily offer a blueprint for corrective action.

Another negative assessment of *The Simpsons* comes from Carl Matheson, who also sees the show as a failure, though for him this is due to a pervasive "hyper-irony," which Matheson believes undermines any purported agendas. In *"The Simpsons, Hyper-Irony, and the Meaning of Life,"* Matheson begins by questioning whether or not *The Simpsons* "uses its humor to promote a moral agenda."[114] Borrowing from ideas articulated in Frederick Jameson's famous essay, "Postmodernism, or the Cultural Logic of Late Capitalism," Matheson reads *The Simpsons* within the context of a postmodern "crisis of authority" and the "death of the idea of progress" and argues that the show is caught up in the endless play of parody, pastiche, and quotationalism. Matheson thus concludes that *The Simpsons* "does not promote anything, because its humor works by putting forward positions only in order to undercut them" through "hyper-ironism."[115] In other words, for Matheson, *The Simpsons* might at first appear to have a moral agenda and a political philosophy, but in the end everything, including the show's supposed endorsement of "family values," is sacrificed for the sake of a joke. Curiously, the episode Matheson cites to support his view—and it is the only episode he discusses in any detail—is "Scenes from the Class Struggle in Springfield." Like Wallace, Matheson has found an easy target. To be fair, I too have problems with this particular episode—it raises some very important questions about classism in American culture but never fully interrogates them—and am thus is accord with Wallace and Matheson on this point. Indeed, as already mentioned, I have broader concerns about how socioeconomic class is dealt with overall on *The Simpsons*, which I will address directly in chapter 5. But I believe it is a mistake to extrapolate, as Wallace and Matheson do, from a few episodes to the entirety of the series.

A slightly different approach is taken by Ted Gournelos, who also offers a rather harsh assessment of the viability of critique on *The Simpsons*. Gournelos notes that the allusive quality of the show that Jonathan Gray analyzes in such depth in *Watching with "The Simpsons"* (which I discussed in the introductory chapter) does help to bypass some of the criticisms levied at most media texts—for example, as good or bad, utopian or dystopian. As Gournelos rightly observes, rather than relying on static texts, authors, and readers, the creators of *The Simpsons* make use of unstable interpretations to create "a stable *community* in which instability is an aesthetic and mode of self-aware critique."[116] Gournelos argues that this community of readers can, at least to a degree, "operate outside a limited capital-user (superstructure-base) binary" and thereby "propose cultural and political change through an education into the modes and techniques by which ideology operates and hegemony is established/maintained."[117] However, Gournelos concludes, *The Simpsons* and its viewers do not escape the capitalist systems in which they operate and are subject to the same kinds of criticisms aimed at irony in the public sphere. He says,

> Interpretive communities, based on intertextual irony or not, are not necessarily aware of their own place within the logic of capital. Even if they are, to be critical of *some* modes of ideology is not necessarily to be aware of *all* of them. This is particularly the case with *The Simpsons*' reliance on a problematic "American every-family," in which the privileged point of view is not questioned (as it often is in other shows, such as *King of the Hill* or *Beavis and Butthead*) but rather gently rendered as more idyllic than the reality of poverty allows (e.g., with frequent expensive vacations and adventures, encounters with Others, etc.). Structural racism, sexism, and a lack of class awareness (among many other issues) are thus completely imbricated into the world of *The Simpsons*, with occasional moments of critique overshadowed by a return to a status quo of harmony and happiness without consequences or enduring social developments. This renders the allusive strategies of the show politically neutral beyond their pedagogical role in media awareness.[118]

To begin with, I think it is quite debatable whether a privileged point of view is questioned in a program like *Beavis and Butthead*. More importantly, it is too simplistic to argue that the return to a "status quo" indicates a failure of the satire on *The Simpsons*. Indeed, this is one of the means by which the show can "reset" itself precisely in order to keep interrogating problems such as racism, sexism, or classism. While I agree that such issues are imbricated in the show, I do not believe they are merely reified, as Gournelos implies, but regularly interrogated (albeit in sometimes contradictory and not unproblematic ways). I would not go so far as to claim the show is "politically neutral," nor would I discount the power of the pedagogical role to be played by the show, given the burgeoning interest in media literacy programs, mass media studies, and popular culture studies at all levels of education in the United States today, a phenomenon perhaps best captured in Karma Waltonen and Denise Du Vernay's recently published book *"The Simpsons" in the Classroom: Embiggening the Learning Experience with the Wisdom of Springfield* (2010). The satire on *The Simpsons* is at times unclear and inconsistent, but in my view the show succeeds more often than not in raising awareness of serious cultural problems and censuring the simplistic, hypocritical, and often persecutory ways these are discussed and dealt with in American society.

Conclusion

The Simpsons is assuredly a sitcom that, like many of its 1990s peers, has self-consciously questioned the idea of a "moral lesson" and has often used this as a basis for both parody and satire. And yet satire itself is, as Dustin Griffin puts it, "a moral art."[119] So how are we to understand these conflicting strains? I began by posing some questions about the satirical status of *The Simpsons*. Can a satire thrive on network television? And, if so, what purposes can it serve? The media scholar Douglas Kellner provides one way for us to think about the answers to such questions. In his essay "TV, Ideology, and Emancipatory Popular Culture," Kellner notes that the images and narratives of television contain contradictory messages, reproducing the conflicts of advanced capitalist society and ideology and thus opening space for what he calls "emancipatory popular culture."[120] By this Kellner means that popular culture artifacts such as television programs can function in oppositional ways. This is an important opening up of the examination of ideology in mass culture, which has been viewed previously in strictly hegemonic terms, particularly in relation to television. As numerous scholars have explained, television is stilled viewed by many, on both the right and the left ends of the political spectrum, as a form of passive indoctrination. This is not to say that mainstream media no longer function as they used to or no longer convey messages designed to keep the populace in line with middle-class norms; rather, it highlights the fact that the system is by no means total-izing or capable of fully policing all of its boundaries and borders. Given that various forms of mass media still have the power to teach us how to fit in with the dominant norms, values, and practices of contemporary American society, it is imperative that we develop a media literacy; this crucial skill is a means of coping with a seductive cultural environment, a method for resisting media manipulation, and an invitation to create forms of emancipatory popular culture. For Kellner, the value of the last of these is quite clear:

> Emancipatory popular culture challenges the institutions and way of life of advanced capitalist society. It generally has the quality of shock, forcing people to see aspects of society that they had previously overlooked, or it focuses attention on the need for change. Emancipatory popular culture subverts ideological codes and stereotypes, and shows the inadequacy of the rigid conceptions that prevent insight into the complexi-ties and changes of social life. It rejects idealizations and rationalizations that apologize for the suffering in the present social system, and, at its best, suggests that another way of life is possible.[121]

What Kellner describes here is akin to the definition of satire given by Griffin, Kercher, and Weisenburger, among others, in that it emphasizes four key elements: awareness, resistance, subversion, and change. This subversive and resistant strain, this questioning of norms and of the dominant order, is one of the qualities that originally drew me to *The Simpsons* many years ago, and it is one of the things that I still find compelling about the show. It is this oppositional stance that I intend to explore in more detail in the following chapters, examining in the process the ways in which the show engages issues and debates central to the ongoing culture war. This engagement with many of the culture war issues certainly makes *The Simpsons* a unique piece of American popular culture. More importantly, though, it also makes *The Simpsons* a valuable barometer of shifting sensibilities and an important resource for better understanding some of the key ideological battles taking place within American culture. Though sometimes farcical and absurd, *The Simpsons* stands apart from almost every other show on network television by offering satirical treatments—and, thereby, some very serious contemplations—of some of the most important and controversial topics of our time.

2

"You're an American Now": Race, Ethnicity, and Nationality on *The Simpsons*

Deep within the word "American" is its association with race.

—Toni Morrison[1]

Concerns over racial and ethnic identity, US immigration policy, and the processes of Americanization were key elements of the culture wars of the 1980s and 1990s. This was evident in nativist phenomena of the era such as the "English only" movement, the restrictions placed on the numbers of legal immigrants, and the related proposals for the literal "walling out" of illegal immigrants, particularly in the southwestern part of the United States in the early 1990s.[2] In November 1997, just as the most heated debates were winding down, the US Commission on Immigration Reform offered Congress its final report, which included three key items: an analysis of the economic impact of recent immigration, a recommendation to restructure the existing immigration system, and a call for "a new Americanization movement."[3] In discussing the three focus areas, Judge Shirley M. Hufstedler, the commission chair, referred to the "Americanization" movement as "the most important of all." What is remarkable about the Hufstedler Commission's report is its eerie echo of a 1911 report by the US Immigration Commission (also known as the Dillingham Commission), which expressed similar concerns about the "desirability" of recent immigrants and initiated a federal campaign to "Americanize" immigrants, to be directed by the new Bureau of Americanization.[4] The Dillingham Commission report helped reinforce the already strong "Anglo-Saxon racialism" of the early part of the twentieth century and helped spur the later passage of exclusionary legislation—most notably the Emergency Quota Act (1921) and the National Origins Act (1924)—which, in effect, led to the triumph of "whiteness" as the normative American identity.[5] This, in turn, led to the incorporation of certain "white ethnics" into the body politic and to the relegation of "nonwhite" immigrants to the margins (the shtetls, barrios, or ghettos) of society. What Judge Hufstedler's comment about Americanization makes clear is that the patterns of fear over increased levels of immigration that were seen in the early decades of the last century had firmly reestablished themselves in the later decades and that the problems associated with racial, ethnic, and national identity are long-standing and as yet unresolved.

This history underscores the ongoing tensions surrounding a process that has been variously referred to as "assimilation," "acculturation," "socialization," "nationalization," and "Americanization." Each of these is a highly contested term, and each is intimately bound up with hotly debated social and legal policies. What the concepts all have in common is a concern with helping immigrants to "fit into" American society in some fashion or, as the 1997 Commission on Immigration Reform put it, "to help immigrants become Americans." But just who is an "American"? And what does it mean to be an "American"? Obviously, there are many factors involved in the shaping of an identity, national or otherwise, and any attempt to address these questions fully is beyond the scope of this volume. This chapter focuses only on the racial and ethnic distinctions apparent on *The Simpsons* and examines how these are portrayed in relation to "American" identity. As noted in the introductory chapter, *The Simpsons* is, in many ways, quintessentially "American." The fictional town of Springfield is designed to be an Everywhere, USA, and the Simpson family itself has been praised by many as a more "realistic" portrait of the "typical American family" than that found on most other television programs. Given the enormous cast of characters who populate the town of Springfield and, more generally, the diegetic space of *The Simpsons* itself, some commentators have given particular emphasis to the diversity of the show, and many see it as a more accurate reflection of American communities than the one offered by almost any other television program today. Such observations lead to a host of questions, among them: How does *The Simpsons* define its "Americanness"? How is this definition related to racial and/or ethnic identity? How is an American national identity configured for members of the Simpson family and other whites as compared to other (and "Othered") nonwhite members of the community? Does *The Simpsons* only reify existing racial and ethnic categories, or does it work to deconstruct them? What is the vision of contemporary American culture offered to viewers? And in what ways does this then shape the viewers' vision of both America and American identity?

An exploration of race and ethnicity on *The Simpsons* is both timely and important, as it helps to illuminate the contemporary figuration of "normative" American identity in mass media, which has long been coded as white, middle class, suburban, and Protestant (i.e., as traditionally WASP). Such an analysis also helps to illustrate the ways in which most mainstream media perpetuate a belief in assimilation as imperative for achieving "Americanness." Of course, representations of race and ethnicity on *The Simpsons* are quite complex, as are the engagements with issues attendant to racial, ethnic, and national identities in American culture. As might be expected, racial and/or ethnic identification is made evident on *The Simpsons* through common markers such as food, language, and clothing, but it is also made clear through the literal coloring of the cartoon characters. Characters are either yellow, which functions here as a signifier of "white" identity, or some shade of brown, which works as a signifier of an "Othered" identity and which, in turn, is tied to specific racial or ethnic groups and thus representative of what we can call a "hyphenated-American" identity.[6] The members of the Simpson family embody the "norm" of television situation comedy as racially unmarked whites and therefore, in many ways, represent a continuation of the tradition of the so-called WASPcoms of the 1950s and 1960s. To examine white identity fully, I first discuss earlier periods of immigration and the integration of certain ethnic groups into "whiteness." However, whiteness itself is problematized on *The Simpsons* in two important ways: first, in the character of Krusty the Clown, who is revealed to be Jewish (both an ethnic and a religious marker) but who has successfully "passed" into the mainstream of racial whiteness; and second, in the characters of Cletus and Brandine Delroy, who are positioned as "poor white trash" and thus far outside the mainstream.[7] Hence, in addition to discussing the historical integration of certain ethnic groups into "whiteness," I will briefly consider the concomitant push for assimilation into middle-class identity. The pressure to assimilate resonates strongly with the contemporary immigrant experience as well, embodied here by Apu Nahasapeemapetilon, proprietor of the local Kwik-E-Mart. I will discuss Apu in connection with assimilation and with the more recent struggles over defining "Americanness." This will lead to an examination of episodes of *The Simpsons* that focus on patriotism, dissent, and national identity and that deal with the lives of Muslim Americans, here dealt with as "racialized Others" as a result of the ready equation in the post-9/11 era between Islam and Arab identity.

As might be expected, *The Simpsons* demonstrates a fair amount of ambivalence about "American" identity and the methods of defining it over the past two decades. As a satire, *The Simpsons* regularly offers sharp critiques of many of the cherished myths of "American" identity (e.g., Horatio Alger–style success and faith in class mobility), and it often expresses opposition to conformity and prejudice. However, explicitly and implicitly, the show also often relies upon the traditions of assimilation and the myth of "the melting pot," and it often appears to advocate the ideal of a meritocracy. Given *The Simpsons*' regular engagement with contemporary issues and its reflection of American cultural traditions, such ambivalence is not surprising— indeed, it strikes me as an accurate reflection of the ambivalence that many citizens have about topics associated with the multiculturalist movement (e.g., affirmative action programs, immigration policy, etc.), about the pursuit of the "American Dream," and about the multiple definitions of "American" identity itself.

Constructing "American" Identity

In a letter entitled "What Is an American?" (1782), J. Hector St. Jean de Crèvecoeur infamously claimed, "Here [in America] all nations are melted into a new race of men, whose labours and posterity will one day cause great changes in the world."[8] Such a view was certainly prescient, if not entirely accurate. But it was not until the early part of the twentieth century that a more specific and much clearer expression of the melting pot metaphor was offered. The metaphor was popularized by Israel Zangwill's 1908 stage play *The Melting Pot*, a melodramatic tale of a romance between David Quixano, a second-generation American Jew, and Vera Revendal, the Christian daughter of an anti-Semitic baron. The play was a commercial hit in its time, and this helped to put the term *melting pot* into wide circulation.[9] As the century progressed—and as new waves of immigrants appeared—the concept took root in the public consciousness, becoming one of the most powerful articulations of the process of "becoming American" and one of the most deeply held convictions among the citizenry. It is no surprise that the metaphor caught hold of the public imagination when it did, as this was coincident with the "Americanization" movement spawned by the Dillingham Commission report of 1911 and embodied in the highly restrictive legislation that soon followed. The metaphor of the melting pot held sway for decades afterward, assisted by the Great Depression, the Second World War, and the postwar suburbanization of America. However, during the socially turbulent 1960s and 1970s, the metaphor was called into question in a number of influential and controversial books, most notably Nathan Glazer and Daniel P. Moynihan's *Beyond the Melting Pot* (1963), Peter Schrag's *The Decline of the Wasp* (1970), and Michael Novak's *The Rise of the Unmeltable Ethnics* (1972).[10]

The Simpsons appeared in the wake of these conversations and in the midst of heated debates over multiculturalism, assimilation, and American identity. During the 1980s and 1990s, commentators from both the left and the right rang in with treatises on these issues, predictably arguing either an assimilationist or a pluralist concept. The left delivered books detailing the value of diversity and arguing for the inclusion of "silenced" voices and marginalized peoples, while the right continued to argue that diversity was the problem and that multiculturalism was "disuniting" the nation and tearing it apart from within. Such sentiments were forcefully articulated by Arthur M. Schlesinger, who somewhat shrilly claimed, "If separatist tendencies go on unchecked, the result can only be the fragmentation, resegregation, and tribalization of American life."[11] Similar views were expressed in books published before Schlesinger's and even more so in those published afterward, when the focus of the debate shifted to castigating multiculturalism and the multiculturalists who advocate it.[12] A very different argument was being made by academics on the left, largely those inside the academy, who were now interrogating white racial privilege and inaugurating what has come to be known as "whiteness studies."[13]

One of the great difficulties in studying whiteness is the fact that, until quite recently, whiteness was an invisible and nonresearched category. As many scholars have noted, most white Americans do not think about their whiteness and do not consider themselves part of a racial category; when the white self is foregrounded, it is often thought of in positive or neutral terms. As the film critic Richard Dyer states it, "Trying to think about the representation of whiteness as an ethnic category in mainstream [media] is difficult, partly because white power secures its dominance by seeming not to be anything in particular."[14] The consequences of this are well expressed by Matt Wray and Annalee Newitz in their introduction to *White Trash: Race and Class in America* (1997), where they state,

> It has been the invisibility (for whites) of whiteness that has enabled white Americans to stand as unmarked, normative bodies and social selves, the standard against which all others are judged (and found wanting). As such, the invisibility of whiteness is an enabling condition for both white supremacy/privilege and race-based prejudice.[15]

Another formidable problem with the conceptualization of whiteness is the casual equation of race with nationality, that is, of "white" with "American." Researchers Thomas K. Nakayama and Robert L. Krizek report that many of the respondents to their survey on white racial identity make the claim that to be white means to be American or that "whiteness means 'that I'm of American descent.'"[16] Of course, according to the (il)logic of white privilege, in order to be considered "truly American," one has to be more than white alone: increasingly, one also has to be middle class. The conflation of whiteness with Americanness therefore invokes class as well as race, which operate simultaneously in American culture not only to maintain power in very specific and asymmetrical ways but also "to instantiate a structured exclusion of certain groups from social arenas of normativity."[17] But as the history of US immigration highlights, whiteness also creates a structured *inclusion* of many groups—primarily those with wealth, even if modest, and therefore with some degree of power—and it is these groups who have long been dominant on television.

The racial and ethnic landscape of *The Simpsons* has been shaped by the ideological codes of whiteness and its popularization via mass media—particularly since the end of the Second World War—as WASP identity.[18] The term *WASP*, an acronym for White Anglo-Saxon Protestant, was first used to describe those of British descent, as opposed to those of Irish, Scottish, or Welsh descent, who had immigrated to the colonies of the "new world" during the eighteenth and nineteenth centuries. In the early part of the twentieth century, when social scientists began to rigorously study the phenomenon of immigration, they charted the complex ways in which "white ethnic" groups negotiated racial and national identity as they attempted to integrate—or, in the parlance of the age, to "melt"—into the larger society. It is important to note that most of the early investigators were themselves WASPs and thus carried with them an inherent bias toward seeing immigrants follow a "straight line" form of assimilation in the direction of being an American, which in large measure meant being a WASP or coming as close to being one as was possible. After 1920, a pattern of "white unity" took place, mainly as a consequence of a large-scale reclassification of "whites" as members of the "Caucasian race" and of the so-called authority conferred upon Caucasian identity by the scientific community; with such reclassification, the "minor" divisions among white ethnics took a back seat to the perceived "major" divisions between white (Caucasian) and nonwhite (now Negroid and Mongoloid) groups, which were increasingly figured in public discourse as a threat to WASP identity and the nation.[19] What remained consistent and what has resonated most strongly in the public imagination, particularly during and after the black civil rights struggles of the 1950s and 1960s, is the overtly "White" character of the "White Anglo-Saxon Protestant" concept. Indeed, by the time E. Digby Baltzell put the term into popular use in the mid-1960s, "whiteness" had solidified itself— regardless of "ethnic" distinctions (which were "racial" distinctions half a century before)—against the perennial Other, "blackness."

The solidification of "whiteness" was greatly assisted in the early part of the twentieth century by what Adorno and Horkheimer infamously called "the culture industry," that is, the aggregation of radio, sound records, print media, advertising, and, most importantly, Hollywood film.[20] Caucasian unity (and the racism attendant to it) was fueled in part by the newly popular visual media. Michael Rogin speaks powerfully of this in his discussion of the first "talkie," *The Jazz Singer*, and his analysis of the transformative moment in the film when Jackie Rabinowitz (Al Jolson) is reborn as Jack Robin by performing in blackface and singing "My Mammy" to his immigrant Jewish mother. According to Rogin, assimilation for Jews (and by extension, other white ethnics) was possible via the mask of blackface, which worked as a potent signifier of "minority" and through which Jews could call attention to their whiteness and thus "ritually enter, even as they helped to create, the American melting pot."[21] Ironically, the entertainment industries of the first decades of the twentieth century—radio and film—were dominated by ethnic identity. Jews, for example, were integral to the success of radio and at the forefront of developing the Hollywood studio system. Jews were also key to the success of television—as writers, performers, producers, and even as founders and owners of the Big Three broadcast networks.[22] In its earliest days, television also featured the talents of Jewish comics such as Milton Bearle, Sid Caesar, Groucho Marx, George Burns, Jack Benny, Phil Silvers, and Carl Reiner since stand-up comedy translated so easily to the new medium.[23] Other racial and ethnic identities were explicitly represented as well in the earliest days of television, often as translations of popular radio programs owned by the networks. For example, the long-running radio show *Amos 'n' Andy* (1928–54), a comedy originally voiced by white actors, was remade as a television show of the same name (1951–53) but with black actors in the title roles. *Fibber McGee and Molly* (1935–59), a popular Irish radio comedy, provided the material for a television spin-off called *Beulah* (1950–53), which centered on the life of the McGee family's black maid. Of course, both *Amos 'n' Andy* and *Beulah* led to controversy over stereotypes and/or racist imagery, and neither lasted very long in the new medium, owing in part to protests from the NAACP and subsequent lack of advertiser sponsorship.[24] Other, less controversial situation comedies included the short-lived *Life with Luigi* (1952), about a working-class Italian American family, and, most successfully, *The Goldbergs* (1949–54). This comedy about a working-class Jewish family in the Bronx was itself the television incarnation of the long-running and highly popular radio show *The Rise of the Goldbergs* (1929–47), one of the biggest hits on radio in the 1930s and 1940s. Thus it was that television initially seemed to be a promising venue for American "minorities." Such diversity suffered, however, from the push toward assimilated whiteness in mid-century media, and so pluralistic a view of American society would not be seen again on television until the premiere of *The Simpsons*.

Simultaneous with the brief visibility of ethnic identity on television in the late 1940s and early 1950s was the real-world "white flight" from urban centers to the newly proliferating suburban communities and a unification of whiteness in WASP identity. Rather quickly, then, ethnic identity in mass media was either transformed or erased. Jewish identity, for example, was increasingly downplayed in television sitcoms, and even the Goldbergs, in their last season on the air, moved from the urban space of the Bronx, their longtime residence while on the radio, to the suburban town of Haverville, in upstate New York. As David Marc rather wryly notes, with the end of *The Goldbergs* in 1954, "only families of Northern European descent were left on television sitcoms (with the exception of course of Ricky Ricardo)."[25] As many cultural historians have noted, shifting social and political mores and changing consumer patterns in the postwar period set the tone for what would and would not appear on television in the late 1950s and early 1960s: the future of the family-centered situation comedy would be left to the "pointedly nonethnic Nelsons and Andersons and Cleavers."[26] The sitcom of the 1950s, which David Marc derisively refers to as the "WASPcom," simply shifted its locale from the urban to the suburban landscape, and "as urban identity faded, ethnic identity waned with it."[27] In other words, the stage was set for the rise and dominance of the WASP nuclear-family situation comedy—and for the cultural preeminence of those who populated these shows: professional, college-educated, middle-class whites whose whiteness was never consciously discussed nor tinged by any hint of previous ethnic affiliation. In short, the new medium of television rather quickly erased ethnic identity and created a unified "whiteness" for American audiences, particularly in the form of the situation comedy. The result, according to David Marc, was that "Television—especially the sitcom—valorized suburbia as democracy's utopia realized, a place where the white middling classes could live in racial serenity, raising children in an engineered environment that contained and regulated the twin dangers of culture and nature."[28] What is important here is Marc's reference to middle-class status, which highlights a problem with the WASP label: its exclusion of economic and social class as elements of "American" identity and the "American Dream." As Herbert Gans points out, "The dirt-poor Appalachian 'hillbillies' were WASPs too, after all, and just as 'Anglo-Saxon' as the elite who controlled the economy, politics and culture."[29] What Gans reminds us of here is how important—and how ignored—the factor of class has been to the construction of the WASP identity in American culture.

Given such facts, it would be wrong to uncritically apply the WASP label to *The Simpsons*. It is too simplistic to read *The Simpsons* as yet another WASPcom in a long line of WASPcoms and too naive to read it as a full-fledged satire upon the WASP sitcoms of a previous era, to which it owes a significant debt. Therefore, it is necessary to reconceptualize the WASP label, which has been something of a misnomer for the past 40 years and a highly problematic term to use these days. Foremost, the casual yoking together of the terms *White* and *Anglo-Saxon* elides the troubled history of whiteness as a racial category and "white" as its signifier. Matthew Frye Jacobson has demonstrated how the word *white* had undergone great shifts in meaning in American culture from the late eighteenth century through the late twentieth century. Further complicating the use of the WASP label is that fact that it encompassed a host of Protestant faiths—among them, Lutheran, Methodist, Episcopal (Anglican), Congregationalist (Puritan), Quaker, Presbyterian, and Northern and Southern Baptist—which were of not only English but also Northern European origin. Another complication arises in the consideration of class. The term WASP makes no direct reference to class status; however, it is clear that in the short time in which the term has been in use, the implied status has been, at a minimum, middle class.[30] This implicit status was made quite clear in Milton Gordon's *Assimilation in American Life* (1964), which powerfully reaffirmed the "melting-pot" metaphor during a period of racial and ethnic unrest. According to Gordon, the first and inevitable step in the process of assimilation was "acculturation," which Gordon defined broadly as the minority group's adoption of the "cultural patterns" of the majority group; and what Gordon saw as the "core culture" in the United States was the "middle-class cultural patterns of, largely, white Protestant, Anglo-Saxon origins."[31]

Reconceiving the WASP label is an important first step in critically examining race, ethnicity, and nationality on *The Simpsons*. At this point, it is necessary to expand the scope of the WASP label and to offer a more accurate descriptor of what it truly represented—and what it perhaps still does. From here on, I will use the term *McWASP*—the Middle-Class White-Assimilated Suburban Protestant—which acknowledges the important factors of class and place, too easily elided by the old WASP label, in addition to those of religion and race.[32] McWASP is both a more accurate model of the "American" identity offered in mainstream mass media, both previously and today, and a more useful lens through which to analyze such identity. In short, the McWASP label reveals three things: first, the classism always inherent in traditional WASP identity (hence the phrase *Middle-Class*, which highlights the presumed "normative" status of this social and economic position); second, the valorization of suburban space, especially after the expansions of the post–World War II era (hence the term *Suburban*, which also takes into account the more recent phenomenon of the "exurbs"); and last, the increased racialization of ethnicity in the latter half of the twentieth century (hence the phrase *White-Assimilated*, which underscores the "normative" character of racial whiteness rather than the ethnically specific but outdated "Anglo-Saxon").

The legacy of McWASP identity on television is an important part of understanding how *The Simpsons* deals with both race and ethnicity in relation to American identity. The nuclear family sitcom came of age at a time when American society was struggling for ideological consensus and uniformity, largely in response to the end of the Second World War and onset of the Cold War, which was fueled by increasing anticommunist sentiment. The McWASP sitcoms of the 1950s were manifestations of the conformity of the Cold War era and reflected, as Gerard Jones explains, a "placidity and changelessness, [and] an eerily homogeneous landscape of spacious houses and smiling, self-satisfied WASP families."[33] For immigrants to America, the push toward assimilation into dominant society was strong and served by a host of civic organizations, as well as radio, film, and television—each of which promoted assimilation and Americanization. Television was an important agent of socialization for immigrants and their American-born progeny who had aspirations to McWASP identity. Indeed, the pointedly ethnic sitcoms of the early 1950s can be viewed as "revisionist explorations of the immigrant experience as seen through the eyes of a middle class not quite sure of its locations within the status hierarchy, yet not distinctly secure enough to laugh about its origins."[34] This was evident in the dialect humor on such programs, which captured the tensions between the older and younger generations. The explicitly nonethnic sitcoms that followed functioned to alleviate such tension by offering the next "logical" step in the process of Americanization: becoming "white." Conditions were good for "ethnic whites" in the 1950s, as the key to acceptance in suburbia was one's appearance: Gerard Jones notes that if you could look, dress, and act like "a solid all-American family, then no one really cared about your roots. Whoever could leave his ethnicity at the gate could be admitted to the paradise of Levittown."[35] Jones's comment here stands out for two reasons. First, it underscores the fact that what hinders most, at least in that time period, is skin color. The history of the twentieth century demonstrates that those with lighter skin color (i.e., skin closer to the "norm" in the society) were able to more readily "melt" or mix in; indeed, many if not most of the "white ethnics" had, by mid-century, assimilated into white racial identity. Hence, being "white-assimilated," as opposed to being "white Anglo-Saxon," was the new key to achieving Americanness. Second, Jones's use of the term "all-American" relies upon the awareness that most readers carry with them of a long-standing equation between American identity and whiteness—indeed, so deeply embedded in the public imagination is this belief that the term "all-American" is now a common signifier of whiteness within consumer culture, in things as disparate as advertisements and personal ads, as well as within everyday vernacular speech.[36]

"Colored People": Racial and Ethnic Identity

In a 1994 episode of *The Simpsons* entitled "New Kid on the Block," we see Bart Simpson taking a bath and preparing for his "date" with the girl who has moved in next door. When Lisa queries him about his sudden willingness to bathe, Bart replies, "Sometimes a guy just likes his skin to look its yellowest." It's a humorous line, and the writers are obviously having fun with the fact that the Simpson family (and many other residents of Springfield) are quite literally yellow. But what are we to make of this information beyond the laugh it provides? Why exactly are the characters yellow? And how might this be important to an examination of racial and ethnic identity? As noted earlier, racial and/or ethnic identifications are made evident on *The Simpsons* through the coloring of the cartoon characters; various colors stand in for skin color, and what yellow represents, of course, is white skin. In a 1995 interview, Matt Groening rather matter-of-factly stated, "The real reason *The Simpsons* are yellow is so that they will look like nothing else on television."[37] David Silverman, a former director for the show, provides a different explanation, acknowledging the influence of the original color stylist, Gyorgi Peluci. In a 1998 interview, Silverman said,

> I think she [Peluci] made *The Simpsons* yellow because Bart, Lisa and Maggie don't have a hairline, so they had to be yellow, otherwise Bart would look like he had a serrated forehead...And if they're yellow, you kind of get used to the fact that it's their hair and their skin colour, once the shock wears off.[38]

Interesting as they are, these comments ignore the racial connotations of "coloring." It is not surprising, however, that there is no commentary on the whiteness of the characters given that whiteness itself is normative, unmarked, and invisible in US culture. When viewed against the backdrop of other racially marked characters on the show, Bart and the rest of the Simpson family are clearly white people. In essence, yellow functions as a mask for white identity on *The Simpsons*, creating a simultaneous presence and absence for whiteness.[39]

In order to fully examine the racial politics of *The Simpsons*, it is important to acknowledge the fact that yellowness is a proxy for whiteness on the show. However, an examination of the function of whiteness within the text of *The Simpsons* should begin with a discussion of its cultural context, specifically with the infamous "Black Bart" Simpson phenomenon. In the summer of 1990, unlicensed T-shirts began to appear with the image of Bart Simpson as a "black" youth, and these became popular in many urban areas. Among the most popular were the "Air Bart," a parody of Michael Jordan in a series of then-common Nike commercials, and a dreadlocked "Rasta Bart."[40] Such cultural appropriations can be understood in numerous ways. After all, this was the summer following the explosive appearance of Spike Lee's seminal film *Do the Right Thing* (1989), the accompanying single "Fight the Power" by the militant-looking rap group Public Enemy, and the subsequent resurgence of black nationalism and black power, which would intensify soon thereafter with the release of John Singleton's *Boyz N the Hood* (1991) and the controversy surrounding the making of another "Spike Lee joint," *Malcolm X* (1992). Amid all of this race-consciousness, *Newsweek* published an editorial on the "Black Bart" Simpson phenomenon that coyly asked, "Who said Bart Simpson was white, anyway?"[41] Only in the yellow press of white America could a mainstream "news" magazine editorial, discussing the phenomenon of a yellow cartoon character rendered in blackface on bootleg T-shirts, open with so naive a question.

In an otherwise insightful examination of ideology on *The Simpsons*, Vincent Brook briefly discusses the "Black Bart" phenomenon and claims that *The Simpsons* itself encourages such "creative colorization"; he states,

> although coded as white folk, the Simpson family's skin pigmentation (and those of other "whites") is not, in that most racist of descriptions, "skin tone"; it is rather a bright

and quite unearthly *yellow*… The Simpsons are already, in other words, quite literally, "people of color."[42]

Perhaps Brook is being playful here, speaking to the desire in the postmodern era for the fluidity of identity categories and the impermanence of boundaries; it is, after all, both fun and funny to refer to the Simpsons as "people of color." And as cartoon characters, yes, they are literally "people of color." But this is a surprisingly simplistic interpretation of *The Simpsons*, especially from someone as informed on matters of race and mass media as Brook. One ought not to read animation in a literal fashion; since animation is inherently "unrealistic," it must be understood in figurative and metaphoric ways. Whereas live-action genres such as the television sitcom strive toward realism, or what Ella Taylor incisively calls "visual naturalism," the cartoon sitcom often moves toward surrealism. As Taylor notes, "The codes of realistic narrative are meant to persuade the viewer that the television depiction of domestic and work settings reflects the human situation more accurately than 'the caricatures of the Disney cartoon.'"[43] The cartoons that have proliferated on television in the wake of *The Simpsons* (e.g., *Beavis and Butt-Head*, *South Park*, *King of the Hill*, and *Family Guy*) quite clearly do not work within the traditional codes of realistic narrative. *The Simpsons*, like its many imitators, needs to be read in a figurative rather than literal manner. *The Simpsons* must also be decoded in this way when viewed as satire, since the art of satire relies so heavily on irony, absurdity, caricature, and exaggeration. One might be inclined to claim that such playful use of color on *The Simpsons* is an indication that the creators of the show are aiming to point out that race is not a biological reality but a social construct—that is, what many people consider to be an "essential" trait is truly nothing more than a difference of "coloring." However, this does not seem to be a logical line of inquiry. If the intention were to offer a vision of some postracial, "color-blind" world, then everyone on *The Simpsons* should be a single, uniform color. This is not the case because the show aims instead to reflect the actual diversity of American society, and a difference in skin color is a factor of that diversity. *The Simpsons* is actually very consistent in its portrayal of color and thereby of ethnicity and race. As Brook acknowledges, the Simpsons are "coded as white"—and white they remain in the landscape of Springfield. Nonwhite characters are a distinct shade of brown, which is used to represent all other racial and ethnic categories. What Brook's comment highlights is the way in which yellowness remains unmarked, much as whiteness does in most of television programming; the Simpsons thereby become an "ordinary"—and ordinarily "American"—family.

Most longtime fans of *The Simpsons* are aware, however, of a least one significant discrepancy regarding "color" (i.e., race) on the show—and thereby of a notorious instance of *marked* whiteness. In "Homer's Odyssey" (an episode from the very first season), Waylon Smithers, a well-known "white" character, appears to be "black" since he is colored a dark shade of brown. Apparently, he was accidentally colored incorrectly by artists at the animation house Klasky-Csupo. As producer David Silverman explains it, Smithers was always intended to be yellow (i.e., white). Silverman's comments are revealing about how race both was and was not considered at the show's inception, and they are worth quoting in full:

> As far as Waylon Smithers, I think [Gyorgi Peluci] didn't read the script. I'm pretty sure she didn't read the script because she never did, she just was sort of like, "Oh I

have to make it multi-ethnic, so I'll make this person white, I'll make this person black, la la la la la" and not really paying attention to what the script was about. No one was really paying attention to that, so when it came back we said "Oh, we didn't really want Waylon Smithers to be black, we want him to be, you know, [Mr. Burns's] white syco-phant, so maybe we should repaint this."[44]

Silverman then humorously suggests that fans should simply imagine Smithers had just come back from a vacation in the Caribbean with a deep tan when the episode took place. One thing Silverman's comment makes clear is that from the start the creators were well aware that yellow was equivalent to white identity and that it was important to have the übercapitalist Burns and his right-hand man Smithers be white. Another interesting aspect of Silverman's comment is the passing reference to Peluci's understanding that in coloring *The Simpsons* she was expected to "make it multi-ethnic." Although I have been unable to find any corroboration of this claim, considering when the show premiered (1989), it is not inconceivable that such an expectation was in place. Given the well-known liberal politics of Matt Groening, the idea might have originated with him. It might also have come from producer James L. Brooks, a man with a history of challenging status-quo ideology on television. Or perhaps it came from FOX executives, who were at that point doing very well by catering to a long-ignored urban/black population with multiracial and black-centered shows such as *In Living Color, Martin,* and *Roc.* Whatever the impetus, it is clear that a degree of multiculturalism did find its way into Springfield—certainly in a much more direct way than in the Springfield of *Father Knows Best*—and this is most likely a simple reflection of the era in which *The Simpsons* appeared and of trends then current within American culture (for example, the emphasis on mul-ticultural educational curricula, pluralistic celebrations of difference, and calls for more diverse representations in mass media).

Given that racial and ethnic identities are clearly distinguished on *The Simpsons,* one has to wonder why the most deeply rooted racial divide in American culture—that between black and white identities—is not overtly addressed on the show. The historical context in which the show arose provides at least a partial explanation. *The Simpsons* indeed appeared on the heels of an ascendant multiculturalism, but it also emerged in the wake of the enormously successful *The Cosby Show* (1984–92), which marked a significant transition in network television's portrayal of black Americans. The pluralistic worldview being promoted in the 1980s helped provide an opening and a comfortable space on network television for *The Cosby Show,* which was dis-tinctly different than many of its predecessors from the 1970s, such as *Good Times, Sanford and Son,* and *What's Happening!* While explicit in their recognition of both race and class, these comedies relied upon a deeply engrained equation between blackness and poverty and thus kept black cultural identity separate and apart from the "normative" order depicted in the domestic sitcom.[45] *The Cosby Show,* on the other hand, offered viewers the more "universal" image of an upper-middle-class family, largely untethered from black cultural identity: indeed, as many critics have noted, *The Cosby Show* worked hard to downplay its "blackness" and to avoid engag-ing the complex and controversial aspects of black life in the United States during the 1980s.[46] Consequently, the show was widely embraced by audiences and worked largely to reaffirm viewers' beliefs in meritocracy, social mobility, and the American Dream.

The black characters most prominent on *The Simpsons*—Dr. Julius Hibbert, Lou the cop, and Carl Carlson—are incorporated in ways that rarely highlight their "racial" status. This is perhaps a consequence of the prevailing emphases on diversity and multiculturalism in the 1980s and of the great success of *The Cosby Show* and its crossover appeal for white audiences. However, I think the reluctance to engage with black-white racial politics is also due to the fact *The Simpsons* appeared just as the intense racial animosities that were suppressed, glossed over, or outright denied by *The Cosby Show*—and, by extension, the American people during the Reagan era—exploded on a national scale. *The Simpsons'* first season, for example, coincided with the popularity of "gangster rap" and the increased visibility of aggressive black masculinity in music videos; with Spike Lee's provocative *Do the Right Thing* being bested by Bruce Beresford's *Driving Miss Daisy* in the contest for Best Picture in 1990; and, most importantly, with the growing disparity between blacks and whites in both economic stability and educational achievement. In March 1991, during *The Simpsons'* second season, the country watched (repeatedly) a videotape of motorist Rodney King being brutally assaulted by four Los Angeles police officers, which provided a new layer of controversy to the debates over so-called "reality" television—a programming trend initiated, ironically enough, by the Fox show *COPS*, which first aired in March 1989—and its exploitation of white racial fears. In October 1991, the nation witnessed the spectacle of the confirmation hearings for Clarence Thomas (whom George Bush Sr. had earlier nominated to replace the retiring justice Thurgood Marshall on the Supreme Court), who was accused of sexual harassment by former colleague Anita Hill. Though effectively an issue of gender, the hearings were caught up in racialized discourse, invoking the specter of black male sexuality with open talk of penises and pubic hairs and with Thomas's own claim to being the victim of a "high-tech lynching." And in April 1992, in the wake of the acquittal of the four officers who had beaten Rodney King a year earlier, the country watched Los Angeles consumed by a six-day-long "riot." In short, the issue of black-white relations in American culture was likely too inflammatory to be fodder for satire on *The Simpsons*, a fledgling program on a still-young network.

Most commonly, the politics of racial or ethnic identity are made apparent on *The Simpsons* in brief moments or in the subplots of episodes, usually in satirical ways. For example, in the episode entitled "Mr. Lisa Goes to Washington" (September 1991), the racial history of the United States is subtly invoked for the sake of satirical commentary. The show begins with Homer's newfound fascination with reading, although only in the form of the condensed *Reading Digest*, which Homer finds a source of "intelligent stuff." Wanting to read his children a true-life adventure story, Homer pulls Bart and Lisa away from the "idiot box," where they are watching a "period" film in which a white preacher is seen telling an "Indian Chief" that the tribe's homeland will be more valuable if they abandon it and allow the whites to "irrigate" it. Although a minor scene, the subject matter highlights how public perceptions of American history and race relations are mediated (and arguably distorted) by mass communication media such as television. The scene also sets the stage for a more direct engagement with the racial politics of "Americanness" as the story progresses. Lisa learns that *Reading Digest* is sponsoring a "Patriots of Tomorrow" essay contest and that the student who writes the best essay—which is to be 300 words and "fiercely pro-American" in sentiment—will win a trip to Washington, DC. Believing herself to be a good and patriotic citizen, Lisa enters. For inspiration, she visits the Springfield

National Forest, where she sees the "purple mountains' majesty" and a very large bald eagle. The result is an essay entitled "The Roots of Democracy," a sweet and patriotic paean to her homeland. A very different view of America is offered by Nelson Muntz, the local school bully, who has also entered the contest. He is rendered as intensely patriotic and nativistic, and his essay, unsurprisingly, concerns the issue of flag burning. In Nelson's simplistic formulation, burning the flag is equivalent to burning one's possessions, such as one's pants, television, and car. Unlike Lisa, Nelson equates democracy and patriotism with capitalism and consumerism. Nelson's nativist sentiments echo those of many right-leaning politicians of the Reagan-Bush era who had, in the late 1980s, opposed flag burning as a form of free speech and who would, in the early 1990s, propose restrictive immigration legislation.[47] Appropriately enough (and with clear satirical intent), the students' essays are scored on clarity, content, and jingoism. Nelson, of course, does quite well, but it is Lisa who wins and gets to compete in the national finals in Washington.

When in Washington, Lisa meets the other two national finalists: Trong Van Din and Maria Dominguez. Although coded by both name and coloring as distinctly "ethnic," no overt comment is made about ethnic or cultural differences, and Lisa bonds with her peers over their shared intellectual abilities. In short, the audience is set up to see all of the finalists as equally "American." However, as Trong tells his family story, we see that it is a typical (although exaggerated) immigrant story: the family had arrived only four months earlier; they spoke no English and had no money, yet they now own a nationwide chain of wheel balancing centers. In essence, Trong's story is a condensed version of the American Dream; not surprisingly, his essay is called "USA A-OK." Trong's place of origin is never specified, so he remains enigmatically "Asian." As such, Trong is what is controversially called a "model minority" and a good example of successful integration, if not assimilation. Although Maria is positioned as Hispanic, and therefore not a "model minority," we do not get an immigration story from her; we are left to assume that she is likely a native-born citizen. However, Maria's faith in old-style assimilation is similarly captured in her essay, which is entitled "Bubble On, O Melting Pot."

The details of the essay contest outlined here are admittedly small moments in the "Mr. Lisa Goes to Washington" episode—which is actually concerned much more with political corruption and governmental malfeasance than with race or ethnicity—but they highlight how "American" identity is foregrounded and commented upon on *The Simpsons*. The writers of the show are well schooled in the racial (and racist) history of the nation, and they often employ this in very satirical ways. They are also well aware of the mythology of the melting pot, the story of the American Dream, and the politics of identity in the contemporary age, and they employ these ideas in quite subtle ways in "Mr. Lisa Goes to Washington," engaging the viewer in a (re) consideration of what defines nationalism—that is, of what it means to be a patriot and an American. Clearly, jingoism and exclusionary nativist sentiments are being held up for censure, but are traditional assimilationist concepts as well? It is, after all, Trong who wins the contest, and this seems to reflect the general belief that the traditional method of integration and/or assimilation is still the "best" method. Such a conclusion is not surprising when one considers the time in which "Mr. Lisa Goes to Washington" was produced and aired (September 1991). The historical and political context for this episode is slyly acknowledged in a scene in which the Simpson family walks past the White House, where we see a small group of "typical" Americans carrying protest-style placards with messages such as "Everything's A-OK," "No Complaints Here," and "Things Are Fine." As Lauren Berlant astutely observes, all of these faux protestors are white; for many white Americans (and for many of the so-called model minorities, such as the Din family, who are often readily embraced by white America), things might have indeed seemed fine in 1991. But this was not the case for many black and Latino Americans, as the so-called riots in Los Angeles only one year later made all too clear. For Berlant, the scene resonates strongly as a satirical stab at "the right-wing cultural agenda of the Reagan-Bush era."[48] Although accurate, this seems a bit overstated: a scene showing whites with nothing to complain about is a small barb tossed toward the White House, not a particularly powerful satirical statement. Nonetheless, the scene does effectively illustrate an awareness of racial politics among the writers and producers of *The Simpsons* in its earliest days and an understanding that in American culture, racial and national identities have been and continue to be shaped in relation to whiteness.

In general, the creators of *The Simpsons* have avoided the thorny issue of race in favor of ethnicity. They have, however, addressed race directly on occasion, and they did so somewhat provocatively in a 2010 episode entitled "The Color Yellow." The episode concerns the efforts of Lisa to find "at least one good Simpson" ancestor when she is assigned a family tree project in Miss Hoover's class. However, when she begins to look into the Simpson's family history, all she finds is a series of scoundrels and criminals, including murderers. "They're all horrible," she exclaims in frustration. Homer nonchalantly replies, "Yeah, the Simpson family is a long line of horse thieves, deadbeats, horse beats, dead thieves and a few alcoholics." Lisa is determined to find a "noble spark" in the family line and so explores the attic, hoping to locate more promising information, and it is there she finds the diary of one Eliza Simpson. Lisa is quite excited to read the first entry, dated 1860, but immediately dismayed when she does. "Dear Diary," Eliza wrote, "Today I get my first slave." That the Simpsons are descended from slave-owners is more than Lisa can bear, but she perseveres, certain that there is more to the story. What she soon discovers is that Eliza was attempting to help the family slave, Virgil, escape to freedom via the Underground Railroad. As the episode progresses, the story unfolds for the audience in a series of flashbacks. The first attempt at escape fails when Eliza and Virgil are spotted by two patrollers. After escaping the clutches of patrollers (with some assistance from Krusty the Clown, who "hides" Virgil in plain sight by dressing him as a clown and literally placing him in whiteface!), Eliza and Virgil go back home to seek the help of Eliza's mother, Mabel. Mabel wants to help, but her husband, Hiram—who had not quite caught "abolition fever," as Mabel states—resists the idea. Hiram is quickly convinced, however, by Virgil's delicious fried "wheel cakes" (doughnuts) and agrees to assist with the escape. After reading of this, Lisa is convinced that the family does indeed have "heroes" and proudly decides to use the diary as part of her presentation for Black History Month. At the end of her speech, however, Lisa's schoolmate Milhouse confronts Lisa and calls her version of events a "fairy tale." He then presents the diary of his ancestor Milford Van Houten, who was tangentially involved in the events. In this alternate story, which we again get in flashback, Hiram, who has promised to keep the secret, breaks under pressure from the evil Colonel Burns and reveals Virgil's whereabouts. Van Houten's diary also explains that Eliza acquiesces to Burns as well when he tells her that she is to be quiet, like a "good girl" of her era should. Lisa is indignant and refuses to believe that Eliza is a "coward."

Determined to prove Milhouse's version wrong, Lisa heads back to the library for further research. Finding nothing in writing, she goes to the film vault, and there she finds a film (made in 1952) of Eliza at age 100 being interviewed about the events of the past. Eliza confesses that she is "haunted by her silence" regarding Virgil. "There's no noble Simpson," Lisa sadly concludes. However, back home Lisa discovers that there is one last version of the story to be told, this time by Abe Simpson (Grandpa). In his version, we find out that Mabel is the hero of the story, surprising Colonel Burns when he arrives and wielding a gun to protect Virgil. She is so mad at Hiram for not following through on his promise that she determines to take Virgil to Canada herself. Since Mabel and Hiram are rendered as nineteenth-century variants of Marge and Homer, the audience is preconditioned to have the episode resolve itself as it often does on *The Simpsons* when Homer and Marge fight—with forgiveness, a reunion, and a happy ending. However, in this case, such expectations are thwarted. In short order, Mabel decides to remain in Canada, divorce Hiram, and marry Virgil. She and Virgil then have a child, Abraham, who we learn is Abe's great-grandfather. What we learn, then, is that the Simpson children are descended from an act of miscegenation and are, as Lisa says, "one sixty-fourth black." They are, therefore, in the parlance commonly used today, "people of color."

A number of things stand out about "The Color Yellow" in relation to the themes I am exploring here. Foremost, perhaps, is that the invocation of the history of slavery in the United States makes quite clear that yellow is indeed a proxy for white, yellowness for whiteness. Racial identity is a reality within the world of *The Simpsons*, not merely a playful conceit or an accident of colorization, as some might have it. The revelations about the Simpsons' racial identity are also intriguing, less I think for what they state within the text of *The Simpsons* than for what they suggest about the context in which this episode appeared in February 2010. Although "The Color Yellow" can be read as a mere nod to Black History Month and yet another set of wacky Simpson family adventures, it strikes me as remarkably in tune with the conversations about race taking place in the era of Barack Obama, particularly the discussion of so-called postracial identity and the explorations of "hybrid" selves and multiethnic or multiracial identities. No figure in recent memory has more fully crystallized and embodied the tensions surrounding racial identity in the United States than President Barack Obama. As Thomas Sugrue points out in *Not Even Past: Barack Obama and the Burden of Race* (2010), it is now commonplace to see the election of Barack Obama as the "opening of a new period in America's long racial history" and a new conversation about the meanings of race and ethnicity.[49] Obviously, Obama represents various points of division, not the least of which is a difference of opinion on the persistence of racism and the future of the nation. Some are very optimistic, believing that Obama heralds the emergence of a new multihued racial order in which static notions of race are obsolete and race-conscious programs such as affirmative action are no longer needed. Such ideas were articulated by scholars throughout the first decade of the new millennium, well in advance of Obama's election.[50] Others are more pessimistic, arguing that deep-seated racial prejudices still exist and that the changing face of the nation does nothing to alter the persistence of a color hierarchy that relegates the darkest-skinned among us to the bottom tier.[51] Sugrue states,

> History today is being shaped by tensions between a historically specific postracial framework, a now broadly accepted discourse of color blindness that has especially

deep appeal to whites, and a still deeply rooted racial consciousness, especially among African Americans.[52]

As many have noted, the ubiquity of color-blind rhetoric today is "testimony to the effectiveness of more than a half century of civil rights activism in de-legitimating overt, public expressions of racial prejudice."[53] Of course, not everyone is satisfied with the rhetoric of colorblindness. Notable in this regard is the work of the antiracism educator Tim Wise, who has in recent years been the most eloquent commentator on the persistence of racial prejudice and the problems of white privilege in American society. In his most recent book, *Colorblind: The Rise of Post-Racial Politics and the Retreat from Racial Equity* (2010), Wise offers a fairly harsh assessment of Obama and of what Wise rather cheekily calls Racism 2.0, by which he means the concept of "enlightened exceptionalism." As Wise explains it, "enlightened exceptionalism manages to accommodate individual people of color, even as it continues to look down upon the large mass of black and brown America with suspicion, fear, and contempt."[54] In other words, in this "updated" version of racism, the larger white majority makes exceptions for certain "unthreatening" individuals while holding the larger black community in low regard and adhering to a number of racist stereotypes about African Americans.

These realities are alluded to in the conclusion of "The Color Yellow." After Lisa announces that she, Bart, and Homer are "one sixty-fourth black," Bart says, "So that's why I'm so cool." "And that's why my jazz is so smooth," Lisa adds. "And that's why I earn less than my white co-workers," Homer quips. Bart and Lisa express and perpetuate notions about black culture that are certainly stereotypical but not particularly offensive—indeed, they are ideas largely embraced within the African American community. Moreover, they refer to characteristics already associated with Bart and Lisa as previously "white" characters. Homer's comment, however, is much more telling, for its purpose is clearly satirical and intended to highlight the very kind of persistent prejudice in the culture that Tim Wise so diligently exposes in *Colorblind*. Grandpa's final comments in this episode are also intriguing. When Lisa asks Grandpa why he had kept the truth from them, he responds, "Well, it's hard to explain this to a young person, but people of my generation are, you know..." "Racist," Lisa suggests. "That's it," he replies. Grandpa's generation, of course, is the target of the satirical jabs at Fox News discussed in chapter 1. Comments such as "Not Racist, But #1 With Racists" and "Unsuitable for Viewers Under 75" are clearly aimed at the primary demographic of Fox viewers. People like Grandpa (old, white, conservative, and male) compose a large portion of the Tea Party movement, of anti-immigration protesters in the South and Southwest, and of those groups that have most forcefully and vocally vilified Barack Obama as an "Other" in terms of his nationality, religion, and race. That the creators of *The Simpsons* were willing to make members of this "all-American" (read: McWASP) family quite literally mixed-race people in order to make a point about racism and white privilege is, in short, remarkable.

Ethnic Whitewashing and Jewish Identity

The relationship between "whiteness" and Jewish identity has been explored in great detail in numerous studies, covering a wide range of topics.[55] What each of these studies points out is that during the late nineteenth and early twentieth centuries, many commentators struggled with understanding and categorizing Jewish identity. As Daniel Itzkovitz succinctly states,

> [I]n an astonishingly wide range of journalistic, literary, and social-scientific texts, the image of "the Jew" developed out of a set of paradoxes—Jews were both White and racially other, American and foreign, deviant and normative, vulgar and highly culti-vated, and seemed to have an uncomfortably unstable relation to gendered difference— all of which made them seem at once inside and inescapably outside of normative White American culture.[56]

The "visible" racial character of Jewishness that was highlighted in the eighteenth and nineteenth centuries had, by the mid-twentieth century, largely disappeared through the processes of secularization, "passing," intermarriage, and amalgama-tion, which worked over time to make visible differences less apparent and/or more ambiguous. As discussed earlier, the newly popular visual entertainment media— especially Hollywood films of the 1920s and 1930s, which offered tales of successful Americanization—were assisting in the assimilationist project, despite the fact that these media were largely owned and operated by Jews. As Vincent Brook points out, during the twentieth century,

> opposing integrationist and separationist tendencies have not only reinforced but also threatened Jews' historically unique insider/outsider status in American society, upset-ting the delicate balance between the senses of "sameness" and "otherness" that has been a defining component of American Jewish identity.[57]

This assimilationist/separatist binary was exemplified by the debate over media rep-resentations that were seen as either "too Jewish," a term legendarily ascribed to the Columbia Studios mogul Harry Cohn to describe what he saw as overtly stereotypi-cal characteristics, or "not Jewish enough," a term used more recently to highlight the commonality of interfaith marriage as a form of assimilation and the increased ambiguity of Jewishness vis-à-vis whiteness. The purpose in reviewing this history here is not to engage the ongoing debate over defining Jewishness (is it a religion, a race, an ethnicity, a culture?) but to examine how the opposing tendencies of "same-ness" and "otherness" have been articulated in mainstream mass media and, more specifically, how Jewish identity has been coded as both "white" and "nonwhite," both visible and invisible, in television situation comedy.

In *The Jews of Prime Time*, David Zurawik argues that conformist and assimilation-ist pressures resulted in "the ethnic whitewashing of television," which, as discussed earlier, paved the way for the McWASP sitcoms of the late 1950s and early 1960s.[58] This also resulted in the large-scale erasure of Jewish identity on television for the next two decades. However, by the late 1980s, things had begun to change once again and overtly Jewish characters and shows began to appear on television. In 1989 alone, there were three new Jewish sitcoms with overtly identified Jews as the lead character (*Chicken Soup, Anything but Love,* and *Seinfeld*) compared to seven in toto in the pre-vious 40 years, and between 1989 and 2001, some 33 sitcoms with Jewish protagonists were on TV.[59] There are at least two factors that help explain such a change. First, the widespread visibility and apparent acceptance of Jews coincides with a multiculturalist thrust in the country and the emphasis on identity politics in the 1980s and 1990s. Second, changes in both technology and the television industry, particularly the rise of cable television networks, have led to a fragmentation of the audience and thus to more niche programming. Although lamented by many executives at the Big Three networks, this fragmentation has been beneficial for upstart stations such as Fox and, more recently, UPN and the WB. Still, within the same time period, continuing commercial imperatives to maximize market share fueled contrary pressures to consolidate entertainment and appeal to broad audience demographics. In other words, the television industry was still designed to conceive of the sitcom as an "art of the middle," to use David Marc's term, and to reproduce it as such ad nauseum.[60]

By the early 1990s, the assimilationist/separatist debate was not only continuing but also intensifying as a result of increased intermarriage and the influence of multiculturalism. Such realities and the tensions surrounding related demographic changes became part of the discussion of the hit sitcom *Seinfeld* (1989–98). Originally opposed by the NBC programming executive Brandon Tartikoff as "too Jewish," the show went on to have great commercial success in the 1990s. However, by the end of its run, it had also received criticism for being too assimilationist and garnered inquiries such as "How Jewish Was It?" (which was the title of an entire issue of the *Jewish Journal* devoted to *Seinfeld*).[61] Given that Jewish identity was increasingly visible and popular (albeit in conflicting and contradictory ways) in the 1990s, what are we to make of its representation on *The Simpsons* and its embodiment in Krusty the Clown, a secularized Jew who has successfully "passed" into mainstream racial whiteness and who has largely adopted the ethos of McWASP identity? In other words, does the show employ negative stereotypes of Jewish identity uncritically, or does it use them in the service of satire? To answer these questions, it is necessary to look at the production of *The Simpsons* and at specific episodes of the show that feature Krusty and/or Jewish themes.

The issues surrounding Jewish identity on *The Simpsons* come to the fore in an early episode entitled "Like Father, Like Clown" (October 1991), a brilliantly conceived parody of *The Jazz Singer* centered around the character Krusty the Clown. At the onset, Krusty, who has been invited to the Simpson home for dinner, is asked to offer grace before the meal. Krusty pauses a moment, apologizes for being "rusty," and then recites the traditional Jewish blessing—the "bracha"—in Hebrew. Homer, as might be expected, laughs at the "funny talk," but Lisa recognizes the language and points out that Krusty must be Jewish. Krusty tells the Simpsons that his real name in Herschel Krustovsky, that he was raised in Springfield's Lower East side, that he is descended from a long line of rabbis, and that his father is the Rabbi Hyman Krustovsky of Temple Beth Springfield. In a flashback sequence, we learn that Krusty was pulled toward comedy as a young boy, but his father, who is quite orthodox, forbade him from following that path because a clown was not "a respected member of the community." Krusty continued to perform clandestinely, but he was eventually found out and then publicly disowned by his father. Through tears, Krusty tells the Simpsons that he and his father have been estranged for 25 years. After leaving the Simpson home, Krusty wanders the streets, sadly reminiscing about the past. He attempts to call his father on the phone, but he cannot bring himself to speak. When we see Krusty again, he is an emotional wreck, unable to control himself during a performance on the *Krusty the Clown Show*. Bart and Lisa, upset by their hero's condition, decide they have to intervene and reunite father and son. What follows is a playful exploration of the confluence of Jewish traditions and secular influences in contemporary American culture.

The Simpson kids first seek out Rabbi Krustovsky and ask to speak with him about his son, but they are summarily rejected: "I have no son!" he shouts and slams the door on them. The next tack is to call in to the radio show that Rabbi Krustovsky does each week on KBBL, along with Reverend Lovejoy and Monsignor Kenneth Daly. Bart calls the show and asks all three religious leaders a question: "If a son defies his father and chooses a career that makes millions of children happy, shouldn't the father forgive the son?" The priest and the minister say yes, but Rabbi Krustovsky adamantly says no. Undeterred, Bart visits a shop called Yiddle's and purchases a costume (one stereotypical of Hasidic Jews) that will allow him to pass as a Jew and infiltrate the rabbi's close circle. Bart passes long enough to pose a question, but his disguise is exposed and he is again sent away. Lisa and Bart then arrange for Krusty and his father to "accidentally" meet by tricking them both into going to Izzy's Deli at the same time. It appears for a moment that they might be able to talk at last, but the rabbi is incensed when he looks at the menu and discovers that although the deli is Jewish, it is not kosher. He is even more incensed when he sees that a sandwich has been named for Krusty—a combination of ham, sausage, bacon, and mayonnaise on white bread! Bart and Lisa next go to the public library, where Lisa reads through books on Judaica so they can use knowledge and scripture to persuade the rabbi. Sadly, these too fail, as the rabbi always has a line of scripture at hand to counter the one Bart offers. As a last resort, Lisa hands Bart a quote from *Yes, I Can*, the autobiography of Sammy Davis Jr., and it is this, ironically, that does the trick. Rabbi Krustovsky goes to Krusty's studio, where the two men embrace, weep, and apologize for their past mistakes. Krusty then brings his father onstage to introduce him to the audience, and the two men then sing a duet of "Oh, Mein Papa." Mike Reiss, a producer and veteran writer on the show, notes that "there have always been a lot of Jewish writers on *The Simpsons*," which presumably has given the show a Jewish "sensibility."[62] Certainly a Jewish sensibility is evident in the humor that surrounds Krusty, who owes a debt to the *tummlers* of the Borscht Belt (i.e., those comedians who worked the Catskills in the 1950s).[63] There is also a large Jewish presence in the geography of Springfield—for example, there is a Jewish hospital, a synagogue, a Lower East Side, and restaurants such as Tannen's Fatty Meats and Izzy's Deli. There are many references to Judaism throughout and a rather liberal use of both Hebrew and Yiddish. Krusty, for example, peppers his speech with Yiddish expressions such as *mishegoyim* (crazy Gentiles), *pisher* (squirt), *tucchus* (butt), *yutz* (empty head), *plotz* (burst), *bupkes* (nothing), *schlemiel* (bungler), and *schmutz* (mess).[64]

At the same time that we see evidence of Jewishness in Springfield, we also see that assimilation has taken place, much as it has in American culture, and that this has helped largely to erase Jewish identity. One sign of such erasure is the alteration of names. As noted, in the episode "Like Father, Like Clown," we learn that Krusty the Clown was born Herschel Krustovsky. Similarly, in another episode, we learn that Kent Brockman, the local TV newsman, began his career as Kenny Brockelstein and that he still wears a pendant around his neck with the Hebrew word *C'hai* (life) inscribed on it. Both Krusty and Brockman have enacted the same sort of self-censorship as the studio moguls in the 1920s and 1930s as a means of fitting into the dominant culture and of gaining success, appropriately enough, in the medium of television. The degree of masking taking place among Jews in the entertainment industry is beautifully captured in a comment by Homer, of all people, in a scene from "Like Father, Like Clown." After Krusty has confessed his heritage to the Simpsons, Lisa explains to Homer that "many famous entertainers are Jewish" and proceeds to offer a short list of names as examples. When she is done, Homer exclaims with great surprise, "Mel Brooks is Jewish?" Again, the writers are having fun here with a knowing audience's own familiarity with Mel Brooks, his brand of humor, and the many overtly Jewish aspects of his comedy. What is important here is not the specific reference to Brooks but the ambiguous nature of Jewish identity in general. Clearly, Homer has mistaken Brooks for "white," which can only be read in this context as unmarked, assimilated whiteness. The show appears to be satirizing here the cultural reliance upon skin color as a reliable marker of racial or ethnic identity. It is no small matter that Krusty (a Jew) looks almost identical to Homer (a McWASP), although in clown makeup.

What The Simpsons is offering in "Like Father, Like Clown" is a parody of The Jazz Singer. However, rather than losing himself in "whiteness," like Jackie Rabinowitz, Krusty maintains his Jewish identity and foregrounds his Jewish heritage. Still, his father is brought into (assimilated into?) a mainstream, secularized view in accepting his son's role as an entertainer. Is this a way of further Americanizing Rabbi Krustovsky? Perhaps. Krusty's Jewishness is employed in minor ways in later episodes, though often as a kind of throwaway joke about the treatment of "his people" or the way that "his kind" have historically felt excluded from mainstream (Anglo) white culture. Krusty remains ambivalent about his religion and his Jewish heritage. In an episode entitled "The Front," which aired just two years later, in 1993, Krusty gets angered when the chef on Krusty's TV show surprises him with news that he has Krusty's mother's recipe for a traditional Passover dish: Krusty snaps, "I don't do the Jewish stuff on the air ... Ixnay on the oojay!" Watching this at home, Lisa comments, "It's so sad that Krusty is ashamed of his roots." Indeed, after all she and Bart went through to help reestablish those roots, it does seem so. Jacobson notes,

> The Jews' version of becoming Caucasian cannot be understood apart from their particular history of special sorrows in the ghettos of Eastern Europe, apart from the deep history of anti-Semitism in Western culture, apart from anti-Semitic stereotypes that date back well before the European arrival on North American shores, or apart, finally and most obviously, from the historic cataclysm of the Holocaust.[65]

And yet on The Simpsons, Jewish identity is largely apart from all of this: it is in many ways dehistoricized and decontextualized, so all that remains is a loose configuration of superficial identifiers of Jewishness that can be comically employed (made visible) and then easily disposed of (rendered invisible). In this sense, Krusty is a continuation of a long line of Jewish characters on television whose identities were tenuous. Much like Seinfeld, its 1990s sitcom competitor, The Simpsons most commonly offers self-deprecating Jewish humor, a variety of less-than-flattering stereotypes of Jewish people, a highly ambivalent Jewish character, and a rather ambiguous sense of Jewish identity in relation to mainstream "white American" identity.

Neonativism and Indian American Identity

Nativism, simply put, is the practice or policy of favoring native-born citizens over immigrants, even those who are naturalized. The United States has of course seen many cycles of nativist sentiment, which have been closely tied to the economic status of the nation: in periods of economic expansion and optimism, the nation has warmly welcomed many immigrants, but in periods of stagnation and pessimism, it has often reviled them. The fear and loathing of immigrants usually intensifies in the midst of war or in economic downturns, during which time native-born citizens seek the safety of social homogeneity and the convenient scapegoat of "alien" enemies. In the early 1990s, simultaneous with the appearance of *The Simpsons*, there was a resurgence of nativism and anti-immigrant activism, expressed as a growing distrust of immigrants already in the country and a desire to keep more from entering.

The issues surrounding nativism and racial identity come to the fore in an episode entitled "Much Apu about Nothing," which centers around Apu Nahasapeemapetilon, the Bengali Indian who is the proprietor of the local Kwik-E-Mart. Primarily concerned with a proposition to deport all illegal immigrants from Springfield, the episode begins with images of wild bears loose in Springfield and a glimpse of the fear this creates among the town's residents—an apt metaphor for the issues to be dealt with in the episode. In the opening sequence, we see Ned Flanders, a quintessentially McWASP character, encounter a bear in the street. Ned is terrified and runs home, screaming hysterically; the bear, however, is quite genial and calm. Of course, Ned's reaction reflects the same kinds of fears expressed by many whites (or those at the centers of power in the United States) about the increase of immigrants, who have been and continue to be perceived as a "threat" to the well-being of the nation. Homer, our resident nativist, is incensed by the threat posed by the bears and leads an angry mob to the mayor's office to demand that something be done. Mayor Quimby establishes a Bear Patrol to (rather brutally) keep order in the streets. But when Homer sees the "Bear Patrol Tax" on his paycheck stub, he is angered and protests once again. Quimby is quick to redirect the focus this time, claiming that Springfieldians' taxes are so high because of "illegal immigration." He then puts forth Proposition 24, a referendum to deport all illegal immigrants, to be voted on in one week. As tensions rise, the show offers us glimpses (with due satire) of the increasing nativism among the residents of Springfield. For example, Uter, a German exchange student legally in the country, is harassed by the other children at school (Nelson ignorantly tells him "Hey German boy, go back to Germania"). Homer and Marge staunchly support Proposition 24 until they discover that Apu is an illegal immigrant and will be deported.

Before discussing "Much Apu about Nothing" in more detail, it is important to acknowledge the context in which the episode appeared. One of the most remarkable qualities of *The Simpsons* is its ability to quickly incorporate and respond to events taking place within American culture, and "Much Apu about Nothing" is a fine example. In 1994, the State of California infamously produced Proposition 187, a bill that would deny state-funded services to illegal immigrants and prevent their enrollment in tax-supported educational institutions. Ostensibly, Proposition 187 was initiated by a concern over the economic circumstances of the state, but the proposition served only to shift the focus off of economics and onto immigration—hence onto questions about race, ethnicity, and "American" identity. Candidates for the state governorship and open senate seats blamed California's poor economic condition on the presence of illegal immigrants, particularly Mexican immigrants, thereby framing the issue of immigration in nativist terms. The picture was not quite so simple, however. History shows us that nativism is cyclical, largely driven by economic forces and not necessarily dependent on race or ethnicity. This was made quite clear by the results of the vote on Proposition 187: Hispanics, who comprise a large portion of the immigrants who would be most directly affected by the measure, strongly opposed Proposition 187, and blacks, who historically have seen themselves in competition with foreign-born immigrants for jobs, strongly supported the proposition.[66]

Only a few years prior, at the start of the 1990s, immigration was on the upswing. The Immigration Act of 1990, introduced jointly by Senator Edward Kennedy and Representative Bruce Morrison, increased the overall ceiling on family-based immigration. However, once the Republican Party gained control of both houses of Congress, things changed rapidly. In the short time between Proposition 187 (1994) and the airing of "Much Apu about Nothing" (1996), the country took a decidedly nativist turn, prompted by the conservative wing of the Republican Party. In 1994, Arizona representative Bob Stump proposed the Immigration Moratorium Act (HR 3862), which sought to eliminate the immigration of parents, adult children, and brothers and sisters of US citizens, as well as the spouses and children of permanent residents until the year 2000. That same year, Alabama senator Richard Shelby introduced the Immigration Moratorium Act in the Senate (S 160). In 1995, California representative Brian Bilbray introduced the Citizenship Reform Act (HR 1363), which would have limited the number of children who automatically become US citizens simply because they are born on US soil. Also in 1995, Wyoming senator Alan Simpson and Texas representative Lamar Smith—then chairmen, respectively, of the Senate and House Subcommittees on Immigration—each backed bills that would have amended the Immigration and Nationality Act to reduce immigration quotas by roughly one-third. Smith also introduced the Immigration in the National Interest Acts (HR 1915 and HR 2202). It is notable that none of this proposed legislation passed. However, on September 30, 1996, President Clinton signed the Illegal Immigrant Reform and Immigrant Responsibility Act of 1996 (IIRIRA 96), an omnibus bill that maintained many of the elements of the proposed legislation and resulted in actions such as doubling the size of the Border Patrol, easing procedures for deporting immigrants convicted of crimes, and increasing the financial obligations of sponsors of legal immigrants.[67]

The fears that lay behind such legislation are exposed and explored in "Much Apu about Nothing." Lisa, of course, is opposed to Proposition 24 because, as she reminds everyone, the United States was founded and built by immigrants. At this point, Grandpa Simpson is prompted to recite the Simpson family history: "The story goes back to the old country," he tells us, but then quickly adds, "I forget which one exactly." In an interesting flashback, we see young Abe Simpson and his father first speaking of the trip to America and then aboard a ship bound for the new land. These scenes reveal the racial background of the Simpsons, namely the unmarked (indeed, unremarked upon) invisibility of their whiteness. Tellingly, Abe and his father are rendered in cartoon form as blonde; unlike Bart and Lisa, whose blondeness is ambiguous since their face and hair are of the same color (yellow) and not separated by visible lines, Abe and his father have hair cuts that make the hair stand out prominently, and it is colored a more pale yellow than their faces. Abe's comment that he cannot remember which country the family hails from is an important acknowledgment of the "melting pot" metaphor and the belief that one could and should lose all sense of previous identity to be remade as an American. Abe's comments also show that the Simpson family has lost ties not only to some unremembered nation but to Europe itself (the "old world"); they have severed their connections to some preexisting ethnic culture and have assimilated fully into "American" identity. Theirs is the great American immigrant tale, coincident with the immigration of millions of people from Northern and Central Europe at the dawn of the twentieth century. In short, ethnic identity has been subsumed by white racial identity, and the Simpson family story is thus the quintessential McWASP story, one that resonates well for many viewers of *The Simpsons* who see themselves and their own pasts reflected in this white immigrant narrative. However, many others—those like Apu, for instance—do not and cannot see themselves in this narrative.

In a following scene, we see Homer, wearing a button supporting Proposition 24, enter the Kwik-E-Mart, where he and Apu have a candid conversation about immigration. Apu confesses to Homer that he is an illegal and will be deported if the referendum passes. Homer pauses to reflect momentarily on their relationship but then simply dismisses the idea and tells Apu he will miss him. The scene closes on a powerful shot of Apu in the foreground, looking forlorn, and an Uncle Sam poster in the background with the phrase "I Want You OUT!"—a poster that Homer staples up. Later, we see protesters outside of the Kwik-E-Mart with signs that display their ignorance (one reads "Get Your Ass Back to Eurasia"). When Marge and the kids visit, Marge and Lisa are much more sympathetic to Apu's dilemma and inquisitive as to the circumstances. Here we are given another flashback sequence, one that offers an immigrant tale very different from—and certainly much more contemporary than—Grandpa Simpson's story. We learn that Apu is originally from Calcutta, where he attended CalTech (Calcutta Institute for Technology) and earned a degree. He was then accepted for graduate study in the United States and enrolled at Springfield Heights Institute of Technology. Tellingly, as he prepares to depart, we see Apu talking with his parents. His mother says, "Never forget who you are," and his father says simply, "Make us proud, son." After nine years, Apu completed his PhD thesis but still had student loans to pay back and "didn't feel right" about leaving the United States without doing so, so he took the job at the Kwik-E-Mart. After Marge hears his tale, she decides to vote no on Proposition 24.

Apu decides that he must "pass" as an American in order to remain in the country he loves, so he seeks out the mob boss Fat Tony to secure fraudulent documents, including a passport, driver's license, and birth certificate. The exchange between them is telling. After receiving the documents, Apu clasps his hands together, bows his head, and says, "Most humble and grateful thanks to you." Fat Tony quickly responds,

> Woah, woah, woah, woah, woah! Can the courtesy, you're an American now. Remember, you were born in Green Bay, your parents were Herb and Judy Nahasapeemapetilon, and if you do not wish to arouse suspicion, I strongly urge you to act American.

Not surprisingly, the mobsters, who themselves as Italians have direct experience with the processes of assimilation, also encourage Apu to assimilate. Interestingly, the "American" identity the mobsters create for Apu is a typically McWASP one: both the location of his birth and the names of his parents are "typically American" in that they represent unmarked whiteness (presumably middle-class and Protestant as well) and create an identity that could easily have been on any sitcom in the 1950s.

In an effort to make himself acceptable, Apu attempts to "Americanize" himself in a variety of ways, all of which speak tellingly of the processes of adaptation and assimilation. When we next see Apu at the Kwik-E-Mart, he is wearing a cowboy hat and a NY Mets baseball shirt; he has draped the store in red, white, and blue ribbons;

and he is listening to country music. Apu himself speaks in what he perceives to be the flat (unmarked) English of Middle America, rather than his famously accented brand of English: "Hey, Homer, how's it hanging?" he asks. In words that are clearly enunciated, Apu proposes that he and Homer watch the baseball game on TV. In short, Apu's identity is made evident in much the same way other ethnic identities are on *The Simpsons*: through language and clothing. Ethnic identity is also offered via religious affiliation. Normally, Apu keeps a shrine to the Hindu god Ganesha on the checkout counter, but in the scene here the shrine is now gone, replaced by a stack of glossy magazines. Homer notices this and asks Apu about it. The sequence that follows satirically articulates the real essence of contemporary American identity: consumerism. In satirical fashion, the show makes clear that religion has been replaced by a consumerist ethos and that capitalism is the reigning belief system in the United States. Apu begins by saying, "Who needs the infinite compassion of Ganesha when I've got Tom Cruise and Nicole Kidman . . .," but he quickly shifts his tone and concludes, "staring at me from the cover of *Entertainment Weekly* with their dead eyes!" Apu then drops the facade. He feels he has betrayed his Indian heritage, as he recalls the words of his parents. "I cannot deny my roots, and I cannot keep up this charade," he says. Moved by Apu's plight and his love for the United States, Homer changes his mind on Proposition 24.

As a solution to Apu's dilemma, Bart suggests that Apu "just marry some American broad." Meanwhile, Lisa is seen reading a book entitled *Backdoors to Citizenship*, looking for a more likely solution. Although the satire on *The Simpsons* is often superb, it is sometimes hard to judge just who or what the target is. The strategies of both Bart and Lisa acknowledge methods of "cheating the system," as each offers a shortcut to citizenship. But are these strategies endorsed or satirized? It is truly hard to say. However, one can see that, at least in regard to Lisa's approach, it is highly ironic, for in the book Lisa discovers a grandfather clause that would grant Apu amnesty and allow him to take the citizenship test, thereby achieving citizenship legally. Excited by the possibility, Homer offers to tutor Apu in American history. This is absurd, of course, at least to anyone who knows something of Homer's intellectual abilities, but it is done to satirically illustrate that Apu, the nonnative, has more knowledge and understanding than Homer, the "native" American. This is reflected quite well in a conversation between Apu and an exam proctor during the oral portion of the citizenship test:

> *Proctor*: All right, here's your last question. What was the cause of the Civil War?
> *Apu*: Actually, there were numerous causes. Aside from the obvious schism between the abolitionists and the anti-abolitionists, there were economic factors, both domestic and international—
> *Proctor*: Wait, wait. Just say slavery.
> *Apu*: Slavery it is, sir.

Having passed the test, Apu gains his citizenship. In response, Homer throws a "Welcome to America" party, at which we find a humorous yet complicated comment on identity politics:

> *Apu*: Today, I am no longer an Indian living in America. I am an Indian-American.
> *Lisa*: You know, Apu, in a way, all Americans are immigrants. Except Native Americans.

Homer: Yeah, native Americans like us.
Lisa: No, I mean American Indians.
Apu: Like me.
Lisa: No, I mean . . .

But Lisa is cut off by Homer, who proposes a toast to Apu. The episode thus ends on a highly ambiguous note. As is often the case, *The Simpsons* does not take a clear position or neatly resolve all issues. Of course, parsing the intricacies of words such as "Native," "American," and "Indian" is far too complex for any television sitcom to handle. Indeed, it is often too complex for *us* as members of the culture to handle. What this leaves us with, at a minimum, is the fact that *The Simpsons* is a product of its own time and, as such, often embodies the ideological conflicts alive in American culture. "Much Apu about Nothing" reflects the fact that in our own world, the knotty issues of Native American/American Indian identity are unresolved and very difficult to talk about.

In his examination of ethnic stereotyping on *The Simpsons*, Duncan Beard argues, "However much the parodic use of mass-media stereotypes in *The Simpsons* may function in destabilizing these [ethnic] conventions, the show's presentation of 'Others' may also be seen as perpetuating rather than alleviating stereotypical visions of foreign national identities."[68] This is an arguable position, and it depends a great deal on how one decodes the intent of the show. With an eye to satire one would read such images as a critique of the stereotypes imposed upon foreigners. However, one could also see the jokes at Apu's expense and read the images then as a perpetuation of stereotypes. Beard also offers an intriguing analysis of "Much Apu about Nothing" and claims that Apu's character comes out a "hybrid 'American-Other'...despite the representational tensions that continually pull his character towards one pole or the other in exploring questions of American identity in a multicultural society."[69] This view is reminiscent of W. E. B. Du Bois's notion of "double-consciousness," which Du Bois claimed resulted in "two warring ideals in one dark body."[70] Considering the representation of black Americans on *The Simpsons*, it might be logical to claim that double-consciousness has transferred itself—at least on the show, if not in American culture at large—from black to brown bodies and/or from native to non-native peoples. As Beard more accurately notes later in his essay, "The key issue with regard to the representations of foreign national identities on *The Simpsons* is the ambiguity and ambivalence that exists concerning the show's endorsement or parody of stereotypes."[71] I would add that this is the key issue in the representation of *any* racial, ethnic, or national identity on *The Simpsons*. The notion of an "American-Other" is quite useful in highlighting the continuing power of McWASP ideology, in both television and American culture, and is applicable perhaps even to those safely ensconced in "whiteness" when their "Americanness" is in question.

"Real Americans": National Identity after 9/11

In the immediate aftermath of the attacks on September 11, 2001, the fear of the racial "Other" transferred itself to those living outside the United States (in the Middle East) and practicing a different, "foreign" religion (Islam). As the post-9/11 era progressed, however, that fear turned itself inward once again, and American nativism was given a perverse new face by the "War on Terror." Native-born Americans of all types—including privileged McWASPs—were now prone to persecution, suspected of being "subversives," vilified for offering dissenting views, or branded as "traitors" to the cause. Irrational fear was stoked by the US government itself with the hasty passage of the so-called Patriot Act, the implementation of color-coded "terror alerts," and the intensification of racial profiling, particularly now of Arabs and Arab Americans.[72] Most people knew very little about the Patriot Act when it was first passed by Congress, less than one month after the attacks on the World Trade Center and the Pentagon, and thus were primed to curtail their own liberties and to later support the expansion of the War on Terror into Iraq, based only on thin and questionable evidence. In "Pursuing Political Persuasion: War and Peace Frames in the United States after September 11th," a fascinating study of the rhetorical frames used by the Bush administration in the discourse surrounding 9/11, the authors Gregory M. Maney, Patrick G. Coy, and Lynn M. Woehrle note that President Bush "took extensive advantage of discursive and emotional opportunities presented by the attacks, reinforcing a sense of threat while crafting messages supportive of war and repression."[73] Because the Bush administration was in an institutionally privileged position for disseminating its message (as compared with antiwar and peace movement organizations), the message resonated loudly with the American public and persuaded people toward repressive ends.[74] As might be expected, the divide between the self-proclaimed "patriots" who supported these efforts and others who did not fell along the same lines designated in other culture war debates: that is, between the Right and the Left, between the "God-fearing" (i.e., Christian) Americans and the "anti-American" secularists. This was simultaneous with the rise of the red-state/blue-state rhetoric, which dominated the discourse of electoral politics from 2002 to 2008 but was particularly pronounced in the presidential election of 2004 and seemed only to deepen the political and cultural divides at that time.

The Simpsons stepped into the fray with the fifteenth-season episode "Bart-Mangled Banner," which aired in May 2004. Although the episode does not deal directly with racial or ethnic identity (except for a few passing allusions), it does deal very directly with nationality and the ideology of patriotism and thus, once again, with questions about what it means to be an "American." The episode is in part a response to the "climate of repression and fear," as Lisa herself describes it in the episode, manufactured by the Bush administration. But "Bart-Mangled Banner" is also a reaction to the real-world controversy surrounding the musical group Dixie Chicks just the year before. At a concert in London in early March 2003, just prior to the US-led invasion of Iraq, the lead singer Natalie Maines told the audience, "Just so you know, we're ashamed the president of the United States is from Texas."[75] This was first reported in the British newspaper *The Guardian* on March 12, 2003; a day later, the Associated Press broke the story in the United States, and it was subsequently picked up by nearly every major newspaper in the nation. In reporting on the controversy, the AP stated that "angry phone calls flooded Nashville radio station WKDF-FM on Thursday, some calling for a boycott of the Texas trio's music."[76] Concurrent with the widespread mainstream media coverage was an intense Internet discussion, primarily on alt.fan.dixiechicks, which was quite heated. Some posters said they agreed with Maines or discussed the nature of dissent in a democracy at a time of war, but many of the posts simply expressed contempt for the musicians: one post described the Dixie Chicks as "stupid anti-American sluts like Jane Fonda,

Barbara Streisand [*sic*], Jeannie Garafalo [*sic*], Hillary Clinton, etc." and (inaccurately) alleged that fans at the London concert burned an American flag.[77] Over the next few weeks, angry country music fans smashed and burned Dixie Chicks CDs, branded the trio as unpatriotic, and demanded that country music radio stations take their songs off the air. Sales plummeted, concerts were cancelled, and the band's career seemed at an end. Rather than force the Dixie Chicks to issue an apology for the comment, the accusations and negative publicity seemed to fuel their passion to stand their ground.[78] As Emil B. Towner notes, "What ensued was not only an attack-and-defend argument over what Maines said and whether she was wrong to say it but more importantly a broader argument over what it means to be an American and to be patriotic during times of war."[79] Change was slow, but on the heels of this and the subsequent revelations that no weapons of mass destruction existed in Saddam Hussein's Iraq, many people began to question the limitations placed upon free speech and dissent by the Bush White House and to examine more closely just how much the civil liberties of US citizens had been eroded by the Patriot Act.

All of this is fodder for the satire presented in "Bart-Mangled Banner." In this episode, Bart winds up accidentally mooning the American flag at an elementary school event. He is readily booed by all for his disrespectful and presumably unpatriotic behavior, and even the local bullies refer to him as a "traitor." The local news editor of the *Springfield Shopper* asks one of his reporters to "overhype" the story, and right afterward we see what is clearly a photoshopped image of Bart, showing him with a nasty leer on his face and now mooning both the flag and the Statue of Liberty, who is depicted as recoiling in horror, all under the caption "U-ASS-A!" Local citizens then proceed to condemn the family: "They hate our country!" one declares. Homer is called "Benedict Arnold" at the miniature golf course and is later shunned by his friends at Moe's bar, which he is told is "only for real Americans." Lisa, who realizes the family members have become "pariahs," reports that she has even received hate spam—the one shown to us calls her a "commie pig." She is also later referred to as "Saddam" by the resident rich Texan. When the Simpsons are invited to go on a cable talk show called *Head Butt* (clearly a parody of CNN's *Crossfire*) to tell their side of the story, they figure it might be the only way to resolve the problem. However, the host of the show, Nash Castor, is overtly judgmental and confrontational from the start. He provokingly asks Bart, "What is it you hate most about this country? Is it the freedom?" Bart, well schooled in the art of bullshit and perhaps aware of the need for media spin, makes a play for sympathy, saying, "Nash, I've realized something. I'm the worst kid in the world, and the last thing I deserve is forgiveness, but [and here he begins to cry] with a little help from Jesus and our fighting men and women overseas . . ." Castor interrupts him, saying, "Alright, so if I hear you correctly, you're saying that America is better than Jesus." He then points to Homer and barks, "Do you agree?" Without pause, he then points to Marge and says, "Uh, before he can answer, do you?" "Well," Marge begins, "America's not perfect." "So, is that why you and your son hate us?" Castor asks. Marge, angered by Castor's bullying and the twisting of her words, responds, "If by 'us' you mean loud-mouth talk show hosts, which everyone seems to be in this country, then yes, I *do* hate Americans!"[80] At this, everyone is momentarily stunned into silence. Nash expresses surprise that she hasn't been run out of town. He then equates her with Springfield and thus concludes that "Springfield hates America." This becomes national news, and Tom Brokaw is seen reporting that Springfield is being denounced around the country. In the midst of his report, we also get a quick cut to a scene of Simpson supporters: it is an image from some-where in the Middle East showing a group of women in black burkas holding photos of the Simpson family, yelling, "Simpsons be praised; Praise be to Springfield," and ululating. Once again, we have a provocative scene that can be variously interpreted. One could see this as playing into and perpetuating the stereotype that followers of Islam and, by extension, Middle Easterners in general are America-hating radicals. However, I believe this to be another example of the show's astute satire. What the writers are underscoring here is the absurdity of political dissent being readily equated not only with anti-American views but, by implication, with terrorism. The vilifica-tion the Simpsons are experiencing at this point in the episode is not all that different from what the Dixie Chicks experienced when exercising their right to free speech.

To distance themselves from the Simpsons, other members of the town try to shore up their patriotism, again in ways that are wildly exaggerated and thus make clear that there is a satirical comment being made. Mayor Quimby, for example, announces that Springfield will be renamed Libertyville; accordingly, everything is draped in American flags and red, white, and blue bunting, and even the colors of the traffic lights are transformed (causing many accidents, of course). Apu, who is self-conscious about his patriotism and his status as an "American," once again transforms his store, decorating it in the same patriotic manner as before and sell-ing rebranded products such as "Homeland Noodles with Uncle Sam Balls" soup. As we have seen, Apu is also well aware of the pressures to assimilate and become less "Other"; to do so this time around, he renames his children. When Marge refers to two of his children by their given names, Apu corrects her, telling her that those were their "pre-witch-hunt names"; his eight children are now known as Freedom, Lincoln, Condoleeza, Coke, Pepsi, Manifest Destiny, Apple Pie, and Superman. "And together," Apu concludes, "we're the McGillicuddys!" In one fell swoop, this brief joke deftly and brilliantly skewers the trite clichés of all-Americanism, right-wing populism, consumerism, heroism, and the Republican Party—which has milked each of these ideologies for all they are worth over the past 40 years. Despite Lisa's recita-tion of a passage from the First Amendment (in church, no less!) and her passionate reminder of the value of the freedom of speech, she and her family are arrested for vio-lation of the "Government Knows Best Act." They are then sent to the Ronald Reagan Re-education Center, where they share space with Michael Moore, Al Franken, the Dixie Chicks, Bill Clinton, and Elmo. The inclusion of Elmo is humorous in a parodic sense, but it also satirically targets the ludicrousness of right-wing suspicions about even the most innocuous aspects of popular culture. While at the center, the Simpsons are deprived of sleep, administered Sodium Pentothal, and shown propa-ganda films—all allusions, of course, to the "interrogation" practices being employed by the US military in detention centers both at home and abroad. Under the pressure of these techniques, Lisa begins to change her views, which prompts Marge to suggest that they need to escape. To do so, they arrange to offer a patriotic song-and-dance show for the inmates. This is merely a ruse, however, to buy them time to escape. Once they escape the prison (i.e., Alcatraz), they still have to swim to freedom. They are rescued by a French boat and invited to France, where they can freely vocalize their "hatred" for America. But in short order, they come to miss their home, mainly because, as Lisa puts it, "that's where all our stuff is." Getting back home seems to pose a problem, but Homer observes, "There's one group that's always welcome in America: immigrants without IDs." Thus, the Simpsons return, in an invocation of the McWASP legacy discussed previously, as immigrants ready to "start a new life."

In his discussion of "Bart-Mangled Banner," John Alberti astutely comments,

> *The Simpsons* reflects an ambivalence and confusion over the war and about post-9/11 America that suggests a mixture of feelings and reactions among a broad cross-section of viewers: a desire for community and mutual support that finds expression in the idea of patriotism along with a deep suspicion of how that desire can be easily exploited for political gain; an attraction to the atavistic patriarchal ideal of the decisive leader who acts boldly in a time of crisis along with the wariness of sound bites and photo opportunities born of a lifetime immersed in the discourse of advertising.[81]

This is an accurate assessment of the feelings of many in the viewing audience and perhaps of the writers as well, for this episode—another with only one storyline—is clearly focused on satirically exposing the way that fear was (and perhaps still is) being exploited and on censuring the repressive strategies used to quell dissent in American society.

The fear that lay behind the harassment of the Simpson family in "Bart-Mangled Banner" is also explored in the 2008 episode "Mypods and Boomsticks," in which we see suspicion directed once again toward nonnative Others—specifically, in this case, toward Muslims.[82] This episode concerns Bart's relationship with a Muslim boy named Bashir, whose family has just moved to Springfield from Jordan, and focuses on Homer's unfounded suspicion that his new Muslim neighbors are terrorists. Surprisingly, *The Simpsons* has been reluctant to engage the problems of anti-Muslim sentiment and Islamophobia in the post-9/11 era—and when it finally does, it does so rather halfheartedly. As noted previously, episodes of *The Simpsons* that address serious culture war issues commonly have a singular storyline (e.g., "Much Apu about Nothing" or "Bart-Mangled Banner"); this episode, however, has both a primary plot and a subplot (an extended parody of Steve Jobs and Apple and an implicit critique of the sheeplike following he and his products command). This is an unfortunate choice, I think, as it detracts from the important political issues being addressed in "Mypods and Boomsticks" and minimizes the time that can be devoted to them. Nevertheless, the episode still offers, in a relatively brief time, a powerful critique of xenophobia and, more specifically, of Islamophobia and the ways in which these ideologies are fed by the ideas and images disseminated by the mass media.

As has been well documented, American mass media has regularly equated Arabs and Muslims with terrorism, in news reports, Hollywood film, and television programming.[83] This could be seen, for example, in news stories on successful terrorist attacks prior to 9/11, such as the 1983 bombing of a marine barracks in Lebanon, the 1993 bombing of the World Trade Center in New York, the 1996 bombing of the Khobar Towers in Saudi Arabia, the 1998 bombings of the US embassies in Kenya and Tanzania, and the 2000 bombing of the USS *Cole* in Yemen. The link between Arabs/Muslims and terrorism could also be found throughout the 1990s in Hollywood films—such as *Navy SEALS* (1990), *True Lies* (1994), *Executive Decision* (1996), and *The Siege* (1998)—and into the new millennium in television shows such as *24* (2001–10), *Sleeper Cell* (2005–6), and *The Unit* (2006–9). In the second edition of *Reel Bad Arabs: How Hollywood Vilifies a People* (2009), Jack Shaheen writes,

> Today's reel bad Arabs are much more bombastic, brutal, and belligerent, much more rich, ruthless, and raunchy. They are portrayed as the civilized world's enemy, fanatic

demons threatening people across the planet. Oily sheikhs finance nuclear wars; Islamic radicals kill innocent civilians; bearded, scruffy "terrorists," men and women, toss their American captives inside caves and filthy, dark rooms and torture them.[84]

Tung Yin makes similar claims in his examination of film and television programming in the post-9/11 era, although his view is somewhat more balanced than Shaheen's. Yin concludes that "the results are mixed," with many images of Arab terrorists on the one hand yet many "good" Muslims as secondary characters on the other. Yin astutely observes, however, that the media has introduced a "sinister new type of terrorist" and archetype: the "sleeper," that is, the "seemingly normal Arab-American who insidiously plots to carry out terrorist attacks from inside the country."[85] This new trope is central to the plot of "Mypods and Boomsticks," and it is key to understanding the censure being offered. For the most part, real-life "sleepers" have not had the sophistication or the level of intended lethality that is commonly depicted in the movies or on television. Exposing this truth, however, is not what concerns the writers of the episode; it is instead the irrational fear of Muslims harbored by many citizens—a fear that is perpetuated and fueled by most forms of mass media.

At first, it seems that "Mypods and Boomsticks" will be about religious tolerance. For example, in an early scene, Bart warns Bashir not to tell anyone he is Muslim because the local bullies (Jimbo, Dolf, and Kearney) will harass him for being "different." When the bullies proceed to do just that—one of them exclaiming, "You're the reason I can't carry toothpaste on an airplane"—Bart tries to offer a lesson in tolerance, pointing out that "everyone's different" and reminding Jimbo that he's Christian, Dolf that he's Jewish, and Kearney that he's a member of "that cult Moe started." However, it is soon clear that the primary focus of the episode is on the fear of the Islamic "Other" and the reactions to this by self-proclaimed "patriots," embodied by Homer of course. Viewers of *The Simpsons* know that Homer's worldview is shaped largely by mass media. As a consumer of Hollywood film and television, Homer is already conditioned to be suspicious of others unlike himself. The writers play upon this preconditioning by having the most innocuous of events and conversations, seen and overheard by Homer, become transformed by his fear and wild imagination into a false reality. When Homer first meets Bashir, he likes him because he is well-mannered and polite. But he begins to have a different perspective after talking with his coworkers, Lenny and Carl, who tease him about Bart's new friend, and with Moe, who first plants the seeds of suspicion by telling Homer, "This is serious. This Bashir kid is Muslim and therefore up to something." To ensure that the viewer does not misunderstand Moe's reasoning, an explicit link is provided: Homer responds to Moe by saying, "Oh, I can't believe that until I see a fictional tv program espousing your point of view," and with that, Moe switches on the television above the bar to reveal an episode of *24* featuring the hero, Jack Bauer, "interrogating" a prisoner named Fayed (coded as Arab through name, coloring, and accent) at knifepoint. Homer is instantly convinced and now wonders what he should do. Carl suggests that if Homer wants to "stop Bashir and his war on American principles," he could "discriminate against his family in employment and housing." "Yeah, that's pretty patriotic," Lenny says, "but I got a better idea. Invite 'em over." "A little dinner," Moe says, "a little dessert, and then you Jack Bauer 'em into giving you all their secrets." They all then laugh conspiratorially.

Although the reference here to Fox's *24* is brief, it is important to an understanding of the political and media contexts in which "Mypods and Boomsticks" appeared. The drama *24* first aired in November 2001, just two months after 9/11 and less than one month after President Bush signed the Patriot Act into law. Given the political climate, it is perhaps not surprising that the show was an immediate success and became one of Fox's most-watched shows. But it also became quite controversial and was accused by many of furthering anti-Arab hatred and providing rationalizations for torture and other ethically dubious activities. As early as the fall of 2004, officials of the Council on American-Islamic Relations (CAIR) had expressed dismay at the depiction of Muslims on *24*, which the organization felt promoted suspicion of all Muslims and advanced Islamophobia.[86] In response, Fox somewhat absurdly announced plans to provide its affiliates with public service announcements showing Muslims in a favorable light. The spots, which were sponsored by CAIR, showcased a diverse group of individuals, who share personal stories and identify themselves as American Muslims. Each PSA ended with the statement, "Muslims are part of the fabric of this great country and are working to build a better America." One of these was even done, at a later date, by the *24* star Kiefer Sutherland.[87] Things settled for a time, but CAIR and many Muslim Americans were upset with developments in the show at the start of season 4, which began in January 2005, because of its depiction of the middle-class family (named Araz) as a suburban "sleeper-cell." Muslim extremists were no longer being portrayed within mass media as antisocial fanatics on the fringes of society. As Sabiha Khan, the communications director for CAIR-Southern California, put it, "[T]he neighbor next door could be a terrorist. Your normal, everyday, average-looking kid could be in a plot to kill everybody."[88] Sadly, it was not only the imagery of *24* one had to be concerned with, for the show became more than just a drama on television—it slowly became part of the national conversation and an influence on the thinking of those responsible for shaping antiterrorism tactics. For example, the former Office of Legal Counsel attorney John Yoo referenced *24* in his book *War by Other Means* (2006), which offered a defense of the Bush administration's interrogation policies.[89] That same year, at a symposium on *24* organized by the Heritage Foundation, the former Homeland Security secretary Michael Chertoff stated that people liked *24* because it "reflects real life."[90] The former CIA director James Woolsey also claimed that *24* is "quite realistic" about the threats it depicts.[91] And in 2007, during a debate among Republican presidential candidates, the US House representative Tom Tancredo responded to a hypothetical question about what to do with a captured would-be suicide bomber by saying, "I'm looking for Jack Bauer at that point, let me tell you."[92] The show *24* also had an impact on the behaviors of certain individuals. In one widely reported incident, the dean of the US Military Academy at West Point asked the producers of *24* to either reduce the amount of torture by Jack Bauer or at least show it backfiring because US military personnel in Iraq were using the torture tactics they had observed on the show.[93]

The air of suspicion promulgated by *24* (as well as the Bush administration and its mouthpiece, Fox News) has a powerful influence on Homer and is thus a key element of the satire offered in "Mypods and Boomsticks." After Homer has made the invitation to Bashir's family, Marge, unaware of Homer's plan, praises him for being open-minded enough to invite "Bart's Muslim friend's Muslim family" for dinner, ironically highlighting again how the family is seen as both separate and different. Marge discovers very quickly, however, that Homer has ulterior motives. During dinner, with virtually no tact or subtlety, Homer first makes reference to science being used to make bombs and then presents the dessert, which is a cake in the form of the American flag. He brandishes a knife and mockingly asks Bashir's father if he cares to cut it. When he declines, Homer exclaims, "What's the matter? Don't like the taste of freedom?" Clearly offended, Bashir's parents politely excuse themselves and leave. Bart then chastises his father: "Dad, these people are my friends. Don't fear them just because they have a different religion, a different culture, and their last name is Bin Laden." Marge adds, "You're teaching Bart a terrible lesson of intolerance." "I'm sorry," Homer says, "it's just so fun and easy to judge people based on religion." Per usual, Marge then demands that he go apologize. But when Homer arrives at the Bin Laden home and sees Bashir's father standing in the garage with a case of dynamite, he immediately concludes, "They are terrorists!" Later that night, Homer dreams of an encounter with a genie (in a hilarious parody of the genie from Disney's *Aladdin*), who tells Homer that he (the genie) will "destroy your decadent Western society." He does so in the dream by transforming the church into a mosque, Reverend Lovejoy into an imam, and all the music at the local record store into Cat Stevens. Homer wakes up screaming. Taking his dream as a premonition and determined to prove himself right, Homer goes to spy on the Bin Laden family. What he overhears of their conversation, in typical sitcom fashion, is only partial and out of context and fits comfortably into Homer's preconceived notions about the threat they pose. For example, he hears Bashir's father talk of blowing up buildings and admitting that he is "killing himself" all for the "profit" (which Homer hears as "prophet"). To gather evidence, Homer worms his way into the house, taking advantage of the hospitality of Bashir's mother. Among other things, he insults her by referring to Allah as Oliver and the Koran as the Corona (perhaps thinking of beer) and, by way of small talk, saying, "Now that we're alone, Death to America, right?" With great reserve and patience, she asks Homer why he is really there. He deflects her questions, makes an excuse to leave the room, and then (perhaps fancying himself Jack Bauer) hacks into the family's computer, where he finds schematics of the Springfield Mall. Convinced that Bashir's father is going to blow up the mall—and the people inside it—Homer then tries to play the hero. What he has missed is the fact that it is the old Springfield Mall, which has been scheduled for demolition. Homer runs into the mall, chanting "USA! USA!" He grabs the dynamite and throws it into the river, thereby destroying the bridge from the Duff Brewery to the mainland. By way of apology for his errors in judgment, Homer invites the Bin Ladens over once more. In the final scene, we see the two families gather together on the back patio, beneath a banner reading "Pardon My Intolerance," which Homer notes has "really paid off over the years."

In "Terrorvision: Race, Nation and Muslimness in Fox's *24*," an impressive study of the Fox drama in relation to post-9/11 politics, Peter Morey astutely argues that *24* enshrines a "neoconservative instrumentalism."[94] Morey's comments are both insightful and remarkably applicable to "Mypods and Boomsticks," given the ways in which I have argued that race, ethnicity, and nationality are regularly framed on *The Simpsons*. Of the "clash of civilizations" being presented on *24* and similar programs, Morey writes, "true 'Americanness' and American values are distinguished from those of the villains via a process of racialization wherein all threatening elements become, in a sense, 'Muslimized' [and] expelled from the bosom of the nation which is here conceived as an extension of the white, blond, Protestant family."[95] As McWASPs, the Simpsons are the stand-ins here for the family Morey speaks of, and Bashir's family is the "Muslimized" other that poses a threat, at least in Homer's eyes.

Of course, it is precisely this kind of "us" against "them" dichotomy that the writers of *The Simpsons* are aiming to satirize. Not unlike the episode "Homer's Phobia," which explores Homer's homophobia (discussed in detail in chapter 4), "Mypods and Boomsticks" uses Homer as a foil to explore how the fear of the "other" is cultivated and promoted in American society.

Conclusion

As noted previously, *The Simpsons* is, in many ways, quintessentially "American." However, as explained at the start of this chapter, throughout much of the twentieth century, normative "American" identity has been narrowly coded as white-assimilated, middle class, suburban, and Protestant—what I have referred to here as McWASP—and much of the mainstream media has helped to perpetuate a belief in assimilation as imperative for achieving "Americanness." Of course, identities are not static, nor are ideas about them. Within the past two decades—the same time period in which *The Simpsons* has been airing—common understandings of American identity have been rapidly changing. The monoculturalist metaphor of the "melting pot" has been increasingly contested by more pluralistic metaphors, such as the "quilt," the "mosaic," and the "salad bowl." By the start of the new millennium, being white had lost some of its cachet, if not its power, and today it seems that being "white-assimilated" is not quite so imperative an element of being or becoming fully "American," owing in no small part to the election of Barack Obama—the first black man (or biracial or African American or "person of color," depending on whom you ask) to hold the office of president of the United States. The shifts in perspective are underscored as well by changing demographics, which we now have a more accurate picture of because of changes to the US Census initiated in 2000. That year, for the very first time in census history, respondents were allowed to select "more than one race" and to additionally specify what they believed to be their "ancestry or ethnic origin."[96] In the 2000 census, seven million people (about 2.4 percent of the population) reported being more than one race; in the 2010 census, the number had increased to nine million people (about 2.9 percent of the population).[97] Such large-scale shifts in identification are clearly changing the way we all see and understand "American" identity today and contributing to what the writer Richard Rodriguez infamously called "the browning of America."[98] In short, we are now in the uncharted waters of what some claim to be a "postethnic" or "postracial" era, dominated by "color-blind" rhetoric.[99]

The creators of *The Simpsons* are well aware of the historical and cultural frames in which they work and, therefore, incorporate situations that satirically highlight the ways in which people in the United States are responding to such large demographic and ideological changes. More specifically, they seem particularly interested in exploring the responses to the shift away from the deeply ingrained equation of "whiteness" with "Americanness." As I have tried to show, I think that the writers of *The Simpsons* are aiming to satirize not only this equation but also the fear that arises when such normative ideas are questioned or challenged. To do so, of course, they have to draw upon some very well-known character types and racial and ethnic stereotypes. In his study of race and comic books, Marc Singer argues that contemporary comics and cartoons often reveal "deceptively soothing stereotypes lurking behind their veneers of diversity."[100] Although Singer is speaking specifically of Marvel and DC comic books, his observation is applicable more broadly to other forms of animation and rings true of *The Simpsons*. The creators of *The Simpsons* remain well aware of the social imperative for diverse representations within mass media. For this reason, the writers begin with a self-consciousness about the portrayal of certain characters—witness, for example, the initial concerns of the writers and producers over the creation of Apu: as the producer Al Jean recalls, "[W]e were worried he might be considered an offensive stereotype."[101] *The Simpsons* does indeed offer a more realistic racial and ethnic portrait of contemporary America than most other shows on network television, and it often displays a refreshingly inclusive attitude toward so-called minorities and recent immigrants. However, *The Simpsons* also demonstrates a reliance upon the codes of McWASP identity and normative whiteness, and these often remain unquestioned in the body of the show. Over the years, it seems that the creators of *The Simpsons* have come to rely (for better and worse) on what Peter Morey calls "ethnonormativity."[102] When the creators wish to explore racial or ethnic prejudice, which they often do, they have recourse to an ethnonormative space—that is, a space in which to explore the tensions between contending groups, commonly depicted as a "host community" and an "alien wedge."[103] In this way, the show is not unlike a great many others on American television, including those considered "conservative" rather than "progressive." In exploring taboo topics and controversial issues, the writers can depend upon ethnonormative identity—of the Simpson family, of a great many residents of Springfield, and perhaps even of a large segment of the viewing audience—as a foundation against which to juxtapose an "Other." This can work in service of satire, as I have tried to demonstrate, but it can also result in the reification of "normative" whiteness, since that particular racial category remains largely unmarked and uninterrogated. In this sense, *The Simpsons* truly is an accurate reflection of contemporary American life.

The situation is more complex with Jewish, Indian, and Muslim identity, perhaps because each of these is ideologically marked as or is closely associated with a non-normative racial or ethnic category in American culture, despite being classified as "white" by the US Census.[104] It is also more complex simply because of the social and political changes that have occurred over the past 20 years: questions about what defined "American" identity pre- and post-9/11 are not quite the same. In some ways, the focus has shifted from a preoccupation with race, which dominated academic discourse in the 1990s, to a preoccupation with religion, which has dominated the conversation since 2001. One strong connecting thread, however, is the concern with patriotism, as can be seen in many of the episodes discussed in this chapter. An examination of racial, ethnic, and national identity on *The Simpsons* is thus very revealing about current attitudes toward these topics in the United States. Not surprisingly, the representations of these various identities on *The Simpsons* are quite complex and at times contradictory. In short, the show reveals a large degree of ambivalence about how to define "American" identity in the last decade of the twentieth century and at the start of the twenty-first. Ultimately, what *The Simpsons* offers its viewers is a highly conflicted perspective—not unlike that held by many US citizens—toward racial, ethnic, and national identity. In other words, *The Simpsons* provides viewers a complex blend of both progressive and traditional attitudes toward immigration, assimilation, and the construction of an "American" identity.

3

"Don't Ask Me, I'm Just a Girl": Feminism, Female Identity, and *The Simpsons*

> Our collective history of interacting with and being shaped by the mass media has engendered in many women a kind of cultural identity crisis. We are ambivalent toward femininity on the one hand and feminism on the other.
>
> —*Susan Douglas*[1]

The second wave of feminist movement in the United States helped usher in many significant changes in American culture and women's everyday experience, and it provided many women with increased social, political, and economic power. In short, it created a much greater equality between men and women, in both the public and private spheres. However, another consequence of such changes, as well as of the shifts in theoretical perspective since the height of second-wave feminism, is that many women's lives are now marked by ambivalence and ambiguity. As Katha Pollitt flatly states in "Feminism at the Millennium," the introduction to her essay collection *Subject to Debate: Sense and Dissents on Women, Politics, and Culture* (2001), "[an] ambivalence marks even the attempt to evaluate how powerful women are."[2] Pollitt's view was shared by many other feminist academics and commentators whose similar claims about the contradictory messages offered to women were well supported by the varied articulations of female "empowerment" in American culture at the turn of the century.[3]

A full decade later, little has changed; understandings of feminism in popular culture are still imbued with a great deal of confusion and contradiction. In her most recent book, *Enlightened Sexism: The Seductive Message That Feminism's Work Is Done* (2010), Susan Douglas notes that women are still "bombarded by overlapping and often colliding streams of progressive and regressive imagery, both of which offer [women] very different fantasies of female power."[4] This statement echoes ideas first presented in *Where the Girls Are: Growing Up Female with the Mass Media* (1994), in which Douglas stated that American women were "a bundle of contradictions," torn between very traditional and stereotypical ideas about who and what they ought to be and rather progressive and liberating concepts of who and what they can be.[5] Douglas admirably demonstrates that much of the confusion about women's "proper place" and roles in the culture derives from the mixed messages to be found in mainstream mass media. As Douglas succinctly puts it in *Where the Girls Are*, "The war that has been raging in the media is not a simplistic war against women but a complex struggle between feminism and antifeminism that has reflected, reinforced, and exaggerated our culture's ambivalence about women's roles for over thirty-five years."[6] In *Enlightened Sexism*, Douglas somewhat modifies the terms she uses, but the struggle she describe remains the same: it is a battle between what she now calls "embedded feminism" and "enlightened sexism"—that is, between the clear successes of the feminist movement and the resurrection of sexist stereotypes under the banner of "equality" and the guise of irony.

That Douglas can make such similar claims in books published more than 15 years apart simply underscores how slow and minimal progress has been. Sadly, the analysis provided in *Where the Girls Are* is as valid now as it was in the mid-1990s. Indeed, if anything the situation has become more complex because of the rise of "third-wave" feminism and the entrenchment of "postfeminism" in the academy and in the public lexicon. As Amanda Lotz has pointed out, there is currently a vast theoretical confusion over what one even means when invoking the term *feminism* since there are an abundance of terms in use today, such as *feminism, antifeminism, second-wave feminism, third-wave feminism, liberal feminism, radical feminism, neofeminism,* and *postfeminism*. I do not have the space here to engage in the ongoing debates over terminology, and doing so would be somewhat tangential to my purposes. Thus, for the sake of simplicity, I will employ the terms *feminism* and *feminist* throughout the chapter, modifying them where appropriate to illustrate a difference in perspective.[7]

The complexities of female identity have been commented upon by a host of contemporary writers, whose works examine a vast array of cultural trends and media texts.[8] A more specific body of scholarship has also developed around feminist theory and representations of women in television.[9] Particularly useful for my purposes in this chapter are those studies that address the phenomenon of postfeminism. One notable example of such scholarship is Bonnie Dow's *Prime-Time Feminism: Television, Media Culture, and the Women's Movement Since 1970* (1996), which explores how television programming contributed to the cultural conversation about feminism in the United States. Dow provides an insightful analysis of the cultural shifts that led television programming away from a progressive liberal feminism in the 1970s and into a (largely) regressive "postfeminism" in the 1990s. The essential idea of postfeminism—an echo of what Susan Faludi had called antifeminism a few years earlier in her book *Backlash: The Undeclared War Against American Women* (1991)—is that feminism has finished its job; that is, feminism created positive change in gender relations (especially in creating access to education and employment for women), but now those opportunities are about nothing more than "individual choice," which Dow argues is postfeminism's most powerful framing device. Postfeminist ideology also blames feminism itself for all kinds of social ills, especially the disruption of traditional domestic gender arrangements and hierarchies of power in the public sphere. According to Dow, postfeminist thought is widely evident in the culture, even in the supposedly "feminist" sitcoms of the 1980s and early 1990s—most prominently, she claims, in *Murphy Brown* (1988–98).[10]

One can certainly critique Dow's argument in *Prime-Time Feminism* for being overly selective and, for example, not discussing the one show to largely buck the trend she outlines, *Roseanne* (1988–97).[11] Nevertheless, Dow's overall thesis is quite sound. Indeed, it appears that in the decade and a half since Dow published her study, little has changed for women on television; if anything, the postfeminist philosophy seems now to be a dominant mode. Those who have written on feminism and television programming have offered decidedly mixed interpretations of the current "cultural conversation about feminism" as represented in mass media. This can be seen by looking at the commentary on two of the most widely studied television programs that featured women in lead roles, *Ally McBeal* (1997–2002) and *Buffy the Vampire Slayer* (1997–2003).[12] So popular and/or controversial was *Ally McBeal* that Ally McBeal earned herself a place on the cover of *Time* magazine in 1998, alongside Susan B. Anthony, Betty Friedan, and Gloria Steinem and the provocative question: "Is Feminism Dead?" In the years since that infamous *Time* magazine cover, *Ally McBeal* and *Buffy the Vampire Slayer*—as well as other popular female-centered shows such as *Xena*, *Alias*, and *Sex and the City*—have received a great deal of critical attention; they have earned both praise and condemnation from feminist scholars, which is a fine indication of the degree to which viewers (and reviewers) are still conflicted about women's roles in society and the efficacy of the feminist movement.[13]

As *The Simpsons* is a product of the 1990s, it can be said to have arisen in a "postfeminist" era. It is, therefore, worthwhile to take a close look at what the show has to say about women's lives today. This chapter specifically explores the representations of women on *The Simpsons* and examines how the show both engages the politics of feminist movement and articulates a feminist sensibility within its satire. *The Simpsons'* engagement with feminism is not simple, however, since the show both reflects and reflects upon the ideological preoccupations of the culture, which are invariably complex. Given *The Simpsons'* regular exploration of contemporary issues and its reflection of American cultural values, it is not surprising that the ambivalence and ambiguity currently surrounding female identity are reflected in characterizations and story lines on the show. What *The Simpsons* offers its viewers is a complex blend of progressive and traditional attitudes toward female identity and feminist movement. As Jessamyn Neuhaus notes, "*The Simpsons* offers a relatively mild critique of domestic gender roles," playfully and humorously questioning the function of the nuclear family and its attendant gender norms, "but it ultimately embraces the centrality of female domesticity to the very definition of family."[14] Of course, such conflicting ideologies and representations are in perfect keeping with the times in which *The Simpsons* appeared, for the 1990s itself was an era of great ambiguity about women's lives and widespread confusion over gender norms. By way of example, witness the challenges to the male-only policies of colleges such as the Citadel and the Virginia Military Institute; the evolution of and debates over "third-wave" feminism, particularly in relation to the rise (and subsequent commodification) of "girl power" rhetoric; the judicial reevaluations of Title IX legislation and the establishment of professional women's sports teams and leagues; and the conflicted representations of women in cultural phenomenon as varied as music (e.g., Madonna, Lilith Fair, the Spice Girls, Pussycat Dolls), television (e.g., *Murphy Brown*, *Roseanne*, *Ally McBeal*, *Sex and the City*), film (e.g., *Thelma and Louise*, *G.I. Jane*, *The Long Kiss Goodnight*, *Charlie's Angels*), and video games (e.g., *Grand Theft Auto*, *Tomb Raider*). The complexities and ambiguities of female identity are also apparent on

The Simpsons in relation to gender roles, both male and female, as can be seen in the show's critiques of the ideological norms surrounding gender in American culture. A full and complete analysis of the issues attendant to feminism and female identity in popular culture and on *The Simpsons* is beyond the scope of this project, as it would require a consideration of other central female characters (e.g., Patty Bouvier and Edna Krabappel) as well as the many peripheral characters who populate the town of Springfield.[15] Therefore, in this chapter, I concentrate only on three of the show's primary female characters—Marge Simpson, Selma Bouvier (Marge's sister), and Lisa Simpson—and discuss select episodes prominently featuring them to examine how each is used to articulate varying levels of a feminist sensibility.

"Family Values" and Gender Norms

The initial success of *The Simpsons* was due mainly to the willful manipulation of the image of Bart Simpson: the show capitalized upon the archetype of the male adolescent rebel and upon the rapid commodification of easily reproducible phrases such as "Don't have a cow, man," "Eat my shorts," and "Ay, caramba!" This, of course, led to controversy in the early 1990s. In short order, many school officials around the country condemned the show, singling out Bart Simpson as a poor role model for children, and some states, such as Ohio and California, went so far as to ban the wearing of a T-shirt bearing Bart's image and the slogan "Underachiever and Proud of It!"[16] The ubiquity of Bart Simpson and his catchphrases focused the nation's attention on youth culture and led to a widespread belief that *The Simpsons* was a "children's cartoon." However, from the very start, *The Simpsons* was concerned with adult themes and with issues relevant to both men and women concerning the relationships they have with one another and with members of their immediate families. As pointed out previously, *The Simpsons* is foremost a satire upon the idealized images of family life depicted by both traditional and contemporary domestic sitcoms. Though the Simpson family is far from the media-constructed norm offered by television shows such as *Leave It to Beaver* or *Father Knows Best* in the 1950s or *The Cosby Show* and *Family Ties* in the 1980s, it is perhaps closer to the actual norm. *The Simpsons* are quite simply more akin to what we are today and more attuned to the realities of contemporary life. Nonetheless, the show has been repeatedly criticized as a threat to "family values," a concept that has had increasingly strong cultural purchase over the last two decades. These criticisms have usually been accompanied by a call from conservative quarters for a return to "traditional family values"—code for compulsory heterosexuality, male dominance, and female submission, among other things—and for an increased presence of such values in mainstream media, particularly television, since it is so integral a part of American home life.

Advocates of "family values" have had a love-hate relationship with *The Simpsons* from the start. Initially, the show was seen by many as an amoral and corruptive influence. In 1990, for example, the former US secretary of education William Bennett, who at that time was America's "drug czar," chastised the residents of a drug rehab facility he was visiting for watching *The Simpsons*, claiming that doing so would not help them reform their lives.[17] Later that same year, in an interview in the October 1, 1990, issue of *People* magazine, First Lady Barbara Bush said she loves *America's Funniest Home Videos* but remains baffled by *The Simpsons*, which she declares to be "the dumbest thing I had ever seen." Her criticism was modified only slightly by her concluding thought: "But it's a family thing, and I guess it's clean."[18] These comments touched off a brief but heated exchange with the creators of the show. James Brooks decided to respond to the criticism and wittily did so in the guise of Marge Simpson, who sent a letter to the First Lady gently chiding her for her comments. In the letter, Brooks tries to emphasize the Simpsons' own "family values," one of which is morality; Marge writes, for example, that she tries to teach her children "to give somebody the benefit of the doubt and not talk badly about them." Oddly, the other elements of the letter seem not to chide but merely to appease conservatives. Brooks (via Marge) notes, for example, the family's faith in mainstream Christianity (by having Marge mention her "current events group at the church") and concludes with an affirmation of traditional gender roles, if not submissive femininity (by having Marge tell Mrs. Bush that they are each "living our lives to serve an exceptional man"). Mrs. Bush quickly mailed a reply to apologize for her earlier comment; viewing an image of the Simpson family camping, Mrs. Bush determines that it is a "nice family scene" and thus concludes, "Clearly you are setting a good example for the rest of the country."[19] As noted in the introduction, *The Simpsons* was also unfavorably compared to *The Waltons* by George H. W. Bush as he was campaigning for the presidency in 1992. However, by the late 1990s, after the initial controversies had settled, there was some reconsideration of *The Simpsons* and an attempt to co-opt the show for the political and religious right under the guise of "family values." This began with Paul Cantor's essay "*The Simpsons*: Atomistic Politics and the Nuclear Family," which was one of the first in academic circles to offer a defense of the show, and culminated in the publication of Mark Pinsky's *The Gospel According to "The Simpsons": The Spiritual Life of the World's Most Animated Family* (2001).

Since I will discuss Pinsky's book at length in chapter 6, I want to focus here only on Cantor's essay and his interpretation of *The Simpsons*. According to Cantor, *The Simpsons* "offers one of the most important images of the family in contemporary American culture, and in particular an image of the nuclear family."[20] More emphatically, Cantor says, "For all its slapstick nature and its mocking of certain aspects of family life, *The Simpsons* has an affirmative side and ends up celebrating the nuclear family as an institution."[21] Such claims certainly appear to embrace the controversial cartoon family and, within the context of the recurrent condemnation of *The Simpsons* in the 1990s, might therefore be appealing to many readers. However, a closer look at Cantor's essay reveals its narrow vision and its conservative agenda. Cantor argues that there is no need to lament the success of *The Simpsons* or to see it, as some have, as representing the decline of family values in the United States given that the show offers us a vision of an intact, albeit slightly "dysfunctional," nuclear family. What Cantor laments is the tendency of television producers to "downplay the importance of the nuclear family," evidence of which he finds in the programming shifts of the 1970s and 1980s that gave rise to single-parent and nonnuclear family sitcoms such as *Alice* (1976–85), *Punky Brewster* (1984–86), and *My Two Dads* (1987–90). For Cantor, such shows "expressed the ideological bent of Hollywood and its impulse to call traditional family values into question" and to "endorse contemporary social trends away from the stable, traditional, nuclear family."[22] As should be clear, there is a casual slippage here between family as a structure and family as an embodiment of certain values, a shift evident in Cantor's repeated usage of the terms "nuclear family" and "family values." Not surprisingly, Cantor never names any specific values—what matters most is only that a nuclear family model is on display. The absurdity of this position and Cantor's manipulative rhetorical strategy are best summed up in the remarkably circular logic of a later claim:

> *The Simpsons* continually makes fun of the traditional American family. But it continually offers an enduring image of the nuclear family in the very act of satirizing it. Many of the traditional values of the American family survive this satire, *above all the value of the nuclear family itself.*[23]

From this Cantor concludes that the show is "more traditional than it may at first appear" and "reasserts the enduring value of the family as an institution."[24] Of course, it is only a nuclear family that has value. In a comment less about *The Simpsons* than his own political perspective, Cantor flatly states, "No matter now dysfunctional it may seem, the nuclear family is an institution worth preserving," and this is so because it rests upon "the same principle that makes the Simpson family itself work—the attachment to one's own, the principle that we best care for something when it belongs to us."[25] Why this maxim would not apply equally to single-parent or other nontraditional families is something Cantor never explains. In short, Cantor's view runs contrary to much of the progressive feminist scholarship cited earlier, which more often than not celebrated the increased independence of women and lamented the hold that "traditional family values"—in particular, the patriarchal structure of the nuclear family and its rigidly defined gender roles—continued to have in the 1980s and 1990s.

I highlight this to provide a context for examining "family values" and its relation to femininity and feminism on *The Simpsons*. From the very start, *The Simpsons* has engaged with the political hot topic of "family values" in numerous ways—most obviously in the way it has problematized the tradition of the postwar nuclear family sitcoms. *The Simpsons* has revived the domestic sitcom and utilized the traditional nuclear family construct (mom, dad, kids, dog, and a house in the suburbs) in order to skewer its conventions. For example, *The Simpsons* undermines the traditionally hermetic nature of family sitcoms by incorporating real-world problems into its stories. *The Simpsons* also highlights the superficiality of the "happy family" by exposing the falseness of tension-free relationships, decenters patriarchal authority by removing it from the traditional realm of the father, and subverts conventions such as the "moral lesson" and the "happy ending" by sometimes refusing narrative closure. In short, *The Simpsons* repeatedly questions the dominant value systems and cultural norms so regularly perpetuated by many other situation comedies. The weaknesses of the traditional family sitcom were made abundantly clear in the media-hyped showdown between *The Simpsons* and *The Cosby Show*, when Fox boldly moved *The Simpsons* to Thursday nights in the fall of 1990. It was a stroke of genius for Fox to put the cartoon up against what Jerry Herron calls "NBC's 2-D *pater familias*," for it exposed *Cosby*'s "informational nullity" and forced a visual showdown that demonstrated "the impoverishment of historically constituted forms."[26] The ratings triumph of *The Simpsons* (and subsequent cancellation of *Cosby*) underscored the fact that the family sitcom in its traditional form and conventional trappings was out of step with the times.

The Simpsons has also broached the issue of "family values" quite notably in the portrayal of Homer and Marge's marriage. For example, in the first season, the show featured two episodes (interestingly aired back-to-back) that dealt openly with infidelity and the potential for extramarital affairs: "Life on the Fast Lane" and "Homer's Night Out." In "Life on the Fast Lane," which aired in March 1990, Homer offends Marge by selfishly giving her a bowling ball as a birthday gift; the selfishness of the gesture is underscored by the fact that Homer has already had his name engraved on it, anticipating that Marge would just give it to him because, as he says, "You don't even know how to bowl." Out of well-controlled anger and spite, Marge decides to teach Homer a lesson: "I'll learn," she says. Shortly thereafter, Marge is taking bowling lessons—and being slowly seduced by her new bowling instructor, Jacques. Meanwhile, Homer is made to feel both jealous and suspicious; it is clear to Homer that something has changed between him and Marge, but he isn't sure how to express it. One evening, when Marge is getting ready for yet another lesson and Homer is dressing, Homer finds a bowling glove that Jacques had given to Marge, and he sadly concludes that she is seeing another man. Things between Marge and Jacques do indeed escalate to the point where Marge not only considers but plans a rendezvous with Jacques at his apartment. On the way there, however, Marge literally comes to a fork in the road and, thinking about her past and her family, reconsiders her choice. Instead of going on to the Fiesta Terrace to meet Jacques, Marge drives to the Springfield Nuclear Power Plant. What we are given next is a beautiful parody of the ending of *An Officer and a Gentleman*, complete with cheesy theme music, although in this situation the gender norms—and, by extension, the conventions of romance in mass media—are inverted, for it is the woman, Marge, who surprises the man, Homer, at the workplace and offers a confession of love.

In "Homer's Night Out," also from March 1990, infidelity is again the issue, but this time the roles are reversed. The problems begin when Bart uses his novelty spy camera to snap a photo of Homer dancing suggestively with a stripper at a friend's stag party. The image is soon photocopied by Bart's friends and quickly circulated around Springfield. When Marge discovers the photo, she is understandably upset and kicks Homer out of the house for the night. When Homer returns, he apologizes to Marge, although it is clear to both her and the viewer that he does not really know what he is apologizing for. As she and Homer discuss the situation, Marge says what bothers her most is that Homer "taught Bart a very bad lesson," and she explains her feelings to Homer as follows: "Your boy idolizes you…and when he sees you treating women as objects, he's going to think it's ok. You owe your son better than that, Homer." What follows in the rest of this episode is an assertion of a feminist sensibility, initiated by Marge but intriguingly voiced through Homer. Marge insists that Homer take Bart to meet the "exotic belly-person" and apologize for the way he has treated her because she wants Bart to see that "this other woman is a real human being with real thoughts and real feelings." Homer finds Princess Kashmir at a local dance club and explains that he is there "to apologize for treating [her] like an object." He then reiterates Marge's sentiments and states, "I also want my boy to find out that you're more than just a belly. I want him to meet the woman behind all the spangles and glitter, and find out that she has thoughts and feelings too." In typical *Simpsons* fashion, nothing remains completely serious for long: as Homer is talking, he is inadvertently lifted up in the air along with Princess Kashmir in the cage in which she will perform and subsequently dropped back onto the stage below. When members of the audience recognize Homer as the "swinging cat" from the photo, they begin to cheer; at this point, the music starts up again, the dancers begin their routine, and Homer spontaneously participates, but when he sees Bart looking on in admiration, he pauses.

Meanwhile, unbeknownst to Homer, Marge appears and is mortified to find that Homer has "sunk even lower." To her surprise, however, Homer stops the music and launches into the following monologue:

> I have something to say to all the sons out there. To all the boys, to all the men, to all of us. It's about women, and how they are not mere objects with curves that make us crazy. No, they are our wives, they are our daughters, our sisters, our grandmas, our aunts, our nieces and nephews—well, not our nephews. They are our mothers. And you know what, as ridiculous as this sounds, I would rather feel the sweet breath of my beautiful wife on the back of my neck while I sleep than stuff dollar bills into some stranger's g-string.

Though somewhat simplistic, Homer's speech touches everyone in the audience: one man comments on how much he loves his wife, another pulls out photographs of his kids, and the emcee leaves to call his mother. With tears running down her face, Marge calls out to Homer and runs onstage, where they hug and kiss.

Obviously, the text of Homer's speech is deeply influenced by a feminist sensibility and a regard for the equality of the sexes. But what is also interesting to note as Homer delivers his monologue are the visual clues of the mise-en-scène: the image, crafted like a low-angle film shot, captures Homer in the foreground to the left of the frame and positions Princess Kashmir in the background, above, inside of her cage. The visual image thus metaphorically underscores the literal message conveyed, that is, the notion that sexism places women in narrow confines, effectively "imprisoning" them within the limited definitions of femininity. Considering the ideological implications of this episode, it is likely that such protofeminism, rather than Bart's antics, fueled the early conservative critiques of the show. In her essay "We're All Pigs: Representations of Masculinity in *The Simpsons*," Karma Waltonen notes that at the beginning of each episode, "[Homer] embodies all that is bad about patriarchy and masculinity," but by the end of those episodes he comes closer to being "the early-twenty-first-century liberal, sensitive man."[27] What is firmly put in place with both "Homer's Night Out" and "Life on the Fast Lane" is what many fans of *The Simpsons* initially latched on to: the serious adult situations that the show engages with and the "realism" of these for the adult viewing audience. Indeed, the themes of lust, temptation, and the potential for romantic affairs highlighted in these two early episodes will be repeated in many subsequent ones over the years. Homer, for example, will be tempted in episodes such as "Colonel Homer," "The War of the Simpsons," and "The Last Temptation of Homer"; and Marge will be tempted (often by Ned Flanders) in episodes such as "A Streetcar Named Marge," "Diatribe of a Mad Housewife," and "The Devil Wears Nada." Despite the leftist politics of the series, at heart *The Simpsons* is a rather sentimental show, one that embraces "family values" more deeply than many of the politicians who so vocally tout them and that defines the concept in a much more authentic way: on *The Simpsons*, "family values" most often means mutual respect and deep compassion for the other members of the family unit. In the two episodes discussed here, neither Homer nor Marge is willing to sacrifice the love of the other or of the family they have developed; instead, they choose to remain together and work through their differences, and this has been a sustained theme throughout the entire run of the show. The situations in both "Homer's Night Out" and "Life on the Fast Lane" are a reminder of how, from the very start, *The Simpsons* has engaged gender politics to explore issues that are important to the adult viewing audience, both male and female.

Selma Bouvier and the Politics of "Choice"

Motherhood, which is a topic of especial concern to female viewers, is continually dealt with on *The Simpsons*, although often in generic or tangential ways. However, in "Selma's Choice" (January 1993), the subject of motherhood and the highly politicized issues that surround it are intimately explored. At the beginning of this episode, Marge Simpson and Selma and Patty Bouvier (Marge's twin sisters) are preparing for the funeral of their Aunt Gladys, a woman who "lived alone, died alone." In the videotaped will that Gladys left for the family, she encourages her childless nieces to raise a family before it's too late: "Don't die lonely like me," she advises them. "Do it now!" With an almost cruel irony, Gladys leaves the twin sisters her grandfather clock, which we hear ticking loudly in the backseat of the car as the Simpson clan drives home, a reminder—to the sisters as well as viewers of *The Simpsons*—of women's so-called biological clock. Of the two sisters, only Selma, always the more sentimental of the twin sisters, seems bothered by the fact that she is both single and childless. To regular viewers of the show, this is not surprising: Selma's desires for both a loving partner and children were first made evident in the second-season episode "Principle Charming" (February 1991). In this episode, Selma is feeling a sense of "emptiness" in her life, and she expects that love can fill this void. Marge, naturally concerned, challenges Homer to help find Selma a man. Notably, within the episode, Selma is not criticized or humiliated for being alone; if anything, the show offers a critique of the men who populate Springfield—and by extension the United States—for being, by and large, slobs, snobs, workaholics, narcissists, or drunks; in short, they are both ineffectual and inappropriate as partners. As Homer finally realizes, "A good man really *is* hard to find."

In "Selma's Choice," the problems are exacerbated, and the satire is even more sophisticated. This is in part because the episode appeared shortly after two key cultural events: the publication of Susan Faludi's *Backlash: The Undeclared War Against American Women* (1991) and the infamous verbal sparring match between Vice President Dan Quayle and the fictional character Murphy Brown (from the television show *Murphy Brown*) regarding the character's decision to have a baby alone. "Selma's Choice" is another fine example of *The Simpsons'* ability to quickly incorporate and respond to events taking place within American culture. In May 1992, as then vice president Dan Quayle was speaking about "family values" to an audience in San Francisco, he rather casually commented, "It doesn't help matters when prime-time TV has Murphy Brown, a character who supposedly epitomizes today's intelligent, highly paid, professional woman, mocking the importance of fathers by bearing a child alone, and calling it just another lifestyle choice."[28] Quayle was referring to the 1992 season finale of *Murphy Brown*, aired in May of that year, in which Murphy, a single professional woman, gives birth to a baby boy. Inadvertently, Quayle placed the thorny issue of "family values" at the center of the national conversation and the 1992 presidential campaign. What followed was a wide-ranging debate in the popular press over the definition of family, the rights of women, and the politics of popular culture. In the subsequent season opener of *Murphy Brown*, which aired on

September 21, 1992, Murphy Brown (or was it actually Candace Bergen? or series creator Diane English?) responded to Quayle's rebuke in a special hour-long episode. In a report on the American family on the fictional *FYI* newsmagazine, Murphy states,

> Unfortunately, the only acceptable definition of a family is a mother, a father, and children. And, in a country where millions of children grow up in nontraditional families, that definition seems painfully unfair. Whether by choice or circumstance, families come in all shapes and sizes. Ultimately, what really defines a family is commitment, caring, and love.

Then, in a scene that beautifully blurs the distinctions between reality and fiction, Murphy Brown (a fictional character) is joined in the fictional *FYI* studio by a group of real-life single-parent families who, she tells the audience, "might not fit into the Vice President's vision of a family, but consider themselves families nonetheless." Despite the "media circus" surrounding these events, the American viewing public was obviously interested in watching this debate unfold: bolstered largely by the controversy, the season premiere of *Murphy Brown* pulled in 44 million viewers.[29]

Unlike Murphy Brown, who had the "luxury" of a man in her life (however intermittently) and whose pregnancy was the result of a sexual encounter with him, Selma Bouvier has to work at finding a suitable partner and potential father; however, for a woman of her age and in her circumstances in American culture, this is still a daunting prospect. In a brilliant montage demonstrating the various means by which both Selma and Patty attempt to secure dates, *The Simpsons* offers a critique of the lingering sexist attitudes in the culture, including those regarding women's personal hygiene and how readily they will "put out" on a date. The sexism is perhaps most powerfully highlighted by Patty's use of a relatively "modern" method of finding a man: the video-dating service. In a particularly pointed satirical moment, we see Groundskeeper Willie (no prize himself in his 1970s-era outfit and gold chains) viewing video profiles and then harshly dismissing Patty with the quip, "Back to the loch with you, Nessie." Although a small moment, it aptly demonstrates the show's critique of the culture's continued emphasis upon a woman's appearance as the singular measure of her worth. This critique is powerfully (and very humorously) articulated again later in the episode, when Bart dons a pair of "beer goggles" ("See the world through the eyes of a drunk!") and sees his aunt Patty momentarily transformed into a voluptuous woman standing in a seductive pose.

As in "Principle Charming," it is clear there are no decent prospects available for Selma or Patty. When Selma again becomes dejected, Lisa wisely suggests a contemporary alternative—the sperm bank. Determined to have a baby, Selma goes to the Springfield Sperm Bank for more information. However, this too does not seem to provide the answer Selma is looking for. She returns home with a brochure entitled "101 Frozen Pops," a catalog of "celebrity sperm," which makes her feel even more lonely and dejected. Marge and Patty are a bit uncomfortable with this avenue, and they question Selma about whether she is sure this is something she wants to do. "I've got a lot of love to give," she tells them and then laments, "All I have now is sperm in a cup." Later on, Selma has an opportunity to play mother to Bart and Lisa when she volunteers to take them to Duff Gardens (a wonderfully rendered parody of Busch Gardens). While on the Beers of the World boat ride, Lisa drinks the water and begins to hallucinate; meanwhile, Bart sneaks onto a rollercoaster and nearly gets killed. Selma is both overwhelmed and undone by all of it; when she returns home, she asks Marge and Homer, "How do you do it?" Although her reasons are never explicitly stated, it is clear that Selma recognizes the difficulties of being a single parent and finally decides that she does not want to pursue having a child. On the surface, this might seem a bit of a cop-out considering the issues at stake here. However, what seems fundamentally important is not the issue of motherhood per se but the issue of choice itself: the "choice" Selma makes at the end of the episode is not to pursue having a child on her own. Selma expects that the choice is hers and hers alone to make, and the show lends support to this position throughout. "Selma's Choice" also ends with an homage to *Murphy Brown*, underscoring the issue of choice: in the final scene, we see Selma through the lens of a video camera nestling her pet iguana, Chub Chub, and singing Carole King's "You Make Me Feel (Like a Natural Woman)." Savvy viewers would recognize this as a direct allusion to the controversial 1992 season finale of *Murphy Brown*; the more important point, however, is the political nature of such an ending, which overtly places the episode within the cultural debate taking place and implicitly offers support for the decisions made by both Murphy and Selma, despite their different outcomes. Ultimately, "Selma's Choice" addresses what are still vexing problems for women in this culture: the inherent conflicts among compulsory heterosexuality, nuclear family "norms," and a woman's right to choose.

Although *The Simpsons* has not addressed this question again, it still is a timely and relevant topic. Early in 2002, a similar stir was made by the publication of Sylvia Ann Hewlett's *Creating a Life: Professional Women and the Quest for Children*, a book that spurred cover stories in *Time* and *Newsweek*, segments on *The Today Show* and *60 Minutes*, and reviews and editorials in newspapers nationwide. In a provocative article in *Salon* magazine, partly inspired by a review of Hewlett's book but more broadly examining the status of women today, Michelle Goldberg bluntly claims, "It is time for another backlash."[30] In a review of Hewlett's book for *Dissent*, Ellen Willis similarly argues that "feminism is barely breathing."[31] As both Goldberg and Willis point out, Hewlett's message is a dire one for single and childless women: reproduce now before it's too late or you will be reduced to a clinically depressed and "empty" being. It is remarkable that a full decade after the airing of "Selma's Choice" and the debates over *Murphy Brown*, the same conversation about women's lives and bodies was taking place. In the prelude to an interview with Susan Faludi in *Mother Jones*, Sue Halpern writes,

> When Susan Faludi published *Backlash* in 1992, the moment seemed ripe for a feminist revival. Bill Clinton had been elected, essentially, by women; Anita Hill had outed Clarence Thomas and sparked a national discussion on sexual harassment and gender inequality in the workplace; and Washington had hosted the largest pro-choice rally ever assembled.[32]

Halpern offers an apt description of the era. The decade that followed indeed seemed to fulfill the promise of the time: we witnessed an increase of women in the workplace as well as colleges and more sexual liberation for many women, visible in part in the large number of female-centered films (both independent and studio) and television shows (both network and pay cable). But of late we seem to have come full circle.

Looking back on the 1980s, Faludi saw a rollback of the many gains made by the feminist movement in the 1960s and 1970s; as she noted, prominent in the backlash was the belief that women, biologically "destined" to bear and raise children, were doing the country a disservice by placing their own needs, desires, and careers ahead of family life. More than a decade later, Sylvia Ann Hewlett's *Creating a Life* is offering the same argument. Similar claims are still being made, in best-selling books such as Caitlin Flanagan's *To Hell with All That: Loving and Loathing Our Inner Housewife* (2006) and Linda Hirshman's *Get to Work: A Manifesto for Women of the World* (2006), which have continued to engage the so-called mommy wars—a phenomenon that NOW president Kim Gandy, in an interview with ABC's Diane Sawyer, called a "false conflict" incited by an irresponsible media.[33] The return to a traditionally conservative perspective on family life and gender roles is troubling; however, the situation today is not completely the same. The 1990s and the first decade of this century seem to be marked not so much by a backlash against feminism as by a continual questioning and contestation of existing ideologies—about both women and men— that are almost constantly in conflict and, indeed, often contradictory.[34]

Marge Simpson, Liminal Lady

When one examines the entire run of *The Simpsons*, the contradictory sense of gender norms and ideologies is displayed quite well, but it is perhaps best embodied by Marge Simpson, a woman who lives in what Lori Landay has called a "liminal" space. More than any other character, Marge exists "betwixt and between" social categories, behaviors, and spaces, and she embodies the ambivalence that still exists regarding female identity and its relation to the public and private spheres. In her examination of *I Love Lucy*, Landay argues that the series articulates an ambivalent attitude about female identity and ultimately "reflects anxieties about woman's place and women's power" in the era in which it appeared.[35] Curiously, the same can be said of *The Simpsons* in its own era in relation to Marge Simpson. The intention here is not to argue that Marge Simpson is a trickster figure but to highlight that Landay's assertion that the trickster "can be seen as an articulation of the contradictory position in which women were placed by the processes of modernity" is perfectly applicable to Marge and her situation.[36] Marge, after all, is a baby-boomer—according to sources on *The Simpsons Archive*, she was born in 1956—and as such she is very much a product of her generation. Although we are not given a very full history of Marge, we have enough glimpses of her past in the series to see that she was raised with a rather proscriptive domestic ideology. As Landay observes, the contradictions of postwar domestic ideology represent marriage as an equal partnership yet insist on "polarized gender roles and a separation of the public and private spheres."[37] In her examination of 1950s suburban sitcoms, Mary Beth Haralovich similarly argues that the middle-class homemaker was defined by "contradictions which held her to a limited social place" and which, paradoxically, made her both central and marginal to the economy.[38] She was central as a homemaker—that is, as the subject of consumer product designers and marketing strategists—yet marginal as a worker within the home because the value of her labor existed outside the means of production. As noted, *The Simpsons* self-consciously adopts the model of the postwar nuclear family evident in the 1950s domestic sitcoms such as *Ozzie and Harriet*,

Father Knows Best, and *Leave It to Beaver*. In discussing the latter two shows, Haralovich claims that Margaret Anderson and June Cleaver "are two representations of the contradictory definitions of the homemaker in that they are simultaneously contained and liberated by domestic space."[39]

In the 1990s, Marge Simpson, not unlike Margaret Anderson and June Cleaver, has established herself as the consummate homemaker, housewife, and mother; her life is primarily defined by private domestic space, and her primary functions revolve around tending to her home, her husband, and her three children. Nonetheless, Marge's formative years are in the 1970s, during the peak of the second-wave feminist movement, and we can see that she has been deeply influenced by the ideas and the cultural events of this time period. In various episodes, we learn that Marge was a feminist in college—in one sequence, for example, a young Marge appears holding a copy of *Ms.* magazine—and that she once had ambitions of being an artist. This is likely why Marge often aspires to something beyond her domestic life. On many occasions, Marge takes on the role of social reformer—for example, in "Itchy & Scratchy & Marge," "Marge vs. the Monorail," "Sweets and Sour Marge," and "The Joy of Sect." To some extent, these activities are still rather traditionally feminine, merely a modern-day extension of the Victorian-era belief that women could participate in the public sphere in their "appropriate" role as moral guardians. However, there are just as many examples of Marge stepping into public space by taking jobs outside of the home, in episodes such as "Marge Gets a Job," "The PTA Disbands," "The Springfield Connection," "In Marge We Trust," "The Twisted World of Marge Simpson," and "Realty Bites." The positioning of Marge in these roles seems to indicate a fair degree of ambivalence about women's place in American culture today. Lori Landay points out that in *I Love Lucy*, Lucy's desire to work outside of the home (i.e., to transcend the limitations of the domestic sphere) is continually questioned and contested by male authority figures, such as her husband, and by the restrictive social codes of the time. In *The Simpsons*, by contrast, Marge's choice to take on outside employment is never questioned; indeed, more often than not, Homer embraces the idea, though mainly because it will provide a second income for the family. Landay also claims that the image of a modern public femininity in the early decades of the twentieth century is both liberatory and containing: liberatory because it expresses women's independence, promotes active participation in the public sphere, and encourages the pursuit of erotic and/or economic satisfaction, yet containing because it also legitimates marriage as a woman's goal, locates pleasure in commodity consumption rather than political freedom, and reifies the sexual division of labor.[40] Strains of this very same tension can be found in many of the female characters on *The Simpsons* but most notably within Marge Simpson. Overall, then, the series maintains Marge within a liminal space in which her own ambivalence about conflicting ideologies is played out on the stage of the show, thus revealing the degree of ambivalence still evident in American culture regarding women's "proper position."

The tensions of contemporary femininity can be seen clearly in a number of specific episodes of *The Simpsons* that feature Marge in situations both inside and outside the home. One of the earliest examples is in the second-season episode "Two Cars in Every Garage, Three Eyes on Every Fish" (November 1990). Although Marge is not central to the overall plot of this episode—which focuses more on corrupt business practices and environmental concerns—she and her femininity are key to the resolution of the plot. The episode involves Montgomery Burns running for governor as a way to spin and control the scandal that ensues after Bart catches a three-eyed fish in the waters near the Springfield Nuclear Plant. Homer is coerced into helping Burns, who is represented to us as the conservative candidate who wants to ease regulations on businesses and, of course, "lower taxes." Marge, however, intends to support and vote for Mary Bailey, the beloved incumbent governor. We don't hear much about Bailey's political positions, so we can't be sure whether or not they are "liberal" in comparison to those of Burns, but we can safely assume so: Marge appears to admire Bailey as much for her policies as for her status as a female in a position of power. One reason is that Bailey herself seems a lot like both Marge and Lisa—intelligent, level-headed, and kind. This can be seen in Bailey's response to her opponent's efforts at manipulating the voters. To do so, Burns runs misleading and manipulative ads about Bailey, which boosts his poll numbers, and then stages a series of photo ops, including one of him holding a jackhammer alongside city street workers and another of him inside a military tank. When asked about Burns's campaign strategies, Bailey says her "worthy opponent" seems to think that the voters of the state are "gullible fools." "I, however, prefer to rely on their intelligence and good judgment," she says.

To assist Burns further, the spin doctors of his campaign decide that he needs to be seen socializing with the "average" worker and so arrange for what one of the handlers calls a "cornball stunt": dinner with the Simpsons. Both Marge and Lisa become frustrated with the role they are asked to play to help Homer court favor with his boss—Marge because she is asked to serve dinner to Burns on the same night she intended to be "ringing doorbells for Mary Bailey," and Lisa because she is asked to pose an inane question for the cameras. When Lisa is first given the question (which reads, "Mr. Burns, your campaign seems to have the momentum of a runaway freight train. Why are you so popular?"), she responds by asking, "Well, as long as I'm asking something, can I ask him to assuage my fears that he's contaminating the planet in a manner that may one day render it uninhabitable?" The answer, of course, is no. Later that evening, Marge tells Homer that she is frustrated and doesn't want to "snuggle" with Homer because he is not willing to allow her to express herself. "But you do get to express yourself," he says, "in the lovely home you keep and the food you serve," articulating the gender norm still in place and yet increasingly contested in the culture when this episode aired. Marge pauses a moment and then says, "That's it. That's how I'm going to express myself. Goodnight." The night of the dinner, the cameras are gathered and awaiting the arrival of Burns. Lisa is visibly disheartened as she reads (in a dull monotone) the trivial question provided to her. She doesn't even stay at the table to hear Burns ramble on about his "integrity" and "incorruptibility." She retreats to the kitchen, where she tells Marge that she "felt awful" about doing that and is concerned she and her family "have become the tools of evil." What Lisa and the viewers of the episode don't yet know is that Marge has a plan to set things right. With a smile, she tells Lisa to give her the benefit of the doubt and then proceeds to the dining room with the entrée, which turns out to be the mutant three-eyed fish. At its presentation, Lisa smiles broadly; others simply gasp. Burns is encouraged by his handlers to keep up the pretense and eat the fish; he tries, but he quite literally cannot swallow his own lies and spits the bit of food out and across the room. As one of the news reporters put it, Burns's political career was "ruined before it hit the ground." In short, Marge craftily uses her domestic skills in an act of protest; she dissembles and plays the role of homemaker and housewife, but in this case she does so in order to subvert the political order.

The contradictions of female identity are made evident as well in "Homer Alone" (February 1992), an episode from season 3. This episode opens with a very harried Marge attempting to get her family ready for their day: in a fast-paced montage, we see Marge feed, change, and burp baby Maggie; prepare lunches for Homer, Bart, and Lisa; make a list of items to get at the market and errands to run; and then drive the kids to school because, in their sloth, they have missed the bus. After doing her shopping, while driving home, Marge is beset on all sides by stress factors—namely, practical jokers on the radio, heavy traffic, a rude tailgater, and finally Maggie, who spills her bottle of milk all over Marge and the car. At this point, Marge lets out a chilling "Noooooooo" and slams on the brakes, stopping her car in the middle of a bridge and creating gridlock in both directions. When another driver approaches her car to see what is wrong, she simply turns and roars at him like an angry animal (appropriately enough, the sound effect used here is infamous roar of the MGM lion). Shortly thereafter, the situation is featured on the local traffic report, and the newsman Kent Brockman shows up to report on the situation. Pointedly, the script here highlights the gender issues in question. According to Brockman, "An overworked and underappreciated housewife has snapped and parked her car on a bridge." The police arrive and cordon off the area with police tape that reads "Distressed Mother—Please Stay Back." Hence, a situation is established that will allow the writers of the show to examine the strains placed upon modern-day mothers and the current position of such women within both the domestic and public spheres.

A short time later, Homer arrives and pleads with his wife to move her car and come home. To secure the deal, Homer promises to "help out" more at home; Marge agrees, although she insists that she first have a vacation away from the family in order to decompress. In a rather typical sitcom reversal—one reminiscent, in fact, of episodes of *I Love Lucy*—Marge goes off to enjoy the amenities at Rancho Relaxo and Homer stays behind to tend to the children and the home. Of course, being ill-prepared to do either task, he is ultimately seen to be incompetent. In a series of juxtapositions, we see Homer's incompetence contrasted to Marge's indulgence in the things one assumes she rarely has time for: tellingly, in one scene, we see Marge soaking in a bubble bath while eating a hot fudge sundae, drinking tequila, and watching *Thelma and Louise*. What one might expect at this point—and might well see in other contemporary domestic sitcoms such as *Home Improvement*—is that Marge would be pulled away from the "dangerous" feminist fantasies of independence and freedom and summoned back to repair the damage done by Homer and restore "proper" order to the domestic realm. Instead, we are given a variation on this theme: Marge completes her vacation, and as she is traveling home, Homer is desperately trying to pull everything together to make it appear that all went well in Marge's absence. Interestingly, the image of domestic harmony that Homer is looking to cultivate—an image long made the responsibility of women within the family—is self-consciously offered to us at the end of the episode, contrasting the ideal and the "real": as the train arrives, Marge holds up a photograph of her family, a typical family portrait in which everyone is well groomed and content; she then lowers the photograph, revealing (to us and to herself) the disheveled group waiting for her on the platform. The episode ends as Marge says that she expects "more help around the house" from the entire family to lessen her stress level, and the family members promise to pitch in.

It is debatable how sincere this promise is, and I think that, despite the variation noted earlier, the episode ends on a rather ambiguous note, again highlighting its ambivalence about women's "proper" place and role. On the one hand, the show seems to fall back upon rather comfortable and well-established gender norms for the resolution of the plot, returning to the traditionally dichotomized gender roles and the separation of the public and private spheres. On the other hand, the resolution of "Homer Alone" seems to be a testament to the labor involved with taking care of the home, labor that has long been devalued or unacknowledged, and thus stands as a validation of women within the domestic sphere.

The other half of women's dichotomous existence—namely, female identity in the public sphere—is fully explored in a sixth-season episode entitled "The Springfield Connection" (May 1995). In this episode, Marge takes a job as a police officer, thus moving out of the traditionally feminized domestic space of the home and into the traditionally masculinized public space of the law. At the onset of the episode, we see that downtown Springfield is a crime-ridden area. As Homer and Marge leave a local theater, they stumble upon the petty-thief Snake conducting a three-card-monte game on the sidewalk. Homer is naive enough to think he can win, but Snake quickly steals his money and runs off. In a sudden and very surprising move, Marge boldly gives chase; unfortunately, she pursues him into a blind alley, where he turns and pulls out a knife. Marge is initially fearful, but with a rush of adrenaline, she grabs a trash can lid and defends herself by striking Snake in the head. After the police and Homer arrive on the scene, Marge describes the experience as "scary but exhilarating." In a condescending tone, Homer says, "Yes, it is exhilarating to see the police get their man and save a hysterical woman." "For crying out loud," Marge replies, exasperated. "Easy now, sweetheart," Homer assures her, "Homey's here." Homer's response is intentionally designed to be patronizing and to indicate to us that he is operating out of a simplistic and outdated notion of patriarchy, one in which women are passive and helpless victims and men are the heroes who rescue them (bear in mind here that Homer watches *a lot* of television).

In the next scene, Marge is back home and tending to the family, but her domestic sphere is not quite as sheltered as it once was, for the very public events of the day have intruded upon it. Lisa, who is quite excited by both the adventure and the attention her mother's actions have attracted, animatedly asks, "Mom, was that the most exciting thing you have ever done? "Yes," Marge tells her, "but celery soup is also exciting." It's clear from Marge's tone, however, that something has changed and that she is trying to convince herself as much as Lisa of the truthfulness of this statement. While shopping the next day, Marge picks up a can of ham, pauses, and reflects, "Hmmm. Regular ham just doesn't thrill"; she then replaces this with a can of deviled ham. A moment later, she is running with her cart down the aisle, recklessly seeking a thrill. Looking over the magazine rack, Marge reaches for the new issue of *Sponge & Vacuum* but then suddenly opts for an issue of *Death Sports*. Finally, after she arrives home, in an inspired moment of derring-do (and in a beautiful allusion to *Raiders of the Lost Ark*), Marge impulsively rolls underneath her garage door a mere moment before it closes. Encouraged perhaps by her own physical capabilities, and assuredly by her newfound desire for "thrills," Marge goes the next day to the Springfield Police Department and tells the men gathered there that she wants to join the police force. There is a momentary pause, and then all of the men laugh out loud—and they laugh a long time. The intent here seems to be to give the viewer time to process the sexist attitude on display and perhaps condemn these men for thinking the idea of a female cop is laughable. However, just as this idea is jelling in the mind, they abruptly stop laughing and Police Chief Wiggum simply says, "Welcome aboard."

Homer's response to the news reveals his narrow-minded views and his belief in polarized gender roles. He says, "Marge, you being a cop makes you the man, which makes me the woman, and I have no interest in that." At this point, Marge plays the role expected of her and to which she has been well conditioned: she reassures Homer that there is no need for him to feel "threatened," a fine acknowledgment of the perceived threat to patriarchy that feminist movement has long represented. However, as we watch Marge train for the force (in a montage that shows her completing an obstacle course, navigating a driving course, and shooting in a target range), she easily outperforms all of the other cadets, as well as the current officers, who are shown to be a perpetually gluttonous, slovenly, and lazy bunch. When we next see Marge, she is in uniform and patrolling her beats in Junkieville and Bumtown. We are led to believe that Marge is the best cop on the force, but we also see that her reputation as such is causing numerous problems. Once again, in its presentation of contemporary femininity, *The Simpsons* is conflicted and determined to have it both ways: the story line in this episode toys with the viewer's expectations and forces interpretation into the same liminal space that Marge inhabits. Whereas one might expect Marge's problems to stem from sexist attitudes within the community about her role in a male-dominated profession, what the residents of Springfield latch on to is her status as a "cop," as an enforcer of the law, and this is what positions her as an outsider. The women in the beauty parlor, for example, are afraid to even gossip for fear of giving up "incriminating" information, and Homer's gambling buddies are afraid to visit Homer and play a game of poker for fear of "breaking the law." Of course, considering the plotline offered and the cultural context in which the episode appears, the issue of gender cannot be fully avoided; fittingly, it is Homer who raises it. After his poker partners run off, Homer tells Marge, "You've become such a cop," a sentiment in accord with that of the entire town. However, unlike the other residents of Springfield, Homer is unable to see beyond the confines of narrowly defined gender roles. He continues his complaint, and in the process he makes clear just where the problem resides, at least for him: "Not that long ago, you were so much more to me. You were a cleaner of pots, a sewer of buttons, an unplugger of hairy clogs." In other words, she was a housewife, both domesticated and servile. Marge replies, "I'm still all those things, only now I'm cleaning up the city, sewing together the social fabric, and unplugging the clogs of our legal system." Homer, locked into a dichotomized view of his and Marge's roles, simply asks, "You're cooking what for dinner?"

Marge's idealism about her role in the public sphere is tempered by a number of experiences, including her first taste of police corruption (a point that is important in the resolution of the episode). This occurs when Marge first enters the local Kwik-E-Mart and proprietor Apu Nahasapeemapetilon, assuming she has come to collect on a bribe, tries to pass her a stack of cash. Her idealism is also challenged by the cool logic and political savvy of Lisa, who at one point asks, "Mom, I know your intentions are good, but aren't the police the protective force that maintains the status quo for the wealthy elite? Don't you think we ought to attack the roots of social problems instead of jamming people into overcrowded prisons?" Marge, unprepared for a debate on public policy, merely tries to distract Lisa with a hand puppet, saying, "Look, Lisa, it's McGruff the Crime Dog." Most significantly, I think, Marge is made to confront the reality of her position when Homer openly and publicly challenges her authority. In this scene, Homer steps out of the Kwik-E-Mart and finds Marge writing a ticket for his car, which he parked across three handicapped spots. "How's my little piglet?" he asks, nonchalantly. Marge, already exhausted and frustrated by her day on the beat, criticizes Homer for being so irresponsible; Homer, appropriately enough, then teases her like a child about her job and claims that she is "not a real cop." During all of this, a crowd begins to gather, and Marge feels embarrassed by the "spectacle" she and Homer are making in public. Homer then grabs the police cap off Marge's head, symbolically disempowering her even more, and begins to verbally mock her, which intensifies the sense of shame and humiliation Marge feels. Pushed to the limit, Marge finally demonstrates the "realness" of her job by arresting Homer. This, of course, causes a variety of tensions at home. Marge later apologizes to Homer for arresting him, but she maintains that she did the right thing. "Someday," she tells him, "when you really need it, you'll be happy there are dedicated cops like me out there." "I have nothing more to say to you, Marge," Homer says. But, in typical *Simpsons* fashion, he does offer more, adding a statement that perfectly encapsulates the gender politics of popular culture in the postwar era: "I'm drawing a line down the center of the house, à la *I Love Lucy*. You stay on your side and I'll stay on my side."

A short time later, we discover that Hermann, one of Homer's poker buddies, is running a counterfeit jeans operation out of Homer's garage. Homer quite literally stumbles upon this information while in search of more beer; Marge, being ever vigilant, is already one step ahead, and she arrives a moment later to arrest the criminals gathered in the garage. Homer, enacting his expected role as male "hero," steps between Marge and Hermann and yells, "Leave the girl out of this," but he is inept in this role and is captured by Hermann. Marge is thus thrust into the position of being the hero and saving the day. What follows is a dramatic chase sequence in which the contradictory messages about female identity and women's "proper place" are very curiously combined. Marge chases Hermann into the Simpson's backyard and then up a tree to Bart's tree house. As she climbs, we see Bart and Lisa in the background cheering her on from the second-floor bedroom window. Marge pauses momentarily and admonishes them to "Get back to bed!" "Don't make me come up there!" she warns. After she has successfully captured the criminal, Homer admits that Marge is a good cop and that he is proud of her. However, as in "Homer Alone," this somewhat progressive ending is placed in check with a quick denouement that returns the characters to their "normal" state: when Marge sees all of the other cops trying on the contraband jeans, she asserts, "There's too much corruption on this force," and she quits.

Once again, the show ends on a rather ambiguous note, highlighting its ambivalence about feminism and female identity. Although the episode returns the characters to their traditionally dichotomized gender roles and separate spheres, it also makes abundantly clear in the process that a female in a traditionally male-dominated profession is not only capable of performing all of the duties of the job but is at times even better at it than those who are considered the "appropriate" jobholders. This seems to be a particularly powerful statement in an era in which women nationwide were challenging the exclusionary practices of police and fire departments, as well as the military. Nonetheless, *The Simpsons* leaves Marge positioned in a liminal space, and she remains in many ways the embodiment of the cultural contradictions of contemporary femininity. A much clearer stance is evident in Lisa

Simpson, who is positioned quite strongly as a young feminist, one more in the second-wave mold than her mother, and there is little ambiguity about where she stands, what she believes, and what she represents.

Lionhearted Lisa Simpson

Lisa Simpson's political sensibilities were on display early in the series. For example, in the episode "Mr. Lisa Goes to Washington" (September 1991), which I discussed briefly in chapter 2, we get a clear sense of her progressive views. Such views are evident again, in a way that connects more closely to concerns with gender, in the fourth-season episode "Lisa the Beauty Queen" (October 1992). After seeing a sketch artist's caricature of her, Lisa becomes convinced that she is "ugly." Concerned about his daughter, Homer decides to help build up Lisa's self-esteem by enrolling her in the Little Miss Springfield pageant. Lisa is at first resistant to the idea, not believing she is pretty enough to compete, but she goes through with it because Homer had sacrificed a ride on the Duff beer blimp, which he won in a raffle, to pay the registration fee. Although the episode doesn't offer a direct critique of child beauty pageants, it does briefly raise concerns about the commercialization of youth and the pressures placed upon very young girls to conform to a beauty standard and to stereotypical gender norms. This is most noticeable with a skilled competitor named Amber Dempsey, whom Lisa admiringly describes as "beautiful" when she first sees her. Not surprisingly, Amber has bleach-blond hair and, we are told, eyelash implants; Amber also confesses that her aspiration in life is to be "a sweetie-pie." Given that this episode aired in advance of the scandal surrounding JonBenét Ramsey in 1996 and long before the advent of reality shows such as *Toddlers & Tiaras* (2009–), the satirical critique offered is quite prescient. The real focus of the episode, however, is on how large corporations—in this case, Laramie Cigarettes, which sponsors the pageant—market to children. Although Amber wins the crown, as expected, Lisa is named the runner-up. After Amber is wounded (fatally, it seems) by a lightning strike, Lisa has the opportunity to use her position as Little Miss Springfield as a bully pulpit to promote her beliefs, which she does as an act of resistance against being a "corporate shill." Declaring that she will "speak out against the evils in society," Lisa first denounces cigarettes and then, among other things, criticizes how college football "diverts funds badly needed for education and the arts." Concerned about this, the pageant officials, in collusion with Mayor Quimby, soon strip Lisa of her title based on a technicality: Homer has made an error on the application form. In the end, Lisa tells Homer that she is glad he entered her in the pageant because it did help her feel better about herself. It is clear to the audience that the experience was beneficial not because it made Lisa feel prettier but because it gave her a public voice.

By its fifth season, which began in the fall of 1993, *The Simpsons* had hit its stride and was receiving enormous amounts of press coverage, both positive and negative, thanks to the "bad-boy" antics of Bart Simpson and, increasingly, of Homer. However, by the end of that season, in the spring of 1994, it was the Simpson women who were making a name for themselves within the culture at large and who were standing out more dramatically than the Simpson men. In honor of Mother's Day that year, for example, Ken Tucker of *Entertainment Weekly* (the newly established arbiter of popular cultural tastes) ranked television's moms and named Marge Simpson as "the best," praising her for being "at once progressive and traditional."[41] More significantly, later that same year, Lisa Simpson appeared in an issue of *Ms.* magazine, alongside notable feminist activists such as Gloria Anzaldúa and Bella Abzug, in a section called "The Many Faces of Feminism." In the article, the editors of *Ms.* magazine claim that Lisa "wages a one-girl revolution against cartoonland patriarchy."[42] This is true, but it is important to point out that Lisa's activism is not really relegated to cartoonland—it is actually a part of our land, the United States—and her concerns transcend the narrow confines of the animation cel or the television screen. It is perhaps no surprise that Lisa appeared in the *Ms.* magazine spread in 1994 when one considers that her battle against patriarchy and sexism was quite powerfully demonstrated in an episode airing that very year.

"Lisa vs. Malibu Stacy," which first aired in February 1994, provides what is perhaps the most overt critique of sexism and patriarchy to ever appear in an episode of *The Simpsons*. In this episode, Lisa is excited about acquiring the new "Talking Malibu Stacy" doll and thus flocks to the mall with the other excited consumers to purchase one on the day of its release. In a section of the store appropriately named the Valley of the Dolls, Lisa warns her mother, "I may get a little crazy, Mom." Before Marge can even finish acknowledging her understanding, Lisa is wrestling another little girl for a Summer Fun Set. The frenzy over and now back at home, Lisa constructs a diorama of what appears to be a mock UN and prepares her audience (i.e., her other dolls and the viewers of *The Simpsons*) for Stacy's grand entrance: "A hush falls over the general assembly as Stacy approaches the podium to deliver what will no doubt be a stirring and memorable address." But when Lisa pulls the string on the back of the doll, Stacy simply says, "I wish they taught shopping in school." Discouraged but not without hope, Lisa tries again. This time, Stacy says, "Let's bake some cookies for the boys." Frustrated, Lisa says, "Come on, Stacy. I've waited my whole life to hear you speak. Don't you have anything relevant to say?" and pulls the cord one last time: "Don't ask me. I'm just a girl [tee hee, tee hee]." Bart flippantly says, "Right on. Say it, sister." In response, Lisa launches into a heartfelt and politically charged monologue:

> It's not funny, Bart. Millions of girls will grow up thinking that this is the right way to act, that they can never be more than vacuous ninnies whose only goal is to look pretty, land a rich husband, and spend all day on the phone with their equally vacuous friends talking about how damn terrific it is to look pretty and have a rich husband!

And with that, Lisa angrily hurls the doll out of her bedroom window.

Before proceeding with a detailed analysis of the episode, it is important to note again the context in which this episode appeared to highlight how *The Simpsons* engages politically with trends in American culture. Malibu Stacy is obviously a fictional stand-in for the immensely popular Barbie doll, and "Lisa vs. Malibu Stacy" was clearly inspired by the furor over the Teen Talk Barbie, introduced in 1992. Teen Talk Barbie was the first talking Barbie doll on the market in 20 years, and it was expected to be a huge hit with consumers who were increasingly jaded by "high-tech" developments in the toy industry. Each doll could speak four of 270 preprogrammed one-liners.[43] Among these, however, was the phrase "Math class is tough," which sparked a heated debate among parents, educators, and concerned citizens. In reaction to the controversy surrounding the Teen Talk Barbie, a small contingent of performance artists based in New York's East Village formed a group called the

Barbie Liberation Organization (BLO). With the appearance of the Talking Duke G.I. Joe doll in 1993, the BLO saw potential for social commentary and began switching the voice boxes of the Teen Talk Barbie and the Talking Duke G.I. Joe and then placing them back on store shelves for unsuspecting consumers. Needless to say, confusion ensued. The group says its aim was to "startle the public into thinking about the Stone-Age worldview that the dolls reflect."[44] Though small-scale and short-lived, this guerilla tactic highlighted a valid point. As one BLO spokesman put it, "We [were] trying to make a statement about the way toys can encourage negative behavior in children, particularly given the rising acts of violence and sexism."[45] Timely as ever, *The Simpsons* capitalized upon this controversy in "Lisa vs. Malibu Stacy" in order to raise similar questions about sexism in American culture and the influence of toys upon such attitudes.

Of course, the person on the show most suited to raising such questions is Lisa Simpson. After her diatribe against the doll in her bedroom, Lisa goes to the playground at school, where she challenges her female peers to examine the import of what Stacy says. Lisa pulls the string on her doll once again, and this time Stacy says, "Let's put on makeup so the boys will like us." Lisa then asks her playmates, "Don't you see anything wrong with what she says?" One girl admits that she does; but when she pulls the string on her doll, we hear Stacy say, "My Spidey sense is tingling. Anyone call for a webslinger?" Admittedly, it is a humorous moment; more significantly, however, it is also a knowing nod to the sabotage enacted upon real-world Barbie and G.I. Joe dolls by the BLO and thus to the serious political nature of the subject at hand. Lisa retorts, "No, Celeste, the things she says are sexist." Sadly, their collective response is to simply giggle and say, "Lisa said a dirty word."

Ever the activist, Lisa is convinced that something has to be done about the situation. However, when she shares this idea with the family, they discourage her from doing so. Here the show displays its own ambivalent position toward political action. Although Marge and Lisa are often united in their beliefs and goals, Marge doesn't readily support Lisa's position. Once again, the show offers a contradictory moment in which it has to rely upon its positioning of Marge as a traditional housewife and homemaker to emphasize her culpability in her own subjugation. Though an ardent feminist in many ways, especially at a younger age, Marge is still a product of her generation, and she often displays an unquestioning acceptance of female identity defined in rather traditional ways (i.e., through service to men, second-class status, and a passive mindset). Marge tells Lisa, "I had a Malibu Stacy when I was your age, and I turned out just fine. Now, let's forget our troubles with a big bowl of strawberry ice cream." Without comment, Lisa pulls the string and makes her point through Stacy, who says, "Now, let's forget our troubles with a big bowl of strawberry ice cream." Clearly, generational differences set Marge and Lisa apart. Whereas Marge is often conflicted in her opinions and vacillates between positions, Lisa has inherited the successes of first- and second-wave feminists and has grown up with a faith in true equality; she is a political activist, a vegetarian, a voice of reason, and an avowed feminist. She is also most often the moral center of the show, which gives her views on gender and feminism special relevance.

Undeterred, Lisa calls the Malibu Stacy hotline to complain and discovers that she can take a factory tour and thus "complain in person." Perhaps in reconsideration of her earlier statement, Marge accompanies Lisa on the tour. Lisa and Marge (the only persons on the tour) watch a brilliantly conceived parody of corporate propaganda films, this one detailing the origins of Malibu Stacy, "America's favorite eight-and-a-half incher." The film ends with Stacy again claiming, "Don't ask me. I'm just a girl [tee hee, tee hee]," and a male voice-over that concludes, "She *sure* is." At this point, the show takes on a number of political concerns, though most prominent are the sexist attitudes that persist in the workplace and women's own responsibility in perpetuating sexism in the culture. When the woman giving the tour asks if there are any questions, Lisa says, "Yes, I have one. Is the remarkably sexist drivel spouted by Malibu Stacy intentional, or just a horrible mistake?" Without missing a beat, the woman says, "Believe me, we're very mindful of such concerns around here," after which a male employee opens a door behind her and calls out, "Hey, Jiggles. Grab a pad and back that gorgeous butt in here." Good naturedly, "Jiggles" giggles, enters the room, and closes the door behind her with her rear end. Marge and Lisa simply grimace: "Mmmmmmm."

Having witnessed sexism in action, Lisa is more determined than ever to do something, so she seeks out the creator of Malibu Stacy, Stacy Lovell, and proposes that they make an alternative talking doll. At first, Lovell is skeptical, but after hearing what the Malibu Stacy doll is saying to an entire generation of little girls (for example, "Thinking too much gives you wrinkles"), she decides to help Lisa design a new doll. In describing her template for the doll, Lisa offers viewers a clear example of her influences and role models: "She'll have the wisdom of Gertrude Stein and the wit of Cathy Guisewite; the tenacity of Nina Totenberg and the common sense of Elizabeth Cady Stanton; and to top it off, the down-to-earth good looks of Eleanor Roosevelt!" In a later scene, in which Lisa is recording statements for her talking doll, we get a telling glimpse of Lisa's political beliefs. She first records the line, "When I get married, I'm keeping my own name" but then pauses to reconsider and says, "Maybe that should be 'If I *choose* to get married.'" Ultimately, the phrase that is settled upon (and repeated twice in the show for emphasis) is "Trust in yourself and you can achieve anything!"—an apt summation of Lisa's own feminist philosophy. In tribute to her inspiration, they name the doll Lisa Lionheart.

Word of the development of Lisa Lionheart soon reaches the ears of executives at Petrochem Chemical Corporation (the makers of Malibu Stacy), and the head of the marketing division, rightly seeing the new doll as a threat, tells his staff that they need to "sink this Lisa Lionheart fast." To do this, the executive says, they have to "reinvent Malibu Stacy for the 90s." Meanwhile, erstwhile reporter Kent Brockman is persuaded by his young daughter to do a news report on the new "talking dolly" ("Well...you were right about the Berlin Wall," he concedes). Brockman's report, as might be expected, fuels even greater interest in Lisa Lionheart, and at the end of the episode we are returned to where we began: outside the Springfield Mall waiting for the doors of the Valley of the Dolls to open. Lisa and Stacy Lovell are there to witness the sale of their new doll, and again, there is a crowd of eager young consumers waiting to get their hands on the newest commodity. However, when the doors open and the children are making a mad dash to the Lisa Lionheart display, an employee rolls out a pallet of Malibu Stacy dolls—"Complete with New Hat"—and blocks their path. They pause momentarily, confused, and then one excited child says, "Look, they've changed Malibu Stacy." Another exclaims, "She's better than ever!" Lisa, aware of the ruse, inserts herself between the crowd and the dolls and tries to explain. "Wait," she says. "She's still the same Malibu Stacy. The only difference is her stupid, cheap hat. She still embodies all of awful stereotypes she did before." Again there is a pause, and then Waylon Smithers ("owner of the world's largest Malibu Stacy collection") shouts, "But she's got a new hat!" and that's all it takes for the crowd to surge forward, claim their Malibu Stacy dolls, and ignore Lisa Lionheart. Lisa sighs and sadly concludes, "I guess you just can't beat big business. There's no room for the little guy." But just as soon as the words are out of her mouth, she hears her own voice saying, "Trust in yourself and you can achieve anything!" and she turns to see one little girl standing before the Lisa Lionheart display, smiling at the doll. Proudly, Lisa then says, "You know, if we get through to just that one little girl, it'll all be worth it." Not content to let liberal pieties go uncontested, the writers have Lovell quietly say, "Yes, particularly if that little girl happens to pay $46,000 for that doll." "What?" Lisa asks. "Oh, nothing," Lovell replies. "Kudos to you, Lisa. Kudos."

How are we to read such an ending? On the one hand, this episode is offering its viewers an image of youthful idealism, can-do individualism, and grassroots activism in the service of contesting prevailing ideologies and providing alternative ones, an image in accord with the progressive politics of *The Simpsons*. On the other hand, in acknowledging capitalism and the reality of a profit-oriented consumer marketplace, the episode is also offering a rather pessimistic view of the ability of individuals (or even small coalitions of individuals) to truly effect social change. In this regard, the politics of the episode is marked by an ambiguity that seems to me in perfect keeping with the times in which it appeared. As noted previously, the 1990s itself was an era of great ambiguity, epitomized by conflicting representations of female "power," changing definitions of masculine and feminine identity, and debates over women's movement into male-dominated professions. The movement of women into traditionally male domains of public life in the 1980s and 1990s obviously generated a great deal of controversy—and subsequently provided *The Simpsons* with fodder for its satire, as we have already seen with Marge Simpson's turn as a police officer in "The Springfield Connection."

Another of the controversial challenges to male power in the early 1990s was the attempt to integrate all-male military schools, namely the Citadel and the Virginia Military Institute (VMI). This began in 1990, when the Civil Rights Division of the US Justice Department filed a suit against the State of Virginia and VMI, claiming that VMI's all-male admission policy violated both Title IV of the Civil Rights Act and women's equal protection under the Fourteenth Amendment, and it demanded that VMI become coeducational.[46] One year later, the high school student Shannon Faulkner applied to and was admitted to the Citadel, but when it was discovered she was female (the application form had no place to identify one's sex, as it was an all-male institution), she was rejected. A discrimination case was brought forward by the ACLU but was joined by the United States as plaintiff-intervener in a potential civil-rights violation.[47] Each of these cases progressed separately, but both were heard on appeal by the US Court of Appeals for the Fourth Circuit, which in 1992 affirmed that the admissions policies at the Citadel and VMI did discriminate against women; the Citadel was then ordered to admit Shannon Faulkner. Each school was also given options to exercise in the interim to potentially avoid such problems in the future. One of these options was to establish separate but equal programs for women, which would allow the schools to comply with the law and yet to remain private and exclusive; both the Citadel and VMI took the option offered by the court and set up parallel programs at neighboring women's colleges.[48] In 1994, in a follow-up to the court order, the Virginia district court and the Circuit Court of Appeals ruled that VMIL was an acceptable alternative and met the demands of the Equal Protection Clause; the Justice Department, however, was not convinced and appealed the decisions to the US Supreme Court in 1996. In June of that year, in a seven-to-one vote, the court made a ruling in *United States v. Virginia*: it declared that VMI did indeed violate the Equal Protection Clause, and it ordered the institution to being enrolling women.[49] Just a few days earlier, the governing board of the Citadel unanimously voted to abolish its all-male admissions policy and open the school to women.

True to form, *The Simpsons* quickly absorbed and incorporated these historic events into an episode that once again offered a timely reflection on contemporary gender issues. "The Secret War of Lisa Simpson," which first aired in May 1997, concerns Lisa's attempts to succeed as the only girl at the all-male military school to which Bart has been sent and which Lisa voluntarily joins. At the start of the episode, we see Bart engaged in a prank, once again with disastrous consequences; Marge and Homer are subsequently convinced that the best course of action is to send him to military school, where he will presumably learn discipline. Meanwhile, we see Lisa suffering the tedium of another day in school—her teacher, Ms. Hoover, is filling the time with dull documentaries on subjects like sand and outdated films about man's desire to walk on the moon. Lisa simply feels unchallenged and desires a more intellectually stimulating environment. When she sees the challenges posed to the boys at Rommelwood, the military school Bart is taken to, she declares that she too is staying. The commander is initially perplexed: "You're a girl?" he asks Lisa. "Yes," she replies. "Gosh darnit," he says, "I just don't understand the situation. You're a girl." "All I want is a chance to prove myself," Lisa declares. The commander points out that in the school's 185-year history they have never had a female cadet, although he then concedes "that seems to be the way the wind is blowin' these days," and with that Lisa is welcomed aboard.

With Lisa's admission so easily secured, it is clear that the writers are less concerned with the barriers to gaining entrance to the school than with exploring what happens to Lisa once she is there, which they do by paralleling to some degree the experiences of Shannon Faulkner, who was harassed by her male peers and hazed to such an extent that she dropped out only a week after joining.[50] As Michael Kimmel explains, schools such as VMI and the Citadel train cadets with what is known as an "adversative" method—the introducing of physical, emotional, and psychological stressors to break down a subject's previous belief systems and thereby more effectively mold the subject in line with the values of the institution—and this strategy often creates an intense bond and a fierce loyalty among male cadets.[51] This is reflected in *The Simpsons*' depiction of Rommelwood, where the focus is on discipline of a highly "masculinized" type, characterized by grueling physical challenges, overtly aggressive behavior, and an exclusion of those who are outsiders. Lisa is immediately resented by the male cadets because their barracks is given over to her, and they are told to share quarters with another company. The male cadets decide that they will have to drive Lisa out—"That's why God invented hazing," one says—and thus put both Lisa and Bart through a series of trials, including doing push-ups in the mud, polishing statues with toothbrushes, and being spun on the propellers of an airplane. Although Bart is initially excluded and subjected to the same humiliations as Lisa, this is just an initiation process for him, and after a time he is accepted into the boys' pack; Lisa, however, remains excluded, despite the fact that she and Bart both completed the same tasks and she was equally successful in performing them.

Lisa, feeling lonely and homesick and now questioning her decision to attend Rommelwood, seeks out the company of her brother, but Bart shuts her out in an effort to maintain solidarity with the boys. Feeling guilty, Bart apologizes to Lisa the following day, admitting to her that he did not want the other boys to think he had "gone soft on the girl issue." "I'm tired of being an issue, Bart," Lisa says—a comment that can be read to mean two things: being a problem for the cadets who have to accommodate her or, more broadly, being a female in a male-dominated world. Lisa then suggests that everyone would be happier if she just quit. "You can't quit," Bart tells her, and he promises to help her get through, although he will do so on the sly, so as to protect his reputation. Though Lisa was seeking intellectual challenges, the big challenge at Rommelwood is the Eliminator, a physically demanding, 150-foot hand-over-hand crawl along a rope ("with a blister factor of twelve") suspended over "a solid British acre of old-growth Connecticut Valley thorn bushes." Lisa is unnerved at the prospect of having to complete this task, but Bart helps her practice so that she is well prepared on the day she has to perform. When the day comes, Lisa is the last to go. All the boys, having successfully completed the crawl, are standing at the far end and hoping to see Lisa fail. When her hold momentarily slips, they begin to chant, "Drop! Drop! Drop!" At this point, Bart steps forward, openly breaking rank with his male peers, and verbally encourages Lisa to help her succeed. Though the cadets promise a painful retaliation for this betrayal, Lisa points out that graduation is only three hours away, and the cadets all rush off to prepare.

"The Secret War of Lisa Simpson" is more sentimentalized and less overtly politicized than "Lisa vs. Malibu Stacy," focusing as it does on the relationship between Lisa and Bart. Nonetheless, the episode engages once again in timely commentary on a topic that was a central part of the mid-1990s culture wars. Again, the emphasis here is upon gender equality, implicitly in the acceptance of Lisa into Rommelwood and explicitly in Lisa's ability to perform in a male-dominated world and a highly masculinized space.[52] The episode also has resonance with both "The Springfield Connection" and "Homer's Night Out." Like Marge, who as a police officer stepped into a male-dominated domain, Lisa chooses to place herself inside a traditionally male sphere. And like her mother, Lisa is disrespected and assumed to be incapable, but she ultimately proves to herself and others that she is just as capable as the males. Similarly, like Homer before him, Bart elects to forego male privilege, at least temporarily, and support gender equality. At the end of "Homer's Night Out," we see Homer in a position to simply join the ranks and participate in the sexual objectification of women; instead, he stops the proceedings and offers an emotional speech about respect for women. Bart is in a similar position at the end of "The Secret War of Lisa Simpson," yet rather than maintain male solidarity, he too allows emotion to come to the fore and risks the wrath of his peers to support Lisa's endeavors. Such moments are not uncommon on *The Simpsons* and are to be read, I believe, as metaphorical comments on the roles of men in supporting women as they challenge gender norms and stereotypes about female ability—that is, on men's role in an ongoing feminist movement. And yet one has to acknowledge that the successes of both Marge and Lisa are still temporary. This can be attributed in part to a convention of the sitcom genre, which effectively dictates that characters return to a previous state, although I think that is too simplistic a way to approach it. Indeed, as I have noted elsewhere, such a convention actually works in service of satire: the conceit of repositioning characters to an earlier state of mind allows the creators to again explore issues such as gender discrimination and sexism. That said, it also seems to me that the resolutions of these *Simpsons* episodes are inexorably entangled with the ideological preoccupations of the culture and thus inevitably influenced by the ambiguities and ambivalences about women's lives discussed at the onset of this chapter.

Conclusion

Ironically enough, considering the largely egalitarian climate in which *The Simpsons* is both set and produced, the show seems to be, in the words of Lori Landay, "at a crossroads of reactionary and liberated definitions of femininity."[53] Some of this can assuredly be attributed to the fact that *The Simpsons* is, after all, a mass media product, produced for and marketed to the largest demographic possible, and as such, it often needs to cater to prevailing ideologies. However, considering how commonly the show functions to contest prevailing ideologies of all sorts, this seems an interpretive sleight of hand. It appears that the creators of *The Simpsons* themselves have mixed feelings regarding feminism and female identity in the contemporary age. One way of understanding the ambiguities inherent in *The Simpsons* is to point out the predominance of men in the creation of the show. By and large, *The Simpsons* is a television show dominated by men: the show is produced by Matt Groening, James L. Brooks, and Sam Simon, and it is overseen by a host of male writers, directors, and animators. This is especially true of the early seasons, when *The Simpsons* writers room was almost exclusively dominated by men.[54] Most notable among this group are George Myer, Al Jean, Mike Reiss, Jon Vitti, Jay Kogen, Conan O'Brien, Jeff Martin, and John Swartzwelder. Not surprisingly, perhaps, the scripts for episodes were focused largely on the antics of Bart and Homer rather than the struggles of Lisa or Marge. The talent of the early writing staff is undeniable—but so is the rather masculine sensibility they brought to the show, and this perspective helped shape and define *The Simpsons* in its formative seasons. As the former writer and producer Wallace Wolodarsky recalls, "The Homer stories were the easiest to write, and then the second easiest were Bart stories, and then Lisa stories. Marge stories were always the toughest, because we were a bunch of boys, really, and nobody had any understanding of what it meant to be a mother or a woman."[55] Not surprisingly, only five women were involved in writing episodes of *The Simpsons* from its premiere in 1989 through the tenth season in 1998, and only two episodes written by women appeared before 1995: the premiere episode, "Simpsons Roasting on an Open Fire," which was written by Mimi Pond, and "One Fish, Two Fish, Blowfish, Blue Fish" (January 1991), which was written by Nell Scovell.[56] Until season 15 (2003–4), the largest number of episodes attributed to a single female writer was only five; these are all the work of Jennifer Crittenden, whose very first effort, "And Maggie Makes Three," appeared in January 1995.

Although these facts might help in part to explain the subtle ambivalence about feminism on *The Simpsons*, essentialist notions of authorship are ultimately quite limiting, and it is naive to say the ambiguities noted in this chapter are the sole result of male creativity. In later years, *The Simpsons* had more contributions by women writers in episodes that focus strongly on the female characters and interrogate the gender politics of their (and our) society. Carolyn Omine, for example, has written "Little Big Mom" (January 1999), in which Lisa temporarily takes over as the mother of the household when Marge is injured in a ski accident; "The Strong Arms of the

Ma" (February 2003), in which Marge begins lifting weights and abusing steroids; "Smart and Smarter" (February 2004), in which Lisa struggles with the fact that baby Maggie's IQ turns out to be higher than her own; and "The Great Wife Hope" (October 2009), in which Marge physically takes on (and beats) the promoter of a popular mixed martial arts contest. To date, Omine has penned a total of nine episodes; she has also been a cowriter on three others, two of which were Halloween specials.[57] However, despite such developments, ambiguities abound on *The Simpsons*, and the ambivalence about women's power and position is still strongly evident in many recent episodes. It is also apparent in the culture at large: witness, for example, Marge's sexed-up appearances in two men's magazines, *Maxim* (April 2004) and *Playboy* (November 2009). The latter appearance coincided with the airing of "The Devil Wears Nada," in which Marge becomes briefly infamous in Springfield—and widely ogled by all of the men and boys of the town—for her risqué photo-spread in a calendar that she and the Springfield Charity Chicks created as a fund-raiser.

The fact remains that *The Simpsons* is primarily produced, written, directed, and even animated by a stable of men—indeed, all of the early episodes that I discussed in detail in this chapter were written by men. "Homer's Night Out" was written by John Vitti; "Life on the Fast Lane" by John Swartzwelder; both "Homer Alone" and "Selma's Choice" by David M. Stern; "The Springfield Connection" by John Collier; and "Lisa vs. Malibu Stacy" by Bill Oakley and Josh Weinstein.[58] This point is offered not as a critique of the possible limitations these individuals might have by virtue of their sex but instead as a reminder of the ability of the show's writers—both male and female—to transcend essentialist notions of authorship and to produce a mainstream television show that contains an overt feminist sensibility. A fine example of this crossover sensibility is the seventeenth-season episode "Girls Just Want to Have Sums" (April 2006), written by Matt Selman and directed by Nancy Kruse, which concerns the division of Springfield Elementary into separate learning spaces for boys and girls and which is clearly designed to challenge the rigidly dichotomized ways of thinking about gender norms, intellectual ability, and educational achievement still prevalent in the culture today. "Girls Just Want to Have Sums" was inspired by the debate generated over comments made by the Harvard University president Lawrence Summers the year before. In January 2005, Summers gave a speech in which he stated that innate differences between the sexes may have something to do with the fact that proportionately fewer women than men hold top positions in science. The uproar over his speech eventually led to his resignation the following month. In "Girls Just Want to Have Sums," Principal Skinner is fired for making a comment ("Boys are better in math and science—the real subjects") that is taken to be sexist, and he is replaced by a female principal who believes strongly in gender-segregated education. The episode offers another example of feminism in action (as well as another example of gender-bending on *The Simpsons*) when Lisa goes undercover in the boys' school (as Jake Boyman) to do "real math"—and to prove her point about gender equality—after discovering that the girls' school will only be discussing the "emotions" of math to help build confidence and self-esteem. After achieving the highest grade in the boys' math class, "Jake" reveals himself to be Lisa, who declares, "I'm glad I'm a girl and I'm glad that I'm good at math."

It seems that the writers have an easier time developing more openly and overtly feminist story lines for Lisa; things are more complicated, however, with Marge. As Jessamyn Neuhaus points out, Marge is much more commonly associated with and yoked to the domestic sphere via her roles as wife and mother. Marge's satisfaction with her marriage, which is powerfully tested on a regular basis, is invariably restored, but "her frustrations with homemaking are somewhat less easily resolved."[59] As noted earlier, Marge has operated as a social reformer many times, and she has been employed outside the home in numerous episodes. However, according to Neuhaus, these episodes of employment, which never last more than one episode and always end with Marge reentering the home and returning to her domestic role, "never provide a lasting solution to Marge's occasional discontent with homemaking" and ultimately demonstrate that Marge's "attempts to dislocate herself from her domestic role fail."[60] I don't dispute that Marge's jobs are short-lived, but to what degree this is a failure is debatable. Homer also holds many other jobs, often for just one episode, and he is returned to his previous status as well. He has also quit or been fired from the nuclear plant numerous times—yet he always returns. I take these strategies to be in service of the satire, not failures of imagination or lack of support for progressive perspectives. If the aim is to deconstruct the myths of the happy homemaker, then Marge has to be put into the role again and again. This allows the writers to find new angles from which to critique contemporary mythologies and ideologies. If Marge were to say in one position, this might not be so effective. To my mind, this is parallel to the conceit that no one ages on the show—by keeping the Simpson children the same age, for example, the writers can repeatedly mock the ineptitude of authority figures and, more importantly, the failings of public education. Such outcomes would be hard to achieve if the people of Springfield—like the actors on traditional live-action sitcoms—were required to "grow and change." To be fair, Neuhaus does acknowledge that Marge challenges the "total acquiescence of 1950s sitcom wives to traditional gender roles" and does, at points, recognize the inherent ambivalence and ambiguity I have been discussing in this chapter. For example, Neuhaus notes that the episode "Marge in Chains" is clearly satirical, "exaggerat[ing] Marge's domestic role to the point of absurdity." In this episode, Marge accidentally shoplifts at the Kwik-E-Mart and has to spend 30 days in jail, thus depriving her family of her consummate domestic skills. As in "Homer Alone," Homer cannot manage the most basic of domestic chores, and in short order the children are a mess and the house in disarray. In this case, however, there is a ripple effect: the problems extend beyond the Simpson home and into Springfield at large, in a preposterous series of events that result in widespread chaos. The absurdity is made clear in Helen Lovejoy's comment, "This never would have happened if Marge Simpson were here." Despite the clear satire here, Neuhaus nevertheless concludes that "*The Simpsons* ultimately does not satirize the role of homemaker as much as it reifies it."[61]

Admittedly, progressive representations of women in American mass media are still quite rare. Indeed, in recent years there appears to have been yet another "backlash" against the image of strong and independent women, brought on in part by the return to a conservative political agenda at the start of the new millennium. However, it is potentially detrimental to cast an examination of media forms into such a dichotomized schema. Living in a largely dichotomized world, we are quick to label representations of women in the mass media as either "positive" or "negative" or, in other words, as "empowered" or "disempowered." But things are rarely so simple, as *The Simpsons* admirably demonstrates. In her provocative examination of women in the mass media, *Madcaps, Screwballs & Con Women*, Lori Landay argues that representations of female "weakness" and "power" are not really contradictory but are instead "two streams of feeling which commingle and feed each other."[62] In other words, traditional and progressive ideologies of "femininity" and "womanhood" exist simultaneously, in both the mass media and the culture itself, and at this particular moment in American history they remain in conflict. As noted earlier, many women's lives today are marked by such conflict, a reality that is reflected—and reflected upon—in the text of *The Simpsons*. As Barry Hodge succinctly claims, "*The Simpsons* doesn't constitute an 'out-and-out' feminist text, but one of a feminine culture asserting its values within and against patriarchy."[63] This seems to be precisely the understanding of the show that the editors of *Ms.* magazine were articulating with their claim that Lisa Simpson "wages a one-girl revolution against cartoonland patriarchy."[64] What *The Simpsons* offers viewers regarding female identity is a complex combination of "strength" and "weakness": in other words, of activism and submission, of protest against and acquiescence to male dominance and patriarchal structures. It is through this lens, then, that we can perhaps best understand *The Simpsons'* representations of female identity and a feminist sensibility.

4

"The Whole World's Gone Gay!": Gay Identity, Queer Culture, and *The Simpsons*

> In the absence of adequate information in their immediate environment, most people—gay or straight—have little choice but to accept the media stereotypes they imagine must be typical of all lesbians and gay men.
>
> —*Larry Gross*[1]

Before the "queer vogue" of recent years, there was a decided lack of visibility for gay, lesbian, bisexual, transgendered, and queer individuals in the media landscape; the visibility that did exist largely comprised long-standing stereotypes and negative portrayals.[2] Of course, this did not mean that there was a lack of concern about gay identity and the queering of American culture. For example, during the late 1980s, the mainstream news media periodically reported, in both positive and negative ways, on the continuing AIDS crisis and on issues such as gay adoption, domestic partnerships, and military service for gays and lesbians.[3] At the same time that gay and lesbian lives were becoming a larger part of the national conversation, queer identity was becoming a more integral part of mass media at the fringes of the mainstream. In the late 1980s and early 1990s, independent films studios were producing an array of films that candidly explored the queer experience, inadvertently launching what B. Ruby Rich would infamously label the "New Queer Cinema." The commercial success of these films led Hollywood to follow suit, and within a few short years, the studios were also producing films with queer subject matter.[4] Additionally, queer phenomena such as drag performance and "vogueing" crossed over into the mainstream via the work of artists such as k. d. lang and Madonna, whose hit single "Vogue" (1990) and accompanying video (directed by David Fincher) did much to popularize the formerly subcultural practice. On network television, by the mid-1990s, gay-themed episodes and references to homosexuality were also plentiful, as Ron Becker points out in *Gay TV and Straight America* (2006), his analysis of America's "obsession" with gayness in the 1990s. According to Becker, between 1994 and 1997, over 40 percent of all prime-time network series produced in this period had at least one gay-themed episode, 19 network shows debuted with recurring gay characters, and "hit shows like *Roseanne, Friends,* and *NYPD Blue* (to name but a few) seemed to include gay jokes and references to homosexuality every week."[5]

Despite the obvious progress, however, the 1990s was also a period of backlash and resistance to queerness. This was made manifest in the "culture wars" of the era, which encompassed a host of issues under the rubric of multiculturalism, many of them discussed in the previous chapters. Debates related to gender, sex, and sexuality—always present but not as heavily emphasized as those related to race and ethnicity—became more frequent and increasingly centered on gay and lesbian life. Some of the debates in this variation on the culture wars were familiar, and others were quite new: among other things, these were driven by concerns over sexually explicit art and pornography; niche publishing aimed at queer consumers; "hate speech" and speech codes; the expansion of educational curricula to include gay and lesbian voices; and the recurring struggles for gay and lesbian civil rights, which included battles over antidiscrimination laws, US military service, and same-sex marriages.[6] A backlash was also apparent in the large-scale, nationwide anxiety over homosexuality, which was seen throughout the decade and into the new millennium in nearly every form of popular media (Hollywood film, television programming, advertising, stand-up comedy, talk radio, rock and rap music, and music videos) and which sometimes resulted in violence, as in the brutal murders of Brandon Teena in 1993, Scott Amerdure in 1995, and Matthew Shepard in 1998.

The media's treatment of queer identities thus calls for a serious critical inquiry among media scholars. The perspective I adopt here for such inquiry is one aligned with the academic discipline of "queer media studies," a merger of well-established film and television studies practices with a queer theory perspective.[7] The antecedents of queer theory can be traced to earlier work on social constructionism found in women's studies and gay and lesbian studies and to poststructuralist literary and cultural theory, but two works in particular have been taken as foundational texts for queer theory: Eve Kosofsky Sedgwick's *Epistemology of the Closet* (1990) and Judith Butler's *Gender Trouble* (1990). Together these works disrupted traditional feminist theory, subverted "commonsense" beliefs about gender, sex, and sexuality (as well as binaristic thinking about these categories), and offered what Karen Kopelson calls "theoretical interventions of the first order."[8] Queer media studies has borrowed from such "interventions" to establish a framework for investigating how images within cultural texts can be examined from various sexed, gendered, and sexualized positions. My thinking on representations of queerness in mass media has been influenced by some of the pioneering studies published in the late 1980s and early 1990s, as well as by the many contributions to the fields of media studies and queer studies, which have expanded exponentially in the years since.[9]

Much of this scholarship has made clear that one of the goals of queer media studies is to challenge the negative representations of the queer experience in mainstream media. As Alan Brookey and Robert Westerfelhaus note, "[T]he mainstream media are an important element of defining and defending [American] culture's center and its boundaries."[10] Of course, television has functioned, at least in part, to establish and promote the notion of a normative American mainstream, which has until quite recently been defined as straight, white, and middle class. However, that norm has been fragmenting over the past three decades, and "normative" Americans have increasingly had to confront "difference" as a result of large-scale social and political changes taking place in the nation. What Ron Becker usefully calls America's "straight panic" in *Gay TV and Straight America* is partially a consequence of these social, cultural, and political changes.[11] Progress assuredly has been made, and the media portrayals of queer identity so prominent now have largely departed from the negative portrayals of previous eras. So if the depiction of gay, lesbian, and queer life is largely "positive," then what is left for a queer media studies project? What other goals must it focus on? Brookey and Westerfelhaus offer two very useful responses to such questions: they argue that those engaged in queer media studies must "examine the impact, [both] potential and realized, of such portrayals in redefining the intersection of gay and mainstream cultures," and then they must work to "identify how such portrayals serve to challenge and/or reinforce the heterosexual bias of American culture."[12] This view aligns with my own thinking and informs the analysis provided in this chapter, which focuses on queer visibility in mass media, the politics of sexuality, and the representations of queer identity on *The Simpsons*. In discussing queer identity on *The Simpsons*, I am mostly referring to gay male life, particularly as it centers on the character Waylon Smithers, as this is what is most commonly depicted on the show; however, I will also briefly refer to gay female life in my discussion of the coming-out of Patty Bouvier, one of Marge's twin sisters, in the 2005 episode "There's Something about Marrying."

Those who are not regular watchers of the show might be inclined to raise an eyebrow at a topic such as queer identity on *The Simpsons*. However, those who are among the faithful are likely to recognize that such a discussion is not inappropriate, considering both the show's cast of characters and its political aims. As discussed previously, *The Simpsons* established itself as a biting satire on American culture, and it commonly works from a leftist political position to lambaste, among other things, "traditional" family values. More often than not, the mainstream media represent gay and lesbian life as existing outside the confines of traditional nuclear family structures and thereby apart from its presumed "values." *The Simpsons* is no exception to this, focusing as it does primarily on the nuclear family; however, because of its satirical bent and its ideological stance, I believe the show enacts a different kind of representation of queer identity. To examine this in more detail, I begin by exploring the ways in which *The Simpsons* establishes a "queer sensibility" for its viewers. This is done in many ways, of course, but primarily through the abundant use of allusions to gay life and sexual orientation, a toying with the fluid nature of sexuality, the incorporation of regular gay characters (especially Waylon Smithers), and, most recently, an engagement with the highly politicized issue of same-sex marriage. This chapter also examines the ideological implications of queerness as portrayed on *The Simpsons*. Via its regular critique of the oppression of sexual "minorities" in American culture, *The Simpsons* appears to promote a progressive political agenda. However, the ways in which issues related to sex and sexuality have been addressed and dealt with on the show raise questions once again about the tensions between political satire and commercial interests and about how satirical messages are received by audiences. Thus, I want to more closely examine how *The Simpsons* employs queerness in service of its satire.

Visibility and Contemporary Mass Media

To fully understand *The Simpsons*' engagement with queer identity, it is necessary to know something of the representations of queerness in mass media, especially television, that preceded the show. Until quite recently, queer identity was not widely reflected in America's popular arts, outside of certain long-standing, easily recognizable, and predominantly negative stereotypes. Over time, therefore, gay men and women have had to look very hard to find representations of themselves. As Andy Medhurst eloquently puts it,

> Denied even the remotest possibility of supportive images of homosexuality within the dominant heterosexual culture, gay people have had to fashion what [they] could out of the imageries of dominance, to snatch illicit meanings from the fabric of normality, to undertake a corrupt decoding for the purposes of satisfying marginalized desires.[13]

In the wake of the Stonewall riots and the organized political movements of the late 1960s and early 1970s, Hollywood made some concession to the presence of gay and lesbian men and women in American culture, and gay characters or gay-themed story lines began to appear in select films. Nonetheless, during this same time period, queer characters in Hollywood film by and large committed suicide or were murdered by another character, often in retaliation against the queer character's own "villainous" or threatening behavior. Examples of this trend can be found in a diverse set of Hollywood films, including *The Children's Hour* (1961), *Advise and Consent* (1962), *Walk on the Wild Side* (1962), *The Best Man* (1964), *The Detective* (1968), *Vanishing Point* (1971), *Freebie and the Bean* (1974), *Midnight Express* (1978), and the controversial *Cruising* (1980).[14] A similar trend was in place on television, in popular dramatic shows such as *Marcus Welby, M.D.* (1969–76), *The Streets of San Francisco* (1972–77), *Police Woman* (1974–78), and *Charlie's Angels* (1976–81).[15] Something slightly different was taking place on situation comedies, however. As John R. Leo points out, during the 1970s, many well-meaning and self-consciously liberal television sitcoms tried to both acknowledge gay life and offer more progressive-minded representations of homosexuality.[16] Notable among these are *All in the Family* (1971–79), *Maude* (1972–78), and *Barney Miller* (1975–82), all of which offered gay-themed story lines. A more overtly queer presence was offered on *Soap* (1977–81), which gave us prime time's first recurring gay character (Jody, played by Billy Crystal), and the short-lived *Love, Sydney* (1979–81), which offered us television's first gay lead character. Gay and lesbian characters also appeared as extras in gay-themed episodes of prime-time dramas such as *Lou Grant* (1977–82), *Trapper John, M.D.* (1979–86), and *L.A. Law* (1986–94) and even as regular cast members, as was the case with *Dynasty* (1981–89), which featured an openly gay character, Steven Carrington.[17] However, more often than not, such shows portrayed gayness as a "problem" to be solved; the incident was inevitably isolated and the story line focused upon a straight character trying to deal with and/or accept someone else's homosexuality. As the 1980s progressed, there was a shift toward heteronormativity; with regard to the sitcom, there was a notable return to the genre's conventional family center and its hermetic, middle-class lifestyle, a movement that coincided with the conservative zeitgeist of the Reagan years. The erasure of gayness from everyday life led to the erasure of gayness within the television world. When it was there, it was increasingly equated with the AIDS epidemic of the late 1980s, which helped reinvigorate the proscribed "roles" for gay people in film and television: namely, victim and villain.

However, in the 1990s, things began to change, and "gay" appeared to be back in vogue. In March 1990, *Newsweek* ran a cover story on "The Future of Gay America," predicting that the 1990s would "reflect a new spirit of anger, activism, and political clout" and concluding that "gays won't let up in their quest for a more visible—and influential—place in American society."[18] In 1993, *The Nation* offered a more sober look at the politics of the gay struggle in its cover story on "The Gay Moment" in America. The author Andrew Kopkind writes,

> The gay moment is unavoidable. It fills the media, charges politics, and saturates popular and elite culture. It is the stuff of everyday conversation and public discourse. Not for thirty years has a class of Americans endured the peculiar pain and exhilaration of having their civil rights and moral worth—their very humanness—debated at every level of public life. Lesbians and gay men today wake up to headlines alternately disputing their claim to equality under the law, supporting their right to family status, denying their desire, affirming their social identity. They fall asleep to TV talk shows where generals call them perverts, liberals plead for tolerance and politicians weigh their votes. "Gay invisibility," the social enforcement of the sexual closet, is hardly the problem anymore. Overexposure is becoming hazardous.[19]

Not long after, in September 1995, *Entertainment Weekly* published a special issue on "The Gay 90s," claiming that entertainment had "come out of the closet." In the cover story, Jess Cagle discusses "gay-friendly" entertainment, which he sees evident everywhere in the 1990s—in advertising, music, and film and on television and Broadway.[20] In light of all this, Cagle quite optimistically crows, "In 1995, the gay stream flows freely into the mainstream."[21] Cagle's claim was perhaps naive in its assumption of wide acceptance for this "gay stream"; the media may well have had a change in attitude by the mid-1990s, but the public at large had not. Although the media opened up significantly during this time period, they did so out of necessity. As Leo notes, this is particularly true of television: faltering network ratings and a loss of revenue resulting from competition from cable and video led to a state in which "what used to be censored as controversial is now welcomed as sensitive theme programming."[22] While Leo's assessment is true to a degree, it does not provide a full picture: the "controversial" depictions of queerness were not so easily welcomed in the 1990s. Those desirous of pushing the boundaries on network television, for example, were in a constant state of worry over how advertisers would react, and this had serious consequences. One example is the ABC series *thirtysomething* (1987–91), which pushed network television boundaries in 1989 with an episode showing two men waking up together in bed, clearly implying a sexual encounter. ABC lost approximately $1.5 million in ad revenue after five of the ten regular sponsors of the series pulled their ads in response to the episode, and the network was inundated with angry phone calls from viewers. The producers of the show, Marshall Herskovitz and Ed Zwick, insisted that such reactions would not prevent them from featuring gay characters again, but "Herskovitz recognized that *thirtysomething*'s ability to include gay material was constrained by the network's commercial imperative."[23] Things began to change rather rapidly, however, after ABC's hit show *Roseanne* began to incorporate gay characters and stories. This started in 1991 with the "outing" of Roseanne's boss, Leon (Martin Mull), and continued in 1992 with Roseanne's friend Nancy (Sandra Bernhard) announcing that she was bisexual. The real turning point, however, came in March 1994 with the controversial episode "Don't Ask, Don't Tell," which featured a same-sex kiss between Roseanne and Nancy's new girlfriend, Sharon (Mariel Hemingway). Roseanne Barr's then-husband Tom Arnold attracted some media attention in advance by claiming that ABC executives were planning to either censor or refuse to air the episode; Roseanne herself then stirred the controversy further by appearing on the late-night talk show circuit to complain about network censorship. Although it was preceded by an advisory warning, the episode aired as scheduled, just in time to be included in the February sweeps, and drew strong ratings. As Becker reports, advertisers did not pull out, the show earned a high Nielsen share of 30, only two of ABC's 225 affiliates refused to carry the episode (both in small markets), and ABC received only 100 calls, 75 percent of which were positive.[24]

As these examples indicate, just at the time *The Simpsons* first appeared in the early 1990s, there was a tentative but growing faith in the media's liberalism, and gay characters began to appear on television with greater frequency. In his essay "Invisibility, Homophobia, and Heterosexism," Fred Fejes argues that such visibility is due to the advancements made in the 1970s and 1980s by gay activists, whose political organization led to demands for increased and more accurate representation.[25] Interestingly, in the same essay, published in 1993, Fejes also avers that homosexuality remains as a subtext on television, that gay characters exist on the periphery, and that "a regular network program with a gay or lesbian main character is far in the future."[26] However, the industry did change dramatically and very rapidly by the mid-1990s, having discovered that queerness was both controversial and profitable, and gay and lesbian lead characters on television were not nearly as unlikely as Fejes predicted, as both *Ellen* and *Will & Grace* would prove only a few years later. By 1995, gay characters were plentiful on television, which lends some credence to their enthusiastic claims about the "gay 90s." During the 1994–95 season, for example, gay characters and gay-themed story lines could be seen on all of the networks, including Fox, in shows such as *NYPD Blue, Northern Exposure, My So-Called Life, Party of Five, Melrose Place, Friends, Frasier, Roc, Seinfeld*, and *The Simpsons*. As the representations increased, so did the scrutiny of these from such organizations as the Gay & Lesbian Alliance Against Defamation (GLAAD). Since 1995, GLAAD has published reports that record the number of gay, lesbian, bisexual, and transgendered characters on television. According to the GLAAD TV Scoreboard for 1996–97, there were 34 gay, lesbian, bisexual, or transgendered characters on television. This is an impressive number, especially compared with the statistics from just a few years earlier. However, the GLAAD report also points out that nearly all of these characters were in minor and/or nonrecurring roles; the following season, queer characters on television numbered just 27—and the only one in a lead role was Ellen DeGeneres on *Ellen*.[27]

Although *The Simpsons* had a clearly established queer sensibility in its early seasons, and regular fans were well aware of the (still implied) sexuality of Waylon Smithers, it was the show *Ellen* (1994–98) that was making headlines and sparking controversy in the mid-1990s. In October 1996, *Entertainment Weekly* published yet another cover story on "Gay TV," this time in direct response to the "controversy" surrounding Ellen DeGeneres, star of ABC's *Ellen*, and speculation that she (and her television doppelgänger) would publicly "come out" in the season 4 finale. The speculation stemmed in part from what was being written about DeGeneres herself in the tabloids. By the second week of the fall television season, DeGeneres made herself visible on various daytime and nighttime talk shows discussing the issue. Notably, she appeared on *The Rosie O'Donnell Show*, where the two women joked at length about Ellen's character being "Lebanese." Of course, there had been similar speculation in the media about the sexual orientation of O'Donnell as well, thus adding an interesting double layer to the joke. The significant point, however, is that they made light of the issue, wanting to admit it without admitting it. This approach was funny, but it was also safe. The question remained: Was America ready for its first lesbian in a lead role on television? It was admittedly a precarious situation for a major network. Apparently, ABC wanted to test the waters, which is probably why the coming out of Ellen progressed so slowly. However, it was soon apparent that network executives were willing to risk the show (and by extension the career of DeGeneres) by allowing Ellen to become "a testcase for the nation's tolerance."[28] Initially it seemed that the risk would pay off and that the nation was ready for such overt representation. On the heels of a great deal of media attention, the infamous "Puppy Episode" of Ellen was finally aired on April 30, 1997, and it pulled in a healthy 36.2 million viewers. However, in its subsequent season, the show was quickly criticized for being "too gay" and didactic, and the show averaged only 12.4 million viewers. Soon afterward, amid some very public squabbling between DeGeneres and ABC executives, Ellen was canceled.[29]

In light of the rather rapid demise of Ellen once DeGeneres came out publicly, I think it important to examine why it seemed so likely at that point to finally have a gay character in a lead role on television and why the response was initially so positive. Prime-time television had a fair number of gay characters in supporting roles but none in a lead role during that time. Ellen DeGeneres was a logical choice for the transition to a gay lead role and ideal for making homosexuality acceptable to the public at large because she was seen as "nonthreatening" to mainstream audiences. In part, DeGeneres was less threatening because Ellen was a situation comedy and DeGeneres herself is a lesbian. As A. J. Jacobs succinctly put it, "[S]he'd be a lesbian instead of a gay man, which, like it or not, makes her more palatable."[30] The aforementioned gay kiss on Roseanne, for example, was also "palatable" because it was both on a sitcom and between two women. As is well known, our culture more readily accepts close female relationships; emotional intimacy is perceived to more easily slip into physical intimacy among women. The so-called "straight" porn industry, for example, is filled with gayness in the form of lesbianism. However, the sexual interaction of women in these movies is filtered through the male gaze and perceived to be part of a straight male fantasy; this effectively erases the "taint" of homosexuality and the threat it poses to masculinity. But unrestrained female (homo)sexuality, overtly put forth and not confined by the male perspective, as was the case with Ellen, is threatening and must be contained. Straight white men, who still hold the majority of power and control in the media, are more often than not still unwilling to offer representations of homosexual relationships—female or male—in the mainstream. This fact, alongside Jacobs's astute observation that gay men are less "palatable" to mainstream America than gay women, should then force us to question the overt prejudice directed at gay males in American culture. Gay males were widely considered social and commercial anathema in the early 1990s; it is no surprise that the greatest inroads of the period were made by straight women sympathetic to gay rights, by gay women themselves, and by men masquerading as women—for example, Roseanne Barr, Melissa Etheridge, and the films Mrs. Doubtfire (1993), To Wong Foo (1995), and The Birdcage (1996). Mainstream images of gay men who are not drag queens or examples of successful gay male relationships were (and, on network television, largely still are) rare in American culture.

The Simpsons has not yet offered a regular gay male relationship, but neither has it adopted the common strategy of handling gay male identity in the popular media, which has been to pair gay men with straight women, thus offering visibility in a "safe" manner. The formula was very successfully employed in *My Best Friend's Wedding* (1997), which paired Rupert Everett with Julia Roberts, and then repeated with similar levels of success in the films *As Good As It Gets* (1997), *The Object of My Affection* (1998), *The Opposite of Sex* (1998), and *The Next Best Thing* (2000). More significantly, this formula was also used as a premise for the NBC sitcom *Will & Grace* (1998–2006). Considering what happened with *Ellen* only the previous year, it seems surprising that NBC would risk losing both advertisers and viewers by placing an openly gay character in a lead role. It also seems surprising that *Will & Grace* did not meet with the same harsh criticism as *Ellen* nor ignite another national debate over homosexuality. But upon closer inspection, it becomes clear why and how this is the case. Although Will and Grace have a platonic relationship and live together only as roommates, their living arrangement provides a pretense of heterosexuality. Not surprisingly, members of an NBC-sponsored focus group who watched the series pilot had no idea that Will was gay until told that he was.[31] Will and Grace are an idealized couple, free of the pains associated with a (hetero)sexual relationship and benign enough to appeal to the largest demographic. In short, NBC's approach packaged gay men in a nonthreatening —and thereby still lucrative—way for Middle America.

Nevertheless, *Will & Grace* proved to be very popular and commercially successful, and it thus paved the way for even greater visibility on television. The other major networks all scrambled to produce shows that might tap into the queer vogue and duplicate the success of *Will & Grace*. But shows such as ABC's *It's All Relative*, NBC's *Coupling*, CBS's *The Guardian*, and Fox's *Normal, Ohio* were unable to find an audience and were soon canceled. The strategy of catering to queer audiences had much greater success in cable programming. In July 2003, the Bravo channel premiered its newest series, *Queer Eye for the Straight Guy* (2003–7). The show benefited from all the media attention it received as a result of appearing in the midst of rancorous debates over gay marriage that summer, and it very quickly became a commercial hit. Although *Queer Eye* garnered the greatest attention during the 2003–4 television season, there were many other cable shows featuring gay and lesbian characters at that time, including *The Wire, Sex and the City*, and *Six Feet Under* on HBO; *Queer as Folk* and *The L Word* on Showtime; and *Nip/Tuck* and *The Shield* on FX. Although queer representation on the networks was minimal by comparison (seen only with the continuing characters on *Will & Grace* and *ER*), queer visibility was high overall in the 2003–4 season. This is not surprising given that queer identity was proving to be profitable—and there was no better example of this than *Queer Eye for the Straight Guy*. Though the show premiered on the cable channel Bravo, it quickly migrated to network television after NBC purchased Bravo that same year. And it was NBC that heavily promoted *Queer Eye*, placing 30-minute versions of the show into its coveted Thursday-night lineup to run behind repeats of *Will & Grace* and ordering new episodes of the show to air that fall, thus making *Queer Eye* into a crossover hit.[32] On the surface, this great expansion of queer visibility would appear to be progress. But, as many commentators pointed out, most often with reference to *Queer Eye*, it is more accurately a crass marketing strategy designed to exploit a small fraction of the gay and lesbian community and a commodification of queer identity as a packageable good. As a September 2003 GLAAD press release on gay and lesbian representation makes clear, despite the abundance of images of gay life on television at that time, these images were very narrow. In the midst of discussions about gay civil rights, GLAAD reminds us that "hit shows like Bravo's *Queer Eye for the Straight Guy* and CBS' *The Amazing Race* offered viewers glimpses of gay life that, while groundbreaking, remained predominantly male, white, affluent and decidedly 'fabulous.'"[33] Of course, long before the co-optation of the word *queer* by commercial forces and the commodification of a narrowly defined queer identity, *The Simpsons* was cultivating and regularly offering its viewers a clearly established queer sensibility.

The Simpsons' Queer Sensibility

When looking over the entire series, one is struck by just how prominent the queer sensibility is on *The Simpsons*; there are abundant allusions to gay life and sexual orientation and numerous examples of high camp.[34] Of course, the incorporation of a queer sensibility seems almost expected if one considers the career of the show's creator, Matt Groening. Groening first yoked the gay and cartoon worlds together in his *Life in Hell* comic in the form of Akbar and Jeff, two characters whose camaraderie was soon read by many as a gay relationship. In response to being pointedly asked during an interview if Akbar and Jeff were gay, Groening said that he designed them as "a comment on all relationships."[35] However, in this same interview, Groening made clear where his sympathies lay. He was raised with what he calls the "good lefty politics" of the 1960s; he has many close gay friends, some of whom he has lost to AIDS over the years; and he is "pissed off" at the lingering injustice he sees in America.[36] Although Groening concedes that there is a lack of representation for gay individuals in the popular media, he emphasizes that there is even more of a lack for gay couples; as he says, "[G]ay men are starved for positive portrayals of lasting love"[37]—hence the creation of Akbar and Jeff, who provided a much-needed palliative for many.

It is thus no surprise that a queer sensibility is a large part of *The Simpsons*. Indeed, it has been there from the start. As the series developed, so too did this sensibility, especially among the show's male characters: although all are strongly positioned as heterosexual, many of them frequently reference gay culture, toy with the notion of same-sex unions, freely hug and kiss, and rather casually participate in drag. This is particularly true among the Simpson family males (Abe, Homer, and Bart), who have each been central to numerous moments of camp and one or more incidents of cross-dressing. Fine examples are to be found in episodes from the show's earliest seasons. An early and subtle camp moment can be seen in "Brush with Greatness" (April 1991), from season 2. In this episode, Marge has been commissioned by Montgomery Burns to paint his portrait. While putting makeup on Burns, preparing him to be immortalized on canvas, Smithers affectionately says, "Now the world will see you as I always have, sir." "Yes, yes, yes," Burns replies. "Now don't be stingy with the blush, Smithers." In "The Front" (April 1993), we are given a sequence in which Grandpa (Abe) Simpson dreams of himself as "a Queen of the Old West" who is torn between the love of two cowboys; in the dream bubble, we see Abe, dressed in red petticoats, run to prevent a gunfight by declaring, "Boys, stop. You can both marry me!" The cowboys cheer and fire their guns in the air just prior to a heart-shaped fade to black accompanied by the theme song to *Love, American Style*. More overtly, in "Lisa the Beauty Queen" (October 1992), Bart gives Lisa advice on how to compete in a local beauty contest. Lisa, who cannot manage the victory walk in high heels, is ready to quit. "There's nothin' to it," Bart quips. "Gimme those heels." As he proceeds to demonstrate the posture, Lisa asks, "Do you really think I can win?" With a swish of the hip, Bart replies, "Hey, I'm starting to think I can win!" In the season 6 episode "Homer vs. Patty and Selma," the show continues challenging rigid gender norms by having Bart partake in ballet, at which he is a natural and with which he impresses his schoolmates in the school recital. Even the bullies Jimbo and Nelson, deeply invested in maintaining a masculine identity, are impressed by Bart's performance—as Jimbo observes while watching Bart dance, "He's graceful yet masculine, so it's ok for me to enjoy this." But it is with Homer that the series has most commonly explored the queer sensibility. Indeed, more than decade before the appearance of *Queer Eye for the Straight Guy* and its popularization of the male makeover, *The Simpsons* offered us a similar motif—though with more sincere emotional intimacy—in the second-season episode "Simpson and Delilah" (October 1990). After being promoted, Homer hires a secretary, Karl (voiced by Harvey Fierstein), who helps Homer dress for success and develop his self-confidence. Just prior to delivering an important speech to the bosses, Homer, still feeling uncertain, refers to himself as a "big fool." "Oh no you're not," Karl tells him. "How do you know?" Homer asks. "Because my mother taught me never to kiss a fool," and with that Karl gives Homer a kiss full on the lips, to which Homer, quite surprised, simply exclaims, "Karl!" Karl then says, "Now go get 'em, tiger," and gives Homer an affectionate pat on the rear as he leaves. A similarly flexible attitude toward sexuality is evident in the season 4 episode "Last Exit to Springfield," in which Homer becomes the union representative at the nuclear plant and has to negotiate with Mr. Burns for a dental plan. When Burns tells Homer, "If you scratch my back, I'll scratch yours," and then suggests (with a chuckle and a wink) that "Negotiations make strange bedfellows," Homer misreads the metaphors as come-on lines and is startled; however, he replies by simply saying, "Sorry, Mr. Burns, but I don't go in for these backdoor shenanigans. Sure, I'm flattered, maybe even a little curious, but the answer is no."

The campiness of *The Simpsons* is perhaps best illustrated in an episode from the seventh season entitled "Radioactive Man" (September 1995). In this episode, Hollywood moguls are in Springfield to make a film version of the exploits of Radioactive Man, comic-book superhero and one-time star of his own television series. As the producers of the film say, they want to "stay as far away from the campy 70s [television] version as possible." We then see a flashback to a scene from *Radioactive Man*, done as an obvious parody of the 1960s *Batman* television show.[38] The writers for *The Simpsons* know full well that the original *Batman* was saturated with a queer sensibility, and they highlight this fact by paralleling Batman with their stand-in for all "real-world" comic-book superheroes, Radioactive Man. *The Simpsons* then takes the queer factor one step further by making the villain that weird combination of pubescent effeminacy and adolescent masculinity: the Boy Scout. The effect is additionally underscored in having the villain (the Scoutmaster) voiced by Paul Lynde, who encourages his henchmen, "Don't be afraid to use your nails, boys." Of course, to create this effect, the show relies on some well-worn and less than favorable stereotypes. As Larry Gross rightly notes, "[M]edia characterizations [typically] use popular stereotypes as a code which they know will be readily understood by the audience."[39] With regard to gay males, Gross has in mind here such stereotypes as lisping speech, limp-wristedness, and the effeminate sashay. I concede the Batman parody employs these stereotypes; indeed, *The Simpsons* uses these for peripheral gay characters on a regular basis.[40] But I think the show does so with an ulterior motive. In his book *The Matter of Images: Essays on Representation* (1993), Richard Dyer reflects on the distinction between "social types" and "stereotypes" in media representations. According to Dyer, the function of stereotypes is "to make visible the invisible, so that there is no danger of it creeping up on us unawares; and to make fast, firm and separate what is in reality fluid and much closer to the norm than the dominant value system cares to admit."[41] One only has to reflect on what has happened in American media since the publication of Dyer's book to see the relevance and applicability of this idea, particularly in relation to the surprising popularity of *Will & Grace*, which relies upon recognizable stereotypes for its version of gay "visibility" and, thereby, for its commercial success. *The Simpsons*, in contrast, most often utilizes stereotypes in service of its satire and to expose fear and prejudice. By rehearsing the patterns of the *Batman* series, it is in effect rearticulating the gayness of the show for mainstream audiences, overtly enacting the same reading that gay men and women have done covertly for years. Stereotypical representations on *The Simpsons* are not at the expense of the gay community but in support of it—a fact most notable, perhaps, in the episodes "Homer's Phobia" and "There's Something about Marrying," which I discuss in detail later.

As I have tried to demonstrate, a queer sensibility is strongly evident on *The Simpsons*, but a discussion of gay life on the show would not be complete if it did not center on its regular gay character, the self-described sycophant, Waylon Smithers. Those who have faithfully watched *The Simpsons* over the course of many years know that there has been a slow but steady coming-out process for Smithers. They also know that the object of his affections is his boss, Mr. Burns. Smithers's concern for the well-being of Burns was well established early on. The aforementioned episode "Brush with Greatness," in which Burns contracts Marge to paint his portrait, provides an example of Smithers's devotion. At the Simpson home, Marge accidentally walks into the bathroom to find Burns exiting from the shower, naked, and Smithers offering him a towel. Marge apologizes for the intrusion and quickly leaves. Smithers asks, "Would you feel more comfortable if I left too, sir?" "Of course not, Smithers. You're...you're like a doctor." The comment positions Smithers in the role of caretaker and has the effect of both desexualizing their contact and affirming Burns's heterosexuality. But, for the viewer, it also provides an indication of both the physical and emotional closeness of the two men, which evidently fuels Smithers's desire. A similar circumstance is found in "Burns Verkaufen der Kraftwerk" (December 1991). After Burns sells the plant to a German consortium, Smithers is saddened by the loss of his job and, subsequently, his ties to Mr. Burns. Burns meanwhile occupies himself with bocce ball and beekeeping. But he too misses the camaraderie, so he invites Smithers for a drink at his estate. When Smithers arrives, Burns politely introduces him to the bees he is tending. Pointing, he says, "That's Buzz, that's Honey, and see that Queen over there? Her name is Smithers." Smithers replies, "That's very flattering, sir." Of course, this is subtle, and understanding how this scene implies a homosexual proclivity requires a certain in-group knowledge of the term "queen," which some viewers might be lacking. Smithers's desire is a bit more overtly on display in "Dog of Death" (March 1992), in which Homer reluctantly turns to Burns for a loan to cover the cost of an operation for Santa's Little Helper, the family dog. Burns cannot understand the attachment and asks Smithers, "Why would anyone spend good money on a dog?" "People like dogs, Mr. Burns," Smithers replies. "Nonsense," says Burns. "Dogs are idiots. Think about it Smithers. If I came into your house and started sniffing at your crotch and slobbering all over your face, what would you do?" Smithers's noncommittal reply: "Mmmmm...if *you* did it, sir?" Presumably, he is savoring the image. The first overt and truly audacious reference to Smithers's sexual orientation—and the one that had many fans viewing the show in a whole new light—was made in "Marge Gets a Job," an episode from season 4, in which Marge goes to work alongside Homer at the Springfield nuclear plant. Like an evil overlord, Mr. Burns watches his employees on the TV monitors installed in his office, berating them all for their shoddy work: "Jackanapes, lolligaggers, noodleheads..." But when he sees Marge, he is captivated: "Enchantress," he exclaims. Infatuated, Burns begins to court Marge and in short order offers her both a raise and the adjacent office, which supplants Smithers. Later on, Burns, acting like a smitten schoolboy, attempts to express to Smithers his depth of feeling for Marge. When Burns asks Smithers, "You know that dream where they fly in through the window?" we are shown a brief depiction of Smithers's own dream—and see for the first time an acknowledgment and direct representation of Smithers's erotic desire, for in his dream, it is Mr. Burns who flies in the window.

By its fifth season (1993–94), *The Simpsons* had moved beyond allusion to gay culture and into a frank acknowledgment of gay identity as an alternative lifestyle, paving the way for the coming-out of Waylon Smithers. An overt representation of Smithers's desire is offered, for example, in "Rosebud," which aired in October 1993. In this episode, Smithers laments not getting what he wants for his birthday: namely, Mr. Burns popping out of an oversized birthday cake, clad in nothing but a sash, and doing a bad impersonation of Marilyn Monroe's breathy rendition of "Happy Birthday." The aforementioned "Lisa vs. Malibu Stacy" (February 1994) provides another fine example of how the show allows gay life its own place and displays a refreshing tolerance for it. When Lisa wishes to launch a campaign against the recently marketed talking doll and presents the idea to her family, she is chastened for her continual activism. Bart, for example, notes that Lisa made the family march in a local gay rights parade, brandishing a copy of the local newspaper to emphasize his point. What interests me here is the fact that it is the level of her activism they criticize ("You've been doing that a little too much lately," Marge reluctantly admonishes) and not the fact that they were photographed alongside gay men in the parade or that this photo wound up on the front page of the Springfield newspaper. As noted before, Lisa seeks out the creator of the Malibu Stacy doll, Stacy Lovell. To find her, Lisa turns to Waylon Smithers, owner of the world's largest Malibu Stacy collection. Smithers, who is writing an article on Stacy Lovell for his next Malibu Stacy newsletter, has her last known whereabouts and offers to print a copy of this for Lisa. When Smithers boots his computer, an image of Burns appears on the screen and says, in a halting computerese, "Hello, Smithers. You're quite good at turning me on." Only mildly embarrassed, Smithers pauses and then says to Lisa, "Umm, you probably should ignore that." Although I find these three sequences intriguing, I also find them a bit disheartening, for they each relegate Smithers's homosexual desire to the realm of fantasy. And the show is often guilty of such relegation. In its earliest seasons, the show did not regularly represent homosexuality as a livable lifestyle; instead it positioned it as unsatisfied sexual desire and/or unrequited love. As Smithers's coming-out process was increasingly foregrounded, the creators of the show increasingly pushed the issue into the periphery by making it literally fantastic.

Though visually and textually overt, the show seemed fearful of being politically overt with the issue of sexuality.

However, the show subsequently offered images that moved queer identity out of the periphery and made it a more substantial aspect of Smithers's "actual" life. Perhaps the best example of this attempt to portray an actual gay lifestyle is from the final episode of season 5, "Secrets of a Successful Marriage" (May 1994), in which Homer teaches a community college class on marriage. Here the producers decided to make it clear—at least to those who could understand the literary allusions—that Smithers is indeed a gay man. Homer initially gets the class to share personal secrets and reveal the failings of their marital relations. Smithers speaks up, saying, "I was married once. But I just couldn't keep it together." We are then given a flashback scene showing Smithers having an argument with his wife over Mr. Burns and Burns himself passionately calling out for Smithers. This flashback, a wonderfully rendered parody of scenes from two of Tennessee Williams's most famous plays, *Cat on a Hot Tin Roof* and *A Streetcar Named Desire*, has great resonance within the context of *The Simpsons*. To fully appreciate it, one must know something not only of the two plays cited but also of Williams himself, of his own struggles with both heterosexual and homosexual desires and the ways in which these struggles were incorporated into his art. The creators of *The Simpsons* offer what I think is a perfect parallel for the relationship between Smithers and Burns by combining Williams's two most notable male characters and their defining characteristics: the suppressed homosexual desire of Brick and desperate dependence of Stanley. I also believe that this scene is significant in that it provides viewers an allusion to past experience, not fantasy. We are meant to read this scene literally, as one of Smithers's memories; it is, in effect, a moment from his "real" life.

It is important to keep in mind the historical context of these overt references to Smithers's sexuality, which did not appear until the show had established itself as a pop culture phenomenon and the political climate began to change after the inauguration of Bill Clinton. We must remember that *The Simpsons* first appeared (as shorts on *The Tracey Ullman Show*) when Ronald Reagan was still in the White House, and it became the phenomenon it is now during the first Bush administration. Thus, the show premiered on the heels of a highly conservative decade, one in which much of the ground made by various political movements in the 1960s and 1970s was lost. This is particularly relevant when we consider the kinds of queer representations available on television during the 1980s, which were few and far between and rarely positive or progressive. *The Simpsons*, along with envelope-pushing shows such as *Roseanne*, filled a void in the media landscape in the early 1990s, offering a greater visibility for queerness and helping to make it more acceptable within the mainstream of American culture.

Queer Politics and *The Simpsons*

At the same time that representations in mass media were increasing, the nation was experiencing an ongoing culture war pitting liberal secular values against conservative religious values, and the flash point in these battles was, more often than not, homosexuality and queer culture. Jeffrey Escoffier succinctly notes,

> Since the 1970s, American political and cultural life has become polarized between
> secular liberalism—increasingly identified with multiculturalism, pluralism, and the

politics of diversity—and religious conservatism. The Religious Right is engaged in a campaign to achieve political and cultural hegemony in American life, and it has built this campaign on the revival of supposedly traditional "family values." Homosexuality is currently a major target of this hegemonic project.[42]

With the battle lines in the culture war starkly drawn, the 1990s thus became an era of simultaneously progressive and regressive movements. In 1993, for example, gay and lesbian activists and supporters watched President Bill Clinton casually betray the progressive-minded promises of his presidential campaign by sanctioning the "Don't Ask, Don't Tell" policy of the armed forces. As a consequence, the pressure to stay closeted, both in the armed services and society at large, remained a strong force throughout the decade. In 1994, the Republican Party gained control of the Congress for the first time in 40 years, riding high on the popularity of Newt Gingrich's "Contract with America" and ushering in a more conservative ideology, one that would make progressive change in the nation even harder to secure. Of course, the most contentious issue of the era was—and, sadly, still is—same-sex marriage. This has been of concern ever since the 1993 Hawaii State Supreme Court decision in *Baehr v. Lewin*, which ruled that refusing marriage licenses to same-sex couples was sex discrimination under Hawaii's state constitution. Although that decision did not ultimately lead, as was expected, to the legalization of same-sex marriages in Hawaii, it put the question of gay civil rights front and center in a national debate. In response, many states around the country began passing legislation or amending state constitutions to prohibit not only same-sex marriage but also civil unions and domestic partnerships. This all culminated in the Defense of Marriage Act (DOMA), which passed Congress by a very wide margin—82 to 14 in the Senate and 342 to 67 in the House—and was signed into law in September 1996 by President Bill Clinton.[43] That same year, the Supreme Court issued its decision in *Romer v. Evans*, declaring unconstitutional the injunction against Colorado's Amendment 2 (first passed in 1992), which had modified the state constitution to prevent any city, town, or county in the state from taking any action to protect homosexuals from discrimination on the basis of their sexual orientation. In just a three-year period following passage of the federal DOMA, 31 states had either enacted legislation or passed ballot initiatives that effectively banned same-sex marriage.[44]

Perhaps in response to this increasingly conservative cultural climate, *The Simpsons* began to be more openly political regarding homosexuality in the mid-1990s. As discussed previously, the show has a generally leftist political vision and, although it regularly presents and juxtaposes both liberal and conservative ideologies, it usually does so as a means of critiquing the latter. "Sideshow Bob Roberts" (October 1994) well illustrates the battle of ideologies on the show and its engagement with the politics of sexuality. In this episode, the conservative candidate Sideshow Bob runs for mayor of Springfield and, with the support of Mr. Burns, wins the election over the liberal candidate, Diamond Joe Quimby. It is clear, however, that Bob did not win the election legitimately. Lisa's subsequent investigation leads her to an anonymous source, who provides her with information to expose the rigged election. After being inadvertently exposed as the source, Smithers confesses his guilt at betraying Mr. Burns. When Lisa observantly asks why he does so, Smithers states, "Unfortunately, Sideshow Bob's ultraconservative views conflict with my choice of, um, lifestyle." There is no mistaking what Smithers means here, nor what the show is saying about the relationship between homosexuality and (ultra)conservative politics: the two cannot coexist. Moreover, whereas in the past Smithers's sexual orientation was private and apolitical, it has now become both public and political.

The first attempt to overtly engage the politics of sexuality on *The Simpsons* appears in "Homer's Phobia" (February 1997). In this episode, the show finally confronts the specter of fear that surrounds gay identity by having the Simpson family befriend a gay man named John, the proprietor of an antiques and collectibles shop at the Springfield Mall. John makes a living selling "kitsch" and items with "camp" appeal, such as old issues of *TV Guide*, 1970s-era toys, and inflatable furniture. Homer is incredulous that anyone would spend hard-earned money on such "junk," but in the hopes of turning a quick buck, he invites John over to the Simpson house because, as he says, "Our place is full of valuable worthless crap." Initially, Homer and John bond over their shared affinity for the "junk" the Simpsons have amassed, and they quickly become friends. The two then spend time talking and laughing together and, in a wonderfully ironic scene, even dancing to Alicia Bridges's disco classic, "I Love the Nightlife." Despite such clear signals, Homer is oblivious to the fact that John is gay. However, Marge and Lisa both intuit this fact, and when they share this information with Homer, his homophobia comes to the fore. Initially, Homer is fearful that others will find out he has befriended a gay man, presumably because this would stigmatize him, so he refuses to go with John and the family on a tour of the sights of Springfield. In response, John is nonchalant—he does not react negatively to Homer's fears, nor does he make any apologies for being gay—and simply tells Homer, "You don't even know what you're afraid of." What is unmistakable to both John and the viewing audience is that Homer expects gays to be readily identifiable, which he makes clear after Marge chastises him for his narrow-mindedness; he says, "You know me, Marge. I like my beer cold, my TV loud, and my homosexuals flaming." In short, Homer is upset at having mistaken a gay person for a straight one and frustrated that gays do not conform to his preconceived stereotypes.

As Homer's phobia escalates, he begins to worry that John might have a negative "influence" on Bart. Homer is further convinced of such influence when he sees Bart begin to behave like John—that is, behave in what appears to be a "gay" manner. With a series of delightfully campy scenes, *The Simpsons* illustrates the telltale signs, which include Bart choosing a pink rather than a brown Hostess cupcake, using the phrase "You're the living end," and wearing a bright Hawaiian shirt that, as Bart innocently tells Homer, "just came out of the closet." The final straw for Homer is when he sees Bart wearing a 1950s-style wig and dancing to a song by the Supremes. At this point, Homer decides to take action. He thus confronts John and very plainly tells him to stay away from Bart. In doing so, Homer displays a classic "us versus them" mentality. When Homer is at a loss for an adjective to describe "them," John prompts him with the word "queer," which launches Homer on yet another tirade. "That's another thing," he says. "I resent *you people* using that word. That's *our* word for making fun of *you*. We need it." With that, Homer proposes to take back both the word and his son. His plan for doing so is to "make a man" of Bart by conditioning him toward heterosexual desire and exposing him to traditionally "masculine" activities. Homer's first attempt at "heterosexualizing" Bart involves placing him for a few hours in front of a billboard that features three bikini-clad women promoting Laramie cigarettes. In a doubly satirical moment, the show demonstrates the absurdity of viewing gayness—indeed, sexuality itself—as a learned behavior while simultaneously showing how easily other behaviors are manipulated through exposure to advertising: when Homer returns and asks Bart how he feels, Bart simply shrugs and says, "I dunno—kind of feel like having a cigarette." In short, this scene echoes the rhetoric of contemporary gay activism and underscores the current and fairly widespread belief that gayness is an innate quality; unlike smoking, being gay (or being straight, for that matter) is neither a learned behavior nor a simple matter of choice. Having failed with his first plan, Homer's next strategy is to take Bart to a steel mill to see "real men" hard at work. Unfortunately for Homer, the men at the steel mill aren't quite what he had expected. As Homer is trying to process what seems "odd" about their appearance and behavior, one of the workers tells Homer, "We work hard and we play hard," and pulls the cord on a steam whistle; with that the entire mill transforms into a giant discotheque, complete with laser lights and a glitter ball, at which point a stunned and exasperated Homer exclaims, "The whole world's gone gay!" Determined to condition Bart toward traditional masculinity, as a last resort Homer decides to take Bart hunting because he believes that killing a deer will make Bart "more of a man." Sadly, the only deer Homer can find are reindeer, and when he orders Bart to shoot one, Bart simply says, "I'm not going to shoot a reindeer in a pen, man." At this point, the reindeer get restless, and the misguided hunting trip results in Homer, Bart, Moe, and Barney being attacked by the angry herd. They are subsequently rescued, however, by John, who scares the reindeer away with a remote-controlled robot version of Santa, "their cruel and evil master." Moe and Barney lament being saved by "a sissy," but Homer, having now confronted his own homophobia, rises to John's defense—albeit in typically bumbling Homer fashion: in an effort to be politically correct, Homer first calls John a "fruit" and then, realizing the term might also be offensive, a "queer." "Queer," he says. "That's what you like to be called, right? Queer?" "Well, that or John," John drolly replies. Regardless of the faux pas, by the end of the episode Homer has come to see John as a fellow person rather than as a *gay* person.

Not surprisingly, "Homer's Phobia" received accolades from the Gay & Lesbian Alliance Against Defamation, which each year awards the best and brightest representations of gay and lesbian individuals and the gay community. At the Ninth Annual Media Awards ceremony in April 1998, "Homer's Phobia" won the award for "Outstanding TV: Individual Episode" for its exploration of homophobia. In her book *All the Rage: The Story of Gay Visibility in America*, Suzanna Walters also praises this episode, along with the earlier "Don't Ask, Don't Tell" episode of *Roseanne*, commending them both for not attempting to make homosexuality accessible and assimilable. She says, "The gay characters are not the problems to be solved here, nor is homophobia the vaguely vile emotions of outside agitators: it is *their* [heterosexuals'] discomfort, homophobia, and bigotry that must be confronted."[45] Before adding to the praise here, I want to reflect briefly on the concept of homophobia itself, as it is not without controversy. In his essay "Homophobia: On the Cultural History of an Idea," Daniel Wickberg argues that the term is misleading and is effectively used to demonize individuals rather than an ideology, unlike terms such as racism and sexism, which both "have a putative neutrality" and are clearly directed at a belief system (an "ism") as opposed to a person. In conclusion, Wickberg writes, "Homophobia and its bearer, the homophobe, are only the latest incarnations of the demon that liberalism loves to hate."[46] This may well be true of *The Simpsons*, whose creators are avowedly leftist in their politics and who, as satirists, intend to censure what they see as narrow-minded, provincial, or simply wrong. However, I believe a careful distinction needs to be made in regard to *The Simpsons*. As a homophobe, Homer Simpson is still lovable, partly because he is familiar to audiences and partly because he is so regularly used to embody beliefs that are the object of satire on the show. It is less Homer the homophobe than Homer's *homophobia* that is being ridiculed in this episode—that is, less the individual than the ideology he has embraced. I concede that the term *homophobia* is problematic, despite its wide usage and commonly understood meaning. And yet, as Wickberg notes, no viable linguistic alternative has caught on. A number of terms could be used to describe Homer and his worldview—antihomosexual, heterocentric, heterosexist, sexual chauvinist—though each of these is awkward and inelegant. The fundamental point is that Homer's worldview is narrow-minded and prejudicial. Homer might be a "psychological aberration in need of a cure," but the agenda of the writers of *The Simpsons* is not to cure what ails him but to cure what ails society: namely, a pervasive distaste for and distrust of the sexual "other," the prejudicial belief that gay men and women are not "normal," and the idea that sex and gender are somehow synonymous.

The award that "Homer's Phobia" received from GLAAD is well deserved, for the episode offers its audience cogent critiques of many of the myths surrounding homosexual identity. Foremost, "Homer's Phobia" critiques what is perhaps the most common misconception about homosexuality: namely, that gayness is a contagious "disease." What the show intends to illustrate with this episode is the speciousness of believing that one can "catch" gayness or learn to be gay according to proximity. This was a timely message considering the then-current "ex-gay" movement taking place in America and the Religious Right's proposition that homosexuality can be "cured."[47] It also fits in well with recent claims from within the gay community (and increasingly from the medical establishment) that a gay identity is not simply a choice one makes. "Homer's Phobia" also critiques the narrow-minded belief that violence and aggressiveness are part and parcel of a (heterosexual) masculine identity. The episode shows that homosexuality is not a threat to such masculinity; indeed, it implies that heterosexual male identity would benefit from the incorporation of certain emotional qualities traditionally associated with gay men. Lastly, I think this episode illustrates that homosexuality itself is not a threat to the family but homophobia is; in essence, homophobia is destructive to both the heterosexual and the homosexual community.

The Culture Wars, Redux

The summer of 2003 proved to be an important time in American cultural history, key to both the increase in queer visibility in mass media and to the intensification of the latest battle in the culture wars: the debate over sexuality and civil rights in the United States. On June 26, 2003, in a 6-3 decision, the US Supreme Court offered its decision in *Lawrence v. Texas*, the landmark case that overturned the 1986 *Bowers v. Hardwick* decision and struck down the Texas state sodomy law, thus rendering sodomy laws throughout the country unconstitutional. A week later, the cover of *Newsweek* simply asked, "Is Gay Marriage Next?" The answer was clearly yes, just as it had been ten years earlier, in the wake of the *Baehr v. Lewin* decision. Just prior to the *Lawrence v. Texas* ruling, the Ontario Court of Appeal in Canada ruled that restricting marriage to heterosexual couples violated the equality provisions of Canadian law, thus effectively legalizing same-sex marriage in the province of Ontario. Same-sex marriage became legal nationwide in Canada with the approval of the Civil Marriage Act on July 20, 2005.[48] This, in turn, inspired speculation about and a renewed fear over what might happen in the United States, echoing the same kinds of concerns that culminated in the passage of the Defense of Marriage Act in 1996. Many activists were inspired by these rulings, and with renewed energy they set about challenging existing state laws barring civil unions, domestic partnerships, and same-sex marriages. In November 2003, the Massachusetts Supreme Judicial Court made another historic ruling: in the case of *Goodridge v. Dept. of Public Health*, the court declared that the constitution of the Commonwealth of Massachusetts required the state to provide same-sex couples with full marriage rights. The state legislature was given 180 days to decide how to go about doing this, and in May 2004, Governor Mitt Romney ordered town clerks to begin issuing marriage licenses, which prepared the way for yet another cultural showdown over same-sex marriage.

The looming battles over same-sex marriage were well anticipated, of course. As Jeffrey Escoffier notes in *American Homo*, by the mid-1990s, "gay issues became the one social issue—even more than abortion—that most polarizes the American electorate," and homosexuals were the primary target of many fundamentalist organizing activities.[49] Escoffier's comments were remarkably prescient. Nothing polarized the electorate more than the issue of gay marriage, as could be seen in the rush to pass DOMA laws throughout the country in the late 1990s and early the next decade: between 1996 and 2002, a full 37 states had adopted DOMA laws that, following the lead of the federal legislation, prohibit same-sex marriages, define marriage as the union of one man and one woman, or deny same-sex couples the rights available to married couples.[50] Almost immediately after the Supreme Court decision in June 2003, the Republican leadership of the US Senate proposed an amendment to the Constitution of the United States to forbid gay marriage. The charge was led by Senator Bill Frist of Tennessee, who said that he believed the Supreme Court's decision "threatens to make the American home a place where criminality is condoned."[51] President George Bush, appearing on *The Today Show* in July that year, claimed that he respects the rights of individuals and believes that this is a "welcoming country"; however, for him, there is no compromise on the issue of gay marriage—as he bluntly put it, "I believe a marriage is between a man and a woman and I believe we must codify that one way or another." Not surprisingly, same-sex marriage—and gay rights in general—became a wedge issue in the presidential race of 2004, pitting the conservative "moral" values of the Religious Right and the Republican Party against the "liberal" values of the Left and the Democratic Party, this time around represented in the simplistic and sound-bite-friendly rhetoric of red and blue states.[52]

Bravo's *Queer Eye for the Straight Guy* premiered less than a month after the Supreme Court's ruling in *Lawrence v. Texas*. As mentioned already, *Queer Eye* benefited from the media attention it received as a result of appearing amid all the political posturing over same-sex marriage, and it quickly became a hit. It also quickly (and perhaps unexpectedly) became a flash point in the culture wars. Writing in *The Advocate* that summer, Bruce Steele notes,

> *Queer Eye for the Straight Guy* debuted just 19 days after the U.S. Supreme Court abolished sodomy laws, 28 days after Canada's prime minister promised marriage to

same-sex couples countrywide. In the weeks since the show's launch, the president of the United States drew a straight line from homosexuality to sin, and the Vatican lashed out at "gravely immoral" homosexual couples. And so it was that Bravo's sleek party boat of a makeover show found itself made over into a battleship in the war for gay rights.[53]

As the GLAAD executive director Joan M. Garry points out, it was quite a contrast to experience the hateful rhetoric and blatant homophobia that followed the Supreme Court's decision in *Lawrence v. Texas* and at the same time to see Americans embrace *Queer Eye*'s Fab Five and other gay images on television. Garry said, "There was a profound disconnect between what viewers saw on television and the real-life issues—such as marriage, parenting, workplace discrimination and religion—facing our community."[54] The sentiment is echoed in Andrew Sullivan's essay "Beware the Straight Backlash," from the August 11, 2003, issue of *Time*, which captures the contradictory nature of the debate and the conservative perspective. He says,

> It seems as if heterosexuals are willing to tolerate homosexuals, but only from a position of power. They have few qualms about providing legal protections, decrying hate crimes, watching gay TV shows, even having a relative bring her female spouse to Thanksgiving dinner. Yet arguing that the lesbian couple is legally or morally indistinguishable from a straight couple is where many draw the line. That's why marriage is such a fundamental issue. Allowing gay marriage is not saying, We Will Tolerate You. It's saying, We Are You. This, it seems, we have a hard time doing.[55]

Indeed, even *The Simpsons*, though invariably ahead of the cultural curve, seemed more tentative in its approach to gay themes, as could be seen in the episode "Three Gays of the Condo." This episode first aired on April 13, 2003, in advance of both the *Lawrence* and *Goodridge* decisions and thus ahead of the more heated arguments over gay life that summer and fall. In keeping with the wider visibility of gay lives on television and the trend toward greater acceptance of queer identity within the culture, "Three Gays of the Condo" largely uses gayness as a backdrop to a central story about marital troubles for Marge and Homer. Unlike "Homer's Phobia," there is not a particular moral or ethical issue being addressed here. While looking for a missing puzzle piece, Homer stumbles upon an angry note Marge wrote one night when Homer was drunk, and he wonders why Marge chose to stay with him if she truly felt he wasn't good enough for her. Dejected, Homer moves out of his house and into a condo in the hip part of Springfield with two openly gay men, Grady and Julio. What is most notable about the episode is a lack of the "crisis" Homer experienced previously in his relationship with John in "Homer's Phobia." In this episode, Homer affects a very blasé attitude toward the entire idea of living with gay men and of partaking in the lifestyle, which in the episode includes leg waxing, shopping (for the trendiest of clothes), drinking (in excess), and dancing (topless at the local gay club). Again, this presentation of gay life is filtered through the generic stereotypes surrounding gay men, but it appears to be done in keeping with the attitude of openness and acceptance—at least of "safe" images of homosexuality—that had been increasingly taking hold in American culture. However, a closer look at the episode does reveal an odd shift in tone. Homer's comfort level is challenged when Grady expresses his interest in Homer and then sweetly kisses him on the mouth. Homer is at first wide-eyed with surprise and remains calmly lying on the bed. "Wow," he says.

"I never realized you felt about me that way. We should really take some time to talk and . . ."—and with that, Homer leaps up and out the bedroom window. This scene can be read in a couple of ways. Some would surely argue that Homer's attitude is open and accepting and that rather than reacting with anger (as he did in the "Homer's Phobia" episode) or with violence, Homer quietly accepts the kiss. This is true, and yet it is important to consider how the humor of this scene works: the joke here lies in Homer fleeing out the window, and this relies upon the willingness of audience members to believe that something is fundamentally wrong here. Though a small moment in the episode, it is nonetheless a significant change from the nonchalance with which Homer received a kiss from Karl in "Simpson and Delilah" a full decade earlier and a significant departure from the oppositional politics articulated—not by Homer but by the writers of *The Simpsons*—in "Homer's Phobia" six years earlier. As observed earlier, *The Simpsons* has been part of creating greater visibility and of mainstreaming the acceptance of queerness in American culture, but it is often done in ways that conform to existing stereotypes, and this is certainly the case in "Three Gays of the Condo."

Another attempt by *The Simpsons* to overtly engage with the political debates surrounding sexuality appears in the episode "There's Something about Marrying" (February 2005), which tackles the issue of same-sex marriage and features the official "coming-out" of Patty Bouvier. Before the episode began, however, a black screen appeared with this disclaimer: "This episode contains discussions of same-sex marriage. Parental discretion is advised." This was the first and only time in the history of *The Simpsons* that such a warning was offered to viewers. Considering the range of topics and targets of satire over the previous 16 years, it might seem odd that this particular topic would merit such a disclaimer. And yet it is really not so peculiar when one sees it in light of the pervasive heteronormativity of mass media. In short, the disclaimer is merely an indicator of the degree to which homosexuality remains "controversial" for programmers and continues to be threatening to American norms. Although James Brooks long ago secured complete creative control for *The Simpsons*, he and his team have had to make concessions to Fox on occasion, as with the Fox News parodies discussed in chapter 1, and it appears that a compromise was once again reached in order to air such "controversial" material.

"There's Something about Marrying" begins with yet another of Bart's pranks—this one played upon Howell Huser, a visiting reporter who travels the country looking for new places to feature in his show on the Soft News Network. As a result of his mistreatment at the hands of Bart and Milhouse, Huser gives Springfield his poorest rating and declares it to be an unfriendly town. Tourism subsequently plummets, and within a month, Springfield is in economic decline; Mayor Quimby thus calls a town meeting to solicit ideas for increasing the tourist trade. Among the many absurd ideas (e.g., stronger beer, gladiator fights, a poetry slam), Lisa quite rationally suggests that Springfield legalize same-sex marriage. Lisa's justification for this view is twofold; as she puts it, "We can attract a growing segment of the marriage market *and* strike a blow for civil rights." The residents of Springfield appear only to hear or be concerned with the first part of Lisa's statement—the opportunity to bring in all the disposable income gay men and women are presumed to have—and no one objects to the plan. "Then it's settled," Quimby states. "We'll legalize gay money—I mean marriage." We then cut to the television commercial produced by the tourism board, which features images of happy gay and lesbian couples walking hand in hand, shopping, and kissing and Mayor Quimby inviting people to come to Springfield or to visit their website (www.springfieldisforloversofgaymarriage. com) for more information. The episode next shows cars full of couples flocking to Springfield to get married. As might be expected, before any marriages take place, a showdown occurs between the religious and the secular forces in Springfield, the former led by Reverend Lovejoy and the latter by Marge Simpson. As a large group of couples approaches the church, Lovejoy is seen rapidly nailing a board over the door. Lovejoy explains to the group assembled, "While I have no opinion for or against your sinful lifestyles, I cannot marry two people of the same sex any more than I can put a hamburger on a hot dog bun." As the dejected crowd disperses, Marge steps up to confront Lovejoy and to challenge the religious viewpoint. She says, "As long as two people love each other, I don't think God cares whether they have the same hoo-hoo or ha-ha." Although couched in the language of emotion, her statement is an implicit defense of civil rights. Lovejoy responds, "The Bible forbids same sex relations." "Which book?" Marge quite rationally asks. Incredulous, Lovejoy exclaims, "Which book? The Bible!" and begins to ring the church bell to silence Marge's protest. One can hear her begin to say, "But Reverend, scriptural scholars disagree on the significance of . . ." Her words are briefly drowned out by Lovejoy's ringing of the church bell, but a moment later one can hear Marge conclude, "Jesus's teachings stress inclusiveness and compassion." Despite her best efforts and her rationality, however, Marge cannot get through to Lovejoy.

When Homer discovers that there is money to be made performing wedding ceremonies, he quickly gets himself ordained as an Episcopal minister (via the Internet Divinity School of the e-Piscopal Church) and begins to perform gay weddings in the L'il Chapel set up in his garage. The difficulties begin when Marge's sister Patty comes to announce that she is getting married. Marge assumes it is to a man but is told Patty is to marry a woman named Veronica. "I'm gay," Patty tells her.[56] At this point, the episode becomes a variation on the "Homer's Phobia" episode, with Marge's own fears and prejudices kicking in now that a gay person is within her family. Patty is angered by Marge's refusal to accept her, despite Marge's "liberal" views, and by what Patty sees as hypocrisy. Marge cannot initially bring herself to support the union, although it seems to be more because Patty has kept her sexuality a secret for many years and is now expecting sudden and complete support. While fretting over what to do on the wedding day, Marge stumbles upon Veronica in the bathroom preparing for the big event. The toilet seat is up and Veronica is shaving her face while singing Aerosmith's "Dude Looks Like a Lady." Now knowing that Veronica is actually a man in disguise, Marge feels lighthearted, anticipating an embarrassing moment for her sister at the altar. Of course, Marge is too decent a person to let things play out that way, so when Homer asks if anyone objects to the marriage, she speaks up and exposes Veronica. Veronica confesses to being a man and explains that he had pretended to be a woman in order to get on the LPGA circuit, long before he met Patty. When asked why he kept up the lie, he tells her, "Because you fell in love with me as a woman, and I didn't want to lose you." Love is in the air, and love is ostensibly very powerful. Love is, after all, what Marge told Lovejoy was the only real concern in uniting two people in a marriage. Therefore, viewers perhaps anticipate the following plea to Patty: "Now I'm asking you, not as Veronica, but as the man I am—Leslie Robin Swisher—Patty, will you marry the real me?" Leslie then falls on one knee, and there is a pause. Patty looks into his eyes and he into hers, and we hear the light, romantic strains of piano music. Patty then shakes her head and firmly says, "Hell, no! I like girls." All in attendance then applaud and cheer.

The ending of "There's Something about Marrying" can certainly be interpreted in different ways, and not all readings of it would necessarily be satisfactory to all viewers—again, one must bear in mind that, in accord with Stuart Hall's model of decoding, our own social positioning shapes how we receive and interpret texts. One could, for example, critique the episode for not "troubling" gender and sexuality, drawing upon the ideas presented in Judith Butler's *Gender Trouble* (1990). There is admittedly a simplistic reliance here upon the kinds of binary oppositions that Butler seeks to question if not undermine—for example, male/female and hetero/homo. The writers do not address, for example, the transgendered identity on display—why does Robin dress as a woman anyway? And why does he pose as a lesbian? One might also claim that the ending here is something of a cop-out, given that what the show seems to promise, a gay marriage, it does not actually deliver.[57] In many ways, however, such questions and criticisms are irrelevant to the clear satirical agenda of this particular episode, which is most evident in the remarkable way it resolves itself. The final scenes create a potential to offer a "safe" heterosexualized ending, such as might be found on *Will & Grace*, and which would comfort mainstream audiences. But rather than take a safe route, the writers allow Patty to freely choose, to affirm her sexuality and preference, and they do not give in to Hollywood clichés. From its very start, *The Simpsons* has been operating within a culture that largely opposes gay marriage, often on religious grounds, and that strongly encourages conformity to heterosexual norms—not to mention the norms of femininity and masculinity. The satirical target in "There's Something about Marrying" is clearly the bias that would keep an openly lesbian woman from pursuing love in an open and honest relationship and codifying that in marriage.

The next episode of *The Simpsons* to deal with homosexuality in a direct manner was "Flaming Moe," which aired in January 2011. Unlike "There's Something about Marrying," this episode garnered no media attention and stirred no controversies, despite incorporating a wide variety of queer characters (including cross-dressers and transsexuals) and tangentially exploring the political power of the queer visibility and activism. Despite its title, the episode largely focuses on the experience of Waylon Smithers, who at the beginning is disheartened to discover that Mr. Burns has cut him out of his will. Although Smithers is, as Burns states it, his "campiest of aides-de-camp," he hasn't earned Burns's respect and is therefore not seen as an equal and not entitled to an inheritance. While moping and wandering the streets, Smithers comes across a gay bar called the League of Extra-Horny Gentlemen. "Here's a place I can feel wanted," he says. However, the bouncer at the door quickly denies Smithers entry because he doesn't fit the übermasculine aesthetic clearly favored at this bar, which can been seen from the depictions of the muscular and handsome men being let in and standing in line. Dejected, Smithers ends up in Moe's bar instead, and it is here that he gets the idea to earn Burns's respect by starting a business—in this case, opening "a men's bar for the average-looking fellow." Smithers proposes to Moe that they transform the bar into "a place for guys like me," a euphemism he then has to clarify. Moe is at first reluctant about "hanging out with swish-kabobs," as he puts it, but his fear is quickly outweighed by his desire to make money. In short order, they transform "Moe's" into "Mo's," a place that welcomes men "with a few extras pounds or a little less hair." Soon after, word has spread and the bar is crowded with people and doing very well.

The problem for Smithers begins when he realizes that the men in the bar assume Moe himself is gay. Moe seems rather oblivious to the fact until Marge points it out to him, at which point he decides to "clear the air." However, he can't bring himself to do so, primarily because the bar is a success and he is making good money. Of course, this means he has to keep up the ruse. When one of the patrons, a big bear of a guy named Grizzly Shaun, takes a liking to Moe and asks him out on a date, Moe makes an excuse to avoid the date but nonetheless flirts with Shaun. Seeing this, Smithers testily asks Moe, "Have you been telling the men here that you're one of them?" Moe simply passes off his "passing" as harmless. Given the views expressed by Moe in "Homer's Phobia" and the generally narrow-minded opinions he offers in many other episodes, his cavalier attitude here is somewhat surprising. Of course, this is also an accurate reflection of changing attitudes within American society over the past decade and a half, a cultural shift with which the writers for *The Simpsons* are quite familiar. Being gay, or even pretending to be, does not carry the same kind of stigma it once did for many people. Such open-mindedness is underscored in passing comments elsewhere in the episode. For example, when Homer, Lenny, and Carl arrive at the newly remodeled Mo's, they quickly realize there is something "different" about the place; as Lenny puts it, "there's a sense of acceptance in the air." Even so, for Smithers at least, there is a fundamental problem with Moe's "gayness": it isn't authentic. Smithers's concern with Moe's pretense intensifies a short time later when Patty and three men come in complaining that they (i.e., Springfield's gays) have been barred from marching in the Springfield Founder's parade. When one of the group states that nothing will change until one of "them" is on the town council, Shaun quickly suggests Moe for the job, calling him "the heart of this town's gay community." "What about it, Moe," another asks. "Will you become Springfield's first openly-gay city councilman?" When he agrees to, Smithers becomes incensed. He asks to speak to Moe in private and berates him for his dishonesty: "You can't be these people's leader if you're lying to them about who you are," he says. "You're not gay!" Moe rejects Smithers, however, and returns to the bar, announcing with a flourish, "Your queen is back!"

The next day, Springfield's queers (a remarkably large and diverse population) turn out for a rally at City Hall, where Moe announces, "My name is Moe Szyzlak, and I'm here to elect me." It is a scene that both parodies Gus Van Sant's *Milk* and invokes the spirit of the San Francisco city councilman Harvey Milk. Beyond being a humorous allusion, I think the scene has great resonance with the theme being explored in this episode. What Milk stood for above all else was the idea of integrity and being true to one's self; more than anyone at the time—and many since—Milk was adamant that gay and lesbian individuals need to step out of "the closet" and "come out" to family, friends, coworkers, and society in general. Only with the visibility generated by such actions could large-scale change take place. Moe, who is merely a pretender to the throne, is likely not aware of this history or the political importance of the truth when it comes to one's sexuality. Smithers is, however. When Smithers arrives at the rally, he thus exposes Moe publicly, declaring before the crowd, "You're not one of them." When Moe denies the allegation, Smithers challenges Moe to kiss him. Reluctant to lose his tenuous power, Moe tries, but he cannot bring himself to do it and so admits, "I ain't gay." He quickly tries to smooth things over by asking, "Who ya gonna vote for, me or a Republican whose record is so anti-gay that he's clearly secretly super-gay?" but the crowd is not persuaded and leaves in disappointment.

By way of condolence, Smithers tells Moe he simply did what he felt had to do. At this point, we have a conclusion not unlike that in "There's Something about Marrying": there is the potential once more for a "safe" ending, one that would reinscribe traditional masculinity and reassert heteronormativity, "justifying" Moe's reluctance to kiss Smithers. However, that is not the route the writers choose; once again, they subvert expectations. Moe pauses, shrugs, and says, "As long as I got nothin' to lose . . ." and with that he grabs Smithers, dips him back, and gives him a kiss. "Not bad," Moe says afterward. "Like Frisbee golf, I'm glad I tried it once." He then leaves, and the final shot is of Smithers standing there with a very large smile on his face.

Conclusion

Generally speaking, queer visibility is quite strong in American mass media today. Even at the time that "There's Something about Marrying" appeared, at the start of 2005, the political climate in America and the dynamics of network television had already shifted considerably, and neither was as hostile to queer subject matter as they likely would have been in 1989, when *The Simpsons* began its run, or even in 1997, when "Homer's Phobia" appeared. I doubt that an episode such as "There's Something about Marrying" could have aired at an earlier time without sparking much greater controversy or hysteria. Aside from some media hype leading up to its airing—mainly in the form of speculation about which character would be "coming out"—there was very little discussion about the issues presented in the episode and even less controversy. The media landscape had clearly changed, and by 2005, queer identity was not only visible but commercially viable. At the end of that year, for example, Ang Lee's *Brokeback Mountain* proved to be a critical and commercial success, winning three Oscars (for director, screenplay, and original music score) and earning $83 million in the United States and another $95 million overseas.[58] Two other critically acclaimed films from 2005 that dealt with queer identity, *Capote* and *Transamerica*, were also commercially successful, relative to their initial budgets. The culture and the media landscape appear to be even more open now than they were then, as can be seen with the success of films such as *Milk* (2008) or *A Single Man* (2009) and in network television shows such as *Grey's Anatomy* (2005–), *Ugly Betty* (2006–10), *Modern Family* (2009–), and *Glee* (2009–), all of which have been critical and commercial successes.

Is it perhaps not surprising, then, that the current representation of gay, lesbian, bisexual, and transgendered people on network television is relatively high, comparatively speaking. GLAAD's analysis of the 2010–11 season, which covers 84 prime-time comedies and dramas scheduled to appear on five broadcast networks (ABC, CBS, NBC, FOX, and the CW), reveals that 23 of the 587 regular lead or supporting characters are queer—an overall total of 3.9 percent, which is up from 3 percent in 2009, 2.6 percent in 2008, and 1.1 percent in 2007.[59] Such numbers seem to indicate that while television executives might not necessarily be desirous of placing queer characters front and center in prime-time programs, they are interested in being inclusive. As the GLAAD president Jarrett Barrios states,

> The increase in lesbian, gay, and bisexual characters on primetime television not only reflects the shift in American culture towards greater awareness and understanding of

our community, but also a new industry standard that a growing number of creators and networks are adopting. The recent critical and commercial success of shows like *Modern Family* and *Glee* clearly indicate that mainstream audiences embrace gay characters and want to see well-crafted stories about our lives.[60]

There is also a greater visibility of gay, lesbian, and transgendered individuals on cable television. GLAAD's 2010–11 report lists a total of 35 GLBT series regulars and an additional 18 semiregular recurring characters on 30 scripted comedies and dramas in cable programming, a significant increase from the 25 regular and 17 recurring characters just the year before.[61]

Nevertheless, as Suzanne Walters reminds us in *All the Rage*, it is necessary to examine not only the *quantity* but also the *quality* of queer images, for visibility itself can be "a road to nowhere, a deceptively smooth path that can knock us off the course of meaningful change."[62] Walters's concern is that the increased visibility of gays and lesbians has tended toward either the "normalizing" of queerness or its commodification, which might ultimately deflect attention from substantive political concerns. As she rightly notes, "The cultural moment is not wholly embracing, nor the political moment wholly rejecting: both realms coexist and interact in an uneasy mix of opportunity and opposition, inclusion and exclusion."[63] Although this claim was made a decade ago, it is still applicable and relevant. To me, Walters's concerns are well founded when one considers some of the representations that have appeared in popular culture since the initial publication of her book. One fine example of problematic visibility is the notorious series of Snickers ads produced for the 2007 Superbowl. In the one ad that aired, two mechanics are shown eating from opposite ends of the same candy bar, and they accidentally end up in a near-kiss. They respond by ripping out fistfuls of chest hair, presumably to reassert their manliness. The ad was coupled with a website that featured pro football players reacting in disgust to the kiss. The website also featured alternative versions of the ad that viewers could vote on, one with the two men physically abusing each other, and another with them drinking motor oil and windshield washer fluid to "cleanse" their mouths.[64] Another example, curiously from the same year, is the comedy film *I Now Pronounce You Chuck and Larry* (2007), starring Kevin James and Adam Sandler as two New York City firefighters who pretend to be a gay couple in order to secure benefits. Although the film was marketed by Universal Studios as a "progressive" comedy, it is actually a deeply ambivalent and heterosexist (if not ultimately homophobic) commercial product.[65]

Thus it is that the praise for the increased representation and apparent attitude of acceptance needs to be tempered by an acknowledgment of the still sad state of affairs for gay men and women. Admittedly, there has been some real progress toward visibility, acceptance, and equal rights in recent years. For example, since Massachusetts extended marriage rights to same-sex couples in 2004, same-sex marriage has been made legal in five states—namely, Connecticut (2008), Vermont (2009), Iowa (2009), New Hampshire (2010), and New York (2011)—and in the District of Columbia (2009). And in 2010, the Obama administration succeeded in overturning the military's "Don't Ask, Don't Tell" policy (albeit rather quietly, during a lame-duck session in December). Nevertheless, it must be acknowledged that even in the wake of such historic changes, many men and women are fearful of the repercussions of coming out to family, friends, and coworkers; that gay bashing, bullying, and hate crimes continue unabated in many cities around the country, most of which still offer no specific legal protections for the victims of such crimes; that 39 states in the United States have Defense of Marriage Act laws that were enacted to prevent recognition of civil unions or marriages from other states; and that negative and regressive images still abound in the mass media.

As stated at the onset of this chapter, I believe that *The Simpsons* aims to critique the mistreatment and exclusion of many so-called minority citizens in American culture, but I realize that this critique is always being negotiated in relation to shifting social and political contexts. Ron Becker notes in the conclusion to *Gay TV and Straight America* that television programming has continually "reflected the ambivalence certain viewers felt about both multiculturalism and homosexuality"; moreover, he argues, the television shows themselves "often reflected such ambivalence, mixing homophobic stereotypes with gay-affirmative narratives."[66] That an ambivalence toward nonnormative identities exists in American culture and is reflected in its popular arts is not in doubt—indeed, this very thing underlies representations of feminism in mass media, as I discussed in chapter 3. However, the degree to which an ambivalence toward queer identity is applicable to *The Simpsons* is debatable. The show does indeed utilize many of the well-worn stereotypes that have been so often exploited in television, particularly those of gay men, but I would be hard-pressed to read these representations as "homophobic"—certainly not in comparison to the examples of "straight panic" Becker offers from shows such as *Friends* and *Seinfeld*. I believe that the appearance of stereotypical representations on *The Simpsons* is not at the expense of the gay and lesbian community but in support of it. Moreover, I contend that by enacting a queer sensibility, *The Simpsons* is rearticulating "queerness" for its audience, thereby making mainstream what is still derisively referred to as an "alternative" lifestyle and contesting how this is generally (mis)understood in American culture. *The Simpsons* continually seeks to expose cultural homophobia, to criticize the institutional apparatuses that maintain it, and to deplore the attendant exclusionary practices based on sexual orientation, as the plotlines of the various episodes discussed in this chapter make clear. These episodes, I believe, also demonstrate that *The Simpsons* ultimately wants both to acknowledge gay and lesbian lives and to support them, which is done by maintaining gay characters in major recurring roles and by overtly politicizing sexual identity in numerous story lines. Waylon Smithers and Patty Bouvier, both integral characters on the show, are allowed to be openly gay and the focal points for *The Simpsons'* critiques of prejudice and oppression in American culture.

5

"Upper-Lower-Middle-Class Types": Socioeconomic Class on *The Simpsons*

Even though the middle class is only about thirty-five percent of the work-force, almost every aspect of politics and popular culture, with help from the media, reinforces the idea that "middle class" is the typical and usual status of Americans.

—*Michael Zweig*[1]

The culture wars in the United States have generally focused on hot-button social and political issues—such as gender equality, immigration reform, and educational policy—and on so-called "moral" issues, such as abortion and same-sex marriage. Oddly, the topic of class is rarely raised in relation to these debates. The absence of class in these discussions is striking, given that many of the culture war issues are intimately connected to money (often in the form of the awarding or the withholding of government funds), and the public policies related to these issues often have disparate impacts on people of differing socioeconomic standing. What might rightly be called the "class war" in American society is a key, although largely unacknowledged, component of the culture war that has been waged over the past 40 years, primarily by those in positions of political and economic power. The search for economic justice has, of course, long been a part of the cultural debate taking place in the United States, but the battle lines have become starker since the "Reagan Revolution" in 1980 and the shift toward neoliberal economic policies during Ronald Reagan's presidency. Since that time, the "class war" in the United States has been increasingly pronounced, manifest in attacks by the rich against the poor, by corporations against workers, and even by members of the working class against others like themselves.[2]

Like other culture war topics, the class war in American does not readily lend itself to a simplistic binary of right and left or conservative and liberal. Indeed, the class struggle in the United States often unites those who might otherwise be divided by identity factors (such as race, ethnicity, or sexuality) or on social issues (such as abortion or gay rights) against those who hold enormous wealth and power. There is perhaps no better symbol of this than the recent Occupy Wall Street movement and its critique of "the one percent"—in short, this is a battle between the proverbial "haves" and "have-nots." Nevertheless, there are still many parallels between the perspectives and political affiliations of those divided by the hot-button culture war issues and those divided by the inequitable distribution of wealth in the nation. For example, the attacks on unions, pensions, teachers, and civil servants seen in recent years in states such as New Jersey, Ohio, and Wisconsin have been initiated by conservative Republican politicians bent on privatizing the public sector and keeping taxes low for their wealthy donors. Moreover, conservatives and others on the political Right have succeeded in rhetorically casting the Left as "elites" (or sometimes "liberal elites") who are pretentious and out of touch with the values of the common (working) man. As Thomas Frank demonstrates in *What's the Matter with Kansas? How Conservatives Won the Heart of America* (2004), the Republican Party has had great success in rebranding itself the party of the "working man," despite the fact that Republican economic policies often do more harm to working people. In Frank's view, the capitalist class, which has been closely aligned with the Republican Party, has succeeded in diverting the anger of workers from the ills inflicted upon them by the free-market system to "the forgettable skirmishes of the never-ending cultural wars."[3]

One powerful tool in the hands of political conservatives and the capitalist class is the mass media. As many scholars continue to point out, analyses of class in mass media remain minimal, and they are too often subordinated to issues of race, gender, or sexuality, despite the fact that class permeates American media content.[4] Gregory Mantsios, in his regularly updated and widely reproduced essay "Class in America," argues that "class is not discussed or debated in public because class identity has been stripped from popular culture."[5] Although provocative, this is not an altogether accurate statement. Class is certainly not absent from television; indeed, it is all over the place. What Mantsios means—and what is evident from any cursory glance at the media landscape today—is that *working-class* identity has been stripped; middle- and upper-class identity are highly visible. Wealth and leisure, perversely coded as "average" and middle class, are regularly on display and glorified. This was the primary imagery of television throughout the boom era of the 1990s, and it has extended well into the new millennium: despite even the economic turmoil of the great recession in 2008, television continues to provide aspirational images, in the form of advertising and financial news, and it continues to glorify the wealthy in a vast array of programming, such as sitcoms, soap operas, dramas, game shows, and so-called "reality" programming. As Joan C. Williams notes, such television programs continue to give us an endless parade of people from the "professional-managerial class"—for example, lawyers, doctors, architects, advertising executives, journalists, and assorted businesspeople, mainly in middle- or upper-management.[6] Quite simply, most of the mass media, including the entertainment media, work to perpetuate the mythology of upward mobility and the belief that everyone in the United States is, at a minimum, middle class (or should be). What is absent in all of this is an honest image of and discussion about the working class.

My aim in this chapter is to explore the complexities of social and economic class as they are dealt with on *The Simpsons*. Surprisingly, very few academics have addressed the topic of class on *The Simpsons*; many allude in passing to the Simpsons as a working-class family, and some comment directly on the prevalence of advertising and consumerism on the show, but no one has offered a sustained analysis of how the series deals with socioeconomic class.[7] This is an irony, to say the least, since when watching *The Simpsons* one simply can *not* be unaware of social and economic class, class stratification, and the inequitable distribution of wealth. Because a full and complete analysis of class on *The Simpsons* is beyond the scope of this chapter, my discussion will of necessity be more selective, concentrating primarily on the representation of working-class identity and the framing of "white trash" identity. In *Framing Class: Media Representations of Wealth and Poverty in America* (2011), an impressive study of class in news media and television programming, Diana Kendall illustrates how television programs contribute to the social construction of reality about class in the United States, including "the manner in which myths and negative stereotypes about the working class and poor create a reality that seemingly justifies the superior positions of the upper-middle and upper classes and establishes them as entitled to their privileged position in the stratification system."[8] I would modify Kendall's claim just slightly, adding the middle class as well, because powerful forces are at work to use negative impressions of workers and the poor as a means to shore up middle-class status—of both the characters in television programs and of the viewing audience at home. The effect of this is the perpetuation of middle-class ideology.

As I have demonstrated elsewhere in this book, *The Simpsons* often works in oppositional ways, but in relation to social and economic class, the show offers a much more conflicted vision. On the one hand, we have a consistently satirical depiction of wealth and greed on the show. Among other things, the show satirizes the excesses of the capitalist class (using the nuclear power plant owner Charles Montgomery Burns as a symbolic representative) and highlights the corrupting influence of unchecked capitalism on society (e.g., on the educational system, democratic government, and the environment). Indeed, one of most common, yet least articulated, ways in which *The Simpsons* engages the culture wars is by exposing how free-market ideology and capitalism, both closely tied to conservative views and Republican Party platforms over the past 30 years, have run roughshod over the "average" family, here represented by the Simpsons. On the other hand, we have a subtle movement of the Simpson family into middle-class identity, socially if not economically, and the embrace of a middle-class aesthetic. This latter element is to some degree merely a consequence of the commercial imperatives of network television and the need for advertising dollars. Yet even here there is a parallel movement away from a working-class milieu. For example, the licensing contracts for *The Simpsons* secured at the start of the 1990s were for products stereotypically associated with the working class and the poor (e.g., fast food and candy, namely, Burger King and Butterfinger), whereas those at the end of the decade were for products associated with the middle class and white-collar professionals (e.g., technology and commerce, namely, Intel and MasterCard).[9] The shifting emphasis in status is also a reflection of the culture at large, which was emerging from an economic downturn in the late 1980s, under George Bush, into a stronger and more stable economy by the mid-1990s, under Bill Clinton. The increased financial stability of many Americans during the Clinton years helped reaffirm the long-standing and widespread desire in the culture to identify as middle class—and perhaps to encourage Americans to seek that out in their entertainment programming.

More problematically, *The Simpsons* offers viewers a variety of mixed messages about middle- and working-class identity and numerous uncritical portrayals of "white trash" identity. Many television viewers, conditioned by the majority of television situation comedies to equate whiteness and suburban life with middle-class identity, often presume that the Simpsons are a middle-class family. I intend to illustrate that the Simpsons are very much within the working class, as made clear from both their social behaviors and their economic status, which are prominent features of many episodes, especially in the earliest seasons. However, as *The Simpsons* grew in popularity, the family's working-class identity was modified in subtle ways and made to appear less working class, if not more middle class. This is offered most overtly through the inclusion of the "white trash" characters Cletus and Brandine Delroy, who are first introduced on the show in 1994 and 1996, respectively. Although the Simpson family is initially positioned as working class, the writers very clearly separate the Simpsons from the Delroys, who are meant to be seen as having a much lower status. In this way, the Delroys function as a marker, or what Pierre Bourdieu calls a "negative reference point," which, as he explains, exists within aesthetic systems simply to reaffirm class distinctions and hierarchies.[10] Within the diegesis of *The Simpsons*, the members of the Simpson family and the Springfield community are able to view Cletus, Brandine, and their children as a negative reference point; outside the diegesis, the writers for the show and the television audience can each do the same.

Understandings of Class, in Context

To fully understand the representations of social and economic class on *The Simpsons*, it is helpful to first consider three things: the televisual history from which the show arose, the historical context in which it first appeared, and the normative understandings of class in the United States today. The history of the television situation comedy has been well documented, so there is no need to rehearse that history here.[11] I will simply point out that the key studies on the sitcom are in accord on at least one point: 1950s television was marked by nothing less than the glorification of McWASP identity, and the Middle-Class White-Assimilated Suburban Protestant was the pinnacle of Americanness. The McWASP sitcoms were also deeply infused with the American dream mythology, particularly its tales of class mobility and its promise of a postwar consumer paradise. Firmly middle-class nuclear-family sitcoms dominated the airwaves in the 1950s and 1960s. The only exceptions were the working-class sitcoms *The Honeymooners* (a critical bomb that ran for only one season, from 1955 to 1956), *Life of Riley* (1953–58), and *The Flintstones* (1960–66). After *The Flintstones* left the air in 1966, no other working-class family series appeared on television until *All in the Family* (1971–79). Developed for television by Norman Lear, *All in the Family* offered an image of working-class life not seen since the days of Chester A. Riley and Ralph Kramden, and in this respect, *All in the Family* was a welcome challenge to the hegemony of McWASP identity on television. However, what differentiated *All in the Family* from its working-class predecessors of the 1950s was the fact that, although emphatic about being a working-class sitcom, "it was equally emphatic about *not* being ethnic," offering the Bunker family to the American public as "*déclassé* Protestants" and thus giving us television's "first explicitly WASP hourly wage-earner."[12] *All in the Family* proved very successful, and it paved the way for a new breed of working-class family sitcoms defined, in part, by an increased "social realism" and an attention to political and politicized issues in American culture during the 1970s, which was a heyday for the working-class sitcom. This was evident at first in spin-offs of *All in the Family*, such as *Maude* (1972–78) and *The Jeffersons* (1975–85), then in shows such as *Sanford and Son* (1972–77) and *Good Times* (1974–78), and finally in the then-controversial *One Day at a Time* (1975–84).[13] As discussed in the introductory chapter, during the 1980s, there was a return of the traditional nuclear-family sitcom popularized in the postwar era: the most popular shows of this decade were firmly middle- and upper-middle-class sitcoms such as *Family Ties* (1982–89), *Growing Pains* (1985–92), and *The Cosby Show* (1984–92). However, by the end of that decade and the start of the 1990s, comedies based in the working class began to return to television, and in a relatively short period of time, it was these types of sitcoms that came to dominate the television landscape. Most notable among these are ABC's *Roseanne* (1988–97) and *Grace Under Fire* (1993–98), both focusing on working-class women, and Fox's *Married... with Children* (1987–97), *The Simpsons* (1989–), and *Roc* (1991–94).

The Simpsons began in the wake of the "Reagan Revolution" and the economic turmoil caused by deregulatory policies and the embrace of free-market ideology in the 1980s. In the early 1980s, for example, the country weathered the collapse and subsequent government bailout of failed savings and loan associations; the so-called S&L crisis was a problem initiated in part by the deregulatory practices of the Reagan administration.[14] The 1980s was also the era of "corporate raiders," who made fortunes by buying weakened companies, "restructuring" them, and selling them (in whole or in parts) for a profit. Such naked greed was captured quite well in Oliver Stone's prescient film *Wall Street* (1987). Admittedly, the economy experienced growth in the middle of the decade, and there was for a time modest unemployment and low inflation, all of which appeared to give credence to what was dubbed "Reaganomics"—or sometimes "trickle-down" economics—which posited that tax relief for the wealthy and for corporations would lead to more savings and investment, resulting in more production, thus stimulating greater economic growth for all. But Reagan's economic policy rested on shaky foundations, and as the 1980s progressed, signs of trouble began to mount. This culminated in "Black Monday" (October 19, 1987), which was the biggest stock sell-off since the 1920s and which created panic both here and abroad. Stock markets around the world crashed that day, and in the United States, the Dow Jones lost over 22 percent of its value.[15] The nation was slow to recover from this, and by 1990, it was facing an economic crisis once again.

Given this information, it is safe to say that *The Simpsons* appeared at the end of a decade that epitomized greed. This ethos was perpetuated within mass media in the gratuitous displays of wealth and decadence in the popular nighttime soap operas *Dallas* (1978–91), *Dynasty* (1981–89), and *Falcon Crest* (1981–90) and in programs such as Robin Leach's *Lifestyles of the Rich and Famous* (1984–95), a show that allowed viewers to fawn over and envy the superrich.[16] Such programming was—and still is—out of joint with the lived experience of most working Americans, for whom the early 1990s were very difficult. When *The Simpsons* appeared as a stand-alone series in the spring of 1990, during the presidency of George H. W. Bush, the nation was in the midst of a mild recession, brought about in part by the legacy of Reagan-era deregulation and government cutbacks. Reaganomics was having a "trickle-down" effect, just not the one promised by capitalists and their political enablers. This was a period of economic turmoil and fear for many Americans because it was a time of increased mergers, downsizing, and layoffs. This grim reality was captured by filmmaker Michael Moore in his first documentary, *Roger & Me* (1989), which deftly explored and exposed the corrupt practices of General Motors (and its CEO, Roger Smith), who claimed to be struggling while profits were soaring.[17] It was also under Reagan that Americans first began to see an acceleration of attacks on unions, the off-shoring of manufacturing jobs, and the stagnation of wages for workers, problems that have only worsened since the 1980s.[18]

The economic climate of the early 1990s was bad enough that it led the producers of *The Simpsons* to speak back to George H. W. Bush's criticism of the show by pointedly mentioning the economic woes of the nation. As mentioned in the introductory chapter, in a speech in 1992, Bush stated, "We need a nation closer to *The Waltons* than *The Simpsons*." Although Bush was speaking to the "family values" debate of the time, the writers used his allusion to the Waltons as ammunition in Bart's comment, "Hey, we're just like the Waltons; we're praying for an end to the depression too!" In short, the writers, well aware of how tough times were for many people because of the Reagan-Bush agenda, highlighted the almost absurd irony of Bush invoking a struggling depression-era family as an example or standard for contemporary American families. Bart's comment about the depression ending was more than a retort to George Bush Sr.; it was also a satirical comment on the Reagan-Bush era and the disproportionate impact the economic policies of those administrations were having on working-class families. Of course, the trends initiated under Reagan and Bush were exacerbated to some degree by the Clinton administration, with the passage of the North American Free Trade Agreement (NAFTA) in 1994 and the Personal Responsibility Act (a welfare reform bill) in 1996.[19] In short, life was tough for many workers in the late 1980s and during the 1990s, a reality reflected in the return of working-class programs, including *The Simpsons*, to the prime-time television schedule.

Before proceeding with a more detailed analysis of *The Simpsons*, I think it is important to reflect briefly on the current understandings of class in the United States. As is well known, many Americans are reluctant to discuss ideas such as class privilege, social stratification, and the inequitable distribution of wealth, preferring to hold instead to the familiar and comforting mythologies of classlessness and upward mobility. The reality, of course, is that Americans are deeply divided along class lines, both socially and economically. As Gregory Mantsios accurately notes, although people in the United States are loath to discuss class privilege or class oppression, they will speak easily and comfortably about the middle class.[20] This has the effect of muting class differences and avoiding the suggestion that there is class conflict or injustice. We also mask references to class with language of "the rich" and "the poor," which are viewed as small extremes to the otherwise broad, typical, and "normal" middle. We thus "mistakenly hold a set of beliefs that obscure the reality of class differences and their impact on people's lives."[21] Mantsios explains that the most common of these beliefs are that the United States is "fundamentally a classless society" and that we are "essentially a middle-class nation."[22] As Michael Zweig points out in the epigraph that begins this chapter, even though the middle class is only about 35 percent of the workforce today, nearly every aspect of the political and cultural landscape reinforces the idea that "middle class" is the typical and usual status of the vast majority of Americans.[23]

For many decades now, the discussion of class in the United States, at least within academic circles, has been dominated by a structural model first presented in the late

1950s by Joseph A. Kahl in his pioneering study *The American Class Structure* (1957). Kahl, who was deeply influenced by the writings of both Karl Marx and Max Weber, divided the United States into six classes, which he labeled "capitalist," (referring to the top 1 percent), "upper-middle," "middle," "working," "working poor," and "underclass" (referring to the poor and homeless).[24] Kahl's work helped define the field of social stratification, and his model of class held sway among sociologists for 25 years. In the early 1980s, Kahl and Dennis L. Gilbert (one of Kahl's former students) refined and updated the model—while leaving the basic structural framework intact—and published the results as *The American Class Structure: A New Synthesis* (1982). The Kahl-Gilbert model, as it has come to be known, was widely adopted by many sociologists and has come to be a standard-bearer in the field. It has thus had a significant impact on contemporary understandings of the US class system. What is most curious about the model is how it has morphed over time and been made to accommodate both the mythology of classlessness and the ideology of consumerism in American culture. This is partly because the popularity of Kahl's original model coincided with post–World War II economic expansion and the popularization of the American dream story. Kahl's claim that only 30 percent of the US population was in the middle class was an accurate figure, but it was increasingly at odds with the stories being manufactured—and widely disseminated through new forms of mass media, such as television—about the consumer paradise and class mobility. Also at odds with the American dream mythology was the phenomenon of "the working poor" and the ugly reality of poverty, elements of the society that were largely ignored until the publication of Michael Harrington's *The Other America: Poverty in the United States* (1962).

By the early 1980s, when Kahl and Gilbert published their updated book, the term *middle class* had come to connote "average" and "typical," and it was understood to be the status of the majority of Americans. However, as Kahl and Gilbert report, the majority of the population at that time (55 percent) comprised people *beneath* the middle class in the socioeconomic hierarchy; these were the people classified as working class, working poor, and the underclass (respectively, 30 percent, 13 percent, and 12 percent of the population). Tellingly, Kahl and Gilbert had used three separate terms (working class, working poor, and underclass) to describe the majority population. But within a single generation, the public discourse on class moved away from these terms, especially "underclass," which helped to pave the way for "middle class" to become normative, as both a concept and an identity. This shift in thinking and terminology coincided with the increasing glorification of wealth in the culture in the 1980s and 1990s, and so what has come to dominate the popular consciousness (despite the statistics of numerous sociologists and economists) is the myth that the United States is a "classless" society or, at worst, a society with a few very rich, a few very poor, and a great majority of people very comfortably in the middle.

The absurdity of our understandings of class in general and of the middle class in particular is captured quite well in a 2008 Pew Center Survey. In this telephone survey, people were asked to specify the social class with which they identified, choosing from the following terms: "the upper class," "the upper-middle class," "the middle class," "the lower-middle class," or "the lower class." Fifty-three percent of the respondents self-identified as precisely "middle class," which led the Pew Center researchers to conclude that "there isn't one American middle class; there are four."[25] Such statistics fit comfortably with most Americans' "commonsense" notions of class and thus are often left unquestioned. However, we should note how skewed this study is from the start:

three-fifths of the labels used incorporate the term "middle class." This is a striking shift from the terms used in the Kahl-Gilbert model, in which only one-third of the terms refer to the middle class and one-third to the working class. It would have been much more interesting had the Pew researchers used the terms "capitalist class" and "working class," in keeping with the Kahl-Gilbert model. The erasure of the term "working class" in the Pew Center study has the effect of forcing those in the working class (or those who might wish to proudly identify as such) to identify instead with the term "lower-class," which many are not wont to do because it is pejorative. Further examination of the Pew Center study reveals even more problems. In the full report, downloadable on the Pew website, the project members note that "for the purposes of this study and reports based on this poll, the upper class is comprised of those who identified with the upper or upper middle class, or 21% of the sample," and "the lower class is defined as those who said they were lower middle or lower class," which was 25 percent of the sample.[26] The fact that the researchers combined categories (for reasons that remain unexplained) creates even more confusion and further skews the results. A footnote in the report reveals the specific numbers: "[S]ome 19% say they are upper middle class and another 19% say they are lower middle class; 6% say they are lower class and 2% say they are upper class."[27] This means that, when accurately presented, a *middle-class affiliation* was on the minds of a whopping 91 percent of respondents! In addition to problematically manipulating data, the Pew Center survey reflects and perpetuates an already common ideology: that the middle class is normative, average, and the status of the majority of Americans. I note this not to criticize the researchers but to illustrate the confused and rather absurd ways in which Americans think about and talk about class, and this study is a particularly striking example.

Similar problems in conceptualizing class appear in other common (and presumably authoritative) sources of information. A fine example is found in John Macionis's *Sociology*, a textbook that is in wide use in colleges and universities around the nation.[28] This text employs the same stratification model first proposed by Joseph Kahl but presents only four major categories: "Upper," "Middle," "Working," and "Lower." Three of the four categories, however, are further subdivided into two parts (creating the awkwardly named categories of "upper-upper," "lower-lower," and "average-middle"), thus giving us a total of seven categories; curiously, the working class category is not further refined. It is notable, if not surprising, that Macionis offers no parallel "lower-middle" category, but what is most remarkable is the way that Macionis's chart also perpetuates the myth of middle-class typicality. At first glance, the numbers offered seem to be more accurate than those in the Pew Center survey, although they still align with our commonplace perceptions about class. For example, the middle class is identified as roughly 40–45 percent of the US population and the working class as a healthy 35 percent. But the percentages are not the whole story here. The working class is shown to have a narrow family income range between $25,000 and $50,000 a year. The lower class, which is 20 percent of the overall population, is also narrowly defined, with a family income below $25,000. The upper class, said to be 5 percent of the population, has a family income of $197,000 and above. The so-called middle class, however, has an extraordinarily large income range of between $50,000 and $197,000.[29] Macionis's "middle class" category also yokes together a rather disparate collection of blue-collar jobs and white-collar professions. It is clear that some of those designated as part of the "middle" here more appropriately belong to the upper class and others to the working class. This, of course, would alter the percentages a great deal.

A very different assessment of the American class structure is provided by economists and sociologists such as Michael Zweig and Stanley Aronowitz. Zweig and Aronowitz are both critics of the middle-class mythology, and they forcefully argue that the United States is primarily a working-class nation. Zweig reads class with a more explicitly Marxist orientation, using the term *capitalist class* to describe the wealthiest segment of society, which he claims is roughly 2 percent of the US population. According to Zweig, the middle class is about 35 percent of the population and the working class is roughly 63 percent.[30] The numbers are about the same for Stanley Aronowitz, who argues that the working-class majority is roughly 60–65 percent of the US population.[31] Quite usefully, Zweig cites a number of previous studies of class identification, conducted at different periods of time, and points out the very real differences that terminology can make. As he notes,

> Researchers at the University of Chicago have consistently found over the past twenty years that, when offered "working class" as a possible identity, along with "middle class," "rich," and "poor," about 45 percent of people think of themselves as working class, the same fraction as middle class.[32]

The statistics provided by Zweig and other researchers are an important counterpoint to those offered in sources such as the Pew Center survey—which did not offer "working class" as an option for respondents—or in mainstream textbooks such as Macionis's *Sociology*. What is even more important than numbers, I think, is Zweig's reminder that class in America is fundamentally about power, not simply income or lifestyle, and that members of the working class have little power or authority in the workplace. As Zweig succinctly puts it, "To be in the working class is to be in a place of relative vulnerability—on the job, in the market, in politics and culture."[33]

A Working-Class Family, a Working-Class Milieu

Many people think of *The Simpsons* as a middle-class sitcom and of the Simpsons as a middle-class family. Indeed, at the start of each semester, when I ask my students what they think is the class status of the Simpsons, they almost universally answer "middle class." When I ask why, students give voice to the usual "evidence" in the iconography of the show: the Simpsons own a home, live in the suburbs, have two cars, and are a "traditional" nuclear family, with the proverbial 2.3 kids. *The Simpsons* can thus be seen as a comfortable continuation of the McWASP tradition in situation comedy that preceded it. The casual observer of *The Simpsons* might also suspect that the Simpsons are comfortably middle class since Homer has had a host of careers (albeit short-lived ones) that would earn him large sums of money, and the family has taken far-flung trips across the world, to places such as England and Australia. In service of its satire, the show remains flexible and plastic in this sense, allowing the family a great many improbable experiences. On closer inspection, however, we can see that an explanation (often a convoluted one) is invariably provided for such extravagances.[34] What remains consistent, particularly in episodes that highlight issues of class, are the struggles that the Simpson family has in making ends meet and the difficulties Homer has as an anonymous "drone" in sector 7G at the Springfield Nuclear Power Plant and thus as a member of the working class.

Although I read *The Simpsons* as a working-class show, the class status of the Simpson family is somewhat nebulous. A search of *The Simpsons Archive*, which contains electronic reprints of many articles originally published in mainstream US newspapers and magazines, reveals a rather conflicted view of America's favorite family: they are variously described as "middle class," "lower-middle class," and "working class." In the episode "The Springfield Connection" (May 1995), Homer Simpson himself cheekily describes the family as "upper-lower-middle class," a phrase that comically captures the very serious problems with conceptualizing class in American culture. Of course, to conceptualize class well, it is necessary to define it in at least two important ways: economically and socially. Economically, the Simpsons are very much within the working class, as evidenced by Homer's income, which we know of from a scene in the episode "Much Apu about Nothing" (May 1996). Here we get a glimpse of Homer's paycheck, which reveals that he earns only $11.95 per hour, or the equivalent of $25,000 per year. This puts the Simpsons family well above the poverty threshold for a family of five for 1990 ($15,989) and slightly above the threshold for 1996 ($18,725).[35] The Simpsons are socially positioned as working class as well, mainly through a variety of activities that are commonly (if rather stereotypically) associated with the working class: watching television, attending auto races and monster truck rallies, bowling, drinking, and eating at fast-food restaurants.

The first episode of *The Simpsons*, "Simpsons Roasting on an Open Fire" (also known as "The Simpsons Christmas Special"), made quite plain that the Simpsons are a struggling working-class family. The family's financial struggles are a key theme of the episode, and money is an issue throughout. We see the relatively impoverished state of the Simpson family in an early scene, which involves Homer decorating the home for Christmas. The lights that Homer puts on his house pale in comparison to those of his next-door neighbor, Ned Flanders, who is positioned in this and many subsequent episodes of *The Simpsons* as comfortably middle class. After Homer has finished putting up his lights (a single string that outlines just the roof of the house), he invites the family outside to see them turned on. When Marge flips the power switch, however, only a few of the bulbs light up; the rest are burned out. Flanders, who is also outdoors, then powers on his display, which features many large, bright lights and an automated Santa that says "Ho ho ho." As the Flanders boys cheer, the Simpson children stare in awe and, in unison, simply say, "Wow." "Show off," Homer grumbles.

A later scene makes clear to us that money is also tight for gift buying. When the family is ready to head to the mall to do some Christmas shopping, Homer asks about "the money jar," which Marge has carefully hidden (in her hair!) and in which she has squirreled away money for presents. We are not told how much in is the jar, but it is a combination of bills and change, so we can safely assume it isn't much. It does indicate, however, a frugalness that is typical of the working class and that will become a consistent component of Marge's character as the show develops. The family expects these meager savings to supplement Homer's yearly bonus and thus provide a merry Christmas. However, things don't go as expected, for Homer finds out later that day that he and the other "semi-skilled workers" at the nuclear plant will not be receiving a Christmas bonus. "Thank God for the big jar," Homer says. Meanwhile, Marge has to use all of the cash in the money jar to pay for the laser removal of the partial tattoo that Bart has had etched on his arm while at the mall. "Thank God for Homer's Christmas bonus," she says. After Homer finds out what happened, he shouts, "We're ruined. Christmas is cancelled. No presents for anyone." When pressed to explain what he means by his outburst, he can't confess the truth and so lies and says it will be "the best Christmas ever." Feeling guilty, he later tells Marge, "I don't deserve you as much as a guy with a fat wallet and a credit card that won't set off that horrible beeping."

To avoid confessing the truth, Homer offers to do all of the Christmas shopping for Marge. We then see Homer at the Circus of Values store, where a large sign in the front window proclaims, "Nothing over $5," and where Homer shops for very inexpensive items—pantyhose for Marge, packets of paper for Bart and Lisa, and a dog's squeaky toy for Maggie. Later, while at Moe's bar, Homer learns that his friend Barney is earning extra money with a part-time job at the mall playing Santa Claus. Homer decides that it is his duty to earn money to give the family a nice holiday, and so he signs on. There is one small problem with his plan, however: to ensure that he follows through, the mall's owners will not pay him until Christmas Eve. Homer is additionally stressed when he comes home, exhausted from working two jobs, and encounters Marge's sisters, Patty and Selma, who have come to visit—and to criticize. Among other things, they point out that there is no Christmas tree in the house. To save face, Homer claims that he was just on his way to go get one, even though, as the viewer knows, he has no money with which to buy a tree. We next see Homer in his car driving past a series of signs, which read, "Trees $75," "Trees $60 and Up," "Trees—slightly irregular $45," and finally "No Trespassing." After this, we hear the sound of a chainsaw, and we immediately realize what Homer is doing; then come the sounds of dogs and gunshots. That Homer feels he must steal a Christmas tree speaks volumes about the lack of resources he has and about the intentions of the writers in crafting *The Simpsons* as a working-class show.

In a later scene, on Christmas Eve, we see Bart at the mall, plotting with his friend Milhouse to embarrass the store Santa. When Bart discovers that it is his father dressed as Santa, he is understandably surprised. Homer confesses the truth and explains, "To keep my family from missing out on Christmas, I'd do anything." Bart is impressed and believes that Homer must really love them if he is willing to "sink so low." Homer, now proud of what he has done and of his son's admiration, goes to get his check, telling Bart that someday he'll know "the satisfaction of earning a big fat check for a job well done." What Homer gets, however, is a check for $13. When he asks about this, the woman explains, "That's 120 gross, less social security, less unemployment insurance, less Santa training, less costume purchase, less beard rental, less Christmas club." It is ironic and humorous, to be sure, but it also reflects a reality for many working people, who are often barely able to scrape by, despite having the proverbial "hard work" ethic.[36] Homer's friend (and fellow Santa) Barney tells Homer he is going to Springfield Downs to bet his meager earnings on a sure thing—a dog named Whirlwind. Homer is at first resistant, saying, "I'm not going to take my kid to a sleazy dog track on Christmas." But Bart persuades him otherwise, in a speech that is at once heartfelt and satirical. He says,

> Aw, come on, Dad. This can be the miracle that saves the Simpsons' Christmas. If TV has taught me anything, it's that miracles always happen to poor kids at Christmas. It happened to Tiny Tim, it happened to Charlie Brown, it happened to the Smurfs, and it's gonna happen to us!

Homer, now convinced, says, "Well, okay, let's go," then adds, "Who's Tiny Tim?" There is no miracle, of course. They do not win any money at the track, but they do adopt the losing dog (whom they name Santa's Little Helper), thus giving Marge, Lisa, and Bart a merry Christmas and providing the audience a happy ending.

Given the context in which the first season of *The Simpsons* aired, which I briefly outlined earlier, it is no surprise that a concern with money is a prominent theme in the premiere episode. This theme is developed throughout the first few seasons with episodes that regularly depict the family's economic struggles and the difficulties they have providing for fairly basic needs. Notably, in the third episode of the first season, "Homer's Odyssey" (January 1990), Homer is fired from his job at the nuclear power plant because of his incompetence. The entire episode is about Homer's struggle with the guilt and shame he feels over no longer being the "breadwinner" of the family—indeed, he is so distraught about being "useless" as a provider that he aims to commit suicide. In the fourth episode, "There's No Disgrace Like Home" (January 1990), Homer decides that his dysfunctional family needs the help of Dr. Marvin Monroe, whose services he sees advertised on television. The therapy sessions, however, cost $250. When Marge says that they simply "can't afford that," Homer suggests tapping into the kids' college fund. We then see the family smash open a piggy bank, in which they find exactly $88.50. "That's it?!" Homer exclaims. Determined to "fix" his family, Homer pawns the television, which is the only asset they appear to have. Though the therapy fails, the outcome is financially beneficial: since Dr. Monroe had guaranteed "family bliss or double your money back," the Simpsons end up with $500. Homer excitedly declares they will use the money to buy a new 21-inch television, which was at that time (1990) one of the latest models and which they could not have afforded otherwise. Perhaps the most pronounced example of the family's economic difficulties appears in the episode "Marge Gets a Job" (November 1992). Here, Marge decides to take on a job outside of the home, not because she is particularly restless as a mother and housewife—as was the case, for example, in "Homer Alone" (February 1992)—but simply out of economic necessity: the Simpson house needs foundation repair, which will cost $8,500. Once again, the writers indicate how little wealth the family has: as Homer explains, they have only $500 in the bank, so Marge decides to get a job to help out with the repair cost. Ironically, she ends up with an entry-level job at the nuclear plant, in sector 7G, right beside Homer.

The economic status of the Simpson family is also represented via class envy and conspicuous consumption, which are prominent themes on the show as well. For example, in "Call of the Simpsons" (February 1990), which features a "keeping up with the Joneses" motif, we see how much of Homer's economic woes are about fulfilling his wants as well as his needs. The episode opens on Bart mowing the lawn with a push mower, which he calls "a piece of junk." We then see Rodd Flanders on a large riding mower, which Bart envies. Homer tells Bart to be happy with what he has, but he quickly changes his tune when he sees Ned Flanders pull up in a brand-new RV, equipped with a "microwave, big screen TV, dishwasher, deep fryer, and satellite dish." Homer is incredulous and asks Ned how he can afford it when he only makes $27 more per week (which Homer knows from having once seen Ned's paycheck). "It's easy," Ned says. "Credit." Like many middle-class Americans at the time, Ned was relying on credit to live the consumer lifestyle. Hoping to do the same, Homer goes to Bob's RV, where he sees "the Ultimate Behemoth," which he wants, but because he has bad credit (so bad that it sets off alarms), he has to settle for a crappy secondhand RV. In "Bart's Dog Gets an F" (March 1991), we see Homer once again coveting something Ned Flanders has—in this case an expensive pair of sneakers known as "Assassins." Although they cost $125, Homer selfishly buys them so he can show them off when out walking, again demonstrating his desire to compete in a conspicuous display of status. Homer's secret comes out when the dog, Santa's Little Helper, gets hold of the sneakers and tears them to shreds. Admittedly, Marge does not make much of the cost of the shoes, but she is angry that Homer bought them without her knowledge because they had agreed to consult one another before making any "major purchases."

Like many Americans, Bart and Homer are consummate consumers, conditioned by television and advertising to impulsively acquire material goods in the pursuit of happiness. The family's lack of resources, however, thwarts their desires to consume and creates a variety of tensions. A fine example of Homer's impulsive desire, as well as of the Simpsons' economic status, is on display in the second-season episode "Simpson and Delilah" (October 1990). While again watching television, Homer sees an ad for Dimoxinil, a "new miracle breakthrough in hair regrowth." Homer then goes to the clinic to get more info, and he is there presented with the Dimoxinil action set (a six-month supply, gravity boots, scalp massager, and t-shirt), which costs $1,000. "I can't afford that!" Homer cries. "Well," says the representative, "we do have a product which is more in your price range," and with that, he hands Homer a large bottle of Hair in a Drum, at a cost of just $19.95. "However," he continues, "I must assure you that any hair growth you experience while using it will be purely coincidental." Frustrated in his quest for hair (and, he expects, a better life), Homer goes to Moe's bar to drown his sorrows in Duff beer. Hearing of his problems, his coworkers Lenny and Carl suggest that Homer just "creatively" fill out some medical insurance forms and charge the product to the company. Inspired, Homer does so, thus committing fraud. Like his father, Bart is conditioned by television and advertising toward consumerism. In "Marge Be Not Proud" (December 1995), Bart wants a videogame called *Bonestorm*, which of course he has seen advertised on television. Marge says, "Sorry, honey, but those games cost up to and including seventy dollars." In fact, we find out later, it actually costs $59.99. Bart is frustrated that his friend Milhouse, whose family is economically better off, already has the game, again highlighting the theme of class envy. At the local Try N' Save, where Bart is admiring the game, he becomes even more frustrated when he sees another kid, Gavin (coded by appearance, speech, and behavior as rich and spoiled), with his mother, who purchases two copies of the game so that Gavin will not have to share with his sister. Like Homer, Bart wants what he can't have; and like Homer, he resorts to illegal ends: prompted by the local bullies, Bart shoplifts. The writers for *The Simpsons* certainly don't condone such behaviors—indeed, Homer is found out and fired from his job, and Bart is caught and punished for his crime—but they do provide viewers a clearer sense of the reasoning behind such actions: these are the reactions of a disempowered class seeking to achieve happiness, as they are told they should, in the American consumer paradise.

Struggling with Class on *The Simpsons*

The most common method of depicting class on *The Simpsons* is to position the Simpson family in between the poles of the upper and lower economic tiers in Springfield, replicating to some degree the middle-class mythology. The upper tier is home to the capitalist class, represented most commonly by Charles Montgomery Burns, and it is against this class that much of the satire on the show is directed. From the start of the series, Mr. Burns has been depicted as a cold, calculating, and venal capitalist. As Dale Snow and James Snow point out,

> Mr. Burns is to a great degree capitalism personified. Most often, Mr. Burns is presented as an exaggerated characterization of the Friedmanesque free-wheeling capitalist whose telos is profit, whose *raison d'etre* is greed. In the character of Mr. Burns we have an effective caricature of the relentless criticisms of the capitalist world-view by exaggerating or magnifying that view. Put another way, Mr. Burns shows us the logical conclusion of the capitalist world-view when it is unchecked by other fundamental moral or social commitments.[37]

Examples of Burns's greed and callousness are legion on the show. One early example is found in "Lisa's Pony" (November 1991), in which Homer, desperate to buy a pony for his daughter, goes to his employee credit union at the nuclear plant to get a loan. There he finds Mr. Burns, who asks Homer if he is acquainted with the state's "stringent usury laws." When Homer indicates that he is not, simply telling Burns that he wants to buy his daughter a pony so she will love him again, Burns quickly tells him to "just sign the form" and then breaks into his evil laugh. A similar example appears in "Last Exit to Springfield" (March 1993), which opens with a powerful invocation of socioeconomic class. Homer and Bart are watching an action film starring Rainier Wolfcastle, in the guise of McBain (a parody of the 1980s action heroes Arnold Swarzenegger, Bruce Willis, and Sylvester Stallone all rolled into one). The villain of the film, who at a previous point offered a toast "to human misery," subdues McBain with a toxic salmon puff and then laughs a maniacal laugh. "That is one evil dude," Bart comments. "It's just a movie, son," Homer assures him. "There's nobody that evil in real life." Cut to Montgomery Burns in his office laughing the same evil laugh as he watches a window washer dangling from a broken platform outside; after the man falls, Burns simply closes the blinds. As *The Simpsons* develops, Burns's heartlessness and greed become stronger and more prominent elements of many episodes. A good example is the two-part cliffhanger, "Who Shot Mr. Burns?" (May 1995), a loose parody of *Dallas* and its infamous "Who Shot J. R.?" episodes. In this episode, Burns sets up a slant drilling operation to mine oil from beneath Springfield Elementary, thereby depriving the school of the revenue it expected to get (and badly needed) when the oil deposit was first discovered. Burns also lays out a plan to block out the sun with a giant space shield so that everyone in Springfield will have to use more of the electricity generated by his nuclear power plant. For such naked villainy, he is despised by everyone in town, who all become suspects when he is shot. Perhaps most perversely, in the episode "Two Dozen and One Greyhounds" (April 1995), we learn that Burns is planning to use the pelts from a litter of puppies to make himself a tuxedo coat.

The satirical treatment of Burns in each of these situations—and in many others I could cite—makes clear for the audience that he is to be condemned for his actions. But what is of more interest to me, given the purposes of this chapter, is Burns's view of the working class, which is clearly designed by the writers to be a reflection of the perception, as they see it, of the economic elite in American society. We are given a sense of Burns's attitudes very early in the series, in "Two Cars in Every Garage,

Three Eyes on Every Fish" (November 1990), which involves Burns trying to put a positive spin on the phenomenon of Blinky, the three-eyed fish, which Bart and Lisa find in a stream near the nuclear plant. To avoid paying $56 million to bring the nuclear plant up to code, Burns decides to run for governor so that he "can decide what is safe and what isn't." His competition is the incumbent, Mary Bailey.[38] The spin doctors Burns has hired him tell him that he is hated and seen as "despicable." Their job, Burns tells them, is to make him seem likable to the "average Joe sixpack" and to turn such voters against Mary Bailey. Throughout the remainder of the episode, Burns refers to blue-collar workers and the average American by a variety of derogatory names, including "Joe meatball," "Sally housecoat," "Eddie punch-clock," and "Johnny lunch-pail." Terms such as these are used over and over again in episodes of The Simpsons to indicate Burns's attitude toward his own workers and the laboring class in general. Of course, the terminology here is also designed to evoke the language so often employed by conservative politicians and the wealthy elite to align themselves with "the average American" and "the working man." Here, however, the language is given a clearly ironic cast, which is meant to satirically highlight the condescending attitude of the political and economic elite, who are increasingly one and the same.

We also have a sense of Burns's worldview from the way he almost literally lords over the workers at the Springfield Nuclear Power Plant. The image of work on The Simpsons, which is seen most often via the employees at the nuclear plant, is quite bleak. Indeed, as Chris Turner notes in Planet Simpson, the image stands in stark contrast to many of the myths of the postindustrial economy—for example, "that work had grown more exciting, more fulfilling, more egalitarian, that corporations had come to hate hierarchy, [and] that gray-suited conformity was as out of date as the ducktail haircut."[39] This was true, of course, for some workers in the 1980s and 1990s, especially those in then-burgeoning high-tech fields. But for many other workers, the situation was actually worsening. This period of time, according to Turner,

saw the greatest redistribution of wealth in the history of capitalism throughout the corporate West—particularly in the United States, where by the late 1990s the richest 1 percent controlled more than 40 percent of the nation's wealth (up from 20 percent in 1979). At the same time, job security for those on the social ladder's lower rungs all but vanished, and working-class workplaces moved by the thousands to the Third World redoubts, where wages were counted in pennies per hour and labor and environmental regulations were so lax that even the Springfield power plant probably couldn't violate them.[40]

Turner claims that this image of labor, which reflected the grim reality of many workers in the 1990s, played a part in making Homer Simpson into a "working-class hero" and Burns a villain for audiences.

This dichotomy is perhaps best shown in "Last Exit to Springfield" (March 1993), one of the few episodes of The Simpsons to overtly deal with social and economic class. "Last Exit to Springfield" primarily concerns a strike by workers at the nuclear power plant. At the start of the episode, Burns is waiting on the union representative to discuss a new contract. Looking over the current contract, Burns laments the "benefits and perks" that, as he sees it, cut into his profits; he then says to his assistant Smithers, "It didn't used to be this way—it didn't used to be this way at all."

We then have a flashback to 1909 (done in a sepia tone appropriate to the era), which provides a very clear picture of Burns's economic philosophy. A young Burns and his grandfather are seen entering the atom smashing plant in Springfield. Workers in this Dickensian environment are (absurdly) smashing atoms with sledgehammers. Burns's grandfather singles out one young worker for inspection and discovers that he is stealing atoms (by smuggling them out in his pockets). Infuriated, the elder Burns calls his thugs to take the young man away. As he is being dragged out, the young man says, "You can't treat the working man this way. One day we'll form a union and get the fair and equitable treatment we deserve. Then we'll go too far, and get corrupt and shiftless, and the Japanese will eat us alive!" This is a moment of what Carl Matheson calls "hyper-irony," which Matheson argues undermines the satire on *The Simpsons*.[41] Admittedly, this is a criticism directed at both capitalists and at unions, which indeed had a history of corruption. But this one moment does not take away from the overall effect of this wildly exaggerated scene, which is clearly designed as a satirical attack on the capitalist class for its labor practices and treatment of workers. Matheson's criticism of this moment (and of this episode in general) also ignores how the narrative develops, that is, how the conflict between owners and workers—hinted at in this flashback and fully explored in the present of the episode—is ultimately resolved.

The conflict in the present ends up centering on the employee dental plan, which Burns is determined to take back from "the greedy union." The dental plan ends up being of importance to Homer because his daughter Lisa needs to have braces.[42] When Marge first tells Homer about this, he tells her not to worry because he and his coworkers (members of the International Brotherhood of Jazz Dancers, Pastry Chefs, and Nuclear Technicians, Local 643) won a dental plan "in the strike of '88." However, the dental plan is threatened by Burns's strategy of bribery. At the union meeting the following day, Carl (the union vice president) tells his fellow workers that the contract they are voting on is "basically the same deal, except we get a free keg of beer for our meeting." At this, everyone cheers. Carl then adds, "In exchange, we have to give up our dental plan." Everyone cheers again and rushes to the keg. Lenny (another coworker) raises a toast and says, "So long, dental plan." Once Homer finally realizes that if they give up the dental plan, he will have to pay for Lisa's braces, he stops the party and reminds everyone of how valuable the dental plan has been to them over the years. He then defiantly tears up the proposed contract, and Carl moves that Homer become the new union president. When Lisa hears of this, she proudly proclaims, "This is your chance to get a fair shake for the working man." Homer instead fantasizes about making "lifelong connections to the world of organized crime."

The remainder of "Last Exit to Springfield" demonstrates the various ways by which Burns (i.e., the capitalist class) seeks to undermine and destroy his employees (i.e., the working class). It also makes very clear that behind this desire lie naked greed and a lust for power. The first round of negotiations between Burns and Homer fails (though only because Homer humorously mistakes the language of negotiation for sexual innuendo and rejects Burns's offer). Burns, believing that Homer is a talented negotiator, then has his "hired goons" drag Homer to his estate, presumably to intimidate him. Burns subtly tries to bribe Homer by showing off his wealth, including "the largest tv in the free world." However, talks fail once again, and the workers call for strike. We then see the workers gather outside the nuclear plant to picket and protest. As might be expected, Lisa draws upon a musical convention (here, the folk song) and becomes the voice of protest. As the workers picket, she plays a guitar and sings: "Come gather round children, it's high time ye learned, about a hero named Homer and a devil named Burns. We'll march 'til we drop, the girls and the fellas, we'll fight to the death, or fold like umbrellas." Frustrated by such defiance, Burns tells Smithers to find him some strikebreakers, "the kind they had in the thirties." The allusion here is not to be lost; Burns is nostalgic for the kind of violent thugs used to brutalize and suppress workers in the days before the National Labor Relations Act (also known as the Wagner Act) of 1935 and the Fair Labor Standards Act of 1938. Since all Smithers can manage to rustle up is a group of old men, including Abe Simpson—who tells Burns, "We can't bust heads the way we used to"—Burns decides that he and Smithers can run the plant themselves. We then have a hilarious montage of them doing so, one that ends with Burns uncrating robot workers, whose crates are stamped "100% Loyal." The moment perfectly captures the capitalist's fantasy. However, the fantasy quickly becomes a nightmare for Burns and Smithers when the robots begin to chase them, intoning, "Crush, kill, destroy." In a last-ditch effort to win the battle, Burns appears on the news program *Smartline*, ostensibly to debate Homer and win public opinion. But Burns can't withhold his anger and instead publicly threatens to "wreak a vengeance" on the city. He does so by stopping the flow of electricity. When the lights go out, everyone pauses momentarily, and it seems like a victory for capital. But then Lisa again begins to sing. In a beautiful homage to the Dr. Seuss classic *How the Grinch Stole Christmas*, the workers then join hands in solidarity and sing, "So we'll march day and night / by the big cooling tower / They have the plant / but we have the power." At this point, Burns (appropriately cast here as the Grinch) decides to concede to the union's demands.

As noted previously, socioeconomic class is openly and directly dealt with in one other episode of *The Simpsons*: "Scenes from the Class Struggle in Springfield" (February 1996). Unlike "Last Exit to Springfield," this episode focuses more on social class and the problem of classism in American culture, although the economic status of the Simpson family is once again underscored. At the start of the episode, Grandpa Simpson breaks the family's treasured television set, so they set off to buy a new one. Because the family "can't afford to shop at any store that has a philosophy," as Marge puts it, they head to the outlet store in neighboring Ogdenville. In the next scene, we have the first appearance of Cletus and Brandine Delroy and thus of "white trash" identity in the episode. I will discuss this representation in full in the next section, but it is important to note it here because of what it says about Marge's own sense of class. As Marge paws through a pile of discount clothing with a look of disdain, she says to Lisa, "I don't think these clothes are us." Lisa asks, "Who are they?" At that point, Cletus appears and holds up a T-shirt with the phrase "Classy Lassy" written across the chest in rhinestones, and he suggests that Brandine wear it to work. She replies, "Oh Cletus, you know I gotta wear the shirt what Dairy Queen gimme." Significantly, no commentary is offered here by Marge or Lisa, the most mature, intelligent, and politically aware characters on the show. It is simply allowed to stand that Cletus and Brandine are uncouth and without "class," meaning middle-class taste. Marge's and Lisa's own tastes are evident in Marge's later discovery of a deeply discounted Chanel suit, on sale for $90, marked down from $2,800. Although Marge likes the suit, she tells Lisa, "We can't afford $90, even if it is a bargain." However, encouraged by Lisa, who tells her mother to do something for herself for once,

Marge decides to buy the suit, rationalizing that "it'll be good for the economy." Later, at the Kwik-E-Mart, Marge runs into Evelyn, a woman Marge knew from high school and who is now obviously very wealthy. Impressed by Marge's skill in pumping gas and her Chanel suit, Evelyn invites Marge to drop by the country club the next day. At home, tensions begin to mount because Marge is now worried about how her family appears to others and how they will behave. Lisa, well aware of the class structure in Springfield, flatly states that she does not want to go, claiming, "That country club is a hotbed of exclusionist snobs and status-seeking social climbers." Marge pressures them into going anyway. When they arrive at the gate outside the country club, Marge, apropos of nothing, says to the gatekeeper, "We're not poor." Everyone else looks at her in silence, obviously surprised. "Well, we're not," Marge insists.

As the episode progresses, we are given a strong sense of the differences between the working class and the elite, which are starkly drawn, and we see that Lisa is in many ways right about the people at the country club. The women Marge meets in the clubhouse, for example, are all vain and shallow, prattling on about their disdain for sales clerks and their preference for mail-order items like Omaha Steaks. Trying to fit in, Marge says that she also gets food through the mail—in the form of recipes in *Good Housekeeping* magazine—and tells the women that "sometimes the most satisfying meal is the one you cook yourself." One of the women, trying to relate, merely demonstrates how far removed from the working class she is by sharing a story about herself and her husband (Whiff) coming home late one night and, deciding to not wake their live-in maid, microwaving their own soup. "Of course, it was a horrible mess. But Iris didn't mind cleaning it up," she chirps. Back home, after this first visit to the country club, Marge tells her family how much she enjoyed the experience. None of the others did, however, particularly Lisa. "The rich are different from you and me," Lisa dryly observes, echoing Fitzgerald. "Yes," Marge says. "They're better." Again, there is a stunned silence. "Socially better," Marge offers. "And if we fit in, we can be better too." A subsequent scene at the country club shows quite clearly that the rich are not socially better. Here, Lisa sees a spoiled little girl berate a servant, shouting, "Fritz, you idiot. I didn't order a baloney sandwich. I ordered an *abalone* sandwich," and then throwing the plate of food at his feet. At this point, Lisa launches into what could and should be a speech denouncing the class system; however, she is distracted as she speaks by seeing another young girl riding a horse. "This whole country club scene is so decadent," Lisa begins. "All these spoiled brats and their smug complacent parents. It just reinforces the unspoken class system of . . ." and here she spins around to watch the girl on the horse ". . . sitting on their high horses . . ." Having lost her train of thought, she says, "I'm sorry I've gotta go!" and runs off. Shortly thereafter, we see Lisa skillfully riding a horse. "Mom, look. I've found something more fun than complaining," she shouts. It is a surprising moment, given Lisa's stance on classism and her activism in previous episodes. It is also another example of the "hyper-irony" Matheson speaks of, and in this case I concur that it is a problematic image, one that undermines the potential critique.

Marge, meanwhile, has been fitting in well, but her comfort level starts to unravel when the one of the women teases her about her Chanel suit, which she has worn each time. Marge self-consciously alters the suit, using her (working-class) sewing skills to modify it into a vest and culottes. This buys her a bit of time but not enough. After Evelyn tells Marge that she wants to sponsor her and the family for membership, Marge knows she needs another "lovely new outfit." She tries once again to modify the Chanel suit, but this time she is distracted by Lisa's excited chatter about horses and her own stress level; she lashes out at Lisa to quiet her and in the process accidentally gets the suit material jammed in the sewing machine; trying to save it, she succeeds only in tearing it to pieces. Now in panic mode, Marge first attempts to get an outfit from her sisters, Patty and Selma, but what they have is both tacky and ill-fitting, so Marge heads back to the outlet mall, hoping for another great bargain. Marge returns and asks the saleswoman there if she has "a Chanel suit or any other high-quality clothes." The woman tells Marge no but then informs her that a shipment of "slightly burnt Sears active-wear" is due that afternoon. Cletus once again appears, out of nowhere, to ask, "What time and how burnt?" The meaning of the "joke" here relies upon the audience associating Sears with a certain class status in American culture (one made distinct from the status of the Simpsons) and thereby seeing the clothing from Sears as unsuitable because it is, by implication, neither high quality nor high class. Now desperate, Marge goes to the Chanel store in downtown Springfield and buys a fancy new gown. When Lisa inquires about the dress and its cost, excited by the idea her mother found two great bargains in one outlet store, Marge is evasive and then angry, and she finally snaps at Lisa, "Why do you always have to question everything I do?" Lisa is cowed into silence by her mother's anger. On this last trip to the country club, Marge won't let Homer drive up to main entrance because she fears people will see the dent in the car and the coat-hanger antenna. She makes him park the car elsewhere, and they begin to walk across the expansive lawn. As they do so, Bart, Homer, and Lisa explain what they are intending to do. Bart and Homer, of course, simply want to cause trouble. Lisa, still the activist, says, "I'm going to ask people if they know their servants' last names, or in the case of butlers, their first." Marge stops at this point and scolds them. "No, no, no," she says. Looking at each in turn, she continues, "No vulgarity, no mischief, no politics. Just be good." Humbled, Homer says, "You kids should thank your mother. Now that she's a better person, we can see how awful we really are." At this point, sentimental music rises up and Marge, now recognizing what she has become, apologizes. She tells Homer that she likes her "old green dress" and is sorry she spent all of their savings on a new one. She then concludes, "I wouldn't want to join any club that would have *this* me as a member." As they walk away, Lisa observes, "[T]hose snobs never would have made us members anyway." The irony is that they did, as we see from an interior scene in which the members of the club are puzzling over the Simpsons' whereabouts. In the final scene, the family is gathered at a local Krusty Burger. The teenager sweeping the floor notices that they are well-dressed and asks if they just came from the prom. Marge simply tells him, "We realized we're more comfortable in a place like this." Presumably, what she means is that they are more comfortable in a working-class milieu. "You're crazy," he says. "This place is a dump."

As noted in chapter 1, one of the more dismissive readings of the representation of class on *The Simpsons* comes from James M. Wallace, who approaches the show from a Marxist perspective in his essay "A (Karl, Not Groucho) Marxist in Springfield." Early on, Wallace does concede that *The Simpsons* is full of "thoughtful laughter," that it uses incongruity to encourage us "to at least think about how we normally see the world," and that it at times "distances us momentarily from the prevailing ideology of capitalist America."[43] However, Wallace ultimately believes that the show fails as a satire, largely because it offers no image of "what the ideal world is supposed to look like" or has "no vision of what the world should be."[44] Lacking this, he says, "*The Simpsons* does little more than string together isolated and transitory comical moments that in the aggregate add up to no discernible, consistent political point of view, let alone a subversive one."[45] Wallace later concludes that *The Simpsons* is "the worst kind of bourgeois satire" since it not only fails to suggest the possibility of a better world but "teases us away from any serious reflection on or criticism of prevailing practices, and, finally, encourages us to believe that the current system, flawed and comical as it sometimes is, is the best one possible."[46] From a rigidly Marxist perspective, Wallace has a fair claim: neither of the two episodes he analyzes—"Scenes from the Class Struggle in Springfield" and "Last Exit to Springfield"—offers the kind of indictment of classism or capitalism that would satisfy a Marxist. Nonetheless, I cannot subscribe to Wallace's interpretation of these episodes or his overall view of *The Simpsons*. One problem with Wallace's reading of the episodes is that he conveniently ignores elements of the narrative that do not support his thesis. For example, in his brief discussion of "Last Exit to Springfield," Wallace focuses only on the "portrait of the workers," which is admittedly unflattering—they are bumbling, foolish, and short-sighted enough to give up their dental plan for a keg of beer. However, that is only where the narrative begins; as it progresses, we see Homer rally his coworkers, become elected president of the union, and negotiate the terms of a settlement with Mr. Burns. We also see the workers vote to strike, picket and protest, stand in solidarity, and ultimately get what they want when Burns gives in to the union's demands. As a portrait of the working class, this seems much more a success than a failure, as the collective effort of the workers actually results in change. One might also argue that the portrait of the owners, represented by Burns and Smithers, is also unflattering and that they too are portrayed as bumbling and foolish. That said, I have to concede that there is something troubling about "Scenes from the Class Struggle in Springfield." For me, this is something of a transitional episode in the series. Although it contains critiques of the class system and classism, these are modified and weakened in a number of ways. Marge's confession at the end is followed by her telling Homer that they will have a $3,300 credit at the Chanel store. His only response is a question: "They have beer and gum, right?" This is a rather blithe attitude to take toward such enormous debt; it is certainly far removed from the concern with expenses expressed four years earlier in "Marge Gets a Job," in which earning money was so paramount. It is, perhaps, simply a reflection of the time, the mid-1990s, and the fact that many Americans were then living high on easy credit. Lisa's voice is also significantly dampened in "Scenes from the Class Struggle in Springfield." Whereas in "Last Exit to Springfield" Lisa was the inspirational bard of protest, here she is easily distracted by the wealth around her, and her valid and valuable critique of classism is dismissed—by her, no less—as mere "complaining." However, most troubling to me is not the lack of a critique of capital—that is done well and often in many other episodes of *The Simpsons*—but rather the lack of a critique at the other end of the socioeconomic spectrum via the uncontested imagery of "white trash" identity, which is used to help audiences more easily see the Simpsons as (in Marge's words) "not poor."

Class and "White Trash" Identity on *The Simpsons*

In his well-known and widely reproduced essay "Ralph, Fred, Archie, and Homer: Why Television Keeps Recreating the White Male Working-Class Buffoon," Richard Butsch argues that television situation comedies have, from the very start, suggested the inferiority of the working class, particularly the working-class male, who is depicted as "dumb, immature, irresponsible or lacking in common sense."[47] According to Butsch, this is the character of the husband in most sitcoms depicting a blue-collar (and white) male head of household, the most representative examples of which are *The Honeymooners*, *The Flintstones*, *All in the Family*, and *The Simpsons*. As Butsch puts it, the working-class male is "typically well-intentioned, even lovable, but no one to respect or emulate."[48] Butsch's claim is valid to a large degree, but I do not think it is a necessarily fair comparison of texts. Neither *The Honeymooners* nor *The Flintstones* was intended to be satire, for example; *All in the Family* was arguably closer in spirit to satire than either of its predecessors, and yet, as a live-action show rather than an animated one, the way in which it could offer satire was restricted, and it often relied more on simply exposing generational conflict. Although I am sympathetic to Butsch's concern about the replication of the "buffoon" image within mass media, and I agree that it is all too commonplace, I think the unique status of *The Simpsons* as both an animated sitcom and a satire calls for greater nuance in the analysis. I would not go as far as Chris Turner, who argues that Homer Simpson is a "working-class hero," but I believe it is important to take a much closer look at the representation of the working class on *The Simpsons*, with particular attention to how it is positioned in relation to so-called "white trash" identity.

In a chapter on the working class and the poor in *Framing Class: Media Representations of Wealth and Poverty in America*, Diana Kendall offers an illuminating discussion of "white trash" images in contemporary media, accurately concluding that these are overwhelmingly negative.[49] She follows this with a section discussing working-class images on television, entitled "TV's Buffoons, Bigots, and Slobs," where she mentions, albeit briefly, *The Simpsons*.[50] Unfortunately, Kendall offers no nuance in her analysis of the show and, in particular, of Homer Simpson; in effect, she mainly reiterates the argument originally advanced by Richard Butsch. What surprises me most, however, is not the assessment of Homer but the fact that on the heels of an insightful reflection on current "white trash" representations in mass media, Kendall makes no mention of this group's depiction in the world of *The Simpsons*. To my mind, the problem here has less to do with the depiction of Homer as a buffoon—mainly because I see this as a strategy of the show's satire, as I have highlighted earlier and in previous chapters—than with the continual efforts by the writers to elevate the status of the Simpson family by contrasting it with "white trash" and thereby providing the soothing illusion of middle-class "normality."

Given the clear presentation of the Simpsons as a working-class family, at least in the early years of the series, it is perhaps not surprising that Reverend Lovejoy's daughter, Jessica, once referred to Bart Simpson as "yellow trash." Jessica's putdown works, in part, because in this particular episode ("Bart's Girlfriend," November 1994) the Simpsons are shown to be in a much lower economic position than the Lovejoys. Jessica's comment also works because many members of the viewing audience carry with them an implicit understanding of what defines "white trash" identity and an expectation of the behaviors associated with it in American society and thus "get" the joke. However, Jessica's comment should not be taken as indicative of the television show's positioning of the Simpson family. Indeed, the show works very hard to portray the Simpsons as "average" Americans and, more often than not, reinforces middle-class American values by positioning the Simpson family as higher than those who are "poor" or who embody "white trash" identity in Springfield. As Matt Wray and

Annalee Newitz helpfully explain in the introduction to *White Trash: Race and Class in America* (1997), current stereotypes of "white trash" can be traced to a series of studies produced around the turn of the twentieth century by the US Eugenics Records Office (ERO), which sought to demonstrate "scientifically" that large numbers of rural poor whites were "genetic defectives."[51] Many of the characteristics associated with these families entered the public imagination and coded rural whites, particularly in the South, as "poor, dirty, drunken, criminally minded, and sexually perverse people."[52] Although the Nazi experiments of the 1930s and 1940s did much to discredit eugenics in the United States, the stereotypes of rural poor whites remain with us to this day, largely through their reproduction within mainstream media. In a more recent work, *Not Quite White: White Trash and the Boundaries of Whiteness* (2006), Matt Wray has usefully called such negative ideas "stigmatypes." According to Wray, stigmatypes such as "white trash" are "stigmatizing boundary terms that simultaneously denote and enact cultural and cognitive divides between in-groups and out-groups, between acceptable and unacceptable identities, and between proper and improper behaviors."[53]

The stereotypes and stigmatypes related to "white trash" identity are often uncritically offered in the world of *The Simpsons*. The very geography of Springfield, for example, helps to reproduce and stabilize (white) class differences. In the season 2 episode "Colonel Homer" (March 1992), Homer inadvertently travels to neighboring Spittle County after having had an argument with Marge. On the way, Homer passes signs for Flaming Pete's steak house (which turns out to be burned down), an assortment of malodorous items (a skunk, a fertilizer plant, the county dump, and a sulfur mine, in that order), and lastly a sign reading "Open Sewers, Next 40 Miles." A host of other stereotypes of rural white identity are offered once Homer arrives at his destination, the Beer-N-Brawl tavern, which Homer quickly labels "a redneck bar." As Homer opens the door, he finds brawls in progress among a group of bearded, tattooed, and flannel-shirt-clad men. Homer is forced to drink a Fudd rather than a Duff beer (the former is apparently "inferior") and listen to the vocal stylings of Yodelin' Zeke. It is here that Homer also meets Lurleen Lumpkin, a waitress with dreams of being a country-and-western singer and escaping life in Spittle County and the Royal King Trailer Park where she lives. Such images and references are readily decoded and understood by audiences. As Duncan Beard argues, although certain episodes of *The Simpsons* do provide "incisive interrogations" of issues surrounding cultural difference, "the presentations of Others that are made in passing seem to utilize cultural stereotypes much less critically."[54] Although Beard is speaking of racial identity and traditional dichotomies (i.e., white and nonwhite Other), his claim is perfectly applicable to white racial identity and the Othering of "white trash" identity on *The Simpsons*, which is embodied most regularly in the characters of Cletus and Brandine Delroy.[55] Cletus and Brandine, the heads of a lower-class family living on the outskirts of Springfield, occasionally appear on the show but mainly in minimal ways and for brief moments and usually in order to create a joke at their own expense. Although satiric strategies such as exaggeration and irony are used in the depictions of the Delroys, the narratives surrounding them do not provide clear targets for censure (e.g., bigotry or class prejudice); instead, we get a replication of the stigmatypes with which viewers are already familiar and to which they likely subscribe. In short, I see Cletus and Brandine being used on *The Simpsons* primarily to provide an affirmation of middle-class status for the Simpsons and to establish middle-class identity as normative.

Cletus made his first brief appearance in the fifth-season episode "Bart Gets an Elephant" (March 1994), in which Bart wins an elephant from a local radio station. In a scene midway through the episode, we see people gathered in the Simpsons' backyard, where Homer has established a makeshift zoo and is trying to capitalize on the elephant (named Stampy by Bart) by charging money for visits and rides. When Helen Lovejoy makes a comment about Stampy's temper, Lisa, sympathetic to the elephant's plight, snaps back, "You'd be grumpy too if you were taken out of your natural habitat and gawked at by a bunch of slack-jawed yokels." At this point, Cletus steps in, points to Lisa, and says, "Hey, Maw, lookit that pointy-hairded little girl." Although his clothing and accent mark him as rural, and perhaps poor, nothing in this brief appearance positions him as "white trash." That is not the case with his next appearance, in the episode "Home Sweet Home-Diddily-Dum-Doodily" (October 1995), in which Marge and Homer are ordered to take a family skills class to learn how to be better parents. Cletus is in the class as well, along with some others who are meant to represent the poor (one, for example, is dressed in a burlap sack). The instructor is seen telling everyone about things that they "should have learned long ago," such as "if you leave milk out, it can go sour. Put it in the refrigerator, or, failing that, a cool wet sack" and "put your garbage in a garbage can, people." The satirical target here is an interventionist welfare state, and we know from the plotline of the episode that this is the consequence of a simple misunderstanding for Homer and Marge, for whom the entire experience is "so humiliating." But we have no explanatory story for Cletus or the others in the class. We are left to infer that these individuals, because they are poor and uneducated, are simply unfit parents.

As mentioned in the previous section, Cletus and Brandine appear together for the first time in the episode "Scenes from the Class Struggle in Springfield" (February 1996). Recall that in this episode, Cletus and Brandine are shopping at the same outlet as Marge and Lisa, who look with disdain on a particular item of clothing (a T-shirt with the phrase "Classy Lassy" written on it). "I don't think these clothes are us," Marge says, and Lisa asks, "Who are they?" The answer, of course, is Cletus and Brandine. By extension, it is also others like them: that is, the poor, whom we are meant to view as uncouth and lacking in "class," which here clearly means middle-class taste. As I noted before, no commentary is offered by Marge or Lisa, the most mature, intelligent characters on *The Simpsons*. Recall as well that when Marge returns to the same store later, seeking another bargain, and is told that a shipment of "slightly burnt Sears active-wear" is due that afternoon, Cletus once again appears and asks, "What time and how burnt?" Again, there is no comment from Marge and nothing in the narrative to contest this imagery; the joke here is completely at Cletus's expense. These brief incorporations of "white trash" identity elide the fact that Marge and Cletus are both shopping at the Ogdenville Outlet Mall; the reality here is that the Simpsons and the Delroys are on equal ground and *economically* very much alike, yet the episode encourages viewers to see them as *socially* very different.

The coding of Cletus, Brandine, and their children as "white trash" is done in numerous ways on *The Simpsons*, and these representations have been both regular and consistent. In "Twenty Two Short Films about Springfield" (April 1996), we have a short vignette devoted to Cletus, who is regularly depicted as having a snake tattoo on his arm, a scraggly mustache, and buck teeth and wearing a tank-style white undershirt. The scene opens with a song, "Cletus the Slack Jawed Yokel," the lyrics of which appear on the screen as the song plays, superimposed over images of

Cletus in scenes from past episodes. The lyrics read, "Some folk'll never eat a skunk / But then again some folk'll / Like Cletus, the slack-jawed yokel. / Most folk'll never lose a toe / And then again some folk'll / Like Cletus, the slack-jawed yokel." Other episodes appear to make light of Cletus and Brandine's poverty. In "Days of Wine and D'oh'ses" (April 2000), for example, in which we see Homer and Bart go "dumpster diving"—in a parody of a remarkably bourgeois "trend" of the 1990s—we also see Cletus and Brandine rummaging through a dumpster. At one point, Cletus holds up some cardboard tubes that he finds and says, "Looky here! Cardy-board tubes!" Brandine replies, "Now we can have indoor plumbing, just like they's got at the women's lockup." Cletus responds, "They spoiled you, Brandine. Sometimes I don't even know who you are anymore." In "Lost Our Lisa" (May 1998), in which Lisa gets lost in an unfamiliar (read: poor) part of Springfield, we see Lisa, walking near a junkyard, come upon a raccoon that has been run over by a car. Cletus suddenly appears, once again out of nowhere and apropos of nothing else, to yell, "I seen it first!" He then scoops up the raccoon with a shovel and tosses it into the back of his pickup truck, which is loaded with roadkill. "Ooh, Girly Sue's gonna have a elegant wedding feast," he says. Lisa then asks Cletus for a ride downtown. Brandine, impatient with the delay, shouts from the truck, "Cletus, what are you beating your gums about?" "Never you mind, Brandine," he responds. "You just go back to birthin' that baby." He then turns back to Lisa and says, "Yeah, I'll fetch you a ride, little missy, hop on in. Mind the skunk, them things can go off even after they's dead." Disgusted, Lisa runs off instead. Among other things, this scene casts Cletus and Brandine as irresponsibly procreative, in keeping with the common "white trash" image. This idea is developed further in other episodes. For example, in the eighth-season episode "The Twisted World of Marge Simpson" (January 1997), we learn that Cletus and Brandine have 26 children. A "joke" is offered in one scene by way of Cletus offering Marge an armful of coupons good for a free pretzel (Marge had not specified "one per customer") and thus being able to feed his entire family: "Hey kids," he shouts, "we're eatin' tonight!" The kids then step out onto the front porch as Cletus names them one by one.[56] Other episodes imply that Cletus and Brandine may be siblings who have an incestuous relationship, thus playing into another prominent "white trash" stigmatype. Although Brandine is generally represented as Cletus's wife, the exact nature of their relationship is kept somewhat vague—and, of course, played for laughs. In "Alone Again, Natura-Diddily" (February 2000), we see the two of them arriving at an auto racing event, where Brandine remarks, "Dang, Cletus! Why'd you have to park so close to my parents?" To this, Cletus responds, "Now honey, they's mah parents too!" Cletus might mean that Brandine's parents are his in-laws, but that is certainly ambiguous here and meant at least to imply an incestuous relationship. Similarly, in "There's Something about Marrying" (February 2005), Cletus and Brandine come before Homer to be married (Homer was ordained over the Internet as a minister). Looking at their paperwork, Homer asks, "Wait a minute...are you two brother and sister?" Brandine replies, "We's all kindsa thangs." To complicate the issue even further, in "The Italian Bob" (December 2005), Brandine says to Cletus, "Yer tha best husband, brother and son I ever did have."

The images of "white trash" outlined here clearly rely upon exaggeration, which is a technique of satire commonly employed on *The Simpsons*. However, I do not see these images working in service of satire. One way of discerning this is to note that there is no critical voice built into the episodes to challenge the images of Cletus and Brandine or the comments made by them. A statement such as "Yer tha best husband, brother and son I ever did have" is absurd, to be sure, but there is nothing in the narrative to explain or contest the statement; it stands alone as a joke at the expense of Cletus and Brandine and for the pleasure of the viewing audience. Even Lisa, the most progressive-minded and tolerant member of the Simpson clan, and someone whom we might expect to be a voice of protest, remains silent. In the encounter with Cletus and Brandine at the outlet mall in "Scenes from the Class Struggle in Springfield," Lisa also says nothing. Recall that in this same episode she is also distracted from her critique of the capitalist class by her desire to ride a horse, which she claims is "more fun than complaining." These are notable shifts away from the class consciousness Lisa exhibited at the start of the series, in episodes such as "Moaning Lisa" (February 1990). Here, we are given a clear indication of Lisa's views on class through the music she embraces (jazz and bebop) and her explanation for these preferences. During a rendition of "My Country 'Tis of Thee" in music class, Lisa's music teacher, Mr. Largo, criticizes Lisa for her improvisations. "But that's what my country is all about," Lisa says. "I'm wailing out for the homeless family living out of its car, the Iowa farmer whose land has been taken away by unfeeling bureaucrats, the West Virginia coal miner . . ." She is interrupted at this point by Largo, who says he doesn't want to hear any more about such "unpleasant people." Lisa's concern with the poor and the working class is not just idle fascination; it is part of her own experience since she is witness to her father's exploitation as an undervalued laborer in the nuclear plant and to her parents' struggle to make a comfortable life for their kids. However, by the time "Scenes from the Class Struggle in Springfield" aired in 1996, Lisa's sense of righteous indignation seems to have disappeared.

Despite Lisa's many admirable qualities, she is often given to class-based prejudice, especially in relation to intellectual ability and educational level. In short, Lisa is frequently an intellectual snob, and her intellectual elitism commonly has a classed component, a reflection, perhaps, of the worldview of many of the writers for *The Simpsons*. It is worth noting here that many of the writers for *The Simpsons*—particularly in its first decade—were products of the Ivy League, especially Harvard. The intellectual pedigree of the writing staff was even emphasized in media accounts during the first decade. For example, in a piece written for *The New York Times* in 1997, James Sterngold notes,

> Prime-time television may be reviled in intellectual circles for its supposedly lowbrow sensibilities, but many people in the medium regard this as a second golden era, both in terms of money and the quality of writing. Few things demonstrate the growing attractiveness of the field more than the presence of dozens of Harvard graduates (as well as many other Ivy Leaguers), particularly in the realm of comedy. Writing staffs of shows like *The Simpsons, King of the Hill, Saturday Night Live*, and *Late Show with David Letterman* have come to look like Harvard alumni clubs.[57]

Among those who attended Harvard and who have worked on *The Simpsons* as writers, producers, or both are Richard Appel, David S. Cohen, George Meyer, Bill Oakley, Jon Vitti, Al Jean, Mike Reiss, Conan O'Brien, Jonathan Collier, and Greg Daniels. The longtime producer Sam Simon went to Stanford, and the writer and show runner Mike Scully was a college dropout.[58] Bill Oakley recalls that between seasons 2 and 8, "there was never a time that there were less than 80 percent Harvard Lampoon graduates on the staff."[59] Tom Martin, who joined *The Simpsons* as a writer and producer in 1999 (for season 9), similarly states that in the years prior to season 9, "it had been pretty much an Ivy League institution."[60] As Diana Kendall rightly states, "[T]elevision writers hold elites and their material possessions in greater awe—and encourage their audiences to do likewise," largely by portraying the poor as "in need of our pity" or "doomed by their own shortcomings."[61] This appears to apply quite well to the writers' use of "white trash" on *The Simpsons*. I don't intend to overemphasize authorial intent here, and it is worth remembering that even though episodes of *The Simpsons* are often credited to one writer, they are also the product of collaborative effort. Nevertheless, I can't help but suspect that some of the class prejudices Lisa exhibits on the show might be a reflection of those held by the writers, whether consciously or unconsciously. Michelle Tokarczyk claims that, even among well-meaning academics, "who would never utter a racial slur," there is a tendency to "casually refer to 'trailer trash' or 'white trash.'"[62]

Lisa's class prejudices are evident in a number of subsequent episodes. In "Lisa the Simpson" (March 1998), for example, Lisa envisions her future in a remarkably biased way. At the start of the episode, Lisa is told that she has inherited "the Simpson gene," which will eventually render her "stupid" as she gets older. While trying to bond with Homer and Bart in their "dumbness," in an effort to accept her fate, Lisa has a vision of her future, and the image offered to us is clearly designed to connote "white trash" identity. We see Lisa, very overweight, lying in a hammock (in the living room) attended to by eight children. The room has wood paneling, a framed picture of Elvis Presley, and a pink flamingo. The coffee table is on a cement block, and a television sits on a three-legged stool. With a Southern drawl, Lisa tells the kids who are trying to get her attention, "Knock it off! Momma's tryin' to watch her stories." Lisa asks her husband (here, Ralph Wiggum) to drive them down to the "li-berry" because she wants to "rent us up some movies." She is so fat, however, that she cannot get herself out of the hammock and asks one of her sons to "get Mama's pryin' bar," which he uses as a wedge to help flip her out of the hammock. Back in reality, Lisa shouts, "No, I don't want to turn out that way," and then runs away from Bart and Homer. The oddest element of this peculiar scene is that Lisa envisions adopting a Southern drawl and poor grammar. In the future, she might well be unemployed or become fat, but why she would associate these things with a lack of intelligence and a certain type of speech is not clear—not until one considers that these fit well with existing ideas in American culture about poor whites, ideas shared by the writers of the show and the audience watching it.

Curiously, there is one rare exception to the images of "white trash" typically presented on *The Simpsons*: the episode "Yokel Chords" (March 2007), which is a partial parody of the Rodgers and Hammerstein musical *The Sound of Music*. Near the start of the episode, Superintendent Chalmers discovers that some of Cletus's children are not attending Springfield Elementary and is rightly confused, since the kids reside in the district. Cletus explains that the kids are being homeschooled, but it is soon clear that they are being intentionally kept out of the school. Principal Skinner, defending the exclusion, tells Chalmers, "Sir, if we let these hillfolk into our school, our test scores would drop so low we'd lose all federal funding." Besides being a jab at the Bush administration's No Child Left Behind policy, the comment indicates Skinner's own bias against "hillfolk" and the assumptions he makes about their abilities. At this point, Lisa appears and, inquiring for the school newspaper, asks if Skinner is "purposely denying education to these children." Chalmers and Skinner are at first evasive, knowing they can't admit to this; to quell the potential scandal, they make an arrangement with Lisa to have her tutor some of the kids. Shortly thereafter, Lisa is introduced to the kids, who are named Whitney, Jitney, Crystal Meth, Dubya, Incest, International Harvester, and Birthday. She begins by trying to teach them the principles of government. When one points out that it is not very practical, wondering how it will help put "dog meat" on her plate, Lisa decides to expose them to the wider world by taking them to downtown Springfield. As she puts it, the city is "a treasure-trove of culture and multi-culture." More accurately, it is the culture of the educated elite, as we see in the subsequent musical number. To the tune of "My Favorite Things," Lisa and the kids are seen drinking coffee in a bookstore, where Comic Book Guy is reading books about Dali, Degas, and Miro, singing "those are the folks that you yokels should know." They are shown Luis Buñuel's *Un Chien Andalou* and "outsider art made by mental defectives" (the cat lady); they also attend the opera, eat tapas, and see a production of *Mame*. Krusty the Clown, who happens to see the kids singing and likes their talent, offers to be their agent and later on hires the entire "Appalachian Dumpling Gang," as he dubs them. At this point, Lisa questions if this is what is best for the kids; for doing so, she is literally thrown from the room. The kids are later introduced on Krusty's television show as the Spuckler Family Singers. In the opening number, the kids sing, "I have eight teeth, going on seven teeth, I have a curvy spine / We live on landfill, and feast on roadkill, while we all drink moonshine." They conclude this number with the line, "You're better than us." At home, Homer laughs at the "dumb hillbillies." Frustrated by his condescension, Lisa says, "Dad, those kids aren't dumb. This show just perpetuates the stereotype that all yokels are hicks"—a comment that might well be a metacommentary on *The Simpsons*. Homer's view remains unchanged, however. Lisa is worried about the kids forgoing their education and tries to protect them from being exploited by Cletus, who gets caught up in the money and fame (e.g., dressing as a pimp and ordering a solid-gold hound dog). The final straw seems to be Cletus's plan to send the kids on the road as part of the No-Collar Comedy Tour. As a last resort, Lisa sends an e-mail to Brandine, who arrives by helicopter (because she is serving a tour in Iraq) and tells Cletus that she refuses to allow to children to go on the bus tour. The kids then thank Lisa for her help, and they all hug. The episode ends, interestingly, with an homage to *The Honeymooners*—a working-class icon—and with Cletus offering the line, "Baby, you're the greatest," with the theme music and a rising moon with Cletus's face on it. In short, the episode ends with a striking appropriation of a working-class image.

"Yokel Chords" is a fascinating and curious episode in many ways. Foremost, it is one of the rare depictions of Cletus and Brandine on *The Simpsons* that allows for more emotional resonance, if not identification. In short, Cletus and Brandine are humanized in this episode in ways they have not been previously. In particular, the resolution of the conflict allows Brandine to demonstrate her fortitude, as well as her loving and protective nature as a mother, which places her on par with Marge Simpson. The episode is also more critical of "white trash" images, self-consciously foregrounding a satirical critique of the stigmatypes so unquestioningly employed in many other episodes. This is done by having Lisa take a stand against the exclusion of the kids from the public school, against their treatment as "hicks" by Skinner, Chalmers, and Homer, and against their exploitation by Krusty and Cletus. All of these things make "Yokel Chords" something of an oddity in *The Simpsons* canon.

One way of understanding the oddity of the episode is to consider its writer. "Yokel Chords" was written by Michael Price, who began working on *The Simpsons* (as both a producer and a writer) in 2003, during the fifteenth season. Unlike many of the other writers for *The Simpsons*, Price grew up in South Plainfield, New Jersey, and attended Montclair State University, where he earned a BA degree in theater arts; he later attended Tulane University, where he earned a master of fine arts degree in directing for the theater.[63] This background makes Price quite different from many of his fellow writers, who were, as noted, products of the Ivy League. Again, I don't wish to overemphasize authorship, but it is remarkable that "Yokel Chords" is so uniquely different, offering viewers representations of Cletus and his family unlike nearly every other, in both earlier and later episodes, many of which are penned by the infamous graduates of Harvard.

While I believe that "Yokel Chords" is much more nuanced and less stigmatizing, it still carries reminders of more negative representations, and it is at times hard to tell what is being satirized. Examples that stand out here are the children's names, the line about eating roadkill in the song they sing, and the fact that (as Brandine reveals) Cletus is the father of only two of the kids. There is also the problematic presumption by Lisa (and by extension, I would argue, of the writer) that the kids need to experience "culture" in order to be better people. Of course, the kind of culture offered is defined almost exclusively by forms of high art, which are associated with the educated and wealthy elite. The very pragmatic question from one of the children about how education is supposed to help put food on the plate is completely ignored by Lisa. Lastly, there is Lisa's own troublesome reference to Cletus's children as hillbillies. When she is given the tutoring position, she sings, to the tune of "The Sound of Music," "The hillbilly tykes will become my tutees." Recall, however, that when Homer later refers to Cletus's kids as "dumb hillbillies," she criticizes him. This makes for some decidedly mixed messages.

In subsequent episodes of *The Simpsons*, the usual depiction of "white trash" returns. For example, in "Marge Gamer" (April 2007), after Homer accuses one of Cletus's daughters of cheating at soccer, an indignant Cletus offers this statement by way of defense: "I have sired a dumb-dumb, a mush-head, a whatsit, a dogboy, and something with a human face and fish body what we called Kevin. But my young'uns is not dirty players!" In response, Homer shouts, "I don't need a soccer lecture from a hillbilly!"[64] The episode "Apocalypse Cow" (April 2008) also features the Delroys in familiar ways. In this episode, Bart joins 4-H and befriends both a scrawny cow name Lou and a girl named Mary, who turns out to be one of Cletus's kids. To save the cow from slaughter, Bart and Lisa decide to take Lou to Mary's because she "lives on a farm." When Bart presents Mary the cow, Cletus gets excited and calls Brandine, who tells Bart that "according to the traditions of the hillfolk, by giving our daughter a cow, you've made a formal proposal of marriage." Though the wedding is planned, Marge stops it from happening. Cletus then laments that his daughter will "taste the bitter agony of being an old maid of eleven." Brandine tries to console Mary by telling her she was 13 when she married, to which Cletus responds, "Yeah, and you'd already been dee-vorced four times." One of the most disturbing images of Cletus and Brandine is offered in the recently aired "500 Keys" (May 2011). Bart, frustrated with all the "good luck" his keys have brought him, takes his oversized novelty key to the city and throws it into the woods, where it lands at Cletus's feet. Excited, Cletus shouts, "Brandine! I think we finally gots us something to cut off that umbrilical cord." The camera then shifts to reveal Brandine in a rocking chair on the porch, an umbilical cord snaking out from her skirt to the belly of a boy (clearly a few years old) idly playing paddleball. "Well then you got one more mouth to feed," Brandine replies.

One means of understanding how limiting and regressive is the representation of "white trash" on *The Simpsons* is to compare and contrast the experiences of Cletus and Brandine with another poor white character on the show, Nelson Muntz. Nelson is a regular character, one much more fully integrated into story lines and given much more of a personality. Nelson first appears in the episode "Bart the General" (February 1990) and is introduced to us as the school bully and Bart's nemesis; however, after a schoolyard battle and a truce negotiated by Marge, Bart and Nelson come to have a grudging respect for one another, and as the show progresses, he and Bart actually develop something of a friendship. Nelson has been at times depicted as having a moral code or acting with noble intentions, which is something we do not normally see with "white trash" representations. For example, in "Bart Gets Famous" (February 1994), in which Bart (quite truthfully, it turns out) claims to have been Krusty the Clown's assistant, Nelson punches him in the stomach, saying, "That's for taking credit for other people's work!" In "Bart's Girlfriend" (November 1994), when Bart tries to flaunt his relationship with Reverend Lovejoy's daughter, Jessica, Nelson punches him and says, "That's for besmirching an innocent girl's name!" In the following episode, "Lisa on Ice" (November 1994), Nelson punches Bart for his misbehavior in Mrs. Krabappel's class, saying, "This is for wasting teacher's valuable time!" From early in the series, there are also regular references to a potential romance between Lisa and Nelson. This is brought to fruition in "Lisa's Date with Density" (December 1996), in which Lisa falls for Nelson's rebellious ways and develops a crush. Though Lisa has an ulterior motive (to reform Nelson and turn him into a model student), there is a good deal of romance and emotion on display: Lisa and Nelson even share a kiss in this episode. "Lisa's Date with Density" was also the first episode to center on Nelson and to provide a backstory for his character, thus helping explain his behaviors. We learn here that Nelson's father abandoned him and his mother when he was young, thereby explaining to some degree their poverty. Although Nelson and his mother are presented in ways that might fit the "white trash" stereotype (e.g., they live in a trailer, speak in uncouth language, and have shabby clothing), we are encouraged to sympathize with their situation, which is often depicted in very emotional terms. Nelson has also been shown to have some personal, emotional relations with older female characters, such as Marge Simpson and the elementary school teacher, Edna Krabappel, who function as mother figures. In "Sleeping with the Enemy" (November 2004), for example, Nelson is adopted by Marge Simpson. In the same episode, Nelson also helps Lisa get even with the girls at school who are teasing her about her "big butt," causing her to become self-conscious about her weight. Most recently, an entire episode was devoted to the relationship between Bart and Nelson, who become best friends in "The Haw-Hawed Couple" (December 2006).

In short, the characterizations of "white trash" identity on *The Simpsons* reify existing ideologies rather than contest them. Admittedly, there is a small degree of ambiguity regarding the portrayals of Cletus and Brandine Delroy. One could read the representations of them as satirical rather than stereotypical—and one might be inclined to do so given the exaggerated nature of these images and amount of satire otherwise evident in the show. However, I think there is a significant difference in the way that "white trash" stereotypes are employed compared to others, such as those surrounding race, ethnicity, gender, or sexuality, as discussed in the preceding chapters. The greatest difference is that the stereotypes of women or homosexuals, for example, are regularly undermined or contested, both within individual episodes of *The Simpsons* and over the course of the series. This is achieved either through the inclusion of other characters, whose thoughts and behaviors contradict the usual stereotypes or, more commonly, through narrative structures that make the misperceptions leading to these stereotypes central to the plot, which allows the writers to overtly satirize them. The way that "white trash" identity is coded on *The Simpsons*, however, depends heavily upon "soothing stereotypes" of the rural poor, and these remain uncontested: there are no other poor, rural characters to balance the representation of "white trash," and Cletus and Brandine are never central to the story lines, only peripheral—even in "Yokel Chords," which centers on Lisa. The biases regarding class reflected on *The Simpsons* might best be described as a form of "dysconsciousness," which the education scholar Joyce E. King defines as "an uncritical habit of mind that justifies inequity and exploitation by accepting the existing order of things as given."[65] Conceptually, dysconsciousness offers a useful lens through which to view prejudices, whether they are related to class or race or both, as in the case of "white trash."

The Simpsons is clearly designed to elicit sympathy for and identification with the members of the Simpson family and their many struggles. This perspective is extended to many of the secondary characters as well, such as Patty and Selma Bouvier, Ned Flanders, Waylon Smithers, Seymour Skinner, Edna Krabappel, Milhouse Van Houten, and Nelson Muntz. But Cletus and Brandine Delroy are mostly excluded from this kind of treatment, and the viewer is consistently denied a means of seeing them in a sympathetic way. That we are encouraged to laugh at Cletus and Brandine and not with them might be a reflection of the writers' own middle-class or McWASP biases, as I discussed briefly earlier, but it might also simply rely upon the classism of the viewing audience—that is, upon the unspoken belief in American culture that it is unacceptable for "average" or mainstream whites (such as the Simpsons and such as the target audience) to dress, speak, and behave in ways that deviate from the "respectable," middle-class norm and thereby be branded working class or, even worse, "white trash."

Conclusion

A 20-year history of *The Simpsons* reveals some very interesting developments in the markers of class status on the show and the ways in which socioeconomic class is understood in the United States today. I stated earlier that class has been one of the least explored themes in scholarship on *The Simpsons*. Curiously, a recent paper by the economics professors Steven Horwitz and Stewart Dompe tries to engage the topic. They argue that *The Simpsons* illustrates that life has improved for the "upper-lower-middle class," citing in particular the shift "from rabbit ears to flat screen" television. The authors claim that despite the seeming lack of upward mobility, the material well-being of the Simpsons family has "nonetheless improved notably."[66] More specifically, they write,

> Even though all of Homer's various get-rich-quick schemes over the years have failed mightily, by simply maintaining his relative place, he has nonetheless become

progressively more able to provide a better life for his family as the productive power of the marketplace has delivered newer and better goods at cheaper prices, especially when calculated in terms of the labor time it takes to purchase them. The Simpsons of 2010 are just as upper-lower-middle class as they were in 1989, but they are notably richer in absolute terms.[67]

The evidence Horwitz and Dompe provide for the well-being of the Simpson family, whom they see as "very representative of the experience of both the average American family and the poorest American families over the last 40 years," rests on the fact that the Simpsons possess consumer goods such as a smartphone, a laptop computer, a digital camera, a microfridge, and a flat-screen TV.[68] This strikes me as a very odd claim. While the creators of *The Simpsons* do incorporate the gadgetry of the modern world into the show, it is more often than not another means for conveying satire. For example, in the 2008 episode "MyPods and Boomsticks," half of the narrative is given over to Lisa's desire for and fascination with MyPod products, which everyone seems to have. Among other things, the episode is satirizing the cultlike worship of Steve Jobs, the obsession with technology, and the unquestioning consumption of material goods. If one looks past the simple presence of these gadgets as "evidence" that the Simpsons are economically better off—as Horwitz and Dompe fail to do—and examines the narrative instead, one can see the satire quite well. In this episode, the writers make clear that Lisa cannot afford the toy she so covets; at the Mapple store in the mall, Lisa can only admire the MyPods, MyPhones, and MyCubes; as she tells the salesgirl, "I can't afford any of your products." When Lisa asks if she can just buy some earbuds (to give the illusion that she is part of the consumer paradise), the Mapple representative offers her fake white earbuds (called MyPhonies); however, even these cost $40, and Lisa can't afford them. The only reason Lisa gets a MyPod is because Krusty, who has money to waste, is frustrated with his and gives it to her. And when she gets a $1,200 MyBill, she has to go to Steve Mobs to beg that the debt be forgiven. The satire is even more evident in this episode with Bart's antics at the mall. Although Bart is pulling yet another prank, he actually articulates what seems to be the writers' view of Apple and Jobs. Bart takes control of the voice portion of a video being shown in the store and featuring Steve Mobs; pretending to be Mobs, Bart says, "You're all losers. You think you're cool because you buy a $500 phone with a picture of a fruit on it? Well, guess what? They cost eight bucks to make and I pee on every one. I have made a fortune off you chumps."[69]

The mass media have long encouraged overconsumption, particularly among those who aspired to live a life of greater comfort and luxury than they could actually afford. With the increased availability of easy credit, many Americans were actually able to do so for quite a while. And they sought to emulate the wealthy, who were and still are depicted within media not as rich but as simply "middle class." The norm of what constitutes average has been so skewed that people have come to think of the upper class as not all that different from "average" folk and their lifestyles somehow attainable. This is the kind of thinking that is regularly satirized on *The Simpsons*. Yes, Homer is a buffoon, one who is repeatedly seduced by the cultural messages received through advertising. The "joke" in many episodes of *The Simpsons* is a reminder that the pursuit of the better life via material goods is an illusion. The writers satirize the absurd promises of advertising—and to a large degree, the increasingly absurd myth of the American dream. This was part of the sympathetic approach taken to the working class; conversely, it was at the root of the critique levied against the capitalist class, in the form of Mr. Burns, when the series started. Mr. Burns is now deeply ingrained in the cultural imagination as the embodiment of rapacious capitalism, and he makes for an easy target: his excesses are absurd and easy to satirize. My concern in this chapter has been less with that strategy than with the ways in which the struggle of the working class is minimized in favor of a middle-class ethos. Overall, the desire, if not the need, to elevate the Simpsons to a level approximating the viewership of the show is very evident. As *The Simpsons* rose in popularity and notoriety, the Simpsons' class identity and the show's class consciousness began to shift. Once *The Simpsons* was a firmly established part of the media landscape and American popular culture, it could no longer mine its working-class agenda in quite the same way, nor articulate its critiques of capital so baldly. As I have tried to demonstrate, images of "white trash" are often used to offset the working-class identity of the Simpsons. The result is a show less aligned with a working-class perspective than when it began and far more likely to replicate the "norm" of middle-class identity found in so many other media products. In "The Geography of the Class Culture War," Lisa R. Pruitt makes the provocative claim that "social progressives reserve their greatest contempt—and increasingly also their ire—for whites in rural America, the vast majority of whom are working class."[70] I'm not convinced this is necessarily true in general, but it is certainly true of the political operatives Pruitt discusses in her essay, and it may well be true for many of the writers for *The Simpsons*, who are obviously progressive on a host of social issues (related to sex, race, gender, sexuality, and religion) but who appear to be—like most Americans—seduced by middle-class mythology; the consequence is that they become complicit in the replication of a pernicious character type known as "white trash."

6

"Gabbin' about God": Religiosity and Secularity on *The Simpsons*

Many people [in America] remain convinced of God's existence but realize increasingly that the reality of their world is secular. Thus, they are constantly coming to terms with this secularity—and suffering the pangs of adjustment associated with acquiring any new status.

—*Robert Wuthnow*[1]

Religion is undeniably at the root of some of the most contentious American culture war battles over the past three decades, and no subject appears to have elicited more commentary from academics and intellectuals across the political spectrum than religion. The past decade alone has seen an incredible outpouring of books, published by both mainstream and academic presses, that closely—and often polemically—examine some aspect of religion in American culture. Scholars working in a variety of fields have recently offered important studies of religion's place in American society, both past and present, and have discussed an array of topics: for example, the historical roots of religion and secular thought in the United States; the faith(s) of the founding fathers and the role this played in developing a new nation; the educational struggle over "intelligent design" and Darwinian evolutionary theory; the status of religious fundamentalism, secularism, and atheism; the bases of "morality" and values; and contemporary political debates over religious freedom and equality.[2] The literature on religion and popular culture, mass media, and television is equally substantial, and the scholarship in these areas has grown significantly in the past 20 years, covering a great diversity of topics, including the rise of Christian radio and the advent of television evangelism; representations of Jewish, Christian, and Muslim faiths in film and television; the framing of religiosity in television news; the development of religious (particularly Christian) media; and the growth of the Christian "lifestyle" industry.[3] Interestingly, much of this material is written from a theological or faith-based perspective, often by academics working in religion departments, and this literature is commonly geared toward two aims: condemning the products of a presumably secularized consumer culture for their antireligious biases or finding ways to redeem these commercial products for the faith, especially for Christianity.[4] Of course, a substantial amount of this literature has been written from a different (and likely more secular) perspective by scholars working in fields such as sociology, history, political science, media studies, and cultural studies.[5]

Given the prominence, if not the popularity, of religion in American culture, it is perhaps not surprising to find religion and questions of faith as such prominent elements of *The Simpsons*: indeed, the highly contentious issues related to these themes are featured in episodes on a regular basis, either centrally or tangentially. It is worthwhile, therefore, to take a closer look at *The Simpsons'* engagement with these topics. As Bruce Forbes and Jeffrey Mahan explain in *Religion and Popular Culture in America* (2005), the interactions between the realms of religion and popular culture have generally been approached in four ways: religion in popular culture, popular culture in religion, popular culture as religion, and religion as popular culture.[6] As might be expected, it is the first approach that I take here. Although many have noted that *The Simpsons* became a viewing experience verging on the "religious" for its most avid fans, especially in its earliest seasons, and although one could certainly analyze *The Simpsons* through this lens—examining the worship of, devotion to, or reverence for the show, as evidenced in ritualized viewing habits or the consumption of *Simpsons* artifacts—that is not a part of my project.[7] Instead, I am interested in examining the representations of religion, spirituality, and secularism on *The Simpsons*. Of course, a truly comprehensive treatment of such themes on *The Simpsons* would require a book-length study itself; my treatment here will be more selective and focused primarily on Christianity rather than the multiplicity of faiths on display in the show, which was briefly discussed in chapter 2, with regard to Protestantism, Judaism, Hinduism, and Islam. The central concern of this chapter is the Judeo-Christian tradition that informs *The Simpsons* and the various ways in which this tradition is understood, represented, and commented upon within the show, once again in relation to the show's satirical aims.

Not surprisingly, no topic on *The Simpsons* has been more widely discussed than religion, and discussions of faith, spirituality, and attendant issues have long been a part of the written commentary on *The Simpsons*. This is evident in a variety of newspaper articles, in numerous scholarly journal articles, in select essay collections on *The Simpsons* and on popular culture more generally, and in the numerous "academic papers" posted on *The Simpsons Archive*.[8] The most sustained treatments of religious themes, however, are found in Mark Pinsky's *The Gospel According to "The Simpsons": The Spiritual Life of the World's Most Animated Family* (2001), and Jamey Heit's *The Springfield Reformation: "The Simpsons," Christianity, and American Culture* (2008). By and large, the shorter articles and essays primarily note that religion and spirituality are regular topics on *The Simpsons*, a fact that marks the show as quite different from most other television programs, which have assiduously avoided such "controversial" topics. Pinsky and Heit, however, are very clear about their claims regarding *The Simpsons*: for them, the show does more than merely reflect that religious life is an integral part of the American experience; it openly supports and to a large extent actively promotes a Christian worldview. To be fair, both Pinsky and Heit acknowledge that *The Simpsons* routinely critiques many aspects of Christianity and regularly satirizes religious extremism, but neither author believes such criticism is a means of devaluing Christianity's role in society; indeed, each sees this as a form of "responsible criticism" of Christianity. As Heit states it, *The Simpsons* is ultimately "helping Christianity retain its cultural relevance."[9] What neither Pinsky nor Heit asks, however, is what seems a rather obvious question: Why does *The Simpsons* so regularly mock religion in general and Christianity in particular? In exploring this question, I will again read episodes of *The Simpsons* in relation to issues present in the cultural context, which in this case means the rise of the Religious Right in the 1980s and the growing strength of religious fundamentalism throughout the 1990s and into the new millennium.

In general, I concur with the view that *The Simpsons* is, overall, a very "spiritual" show; however, this does not necessarily make it a "religious" program, a distinction I will elaborate upon in the remainder of this chapter.[10] Although the Simpson family is associated by tradition with Christianity and Protestantism, this is modified in significant ways over the run of the show. Marge and Lisa, who are inevitably the moral centers of the show, sometimes behave in accordance with Judeo-Christian religious beliefs; however, more often than not, they both operate from a philosophical and secularized perspective. And although one can find examples of what appear to be "Christian" beliefs on the show, one must acknowledge that these examples can just as easily be seen as humanist, since the more beneficent tenets of New Testament Christianity—for example, compassion, brotherhood, and love—run parallel to those of secular humanism. Of course, *humanist* and *humanism* are themselves highly contested terms with lengthy and varying histories, and a full discussion of them is beyond the scope of this chapter. For the sake of clarity, I will simply note that I understand secular humanism as an ethical, scientific, and philosophical outlook that rejects theistic and supernatural beliefs in favor of reason, objectivity, and scientific inquiry and that is dedicated to democracy, equality, social justice, human rights, and the overall improvement of the human condition.[11] I do not presume to speak for Matt Groening or for the various writers and producers of *The Simpsons* regarding their personal religious or spiritual beliefs. In general, they have been reluctant to express their own beliefs, although many of them have stated that they are Jewish, and some have admitted in interviews to being former Catholics or atheists. Steve Tompkins, who was a writer for *The Simpsons* for three seasons and who worked as a coproducer alongside George Meyer and Mike Scully, has been most overt about such affiliations: he claims that *The Simpsons'* writers were "atheist Jews or atheist Christians" and that during his tenure with the show, only two writers were "churchgoing Christians."[12]

Regardless of the individual faiths of those involved in the creation of the show, there is a predominant worldview on display in *The Simpsons*, and this is generally in accord with the worldly, progressive, and left-leaning position the show takes on many issues, as discussed in the previous chapters. One quality that has kept *The Simpsons* so successful is its chameleon-like ability to blur boundaries, and its treatment of religion and spirituality is an excellent example. If one looks carefully at *The Simpsons*, one can see that alongside religion lie a basic faith in humankind and a moral and ethical stance that is more often than not based in reason and rationality rather than religious doctrine. Though I understand how the subtlety of the humor on *The Simpsons* can prod the believer into seeing some aspect of his or her faith reflected, if not validated, I am less inclined to see the show redeeming Christianity as a faith system or aiming to help bring it back to "purer" origins. Indeed, I believe *The Simpsons* aims to lessen the authority of Christianity through its satirical attacks upon institutional religion and to promote a more ecumenical, individual, and secularized worldview. The satirical critiques of the excesses of fundamentalist belief are the most obvious means of accomplishing this goal, but the writers have less obvious ways of offering their satire as well: namely, by exposing religious hypocrisy, undermining belief in the supernatural, and mocking the disconnect between religion and modern, scientific culture. Reading *The Simpsons* as satire, I see the religious critique offered by the show working not to shore up or repair a weakened faith system but to rigorously question its authority and power in the culture.

Culture Wars and American Religiosity

The conflict between religiosity and secularity that is so regularly displayed and reflected upon in episodes of *The Simpsons* is perhaps the most entrenched and intractable element of America's ongoing culture war. As James Hunter succinctly states, "[T]he culture war that has unfolded over the last several decades has been a proxy for the conflict between the sacred and the secular."[13] Of course, the debate between religious and secular forces is very old, effectively predating the establishment of the nation itself, and its intensity waxed and waned throughout the eighteenth and nineteenth centuries. The debate was given a renewed life, however, in the second half of the twentieth century, partly because of the advent of television, which provided a new and powerful means by which both religious and secular groups could disseminate messages, but primarily because of the social and political upheavals of the late 1950s and 1960s. In general, since the end of the Second World War, evangelicals and religious fundamentalists have been concerned about many "secularizing" trends in the United States—for example, racial integration, affirmative action, social welfare, prayer in schools, evolutionary theory, voluntary euthanasia, abortion, feminism, and gay rights—that have, in their view, moved the nation further toward pluralistic and relativistic perspectives. Over the past 40 years in the United States, there has been a slow but steady movement away from traditional organized religions and toward a variety of more secular perspectives and activities. This trend is borne out by studies of religious affiliation and belief, such as the 2001 American Religious Identification Survey, conducted by the Graduate Center of the City University of New York, and the 2008 US Religious Landscape Survey, conducted by the Pew Forum on Religion and Public Life, both of which confirm that the United States is on the verge of becoming a minority Protestant country. The number of Americans who report that they are members of Protestant churches now stands at just 51.3 percent.[14] Interestingly, individuals who are not affiliated with any particular religion now make up about one-sixth (16.1 percent) of the adult population and thus comprise the fourth-largest "religious" tradition in the country. Although the United States is still approximately 78 percent Christian, more than one-quarter of American adults (28 percent) have left the faith in which they were raised in favor of another religion or no religion at all, and roughly one in four Americans aged 18–29 say they are not currently affiliated with any particular religion.[15] It is, of course, these very kinds of "secularizing" trends that initially inspired—and in many ways, continue to fuel—the culture wars of the post–civil rights era. Some of the emphasis in these cultural debates has been on the way that certain values or belief systems are reflected in or excluded from the mainstream media, including television. In a now-famous study of the representation of religion and spirituality on American network television in the early 1990s, Thomas Skill and his colleagues determined that religion was "a rather invisible institution" in prime-time television.[16] In a more recent study, the researcher Scott Clarke showed that prime-time characters were more than twice as likely as the general public to belong to a religion other than Christianity or to embrace a more individualized "spirituality."[17] Although Clarke's study makes clear that religion remains "rather invisible" on prime-time network television today, it also points to the fact that Christianity continues to be, by default, a "normative" religion on television, whereas non-Christian religions are often overtly identified. *The Simpsons* is unique in that both Christian and non-Christian religion, as well as forms of secular spirituality, are not only visible but consciously foregrounded as important aspects of the geography of Springfield, the daily lives of many of the show's characters, and the plots of innumerable episodes.

That religion figures so prominently in *The Simpsons* is not surprising when one considers the context in which the show developed. Although *The Simpsons* debuted as a television series in 1990, the Simpson family was created by Matt Groening in 1985 and first offered to viewers (as part of Fox's *Tracey Ullman Show*) in 1987. Hence, *The Simpsons* appeared in the midst of the Reagan-Bush era, a time during which there was a revival and intensification of evangelical and fundamentalist religiosity in the United States. Among other things, the 1970s and 1980s were witness to the rise of the Religious Right (sometimes called the Christian Right) and the advent of the culture wars, which were often, although not exclusively, divided by the differing positions taken by religious and secular camps on a variety of "moral" and legal issues. A powerful evangelical tradition was, of course, in place in the United States in the earliest decades of the twentieth century, making use of radio to reach new audiences, and this continued well into the mid-century, largely via the new medium of television, but this tradition historically operated largely outside of the political sphere.[18] The development of a more politically engaged evangelism began with the responses of certain fundamentalist leaders, such as Pat Robertson and Jerry Falwell, to the Supreme Court rulings in *Engel v. Vitale* (1962) and *Abington School District v. Schempp* (1963), decisions that banned prayer and Bible reading from public schools. However, the criticism from religious fundamentalists remained rather small-scale throughout the 1960s; as George Marsden points out, even as late as the early 1970s, "fundamentalism was essentially a separatist and sectarian movement on the fringes of American church life and society."[19] This began to change, however, in the wake of the Supreme Court's decision in *Roe v. Wade* (1973), and it intensified in each of the subsequent decades. Collectively, the Supreme Court rulings, in addition to other secularizing trends in the culture, provided the impetus for the formation of Religious Right groups such as the Catholic League (1973), Focus on the Family (1977), the American Family Association (1977), the Moral Majority (1979), the Traditional Values Coalition (1980), the Freedom Council (1981), the Family Research Council (1983), and the Christian Coalition (1990); these organizations in turn provided for the rise to national prominence of leaders such as Jerry Falwell, Pat Robertson, James Dobson, Don Wildmon, Louis Sheldon, Gary Bauer, Ralph Reed, and William Donohue, who increasingly turned their attention to national politics.[20]

The social and political influence of Religious Right leaders and organizations in the 1970s and 1980s, particularly during the Reagan-Bush era, marked a significant shift in American culture. During this same time period, Matt Groening was still struggling with his *Life in Hell* comic, and many of the writers for *The Simpsons* were still honing their skills writing for such programs as *Late Night with David Letterman*, *Not Necessarily the News*, and *Saturday Night Live*. By the late 1980s, when the work of turning *The Simpsons* into a series was begun, the creators of the show were working in a context in which evangelical and fundamentalist religiosity was a dominant part of the cultural and political landscape of the United States. As George Marsden notes, for the pious, "secular humanism" came to be the conceptual framework for understanding the convergence of the many secularizing trends and thus "code for the enemy forces in the dichotomized world of the culture wars."[21] The tenor of this cultural conflict in the early 1990s was perhaps best epitomized by Patrick Buchanan's fiery (and bombastic) statement at the Republican National Convention in 1992. "There is a religious war going on in this country," Buchanan said, "a cultural war as critical to the kind of nation we shall be as the Cold War itself, for this war is for the soul of America."[22]

It was inevitable that *The Simpsons* would become engaged in this "war," partly because of its status as a social satire and partly because of the condemnation it almost immediately received from conservative political and religious quarters after its debut in the spring of 1990. As noted in chapter 3, for example, the former US secretary of education William Bennett—who in the early 1990s published books such as *The De-Valuing of America: The Fight for Our Culture and Our Children* (1992) and *The Book of Virtues: A Treasury of Great Moral Stories* (1993)—once chastised the young residents of a drug rehab facility he was visiting for watching *The Simpsons*, claiming that doing so would not help them reform their lives.[23] Regardless of the early perceptions of *The Simpsons* as "immoral," "dysfunctional," and even "blasphemous," the show continued to offer a regular presentation of religious thought and practice. In doing so, *The Simpsons* was—and still is—intervening in the cultural conversation taking place between secular and religious forces in the United States, offering a satirical critique of the conservative challenge to the spread of secularism in American culture. Although *The Simpsons* does not explicitly reference Religious Right leaders or organizations, their collective influence is reflected in the show in numerous ways, including the characterization of religious believers, such as Reverend Lovejoy and Ned Flanders, and the framing of many episodes around the hot-button "moral" issues that have been politicized by those on either side of the culture war debates. As E. J. Dionne explains in *Souled Out: Reclaiming Faith and Politics after the Religious Right* (2008), the culture wars have continued with such intensity in part because we have underestimated the extent to which politics has invaded our discussion of religion and morality. The core divisions among religious Americans, Dionne argues, are no longer defined by theological issues—for example, the Virgin Birth, the Eucharist, the nature of the Trinity—but by social issues such as abortion and gay marriage.[24] These and many other controversial issues make their way into the scripts of *The Simpsons*, in both large and small ways, and they are often positioned within the plotlines so that they directly engage with and question, if not censure, religious traditions and dogma. In short, provocative cultural issues are brought into the world of *The Simpsons*—and into the homes of the show's viewers—for satirical purposes: namely, to showcase and satirize the hypocrisy, bigotry, and narrow-mindedness of institutional Christianity and to censure the zealotry of religious fundamentalism.

The Simpsons and Christianity

Given its regular presentation of prayer, church attendance, and other religious activities, in addition to its engagement with moral and theological issues, it is not surprising that some have claimed *The Simpsons* to be a "Christian" show. In its earliest seasons, *The Simpsons* did indeed appear to be aligned with mainstream Protestantism, and it generally reflected the mores and behaviors typical of those following the Judeo-Christian tradition, despite the antics of Bart Simpson. For example, in the second-season episode "Homer vs. Lisa and the 8th Commandment," we are presented with a story that explicitly links morality and religion. The religious theme is put in place in the opening scene, a dream sequence, in which we see Homer (here called "Homer the Thief") at the base of Mount Sinai, talking with his friends (one a "carver of graven images," the other an "adulterer") just before Moses appears and proceeds to read the Ten Commandments. Homer is awakened from his dream by the sounds of his neighbor Ned Flanders chasing off a cable television installer who has offered him an illegal hookup. As one might expect, Homer makes the decision to get an illegal cable connection, which upsets both Marge and Lisa, although to different degrees. In Sunday school the following week, Lisa listens to a lecture on the Ten Commandments; when the teacher gets to "Thou Shalt Not Steal," Lisa has a vision of her family plunging into a fiery hell, joined by the Devil himself, and she runs screaming from the room. Thereafter, Lisa is concerned about the consequences of violating the eighth commandment. Homer willfully ignores her questions, while Marge is distracted by the programming on the new "women's network," so Lisa turns to Reverend Lovejoy for assistance. Lovejoy recommends that she quietly protest by refusing to watch the "offending cable" and thus set an example for her family. After Marge witnesses the cable installer pick a door lock and casually let himself into the Simpson home, she decides there are too many risks involved in having the illegal cable hookup and joins Lisa in protest. In the final scenes, we see Lisa and Marge on the front lawn while Homer and a large group of friends and coworkers are inside watching the heavily hyped heavyweight boxing match of the year. When two police officers arrive and inquire about Homer's cable access, Homer fears that he will be arrested; however, they assure him that they only came to watch the fight. In a prefight interview, we see boxer Drederick Tatum discuss his time in prison; Homer, already nervous about his crime, imagines himself in a similar position, behind bars and cut off from his family. With a final forlorn glance out the window at Lisa and Marge, Homer decides to cut the cable connection.

In her essay "Homer Erectus: Homer Simpson as Everyman...and Every Woman," Valerie Chow briefly discusses "Homer vs. Lisa and the 8th Commandment," yet she makes no mention of religion at all, reading the episode merely as a conflict between Homer's desire to selfishly consume and his responsibilities as a husband and father. In short, Chow offers a rather secular reading of the episode, seeing Lisa's concerns as simply a question about "the ethics of stealing cable" and Homer's decision to disconnect the cable driven by "the thought that he could be jailed for his theft and barred from his family."[25] Mark Pinsky, on the other hand, views "Homer vs. Lisa and the 8th Commandment" as "an exquisitely crafted, twenty-two-minute sermon" and a lesson in morality.[26] My own take on this episode is somewhere in between these two extremes. While it is clear that the moral position adopted by Lisa derives directly from Judeo-Christian religious doctrine, it is also clear that Marge's change of heart and Homer's final decision do not. Neither is motivated by any sense of the immorality of stealing; Marge is motivated out of fear for her family's safety and Homer by the potential consequences of violating the secular law and the ramifications this has for his family life.

Interestingly, stealing is the only "moral" issue explicitly related to religion in any of the episodes from the first two seasons. As theft is easy to condemn from a religious or a secular perspective, it was not a key element of the culture wars in the 1980s and 1990s. What has been a key element in the battles between religious and secular forces is "family values"—or, in this case, the value of fidelity in marriage. But the two episodes of *The Simpsons* that openly explore this theme in the first season—"Life on the Fast Lane" and "Homer's Night Out," which I discussed in relation to feminism in chapter 3—make no mention of religion at all. This fact, however, does not prevent some from discussing the episodes as if they did. Mark Pinsky, for example, in a section of his book focused on adultery, discusses these and two later episodes dealing with the same theme ("Colonel Homer," from season 3, and "The Last Temptation of Homer," from season 5) and concludes that in each of these stories of temptation, "the sanctity of the marriage vow is tested fundamentally—and preserved. Another victory for traditional family values."[27] Curiously, Pinsky does not discuss in this section another season 2 episode that depicts marriage troubles for Marge and Homer and that explicitly links "family values" to religion: "The War of the Simpsons." This episode revolves around Marge's attempts to repair some of the problems in her relationship with Homer by attending Reverend Lovejoy's weekend marriage retreat. Like many similar retreats offered by religious organizations throughout the United States, Lovejoy's relies upon the belief that religion itself is a panacea for broken marriages and fractured families. Such a belief does not go unchallenged in the irony-laden world of *The Simpsons*, however, and in this case, the challenge comes through Reverend Lovejoy's own words and actions. At one point, he tells Marge, "This is the first instance where I've told one partner that they were one hundred percent right. But it's all his fault. I'm willing to put that on a certificate you can frame." Marge and Homer reconcile, as they invariably do, but this is not because of anything done by Lovejoy or the religious institution he represents; indeed, Lovejoy's advice that Marge leave Homer would lead to disunion rather than union, which would be contrary to the faith in "traditional family values" and is perhaps why Pinsky avoids discussing this episode.

Although I can see how one might want to label *The Simpsons* as "Christian," it would be much more accurate to describe the worldview of *The Simpsons* as Judaic: while the generic Protestantism of Springfield does derive from a Judeo-Christian tradition, it is the Old Testament that is most frequently referred to, quoted, parodied, and satirized on the show. As Jamey Heit accurately notes, "A general tendency within Springfield is to focus heavily on the issues of prohibition, judgment, and God's punishment that pervade the Old Testament."[28] I would argue that this is a general tendency among the writers for *The Simpsons* (many of whom are Jewish, former Catholics, or atheists), who are highlighting and satirizing the continued emphasis on God's wrath in the rhetoric of Christian fundamentalists today. This focus is evident in many episodes that feature religion as either a central theme or a passing reference, as well as in the worldview of many of the show's characters. Homer, of course, views his religion simplistically, and his God is the vengeful God (the Yahweh) of the Old Testament. God has been portrayed on *The Simpsons* many times but always in the form of a white-haired and bearded man dressed in flowing white robes. This image, rooted perhaps in the depiction of God in Michelangelo's *The Creation of Adam* and popularized in many subsequent artworks, remains quite common in the West and is easily recognizable for many viewers of *The Simpsons*. As many have noted, God is treated rather respectfully on the show—for example, his face is never shown, and he is depicted as having five fingers on each hand rather than four. But it is not so much God himself as it is people's understanding of what God can or cannot do for humankind—that is, the ways in which he does or does not intervene in people's daily lives—that is the object of the show's satire.

A fine example of this perspective is *The Simpsons'* take on prayer—particularly the contrasting representations of the (in)efficacy of prayer for Reverend Lovejoy and Ned Flanders. Notably, some of the most satirical examples of the futility of prayer are associated with Reverend Lovejoy, whose words and actions help illuminate the secular worldview that underlies *The Simpsons*. For example, in the episode "She of Little Faith" (December 2001), after Homer inadvertently destroys the First Church of Springfield, Lovejoy convenes the church council to assess the damage. "Fixing all that damage is going to be very expensive," Marge says. "Yes," Lovejoy responds, "barring some sort of miracle," at which point he looks heavenward and expectantly waits a few beats. When nothing happens, he turns back and says, with a hint of resentment, "All right, we'll help ourselves...yet again." In stark contrast, we see that Ned Flanders's prayers, no matter how trivial, are answered immediately. In "A Star Is Burns" (March 1995), Ned is filming a scene from Exodus for the Springfield Film Festival, using his son Todd to replicate the scene in which Moses's mother places her baby in a basket in the river. Here, a sudden strong current grabs the basket and threatens to send it far downriver. Ned hastily prays, "Flanders to God, Flanders to God, get off your cloud and save my Todd." Immediately, lightning strikes a tree and a branch falls into the river to block the path of the basket. "Thanks, God," Ned says. Another example appears in the episode "Team Homer" (January 1996), in which Ned's bowling team, the Holy Rollers, plays Homer's team, the Pin Pals. Here we see Homer taunt and distract Ned, causing him to miss a strike by one pin. Homer then mocks Ned, saying, "God-boy couldn't get a strike." In response, Ned turns his eyes skyward and simply says, "It's me, Ned," and with that the last pin falls. In *The Springfield Reformation*, Jamey Heit concedes that such scenes are "contrived," but he disregards any satirical intent by claiming that these examples suggest "that prayer, when appropriately presented, has efficacy."[29] I interpret the many examples of God immediately responding to Ned's prayers as moments of absurdity on the show and thus candidates for satire, not sincerity. The highly exaggerated way in which Flanders's faith is portrayed is an indication that the writers are satirizing the presumption that, through prayer, one has the power to effect immediate change in one's physical environment.

To fully understand how the representation of prayer is satirical, it is important to again consider the context in which it arises. Many of the religious leaders prominent in the 1990s claimed to communicate directly with God and that their prayers could, among other things, avert or even cause a variety of natural disasters. Pat Robertson, for example, claimed in 1995 that his prayers to God helped steer Hurricane Felix away from coastal Virginia (which happens to be where his Christian Broadcasting Network is headquartered).[30] In due form, the writers of *The Simpsons* incorporated such cultural elements for satirical ends. Only a year after Robertson's claims, *The Simpsons* premiered an episode entitled "Hurricane Neddy" (December 1996) in which Ned Flanders's house is destroyed by a hurricane and Ned momentarily questions his faith in God. "Hurricane Neddy" is quite revealing about how both faith and prayer are dealt with on *The Simpsons*. Prior to the storm, the Simpson family gathers in the cellar of their home, where Marge prays to God to spare their house. After the storm passes, they emerge to find their house intact. Pleased, Marge says, "It just goes to show you that everything will work out if you have faith." Clearly, however, that is not the case, as Flanders's house has been utterly destroyed. Ned, who sees himself as a devout Christian, assumes that he is being punished by God, although he cannot fathom why—as he notes, he does "everything the Bible says, even the stuff that contradicts the other stuff." Such contradictions are what the writers of *The Simpson* latch on to in order to satirize religiosity. In this and other episodes, it is clear that they are intending to mock a number of beliefs, including the idea that the "reverent" have some exclusive access to God; the belief that God would, at their behest, micromanage the lives of individuals; and the notion that the "faithful" would be treated in some preferential way. "Hurricane Neddy" also underscores the fact that even Ned Flanders, the show's most pious Christian, is beholden to a concept of God that derives mainly from the Old Testament—that God is wrathful and inscrutably punishes human beings.

The most significant difference between the Old and New Testament understandings of God (and thus between Judaism and Christianity) of course rests upon the figure of Jesus Christ. However, Jesus has rarely and only briefly been portrayed on *The Simpsons*. Indeed, Jesus was not represented in cartoon form on *The Simpsons* until 1999, in an episode entitled "Simpsons Bible Stories" (April 1999), and this brief appearance was only in the context of a dream sequence. In one segment of the episode, Homer imagines himself as King Solomon, before whom is brought the case of "Jesus Christ vs. Checker Chariot"; as the theme music of *The People's Court* plays, we see the "defendants" enter, Jesus wearing a suit and a neck brace. Jesus appeared more recently, but just as briefly, in the episode "The Father, the Son, and the Holy Guest Star" (May 2005), as part of a scene in which Marge imagines the differences between Protestant and Catholic heaven. Marge pictures Protestant heaven as a WASP (i.e., McWASP)[31] environment, where the people dress in pastel colors, play croquet, and speak with an "upper-crust" accent; Catholic heaven, on the other hand, is ethnically diverse and filled with people drinking, dancing, and fighting. When Marge asks about Jesus, one of the preppies tells her that "he's gone native" and the scene cuts back to Catholic heaven, where we see Bart and Homer tossing a laughing Jesus on a blanket. Just how blasphemous or offensive this depiction of Jesus might be for some viewers is open to debate, although it seems fair to say that the image was not borne of piety or reverence. In short, Jesus does not figure into plotlines on *The Simpsons* in the way that God (Yahweh) often does, and Jesus himself is rarely portrayed on the show.[32] Jesus's name is regularly mentioned in the show, although this is not done in a theistic sense; his name is usually offered as an allusion, as part of a quasi-blasphemous statement, or for parodic or satiric effect. One example of the parodic use of Jesus's name is found in the episode "Homer's Barbershop Quartet" (September 1993), in which Homer claims that his group, the B-Sharps, is "bigger than Jesus," alluding to John Lennon's infamous claim about the Beatles. An example of the satiric use of Jesus's name is offered in the aforementioned "Team Homer," in which we see Bart and Milhouse play the "fold-in" game in an issue of *MAD* magazine; this requires them to first guess the answer to the question posed: "What higher power do TV evangelists worship?" "I'll say God," Bart offers. "I'll say Jesus," Milhouse replies. Once folded, the page reveals the answer: the Almighty Dollar.

The view of God that predominates on *The Simpsons* can be seen quite well in "Homer the Heretic," which first aired in October 1992 and which is perhaps the most widely analyzed and commented upon episode of *The Simpsons*. One freezing cold Sunday morning, Homer makes the decision to skip church. While his family and neighbors suffer the cold (the heat in the church is not working), warmed only by the fire-and-brimstone sermon delivered by Reverend Lovejoy, Homer cranks up the heat at home and entertains himself with a variety of self-indulgent pleasures. When Marge and the kids return home, cold, weary, and frustrated, Homer announces that he has had the best day of his life and that he is "never going back to church again." For Marge, this is equivalent to giving up on his faith, and she is concerned about the impact on Bart and Lisa. Homer uses the church's own double-talk to rationalize his choice: "What's the big deal about going to some building every Sunday? I mean, isn't God everywhere?" he asks. Such sentiments are shared by many people today, even those who still consider themselves "religious" as opposed to "spiritual," as made clear in studies of religious belief and affiliation, such as the American Religious Identification Survey and the US Religious Landscape Survey, which I discussed previously.[33] Of course, these same sentiments (as well as the overall trend away from institutional religion in the 1970s and 1980s) are what fueled the rise of the Religious Right, which by 1992, when "Homer the Heretic" appeared, had secured itself a prominent and powerful place in American culture. Interestingly, God himself appears to share Homer's belief about worship. In what many read as a dream but what Homer later calls a "vision," God and Homer meet and discuss Homer's aversion to church. God at first appears in his wrathful guise: "Thou hast forsaken my church!" he thunders, tearing the roof off the Simpson's house. "I'm not a bad guy," Homer says to him. "I work hard and I love my kids. So why should I spend half my Sunday hearing about how I'm going to hell?" "Hmmm, you've got a point there," God replies, settling down beside Homer. God admits that he would sometimes rather be watching football and that Lovejoy's sermons are tedious and boring. God agrees to allow Homer to worship in his own way and then departs, saying, "Now, if you'll excuse me, I have to appear on a tortilla in Mexico," clearly another satiric jab at Catholicism and those who believe in such "miracles."

Word spreads of Homer's decision, and soon nearly everyone in town is trying to convince Homer to return to the church. Marge, who is strongly positioned as a faithful Christian in this episode, labels Homer's actions "wicked" and flatly tells him, "Don't make me choose between my man and my God, because you just can't win." At Marge's request, Reverend Lovejoy makes a visit to try to persuade Homer to give church another chance, but he remains unmoved. The last to try is Ned Flanders, whose actions are powerfully criticized in a short, satirical sequence. Ned and his family first appear at the Simpsons' front door, where Ned tells Homer, "Neighbor, I heard about your heresy and we've made it our mission to win you back to the flock." To show Homer that Christianity can be "fun," the Flanders family begins to sing a song about Noah and the Ark ("God said to Noah, there's going to be a floody, floody"); Homer simply slams the door shut on them. In the next scene, we see Homer at work; the phone rings, he picks it up, and we hear the Flanders family singing the second verse. Lastly, we see Homer driving his car; Ned and his family pull alongside Homer and signal him to roll down his window, at which point they sing the third verse. "Leave me alone," Homer says and speeds up to get away. At this point, the tone of the scene changes. "Dad," Todd says, "the heathen's getting away." "I see him, son," Ned says, narrowing his eyes, and with a determined look, he pushes down on the gas pedal and engages in a high-speed chase. What follows is a humorous parody of the car chases so common to television police shows, but, more importantly, it is also a strongly satirical critique of the missionary zeal of fundamentalist Christians. Homer, desperate to get away, sees an opportunity at a railroad crossing and so accelerates his car to cross just in advance of the approaching train. Surprisingly, Ned also accelerates his car rather than stopping, despite the fact that the train is now blocking the road; as in many Hollywood films, however, Ned's car safely leaps though an empty gap and the pursuit continues. Given the wide range of viewing positions, it is conceivable that someone could interpret this moment an act of "divine intervention." But to do so, one again has to ignore the markers of satire. The scene is highly exaggerated, bordering on the absurd, which makes it clear that we are in the realm of satire. Considering the Flanders family's earlier harassment of Homer and the casting of him as a "heathen," not to mention the generally satirical aims of *The Simpsons*, this scene is most appropriately read as a condemnation of zealotry. That the otherwise intelligent and caring Ned Flanders would risk the lives of his family in order to "save" the "heathen" soul is somewhat surprising, given that Flanders is normally more mild-mannered. Ned's behavior is a clear and representative example of the zealot's blind faith, which the writer is aiming to satirize. It is worth noting at this point that "Homer the Heretic" was written by George Meyer, an avowed atheist who was raised in a strict Catholic home.[34] As a large body of scholarship demonstrates, authorial intent clearly does not dictate meaning, as audiences can and do decode texts in a multiplicity of ways; however, it would be remiss to ignore intentionality in a discussion of satire and to simply disregard the way in which Meyer's views help shape the satirical attack on religiosity in this episode.

Remarkably, *none* of the commentary on "Homer the Heretic" includes a discussion of the car-chase scene; what most commentators focus on instead is Ned's later efforts to save Homer in a physical sense, after Homer inadvertently sets his house on fire. Ned is the first to respond to the fire, and he does "the Christian thing" by entering the house, risking his own life, and dragging Homer to safety. Shortly thereafter, the volunteer fire department, which includes Krusty and Apu, arrives to put out the fire. As they do so, Homer and Lisa stand watching. "Truly, this was an act of God," Lisa says, still invested, like Homer, in the concept of a vengeful God. At this point, the flames from the roof leap over to Flanders's rooftop. "Hey, wait a minute," Homer says, "Flanders is a regular Charlie Church, and God didn't save his house." With that, a dark cloud appears above Flanders's house and, to the strains of a pipe organ, releases rain to douse the fire, after which a rainbow appears. "D'oh!" Homer exclaims. As with the scenes discussed earlier involving prayer, we once again have a moment that is open to multiple interpretations, highly dependent on the viewer's social position, experiences, and beliefs. One can see how a religious "believer" might read the scene in "Homer the Heretic" as affirming the idea that God plays favorites, punishing Homer for his heresy and rewarding Flanders for his faith. However, to read the text in this way is to ignore the blatant irony and the gratuitous exaggeration and thus to miss the satirical critique being offered.

In the final scene of "Homer the Heretic," everyone is gathered in the Simpsons' kitchen, where they in effect discuss the "moral" of Homer's experience. Asked by Marge if he has learned his lesson, Homer replies that he has learned that God is vengeful. "Oh spiteful one," Homer says, falling to his knees and looking upward, "tell me who to smite and they shall be smoten." Lovejoy laughs and tells Homer that God didn't set his house on fire. "But he was working in the hearts of your friends and neighbors," Lovejoy says, gesturing toward Ned, Krusty, and Apu, and then continuing, "whether they be Christian, Jew, or...miscellaneous." "Hindu," Apu retorts. "There are seven hundred million of us, you know." "Aw, that's super," Lovejoy responds. Oddly, Lovejoy's dismissive observation and condescending reply to Apu are also not examined in any of the analyses of "Homer the Heretic." Dalton, Mazur, and Siems subordinate Lovejoy's comments to a parenthetical phrase, offering no reflection on them whatsoever, yet they later claim that Lovejoy's overall view "represents the sort of generic Christianity prevalent in today's mainline Protestant churches and in most television portrayals of religion."[35] Based on Lovejoy's attitude toward Hindus (and presumably other faiths outside the Judeo-Christian tradition), it would be more accurate for the authors to add that Lovejoy represents a generic ignorance and prejudice, which is also prevalent in certain mainline churches today and which is clearly the target of the satire in "Homer the Heretic." In *Understanding Theology and Popular Culture*, Gordon Lynch briefly discusses "Homer the Heretic," in a chapter on text-based approaches to popular culture, and he does note that Lovejoy represents a "morbid and punitive form of religious faith."[36] However, Lynch claims that in the end, Lovejoy "voices a more humane and tolerant vision of religion when he observes that God's action in the world is demonstrated through those who saved Homer's life," altogether ignoring Lovejoy's rather intolerant dismissal of Apu's faith as "miscellaneous."[37] "Homer the Heretic" might be "fundamentally concerned with the question of whether and why people should be involved in organized religion," as Lynch claims, but, considering how the narrative resolves itself, it is a mistake to argue that "the narrative tends towards a view that organized religion is a good thing in so far as it makes people more humane and concerned for those around them."[38] Organized religion had nothing to do with the compassion extended to Homer: he was saved by the collective efforts of Ned Flanders and the Springfield volunteer fire department, which includes Krusty the Clown (a secularized Jew who does not practice Judaism) and Apu (a Hindu who is not part of an institutionalized tradition in Springfield). It is quite a stretch to say that the humanity of Krusty and Apu has derived from organized religion and thereby to dismiss the satirical critiques of fundamentalism and intolerance offered in this episode.

The Satirical and the Spiritual

After the publication of Mark Pinsky's *The Gospel According to "The Simpsons"* in 2001, there was a reconsideration of *The Simpsons* by religious and political conservatives, who had initially seen the show as amoral and a corruptive influence in American culture. Since that time, there has been an attempt to (re)claim *The Simpsons* for religious believers. However, given that the show is often less than flattering to religion—even Pinsky admits that "*The Simpsons* is consistently irreverent toward organized religion's failings and excesses"—this reclamation of *The Simpson* came in the guise of "family values," which, as noted in previous chapters, remains code for religious conservatism in the culture.[39] In the foreword to Pinsky's book, for example, Professor Tony Campolo claims, "Contrary to what some critics say, the Simpsons are basically a decent family with good values. They go to church on Sunday."[40] The syntax here is quite revealing: Campolo clearly implies a connection between church attendance and possessing "good values," thereby dismissing the idea that their values could possibly derive from something or somewhere else.

This strikes me as a remarkably simplistic link, and yet it is a central tenet of the "family values" and "pro-family" Religious Right. Indeed, it echoes the tacit approval First Lady Barbara Bush gave *The Simpsons* in 1990, prior to the dustup over her husband's comment comparing the Simpson family to the Waltons, by claiming the show was "a family thing" and, therefore, a good example for the nation.[41] In short, because the Simpsons represented a traditional nuclear family, it was given a pass by Mrs. Bush and others of a similar ideological stripe.

As stated at the onset, *The Simpsons* has a strong spirituality overall, demonstrating a sincere compassion for others and a faith in both family and community. However, the show does not present such qualities (in effect, the "goodness" of the Simpsons) as deriving from religion. Indeed, institutional religion (Christianity, in particular) is most often present on *The Simpsons* only to be satirized—usually via the comments and behaviors of the two representatives of religion, Reverend Lovejoy and Ned Flanders. As Chris Turner accurately notes, after the first few seasons, Ned Flanders and his family had become "an extended satirical study in American evangelical Christianity."[42] The evangelical and fundamentalist aspects of the Flanders family are portrayed and satirized quite effectively in "Home Sweet Home-Diddily-Dum-Doodily," which first aired in October 1995. Owing to a variety of mishaps and misunderstandings, the Simpson children are taken away from Marge and Homer by Child Protective Services and placed in foster care with the Flanders family. When the kids first arrive, Maude Flanders says, "I don't judge Homer and Marge. That's for a vengeful God to do." After this, Bart and Lisa are subjected to the very sheltered life of the Flanders family—they are fed "nachos, Flanders style" (cucumber and cottage cheese), they are not allowed to watch television, and they are made to go to bed before sundown. For fun, Ned involves the Simpson kids in a game called "Bombardment... of Bible Trivia," which is played with one of the many editions of the Bible that Flanders owns—in this case, with the Vulgate of Saint Jerome. In the next scene, we see Rod and Todd with small stars stuck all over their faces, indicating they have correctly answered numerous trivia questions. Bart and Lisa, however, have none. Wanting to give them a chance, Ned offers another question, one he considers easy. "We give up," Lisa says. "Well, guess!" Ned encourages. "Book of Revelations, fire-breathing lion's head, tail made out of snakes...who else is it going to be?" "Jesus?" Bart ventures. "Jesus!" Ned exclaims, exasperated. "Don't you kids know anything? The Serpent of Rehaboam? The Well of Zohassadar? The Bridal Feast of Beth Chedruharazzeb?" With each question, Bart and Lisa only give him a blank look. "Why, that's the kind of thing you should start learning at baptism," Maude says. "Um, actually," Lisa stammers, "we were never baptized." With that, Flanders faints. After he awakens, Flanders takes it upon himself to baptize the kids.

Once again, we see Ned's zealotry take over, and once again we see it satirized. On the way to the Springfield River, where Ned will perform an old-fashioned immersion baptism, Ned says, "Until this, I never thought Homer and Marge were bad parents, but now I know you kids need a less hellbound family!" Meanwhile, Marge and Homer, having successfully completed their state-mandated parenting course, arrive at the Flanders's house to pick up the kids, only to be confronted by a sign reading "Gone Baptizin'" stuck to the front door. Marge and Homer are both angered by Ned's actions and race to the river to stop him. They arrive there just in time to see Ned about to anoint Bart with a drop of holy water. "Noooo!" Homer cries, and in a slow-motion sequence (in what appears to be a parody of a monster movie), we see Homer dive toward Bart and knock him out of the way. In the process, however, Homer himself is hit by the droplet of holy water, at which point we hear an audible hiss, and Homer begins to writhe and thrash in water, presumably because his demonic self is being seared by the power of God. Bart runs to Homer and says, "Wow, Dad, you took a baptismal for me. How do you feel?" Homer, in a reverent tone, replies, "Oh, Bartholomew, I feel like St. Augustine of Hippo after his conversion by Ambrose of Milan." Ned, understandably shocked, asks, "Homer, what did you just say?" "I said shut your ugly face, Flanders!" Homer yells, clearly now past his momentary conversion. The ridiculousness of this scene indicates that the writers are intending to satirize a variety of things, including Ned's view of the world as a stark contrast between good and evil, the belief that holy water has some kind of power to fight evil, and the idea that religious conversion can be so easily attained. Above all of this, however, the episode is most invested in satirizing the actions of religious fundamentalists, represented by Ned, who operate out of sheer zealotry, without regard for the beliefs and values of those whom they condemn or proselytize.

With characters such as Ned Flanders and Reverend Lovejoy, and with stories that involve them in the lives of the Simpsons in intimate ways, *The Simpsons* is able to fully examine and powerfully satirize institutional religion and Christianity on a regular basis. However, *The Simpsons* also engages with more secular, spiritual matters. As Dalton, Mazur, and Siems argue, the show "implicitly affirms an America in which institutional religion has lost its position of authority and where personal expressions of spirituality have come to dominate popular religious culture."[43] One of the most deeply spiritual episodes of *The Simpson* is "Bart Sells His Soul," which aired just one week after "Home Sweet Home-Diddily-Dum-Doodily," in October 1995. While this episode again offers some satirical critiques of institutional Christianity, primarily in its first act, its central concern is with an existential question, which it explores, via both theology and philosophy, with great sophistication. "Bart Sells His Soul" addresses what could be a very controversial topic, but in this episode the theological and philosophical are positioned along such closely parallel lines that it can readily be interpreted to support a religious or a secular view. The episode begins with Bart substituting the lyrics for a church hymn, "In the Garden of Eden," with those for Iron Butterfly's rock anthem "In-a-Gadda-Da-Vida." After a full 17 minutes, Reverend Lovejoy finally recognizes the music as "rock and/or roll" and gathers the children to find out who was behind the prank. In order to extract a confession, Lovejoy uses a fear tactic and instructs the children to recite a litany they clearly know very well. "I know one of you is responsible for this," Lovejoy says. "So repeat after me: If I withhold the truth, may I go straight to Hell where I will eat naught but burning hot coals and drink naught but burning hot cola . . ." In unison, the children recite the remaining lines, including the phrases "where fiery demons will punch me in the back" and "where my tongue will be torn out by ravenous birds." The camera focuses, however, on just three individuals, with the soundtrack emphasizing their voices on particular phrases. When we see Bart, who has a very bored look on his face, clearly familiar with the incantation and unconvinced of the truth of these claims, we hear him say, "where my soul will be chopped into confetti and be strewn upon a parade of murderers and single mothers." This moment is both shocking and funny, but it also is a clear reminder of the view the writers have taken of the Religious Right's demonization of single motherhood in the 1990s—for example, when Vice President Dan Quayle publicly chastised single mothers in 1992 via his criticism of the television character Murphy Brown, as discussed in chapter 3 in the context of the backlash against feminism.[44] Milhouse, unnerved by the fearful images being conjured, confesses, "Bart did it!" As punishment, Lovejoy makes them both clean the pipe organ. When Milhouse explains that he was concerned about the fate of his soul, Bart flatly declares, "There's no such thing as the soul." "But every religion says there's a soul, Bart," Milhouse protests. Milhouse then challenges Bart's belief (or lack thereof, to be more accurate) by asking him to sell his soul. Bart does so, writing "Bart Simpson's Soul" on a piece of church stationary and exchanging it for the $5 Milhouse offered. When Lisa finds out what Bart has done, she is both surprised and worried: "How could you do that? Your soul is the most valuable part of you." "You believe in that junk?" Bart asks. "Well, whether or not the soul is physically real, Bart, it's the symbol of everything fine inside us." Although Lisa offers a view of the soul as symbolic, Jamey Heit reads her statement in alignment with Christian theology. Heit says,

> Lisa's words express a fundamental Christian belief: the soul is the fundamental part of one's spiritual identity. Even though Lisa does not embrace Christianity, she articulates a conception of the soul that resonates strongly with traditional and popular Christian thought.[45]

It is significant, I think, that Lisa explicitly refers to the soul as a *symbol*, not a presence or essence, which at a minimum contradicts fundamentalist interpretations of the nature of the soul. The belief in a soul is most certainly not exclusive to Christianity, as Heit implies here. And although the concept does resonate with Christian thought, it also resonates with many other religious traditions, as well as with humanism and secular philosophy. As Hendrik Lorenz explains, in the ordinary language of ancient Greece, having a soul simply meant being alive; hence the emergence at the time (roughly, the fifth century BCE) of the word "ensouled" (*empsuchos*) as the standard word meaning "alive," which was applied not just to human beings but to other living things as well.[46] The concept of soul was also prominent in the work of Greek philosophers such as Plato and Aristotle. Indeed, it is key to Plato's notion of "substance dualism," which has had a profound influence on religious and philosophical traditions in the West. The problems attendant to conceiving of the soul are in large part a consequence of the dichotomized worldview underlying the major monotheistic religions (Judaism, Christianity, and Islam), which all posit a distinction between a Creator and his creation—that is, between God and Man. Such dualistic thinking has also been a part of Western philosophy, particularly after Descartes's rearticulation of substance dualism in his *Meditations* (1641), which left us with the conundrum of the "mind-body problem."[47] There is, of course, no simple way to describe or define the soul, but one can easily aver that it is not the sole province of religion, however much the adherents of institutional religions would like it to be. As with the definitions of terms in the previous section, I posit a secular and spiritual understanding of the term *soul* rather than a religious one. This view derives partly from the concept of Oneness in Buddhism and partly from the notion of "Over-Soul," as Emerson called it, in American transcendentalism, which was itself deeply influenced by Eastern thought. In short, the secular "soul" is simply the animating spirit, the "life force," that is common to all living things.[48]

This secular and spiritual understanding of the soul underlies the entirety of "Bart Sells His Soul." The secular view is furthered, as one would expect, by Lisa, who refers to both poetry and philosophy in her attempts to help Bart understand the meaning of *soul*. After selling his soul, Bart begins to notice strange things happening to him: the automatic doors at the Kwik-E-Mart won't open for him, his breath will not fog the glass of an ice-cream case at the store, and at home, the cat and dog now both shun him. Later, we see Bart and Lisa watching an *Itchy & Scratchy* cartoon, Lisa laughing aloud while Bart just stares silently at the television. "I know that's funny," Bart says, "but I'm just not laughing." "Hmmm," Lisa muses, "Pablo Neruda says 'Laughter is the language of the soul.'" She then suggests they test the status of Bart's soul by playing a joke on Homer. Homer takes the bait, falls down the stairs, and gets his head wedged between the rails of the banister, after which the dog begins to bite his rear end. Again, Lisa laughs wildly, but Bart has no reaction. "That's creepy, Bart," Lisa says. "I think you really did lose your soul." Now quite worried, Bart returns to Milhouse and offers to buy back his soul, but Milhouse demands an exorbitant $50. Depressed, Bart returns home, where he falls asleep and dreams about his predicament. In his dream, he is on a hillside with many of his schoolmates, all of whom are accompanied by translucent versions of themselves—presumably their souls. The children all play with their soul-selves, giving the impression that they are "complete" in this pairing; Bart is not, however, and they mock him for lacking a soul. Near the end of the dream sequence, everyone runs hand-in-hand with his or her soul to the edge of a lake, where they hop into rowboats and row off toward a glowing green castle in the distance. Bart jumps in a boat and starts rowing by himself, but he succeeds only in going in circles. At this point, he awakens from the dream, screaming. Bart decides to pay Milhouse whatever he wants, but when Bart finally tracks him down, he discovers that Milhouse has traded the receipt for Bart's soul for a set of POGS at the local comic-book store. Bart goes to the store, finds it closed, and so settles on the stoop to wait. The next morning, the Comic Book Guy arrives and tells Bart that he is too late—he sold Bart's soul the night before to a party he will not name. Defeated, Bart returns home, where he goes to his bedroom, kneels beside his bed, and begins to pray:

> Are you there, God? It's me, Bart Simpson. I know I never paid too much attention in church, but I could really use some of that good stuff now. I'm afraid. I'm afraid some weirdo's got my soul and I don't know what they're doing to it! I just want it back. Please? I hope you can hear this.

As Bart hangs his head and begins to cry, a piece of paper gently floats down from above. The camera then pulls back to reveal Lisa standing behind Bart, her left hand still held high above his head. "*You* bought this?" Bart asks. "Happy to do it," Lisa says as Bart hugs and kisses her. "But you know, Bart, some philosophers believe that nobody is born with a soul, that you have to earn one through suffering and thought and prayer, like you did last night." "Uh huh," Bart mumbles as he stuffs the paper in his mouth and swallows.

As noted earlier, theology and philosophy run along such parallel tracks on *The Simpsons* that there can be both religious and secular readings of many episodes. However, I believe the secular reading of "Bart Sells His Soul" is more justified. To begin with, it is important to note that Bart does not turn for assistance to the church or its representative, Reverend Lovejoy, as did Lisa in "Homer vs. Lisa and the 8th Commandment." As the writers have repeatedly demonstrated in the four seasons between that episode and "Bart Sells His Soul," Lovejoy is not exactly an authority on theological issues and his advice is often useless. Moreover, the institution itself, as we saw at the start of the episode, offers only fear and penance to its congregation, not spiritual nurturance. Another significant element of "Bart Sells His Soul" is the lack of the religious iconography typically used on *The Simpsons*. As discussed earlier, the Judeo-Christian tradition is depicted on *The Simpsons* in quite common ways: God is an old white man with white hair and beard; Heaven sits atop puffy white clouds, is entered through golden gates, and is populated by winged angels in white robes; and Hell is a subterranean realm of lava flows, torture devices, and demons with hooves and pointed tails. Such imagery, common and familiar in the public consciousness, is a regular part of the show and is consistent from season to season. Yet none of this imagery exists in "Bart Sells His Soul." In Bart's dream, for example, the gleaming green castle in the distance resembles nothing more than the Emerald City of *The Wizard of Oz*. Whether this image is considered to be Bart's view or the writer's makes little difference: this is not a depiction of Heaven, and one can only interpret it as such by reading it metaphorically, which would be inconsistent with and contrary to the way the Judeo-Christian tradition is regularly presented on *The Simpsons*. The writers and artists are also quite specific about revealing the source of Bart's returned soul: it is Lisa and her earthly endeavors. One could, of course, offer the usual defense that "God works in mysterious ways" and attempt to explain Lisa's actions as covertly directed by God. However, I am not persuaded by such an argument, in large part because it replicates the situation presented by the depiction of prayer on *The Simpsons* but also because this episode works so hard to avoid religious iconography and to stress the individualized spiritual journey Bart takes. Although "Bart Sells His Soul" excludes organized religion, it is not dismissive of faith; indeed, the episode is very "spiritual" in that is stresses how important the "soul" is for a person to feel whole, complete, or truly alive. And in this regard, the episode is in perfect keeping with the cultural milieu of the mid-1990s, reflecting a model of belief or faith that can resonate quite strongly with those audience members who are what Robert Wuthnow calls "spiritual seekers"—that is, those in contemporary society who describe themselves as "spiritual but not religious," maintaining a belief in the divine (symbolized perhaps by the notion of "soul") but removed from the institutional apparatus of organized (and primarily Christian) religion.[49]

Secularism and *The Simpsons*

As might be expected, Lisa Simpson is the most overtly secular voice on the show and, eventually, the most vocal critic of institutional religion. Although Lisa was closely aligned with the Judeo-Christian tradition at the start of the series, as discussed previously, she moves toward a more rationalist and skeptical position as the series progresses—ultimately rejecting Christianity altogether and converting to Buddhism in the 2001 episode "She of Little Faith"—demonstrating along the way that her views are shaped primarily by the traditions of Enlightenment philosophy, rationality, and scientific inquiry. Lisa's scientific rationality is the centerpiece of the episode "Lisa the Skeptic," which first aired in November 1997 and which pits faith and science against one another in a very direct manner. While on an archaeological dig—arranged by Lisa as a last-minute effort to locate fossils in Sabertooth Meadow, which is set to be cleared for a new "mega-mall"—Lisa and her classmates uncover an unusual-looking skeleton, which is quickly presumed to be the remains of an angel. As Lisa, Ned Flanders, Dr. Hibbert, and others debate what to do, Homer snatches the skeleton and takes it home, planning to cash in on it later. We then see a series of Springfield residents come to the Simpson home to visit the skeleton, which Homer has displayed in the garage. Ned Flanders brings his sons to pray with the "angel," while other more superstitious folks come to touch it "for good luck." Lisa is bothered that everyone unquestioningly views the skeleton as an angel and, therefore, proposes to take it to the Springfield museum for scientific testing to prove that it is not. Homer refuses to let her, so late at night Lisa sneaks into the garage and breaks off a fragment of the angel's toe to take to the museum for analysis. The resident scientist there happens to be the evolutionary biologist Stephen Jay Gould (guest starring in this episode), who agrees with Lisa that to consider the skeleton an angel is "preposterous." The following day, Gould informs a small group of people gathered in the Simpsons' garage that the results were "inconclusive" (though we later learn that he never ran the tests at all). Reverend Lovejoy gloatingly says, "Well, it appears science has failed again, in front of overwhelming religious evidence." Lisa, still convinced that science will prove her right, continues to challenge people's belief by offering a variety of plausible explanations for the skeleton, including that it could be a mutant created by the Springfield Nuclear Power Plant. Frustrated, Lisa then complains to her mother about the "morons" in town who refuse to listen. Marge, however, does not take Lisa's side, as she is positioned once again as a believer. The dialogue between Lisa and Marge that follows encapsulates the divisive conflict between religion and science that is the centerpiece of this episode, although the debate rests here upon the vague and ambiguous concept of "faith":

> *Marge:* I'd appreciate it if you didn't call them "morons."
> *Lisa:* But they are morons. What grown person could believe in angels?
> *Marge:* Well, your mother, for one.
> *Lisa:* You? But you're an intelligent person, mom.
> *Marge:* There has to be more to life that just what we see, Lisa. Everyone needs something to believe in.
> *Lisa:* It's not that I don't have a spiritual side, I just find it hard to believe there's a dead angel hanging in our garage.
> *Marge:* Oh, my poor Lisa, if you can't make a leap of faith now and then, well, I feel sorry for you.
> *Lisa:* Don't feel sorry for me, mom. I feel sorry for you.

More determined than before, Lisa appears on the television show *Smartline* to present her case. The host Kent Brockman asks her, "Miss Simpson, how can you maintain your skepticism despite the fact that this thing really really looks like an angel?" "I just think it's a fantasy," Lisa says. "If you believe in angels, then why not unicorns, sea-monsters and leprechauns?" "Oh, that's a bunch of baloney, Lisa," Brockman replies. "Everyone knows that leprechauns are extinct." "Look," Lisa states matter-of-factly, "you can either accept science and face reality or you can believe in angels and live in a childish dream world." At Moe's bar, where some of the town's residents are watching *Smartline*, Ned Flanders complains, "Science is like a blabber mouth who ruins a movie by telling you how it ends. Well, I say that there are some things we don't want to know. Important things!" And with that, the group turns into an angry mob that sets out to demolish the town's science buildings. As Kent Brockman later reports, "Technocrats are learning a lesson in humility tonight as angel supporters lay waste to Springfield's scientific institutions." In an effort to direct the violence away from science, Lisa vows to do violence to faith and sets off to destroy the angel. When she gets to the garage at home, however, she finds that the angel has been stolen. Tensions run high as the townsfolk suspect "the unbeliever" of destroying the angel, but Lisa fortunately spies the angel on a hillside near the original dig site. When everyone reaches the relic, they discover a message carved upon it reading "The End Will Come at Sundown." The mob now assumes, readily and blindly, that the apocalypse is nigh, and everyone begins to count down the remaining time. However, at sundown nothing happens. Then, suddenly, the angel rises and floats above everyone while a "heavenly" voice intones, "Prepare for the end...of high prices! Behold, the grand opening of the Heavenly Hills Mall!" The mall lights up in the distance, and it is revealed that the angel is merely part of an elaborate publicity stunt. The episode ends with Lisa attempting to channel the outrage she expects the faithful might harbor at being exploited in this way, but the townsfolk don't even hear her; good consumers all, they rush headlong to the mall, having already forgotten their religious devotion. With such an ending, the writers are simultaneously satirizing the substitution of one religion for another—here, consumerism (another regular target of the show's satire) for theism—but it should not be forgotten that the primary concern of the episode is with Lisa's rationality and faith in scientific explanation and that her view is vindicated in the end.

The question of faith is also explored in "I'm Going to Praiseland," which aired in May 2001 and centers on Ned Flanders and his efforts to build a Christian-themed amusement park in honor of his dead wife, Maude.[50] The episode was most likely inspired by the controversies surrounding the plans for and the subsequent development of the Holy Land Experience, a biblical theme park that opened in Orlando, Florida, in February 2001.[51] Ned is inspired to build Praiseland by drawings he finds in a sketchbook once belonging to Maude. To fulfill her dream, Flanders buys the old Storytime Village and, with the help of the Simpsons, builds the theme park, erecting a statue of Maude at the entrance as a tribute. Prior to the park's grand opening, Ned pledges to show Springfield "that faith and devotion are the wildest thrill-rides of all!" However, once there, the visitors find that the park is primarily designed to proselytize and is thus less than enjoyable: Bart and Milhouse, for example, take King David's Wild Ride only to discover that it involves listening to a likeness of King David read his 150 Psalms; Nelson, standing before a game of Whack-a-Satan and puzzled because there is no mallet, is told by Ned, "You can stop Satan with your faith"; Chief Wiggum and his son Ralph learn that the candy in the park is all one flavor (plain); and Lenny, Carl, and the other adults realize that no alcohol is being served. Soon, everyone begins to leave, complaining of the park's tedium, and Flanders concludes that his tribute to Maude's dream is a failure. But then something unexpected happens: the Maude Flanders novelty mask that Ned had dejectedly tossed in front of the statue of Maude rises into the air and hovers before the statue's face. "It's a miracle," Marge says, as everyone gasps. Immediately, interest is piqued once again. The statue quickly becomes known as Miracle Maude, and people begin coming to Praiseland to pray before it. Then, even more "miracles" occur: Principal Skinner, who aims to rationally dismiss the phenomenon, suddenly falls down before the statue, writhing, and begins "speaking in tongues." After Skinner recovers and explains his "vision" to everyone, Reverend Lovejoy rather sacrilegiously says, "Truly, this was the will of Maude." Homer, always on the lookout for a way to make money, decides to charge people $10 to experience a vision. Ned is at first reluctant to "exploit a divine manifestation," but Marge suggests they give the money to the local orphanage, which he decides to do after seeing one of the sickly orphans. People then clamor to have Maude give them visions, which she indeed appears to do for anyone who stands before the statue. When Rod inquires, "Why is everybody having visions, Daddy?" Ned replies, "There's no explaining God's will, Roddy. That's like explaining how an airplane flies." As usual, Ned's faith knows no limits and cannot be undone by science, which certainly can explain how an airplane flies. We are treated with the humorous and wacky visions of a few of Springfield's residents before we are shown Homer, at a food stand off to the left, struggling to light a grill. Lisa observes that there is a leak in the gas line. Curious, Ned follows the line and discovers that the leak is right in front of Maude's statue. He then realizes that this isn't "a divine miracle" at all—as he puts it, "everyone's just getting goofy from the gas." Ned then decides he has to close Praiseland. Strangely, the writers redirect the focus at the end so Ned never has to confess that the "miracles" are not real. Instead, we are given some rather slapstick humor involving two orphan boys lighting candles near the statue and Homer and Ned leaping in to stop them. Although they prevent an explosion and save everyone, they are chastised for their behavior. The townsfolk are appalled to see "adults attacking orphans" and, taking the high moral ground, abandon Praiseland. Given the satire offered throughout the episode, this is a rather surprising resolution, one that largely lets religion off the hook, unlike the ending of "Lisa the Skeptic," which challenges religion and faith more directly. Nevertheless, "I'm Going to Praiseland," does effectively censure missionary zeal, and it offers another strong critique of blind faith by providing, once more, a rational explanation for the supposedly "miraculous."

Although the religious satire of *The Simpsons* commonly targets a generic form of Protestantism—what Reverend Lovejoy once humorously identified as "Presbylutheran"—some of the more pointed satirical barbs in recent years have been aimed specifically at Catholicism. For example, in "Sunday, Cruddy Sunday," which aired on January 31, 1999, immediately following the Super Bowl telecast that year, *The Simpsons* offered a parody of Super Bowl commercials (in this case, of a GoDaddy.com ad) that apparently crossed a line for many Catholic viewers and for Roland McFarland, Fox's vice president of broadcast standards, who had already dealt with complaints from the Catholic League over some of the jokes in previous episodes. In the commercial parody, we see a car pull up to the pumps at an abandoned-looking gas station; a rather nerdy driver gets out, looks around, and then hits the horn for service. From the gas station appear three scantily clad women (a blonde, a brunette, and a redhead) who, to the tune of ZZ Top's "She's Got Legs," begin to service the car while gyrating to the music and seductively eying the man. One pops up the car's hood, another provocatively leans across the windshield with a squeegee, and the last very suggestively plunges the gas pump nozzle into the hole on the side of the car to fill the tank. The final shot features the first woman (the blonde) bent over the hood of the car, displaying her ample cleavage, and then the camera zooms in for a close-up on the silver cross dangling between her breasts. In a voice-over, one hears, "The Catholic Church. We've made a few changes." Clearly the parody is designed to mock that genre of advertisements (often for beer and often aired during the Super

Bowl) that featured women magically appearing from nowhere and offering themselves as objects of pleasure, presumably for the male viewer/consumer. Critiques of the objectification of women such as this are common in commercial parodies on *The Simpsons,* but this parody goes a step beyond, mocking as well the branding and marketing techniques being employed by the Catholic Church to appeal to parishioners, old and new.[52] Mike Scully, who has been with *The Simpsons* for many years and has served as an executive producer since 1996, claims that the joke was "an observation on crazy Super Bowl commercials, not a comment on the Catholic Church."[53] As Scully explained, "We had the idea for the content of the commercial first. Then we pitched several tag lines. One of the writers pitched the Catholic Church line, and it got the biggest laugh."[54] Nonetheless, McFarland told Scully to edit the sequence. When Scully balked at the idea, McFarland advised changing Catholic to "Methodist, Presbyterian, or Baptist," which to Scully seemed no different since changing it to another religious denomination would just be offending another group of people. McFarland's response to this was that "Fox had already had trouble with Catholics earlier this season." After the episode aired, the Catholic League for Religious and Civil Rights organized written protests against *The Simpsons.* According to Scully, Fox was at first supportive but caved in after the second batch of complaints, and so when "Sunday, Cruddy Sunday" was rebroadcast later in the year, it contained a small but crucial edit imposed by the network: the word "Catholic" was deleted from the voice-over, leaving only the words "the church."

Such specific targeting of Catholicism is a regular but relatively small part of the satire on *The Simpsons*: as noted previously, the satire is commonly aimed at the Protestantism practiced by the majority of people in Springfield (and in the United States). However, as the seasons have progressed, the satire has been more specifically directed against evangelical Protestantism and the religious fundamentalism this often generates, and the tone has become increasingly harsh. In *Planet Simpson* (2004), Chris Turner states, "*The Simpsons*' writers have lost patience with the Flanders brand of fundamentalist Christianity in recent years, their somewhat playful ribbing turning into palpable disgust."[55] A fine example of this appears in the season 12 episode "HOMR," which aired in January 2001. Although the central narrative of this episode is not concerned specifically with religious issues, there are two very potent satirical scenes that express the heightened frustration with fundamentalism that Turner speaks of. In one scene, we see the Flanders boys, Rod and Todd, watching a show called *Gravey and Jobriath,* a parody of the 1960s Christian children's program *Davey and Goliath.* Although Flanders is often opposed to television and to children's cartoons in particular, he allows his children to watch this one because "it's approved by the Council of Presbylutheran Ministers." The segment of *Gravey and Jobriath* shown features Gravey busily making something in the garage. "Whatcha making there, Gravey?" Jobriath asks. "It's a pipe bomb, Jobriath, for to blow up Planned Parenthood," Gravey says. When Jobriath expresses some doubt about this action, Gravey shouts, "I'm sick of your lack of faith," and then lights the bomb and stuffs it into Jobriath's mouth. An explosion is heard, and Rod and Todd righteously cheer "Yay!" By 2001, bombings of abortion clinics were no longer as commonplace as in the 1990s; however, other forms of violence were and continue to be a problem. For example, the National Clinic Violence Survey, conducted by the Feminist Majority Foundation, reports that since 2008 attacks on women's health clinics and abortion providers has been on the increase, the most notorious of which was the murder of

Dr. George Tiller in 2009; moreover, by 2010, more than one in five clinics through-out the country was still targeted with antiabortion violence, including "blockades, invasions, arsons, bombings, chemical attacks, stalking, gunfire, physical assaults, and threats of death, bomb, or arson."[56] Such realities make the satire presented in "HOMR" even more relevant now than when the episode first aired. We also learn in "HOMR" that Homer was once quite intelligent (he only became stupid after sticking a crayon up his nose). In a flashback, we see Homer discussing his work with Ned. While working on a new tax-code plan, Homer stumbled upon a mathematical proof that definitively shows God does not exist. Skeptical, Ned reviews the proof, deter-mines it is accurate, and then whips out a lighter and sets the proof on fire. "Can't let this little doozy get out," Ned says. The satire here ought to be clear, as it is consis-tent with a point raised repeatedly on *The Simpsons*: reason and rationality have the potential to undermine the belief system fundamental to Christianity, which is why they and the evidence they produce are so often suppressed by religious believers. Ned recognizes the truth of this and, like many of those before him, feels threatened and so destroys the evidence, in another example of the extremes to which believers will go to maintain the mystique of religion.

The indoctrination of the Flanders children into a fundamentalist worldview is also satirically broached in a brief but telling scene in the 2006 episode "Bart Has Two Mommies," which involved Marge babysitting Flanders's kids for a short time. When Ned returns home, he is shocked to discover that Todd has a cut on his finger. Todd tells his father that he cut himself on a knife while playing the game *Christian Clue*. Then, in a very quick sequence, his brother Rod explains the cause, flashing the appropriate cards for the audience: "The secular humanist did it in the schoolhouse with misinformation." The secular humanist card shows a bearded man wearing glasses and a Yale sweatshirt; the schoolhouse card shows an old-fashioned little red schoolhouse; and the misinformation card simply depicts a dinosaur (a brontosau-rus). The narrow fundamentalist worldview is also satirized in a brief scene in the 2010 episode "Judge Me Tender," which slyly toys with creationist doctrine. While at the Springfield Pet Fair, Lisa spies Ned Flanders's "Jesus Fish" booth. In the tank are yellow and black striped fish whose wavy vertical stripes, when seen in profile, spell the word Jesus. When she asks Flanders how he made these amazing fish, he chuckles and says, "Actually, God made some fish that were pretty close to these, so naturally we selected those for further breeding." "So," Lisa asks, giving her words particular emphasis, "*natural* selection was the *origin* of this *species*?" "Yes, that's exactly...Woah ho ho, you almost got me," Ned laughs. At that moment, one of the fish leaps to the rim of the tank. This particular fish is seen with four legs where its pectoral fins should be. As it gasps for breath, Ned sweeps it back into the tank and closes the lid, saying, "Not on my watch!"

The critique of religious fundamentalism is a more central part of postmillennial episodes of *The Simpsons*, most notably in "Thank God, It's Doomsday" (May 2005), "The Father, the Son, and the Holy Guest Star" (May 2005), and "The Monkey Suit" (May 2006). "Thank God, It's Doomsday" begins with a series of mishaps that lead to Homer, Bart, and Lisa seeking refuge in the local Googolplex, where they see a film about the Rapture called *Left Below* (a parodic take on Tim LaHaye's *Left Behind* series of books). Homer is unnerved by the idea of being "left below" because he has not led a good life. When he expresses his concern to Marge, she consoles him by saying that God wouldn't just "spring this on people" but would provide warnings.

Homer feels calmed until he witnesses some ominous signs: he is approached by a devil, who intones "follow me," and he sees blood raining from the sky. Of course, these things have logical explanations, which the viewer gets to see: the devil is a man in an outfit promoting a local devil's food cake store, and the blood is coming from a harpooned whale that is being transported to safety by helicopter. Now convinced that the Rapture is near, Homer is motivated to read up on the subject, after which he performs a series of calculations and concludes that the Rapture is due in one week's time. Homer then hits the street—with a bell and a placard reading "The End Is Near"—to warn his fellow citizens. Homer is at first dismissed as crazy and deluded—reporter Kent Brockman, for example, calls him a "mad monk" on the local news broadcast. Lisa is of course skeptical, but so is Marge, who tells Homer he is acting "crazy." Collectively, Marge, Lisa, and Bart express their concern, telling Homer they don't believe the world is coming to an end and asking him to "lighten up on the left below stuff." Homer does so momentarily, but then he sees on television what he takes as another sign: "stars" falling from the sky (in this case, Krusty the Clown and some other entertainers plummeting from a damaged Duff Beer blimp). In the next scene, we see Homer and some townsfolk gathered in the Simpson home to discuss the impending end. As usual, the residents of Springfield exhibit a group-think mentality and are surprisingly blasé about the fact that, as Homer shrilly puts it, "God loves you; he's gonna kill you!" Homer is an unlikely (and ultimately unreliable) prophet, yet they are willing to listen to his advice, paralleling the behavior of many devout believers in American culture today who unquestioningly follow the lead of self-proclaimed prophets of the apocalypse.

The very notion of the apocalypse—of the end-time and the Rapture of the faithful—is being powerfully ridiculed in "Thank God, It's Doomsday," as is clear from the remainder of the episode. On Judgment Day, Springfield's residents gather, as instructed by Homer, to take a bus to Springfield Mesa, where they will await the Rapture. Prior to leaving, Lisa, who is always a voice of reason, pleads with Homer: "Dad, please don't go through with this. All through history, self-anointed seers have predicted the end of the world, and they've always been wrong." Naturally, Homer refuses to listen. On the way to the Mesa, those aboard the bus sing a parody of "99 Bottles of Beer," which includes these lines: "99 minutes until we're all saved, 99 minutes to go. Unless it turns out that you're not devout, then you'll be left down below. 98 minutes until we're all saved . . ." Of course, at the appointed time specified by Homer, nothing happens: there is no Rapture. Everyone patiently waits, first a few minutes, then a few hours, but they finally realize that the end is not coming and then leave, muttering angry curses at Homer. Later, while at home cleaning up, Homer stumbles up on a replica of Leonardo Da Vinci's *The Last Supper* and notes that there were 13 people in attendance, not 12: he had forgotten to count Jesus. Homer recalculates and concludes that the Rapture is now due later that same day. At this point, however, no one is willing to listen to him. Convinced that he is right this time, Homer goes alone to the Mesa and settles in to await the Judgment. He soon falls asleep and dreams of the Rapture. In Homer's dream, heaven is like a resort spa, complete with concierge, hotel rooms, and entertaining activities. It is also a place where every wish is granted. Homer enjoys himself until he inquires about those "left below." He is then shown (on a large-screen television) an image of his suffering family, surrounded by a lake of fire and being tormented by the devil. Disturbed, Homer goes to speak to God about the situation. "God," Homer says, "you've got a first-class destination resort here—really top-notch—but I can't enjoy myself know-ing my family is suffering." "Oh, don't tell me about family suffering," God replies. "My son went down to Earth once. I don't know what you people did to him, but he hasn't been the same since." The camera then pans over to an image of Jesus sitting alone on a swing set, spinning aimlessly in his seat with a blank look on his face. This is a curious moment in the episode. The depiction of Jesus is again very brief, but the tone here is strikingly different than those I discussed earlier, and the moment seems designed to provoke serious thought rather than lighthearted laughter. It certainly raises some provocative questions about theology and humanity. Jesus appears to be psychologically and/or emotionally damaged, much like a human being, which calls into question the "divine" nature of Jesus. Moreover, God's comments imply that he did not send Jesus to Earth and that he is not aware of what happened to Jesus while there, which calls into question both the omnipotence and the omniscience of God. Finally, and perhaps most importantly, considering the concerns of the show's writers, the responsibility for the damage done to Jesus is upon humankind—"you people," as God puts it—which could be read as a metaphorical indictment of the perversions of Christian doctrine (the harm done to the faith) or of the cruelties com-mitted in its name (the harm done to fellow beings). Of course, Homer casually (and callously) dismisses Jesus's condition. "Oh, he'll be fine," he says and then demands that God spare his family. When God refuses, Homer goes on a rampage, destroying the "resort" as much as possible. Like a frustrated father with an incorrigible child, God reprimands Homer and then asks him what he wants. What Homer wants, of course, is for things to return to the way they were. "To do what you're asking, I'd have to turn back time," God says. "Superman did it," Homer taunts, interestingly pitting a secular "all-powerful" being against a religious one. "Fine, mister smarty-pants," God says. "I will undo the Apocalypse." God then intones "Deus ex Machina" and claps his hands, and we are returned to Homer asleep on the Mesa. "It was all just a dream," Homer says with relief, just as his family arrives. In the final scene, Homer returns to Moe's bar to be with his friends. Seated at the bar and sipping a beer, Homer quietly says, "This is heaven." At this point, the camera slowly pulls back to reveal a parodic replication of Da Vinci's The Last Supper, with Homer seated at the center of the iconic image, in lieu of Jesus, accompanied by a chorus of voices sing-ing "Hallelujah." This is a remarkably secular intervention into the iconic imagery of religious art, and it puts a final and clear punctuation point on the statements made in this episode: the Rapture is nothing more than the wild imagining of false prophets, and focusing so zealously on "the end-time" prevents people from appreciating and enjoying what they have in the here and now, such as a loving family, good friends, or a cold bottle of Duff.

Religious zealotry is also openly dealt with in "The Father, the Son, and the Holy Guest Star," which aired just two weeks after "Thank God, It's Doomsday," in May 2005. In "The Father, the Son, and the Holy Guest Star," Bart is expelled from Springfield Elementary and subsequently enrolled in St. Jerome's Catholic School. Although the episode again offers some pointed critiques of Catholicism, the larger targets of the satire are the practice of Christianity itself, the sectarian battles that believers engage in, and the intolerance that underlies the faith. On his first day in Catholic school, Bart behaves just as he does in public school, but he quickly discov-ers that the discipline at St. Jerome's is strict, and corporal punishment in still in effect. The nun teaching the class first punishes Bart by smacking his knuckles with a yardstick and then taking him into the hall and having him extend his arms ("like our Lord Jesus Christ on the cross") to hold two heavy dictionaries. The irony isn't lost on Bart, who feels himself to be persecuted. "I'm the *real* Jesus here," he says. His "sacrilegious" comment attracts the attention of Father Sean, who sees a kindred spirit in Bart and a chance to help. Father Sean begins by giving Bart a "Lives of the Saints" comic; the appeal of this for Bart is not the historical information but his own fondness for blood and carnage, which the comic offers in brightly colored detail. "Catholics Rock!" Bart exclaims. When Marge questions his newfound allegiance to Catholicism—pointing out that the church doesn't allow for birth control, for example—Bart accuses her of "blasphemy" and offers to say a rosary for her. After hearing Bart offer grace in Latin, Homer decides he too has had enough of the Catholic influence and determines to pull Bart out of St. Jerome's. However, once at the school, Homer is seduced by a pancake breakfast, a bingo game, and finally, the concept of absolution. Enamored of the ease with which he can be forgiven of his sins (which he enumerates for Father Sean), Homer decides to convert. This, of course, creates a bit of a scandal, both at home and in the community (a humorous montage showing Homer and Bart partaking of Catholic church activities is preceded by a newspaper headline exclaiming "Local Father, Son May Switch Religions"). The following Sunday, Marge stands uncomfortably alone at church listening to her neighbors whisper disapproval and condemnation. Reverend Lovejoy confronts Marge, claiming that Homer and Bart are "under the spell of a man in a pointy white hat." Marge initially tries to defend their choice as "an interest in spirituality," but Lovejoy tells her that "a different faith means a different afterlife." Frightened by this prospect and now determined to win Homer and Bart back, Marge teams up with Ned Flanders and Reverend Lovejoy, and they descend upon St. Jerome's, interrupting the "First Communion 101" class Father Sean is teaching. When Marge demands that Homer and Bart come back with her, Bart astutely says, "This is the Catholic church. Chicks don't have any authority here." Bart is angry about the intervention, and on the ride home he complains to Marge: "You're always telling me to go to church, and now that I am, it's the wrong one." Lovejoy responds, "We're here to bring you back to the one true faith—the Western Branch of American Reform Presbylutheranism."

The remainder of "The Father, the Son, and the Holy Guest Star" makes abundantly clear that *The Simpsons* aims to satirize the idea of "one true faith" and the intolerance this breeds, even among Christians themselves. In an effort to show Bart that "Protestants can be hip too," Marge takes him to a Protestant youth festival. Bart is unimpressed until he sees the Onward Paintball Soldiers tent. With gun in hand, Bart proceeds to wreak havoc, splattering a nativity scene with red paint and "shooting" Rod and Todd Flanders. When Father Sean and Homer arrive, sporting their own paintball guns, Homer is determined to show Marge that "our God kicks your God's butt." Homer then cocks and aims his gun, and everyone around him follows suit, ready for battle. At this point, Bart steps up and says, "Easy on the zeal, church-os. I've got something to say. Don't you get it? It's all Christianity, people. The little stupid differences are nothing compared to the big stupid similarities." "He's right," Flanders says. "Can't we all get together and concentrate on our real enemies: monogamous gays and stem cells?" Father Sean agrees, and he shakes hands with Flanders. Lovejoy concedes that Bart has taught them all a valuable lesson, saying, "We Christians have been niggling over details for far too long." "Amen," Father Sean says. "And from this day forward, I hope we all learn to take Bart's message of tolerance and understanding to heart." On the heels of Father Sean's statement, we see the words "1000 Years Later" superimposed over dark clouds and set to ominous music. The camera then pans down to reveal two rival factions, both followers of "God's last prophet, Bart Simpson," facing one another on a battlefield and arguing over the message of "the holy Bartman": one group claims that he "preached a message of tolerance and love," the other that he "preached a message of understanding and peace." With shouts of "Eat Our Shorts!" and "Cowabunga!" the rival groups rush into battle, and the end credits roll. The irony of the ending should not be lost on anyone, nor should the satirical critique of religious zealotry.

The Simpsons continued to satirize religious fundamentalism in "The Monkey Suit," although more specifically focusing on its general anti-intellectualism and its opposition to scientific inquiry. "The Monkey Suit," which aired in May 2006, was inspired by the events leading up to the 2005 decision in *Kitzmiller v. Dover*, a federal court case that settled a rancorous debate over science curricula in the small town of Dover, Pennsylvania. The controversy that led to *Kitzmiller* began in October 2004, when the Dover Area School Board adopted a resolution providing that students in science courses "will be made aware of gaps/problems in Darwin's theory and of other theories of evolution including, but not limited to, intelligent design." A month later, the district announced that as of January 2005, high school biology teachers would be required to read to their students a disclaimer pointing out that Darwin's theory of natural selection was only a theory and not fact. Parents of some students sued, alleging that the board's policy violated their constitutional rights under the establishment clause.[57] Of course, the case was as much about the battle between religious and secular worldviews as it was about civil rights. It was also a rather surprising replay of the debates over creationism and evolution that culminated in the infamous Scopes "Monkey" Trial 80 years before. For many, the Scopes trial had seemed to mark the final defeat of nineteenth-century evangelical and fundamentalist religion. Although William Jennings Bryan won the case, many felt that the larger cultural war had been lost and that religious fundamentalism was severely wounded. Clarence Darrow had made Bryan look foolish and reactionary, and the press coverage of the trial (much of it by the journalist H. L. Mencken) made fundamentalists appear anti-intellectual and quite unmodern. As William Martin puts it,

> At the end of the decade of the twenties, fundamentalism appeared to have been defeated and relegated to a minor position. It had not only lost virtually every confrontation it had created but had been exposed to ridicule by its tendency toward intellectual rigidity and obscurantism, by its intemperate actions, by its propensity for attracting and lending support to anti-Semitic, anti-Catholic, and other nativist and right-wing political elements, and by its assertion that only Christians could be 100-percent American.[58]

And yet religious fundamentalism continued to thrive—so much so that come the new millennium, the debate between evolutionary science and creationist belief was raging once again as school boards around the country attempted to insert creationism (also known as "intelligent design") into science curricula and/or to remove the teaching of evolutionary theory. True to form, *The Simpsons* incorporated this contemporary debate for satirical ends.

"The Monkey Suit" begins with a trip to the Springfield Museum of Natural History, where Ned and his sons stumble into the Hall of Man and an exhibit on evolution. Shocked by what he sees, Ned covers his sons' eyes and confronts the docent, asking, "Excuse me, but how can you have an exhibit on the origins of man and not have one mention of the Bible?" "Oh, we do," he replies, pointing to a rather low-tech exhibit labeled "The Myth of Creation," which features the finger of God reaching down from a cloud to create a tree, a rabbit, a sheep, and Adam and Eve—all to the tune of the Doobie Brothers' song "What a Fool Believes." Unnerved by the idea that his cherished beliefs are a "myth" and angered at the idea that he and others are descended from apes, Ned consults with Reverend Lovejoy for advice. Lovejoy, as usual, is dismissive—"Ned, you have to take this thing with a grain of salt," he says, brandishing a Bible—but Lovejoy's wife, Helen, convinces him that a controversy would help reverse the dwindling membership in the church. As she says, "Evolution is the hot button issue we need to mobilize our flock." Ned and Lovejoy then approach Principal Skinner and ask that an alternative to evolutionary theory be taught in the school. Skinner at first refuses but reconsiders when Lovejoy threatens to burn the lease policy (and the "once in a lifetime APR") Skinner has with Christian Brothers Auto. The following day, Skinner tells Lisa's class that they will now be taught an alternative theory on the origins of man while the teacher, Miss Hoover, writes "creationism" on the board. Lisa, of course, protests, saying that creationism is not science. To mollify her, Skinner shows a videotape, a blatant propaganda piece called "So You're Calling God a Liar," which provides an "unbiased" comparison of evolutionism and creationism. According to the video, the Bible was written by "our Lord," whereas *The Origin of Species* "was written by a cowardly drunk, Charles Darwin," who is then shown making out with Satan. When Lisa attempts to rationally counter the slander—explaining that "evolution is a widely acknowledged scientific fact" and is even accepted by "prominent conservatives such as George Will and the late Pope John Paul"—Skinner instructs the children to drown her out with whistling and "arm-flatulence." When Lisa complains at a town meeting that there should only be one theory taught in the schools, Mayor Quimby agrees and bans the teaching of evolution. Lisa subsequently attempts to conduct a secret class for the scientifically "faithful," in which she reads passages from Darwin's book, but she is arrested for her actions and placed on trial. At the trial, which Kent Brockman dubs *God vs. Lisa Simpson*, Lisa is represented by "ACLU appointed liberal Clarice Drummond," a clear stand-in for Clarence Darrow. Prosecuting the case is "humble country lawyer Wallace Brady." Brady's first witness, a "scientist" who says that he has "a PhD in truthology from Christian Tech," dismisses evolution as "pure hogwash" because the evolutionary record contains a "missing link." The key witness winds up being Ned Flanders, who claims that he is positive that man and ape cannot be related—that is, until Homer, unsuccessfully trying to open a bottle of Duff beer, tests Ned's patience to the point that Ned bursts out, "Would you shut your yap, you big monkey-faced gorilla." Clarice Drummond uses this as a wedge and gets Ned to confess that Homer (and thereby, Man) could possibly be related to an ape, and the judge then orders the repeal of the law banning the teaching of evolution.

Admittedly, the satirical perspective at the end of "The Monkey Suit" is neither as strong nor as unidirectional as it is in other episodes of *The Simpsons* dealing with religion. As Ted Gournelos rightly notes, the "resolution" proposed by the judge "relies upon, rather than displaces, subject positioning"; in other words, devout Christians exist alongside devoted secularists, and both parties are able to sincerely refer to the "truth" as they see it.[59] Moreover, the reliance upon parody and irony in the depiction of the trial lawyers and witnesses makes targets of them all and thus (at least implicitly) criticizes those on both sides of the creationism debate. This creates a more open-ended resolution, which allows viewers on either side of the debate to see their own beliefs reaffirmed. Gournelos explains,

> Ironic treatments of the absurdity of religious discourse allow "liberal" communities distance from evangelicals, and similar treatments of whining "activists" allow conservative communities distance from historical objections to (and failures of) creationism in state institutions. The center-left is thus able to sneer as they enjoy the episode, and the right is able to affirm their own (victim-based) identity claims. The lack of sustained dissonance thus creates a community based on allusions without challenging the underlying pathways and patterns of discourse or the terms of debate. Without challenging anyone, therefore, the episode's masterful construction retains a patina of political engagement.[60]

While I concur with Gournelos's assessment of the ending of "The Monkey Suit"— and find myself wishing the writers had taken a clearer stand in favor of the separation of church and state—I cannot dismiss the episode as readily as he does; I don't read it as quite so apolitical. To my mind, the episode fits in very well with the others I have discussed so far in this chapter as satirical attacks on Christianity and fundamentalist zeal, primarily because of the satire offered in earlier parts of the episode, such as the assertion that the biblical story of creation is a "myth" and the censuring of the blatant propaganda techniques used by "people of faith" in public education settings.

Another important target of the religious satire on *The Simpsons* is the widespread belief in an exclusive link between religion and morality. In *Planet Simpson*, Chris Turner accurately notes that religion does not dictate the morality of the Simpson family: "There is a general sense of right and wrong in the Simpson household that is as much a product of Marge's belief in the sanctity of family and Lisa's deeply held humanistic ethics as it is of any particular gospel."[61] That morality and religion are not synonymous is something many people—particularly those within the Judeo-Christian tradition—have a hard time comprehending, as they have often been trained to see the two as inextricably linked. Many such individuals believe that their morality derives from religious doctrine—that is, they subscribe to the divine command theory—and that ethical choices can only be made with reference to religious texts and tenets. However, as James Rachels eloquently explains in *The Elements of Moral Philosophy*, this is not the case. Although the divine command theory holds great appeal, the theory is weak in numerous ways. Christian and secular philosophers have long wrestled with questions of doctrine and morality and have come to see the flaws of the divine command theory. First, God's commands can be shown to be arbitrary, since God could have given different commands (e.g., commanding lying to be good rather than truthfulness). As the Enlightenment led to further scientific discoveries and to a better understanding of the world and of human nature, the reigning theory came to be that moral judgments are, in the words of Saint Thomas Aquinas, "the dictates of reason." Many philosophers have thus abandoned a theological view of morality, hypothesizing instead that "God commands it because it is right," which leads to the conclusion that "there is some standard of right and wrong that is independent of God's will."[62]

Marge Simpson is a Christian, and she appears to abide by the laws of that faith. But Marge is also a rationalist, and her choices do not always align with doctrine—indeed, they often contradict it. In the aforementioned "Homer vs. Lisa and the 8th Commandment," for example, Marge is at a loss to identify the rule she is breaking when she pilfers two grapes at the local grocery store. Lisa, at this point rather intensely focused on sin and damnation, asks Marge, "Don't you remember the eighth commandment?" "Of course," Marge replies. "It's 'Thou shall not...um...covet graven images'—something about covet." "It's 'Thou shall not steal!'" Lisa shouts. Marge's more secularist position is also seen in the season 8 episode "In Marge We Trust," in which Marge becomes the "Listen Lady" of the First Church of Springfield after Reverend Lovejoy loses interest in helping his parishioners. As she tells Reverend Lovejoy, "Sermons about 'constancy' and 'prudissitude' are all well and good, but the church could be doing so much more to reach out to people." What Marge proceeds to do is offer friendly, commonsense advice rather than scripture to the troubled citizens of Springfield who call her show. In short, Marge Simpson straddles the religious and secular realms, drawing upon the strengths of both and using what is most appropriate from either in response to a given situation. According to Gerald Erion and Joseph Zeccardi, in their essay "Marge's Moral Motivation," this quality classifies Marge as a "Christian-flavored Aristotelian." Marge is a good and virtuous person, and the character traits that make her so—for example, friendliness, honesty, and compassion—are as much a consequence of adhering to certain tenets of Christianity as they are of employing reason and rationality. The important distinction that Erion and Zeccardi draw is between theological moralism and philosophical ethics—that is, between the divine command theory and secular humanism. As the authors state, "To resolve her moral dilemmas, Marge simply allows reason to guide her conduct to a thoughtful and admirable balance between extremes"—the extremes here being the secular amorality of Mayor Quimby and the religious fundamentalism of Ned Flanders.[63]

One of the finest examples of Marge's moral reasoning is in the episode "There's Something about Marrying," which I discuss in chapter 4. As my focus in that chapter is on sexuality and civil rights, I do not delve into the religious aspects of Marge's confrontation with Reverend Lovejoy in front of the church. I do so here because the scene is important to appreciating Marge as a rational character and to understanding the secularized perspective of *The Simpsons*. Recall that Lovejoy had nailed shut the doors to the First Church of Springfield and declared that he could not (though, more accurately, would not) perform same-sex marriages. Marge quite rationally states, "As long as two people love each other, I don't think God cares whether they have the same hoo-hoo or ha-ha." Marge is clearly "striking a blow for civil rights," as Lisa put it, but she is also quite directly challenging Lovejoy's perspective and thereby challenging the authority of religion as an arbiter of morality. When Lovejoy tells her, "The Bible forbids same sex relations," she reasonably asks, "Which book?" The writers are making an important point here about the selective interpretation of the Bible to justify persecution, knowing many viewers would be well aware that the book most likely to be cited is Leviticus; but for Lovejoy, it is all one book: "Which book?" he incredulously repeats. "The Bible!" Lovejoy then begins to ring the church bell to silence Marge's protest. Over the sound of the bell, one can hear Marge begin to say, "But Reverend, scriptural scholars disagree on the significance of . . ." Her words are briefly drowned out by Lovejoy's actions, but a moment later one can hear

Marge conclude, ". . . Jesus's teachings stress inclusiveness and compassion." Marge's comments underscore what is fundamental to the view of religion on display on *The Simpsons*: a distinction between Old Testament and New Testament worldviews. The intolerance practiced by the pious and the religious is "justified" for believers by scripture, but that scripture is invariably in the Old Testament. As is well known, that half of the Bible was long used to justify slavery, abuse, torture, and the subjugation of women, among other things. In light of the social and political changes wrought by the modern civil rights movement, such texts are rarely referred to today outside of more fundamentalist circles. In general, Christianity has largely shifted its focus to the New Testament, to the teaching of Jesus, and to the very virtues that Marge Simpson embodies—virtues that, as she attempts to remind Reverend Lovejoy, are a part of the Christian faith. Of course, the dichotomized view of the Bible presented by *The Simpsons* is an oversimplification of matters; the New Testament remains in many ways as troublesome and problematic as the Old Testament—for example, in its continuing support of patriarchal structures of dominance. But the creators of *The Simpsons* are simplifying things with a purpose: in this case, to condemn the recourse to fear, hatred, and violence so often promoted by Old Testament texts and a strictly religious worldview and to highlight the potential links between New Testament teachings and a more humanistic worldview, which are evident in their shared emphases on qualities such as compassion, brotherhood, and love.

Conclusion

As pointed out previously, the distinction between Old and New Testament world-views has been largely ignored by many of those who have written at length about religion and *The Simpsons*, even though it is clearly key to understanding the positions the show takes on "moral" issues, such as gay marriage. To be fair, Mark Pinsky's book *The Gospel According to "The Simpsons"* was originally published well in advance of "There's Something about Marrying," so the episode could not have been addressed. However, in 2007, Pinsky released a second edition of his book, with the subtitle *Bigger and Possibly Even Better! Edition*, in which he included a chapter (of a mere seven pages) entitled "Gay Marriage: Out of the Closet, Left at the Altar." In summary, Pinsky sees "There's Something about Marrying" as part of a cultural trend catering to gay consumers, citing the "Gay Days" event at Disney World in 2006 as an example. Oddly, Pinsky then cites Marty Kaplan, the associate dean of the Annenberg School of Communication at the University of Southern California, who was interviewed by *The New York Times* about "There's Something about Marrying." Kaplan stated that he believed the episode was addressing the Religious Right, who seem "hell-bent" on demonizing the "homosexualist agenda," and was telling them to "lighten up" and "get out of town" because "these people are your neighbors in the Springfield that is America."[64] Perhaps for balance, Pinsky also quotes the comments of the producer and veteran writer Mike Reiss, who told *Encore Magazine* (an Australian publication), "Gay people came out very much in favour of it and were very happy with the episode. But arch conservatives and right wing Christians loved the episode too because they seemed to think we were making fun of gay people. We really had it both ways."[65] Beyond this, Pinsky offers no insights about "There's Something about Marrying": instead, the phrase "left at the altar" in the title is used to imply a smug satisfaction with the fact that the central gay marriage in the episode was not brought to fruition—presumably another "victory" for family values.

Jamey Heit similarly dismisses the topic of homosexuality in *The Springfield Reformation: "The Simpsons," Christianity, and American Culture*, although in this case by not addressing the issue at all. Although Heit's book is timely enough to include lengthy observations of *The Simpsons Movie*, released in the summer of 2007, there is *not a single mention* of the episode "There's Something about Marrying" (which aired in 2005) or, for that matter, of "Homer's Phobia" or "Three Gays of the Condo." Nor is there any discussion of Waylon Smithers. I can only assume that Heit could find nothing in these episodes and nothing about Smithers's life that could work in service of his thesis. In his "Concluding Trumpet Blast," Heit makes his larger concern perfectly clear: "While the extent to which *The Simpsons* is critical of American Christianity suggests that the faith tradition has lost its ability to be relevant in American culture, one can see in the show's inevitable emphasis on coming together that *The Simpsons* does not give up on Christianity."[66] A similar sentiment is expressed in Pinsky's concluding chapter, the title of which poses a question about *The Simpsons*: "Cloaking the Sacred with the Profane?" For Pinsky, the answer is clearly "yes." However, as even Pinsky acknowledges, "whether the series, once considered so antiauthoritarian, is subversive or supportive of faith is largely in the eye of the beholder."[67] Indeed it is, and one's interpretation is dependent on many factors, not the least of which is what one means by a term such as *faith*. Pinsky's statement echoes the views of William Romanowski, the author of *Pop Culture Wars: Religion & the Role of Entertainment in American Life* (1996), who claims that episodes of *The Simpsons* "generally leave the matter of God and religion open to multiple interpretations, perhaps so as not to potentially alienate audience members, but also as a reflection of American attitudes."[68]

For all the dogmatic quoting of scripture in Pinsky's and Heit's texts, their claims boil down to three things: family, brotherhood, and love, which they find in abundance on *The Simpsons*. Does Christianity have an exclusive claim to these values? Of course not. As I noted previously, the aims of mainline Christianity and humanism run along parallel tracks, and this is reflected in many episodes of *The Simpsons*. But it is not enough to simply note that a degree of ambiguity exists and that viewers can often read the show in accord with their own beliefs. Above all, *The Simpsons* is a satire, and as such it has a particular take on those elements of the culture seen to be problematic. What the show regularly satirizes are elements of a far-right religious fundamentalism, an outgrowth of Religious Right perspectives that have come to have a powerful influence in American culture. As Kevin Phillips notes in *American Theocracy* (2006), "[T]he radical side of U.S. religion has embraced cultural anti-modernism, war hawkishness, Armageddon prophecy, and in the case of conservative fundamentalists, a demand for government by literal biblical interpretation."[69] Religious organizations such as the Moral Majority, the Christian Coalition, the Southern Baptist Convention, and Focus on the Family have had an enormous impact on the American political system over the past three decades: they have shaped the national conversation over "moral issues" that have been centerpieces of the culture wars for the past 40 years, and they have been very successful in prompting the populace to react to these issues with emotion rather than reason. As Phillips further argues, changes in affiliation away from mainline Protestantism and toward more "radical" sects has pushed the United States toward a "national Disenlightenment."[70]

Such a claim is not new, of course. Richard Hofstadter explored a similar theme in his seminal *Anti-Intellectualism in American Life* (1963), which described the three pillars of anti-intellectualism that he believed to be widespread in the postwar era: evangelical religion, practical-minded business, and a populist political style. As Todd Gitlin noted in 2000, amid the debacle of the presidential race between George Bush Jr. and Al Gore, "Those pillars stand."[71] I think it is fair to say that Gitlin's claim and Hofstader's earlier insights still ring true, as evidenced by the publication of books such as Charles Freeman's *The Closing of the Western Mind: The Rise of Faith and the Fall of Reason* (2003), Al Gore's *The Assault on Reason* (2007), and Susan Jacoby's *The Age of American Unreason* (2008).[72]

Such righteous moralizing and anti-intellectualism are widely evident in Springfield, which is representative of America in general, and *The Simpsons* displays them to be satirized. The impatience with religion that has been building over many years is evident in the very blunt way it is dismissed in "Bart Has Two Mommies," which aired in March 2006. This episode opens with the Simpson family entering the grounds of the church fund-raiser (which, according to the banner at the entrance, "Does Not Count as Church"), where they pass by fund-raising games such as Whack-a-Moses, Holy Roller-Coaster, and the Tunnel of Abstinence. One scene shows Lenny and Carl playing "Halo Toss," a game in which they toss rings onto the heads of saints. Like any carnival game, it's rigged such that the odds are against the player. Frustrated, Lenny says, "Who knew saints had such big heads?" Carl asserts, "Ah, it's all a big scam." "This booth?" Lenny asks. "No, religion in general," Carl replies. Of course, it is safe to put this view into the mouths of somewhat peripheral characters rather than members of the Simpsons family, even Lisa. Nonetheless, there is a thread running through the narrative of this episode—indeed, as I have tried to demonstrate in this chapter, through the entirety of *The Simpsons* as a series—that underscores the idea that religion, particularly Christianity, is a sham. This lends support to the view that the critique offered by Lenny and Carl is not just the opinion of two minor characters but of the creative voices behind *The Simpsons* as well.

Conclusion

American Culture, Satire, and
The Simpsons

Oh, Marge, cartoons don't have any deep meaning. They're just stupid drawings that give you a cheap laugh.

—*Homer Simpson*[1]

As noted in the introductory chapter, the early 1990s debate over the "culture war" has carried on in the new millennium, largely among the concept's progenitor, James Hunter, and the political scientists Alan Wolfe and Morris Fiorina. This was made most evident with the publication of *Is There a Culture War? A Dialogue on Values and American Life* (2006), which Hunter and Wolfe coedited and to which Fiorina contributed. Although Hunter has continued to use the culture war metaphor, he now concedes that the divisions among people within the nation are not as stark or as binary as the culture war thesis once made it seem. Nevertheless, Hunter and many other scholars remain convinced that a battle still exists. As I have tried to demonstrate in the preceding chapters, I do as well. The powerful clash of worldviews evident in American society today is part of an ongoing struggle, one concerned not only with which worldview will predominate—the more conservative or the more progressive—but also with how the various skirmishes in the culture war will shape the very definition of "American" identity for the future. In a recent essay on this topic, James Hunter accurately notes that there is some common ground in the culture war: both sides of the debate, for example, embrace the "symbolic identity of America as *e pluribus unum*"; what the opponents differ on, Hunter notes, has to do with the limits and range of the pluralism implied by that famous phrase.[2] Hunter continues,

> In our time, what does exist of a dominant culture is attenuated. Indeed, if there is a center in American culture and politics today, it is certainly not "the vital center" that Arthur Schlesinger, Jr. described and hoped for at mid-century. In fact, it is probably fair to say that Schlesinger's "vital center" and the WASP consensus that underwrote it may have begun to erode the moment he declared its triumph.[3]

The culture wars persist today in part because there is no clear center any longer, and we are all struggling for a way to redefine ourselves and our nation. The center

Schlesinger so confidently spoke of—or at least the unquestioning presumption and acceptance of it—had most certainly begun to erode by the time *The Simpsons* appeared in 1989, on the heels of the social unrest of the 1960s, the political turmoil of the 1970s, and the cultural struggles of the 1980s. And it is this center—this sense of "normative" American identity, whether in regard to race and ethnicity, gender, sexuality, class status, or religion—that *The Simpsons* so rigorously questions and satirically critiques on a regular basis.

The Simpsons has had a remarkable impact on the television landscape, most notably in paving the way for further experiments in satirical comedy, on both network and cable channels. Indeed, as the editors of *Satire TV* rightly claim, "no single program is as important in creating the televisual space for the satire TV boom as *The Simpsons*."[4] There is no doubt that satire has become more popular and more mainstream in American culture since the advent of *The Simpsons*, as evident from the growth of Comedy Central and the success of shows such as *South Park*, *Politically Correct*, *The Daily Show with Jon Stewart*, and *The Colbert Report*. Of course, the greater visibility of satire does not necessarily mean that it is better appreciated or understood by audiences. Satire is a complex comedic art form, heavily reliant on irony, and it can quite easily be misunderstood; in short, audiences can and do often "miss the joke." This is not to say that certain audience members are somehow incapable of "getting" satirical humor. Paul Simpson reminds us, "While satire may be relatively complexly ordered and structured, that complexity does not place it beyond the ken of ordinary participants in discourse."[5] Nonetheless, understanding satire does require significant effort—often much more than many audience members have been conditioned to give. As the authors of "Missing the Joke: A Reception Analysis of Satirical Texts" astutely observe,

> Satirical content relies on readers being in the know, and it is easy to judge those who do not get the joke as ignorant of the premise or not smart enough to understand the humor. However, as the tradition of audience research tells us, audience members are active, selective, and motivated by interests that do not necessarily line up with those of a text's author. Audience readings hold the possibility of a variety of readings, some highly idiosyncratic and others sharing common features.[6]

The difficulties with satire stem partly from the fact that the satirist must, of necessity, put on display those elements of the culture that are up for ridicule and censure. In other words, in order to satirize something, the artist must show it. This simple fact has led to a great deal of misinterpretation over the years. It has, for example, plagued Mark Twain's *Huckleberry Finn*, which was—and still is—criticized and suppressed by censors and other moralists who only superficially read the text, missing its nuances and ironies and, ultimately, its condemnation of racism and racial segregation. As William Savage correctly points out in his discussion of satire and censorship, satire depends upon "multiple levels of signification and the reader's willingness to participate in serious interpretive behavior, to read deeply."[7] Censors and other moralists, however, typically read on a singular and superficial level. This is a problem faced by many contemporary satirists, who often try to address the potential for misinterpretation. The filmmaker Kevin Smith, for example, employed tongue-in-cheek humor at the start of his film *Dogma* (1999), a satire on Catholicism and commercialism. Perhaps aware that many people today are, as Michael Moore once put it, "ironically illiterate," Smith opens *Dogma* with a series of disclaimers, beginning with the phrase "Not to be taken seriously" and concluding with this statement:

> To insist that any of what follows is incendiary or inflammatory is to miss our intention. Please—before you think about hurting someone over this trifle of a film, remember: even God has a sense of humor. Just look at the Platypus. Thank you and enjoy the show.[8]

A very different approach was taken by the filmmaker Spike Lee for *Bamboozled* (2000), his astute satire on contemporary race relations. Knowing that many people would simply see images of blackface performance (by both black and white actors) and then simplistically condemn his film as "racist," Lee more bluntly opted to append a dictionary definition of satire to the start of the film.[9] Artists such as Moore, Smith, and Lee obviously understand that in order to satirize something effectively, one has to show it. Satire reveals ugly truths—and it often requires that such ugliness be presented to audiences. This is not to say that everything displayed by the satirist is up for censure; the key is in knowing the difference between what is targeted for ridicule and what is treated with sincerity, and this depends on the viewer's ability to "read deeply," as William Savage states. The interpretation of satirical art also depends on audiences understanding the subtleties of tone (the use of sarcasm, for example) and recognizing some of the key markers of satire (e.g., irony, exaggeration, and juxtaposition). Nevertheless, satirical art can and will be interpreted in a variety of ways and not always in alignment with what the artist meant to convey.

One excellent example of the difficulties of interpretation is the "satirical" cartoon that appeared on the cover of the July 21, 2008, issue of *The New Yorker*. The cover featured a cartoon rendering of Barack Obama and his wife, Michelle, standing in the Oval Office, he in a turban and she in combat gear and toting a machine gun, giving one another a "fist-bump" while an American flag burns in a fireplace, just beneath the prominently displayed portrait of Osama Bin Laden. The image, by illustrator Barry Blitt, was entitled "The Politics of Fear," although the title of the cartoon did not appear on the magazine's cover.[10] The release of the magazine immediately touched off a controversy, and the ensuing debate spilled onto the pages of major newspapers and into the coverage of the cable news channels. The *New Yorker* editor David Remnick, who suddenly found himself on the defensive, tried to explain that the cartoon was intended to be satirical. In an interview with *The Huffington Post*, Remnick said,

> I respect people's reactions. I'm just trying as calmly and as clearly as possible to talk about what this image means and what it was intended to mean and what I think most people will see, when they think it through, that it means. The fact is, it's not a satire about Obama; it's a satire about the distortions and misconceptions and prejudices *about* Obama.[11]

There were few people, however, who saw it as a satire in this way; many people—curiously, on both the political right and the political left—simply saw it as slander. The Obama campaign chastised *The New Yorker*, calling the cartoon "tasteless and offensive," a claim with which even Obama's opponent, John McCain, agreed.[12] In an interview with CNN's Larry King, Obama himself more mildly stated, "I do think that in attempting to satirize something, they probably fueled some misconceptions about me instead. But that was their editorial judgment, and as I said, ultimately, it is a cartoon. It's not what the American people are spending a lot of their time thinking about."[13]

The controversy over *The New Yorker* cover highlights at least two things relevant to my study of *The Simpsons*. First, it reminds us of the deeply held belief that cartoons hold little or no meaning for serious-minded adults. Even Barack Obama, who admits that the cartoon has real-world effects—that is, that the implied associations it depicts might fuel misconceptions about him or tarnish his public image—was nonetheless quick to dismiss the image as "just a cartoon." As I hope to have shown throughout this book, *The Simpsons* is much more than a cartoon or, as Homer puts it, "stupid drawings that give you a cheap laugh." The show engages a number of important social, political, and cultural issues, seeking to satirically critique many problems in today's world. More specifically, as I have tried to demonstrate in the preceding chapters, *The Simpsons* is a thought-provoking satire, aimed at exposing not only stupidity, hypocrisy, and ineptitude but also—and even more importantly—the potential dangers of a host of powerful ideologies intimately connected to the American culture wars. Second, the incident with *The New Yorker* reminds us that satire is a complex mode of humor, both hard to execute and hard to control. The truth of this was clear in the commentary that appeared in the editorial pages of newspapers such as *The Washington Post*, *The Los Angeles Times*, *The Boston Globe*, and *The New York Times*, all of which highlighted the fact that the Obama cartoon was interpreted by different audiences in vastly different ways.[14] The point was underscored further, although in a much more humorous way, by *The Daily Show*, which sent its team of "reporters" out on the streets of New York to see what the average person thought about the *New Yorker* cover and what they understood about satire. As might be expected, people responded to and interpreted the magazine image in very different ways; they also made quite clear in the process that they knew very little about the art of satire.[15]

Such variance in interpretation is, of course, expected in response to any satirical text, including a television show such as *The Simpsons*. As I have illustrated throughout the preceding chapters, there is no guarantee about how episodes of the show will be interpreted by audiences or about what they see as either ridiculed or validated. In this regard, *The Simpsons* is not unlike one of its precursors, *All in the Family*. As Josh Ozersky notes in his study of the show, reactions to and commentaries on *All in the Family* were very divided. Some believed the "new realism" of Lear's sitcom was a step forward, "an emancipation from the see-no-evil escapism of 1960s television," whereas others saw it as a step backward and "an introduction of potent toxins into the main artery of American social life."[16] And, of course, both sides could find ample evidence within episodes of *All in the Family* to support their interpretations. Ozersky points out, for example, that a study conducted by two social scientists not long after the show premiered concluded that "both liberals and conservatives came away from *All in the Family* with their perspectives intact."[17] Reactions to *The Simpsons* have operated in much the same way, and the show has been both widely praised and widely condemned.

Curiously, just as I was putting the finishing touches on this book, *The Simpsons* aired yet another episode that sparked a minor controversy. This one, like the one surrounding the *New Yorker* cover, involves both Muslims and fear-mongering. In the episode "Holidays of Future Passed," which aired on December 11, 2011, the show offers a glimpse of a future in which a married Lisa Simpson helps her husband, Milhouse, deal with his seasonal allergies, which make him allergic to Christmas-related objects such as holly. In discussing the problem, Milhouse suggests to Lisa, "I could nurse my allergies in one of the non-Christmas celebrating states." Lisa suggests, "You could go back to Michigan. It's still under Sharia law." "Yeah," Milhouse replies, "but they always make me wear a veil." We then see a picture of Milhouse standing before a sign for the University of Michigan-Dearborn and wearing a body-covering dress known as a niqab, which covers the entire body and face except for the eyes. Behind him are two men who appear to be Muslim.

Some viewers might be puzzled by these brief comments and images, but those in the know would recognize the allusion to ongoing debates, both in Michigan and around the nation, regarding Islam and the role of Islamic law—debates that have been a staple of the post-9/11 era but that have intensified since 2008 and the election of Barack Obama. As mentioned, the cover of *The New Yorker* focused people's attention on assertions that were in wide circulation during the 2008 presidential campaign season: namely, that Barack Obama was a "secret Muslim" and anti-American. This rhetoric only worsened after the election, once Obama stepped into the quagmire in the Middle East created by George Bush and began to openly confront Republicans on domestic policy, most notably on health care. The resistance to Obama and the concomitant anti-Muslim sentiment intensified even more as the nation approached the 2010 midterm elections, as evident from the rise of the Tea Party movement and of the "birthers" within it, who made an issue of Obama's birth certificate, thereby conflating questions of national identity, religion, and race—perhaps not a surprise in a nation that has long equated whiteness and Christianity with patriotic American identity. Anti-Muslim attitudes were also evident during the summer of 2010 in the furor over the so-called Ground Zero Mosque in New York City and in the arrest of four Christian evangelists (the Dearborn Four) at the annual Arab festival in Dearborn, Michigan.[18] Most notably, anti-Islamic sentiment has been a part of the shrill and oft-repeated claims of a host of conservative politicians that the United States will soon be taken over by "stealth jihadis" intent on imposing Sharia (Islamic) law.[19] The most vocal of these has been Newt Gingrich, who first sounded the alarm about Sharia law in a speech given at the American Enterprise Institute in July 2010. Gingrich told his audience, "Stealth jihadis use political, cultural, societal, religious, intellectual tools; violent jihadis use violence. But in fact they're both engaged in jihad, and they're both seeking to impose the same end state, which is to replace Western civilization with a radical imposition of Shariah."[20] Not surprisingly, Gingrich referred specifically to Dearborn, Michigan, since it has one of the largest populations of Muslims in the United States today.

With "Holidays of Future Passed," we can see once again how cultural trends quickly become incorporated into *The Simpsons*. Of course, given the lead time necessary to develop and produce an episode of *The Simpsons*, the timing of this episode is even more remarkable: it aired almost immediately on the heels of *All-American Muslim*, a new television series on TLC (The Learning Channel) that itself caused controversy and sparked another wave of debate about Muslims in America.[21] *All-American Muslim*, which premiered in November 2011, follows the lives of five Muslim American families in Dearborn, Michigan, ostensibly in an effort to make

Muslims seem less threatening to "average" Americans. Although the show is inoffensive to the point of being bland, it nonetheless spurred a number of advertisers to quickly withdraw their support; among those that did were Kayak, the travel website, and Lowe's, the home-improvement retailer.[22] The passing reference to Dearborn, Michigan, in "Holidays of Future Passed" is obviously not a direct allusion to *All-American Muslim*, but it is clearly designed to mock the idea that Dearborn—or any other US city, for that matter—will soon be under Sharia law, as some have alleged. It is also clearly meant to censure the Islamophobia that has become so visible and widespread in the United States over the past decade. In her aptly titled essay "Fear of a Muslim America," Cathy Young points out that

> anti-Islamic bigotry has become a visible presence in Republican politics and the respectable conservative media. All around the country, right-of-center activists and politicians are trying to use government force to limit the property rights of Muslims and repel the alleged menace of Shariah law. Islamophobia has crossed the line from fringe rhetorical hysteria to active discrimination against U.S. citizens of the Islamic faith.[23]

That *The Simpsons* would step into this heated territory speaks again to the political nature of the show, but it also reminds us of the difficulties of presenting satire. Curiously, the Fox affiliate in Detroit (WJBK) sent a reporter, Bill Gallagher, to the University of Michigan-Dearborn to ask students about "Holidays of Future Passed" and their reactions to its jokes about Islam.[24] Their responses are illuminating. "It was funny seeing it as a cartoon," said one female student, Leann Beydoun. "I didn't know whether to laugh about it or to be upset about it." Another female student, Betool Garbie, said, "It's pretty cool showing how ridiculous the hate is. I think it's pretty funny." Mouhamed Bislih agreed: "*The Simpsons* make fun of everybody," he said. "It was funny. It wasn't offensive, I guess." However, one student (his name was not given) argued that ridiculing anti-Islamic bigotry may not be effective. "Trying to change their opinions—this is not a good thing—I don't think it's a good thing," he said, continuing to state that "we can change [opinions] by talking, not making fun." Dawud Walid, the head of the Council on American Islamic Relations, found the Dearborn references humorous: "*The Simpsons* is a very prolific show," he said. "Now *The Simpsons* is addressing this anti-Sharia fear mongering issue, and perhaps it may gain some currency and more people will make fun of it." Suhehalia Amen, president of the Lebanese-American Club at the university, agreed, saying, "Every group really vies for that type of attention, and when you make it to *The Simpsons*, you've really hit high ground."

Such comments make clear that, as with the cover of *The New Yorker* magazine, there is a great variance of interpretation among audiences, not only over an episode such as "Holidays of Future Passed" but also over *The Simpsons* itself. This is because satire is a form of discourse without "clear-cut digestible meanings"; indeed, it can be hard "work" for viewers, as it requires a certain level of sophistication, and it demands both "a heightened state of awareness and mental participation."[25] To my mind, the reference to current debates about Islam in the United States in "Holidays of Future Passed" underscores above all that the sympathies of the creators of *The Simpsons* lie mainly with the liberal left and in opposition to the hysteria, fear-mongering, and scapegoating so often propagated by the conservative right. The joke about Sharia law in the episode is a reminder of how the creators of *The Simpsons* engage with thorny political topics such as ethnicity, nationality, and religion, as I explore in some detail in both chapter 2 and chapter 6. It is also a reminder of how deftly the creators of *The Simpsons* can satirize cultural issues. Although the lag time necessary for creating an episode doesn't give them the ability to respond as readily as *South Park* or "fake news" programs such as *The Daily Show* or *The Colbert Report*, "Holidays of Future Passed" shows how attuned the writers are to the ongoing culture war debates and how adept they are at weaving these into the texts of episodes for satirical commentary.

As I stated in the introductory chapter, my intention in this book was to explore *The Simpsons'* satirical engagement with some of the more highly politicized issues in the culture war debates in American society and to examine the potential difficulties in doing so given the show's status as a profit-generating product of a multinational media empire. Although *The Simpsons* is a sharp and sophisticated satire, it is also a commercial entity, beholden to the imperatives of the television industry and to the desires of its parent company, one of which is to maximize profit. As a result, the show is sometimes complicit in perpetuating rather than challenging certain dominant ideologies. Given the economics of both the industry and *The Simpsons*, it is perhaps not surprising that the topic on which the satire most wavers is socioeconomic class, as discussed in chapter 5. That said, I would still assert that overall *The Simpsons* succeeds as satire. As I hope to have made clear in the preceding chapters, the show offers viewers important critiques of very serious problems in American society—for example, sexism, nativism, xenophobia, homophobia, and religious fundamentalism. In short, *The Simpsons* stands apart from almost every other show on television by refusing to accept the status quo and by regularly—although not exclusively—challenging prevailing beliefs. When viewed as satire, it becomes clear that *The Simpsons* is a show that continually challenges us to think seriously about our lives today, to question our existing beliefs, to examine our current values, and to imagine the ways in which we all might help to make the world a better place.

Notes

Introduction: *The Simpsons*, Satire, and American Culture

1. Robert J. Thompson, *Television's Second Golden Age: From Hill Street Blues to ER* (New York: Continuum, 1996), 19.
2. "Simpsons Roasting on an Open Fire" (#7G08) ranked thirtieth for its timeslot the night it premiered and earned Fox a 22 percent share and a 14.5 rating. See "Nielsens," *USA Today*, December 20, 1989, 3D, Lexis-Nexis Academic, October 2, 2003.
3. "Bart the Genius" (#7G02) ranked forty-eighth for its timeslot and earned Fox a 19 percent share and a 12.7 rating. See "Nielsens," *USA Today*, January 17, 1990, 3D, Lexis-Nexis Academic, October 2, 2003.
4. Harry F. Waters, "Family Feuds," *Newsweek*, April 23, 1990, 58.
5. Although *The Simpsons* often ranked within the top ten for weekly or monthly Nielsen totals, the show has not ranked high overall: at the end of the 1989–90 season, its first full season on the air, *The Simpsons* ranked only thirtieth. See "Final Season Ratings," *Electronic Media*, April 23, 1990, 36, Lexis-Nexis Academic, October 2, 2003. http:// web.lexis-nexis.com/universe. Curiously, the show has never been among the top 25 in the Nielsen seasonal totals. It is no longer the ratings juggernaut it once was, but new episodes of *The Simpsons* still rank in the Nielsen top 50 among prime-time television shows and often in the top 20 among shows in syndication. Tim Brooks and Earle Marsh, *The Complete Directory to Prime Time Network and Cable TV Shows, 1946–Present*, 8th ed. (New York: Ballantine, 2003), 1073–74. Also see *Nielsen Report on Television*, Nielsen Media Research (Northbrook, IL: A. C. Nielsen Company, 1998).
6. Note that it has only beaten *Gunsmoke* in the number of years on the air, not the total number of episodes made. *Gunsmoke* still holds the record with 635 episodes.
7. Joanna Doonar, "Homer's Brand Odyssey," *Brand Strategy*, February 2004, 20.
8. Alyson Grala, "A Salute to *The Simpsons*," *License! Global* May 16, 2007. http:// www.licensemag.com/licensemag/data/articlestandard//licensemag/192007/425752 /article.pdf.
9. In the first week of its release, in late June 2007, *The Simpsons Movie* had earned $110,979,172 in domestic ticket sales; the total worldwide gross for the film eventually surpassed half a billion dollars—it made $183,135,014 domestically and another $343,610,123 in foreign markets, for a total earnings of $526,745,137. "The Simpsons Movie," *Box Office Mojo*, Box Office Mojo, LLC, March 10, 2008, http://www. boxofficemojo.com/movies/?id=simpsons.htm.
10. For more, see Gerald Graff, *Beyond the Culture Wars: How Teaching the Conflicts Can Revitalize American Education* (New York: W. W. Norton, 1992); Henry Louis Gates Jr., *Loose Canons: Notes on the Culture Wars* (New York: Oxford University Press, 1992); Todd Gitlin, *The Twilight of Common Dreams: Why America is Wracked*

by Culture Wars (New York: Metropolitan, 1995); Paul DiMaggio, John Evans, and Bethany Bryson, "Have Americans' Social Attitudes Become More Polarized?" *American Journal of Sociology* 102 (1996): 690–755; Nancy J. Davis and Robert V. Robinson, "Are the Rumors of War Exaggerated? Religious Orthodoxy and Moral Progressivism," *American Journal of Sociology* 102 (1996): 756–787; and Gertrude Himmelfarb, *One Nation, Two Cultures* (New York: Knopf, 1999).

11. The full title of Wolfe's book is *One Nation, After All: What Middle-Class Americans Really Think about God, Country, Family, Racism, Welfare, Immigration, Homosexuality, the Right, the Left, and Each Other* (New York: Viking, 1998).

12. Morris P. Fiorina, Samuel J. Abrams, and Jeremy C. Pope, *Culture War? The Myth of a Polarized America*, 3rd. ed. (New York: Longman, 2008), 9.

13. Ibid., 19.

14. Irene Taviss Thompson, *Culture Wars and Enduring American Dilemmas* (Ann Arbor: University of Michigan Press, 2010), 1. Thompson's study rests upon the analysis of 436 articles dealing with culture war issues in the pages of *National Review, The New Republic, Time,* and *The Nation* between 1980 and 2000.

15. Fiorina et al., *Culture War?*, 14.

16. Thompson, *Culture Wars and Enduring American Dilemmas*, 2.

17. James Q. Wilson, "How Divided Are We?" *Commentary*, February 2006: 19.

18. Ibid. In recent years, there has been a growth in scholarship rejecting earlier analyses and affirming the idea of a polarized populace. For more, see Alan I. Abramowitz and Kyle L. Saunders, "Is Polarization a Myth?" *Journal of Politics* 70, no. 2 (2008): 542–55.

19. The debate over the culture war concept has been carried on largely among James Hunter, Alan Wolfe, and Morris Fiorina, as evidenced by the publication of *Is There a Culture War? A Dialogue on Values and American Public Life* (Washington, DC: Brookings Institution Press, 2006), which Hunter and Wolfe coedited and to which Fiorina contributed. See, in particular, the contributions in this volume of Hunter, "The Enduring Culture War," 10–40; Wolfe, "The Culture War that Never Came," 41–73; and Fiorina, "Comment: Further Reflections on the Culture War Thesis," 83–89. Hunter has continued to use the culture war metaphor, most recently in relation to religion in the essay "The Culture War and the Sacred/Secular Divide: The Problem of Pluralism and Weak Hegemony," *Social Research* 76, no. 4 (2009): 1307–22.

20. Darrell Y. Hamamoto, *Nervous Laughter: Television Situation Comedy and Liberal Democratic Ideology* (New York: Praeger, 1989), 10.

21. It should be noted that with many of the culture war issues addressed in various episodes of *The Simpsons*, the writers often devote the entire time to a single storyline rather than dividing it, in typical sitcom fashion, between a plot and a subplot. This is true of episodes such as "Like Father, Like Clown," "Much Apu About Nothing," and "Mypods and Boomsticks," which I discuss in chapter 2; "Homer's Night Out," "The Springfield Connection," and "Lisa vs. Malibu Stacy," which I address in chapter 3; "Homer's Phobia" and "There's Something About Marrying," discussed in chapter 4; "Last Exit to Springfield" and "Scenes from the Class Struggle in Springfield," which I discuss in chapter 5; and "Homer the Heretic" and "Lisa the Skeptic," examined in chapter 6.

22. Waters, "Family Feuds," 59.

23. Joe Rhodes, "The Making of *The Simpsons*: Behind the Scenes at America's Funniest Homer Video," *Entertainment Weekly*, May 18, 1990: 5.

24. Tom Shales, "They're Scrapping Again—But This Time It's a Ratings Fight," *Washington Post*, October 11, 1990: C1.

25. See, for example, "Simpsons Just a Cartoon to TV Academy," *USA Today*, February 21, 1992, 1D; Richard Zoglin, "Where Fathers and Mothers Know Best," *Time*, June 1, 1992, 33; B. Zehme, "The Only Real People on TV," *Rolling Stone*, June 28, 1990, 40–43; Mark Muro, "Harvard's Laugh Track," *Boston Globe*, August 7, 1992, L25; John O'Connor, "The Misadventures of the Simpsons," *New York Times*, September 24, 1992, 18; Tom Shales, "America's Most Animated Family," *Washington Post*, September 24, 1992, C1; Ken Tucker, "Toon Terrific," *Entertainment Weekly*, March 12, 1993, 48–50; Tom Shales, "The Groening of America," *Washington Post*, May 13, 1993: C1; and Barbara Ehrenreich, "Oh Those Family Values," *Time*, June 18, 1994, 62.

26. Bruce Gomes, "Awards and Honours," *The Simpsons Archive*, November 5, 2007, http://snpp.com/guides/awards.html.

27. Paul Simpson, *On the Discourse of Satire: Towards a Stylistic Model of Satirical Humour* (Philadelphia: John Benjamins, 2003), 1. It should be noted that Simpson approaches satire from a largely traditional literary and linguistic perspective. However, he also acknowledges that satire is "a culturally situated discursive practice" inextricably bound up with social context and "frameworks of knowledge." His ideas thus remain quite flexible and applicable to predominately visual mass media texts such as *The Simpsons*. For more on this definition, see Simpson's chapter 1, 1–14.

28. David Marc, *Comic Visions: Television Comedy and American Culture*, 2nd ed. (Malden, MA: Blackwell, 1997), 13.

29. *The Flintstones* was the first prime-time cartoon made for television and previously the longest-running animated series in prime-time history. *The Jetsons*, modeled upon *The Flintstones* and designed to capitalize upon its success, failed as a prime-time show and ran only one year, from 1962 to 1963—it only later became popular as a Saturday-morning children's show. Brooks and Marsh, *Complete Directory*, 417–18 and 607. It should be noted that *The Simpsons* also owes a great debt to the animated films that preceded it, such as those produced by Disney, Warner Brothers, and Hanna-Barbera. *The Simpsons'* "Itchy and Scratchy" cartoon, for example, is unthinkable without the precedent of Hanna-Barbera's "Tom and Jerry."

30. An examination of *The Simpsons'* many predecessors and followers is far beyond the scope of this project. For a fine overview of the history touched on here, see Wendy Hilton-Morrow and David T. McMahan, "*The Flintstones* to *Futurama*: Networks and Prime Time Animation," in *Prime Time Animation: Television Animation and American Culture*, edited by Carol A. Stabile and Mark Harrison (New York: Routledge, 2003), 74–88.

31. Jonathan Gray, Jeffrey P. Jones, and Ethan Thompson, eds., *Satire TV: Politics and Comedy in the Post-Network Era* (New York: New York University Press, 2009), 25.

32. Harry Stein, "Our Times," *TV Guide*, May 23–29, 1992, 31.

33. Jessamyn Neuhaus, "Marge Simpson, Blue-Haired Housewife: Defining Domesticity on *The Simpsons*," *Journal of Popular Culture* 43, no. 4 (2010): 761.

34. My understanding of this tradition is informed by many sources but primarily by George Test's *Satire: Spirit and Art* (Tampa: University of South Florida Press, 1991), Dustin Griffin's *Satire: A Critical Reintroduction* (Lexington: University Press of Kentucky, 1994), Steven C. Weisenburger's *Fables of Subversion: Satire and the American Novel* (Athens: University of Georgia Press, 1995), and Stephan E. Kercher's invaluable *Revel with a Cause: Liberal Satire in Postwar America* (Chicago: University of Chicago Press, 2006).

35. Many more books were published on the topic of satire during this same period; however, few of these were generalized studies: the majority of them were more specifically about early forms of Greek and Roman satire—in the works of Horace,

Juvenal, Persius, and Lucian—or about British and European literature—in the works of writers such as Pope, Donne, Dryden, and Swift. For a comprehensive overview of these materials, see the introductory chapter of Griffin's *Satire: A Critical Reintroduction*.

36. Kernan and Frye quoted in Griffin, *Satire*, 35.
37. Griffin, *Satire*, 64.
38. *The Daily Show* has recently drawn a great deal of critical and scholarly attention. For analyses, see Geoffrey Baym, "*The Daily Show*: Discursive Integration and the Reinvention of Political Journalism," *Political Communication* 22, no. 3 (2005): 259–76; Aaron McKain, "Not Necessarily Not the News: Gatekeeping, Remediation, and *The Daily Show*," *Journal of American Culture* 28, no. 4 (2005): 415–30; Michael L. Ross and Lorraine York, "'First, They're Foreigners': *The Daily Show with Jon Stewart* and the Limits of Dissident Laughter," *Canadian Review of American Studies* 37, no. 3 (2007): 351–70; Paul R. Brewer and Emily Marquardt, "Mock News and Democracy: Analyzing *The Daily Show*," *Atlantic Journal of Communication* 15, no. 4 (2007): 249–67; "Journalism, Satire or Just Laughs? *The Daily Show with Jon Stewart*, Examined," Project for Excellence in Journalism, PEW Research Center, May 8, 2008, http://journalism.org/node/10953; Lisa Colletta, "Political Satire and Postmodern Irony in the Age of Stephen Colbert and Jon Stewart," *Journal of Popular Culture* 42, no. 5 (2009): 856–74; Gray et al., *Satire TV*; Jeffrey P. Jones, *Entertaining Politics: Satiric Television and Political Engagement* (Lanham, MD: Rowman & Littlefield, 2010); and Amarnath Amarasingam, ed., *The Stewart/Colbert Effect: Essays on the Real Impacts of Fake News* (Jefferson, NC: McFarland, 2011).
39. Brian Doherty, "Matt Groening," Interview, *Mother Jones* 24, no. 2 (March/April 1999): 35.
40. Linda Hutcheon, *A Theory of Parody: The Teachings of Twentieth-Century Art Forms* (Urbana: University of Illinois Press, 2000), 6.
41. Ibid., 11.
42. Ibid., 16.
43. Ibid., 37.
44. Ibid., 43.
45. The abundant use of parody on *The Simpsons* also helps to explain its longevity. Parody works particularly well in a media-saturated environment like our own, in which quick and easy references (primarily visual ones) can be made and can be assumed to be recognizable. Of course, this is also a very ephemeral type of humor, as the torrent of images and references that confront the reader/viewer are constantly supplanted by others.
46. Jonathan Gray, *Watching with "The Simpsons": Television, Parody, and Intertextuality* (New York: Routledge, 2006), 2.
47. Hugh Holman, "Satire," in *A Handbook to Literature*, 10th ed., ed. Hugh Holman and William Harmon (New York: Prentice Hall, 2005), 107.
48. Gray, *Watching with "The Simpsons,"* 2.
49. Ibid., 5.
50. Ibid., 8.
51. Ibid., 47.
52. Gray et al., *Satire TV*, 19.
53. Ibid., 49.
54. Horace Newcomb, ed., *Television: The Critical View*, 6th ed. (New York: Oxford University Press, 2000), 3–4.
55. Charlotte Brunsdon, "What Is the 'Television' in Television Studies?" in Newcomb, *Television: The Critical View*, 620–21.

56. John Fiske and John Hartley, *Reading Television* (London: Methuen, 1978), 36.

57. Notable examples of this are Henry Jenkins, *Textual Poachers: Television Fans and Visual Culture* (New York: Routledge, 1992); Lisa Lewis, *The Adoring Audience: Fan Culture and Popular Media* (New York: Routledge, 1992); David Morley, *Television, Audiences and Cultural Studies* (New York: Routledge, 1992); and Sut Jhally and Justin Lewis, *Enlightened Racism: The Cosby Show, Audiences, and the Myth of the American Dream* (New York: Westview, 1992).

58. Gray, *Watching with "The Simpsons,"* 119.

59. Ibid., 122.

60. Ibid., 120.

61. Ibid., 126–29.

62. Ibid., 131.

63. Ibid.

64. Ibid.

65. The remaining students did not identify in ways that fit neatly into the five generic categories listed here and instead used unique and creative identifiers: three students identified as "Arab", one as "White/Middle Eastern", one as "Middle Eastern", one as "Mixed", one as "Black/White", one as "African", one as Filipino, one as Vietnamese, two as Chinese, one as Chinese-American, one as Pacific Islander, one as Cuban-American, one as Mexican, and one as "Other."

66. Simone Knox, "Reading the Ungraspable Double-Codedness of *The Simpsons*," *Journal of Popular Film and Television* 34, no. 2 (2006): 72.

67. Chris Turner, *Planet Simpson: How a Cartoon Masterpiece Defined a Generation* (Cambridge, MA: Da Capo, 2004), 320.

68. Ibid.

69. Simpson, *On the Discourse of Satire*, 10.

70. The term *WASP* is highly problematic in this context because it is uncritically used in most studies of the television sitcom (see Marc, Jones, and Hamamoto). I cannot accept the term at face value and, therefore, will not employ it uncritically nor attempt to apply it transhistorically. I will discuss the concept more fully in chapter 2 in order to critically analyze its origins and usage, to argue that it is now both impractical and outdated, and to propose an alternative term.

1   "Entertain and Subvert": Fox Television, Satirical Comedy, and *The Simpsons*

1. Vladimir Nabokov, *Strong Opinions* (New York: McGraw-Hill, 1973), 75.

2. Fox dropped the suit a few days later. The publicity surrounding this only helped Franken: his book shot to the top of the Amazon.com bestseller list, and Penguin ordered a second print run of 50,000 copies. See "Fox Drops Suit vs. Franken over Book," *Book Publishing Report* 28, no. 33 (September 2003): 6.

3. Jeff Guinn, "Al Franken Celebrates a Well-Timed Lawsuit with New Book," *Fort Worth Star-Telegram*, September 5, 2003, 1.

4. Matt Groening, "*Simpsons* Creator Matt Groening," interview with Terry Gross, *Fresh Air*, National Public Radio, October 23, 2003, http://freshair.npr.org/day_fa.jht ml?display=day&todayDate=10/23/2003.

5. Matt Groening, interview with Jon Stewart, *The Daily Show with Jon Stewart*, Comedy Central, July 18, 2007, http://www.thedailyshow.com/video/index.jhtml?videoId=90145.

6. Paul Harris, "In the Yellow Corner: Simpsons and Fox Slug It Out over 'Racism' Jibe," *Guardian*, December 1, 2010, 25.

7. Dave Itzkoff, "Friendly Enemies on Fox: *Simpsons* and O'Reilly," *New York Times*, December 1, 2010, C3.

8. Amanda Lotz, "Textual (Im)Possibilities in the U.S. Post-Network Era: Negotiating Production and Promotion Processes on Lifetime's *Any Day Now*," *Critical Studies in Media Communication* 21, no. 1 (2004): 23.

9. Laurie Thomas and Barry R. Litman, "Fox Broadcasting Company, Why Now? An Economic Study of the Rise of the Fourth Broadcast 'Network,'" *Journal of Broadcasting & Electronic Media* 35, no. 2 (1991): 140.

10. In 1945, the FCC, obligated by statute to distribute broadcast licenses and frequencies for television service, established a table allocating the VHF channels to the country's 140 largest markets. In 1948, beset by the tremendous postwar flood of applications for new licenses, the commission issued a "freeze order" suspending all action on such applications until further study had been made of the channel-allocation problem. In 1952, the FCC lifted the freeze order and adopted its *Sixth Report and Order*; this established a nationwide city-by-city table of television channel assignments, which provided for the use of both VHF and unused UHF channels, in a practice known as "intermixture." These decisions resulted in the concentration of broadcasting within the narrow confines of the VHF band (channels 2–13). Various technical and economic problems prevented the extensive use of the UHF band (channels 14–83) until 1961, when Congress passed the All-Channel Receiver Bill, which ensured greater access to UHF signals and led to the slow but steady growth of UHF stations throughout the country. For a very thorough history of this, see Hugh Slotten, *Radio and Television Regulation: Broadcast Technology in the United States, 1920–1960* (Baltimore: Johns Hopkins University Press, 2000), chapter 5, "VHF and UHF: Establishing a Nationwide Television System 1945–1960," 145–88.

11. Thomas and Litman, "Fox Broadcasting Company," 140.

12. Christopher H. Sterling and John Michael Kittross, *Stay Tuned: A History of American Broadcasting*, 3rd ed. (London: Lawrence Erlbaum Associates, 2002), 871.

13. For a detailed history, see William Shawcross, *Murdoch* (New York: Simon & Schuster, 1997), 201–38.

14. Ironically, the Metromedia stations were largely the remnants of the old DuMont network. After Dumont Laboratories shut down its DuMont network, it spun off some of its holdings into the Metropolitan Broadcasting Company, which included two television stations that DuMont had owned outright. Metropolitan was later purchased by investor John Kluge, renamed Metromedia, and turned into a profitable business that specialized in airing syndicated network shows. For a more detailed history, see Daniel M. Kimmel, *The Fourth Network: How Fox Broke the Rules and Reinvented Television* (Chicago: Ivan Dee, 2004), 6–13.

15. Thomas and Litman, "Fox Broadcasting Company," 145.

16. Jonathan Mahler, "What Rupert Wrought," *New York*, May 21, 2005, http://nymag.com/nymetro/news/people/features/11673/.

17. John Cassidy, "Murdoch's Game," *New Yorker*, October 16, 2006, 70.

18. David McKnight, "'A World Hungry for a New Philosophy': Rupert Murdoch and the Rise of Neo-liberalism," *Journalism Studies* 4, no. 3 (2003): 348.

19. Quoted in Cassidy, "Murdoch's Game," 77.

20. Jeff Chester notes that between 1999 and 2002, News Corporation spent almost $10 million on lobbying, much of it directed at the FCC. Murdoch's company donated nearly $1.8 million to political parties in the 2000 and 2002 election cycles, with the majority of its funds going to the GOP, and, as of December 2003, had already made over $200,000 in contributions into the 2004 election. Chester, "A Present for

Murdoch," *Nation*, December 22, 2003, 26. The amount of money being spent has increased substantially since this time. Most recently, Murdoch made headlines one again with his unprecedented $1 million donation to the Republican Governor's Association. See Eric Lichtblau and Brian Stetler, "News Corp. Gives Republicans $1 Million," *New York Times*, August 18, 2010, A13.

21. Quoted in McKnight, "World Hungry," 349.

22. Neil Chenoweth, *Rupert Murdoch: The Untold Story of the World's Greatest Media Wizard* (New York: Crown Business, 2001), 200.

23. Quoted in David Carr, "White House Listens When Weekly Speaks," *New York Times*, March 11, 2003, E1.

24. O'Reilly's show was originally called *The O'Reilly Report*; it was renamed in 1998. See John Colapinto, "Mad Dog," *Rolling Stone*, September 2, 2004, 104–11. For more on Ailes's career, see Tim Dickinson, "The Fox News Fear Factory," *Rolling Stone*, June 9, 2011, 54–84. For more on his role at Fox News, see Jennifer M. Proffitt, "Challenges to Democratic Discourse: Media Concentration and the Marginalization of Dissent," *Review of Education, Pedagogy, and Cultural Studies* 29 (2007): 65–84.

25. Jeffrey P. Jones, *Entertaining Politics: Satiric Television and Political Engagement* (Lanham, MD: Rowman & Littlefield, 2010), 59.

26. Diller himself had a background in Hollywood film as well as television, functioning as chairman of Paramount Pictures from 1974 to 1984. Diller also flirted briefly with establishing a fourth network, in 1977, while still at Paramount. The Paramount bid was for Saturday evening programming, but the plan never took off because of the unreliability of UHF signals and poor advertiser response, among other things. Ben Grossman, "The First Twenty Years," *Broadcasting & Cable*, November 13, 2006, 18.

27. Quoted in ibid., 19.

28. Alex Ben Block, *Outfoxed: Marvin Davis, Barry Diller, Rupert Murdoch, Joan Rivers, and the Inside Story of America's Fourth Television Network* (New York: St. Martin's Press, 1990), 169.

29. Mark Morrison, "Year of the Fox," *Rolling Stone*, October 4, 1990, 76.

30. Ibid., 76.

31. A large part of the problem stemmed from the fact that *The Late Show* was conceived as a live television program and the first hour of the show would be live on the East Coast. The premiere of the show was delayed because Fox had to purchase a time-delay device for censoring material for live broadcast. This, of course, didn't impact the live broadcast on the East, and Rivers once accidentally said "shit" on the air. Although Fox had given Rivers and her team creative control, Fox had a censor in place from the start, Don Bay, who functioned as a standards and practices "consultant." Block, *Outfoxed*, 216. One has to use the term *censor* loosely here, but the fact remains that Bay was responsible for overseeing the broadcast standards at Fox. Bay was replaced in February 1993 by Roland McFarland, who served as "director" of the broadcast standards area until being named vice president of the Broadcast Standards Department in October 1994. As Jim Impoco reports, although Fox touted itself as a network without censors, by 1995 there were seven active censors working under McFarland. Impoco, "The Bundys Meet the Censors at Fox," *U.S. News & World Report*, September 11, 1995, 68.

32. Block, *Outfoxed*, 220.

33. Joan Stuller-Giglione, "Married with Children," *Encyclopedia of Television*, Museum of Broadcast Communications, http://www.museum.tv/eotvsection. php?entrycode=marriedw.

34. At about the same time, Peggy Charon founded the advocacy group Action for Children's Television (ACT) in an effort to improve the programming aimed at young children. Soon after, Rakolta cited *Teenage Mutant Ninja Turtles*, which was the latest rage among school kids, as excessively violent and called again for governmental action. This time she was more successful: in 1991, Congress passed the Children's Television Act, which ordered that television programming meet the educational and informational needs of children. The terms used, however, were highly ambiguous, and it was unclear precisely who and what would define educational and informational merit. For a thorough overview of the legacy of this legislation, see the *Journal of Applied Developmental Psychology* 24, no. 3 (August 2003), which is a special issue devoted to assessing the impact of the Children's Television Act.

35. Block, *Outfoxed*, 213.

36. Ronald Grover, "The Fourth Network," *Business Week*, September 17, 1990, 114–17.

37. Morrison, "Year of the Fox," 76.

38. Matt Groening, "Matt Groening," in *Current Biography Yearbook, 1990*, ed. Charles Mortiz (New York: H. W. Wilson Co., 1990), 288.

39. Harry F. Waters, "Family Feuds," *Newsweek*, April 23, 1990, 61.

40. Richard Zoglin, "The Fox Trots Faster," *Time*, August 27, 1990, 64.

41. William Savage, "'So Television's Responsible!': Oppositionality and the Interpretive Logic of Satire and Censorship in *The Simpsons* and *South Park*," in *Leaving Springfield: "The Simpsons" and the Possibilities of Oppositional Television*, ed. John Alberti (Detroit: Wayne State University Press, 2004), 220.

42. See, for example, Jerome Klinowitz, *Literary Subversions: New American Fiction and the Practice of Criticism* (Carbondale: Southern Illinois University Press, 1985); Brian McHale, *Postmodernist Fiction* (New York: Methuen, 1987); Steven Weisenburger, *Fables of Subversion: Satire and the American Novel, 1930–1980* (Athens: University of Georgia Press, 1995); and Darryl Dickson-Carr *African American Satire: The Sacredly Profane Novel* (Columbia: University of Missouri Press, 2001).

43. Chris Lamb, *Drawn to Extremes: The Use and Abuse of Editorial Cartoons* (New York: Columbia University Press, 2004), 43.

44. Donald Dewey, *The Art of Ill Will: The Story of American Political Cartoons* (New York: New York University Press, 2007), 5–6.

45. Richard E. Marschall, "The Century in Political Cartoons," *Columbia Journalism Review*, May/June 1999, 54.

46. Dewey, *Art of Ill Will*, 36.

47. Two of the earliest examples are "The Katzenjammer Kids," which appeared in Hearst's *New York Journal*, and "A. Mutt" (later known as "Mutt and Jeff"), which appeared in Hearst's *San Francisco Examiner*. These, however, were not satirical cartoons. For more, see Dewey, *Art of Ill Will*, 39–41.

48. While both artists began offering their critiques from a generally populist and leftist position, by the early 1960s, Capp had moved to the far right politically. Dewey, *Art of Ill Will*, 63. For an informative overview of Capp and Kelly's work, see Kalman Goldstein, "Al Capp and Walt Kelly: Pioneers of Political and Social Satire in the Comics," *Journal of Popular Culture* 25, no. 4 (1992): 81–95.

49. Kristin L. Matthews, "A Mad Proposition in Postwar America," *Journal of American Culture* 30, no. 2 (2007): 212.

50. Stephan E. Kercher, *Revel with a Cause: Liberal Satire in Postwar America* (Chicago: University of Chicago Press, 2006), 108 and 118.

51. Lamb, *Drawn to Extremes*, 31–32.

52. John Nichols, "Huey Freeman: American Hero," *Nation*, January 10, 2001, http://www.thenation.com/doc/20020128/nichols.

53. For more on Trudeau, see Lamb, *Drawn to Extremes*, chapter 2, "President Bush Has Been Reading Doonesbury and Taking It Much Too Seriously," 30–56. For more on McGruder, see Ben McGrath, "The Radical: Why Do Editors Keep Throwing *The Boondocks* Off the Funnies Page?" *New Yorker*, April 19, 2004, 152–161. For excellent overviews, with reference to all of the artists cited, see Edward J. Lordan, *Politics, Ink: How Cartoonists Skewer America's Politicians, from King George III to George Dubya* (Lanham, MD: Rowman & Littlefield, 2005).

54. An important contribution to the discussion of satire on film is Donald McCaffrey's *Assault on Society: Satirical Literature to Film* (Metuchen, NJ: Scarecrow Press, 1992), which examines selected films of the 1960s and 1970s that were adaptations of literary works. McCaffrey's section on Kubrick, which discusses both *Dr. Strangelove* and *A Clockwork Orange* (1971), is particularly illuminating. For more on the independent filmmakers, see Emanuel Levy, *Cinema of Outsiders: The Rise of American Independent Film* (New York: New York University Press, 2001), especially chapter 7, "Comedy and Satire: Tackling Taboos," 249–81.

55. It should be noted that filmmaker Robert Altman and cartoonist Gary Trudeau made a foray into television with the HBO series *Tanner '88* (1988), a satirical take on presidential politics. Altman and Trudeau teamed up again in 2004 to produce a sequel, called *Tanner on Tanner*, which focused on the Democratic presidential race that year. The four 30-minute episodes of *Tanner on Tanner* ran on the Sundance Channel in the fall of 2004, just prior to Election Day. See Jill Abramson, "A New *Tanner* Joins the Race," *New York Times*, September 26, 2004, late ed., sec. 2, p. 26. My focus in this chapter will remain on network television.

56. Kercher, *Revel with a Cause*, 345.

57. Carol A. Stabile and Mark Harrison, eds., *Prime Time Animation: Television Animation and American Culture* (New York: Routledge, 2003), 8.

58. Kercher, *Revel with a Cause*, 354.

59. For more, see Aniko Bodroghkozy, "*The Smothers Brothers Comedy Hour* and the Youth Rebellion," in *The Revolution Wasn't Televised: Sixties Television and Social Conflict*, ed. Lynn Spigel and Michael Curtin (New York: Routledge, 1997), 201–20; Steven Allen Carr, "On the Edge of Tastelessness: CBS, the Smothers Brothers and the Struggle for Control," *Cinema Journal* 31, no. 4 (1992): 3–24; and the documentary film *Smothered: The Censorship Struggles of "The Smothers Brothers Comedy Hour,"* directed by Maureen Muldaur (New Video Group, 2003).

60. *In Living Color* is but one example of Fox's success in appealing to the coveted demographic of ethnic minorities. As Kristal Brent Zook points out in *Color by Fox: The Fox Network and the Revolution in Black Television* (New York: Oxford University Press, 1999), Fox helped open the door to a broader representation of ethnic minorities, particularly blacks, on American television. Fox executives' willingness to give greater creative control led to opportunities that were simply unavailable from the Big Three and lent a new importance to the "urban" audiences who up to that point had not been well served by the major networks. Fox "inadvertently fostered a space for black authorship in television" by giving creative control over to entertainers such as Keenan Ivory Wayans, Charles Dutton, and Martin Lawrence, the creators and/or producers of *In Living Color* (1990–94), *Roc* (1991–94), and *Martin* (1992–97), respectively, which were all very successful vehicles for Fox. By 1993, Fox was airing "the largest single crop of black-produced shows in television history. And by 1995, black Americans (some 12 percent of the total U.S. population) were a striking 25 percent of Fox's market." Zook, *Color by Fox*, 3–4.

61. Gerard Jones, *Honey, I'm Home! Sitcoms: Selling the American Dream* (New York: St. Martin's, 1992), 97.

62. Ibid., 100.
63. John D. Rich and Robert W. Weisberg, "Creating *All in the Family*: A Case Study in Creative Thinking," *Creativity Research Journal* 16, nos. 2/3 (2004): 248.
64. David Marc, *Comic Visions: Television Comedy and American Culture*, 2nd ed. (Malden, MA: Blackwell, 1997), 199–200.
65. Arnold Hano, "Can Archie Bunker Give Bigotry a Bad Name?" *New York Times*, April 12, 1972, SM33.
66. Darrell Y. Hamamoto, *Nervous Laughter: Television Situation Comedy and Liberal Democratic Ideology* (New York: Praeger, 1989), 10.
67. Michael V. Tueth, "Back to the Drawing Board: The Family in Animated Television Comedy," in Stabile and Harrison, *Prime Time Animation*, 133.
68. Rebecca Farley, "From Fred and Wilma to Ren and Stimpy: What Makes a Cartoon Prime-Time?" in Stabile and Harrison, *Prime Time Animation*, 151.
69. Alfred Appel, *The Annotated Lolita* (New York: Vintage, 1991), xlix.
70. Nabokov, *Strong Opinions*, 22. For more on Nabokov's views on parody and satire, see the relevant sections in Brian Stonehill, *The Self-Conscious Novel: Artifice in Fiction from Joyce to Pynchon* (Philadelphia: University of Pennsylvania Press, 1989); Linda Hutcheon, *A Theory of Parody: The Teachings of Twentieth-Century Art Forms* (Urbana: University of Illinois Press, 2000); David H. J. Larmour, *Discourse and Ideology in Nabokov's Prose* (New York: Routledge, 2002); Charles A. Knight, *The Literature of Satire* (Cambridge: Cambridge University Press, 2007); and Robert Lang, *Parody: The Art that Plays with Art* (New York: Peter Lang, 2010).
71. Nabokov, *Strong Opinions*, 33.
72. Joanne Ostrow, "HBO Leads the Pack in Bringing Satire Back," *Denver Post*, June 8, 1997, H01.
73. Matthew Gilbert, "Satirical Yet Sweet, *Simpsons* Remains America's Favorite Nuclear Family," *Boston Globe*, February 16, 2003, N1.
74. Paul Cantor, "*The Simpsons*: Atomistic Politics and the Nuclear Family," *Political Theory* 27, no. 6 (1999): 734.
75. William Irwin and J. R. Lombardo, "*The Simpsons* and Allusion: 'Worst Essay Ever,'" in *"The Simpsons" and Philosophy: The D'oh of Homer*, ed. William Irwin, Mark T. Conrad, and Aeon J. Skoble (Chicago: Open Court Press, 2000), 82.
76. Alberti, *Leaving Springfield*, xiv.
77. Jamie J. Weinman, "Worst Episode Ever," *Salon*, January 24, 2000, http://www.salon.com/2000/01/24/simpsons_2/.
78. Ibid.
79. Ibid.
80. Ibid.
81. For a more detailed discussion, see "Virtual Springfield: *The Simpsons* on the Interweb," in Chris Turner, *Planet Simpson: How a Cartoon Masterpiece Defined a Generation* (Cambridge, MA: Da Capo, 2004), 286–94.
82. Jon Bonné, "*The Simpsons* Has Lost Its Cool," MSNBC, October 2, 2002, http://www.msnbc.com/news/419648.asp.
83. Melinda Penkava, "Effects of *The Simpsons* on Television and Culture as the Show Marks Its 300th Episode," *Talk of the Nation*, National Public Radio, February 13, 2003, http://www.npr.org/templates/story/story.php?storyId=1160554.
84. Jon Bonné, "*The Simpsons*, Back from the Pit," MSNBC, November 7, 2003, http://www.msnbc.com/news/988733.asp.
85. David Carr, "Is Animation Funnier than Live Action?" *New York Times*, July 6, 2003, AR18.
86. Ostrow, "HBO Leads the Pack," H01.

87. Ibid.
88. Douglas Kellner, "TV, Ideology, and Emancipatory Popular Culture," in *Television: The Critical View*, 4th ed., ed. Horace Newcomb (New York: Oxford University Press, 1987), 487.
89. "Michael Moore Discusses His New Series, *The Awful Truth*," interview with Scott Simpson, *Weekend Edition*, National Public Radio, April 10, 1999, http://www.npr.org/templates/story/story.php?storyId=1048125.
90. Ostrow, "HBO Leads the Pack," H01.
91. Stabile and Harrison, *Prime Time Animation*, 2.
92. Trish Hamilton, "Rabbit Punch," *Rolling Stone*, September 1988, 81.
93. Jeremy Gerard, "Bad Language, Hurt Feelings and Success," *New York Times*, February 21, 1990, late ed., C18.
94. Ibid.
95. Brian Viner, "D'oh! I Made Murdoch a Billion Dollars," *Independent*, September 2, 2000, 8.
96. Sanjiv Bhattacharya, "Homer's Odyssey," *Sunday Herald Sun*, August 27, 2000, Z12.
97. Douglas Rushkoff, *Media Virus* (1994; repr., New York: Ballantine, 1996), 7.
98. Ibid.
99. Ibid., 115.
100. Ibid.
101. David L. G. Arnold, "'Use a Pen, Sideshow Bob': *The Simpsons* and the Threat of High Culture," in Alberti, *Leaving Springfield*, 26.
102. Brian Doherty, "Matt Groening," interview, *Mother Jones* 24, no. 2 (March/April 1999): 35.
103. Bhattacharya, "Homer's Odyssey," Z12.
104. Tom Shales, "They're Scrapping Again—But This Time It's a Ratings Fight," *Washington Post*, October 11, 1990, C1.
105. Rushkoff, *Media Virus*, 115.
106. M. S. Mason, "*Simpsons* Creator on Poking Fun," *Christian Science Monitor*, April 17, 1998, B7.
107. James M. Wallace, "A (Karl, Not Groucho) Marxist in Springfield," in Irwin et al., *"The Simpsons" and Philosophy*, 237 and 239.
108. Ibid., 238 and 246.
109. Ibid., 246.
110. Ibid., 250.
111. Brian A. Connery and Kirk Combe, *Theorizing Satire: Essays in Literary Criticism* (New York: St. Martin's, 1995), 5.
112. Dustin Griffin, *Satire: A Critical Reintroduction* (Lexington: University Press of Kentucky, 1994), 186.
113. Steven C. Weisenburger, *Fables of Subversion: Satire and the American Novel* (Athens: University of Georgia Press, 1995), 3.
114. Carl Matheson, "*The Simpsons*, Hyper-Irony, and the Meaning of Life," in Irwin et al., *"The Simpsons" and Philosophy*, 113.
115. Ibid., 118.
116. Ted Gournelos, *Popular Culture and the Future of Politics: Cultural Studies and the Tao of South Park* (Lanham, MD: Lexington, 2009), 88.
117. Ibid.
118. Ibid.
119. Griffin, *Satire*, 1.
120. Kellner, "TV, Ideology, and Emancipatory Popular Culture," 473.
121. Ibid., 489.

2   "You're an American Now": Race, Ethnicity, and Nationality on *The Simpsons*

1. Toni Morrison, *Playing in the Dark: Whiteness and the Literary Imagination* (New York: Vintage, 1992), 47.
2. On these topics, see Denis Baron, *The English-Only Question: An Official Language for Americans?* (New Haven, CT: Yale University Press, 1992); Raymond Tatalovich, *Nativism Reborn? The Official English Language Movement and the American States* (Lexington: University Press of Kentucky, 1995); Juan F. Perea, ed., *Immigrants Out! The New Nativism and the Anti-Immigrant Impulse in the United States* (New York: New York University Press, 1997); David M. Reimers, *Unwelcome Strangers: American Identity and the Turn Against Immigration* (New York: Columbia University Press, 1998); Gerald D. Jaynes, ed., *Immigration and Race: New Challenges for American Democracy* (New Haven, CT: Yale University Press, 2000); and Carol L. Schmid, *The Politics of Language: Conflict, Identity and Cultural Pluralism in Comparative Perspective* (New York: Oxford University Press, 2001).
3. The commission's report is available online. See US House Hearing Before the Subcommittee on Immigration and Claims of the Committee on the Judiciary, *Final Report of the Commission on Immigration Reform*, 105th Congress, 1st sess., November, 7, 1997, http://commdocs.house.gov/committees/judiciary/hju57062.000 /hju57062_0.htm.
4. Among other things, the Bureau of Americanization encouraged employers to make English classes compulsory for foreign-born workers; many states followed the federal government's lead and soon banned schooling in other languages and, in some places, prohibited the study of foreign languages altogether. The entirety of the US Immigration Commission report is available online. See "The Dillingham Commission Reports," Stanford University Digital Library Program, http://library .stanford.edu/catdb/e_resources/ebrary/dillingham/body.shtml.
5. Matthew Frye Jacobson, *Whiteness of a Different Color: European Immigrants and the Alchemy of Race* (Cambridge, MA: Harvard University Press, 1998), 24.
6. For discussions of various hyphenated American identities, see Donna R. Gabaccia, "Race, Nation, Hyphen: Italian-Americans and American Multiculturalism in Comparative Perspective," in *Are Italians White? How Race Is Made in America*, ed. Jennifer Guglielmo and Salvatore Salerno (New York: Routledge, 2003), 44–59; Tamar Jacoby, "Defining Assimilation for the 21st Century," in *Reinventing the Melting Pot: The New Immigrants and What It Means to Be American*, ed. Tamar Jacoby (New York: Basic, 2004), 3–16; Margot Seeto, "Caught Between Cultures: Identity, Choice, and the Hyphenated American," in *Asian American X: An Intersection of Twenty-First-Century Asian American Voices*, ed. Arar Han and John Hsu (Ann Arbor: University of Michigan Press, 2004), 231–38; Berel Lang, "Hyphenated Jew and the Anxiety of Identity," *Jewish Social Studies* 12, no. 1 (Fall 2005): 1–15; and Tanya Golash-Boza, "Dropping the Hyphen? Becoming Latino(a)-American through Racialized Assimilation," *Social Forces* 85, no. 1 (2006): 27–55.
7. I will discuss Cletus and Brandine Delroy and "white trash" identity in much greater depth and detail in chapter 5, which focuses specifically on socioeconomic class on *The Simpsons*.
8. J. Hector St. Jean de Crèvecoeur, Letter III, "What Is an American?" *Letters from an American Farmer*, University of Virginia Hypertexts, http://xroads.virginia. edu/~hyper/crev/letter03.html.
9. Edna Nahshon, ed., *From the Ghetto to the Melting Pot: Israel Zangwill's Jewish Plays* (Detroit: Wayne State University Press, 2006), 13.

10. The twenty-fifth anniversary edition of Novak's book, which was published with the title *Unmeltable Ethnics: Politics and Culture in American Life* (New Brunswick, NJ: Transaction, 1995), contained significant updates and additions and offered a clearer embrace of cultural pluralism.

11. Arthur M. Schlesinger, *The Disuniting of America: Reflections of a Multicultural Society* (New York: Norton, 1992), 18.

12. An explicit focus on WASP identity was offered in texts such as Robert C. Christopher, *Crashing the Gates: The De-WASPing of America's Power Elite* (New York: Simon and Schuster, 1989); and Richard Brookhiser, *The Way of the WASP: How It Made America, and How It Can Save It, So to Speak* (New York: Free Press, 1991). The focus on multiculturalism and "Americanness" was more forcefully articulated in books such as David Hollinger, *Postethnic America: Beyond Multiculturalism* (New York: Basic, 1995); Dinesh D'Souza, *The End of Racism: Principles for a Multiracial Society* (New York: Free Press, 1996); and John J. Miller, *The Unmaking of Americans: How Multiculturalism Has Undermined the Assimilation Ethic* (New York: Free Press, 1998).

13. Early texts in this field include David Roediger, *The Wages of Whiteness: Race and the Making of the American Working Class* (New York: Verso, 1991); Morrison, *Playing in the Dark*; Ruth Frankenberg, *The Social Construction of Whiteness: White Women, Race Matters* (Minneapolis: University of Minnesota Press, 1993); and Theodore Allen, *The Invention of the White Race* (New York: Verso, 1994). Other important texts include Richard Dyer, *White* (New York: Routledge, 1997); Matt Wray and Annalee Newitz, eds., *White Trash: Race and Class in America* (New York: Routledge, 1997); Jacobson, *Whiteness of a Different Color*; Joe L. Kincheloe et al., eds., *White Reign: Deploying Whiteness in America* (New York: St. Martin's, 1998); and George Lipsitz, *The Possessive Investment in Whiteness: How White People Profit from Identity Politics* (Philadelphia: Temple University Press, 1998).

14. Richard Dyer, *The Matter of Images: Essays on Representation* (New York: Routledge, 1993), 44.

15. Wray and Newitz, *White Trash*, 3.

16. Thomas K. Nakayama and Robert L. Krizek, "Whiteness: A Strategic Rhetoric," *Quarterly Journal of Speech* 81, no. 3 (1995): 300.

17. Peter McLaren, "Whiteness Is…The Struggle for Postcolonial Hybridity," in Kincheloe et al., *White Reign*, 67.

18. The term *WASP* is generally considered to have been coined by E. Digby Baltzell in his 1964 book *The Protestant Establishment: Aristocracy & Caste in America*. Some debate continues over the origins of the term in print; as Robert C. Christopher notes, the term WASP had appeared earlier in an article by E. B. Palmore published in the *American Journal of Sociology* in 1962. See Robert C. Christopher, *Crashing the Gates: The De-WASPing of America's Power Elite* (New York: Simon and Schuster, 1989), 23.

19. For an excellent and very detailed history of these developments in the late nineteenth and early twentieth centuries, see chapters 2 and 3 in Jacobson, *Whiteness of a Different Color*, 39–136.

20. Theodor Adorno and Max Horkheimer, "The Culture Industry: Enlightenment as Mass Deception," in *Media and Cultural Studies: Key Works*, ed. Meenakshi Gigi Durham and Douglas Kellner (Malden, MA: Blackwell, 1999), 72.

21. Michael Rogin, *Blackface, White Noise: Jewish Immigrants in the Hollywood Melting Pot* (Berkeley: University of California Press, 1996), 53.

22. William Paley founded and owned controlling interest in CBS until 1986, when the network was sold to Loews Corporation; David Sarnoff founded and ran NBC until 1970, when he was succeeded by his son, Robert, who then ran the network until

1985, when it was sold to General Electric; Leonard Goldenson was the "top officer" at ABC from 1953 until 1986, which was shortly after the network was sold to Capital Cities Communications. See David Zurawik, *The Jews of Prime Time* (Hanover, NH: Brandeis University Press, 2003), 1–15.

23. Not all these performers were overtly Jewish, however; indeed, in deference to the historical and political contours of the era—World War II and its aftermath, the rapid expansion of suburbia, and the solidification of whiteness in mass culture—many of these performers altered their ethnic-sounding names to better assimilate. For example, Milton Berle was once Milton Berlinger, George Burns was Nathaniel Birnbaum, Red Buttons was Aaron Chwatt, Jackie Mason was Jacob Masler (variously Mazer), and Jack Benny was Benjamin Kublesky. See Zurawik, *Jews of Prime Time*, 7.

24. Detailed analyses of the *Amos 'n' Andy* phenomenon, on both radio and television, can be found in Robin R. Means Coleman, *African American Viewers and the Black Situation Comedy: Situating Racial Humor* (New York: Garland, 2000); and Donald Bogle, *Primetime Blues: African Americans on Network Television* (New York: Farrar, Straus and Giroux, 2001).

25. David Marc, *Comic Visions: Television Comedy and American Culture*, 2nd ed. (Malden, MA: Blackwell, 1997), 36.

26. Gerard Jones, *Honey, I'm Home! Sitcoms: Selling the American Dream* (New York: St. Martin's, 1992), 46.

27. Marc, *Comic Visions*, 43.

28. Ibid., 42.

29. Herbert Gans, "The American Kaleidoscope, Then and Now," in *Reinventing the Melting Pot: The New Immigrants and What It Means to Be American*, ed. Tamar Jacoby (New York: Basic, 2004), 38.

30. One could argue that the status is more accurately upper middle class, as the term *WASP* is most commonly used in association with preparatory schools, Ivy League colleges, and the professions of law and medicine, and it is often invoked within mass media in relation to those (whites) who have a great deal of wealth.

31. Milton Gordon, *Assimilation in American Life: The Role of Race, Religion, and National Origins* (New York: Oxford University Press, 1964), 72.

32. I am indebted to my friend and colleague Lesley Bogad for inspiring the development of McWASP. The idea originated with classroom materials she once shared with me, in which she had similarly modified *WASP* to give students a more accurate sense of what that concept represented.

33. Jones, *Honey, I'm Home!*, 87.

34. Darrell Y. Hamamoto, *Nervous Laughter: Television Situation Comedy and Liberal Democratic Ideology* (New York: Praeger, 1989), 37.

35. Jones, *Honey, I'm Home!*, 90.

36. On issues of race in personal ads, see Les Back, "Aryans Reading Adorno: Cyberculture and Twenty-first Century Racism," *Ethnic and Racial Studies* 25, no. 4 (2002): 628–52; and Joy Bennett Kinnon, "Is Skin Color Still an Issue in Black America?" *Ebony*, April 2000, 52–55. On race in advertising, see Alan J. Bush et al., "The Influence of Consumer Socialization Variables on Attitude Toward Advertising: A Comparison of African-Americans and Caucasians," *Journal of Advertising* 28, no. 3 (1999): 13–25; and Leon E. Wynter, *American Skin: Pop Culture, Big Business & the End of White America* (New York: Crown, 2002). The phrase "all-American" was also a key part of the controversy over Korean American Margaret Cho's 1994 situation comedy (a suburban nuclear family comedy at that!), ironically and provocatively entitled *All-American Girl*. For more information, see Leon E. Wynter, "*All-American*

Girl Puts Asians on the Dial," *Wall Street Journal*, June 15, 1994, B1; Bruce Fretts, "The Cho Must Go On," *Entertainment Weekly*, September 16, 1994, 98; and Martha Southgate, "A Funny Thing Happened on the Way to Prime Time," *New York Times Magazine*, October 30, 1994, 52–56.

37. Alan Paul, "Life in Hell," interview with Matt Groening, *Flux Magazine*, September 30, 1995, repr. in *The Simpsons Archive*, November 7, 1999, http://www.snpp.com /other/interviews/groening95.html.

38. Tammy Hocking and Matt Rose, "Section II: Series Background," L.I.S.A. (List of Inquiries and Substantive Answers), *The Simpsons Archive*, March 17, 2004, http:// www.snpp.com/guides/lisa-2.html. Gyorgi Peluci worked for the Hollywood anima- tion house Klasky-Csupo, which was in charge of animation for *The Simpsons* at its inception. Gabor Csupo, part owner of the animation studio, wanted full creative control and was thus unhappy with the decision by Fox executives to bring in new producers for the fourth season of *The Simpsons*. In 1992, Gracie Films, which pro- duces *The Simpsons* for FOX, announced that Film Roman, Inc. of Los Angeles would replace Klasky-Csupo, although it hired many of the animators laid off by Klasky- Csupo. Film Roman, Inc. has been in charge of animating *The Simpsons* since season 4. See Hocking and Rose, "Section IV: Cast, Staff and Production," L.I.S.A. (List of Inquiries and Substantive Answers), *The Simpsons Archive*, March 17, 2004, http:// www.snpp.com/guides/lisa-4.html.

39. This is an ironic inversion of how color has been used to designate race, since yellow had long been associated with Asian identity. Both *yellow* and *red* have fallen out of favor (a consequence, perhaps, of political correctness), unlike *black*, *brown*, and *white*, which continue to be freely used. Some scholars have attempted to deal with these terms and related issues, often in very complex ways. See Craig Womack, *Red on Red: Native American Literary Separatism* (Minneapolis: University of Minnesota Press, 1999); Richard Rodriguez, *Brown: The Last Discovery of America* (New York: Penguin, 2003); and Frank H. Wu, *Yellow: Race in America Beyond Black and White* (New York: Basic, 2003).

40. For more, see Peter Parisi, "'Black Bart' Simpson: Appropriation and Revitalization in Commodity Culture," *Journal of Popular Culture* 27, no. 1 (1993): 125–35.

41. Editorial, *Newsweek*, July 23, 1990, 61.

42. Vincent Brook, "Myth or Consequences: Ideological Fault Lines in *The Simpsons*," in *Leaving Springfield: "The Simpsons" and the Possibilities of Oppositional Television*, ed. John Alberti (Detroit: Wayne State University Press, 2004), 259.

43. Ella Taylor, *Prime-Time Families: Television Culture in Postwar America* (Berkeley: University of California Press, 1989), 38.

44. Tammy Hocking and Matt Rose, "Section III: Characters, Event and Places," L.I.S.A. (List of Inquiries and Substantive Answers), *The Simpsons Archive*, March 17, 2004, http://www.snpp.com/guides/lisa-3.html.

45. For more on representations of African American identity, see Herman Gray, *Watching Race: Television and the Struggle for "Blackness"* (Minneapolis: University of Minnesota Press, 1995).

46. In this regard, *The Cosby Show* was strikingly different from other sitcoms that began during its run, such as NBC's *A Different World* (1987–93), a *Cosby* spinoff, and *The Fresh Prince of Bel Air* (1990–96) or Fox's *Martin* (1992–97). As Lauren R. Tucker notes, "The television criticism about *The Cosby Show* is a site on which the struggle over the meaning of race and racial difference takes place," a truth played out in the divergent interpretations of the show as both revolutionary and accommodationist. See Tucker, "Was the Revolution Televised?: Professional Criticism about *The Cosby*

Show and the Essentialization of Black Cultural Expression," *Journal of Broadcasting & Electronic Media* 41, no. 1 (1997): 90–109.

47. In *Texas v. Johnson* (1989), the US Supreme Court ruled in favor of Gregory Johnson, who had been convicted of violating a Texas law by burning a US flag during the Republican convention in Dallas. In the early 1990s, a number of bills were proposed in Congress to amend the Immigration Act of 1990; among them were the Immigration Moratorium Act, the Citizenship Reform Act, and Immigration in the National Interest Act. Each of these is discussed in more detail in a later section of this chapter.

48. Lauren Berlant, "The Theory of Infantile Citizenship," *Public Culture* 5, no. 3 (1993), 407.

49. Thomas J. Sugrue, *Not Even Past: Barack Obama and the Burden of Race* (Princeton, NJ: Princeton University Press, 2010), 1.

50. See, for example, Dinesh D'Souza, *What's So Great about America* (Washington, DC: Regnery, 2002); Walter Benn Michaels, *The Trouble with Diversity: How We Learned to Love Identity and Ignore Inequality* (Princeton, NJ: Princeton University Press, 2004); and Shelby Steele, *White Guilt: How Blacks and Whites Together Destroyed the Promise of the Civil Rights Era* (New York: Harper, 2006).

51. See, for example, Rodriguez, *Brown*; Eduardo Bonilla-Silva, *Racism without Racists: Color-Blind Racism and the Persistence of Racial Inequality in the United States*, 2nd ed. (New York: Rowman, 2006); and Ronald R. Sundstrom, *The Browning of America and the Evasion of Social Justice* (New York: SUNY Press, 2008).

52. Sugrue, *Not Even Past*, 96.

53. Ibid., 110.

54. Tim Wise, *Colorblind: The Rise of Post-Racial Politics and the Retreat from Racial Equity* (San Francisco: City Lights Books, 2010), 23.

55. Jewish racial and national identity are fully explored in Robert M. Seltzer and Norman J. Cohen's *The Americanization of the Jews* (New York: New York University Press, 1995), Karen Brodkin's *How the Jews Became White Folks...and What That Says about Race in America* (New Brunswick, NJ: Rutgers University Press, 1998), and George Lipsitz's *The Possessive Investment in Whiteness: How White People Profit from Identity Politics* (Philadelphia: Temple University Press, 1998). Jewish involvement in US media has also been well documented in books such as Neal Gabler's *An Empire of Their Own: How the Jews Invented Hollywood* (New York: Random, 1990) and Rogin's *Blackface, White Noise*, an insightful analysis of Jewish cultural assimilation. An even more specific focus on the television industry has been offered in Zurawik's *Jews of Prime Time* and Vincent Brook's indispensable text *Something Ain't Kosher Here: The Rise of the "Jewish" Sitcom* (New Brunswick, NJ: Rutgers University Press, 2003). Tellingly, Brook's book is an outgrowth of his dissertation project, which was more appropriately titled "Wrestling with Whiteness: Assimilation, Multiculturalism, and the 'Jewish' Sitcom Trend (1989–2001)" (PhD diss., University of California, 2001), DAI-A 62/02: 375, ISBN 0–493–15103–6, AAT 3005935. For more on Jewish identity and whiteness, see David R. Roediger, *Working Toward Whiteness: How America's Immigrants Became White* (New York: Basic, 2006).

56. Daniel Itzkovitz, "Passing Like Me," *South Atlantic Quarterly* 98, nos. 1/2 (Winter/Spring 1999): 38.

57. Brook, *Something Ain't Kosher Here*, 2.

58. Zurawik, *Jews of Prime Time*, 9.

59. Brook, *Something Ain't Kosher Here*, 3.

60. Marc, *Comic Visions*, 12.

61. For more, see Albert Auster, "'Funny, You Don't Look Jewish'.... The Image of Jews on Contemporary American Television," *Television Quarterly* 26, no. 3 (1993): 65+; and Rosalin Krieger, "'Does He Actually Say the Word *Jewish*?'—Jewish Representations in *Seinfeld*," *Journal for Cultural Research* 7, no. 4 (2003): 387–95.

62. Mark I. Pinsky, *The Gospel According to "The Simpsons": The Spiritual Life of the World's Most Animated Family* (Louisville, KY: Westminster John Knox Press, 2001), 109.

63. The stand-up comedy tradition of the *tummler*, strongly associated with the comedians who worked the so-called Borscht Belt in the Catskills Mountains in the 1930s, translated easily to both radio and television formats and provided homes for the "old guard" Jewish comedians, such as Red Buttons, Jackie Mason, Henny Youngman, Jerry Lewis, Buddy Hackett, and Shecky Green. A more detailed history of the time period and the performers associated with the Catskill resorts is provided in Lawrence J. Epstein, *The Haunted Smile: The Story of Jewish Comedians in America* (New York: Public Affairs, 2001), chapter 5, "The Jewish Alps: The Rise of the Borscht Belt," 104–25.

64. Pinsky, *Gospel According to "The Simpsons,"* 120.

65. Jacobson, *Whiteness of a Different Color*, 172.

66. Michael R. Alvarez and Tara L. Butterfield, "The Resurgence of Nativism in California? The Case of Proposition 187 and Illegal Immigration," *Social Science Quarterly* 81, no. 1 (2000): 176.

67. Detailed information on all of these proposals can be found online in the archives of *The National Immigration Forum* at http://www.immigrationforum.org/index.

68. Duncan Stuart Beard, "Local Satire with a Global Reach: Ethnic Stereotyping and Cross-Cultural Conflicts in *The Simpsons*," In Alberti, *Leaving Springfield*, 282.

69. Ibid., 283.

70. W. E. B. Du Bois, *The Souls of Black Folk*, 1903, Modern Library Centennial Edition, introduction by David Levering Lewis (New York: Random, 2003), 5.

71. Beard, "Local Satire," 285.

72. The innocuous-sounding Patriot Act is a disturbing and nearly Orwellian piece of legislation; its name is an acronym for its aims (Providing Appropriate Tools Required to Intercept and Obstruct Terrorism), and it provided for some very unpatriotic and antidemocratic limitations on civil liberties.

73. Gregory M. Maney, Patrick G. Coy, and Lynn M. Woehrle, "Pursuing Political Persuasion: War and Peace Frames in the United States after September 11th," *Social Movement Studies* 8, no. 4 (2009): 300.

74. Ibid. On the expansion of presidential power, see Matthew A. Crenson and Benjamin Ginsberg, "Downsizing Democracy, Upsizing the Presidency," *South Atlantic Quarterly* 105, no. 1 (Winter 2006): 207–16; and David Gray Adler, "George Bush and the Abuse of History: The Constitution and Presidential Power in Foreign Affairs," *UCLA Journal of International Law & Foreign Affairs* 12, no. 1 (2007): 75–144.

75. Joe Gross, "Singer's Remarks Stir Up Country," *Austin (TX) American-Statesman*, March 15, 2003, A1.

76. Ibid.

77. Gabriel Rossman, "Elites, Masses, and Media Blacklists: The Dixie Chicks Controversy," *Social Forces* 83, no. 1 (2004): 62.

78. For more on the controversy, see Jeffrey Gilbert, "The Dixie Chicks: A Case Study for the Politics of Hollywood," *Texas Review of Entertainment and Sports Law* 9, no. 2 (2008): 307–34; Claire Katz, "'The Eternal Irony of the Community': Prophecy, Patriotism, and the Dixie Chicks," *Shofar: An Interdisciplinary Journal of Jewish Studies* 26, no. 4 (2008): 139–60; and Emil B. Towner, "A <Patriotic> Apologia: The Transcendence of

the Dixie Chicks," *Rhetoric Review* 29, no. 3 (2010): 293–309. The entire saga is also explored in the documentary film *Shut Up & Sing*, directed by Barbara Kopple and Cecilia Peck (Weinstein Company, 2006).

79. Towner, "A <Patriotic> Apologia," 294.

80. Note that this critique of "news" media appeared in advance of Jon Stewart's evisceration of CNN's *Crossfire* and its hosts, Paul Belaga and Tucker Carlson, during his appearance in October 2004. In January 2005, CNN announced that it was cancelling *Crossfire*. For a concise overview of Stewart's comments, see Lisa Colletta, "Political Satire and Postmodern Irony in the Age of Stephen Colbert and Jon Stewart," *Journal of Popular Culture* 42, no. 5 (2009): 870–73; and Amber Day, *Satire and Dissent: Interventions in Contemporary Political Debate* (Bloomington: Indiana University Press, 2011), 78.

81. John Alberti, "'War Is Not the Answer…Except for All of America's Problems': *The Simpsons* and the War on Terror" (paper presented at the Cultural Studies Association conference, Tucson, Arizona, April 2005).

82. It is worth noting here that in 2005, *The Simpsons* debuted on the Saudi-backed Arab satellite TV network MBC as *Al Shamshoons*. Homer was renamed Omar, Bart became Badr, and the show was stripped of any content deemed offensive to local sensibilities. Four days after the end of Ramadan 2005, only 34 episodes into a 52-episode run, *Al Shamshoons* was pulled from MBC. See Richard Poplak, "Homer's Odyssey: Why *The Simpsons* Flopped in the Middle East," Canadian Broadcasting Corporation, July 25, 2007, http://www.cbc.ca/arts/tv/dubai.html (site discontinuted); reprinted, http://www.nowpublic.com/why_simpsons_flopped_middle_east.

83. This has been most forcefully documented by Jack Shaheen. In *Reel Bad Arabs: How Hollywood Vilifies a People* (2001; repr., Northampton, MA: Olive Branch Press, 2009), Shaheen demonstrates that long before 9/11, stereotypical depictions of Arabs and Arab Americans were already plentiful in the mass media. That book was the basis of Sut Jhally's equally powerful documentary film *Reel Bad Arabs* (Northampton, MA: Media Education Foundation, 2006). Shaheen has continued to analyze the images of Arabs in media and has recently argued that such images have worsened since the 9/11 attacks. For more, see Jack Shaheen, *Guilty: Hollywood's Verdict on Arabs after 9/11* (Northampton, MA: Olive Branch Press, 2008).

84. Shaheen, *Reel Bad Arabs*, 4.

85. Tung Yin, "Through a Screen Darkly: Hollywood as a Measure of Discrimination Against Arabs and Muslims," *Duke Forum for Law & Social Change* 2, no. 1 (2010): 104.

86. Abu Sadat Nurullah, "Portrayal of Muslims in the Media: *24* and the 'Othering' Process." *International Journal of Human Sciences* 7, no. 1 (2010): 1041.

87. In his PSA, Sutherland urged viewers to keep in mind that the show's villains are not representative of all Muslims, saying, "Hi. My name is Kiefer Sutherland. And I play counter-terrorist agent Jack Bauer on Fox's *24*. I would like to take a moment to talk to you about something that I think is very important. Now while terrorism is obviously one of the most critical challenges facing our nation and the world, it is important to recognize that the American Muslim community stands firmly beside their fellow Americans in denouncing and resisting all forms of terrorism. So in watching *24*, please, bear that in mind." Nurullah, "Portrayal of Muslims," 1041.

88. Virginia Rohan, "Defining the Face of Evil," (Bergen County, NJ) *Record*, January 23, 2005, E01.

89. Nurullah, "Portrayal of Muslims," 1043.

90. Michael Chertoff, "Reflections on 24 and the Real World," in *Secrets of 24: The Unauthorized Guide to the Political & Moral Issues Behind TV's Most Riveting Drama*, by Dan Burstein and Arne J. de Keijzer (New York: Sterling, 2008), 160–63.

91. Dan Burstein and Arne J. de Keijzer, interview with James Woolsey, in *Secrets of 24*, 164–69.
92. Nurullah, "Portrayal of Muslims," 1043.
93. Jane Mayer, "Whatever It Takes: The Politics of the Man Behind *24*," *New Yorker*, February 19, 2007, 66.
94. Peter Morey, "Terrorvision: Race, Nation and Muslimness in Fox's *24*," *Interventions: The International Journal of Postcolonial Studies* 12, no. 2 (2010): 258.
95. Ibid., 255.
96. The place for indicating one's "ancestry or ethnic origin" only appeared on the long form of the 2000 census and not the short form that most (i.e., five out of every six) Americans completed. The question on ethnic origin is also included in the yearly American Community Survey, which is a smaller sampling of data but which has revealed a fairly accurate picture of many ethnic communities in the United States. The question did not reappear on the 2010 census, which was developed only in a "short" form because too many people complained about the length of the long form. Because of this, anyone who does not self-identify with one of the Census Bureau's predesignated racial categories will be forced to use the "some other race" option.
97. Susan Saulny, "Black? White? Asian? More Young Americans Choose All of the Above," *New York Times*, January 29, 2011, http://www.nytimes.com/2011/01/30/us/30mixed.html?ref=us.
98. Rodriguez, *Brown*, 1. This idea has been taken up more recently by Sundstrom in *The Browning of America*.
99. For advocacy of the "postracial" and "postethnic" viewpoint, see Shelby Steele, "America's Post-Racial Promise," *Los Angeles Times*, November 5, 2008, http://www.latimes.com/news/opinion/opinionla/la-oe-steele5-2008nov05,0,6049031.story; and David Hollinger, "Obama, the Instability of Color Lines, and the Promise of a Postethnic Future," *Callaloo* 31, no. 4 (2008): 1033–37. For a critique of "colorblindness," see Wise, *Colorblind*.
100. Marc Singer, "'Black Skins' and White Masks: Comic Books and the Secret of Race," *African American Review* 36, no. 1 (2002): 107.
101. Joe Rhodes, "Flash! 24 Simpsons Stars Reveal Themselves," *TV Guide*, October 21, 2000, 17–34; repr. in *The Simpsons Archive*, December 6, 2000, http://www.snpp.com/other/articles/flash.html.
102. Morey, "Terrorvision," 252.
103. Ibid.
104. The situation with Muslims is actually quite complex. The association with racial identity (Arab) is mainly ideological and a consequence of media propaganda. According to data from the US Census in 2000, 1.2 million people reported being of Arab ancestry, with the top three ethnic backgrounds identified as Lebanese, Syrian, and Egyptian. As noted before, the ability to specify "ancestry or ethnic origin" was removed from the 2010 census. Thus, anyone who does not self-identify with one of the Census Bureau's predesignated racial categories will be forced to use the "some other race" option. This is, however, a rather pointless exercise because US Census Bureau regulations stipulate that all people must be placed into an official racial category. In the still very binary "logic" employed by the US Census, persons from the Middle East would be categorized as either black or white, racially speaking. Someone who does not conveniently fit these categories—someone who is, say, Jordanian—and who specified that nationality in the "Other race" box (as many Asians are explicitly encouraged to do and as many African immigrants do anyway) would simply be tabulated as "white." In short, according to the US Census Bureau, all "Arabs" are racially white.

3   "Don't Ask Me, I'm Just a Girl": Feminism, Female Identity, and *The Simpsons*

1. Susan J. Douglas, *Where the Girls Are: Growing Up Female with the Mass Media* (New York: Random House, 1994), 8.
2. Katha Pollitt, *Subject to Debate: Sense and Dissents on Women, Politics, and Culture* (New York: Modern Library, 2001), xvi.
3. For a good overview, see Ellen Riordan, "Commodified Agents and Empowered Girls: Producing and Consuming Feminism," *Journal of Communication Inquiry* 25, no. 3 (2001): 279–97.
4. Susan J. Douglas, *Enlightened Sexism: The Seductive Message That Feminism's Work Is Done* (New York: Times Books, 2010), 15.
5. Douglas, *Where the Girls Are*, 9.
6. Ibid., 12–13.
7. For a full examination of the complexity of the terms surrounding female identity and feminism, see Amanda Lotz, "Postfeminist Television Criticism: Rehabilitating Critical Terms and Identifying Postfeminist Attributes," *Feminist Media Studies* 1, no. 1 (2001): 105–21.
8. See, for example, Susan Faludi, *Backlash: The Undeclared War Against American Women* (New York: Crown, 1991); Naomi Wolf, *The Beauty Myth: How Images of Beauty Are Used Against Women* (New York: Morrow, 1991); bell hooks, *Feminism Is for Everybody: Passionate Politics* (Boston: South End Press, 2000); Kristin Rowe-Finkbeiner, *The F-Word: Feminism in Jeopardy—Women, Politics and the Future* (New York: Seal Press, 2004); and Ariel Levy, *Female Chauvinist Pigs: Women and the Rise of Raunch Culture* (New York: Free Press, 2006).
9. See Julie D'Acci, *Defining Women: Television and the Case of Cagney and Lacey* (Chapel Hill: University of North Carolina Press, 1992); Lynn Spigel and Denise Mann, eds., *Private Screenings: Television and the Female Consumer* (Minneapolis: University of Minnesota Press, 1992); Bonnie J. Dow, *Prime-Time Feminism: Television, Media Culture, and the Women's Movement Since 1970* (Philadelphia: University of Pennsylvania Press, 1996); Charlotte Brunsdon, Julie D'Acci, and Lynn Spigel, eds., *Feminist Television Criticism: A Reader* (New York: Oxford University Press, 1997); Mary Beth Haralovich and Lauren Rabinovitz, eds., *Television, History, and American Culture* (Durham, NC: Duke University Press, 1999); Amanda Lotz, *Redesigning Women: Television after the Network Era* (Urbana: University of Illinois Press, 2006); Lynn C. Spangler, *Television Women from Lucy to Friends: Fifty Years of Sitcoms and Feminism* (Westport, CT: Praeger, 2003); and Merri Lisa Johnson, ed., *Third Wave Feminism and Television: Jane Puts It in a Box* (New York: I. B. Tauris, 2007).
10. For more recent discussions of feminism, postfeminism, and American culture, see the essays collected in Yvonne Tasker and Diane Negra, eds., *Interrogating Postfeminism: Gender and the Politics of Popular Culture* (Durham, NC: Duke University Press, 2007).
11. Though *Roseanne* has received plenty of scholarly attention, much of this is focused on the show's working-class milieu as well as its feminist concerns. For more on both issues, see Kathleen Rowe, "*Roseanne*: Unruly Woman as Domestic Goddess," *Screen* 31, no. 4 (Winter 1990): 408–19, repr. in *Critiquing the Sitcom: A Reader*, ed. Joanne Morreale (Syracuse: Syracuse University Press, 2003), 251–61; Judine Mayerle, "*Roseanne*—How Did You Get Inside My House? A Case Study of a Hit Blue-Collar Situation Comedy," *Journal of Popular Culture* 24, no. 4 (1991): 71–88; Janet Lee, "Subversive Sitcoms: *Roseanne* as Inspiration for Feminist Resistance," *Women's Studies* 21, no. 1 (1992): 87–101; and Julie Bettie, "Class Dismissed? *Roseanne* and

the Changing Face of Working-Class Iconography," *Social Text* 45 (Winter 1995): 125–49.

12. For academic analyses of *Ally McBeal*, see Rachel Moseley and Jacinda Read, "Having It Ally: Popular Television (Post-)Feminism," *Feminist Media Studies* 2, no. 2 (2002): 231–49; Laurie Ouelette, "Victims No More: Postfeminism, Television, and Ally McBeal," *Communication Review* 5, no. 4 (2002): 315–36; Bonnie Dow, "Ally McBeal, Lifestyle Feminism, and the Politics of Personal Happiness," *Communication Review* 5, no. 4 (2002): 259–65; Jonathan Cohen and Rivka Ribek, "Sex Differences in Pleasure from Television Texts: The Case of Ally McBeal," *Women's Studies in Communication* 26, no. 1 (Spring 2003): 118–34; and Michelle Hammers, "Cautionary Tales of Liberation and Female Professionalism: The Case Against Ally McBeal," *Western Journal of Communication* 69, no. 2 (2005): 167–82. The commentary on *Buffy* is enormous, and it has become something of a cottage industry among academics. As a result of the overwhelming number of submissions to their call for contributions to an essay collection on *Buffy* in 2001, Professors David Lavery and Rhonda Wilcox created *Slayage: The Online International Journal of Buffy Studies* to accommodate submissions. For a bibliography of scholarship on *Buffy*, see *Slayage* online at http://slayageonline.com.

13. Commentary on *Sex and the City* now rivals that of *Ally McBeal* and *Buffy the Vampire Slayer*, and the interpretations are just as varied. For more, see Rebecca Brasfield, "Rereading *Sex and the City*: Exposing the Hegemonic Feminist Narrative," *Journal of Popular Film & Television* 34, no. 3 (Fall 2006): 130–39; Laura Tropp, "'Faking a Sonogram': Representations of Motherhood on *Sex and the City*," *Journal of Popular Culture* 39, no. 5 (2006): 861–77; Janet Kramer, "Discourses of Sexual Morality in *Sex and the City* and *Queer as Folk*," *Journal of Popular Culture* 40, no. 3 (2007): 409–32; Belinda Stillion-Southard, "Beyond the Backlash: *Sex and the City* and Three Feminist Struggles," *Communication Quarterly* 56, no. 2 (2008): 149–67; Gail Markle, "Can Women Have Sex Like a Man? Sexual Scripts in *Sex and the City*," *Sexuality and Culture* 12, no. 1 (Winter 2008): 45–57; Jane Arthurs, "*Sex and the City* and Consumer Culture: Remediating Postfeminist Drama," in Brunsdon et al., *Feminist Television Criticism: A Reader*, 41–56; Judith Baxter, "Constructions of Active Womanhood and New Femininities: From a Feminist Linguistic Perspective, Is *Sex and the City* a Modernist or a Post-Modernist TV Text?" *Women & Language* 32, no. 1 (2009): 91–98; and Deborha Jermyn, *Sex and the City* (Detroit: Wayne State University Press, 2009). Also see the special issue of *Scholar & Feminist Online* 34, no. 1 (Fall 2004), devoted to *Sex and the City*; the site is hosted by the Barnard Center for Research on Women and available at http://www.barnard.edu/sfonline/.

14. Jessamyn Neuhaus, "Marge Simpson, Blue-Haired Housewife: Defining Domesticity on *The Simpsons*," *Journal of Popular Culture* 43, no. 4 (2010): 762.

15. I will talk about Patty Bouvier in more detail in chapter 4, in my discussion of homosexuality on *The Simpsons*, which is one of the reasons she is not included here. An interesting, if flawed, reflection on the lives of peripheral female characters can be found in Dale E. Snow and James J. Snow, "Simpsonian Sexual Politics," in *"The Simpsons" and Philosophy: The D'oh of Homer*, ed. William Irwin, Mark T. Conrad, and Aeon J. Skoble (Chicago: Open Court Press, 2000), 126–44.

16. Victoria A. Rebeck, "Recognizing Ourselves in *The Simpsons*," *Christian Century*, June 27, 1990, 622.

17. Chris Turner, *Planet Simpson: How a Cartoon Masterpiece Defined a Generation* (Cambridge, MA: Da Capo, 2004), 26.

18. Paula Chin, "In the Eye of the Storm," *People*, October 1, 1990, 82.

19. The producer James Brooks discusses this incident at length in a supplemental featurette, *Bush vs. Simpsons*, on disc 1 of the season 4 DVD box set (Fox Home Entertainment, 2004). A brief discussion of these events also appears in Turner, *Planet Simpson*, 231–33.

20. Paul Cantor, "*The Simpsons*: Atomistic Politics and the Nuclear Family," *Political Theory* 27, no. 6 (1999): 735.

21. Ibid., 735–36.

22. Ibid., 736.

23. Ibid., 737; my emphasis.

24. Ibid., 738 and 741.

25. Ibid., 745.

26. Jerry Herron, "Homer Simpson's Eyes and the Culture of Late Nostalgia," *Representations* 43 (1993): 18.

27. Karma Waltonen, "We're All Pigs: Representations of Masculinity in *The Simpsons*," paper presented at the Northeast Modern Language Association Conference in Buffalo, NY, April 2000; posted on *The Simpsons Archive*, September 16, 2001, http://www.snpp.com/other/papers/kw.paper.html.

28. J. E. Yang, "Quayle: 'Hollywood Doesn't Get It,'" *Washington Post*, May 21, 1992, A1.

29. "Murphy to Dan: Read My Ratings," *Time*, October 5, 1992, 25.

30. Michelle Goldberg, "A Woman's Place," *Salon*, April 23, 2002, http://www.salon.com/mwt/feature/2002/04/23/childless_women.

31. Ellen Willis, "Giving Feminism Life," review of *Creating a Life: Professional Women and the Quest for Children*, by Sylvia Hewlett, *Dissent* 49, no. 4 (Fall 2002): 95–100, http://www.dissentmagazine.org/archive/fa02/willis.shtml.

32. Sue Halpern, "Susan Faludi: The Mother Jones Interview," *Mother Jones*, September/October 1999, http://www.motherjones.com/media/1999/09/susan-faludi-mother-jones-interview.

33. Kim Gandy, "'Mommy Wars' Incited by Irresponsible Media," *National Organization for Women*, March 8, 2006, http://www.now.org/issues/media/mommywarsupdate.html. For useful critiques of the ideas offered by Hewlett, Flanagan, and Hirshman, see Susan Douglas, *The Mommy Myth: The Idealization of Motherhood and How It Has Undermined All Women* (New York: Free Press, 2004); Miriam Peskowitz, *The Truth Behind the "Mommy Wars": Who Decides What Makes a Good Mother?* (New York: Seal Press, 2005); Judith Warner, *Perfect Madness: Motherhood in the Age of Anxiety* (New York: Penguin, 2005); Leslie Morgan Steiner, ed., *Mommy Wars: Stay-at-Home and Career Moms Face Off on Their Choices, Their Lives, Their Families* (New York: Random, 2007).

34. For more on these issues, see "Epilogue: Beyond Backlash" in the revised edition of Ruth Rosen, *The World Split Open: How the Modern Women's Movement Changed America* (New York: Penguin, 2007), 331–44.

35. Lori Landay, *Madcaps, Screwballs & Con Women: The Female Trickster in American Culture* (Philadelphia: University of Pennsylvania Press, 1998), 161.

36. Ibid., 92.

37. Ibid., 166.

38. Mary Beth Haralovich, "Sit-coms and Suburbs: Positioning the 1950s Homemaker," in *Private Screenings: Television and the Female Consumer*," ed. Lynn Spigel and Denise Mann (Minneapolis: University of Minnesota Press, 1992), 111.

39. Ibid., 112.

40. Landay, *Madcaps, Screwballs*, 92.

41. Ken Tucker, "Yea, Mamas," *Entertainment Weekly*, May 13, 1994, 68.

42. "The Many Faces of Feminism," *Ms.* 5, no. 1 (July 1994): 33.

43. John Leo, "The Indignation of Barbie," *U.S. News & World Report*, October 12, 1992, 25.

44. David Firestone, "While Barbie Talks Tough, G.I. Joe Goes Shopping," *New York Times*, December 31, 1993, A12.

45. Ibid.

46. Michael S. Kimmel, "Saving the Males: The Sociological Implications of the Virginia Military Institute and the Citadel," *Gender & Society* 14, no. 4 (2000): 495.

47. Ibid.

48. The programs were to provide the same educational benefits and training in leadership. The Citadel set up the South Carolina Institute for Leadership (SCIL) at Converse College, and VMI established the Virginia Women's Institute for Leadership (VWIL) at Mary Baldwin College. For details, see Kimmel, "Saving the Males," 494–516.

49. Katie Gibson, "*United States* v. *Virginia*: A Rhetorical Battle between Progress and Preservation," *Women's Studies in Communication* 29, no. 2 (Fall 2006): 140.

50. For a full history of the case, see Catherine S. Manegold, *In Glory's Shadow: Shannon Faulkner, the Citadel and a Changing America* (New York: Knopf, 2000). For an illuminating study of how essentialist notions of gender impacted the case, see Kristina Schriver, "Rhetorical Pathologies and Gender Difference: An Ideological Examination of Cultural Discourse in *Faulkner v. The Citadel*," *Women's Studies in Communication* 26, no. 1 (2003): 27–59.

51. Kimmel, "Saving the Males," 498.

52. Similar issues were explored in Ridley Scott's *G.I. Jane* (1997), which appeared in August, just a few months after "The Secret War of Lisa Simpson." *G.I. Jane* tells the fictional story of navy officer Lt. Jordan O'Neil (Demi Moore), the first female to be selected for training in the elite Navy Combined Reconnaissance Team (loosely based on the real Navy SEAL program).

53. Landay, *Madcaps, Screwballs*, 192.

54. A useful compendium of commentary from each of these men—as well as many other people involved with the creation and production of *The Simpsons*—is the oral history compiled by John Ortved, *"The Simpsons": An Uncensored, Unauthorized History* (New York: Faber, 2009).

55. Quoted in ibid., 119.

56. Many are surprised to learn that the very first *Simpsons* episode, "Simpsons Roasting on an Open Fire," was not written by Matt Groening. Mimi Pond, who made a name for herself writing for the sitcom *Designing Women*, also works as a cartoonist. Ironically, Pond has never worked again on *The Simpsons*. Steve Williams and Ian Jones, "Cartoons Have Writers?" *Off the Telly*, May 2002, http://offthetelly.users. btopenworld.com/comedy/simpsons/history.htm. See also "Episodes by Writer," *The Simpsons Archive*, May 5, 2003, http://www.snpp.com/guides/epsbywriter.html.

57. It should be noted that one woman, Nancy Kruse, has functioned as a director of numerous episodes of *The Simpsons*. Kruse began her tenure on the show in season 10, with the episode "Simpsons Bible Stories" (episode #AABF14, aired April 4, 1999); she has subsequently directed an additional 18 episodes, including the controversial "There's Something about Marrying," which I discuss in more detail in chapter 6. See "The Writers & Directors List," *The Simpsons Archive*, July 20, 2011, http://www.snpp .com/guides/writers.directors.html.

58. See "Episodes by Writer."

59. Neuhaus, "Marge Simpson," 770.

60. Ibid.

61. Neuhaus, "Marge Simpson," 772–73.
62. Landay, *Madcaps, Screwballs*, 192.
63. Barry Hodge, "King Size Homer: Ideology and Representation," *The Simpsons Archive*, 1996, http://www.snpp.com/other/papers/bh.paper.html.
64. "Many Faces of Feminism," 48.

4   "The Whole World's Gone Gay!": Gay Identity, Queer Culture, and *The Simpsons*

1. Larry Gross, *Up from Invisibility: Lesbians, Gay Men, and the Media in America* (New York: Columbia University Press, 2001), 16.
2. Like many words, the word *gay* comes to us "trailing clouds of connotation," as Richard Dyer puts it. Dyer, *The Matter of Images: Essays on Representation* (New York: Routledge, 1993), 8. There are also many practical limitations to its use. I prefer the term *queer* over the phrase "gay and lesbian" or the cumbersome acronyms GLBT or GLBTQ. *Queer* is to be understood here as an all-encompassing term, one that refers to the variety of identities associated with sex, gender, and sexual orientation—e.g., gay, lesbian, and bisexual, as well as transvestite, transgender, and transsexual. I make frequent use of the term *queer* in this chapter; however, in deference to many of my sources, I also regularly use the terms *gay* and *lesbian*.
3. For more on news media, see Edward Alwood, *Straight News: Gays, Lesbians and the News Media* (New York: Columbia University Press, 1996); and Laura Castañeda and Shannon Campbell, *News and Sexuality: Media Portraits of Diversity* (Thousand Oaks, CA: Sage, 2006).
4. B. Ruby Rich, "New Queer Cinema," *Sight & Sound*, September 1992, 30–34. Important films of the period include Bill Sherwood's *Parting Glances* (1986), Isaac Julien's *Looking for Langston* (1988), Marlon Riggs's *Tongues Untied* (1990), Gus Van Sant's *My Own Private Idaho* (1991), Derek Jarman's *Edward II* (1991), Jennie Livingston's *Paris Is Burning* (1991), Greg Araki's *The Living End* (1992), and Todd Kalin's *Swoon* (1992). Hollywood films of the period include Jonathan Demme's *Philadelphia* (1993), Beeban Kidron's *To Wong Foo, Thanks for Everything! Julie Newmar* (1995), and Mike Nichols's *The Birdcage* (1996). For more detail, see Harry M. Benshoff and Sean Griffin, eds., *Queer Images: A History of Gay and Lesbian Film in America* (Lanham, MD: Rowman & Littlefield, 2006).
5. Ron Becker, *Gay TV and Straight America* (New Brunswick, NJ: Rutgers University Press, 2006), 3. Oddly, Becker only makes passing mention of *The Simpsons*, not even discussing a single episode at length, which is an unfortunate oversight in an otherwise comprehensive and admirable work. *The Simpsons*, as I argue in this chapter, also contributed significantly to the representation of gay identity on television during the 1990s and beyond.
6. For more on the culture wars, see James D. Hunter, *Culture Wars: The Struggle to Define America* (New York: Basic, 1991); Jeffrey Escoffier, *American Homo: Community and Perversity* (Berkeley: University of California Press, 1998); and Jonathan Zimmerman, *Whose America? Culture Wars in the Public Schools* (Cambridge, MA: Harvard University Press, 2005). On niche marketing, see Alexandra Chasin, *Selling Out: The Gay and Lesbian Movement Goes to Market* (New York: Palgrave Macmillan, 2000).
7. Teresa de Lauretis is credited with coining the term *queer theory* in a special issue of the feminist journal *differences* that she edited; see "Queer Theory: Lesbian and Gay Sexualities," *differences* 3, no. 2 (1991): iii–xviii. The provenance of the term is not

as important, however, as the dramatic shifts created within the academy by queer theory, which offered a more intensified focus on issues of sex, gender, and sexuality than had been evident in both feminist and gay and lesbian studies up to that point. For a brief (and unsympathetic) history of the institutionalization of queer theory, see David Halperin, "The Normalization of Queer Theory," *Journal of Homosexuality* 45, nos. 2–4 (2003): 339–43. A more comprehensive history is found in William B. Turner, *A Genealogy of Queer Theory* (Philadelphia: Temple University Press, 2000).

8. Karen Kopelson, "Dis/Integrating the Gay/Queer Binary: 'Reconstructed Identity Politics' for a Performative Pedagogy," *College English* 65, no. 1 (September 2002): 17.

9. Pioneering texts include Vito Russo, *The Celluloid Closet: Homosexuality in the Movies*, rev. ed. (1981; repr., New York: Harper & Row, 1987); Alexander Doty, *Making Things Perfectly Queer: Interpreting Mass Culture* (Minneapolis: University of Minnesota Press, 1993); Dyer, *Matter of Images*; Michelangelo Signorile, *Queer in America: Sex, the Media, and the Closets of Power* (New York: Random House, 1993); and Michael Warner, ed., *Fear of a Queer Planet: Queer Politics and Social Theory* (Minneapolis: University of Minnesota Press, 1993). Three texts that have been particularly useful for their focuses on television and mass media and have thus informed much of what follows in this chapter are Suzanna Danuta Walters, *All the Rage: The Story of Gay Visibility in America* (Chicago: University of Chicago Press, 2001); Gross, *Up from Invisibility*; and Becker, *Gay TV*. Other useful collections include Alexander Doty and Corey Creekmur, eds., *Out in Culture: Gay, Lesbian, and Queer Essays on Popular Culture* (Durham, NC: Duke University Press, 1995); Martha Gever, John Greyson, and Pratibha Parmar, eds., *Queer Looks: Perspectives on Lesbian and Gay Film and Video* (New York: Routledge, 1993); Ellis Hanson, ed., *Out Takes: Essays on Queer Theory and Film* (Durham, NC: Duke University Press, 1999); and Michele Aaron, ed., *New Queer Cinema: A Critical Reader* (New Brunswick, NJ: Rutgers University Press, 2004).

10. Alan Brookey and Robert Westerfelhaus, "Pistols and Petticoats, Piety and Purity: *To Wong Foo*, the Queering of American Monomyth and the Marginalizing Discourse of Deification," *Critical Studies in Media Communication* 18, no. 2 (2001): 142.

11. Becker, *Gay TV*, 15. A similar "panic" can be understood as a motivating factor in the "backlash" against feminism in the 1980s documented by Susan Faludi or in the rising nativist movement in the 1990s, as discussed in detail in chapter 3.

12. Brookey and Westerfelhaus, "Pistols and Petticoats," 143.

13. Andy Medhurst, "Batman, Deviance, and Camp," in *Signs of Life in the USA*, ed. Sonia Maasik and Jack Solomon (Boston: Bedford, 1994), 328.

14. This phenomenon is explored fully in the 1995 documentary film *The Celluloid Closet*, directed by Rob Epstein and Jeffrey Friedman and based on Vito Russo's book *Celluloid Closet*. The trend continued into the 1980s, as Russo documents in the revised edition of his book, published in 1987.

15. For a more detailed discussion of these shows, see Steven Capsuto, *Alternate Channels: The Uncensored Story of Gay and Lesbian Images on Radio and Television, 1930s to the Present* (New York: Ballantine, 2000), 106–18.

16. John R. Leo, "The Familialism of 'Man' in American Television Drama," *South Atlantic Quarterly* 88, no. 1 (1989): 31.

17. Whether Steven Carrington is gay, bisexual, or straight is open for debate. His sexuality was constantly shifting: in the first season, Steven, who is first introduced as a homosexual, becomes involved in a sexual affair with a woman. For the next six seasons, Steven struggles with his desires for both men and women; during that time, he is involved in relationships with a man, Ted, and with two women, Claudia and Sammy Jo. See Capsuto, *Alternate Channels*, 177–78.

18. E. Salholz and T. Clifton, "The Future of Gay America," *Newsweek*, March 12, 1990, 21, 25.

19. Andrew Kopkind, "The Gay Moment," *Nation*, May 3, 1993, 577.

20. Jess Cagle, "America Sees Shades of Gay," *Entertainment Weekly*, September 8, 1995, 20.

21. Ibid., 23.

22. Leo, "Familialism of 'Man,'" 39.

23. Becker, *Gay TV*, 138. This remained true for ABC, as well as for NBC, which over the next few years ran into similar resistance from advertisers for gay-themed episodes of the dramas *Lifestories*, *L.A. Law*, and *Quantum Leap*, and for CBS, which was unable to secure enough advertisers for a planned sitcom starring Harvey Fierstein as an openly gay lead character. For more, see Becker, *Gay TV*, 142–43.

24. Becker, *Gay TV*, 155. A Nielsen share of 30 indicates that 30 percent of televisions in use (in households equipped with Nielsen monitoring systems) were tuned in to this episode of *Roseanne*.

25. Fred Fejes, "Invisibility, Homophobia, and Heterosexism," *Critical Studies in Mass Communications* 10, no. 4 (1993): 400.

26. Ibid., 402.

27. See "Where We Are on TV: 1996–1997 Season," GLAAD: The Gay & Lesbian Alliance Against Defamation, March 12, 2008, http://archive.glaad.org/eye/ontv /past/1996_1997.php; and "Where We Are on TV: 1997–1998 Season," GLAAD: The Gay & Lesbian Alliance Against Defamation, March 12, 2008, http://archive.glaad .org/eye/ontv/past/1997_1998.php. For more information, see the "Where We Are on TV" reports for each television season.

28. Cagle, "Shades of Gay," 28.

29. Ibid., 28–29. Bonnie J. Dow provides a useful overview of the rise and demise of the show in "*Ellen*, Television, and the Politics of Gay and Lesbian Visibility," *Critical Studies in Media Communication* 18, no. 2 (2001): 123–40. Also see Susan J. Hubert, "What's Wrong with This Picture? The Politics of Ellen's Coming Out Party," *Journal of Popular Culture* 33, no. 2 (1999): 31–36; Didi Herman, "'I'm Gay': Declarations, Desire, and Coming Out on Prime-Time Television," *Sexualities* 8, no. 1 (2005): 7–29; and Jennifer Reed, "Ellen DeGeneres: Public Lesbian Number One," *Feminist Media Studies* 5, no. 1 (2005): 23–36.

30. A. J. Jacobs, "Out?" *Entertainment Weekly*, October 4, 1996, 23.

31. A. J. Jacobs, "When Gay Men Happen to Straight Women," *Entertainment Weekly*, October 23, 1998, 23.

32. Dana Heller, "Taking the Nation 'From Drab to Fab': *Queer Eye for the Straight Guy*," *Feminist Media Studies* 4, no. 3 (2004): 350.

33. Damon Romine, "Families Matter: GLAAD Examines the 2003–04 Primetime Network Lineup," GLAAD: The Gay & Lesbian Alliance Against Defamation, September 15, 2003, http://archive.glaad.org/media/release_detail.php?id=3489.

34. The term *camp* is notoriously hard to define, as Susan Sontag explains in her now-famous "Notes on Camp." I am particularly fond of her claim that camp "sees everything in quotation marks," and I believe that is a useful way to understand how it is employed on *The Simpsons* to develop a queer sensibility. In short, *The Simpsons* borrows heavily from the ironic camp that is most frequently associated with gay males, female movie icons, and drag performance.

35. Doug Sadownick, "Groening Against the Grain," interview, *Advocate*, February 26, 1991, 32.

36. Ibid.

37. Ibid., 33.

38. In "Batman, Deviance, and Camp," Andy Medhurst meticulously illustrates the queer content of the *Batman* TV show and argues that what has happened since the 1960s is the "painstaking reheterosexualization" of Batman, which he traces in the *Batman* comic books, the subsequent *Dark Knight* graphic novels, and Tim Burton's 1989 film, *Batman*. Medhurst argues that by the late 1980s, in deference to the conservative mood of the nation, the camp connotations put in place by the earlier television series had been "fully purged." Medhurst, "Batman, Deviance, and Camp," 335–36. Medhurst's quite valid claim has direct bearing on my own claims for the camp sensibility of *The Simpsons*, as illustrated by the season 4 episode "Mr. Plow" (#9F07, November 19, 1992). The subplot of this episode involves Bart's attendance at a comic book convention, where he meets the guest of honor, one Adam "Batman" West. Bart, as a child of the 1980s, is unfamiliar with the 1960s TV show, and in response to West's attempts to remind the young crowd who he once was, Bart candidly asks, "Who the hell is Robin?" As Medhurst has noted, by that point Batman had been remade into a lone and heterosexual crime fighter.
39. Larry Gross, "Out of the Mainstream: Sexual Minorities and the Mass Media," *Journal of Homosexuality* 21, nos. 1–2 (1991): 27.
40. Some examples are characters appearing as art instructors, theater directors, and ballet dancers or as miscellaneous men on the street wearing brightly colored clothing (frequently with neck scarves) or dressed in short shorts and tank tops, often with a multicolored rainbow image. One of the more memorable characters is Llewelyn Sinclair (voiced by Jon Lovitz), a flamboyant theater director brought in to direct *Oh, Streetcar!* (a musical version of *A Streetcar Named Desire*) for the Springfield Community Center. The Village People also made a guest appearance on the show in "Simpson Tide" (#3G04, March 29, 1998). For a detailed list of references, see the "Homosexuality References in *The Simpsons*" page of *The Simpsons Archive*, http://www.snpp.com/guides/homosexuality.html.
41. Dyer, *Matter of Images*, 16.
42. Escoffier, *American Homo*, 205.
43. Becker, *Gay TV*, 219.
44. Anna Marie Smith, "The Politicization of Marriage in Contemporary American Public Policy: The Defense of Marriage Act and the Personal Responsibility Act," *Citizenship Studies* 5, no. 3 (2001): 310.
45. Walters, *All the Rage*, 74.
46. Daniel Wickberg, "Homophobia: On the Cultural History of an Idea," *Critical Inquiry* 27 (Autumn 2000): 57.
47. The debate over whether one's sexuality is a "choice" and, therefore, changeable is long-standing, but it intensified after the American Psychiatric Association declassified homosexuality as a mental disorder in 1973. Since that time, a cottage industry has grown around the notion of "reparative therapy" or "conversion therapy," both within the mental health community and among Christian fundamentalists groups, which gave birth to the "ex-gay" movement in the 1990s. The debate became even more heated after a 2001 presentation by Dr. Robert Spitzer, a respected member of the APA, which claimed that sexual orientation could be changed. The Spitzer Study, as it is known, was published in *Archives of Sexual Behavior* in 2003 and has been a source of intense debate ever since. For more, see the *Archives of Sexual Behavior* 32, no. 5 (October 2003), the special issue of the journal that includes Spitzer's paper as well as responses from many other medical professionals. Also see Wayne R. Besen, *Anything but Straight: Unmasking the Scandals and Lies Behind the Ex-Gay Myth* (New York: Routledge, 2003); and Tanya Erzen, *Straight to Jesus: Sexual and*

Christian Conversions in the Ex-Gay Movement (Berkeley: University of California Press, 2006).

48. Clifford Krauss, "Gay Marriage Is Extended Nationwide in Canada," *New York Times*, June 29, 2005, A4.

49. Escoffier, *American Homo*, 208.

50. Danielle O'Connell, "Federal and State DOMA Language," Report to the Judiciary Committee, Report 2002-R-0957, Office of Legislative Research, Connecticut General Assembly, December 6, 2002, http://www.cga.ct.gov/2002/olrdata/jud/rpt/2002-R-0957.htm.

51. "Frist Backs Constitutional Ban On Gay Marriage," *USA Today*, June 29, 2003, http://www.usatoday.com/news/washington/2003-06-29-frist-gay-marriage_x.htm.

52. This partisan divide has been commented upon by many. For more, see George Lakoff, *Moral Politics: How Liberals and Conservatives Think* (Chicago: University of Chicago Press, 2002); Thomas Frank, *What's the Matter with Kansas? How Conservatives Won the Heart of America* (New York: Metropolitan, 2004); and Stephen T. Mockabee, "A Question of Authority: Religion and Cultural Conflict in the 2004 Election," *Political Behavior* 29 (2007): 221–48.

53. Bruce Steele, "The Gay Rights Makeover," *Advocate*, September 2, 2003, 42.

54. Romine, "Families Matter."

55. Andrew Sullivan, "Beware the Straight Backlash," *Time*, August 11, 2003, 35.

56. Hints of Patty's sexuality can be found in earlier episodes of the series. For example, in "Selma's Choice" (#9F11, January 21, 1993), ironically enough, while Marge, Patty, and Selma are discussing potential sperm donors, Homer goes streaking naked through the kitchen; when Patty sees this, she says, "There goes the last shred of my heterosexuality."

57. A rebuttal to such criticisms is certainly possible. Though this is not a primary concern for me here, I'll note that there is a large body of literature documenting that cross-dressing is common among heterosexual males. For overviews, see Richard Elkins, *Male Femaling: A Grounded Approach to Cross-Dressing and Sex-Changing* (New York: Routledge, 1997); and Marjorie Garber, *Vested Interests: Crossdressing and Cultural Anxiety* (New York: Routledge, 1997). Robin's ruse is fueled by his (heterosexual) desire for Patty; since she initially saw him as a fellow lesbian, the ruse is maintained. Lastly, it must be noted that Homer actually performs a great many gay weddings for other people in the course of the episode.

58. "Brokeback Mountain," *Box Office Mojo*, March 10, 2008, http://www.boxofficemojo.com/movies/?id=brokebackmountain.htm.

59. "Where We Are on TV Report, 2010–2011," GLAAD: The Gay & Lesbian Alliance Against Defamation, September 2008, http://www.glaad.org/publications/whereweareontv11.

60. Ibid.

61. Ibid.

62. Walters, *All the Rage*, 12.

63. Ibid., 14.

64. As might be expected, protests were launched by the Gay & Lesbian Alliance Against Defamation and the Human Rights Campaign. These were successful in getting the Mars Corporation to pull the ad and shut down the website. See Matthew Creamer, "Marketing's Era of Outrage," *Advertising Age*, February 12, 2007, 1–2; Guy Trebay, "A Kiss Too Far?" *New York Times*, February 18, 2007, late ed., sec. 9, 1; and "We Are Not Amused" (editorial), *Advocate*, March 13, 2007, 4.

65. Although it was almost universally panned by critics (labeled as, among other things, "sexist," "racist," and "offensive"), the reviews did not stop the film from doing well financially: in its three-month theatrical run *Chuck and Larry* earned a worldwide

gross of just over $186 million—$120,059,556 domestically and $65,994,597 in for-eign markets. "I Now Pronounce You Chuck and Larry," *Box Office Mojo*, March 10, 2008, http://www.boxofficemojo.com/movies/?id=chuckandlarry.htm. For detailed critiques, see Manohla Dargis, "Dude (Nyuck-Nyuck), I Love You (as If!)," *New York Times*, July 20, 2007, 17; and David Noh, review of *I Now Pronounce You Chuck and Larry, Film Journal International*, September 2007, 59.

66. Becker, *Gay TV*, 212–13.

5   "Upper-Lower-Middle-Class Types": Socioeconomic Class on *The Simpsons*

1. Michael Zweig, *The Working Class Majority: America's Best Kept Secret*, 2nd ed. (2000; repr., Ithaca, NY: Cornell University Press, 2012), Kindle edition, Kindle loca-tions 964–66.

2. For more on the class war, see the articles in Bill Keller et al., *Class Matters* (New York: Henry Holt, 2005). The book is a compilation of articles originally printed in *The New York Times* as part of its investigative series on social class in America. Also see Larry M. Bartels, *Unequal Democracy: The Political Economy of the New Gilded Age* (Princeton, NJ: Princeton University Press, 2010). For a rebuttal of the class war the-sis, see Benjamin I. Page and Lawrence R. Jacobs, *Class War? What Americans Really Think about Economic Inequality* (Chicago: University of Chicago Press, 2009).

3. Thomas Frank, *What's the Matter with Kansas? How Conservatives Won the Heart of America* (New York: Metropolitan, 2004), 5.

4. David Croteau, William Hoynes, and Stefania Milan, *Media/Society: Industries, Images, and Audiences*, 4th ed. (Los Angeles: Sage, 2012), 205.

5. Gregory Mantsios, "Class in America—2009," in *Race, Class, and Gender in the United States: An Integrated Study*, 8th ed., ed. Paula S. Rothenberg (New York: Worth, 2009), 177.

6. Joan C. Williams, *Reshaping the Work-Family Debate: Why Men and Class Matter* (Cambridge, MA: Harvard University Press, 2010), 155.

7. Those who do speak of class on *The Simpsons* almost invariable refer to two specific episodes, "Last Exit to Springfield" and "Scenes from the Class Struggle in Springfield," because they address social and economic class very directly. I will discuss each of these episodes in detail later. For an examination of class in relation to the American dream, see J. Michael Blitzer, "Political Culture and Public Opinion: The American Dream on Springfield's Evergreen Terrace," in *Homer Simpson Goes to Washington: American Politics through Popular Culture*, ed. Joseph J. Foy (Lexington: University Press of Kentucky, 2008), 41–60. The topic of class is touched on, albeit somewhat tangentially, by Chris Turner in *Planet Simpson: How a Cartoon Masterpiece Defined a Generation* (Cambridge, MA: Da Capo, 2004); in particular, see Turner's discussion of consumerism (105–9) and his chapter on Montgomery Burns ("Citizen Burns," 151–88). Also see Diane Alter's fascinating small-scale ethnographic study of the viewing habits of two families and their thoughts on class, taste, and *The Simpsons*. Diane Alters, "'We Hardly Watch That Rude, Crude Show': Class and Taste in *The Simpsons*," in *Prime Time Animation: Television Animation and American Culture*, ed. Carol A. Stabile and Mark Harrison (New York: Routledge, 2003), 165–84.

8. Diana Kendall, *Framing Class: Media Representations of Wealth and Poverty in America*, 2nd ed. (Lanham, MD: Rowman and Littlefield, 2011), 2.

9. Contracts with Burger King were secured in 1990. See "Burger King Nabs *The Simpsons*," *Advertising Age*, April 30, 1990, 3. Contracts with Nestlé (for Butterfinger

candy bars) were secured in 1993. See Fara Werner and Terry Lefton, "Bart Inks Sweet New Deal," *Brandweek*, March 22, 1993, 4. Intel Corporation signed a deal to use Homer Simpson in a television campaign for the Pentium II processor in 1998. See Terry Stanley and Tobi Elkin, "Intel Hires Homer to Push Pentium," *Adweek Western Edition*, November 2, 1998, 4. Other promotional partners have included KFC, Kellogg's, Kraft, Proctor & Gamble, Reebok, and MasterCard. For more information, see Joanna Doonar, "Homer's Brand Odyssey," *Brand Strategy*, February 2004, 20–23.

10. Pierre Bourdieu, *Distinction: A Social Critique of the Judgment of Taste*, trans. Richard Nice (1979; repr., Cambridge, MA: Harvard University Press, 1984), 57.

11. See, for example, David Marc, *Comic Visions: Television Comedy and American Culture*, 2nd ed. (Malden, MA: Blackwell, 1997); Darrell Y. Hamamoto, *Nervous Laughter: Television Situation Comedy and Liberal Democratic Ideology* (New York: Praeger, 1989); Gerard Jones, *Honey, I'm Home! Sitcoms: Selling the American Dream* (New York: St. Martin's, 1992); Lynn Spigel, *Make Room for TV: Television and the Family Ideal in Postwar America* (Chicago: University of Chicago Press, 1992); Janet Staiger, *Blockbuster TV: Must-See Sitcoms in the Network Era* (New York: New York University Press, 2000); Robin R. Means Coleman, *African American Viewers and the Black Situation Comedy: Situating Racial Humor* (New York: Garland, 2000); and Vincent Brook, *Something Ain't Kosher Here: The Rise of the "Jewish" Sitcom* (New Brunswick, NJ: Rutgers University Press, 2003).

12. Marc, *Comic Visions*, 147.

13. It should be noted that *The Jeffersons*, *Sanford and Son*, and *Good Times* were also specifically rooted in black culture, which additionally worked to break down the racial barriers and stereotypes imposed by the McWASP tradition.

14. The S&L crisis had effects throughout the decade and negatively impacted the welfare of many American households; the subsequent bailout of the Federal Savings and Loan Insurance Corporation (FSLIC), which insured the deposits in failed S&Ls, has been an enormous cost to taxpayers: current estimates project the final cost of the bailout to exceed $160 billion. James R. Barth, Susanne Trimbath, Glenn Yago, eds., *The Savings and Loan Crisis: Lessons from a Regulatory Failure* (New York: Springer, 2004), 25.

15. Carl Walsh, "What Caused the 1990–1991 Recession?" *Economic Review of the Federal Reserve Bank of San Francisco* 2 (1993): 34–48.

16. *Lifestyles of the Rich and Famous* was created by Leach, who was himself an example of the American dream, having risen from shoe salesman to television personality. *Lifestyles*, which aired in over 30 countries worldwide, ran for 13 seasons. It continues to air in syndication and lives on today as a video game. Kendall, *Framing Class*, 48. The premise of *Lifestyles* never died; it was subsequently carried on in programs such as MTV's *Cribs* (2000–), VH1's *The Fabulous Life* (2003–), and most of the so-called "reality" television programs popular today, which largely depict the lifestyles of the rich and famous.

17. Moore continued his critique in the book *Downsize This! Random Threats from an Unarmed American* (1996) and the film *The Big One* (1998), which was filmed on the road while promoting *Downsize This!* In *The Big One*, Moore turns his scorn on corporations such as Nike, which has caused a scandal by sending jobs offshore and using child labor, and on Nike's CEO, Phil Knight. Though accused of being a partisan, Moore was (and continues to be) just as angry with those on the political left as those on the right. His films of the period also indict the Clinton administration for continuing some of the worst economic policies of Reagan-Bush era. For more on

Moore, see the essays collected in Matthew Bernstein, ed., *Michael Moore: Filmmaker, Newsmaker, Cultural Icon* (Ann Arbor: University of Michigan Press, 2010).

18. The struggle of workers in this period was also captured by Barbara Kopple in her Oscar-winning film *American Dream* (1990), which documented a workers' strike at Hormel Foods in Austin, Minnesota, 1985–86. It is worth noting here that Kopple had explored similar territory in her earlier Oscar-winning film, *Harlan County, USA* (1976), which focused on a 1972 strike by Kentucky coal miners. For more on Kopple's work, see James McEnteer, "Barbara Kopple: Intrepid Pioneer on the Front Lines," chapter 4 of *Shooting the Truth: The Rise of American Political Documentaries* (New York: Praeger, 2006), 63–78.

19. For more on the effects of NAFTA, see Mary E. Burfisher, Sherman Robinson, and Karen Thierfelder, "The Impact of NAFTA on the United States," *Journal of Economic Perspectives* 15, no. 1 (2001): 125–44. On the effects of welfare reform, see Gwendolyn Mink, *Welfare's End* (Ithaca, NY: Cornell University Press, 2002); and Jason DeParle, *American Dream: Three Women, Ten Kids, and a Nation's Drive to End Welfare* (New York: Viking, 2004).

20. Mantsios, "Class in America—2009," 178.

21. Ibid.

22. Ibid.

23. Zweig, *Working Class Majority*, Kindle locations 964–66.

24. Dennis L. Gilbert, *The American Class Structure in an Age of Growing Inequality* (Thousand Oaks, CA: Pine Forge, 2010), 14. Also see Joseph A. Kahl, *The American Class Structure* (New York: Rinehart, 1957).

25. The survey was of a nationally representative sample of 2,413 adults; there were 1,038 respondents. Researchers break the 53 percent of middle-class persons into four categories, which they label "Top of the Class," "The Satisfied Middle," "The Anxious Middle, and "The Struggling Middle." Within the Top of the Class group, 32 percent had family incomes over $100,000 per year; the remaining 68 percent had family incomes between $50,000 and $99,000. In the lowest group, those labeled "struggling," all have income less than $50,000, but a full 58 percent of them have income less than $20,000 per year. Richard Morin, "America's Four Middle Classes," Pew Social & Demographic Trends, *Pew Research Center*, July 29, 2008, 1, http://www .pewsocialtrends.org/2008/07/29/americas-four-middle-classes/2/.

26. Paul Taylor et al., "Inside the Middle Class: Bad Times Hit the Good Life," Pew Social & Demographic Trends, *Pew Research Center*, April 9, 2008, 8, http://www .pewsocialtrends.org/2008/04/09/inside-the-middle-class-bad-times-hit-the-good-life/.

27. Ibid.

28. Macionis's webpage at Kenyon college proclaims that he is the author of "the most widely used textbooks in sociology." "John J. Macionis," http://www.kenyon.edu/ x41416.xml. As of 2010, *Sociology* is in its thirteenth edition. The figures and statistics that follow come from this edition. See John Macionis, *Sociology*, 13th ed. (New York: Prentice Hall, 2010).

29. Macionis, *Sociology*, 275. For more, see chapter 11, 271–95.

30. Zweig, *Working Class Majority*, Kindle location 767.

31. Stanley Aronowitz, *How Class Works: Power and Social Movement* (New Haven, CT: Yale University Press, 2003), 29. Looking at the information presented by Macionis in *Sociology*, it is fairly easy to come up with the numbers claimed by both Zweig and Aronowitz. Taking only half of the so-called "average-middles" (just 15 percent of the 30 percent specified) and adding that to both the working class (35 percent) and the "working poor" (what Macionis calls "upper-lowers," another 10 percent), we have the 60

percent figure that economists and labor leaders regularly cite. This working-class majority would have incomes that range from close to the poverty line (in 2009, $22,050 for a family of four) to $81,000, which still seems a large range, but it is nowhere near as large as that offered by Macionis or the Pew Research Center study.

32. Zweig, *Working Class Majority*, Kindle locations 1383–1386.
33. Ibid., Kindle locations 305–6.
34. For example, in "Deep Space Homer" (February 1994), in which Homer becomes an astronaut, Homer is recruited by NASA because he is a stark contrast to the typical recruits, "clean-cut, athletic go-getters," which the public apparently no longer likes; to get the public interested in space exploration once again, NASA needed a "blue-collar slob." In "Bart vs. Australia" (February 1995), in which the Simpsons travel to Australia, we see that the trip is funded by the US State Department in order to smooth relations between the United States and Australia after Bart is indicted for fraud (for an unpaid international telephone bill) and publicly mocks Australia. In "The Regina Monologues" (November 2003), the family travels to London. In this case, they do pay for the trip, but the episode provides an elaborate series of events to explain how the family secures the money for it. In short, Bart earns $3,000 in entrance fees to his "The Museum of Modern Bart," which displays a $1,000 bill that he accidentally came to possess.
35. "Poverty Thresholds," US Census Bureau, United States. http://www.census.gov/hhes/www/poverty/data/threshld/index.html. I mention both dates, since assessing historical statistics is also complex on *The Simpsons*, given the oddly static nature of its timeframe; the characters have not aged since the start of the show (despite occasional birthdays, grade advancements, and repeated holidays), so one can use statistics that coincide with its "actual" timeframe—1990, when the series began—or 1996, which is when this episode aired.
36. On the struggle to get by in America, see Barbara Ehrenreich, *Nickel and Dimed: On (Not) Getting By in America* (New York: Metropolitan, 2001); and David K. Shipler, *The Working Poor: Invisible in America* (New York: Knopf, 2004).
37. Dale E. Snow and James J. Snow, "Simpsonian Sexual Politics," in *"The Simpsons" and Philosophy: The D'oh of Homer*, ed. William Irwin, Mark T. Conrad, and Aeon J. Skoble (Chicago: Open Court Press, 2000), 140.
38. Bailey is implied to be a liberal candidate. Not much is said about Burns's political affiliation in this episode, but it is not surprising that Burns is cast as the more conservative politician here (and, in later episodes, as a member of the Republican Party) since this aligns him more clearly with the neoliberal economic agenda then being promoted by the Reagan administration.
39. Turner, *Planet Simpson*, 163–64.
40. Ibid.
41. See Carl Matheson, "The Simpsons, Hyper-Irony, and the Meaning of Life," in Irwin et al., *"The Simpsons" and Philosophy*, 108–25.
42. The dental plan motif of the episode is clearly connected to economics, but it also interestingly raises the topic of social class via brand identity. When Lisa returns to the dentist, poststrike, to get her braces, Dr. Wolf shows her a set of designer braces, which are "invisible, painless, and periodically release a delightful burst of Calvin Klein's Obsession—for teeth." Marge grimaces and says, "We don't have a dental plan so we need something a little bit more affordable." The dentist then holds up a clanging mess of metal and cobwebs. "These predate stainless steel," he says, "so you can't get them wet."
43. James M. Wallace, "A (Karl, Not Groucho) Marxist in Springfield," in Irwin et al., *"The Simpsons" and Philosophy*, 237 and 239.

44. Ibid., 238 and 246.

45. Ibid., 246.

46. Ibid., 250.

47. Richard Butsch, "Ralph, Fred, Archie, and Homer: Why Television Keeps Recreating the White Male Working-Class Buffoon," in *Gender, Race, and Class in Media*, 2nd ed., ed. Gail Dines and Jean M. Humez (Thousand Oaks, CA: Sage, 2003), 576. Note that the essay was originally published in 1995.

48. Ibid.

49. See Kendall, *Framing Class*, 142–46.

50. See ibid., 146–53.

51. Matt Wray and Annalee Newitz, eds., *White Trash: Race and Class in America* (New York: Routledge, 1997), 2.

52. Ibid.

53. Matt Wray, *Not Quite White: White Trash and the Boundaries of Whiteness* (Durham, NC: Duke University Press, 2006), 23.

54. Duncan Stuart Beard, "Local Satire with a Global Reach: Ethnic Stereotyping and Cross-Cultural Conflicts in *The Simpsons*," in *Leaving Springfield: "The Simpsons" and the Possibilities of Oppositional Television*, ed. John Alberti (Detroit: Wayne State University Press, 2004), 282.

55. There is some confusion about Cletus's last name. Cletus is identified early in the series as Cletus Delroy, but in the 2002 episode "Sweets and Sour Marge," he is seen signing his name on a petition as Cletus Spuckler, and in the 2007 episode "Yokel Chords," it is implied that Delroy is his middle name and Spuckler his last name. Cletus is not listed in the character files in the Hall of Records on the official *Simpsons* website (http://www.thesimpsons.com/#/characters), so an uncertainty remains. I will refer to Cletus as Delroy, in part because that is how I first came to know him as a character and in part because I relish the irony of the name. For more on the character, see the "Cletus Spuckler" file on WikiSimpsons. Accessed at http://simpsons.wikia.com/wiki/Cletus_Spuckler.

56. The kids are Tiffany, Heather, Cody, Dylan, Dermot, Jordan, Taylor, Brittany, Wesley, Rumor, Scout, Cassidy, Zo (Zoë), Clo (Chloë), Max, Hunter, Kendall, Caitlin, Noah, Sasha, Morgan, Kyra, Ian, Lauren, Q-bert, and Phil. *The Simpsons Archive*, February 6, 2004, http://www.snpp.com/guides/castlist.html.

57. James Sterngold, "As Writers and Producers, Young Alumni Find They Can Make a Lot of Money Fast," *New York Times*, August 26, 1997, C11.

58. John Ortved, *"The Simpsons": An Uncensored, Unauthorized History* (New York: Faber, 2009), 146. For more, see chapter 10, 145–57.

59. Ibid., 146.

60. Ibid.

61. Kendall, *Framing Class*, 3–4.

62. Michelle Tokarczyk, "Promises to Keep: Working Class Students and Higher Education," in Michael Zweig, ed., *What's Class Got to Do with It? American Society in the Twenty-First Century* (Ithaca, NY: Cornell University Press, 2004), 166.

63. See biographies of Price on both Wikipedia, at http://en.wikipedia.org/wiki/Michael_Price_(writer), and WikiSimpsons, at http://simpsonswiki.net/wiki/Michael_Price.

64. Curiously, the word *hillbilly* has appeared with greater frequency on *The Simpsons* in recent years. In *Hillbilly: A Cultural History of an American Icon* (New York: Oxford University Press, 2004), Anthony Harkins argues that the term *hillbilly* doesn't have the same negative connotations as *white trash*. Although *hillbilly*—much like *cracker*, *redneck*, or *white trash*—designates poor rural whites, for Harkin the term has a more

positive dimension because if its connections to "pioneer self-sufficiency, mountain-
eer survival skills, and Anglo-Saxon ancestry." Harkins, *Hillbilly*, 6. While this is
likely true for scholars, who can parse the nuances of words and understand them
in historical contexts, I suspect that the word is received quite differently by the general public. Each of these terms—though "semantically malleable," as Harkins puts
it—are still understood as pejoratives.

65. Joyce E. King, "Dysconscious Racism: Ideology, Identity, and the Miseducation of
Teachers," *Journal of Negro Education* 60, no. 1 (1991): 135.

66. Steven Horwitz and Stewart Dompe, "From Rabbit Ears to Flat Screen: It's Getting
Better All the Time!" *Social Science Research Network*, December 5, 2010, 1, http://
papers.ssrn.com/sol3/papers.cfm?abstract_id=1720060. According to a headnote
on the file, this is a working draft, prepared for a book entitled *Homer Economicus:
The Simpsons and Economics*, edited by Joshua Hall and forthcoming from Springer.
I have been unable to locate more information about this text. However, Hall has
published on the same topic in two other venues. See Joshua C. Hall, "Homer
Economicus: Using *The Simpsons* to Teach Economics," *Journal of Private Enterprise*
20, no. 2 (2005): 165–76; and Mark T. Gillis and Joshua Hall, "Using *The Simpsons* to
Improve Economic Instruction through Policy Analysis," *American Economist* 54,
no. 1 (2010): 84–92.

67. Horwitz and Dompe, "From Rabbit Ears to Flat Screen," 2. One means of arguing
that the standard of living of the average American family has increased in the last
several decades is to point to data collected by the US Census Bureau in its Extended
Measures of Well-Being survey. This notes, among other things, that more than 98
percent of households have a stove, a refrigerator, and a color TV. Conservatives often
try to deny poverty and the class struggle by pointing to such possessions. What is
often left out of this is the fact that in many cases appliances such as stoves and refrig-
erators are supplied in apartment units, in which roughly 30 percent of the population lives. Unless the cost of those items is somehow factored into the rent being paid,
their existence alone tells us nothing about the financial well-being of the family.

68. Ibid., 3. It should be pointed out that the flat-screen TV that the Simpsons own first
appeared in the title sequence of "Take My Life, Please" (aired February 15, 2009) as
a nod to the fact that the show was being broadcast in high definition. Two episodes
later, in "No Loan Again, Naturally," we see a very clear shot of the television, and it
is the same one we are familiar with: a large box shape, with round control knobs, a
VCR on top, and rabbit ears. In the final episode from that same season, "Coming to
Homerica," we see the family gathered before the television, and again the thickness
of the set and the rabbit ears are visible. In "The Great Wife Hope," from season 21,
the television is different. The screen is clearly in a letterbox format (16:9 ratio) for
widescreen entertainment. Curiously, however, there is a device perched on top of the
set that looks suspiciously like a VCR (although it could also be a DVR), and on top of
that are still the rabbit ear antennae!

69. Note that this episode appeared well in advance of the recent exposés of labor practices in China, particularly of the suicides at the Foxconn factory in Shenzhen city.
For more, see David Barboza, "Deaths Shake a Titan in China," *New York Times*, May
27, 2010, B1. Not surprisingly, very little of the "dark side" of Apple is discussed in
Walter Isaacson's recent biography *Steve Jobs* (New York: Simon and Schuster, 2011),
which largely glorifies Jobs and his company. See Eric Alterman, "Steve Jobs—an
America 'Disgrace,'" *Nation*, November 28, 2011, 9, and Malcolm Gladwell, "The
Tweaker," *New Yorker*, November 14, 2011, 32–35.

70. Lisa R. Pruitt, "The Geography of the Class Culture War," *Seattle University Law
Review* 34 (2011): 769.

6   "Gabbin' about God": Religiosity and Secularity on *The Simpsons*

1. Robert Wuthnow, *After Heaven: Spirituality in America since the 1950s* (Berkeley: University of California Press, 1998), 10.
2. On these topics, see Susan Jacoby, *Freethinkers: A History of American Secularism* (New York: Metropolitan, 2004); Barbara Forrest and Paul Gross, *Creationism's Trojan Horse: The Wedge of Intelligent Design* (New York: Oxford University Press, 2004); Eugenia Scott, *Evolution vs. Creationism: An Introduction* (Berkeley: University of California Press, 2005); Sam Harris, *The End of Faith: Religion, Terror and the Future of Reason* (New York: Norton, 2005); Karen Armstrong, *The Great Transformation: The Beginning of Our Religious Traditions* (New York: Knopf, 2006); Daniel C. Dennett, *Breaking the Spell: Religion as a Natural Phenomenon* (New York: Viking, 2006); Richard Dawkins, *The God Delusion* (New York: Houghton, 2006); David L. Holmes, *The Faiths of the Founding Fathers* (New York: Oxford, 2006); Kevin Phillips, *American Theocracy: The Peril and Politics of Radical Religion, Oil, and Borrowed Money in the 21st Century* (New York: Viking, 2006); Jon Meacham, *American Gospel: God, the Founding Fathers, and the Making of a Nation* (New York: Random House, 2006); Damon Linker, *The Theocons: Secular America Under Siege* (New York: Doubleday, 2006); John Danforth, *Faith and Politics: How the "Moral Values" Debate Divides America and How to Move Forward Together* (New York: Viking, 2006); Noah Feldman, *Divided by God: America's Church-State Problem— and What We Should Do about It* (New York: Farrar, Straus, and Giroux, 2006); Christopher Hitchens, *God Is Not Great: How Religion Poisons Everything* (New York: Twelve, 2007); Dan Gilgoff, *The Jesus Machine: How James Dobson, Focus on the Family, and Evangelical America are Winning the Culture War* (New York: St. Martin's, 2007); Mark Lilla, *The Stillborn God: Religion, Politics, and the Modern West* (New York: Knopf, 2007); Peter Irons, *God on Trial: Dispatches from America's Religious Battlegrounds* (New York: Viking, 2007); Steven Waldman, *Founding Faith: Providence, Politics, and the Birth of Religious Freedom in America* (New York: Random House, 2008); Martha Nussbaum, *Liberty of Conscience: In Defense of America's Tradition of Religious Equality* (New York: Basic, 2008); and E. J. Dionne Jr., *Souled Out: Reclaiming Faith and Politics after the Religious Right* (Princeton, NJ: Princeton University Press, 2008).
3. On radio, see Tona J. Hangen, *Redeeming the Dial: Radio, Religion, and Popular Culture in America* (Chapel Hill: University of North Carolina Press, 2002); and Heather Hendershot, "God's Angriest Man: Carl McIntire, Cold War Fundamentalism, and Right-Wing Broadcasting," *American Quarterly* 59, no. 2 (June 2007): 373–96. On television, see Steve Bruce, *Pray TV: Televangelism in America* (New York: Routledge, 1990); Joel Carpenter, *Revive Us Again: The Reawakening of American Fundamentalism* (New York: Oxford University Press, 1997); and Christian Smith, *American Evangelicalism: Embattled and Thriving* (Chicago: University of Chicago Press, 1998). On Christian media, see Linda Kintz and Julia Lesage, eds., *Media, Culture, and the Religious Right* (Minneapolis: University of Minnesota Press, 1998). On news, see Peter A. Kerr, "The Framing of Fundamentalist Christians: Network Television News, 1980–2000," *Journal of Media and Religion* 2, no. 4 (2003): 203–35; and Diane Winston, "Back to the Future: Religion, Politics, and the Media," *American Quarterly* 59, no. 3 (September 2007): 969–89. On the lifestyle industry, see Heather Hendershot, *Shaking the World for Jesus: Media and Conservative Evangelical Culture* (Chicago: University of Chicago Press, 2004).
4. The condemnatory approach can be seen in works such as Martha Smith Tatarnic's "The Mass Media and Faith: The Potentialities and Problems for the Church in

Our Television Culture," *Anglican Theological Review* 87, no. 3 (2005): 447–65. For examples of the redemptive approach, see the essays collected in Peter Horsfield, Mary E. Hess, and Adam M. Medrano, eds., *Belief in Media: Cultural Perspectives on Media and Christianity* (Burlington, VT: Ashgate, 2004). Also see Gordon Lynch, *Understanding Theology and Popular Culture* (Malden, MA: Blackwell, 2005), and Quentin J. Schultze, *Christianity and the Mass Media in America: Toward a Democratic Accommodation* (Lansing: Michigan State University Press, 2006).

5. See Stephen Prothero, *American Jesus: How the Son of God Became a National Icon* (New York: Farrar, Straus and Giroux, 2003); David Paul Nord, *Faith in Reading: Religious Publishing and the Birth of Mass Media in America* (New York: Oxford University Press, 2004); David Chidester, *Authentic Fakes: Religion and American Popular Culture* (Berkeley: University of California Press, 2005); Glenn W. Shuck, *Marks of the Beast: The Left Behind Novels and the Struggle for Evangelical Identity* (New York: New York University Press, 2005); and Stewart M. Hoover, *Religion in the Media Age* (New York: Routledge, 2006). For anthologies, see Eric Michael Mazur and Kate McCarthy, eds., *God in the Details: American Religion in Popular Culture* (New York: Routledge, 2001); Bruce David Forbes and Jeffrey H. Mahan, eds., *Religion and Popular Culture in America* (Berkeley: University of California Press, 2005); and Birgit Meyer and Annelies Moors, eds., *Religion, Media, and the Public Sphere* (Bloomington: Indiana University Press, 2005).

6. Forbes and Mahan, *Religion and Popular Culture*, 10.

7. For a brief examination of *The Simpsons* as a religion—and the general worship of popular culture in America—see the section entitled "The First Church of *The Simpsons*" in Chris Turner, *Planet Simpson: How a Cartoon Masterpiece Defined a Generation* (Cambridge, MA: Da Capo, 2004), 269–78.

8. See Victoria A. Rebeck, "Recognizing Ourselves in *The Simpsons*," *Christian Century*, June 27, 1990, 622; John Dart, "Simpsons Have Soul," *Christian Century*, January 31, 2001, 12–14; Lisa Frank, "The Evolution of the Seven Deadly Sins: From God to *The Simpsons*," *Journal of Popular Culture* 35, no. 1 (Summer 2001): 95–106; and Todd V. Lewis, "Religious Rhetoric and the Comic Frame in *The Simpsons*," *Journal of Media and Religion* 1, no. 3 (2002): 153–65. For collections, see William Irwin, Mark T. Conrad, and Aeon J. Skoble, eds., *"The Simpsons" and Philosophy: The D'oh of Homer* (Chicago: Open Court Press, 2000); John Alberti, ed., *Leaving Springfield: "The Simpsons" and the Possibilities of Oppositional Television* (Detroit: Wayne State University Press, 2004); and Timothy M. Dale and Joseph J. Foy, eds., *Homer Simpson Marches on Washington: Dissent through American Popular Culture* (Lexington: University Press of Kentucky, 2010). *The Simpsons Archive* is available at http://www.snpp.com/.

9. Jamey Heit, *The Springfield Reformation: "The Simpsons," Christianity, and American Culture* (New York: Continuum, 2008), 21.

10. The complexities of religious and spiritual beliefs, even within a specifically Judeo-Christian context, have led to a great deal of debate over the terminology. Therefore, I provide here some brief definitions of the key terms to be used in this chapter. For my purposes, *religion* refers to any theistic belief system that is organized and insti-tutionalized by apparatus such as places of worship, holy texts, and specific rituals and traditions. The terms *religion* and *religious* will be used throughout primarily to describe Judaism and Christianity. Following scholars such as Robert Wuthnow, Eric Leigh Schmidt, and Gregory C. Stanczak, I use the terms *spirit*, *spiritual*, and *spiritu-ality* to designate beliefs that are more personalized and individualized, not codified by texts or rituals and not associated with any particular theistic system. *Spirituality* will thus be treated here as a secular phenomenon, as part of the philosophical

tradition and humanist perspective that I believe underlie *The Simpsons*. The terms *evangelical* and *fundamentalist* will be used in accord with the definitions provided by scholars such as George Marsden, Joel Carpenter, and D. Michael Lindsay, who see *evangelical* as a broad term, designating faith groups that arose from a "conversionist" Protestantism in the nineteenth century, and *fundamentalist* as a narrower term, designating smaller subsets of intensely devout religious groups, who are often adamantly opposed to secular institutions and behaviors.

11. This view aligns with the position currently promoted by the American Humanist Association and the Council for Secular Humanism, among others. For an excellent and concise overview of the history of humanism, see Tony Davies, *Humanism* (New York: Routledge, 1997). For more on the humanist project, see Paul Kurtz, *Humanist Manifesto 2000* (Amherst, NY: Prometheus, 2000).

12. Dart, "Simpsons Have Soul," 14.

13. James D. Hunter, "The Culture War and the Sacred/Secular Divide: The Problem of Pluralism and Weak Hegemony," *Social Research* 76, no. 4 (2009): 1307.

14. Luis Lugo et al., "2008 U.S. Religious Landscape Survey," Pew Forum on Religion and Public Life, February 2008, http://religions.pewforum.org/. Protestantism is not homogeneous; it is divided into three fairly distinct religious traditions—evangelical Protestant (26.3 percent), mainline Protestant (18.1 percent), and historically black Protestant (6.9 percent)—which are marked by significant internal diversity and fragmentation, resulting in literally hundreds of different Protestant denominations. See the "Affiliations" section on the Pew Forum website at http://religions.pewforum.org/affiliations.

15. Ibid.

16. Thomas Skill et al., "The Portrayal of Religion and Spirituality on Fictional Network Television." *Review of Religious Research* 35 (March 1994): 265. This study, published in the *Review of Religious Research* in 1994, was commissioned by the American Family Association in 1990. It was based on a five-week analysis of religious behaviors on prime-time shows and the examination of more than 1,400 characters on 100 different programs, and it showed that less than 6 percent of characters had an identifiable religious affiliation.

17. Scott H. Clarke, "Created in Whose Image? Religious Characters on Network Television," *Journal of Media and Religion* 4, no. 3 (2005): 137. This study focused only on the three top-rated comedies and dramas presented by seven networks during one week in 2002. Based on an analysis of 549 speaking characters on 42 different programs, Clarke concluded that only 32 characters in the sample (5.8 percent) could be identified as religious, which replicated the findings in Skill's study from the early 1990s. Only 25 characters could be associated with a specific religion, and of these, just 15 were Christian—and exclusively Protestant.

18. New communications technologies were fundamental to the growth of evangelicalism in the United States. By 1925, one in ten of the 600-plus radio stations in America was owned and operated by a church or other religious organization. Licensing regulations imposed in 1934 resulted in many of these stations being sold, but many fundamentalist preachers continued to have successful radio ministries. Notable among these are the Roman Catholic priest Charles Coughlin's broadcasts, begun in 1926; Charles E. Fuller's *Old Fashioned Revival Hour*, begun in 1937; and Archbishop Fulton J. Sheen's *The Catholic Hour*, which ran from 1930 to 1952, reaching approximately four million listeners at its peak. Radio was effectively used in the post–World War II era by the Reverend Billy Graham, whose weekly *Hour of Decision* radio program, started in 1950, is still heard today and is now broadcast around the world. Sheen and Graham also made use of television as a vehicle for spreading the gospel:

for Sheen, through his *Life Is Worth Living* program (1951–57), and for Graham, via ongoing televisual "crusades" starting in 1957. Televangelism as we know it today is essentially the product of Pat Robertson's Christian Broadcasting Network, started in 1961, and its flagship program, *The 700 Club*, started in 1966. For more, see William Martin, *With God on Our Side: The Rise of the Religious Right in America* (New York: Broadway, 1996), 18–31, and Tona J. Hangen, "Evangelists/Evangelical Radio: Conservative Protestant Religious Stations and Programs," in *Museum of Broadcast Communications Encyclopedia of Radio*, vol. 1, ed. Christopher H. Sterling (New York: Routledge, 2004), 555–58.

19. George M. Marsden, *Fundamentalism and American Culture*, 2nd ed. (1980; repr., New York: Oxford University Press, 2006), 231.

20. For more detailed histories of the rise of the Religious Right, see Martin, *With God on Our Side*, and Gilgoff, *Jesus Machine*.

21. Marsden, *Fundamentalism*, 245.

22. The full text of the "1992 Republican National Convention Speech" can be found on Buchanan's official website: http://buchanan.org/blog/1992-republican-national-convention-speech-148.

23. Turner, *Planet Simpson*, 26.

24. Dionne, *Souled Out*, 71.

25. Valerie Weilunn Chow, "Homer Erectus: Homer Simpson as Everyman...and Every Woman," in Alberti, *Leaving Springfield*, 122.

26. Mark Pinsky, *The Gospel According to "The Simpsons": The Spiritual Life of the World's Most Animated Family* (Louisville, KY: Westminster John Knox Press, 2001), 84.

27. Ibid., 94. Despite the allusion in the title to Martin Scorsese's *The Last Temptation of Christ* (1988), there are no other religious elements in this episode. The discussions revolve around generic ideas such as love, family, and marriage. Homer's conscience notably appears to him in the highly secularized form of Colonel Klink, from the television show *Hogan's Heroes*.

28. Heit, *Springfield Reformation*, 57.

29. Ibid., 31.

30. David S. New, *Holy War: The Rise of Militant Christian, Jewish, and Islamic Fundamentalism* (Jefferson, NC: McFarland, 2002), 110.

31. McWASP stands for Middle-Class White-Assimilated Suburban Protestant. See my discussion of this term in chapter 2.

32. Jesus also briefly appears in the episode "Thank God, It's Doomsday," which aired two weeks prior to "The Father, the Son, and the Holy Guest Star." However, the depiction in "Thank God, It's Doomsday" is much less lighthearted and more integral to the satire in the episode. I will discuss this in the following section, as part of the analysis of "Thank God, It's Doomsday."

33. The 2001 American Religious Identification Survey (ARIS) was based on a random telephone survey of 50,281 American households in the continental United States and replicated the pioneering 1990 National Survey of Religious Identification (NSRI), also carried out by the Graduate Center of CUNY, which surveyed 113,723 persons about their religious preferences. Both reports are available on the Graduate Center CUNY website: http://www.gc.cuny.edu/faculty/research_studies.htm. The Pew Forum Religious Landscape Survey was based on extensive interviews with a representative sample of more than 35,000 Americans age 18 and older. The full report can be accessed on the Pew Forum website: http://religions.pewforum.org/.

34. David Owen, "Taking Humor Seriously," *New Yorker*, March 13, 2000, 68.

35. Lisle Dalton, Eric Michael Mazur, and Monica Siems, "Homer the Heretic and Charlie Church: Parody, Piety, and Pluralism in *The Simpsons*," in *God in the Details:*

American Religion in Popular Culture, ed. Eric Michael Mazur and Kate McCarthy (New York: Routledge, 2001), 240.

36. Gordon Lynch, *Understanding Theology and Popular Culture* (Malden, MA: Blackwell, 2005), 153.

37. Ibid.

38. Ibid., 153–54.

39. Pinsky, *Gospel According to "The Simpsons,"* 6.

40. Quoted in ibid., ix.

41. Paula Chin, "In the Eye of the Storm," *People*, October 1, 1990, 82. Also see my more detailed discussion of this incident in the first section of chapter 3.

42. Turner, *Planet Simpson*, 265.

43. Dalton, Mazur, and Siems, "Homer the Heretic," 232.

44. Quayle's criticism was perhaps the opening salvo in the mid-1990s battles over welfare—which, according to those on the political right, was being exploited by "welfare queens"—and the push toward so-called workfare, which was codified in the Personal Responsibility and Work Opportunity Reconciliation Act of 1996. For more on the impact of this legislation, see Barbara Ehrenreich, *Nickel and Dimed: On (Not) Getting By in America* (New York: Metropolitan, 2001).

45. Heit, *Springfield Reformation*, 121.

46. Hendrik Lorenz, "Ancient Theories of Soul," in *Stanford Encyclopedia of Philosophy*, The Metaphysics Research Lab, Stanford University, October 23, 2003, http://plato.stanford.edu/entries/ancient-soul/.

47. Descartes added to the complexities by shifting the focus from "soul" to "mind" and consciousness. An entirely separate body of scholarship has arisen to address the conundrum of whether mind and soul, consciousness and spirit, are one and the same. I do not wish to overcomplicate things here and so will not delve into that philosophical debate. For more on this topic, see Lilli Alanen, *Descartes's Concept of Mind* (Cambridge, MA: Harvard University Press, 2003).

48. For more on Emerson and American transcendentalism, see Leigh Eric Schmidt, *Restless Souls: The Making of American Spirituality* (New York: Harper, 2005). For more on the soul and spirituality, see Robert Wuthnow, *After Heaven: Spirituality in America since the 1950s* (Berkeley: University of California Press, 1998); and Gregory C. Stanczak, *Engaged Spirituality: Social Change and American Religion* (New Brunswick, NJ: Rutgers University Press, 2006).

49. Wuthnow, *After Heaven*, 5.

50. Maude Flanders was killed off as a character because of a contract dispute between Fox and the voice actress Maggie Roswell. Maude dies in a freak accident (essentially caused by Homer) in the episode "Alone Again, Natura-Diddly," which aired on February 13, 2000.

51. The Holy Land Experience was the brainchild of Marvin Rosenthal, a Jew (and the grandson of Orthodox Jews) who converted to Christianity as a teenager and later became an ordained Baptist minister. The project cost an estimated $16 million and was funded by Rosenthal's Zion's Hope, a Christian ministry that specializes in proselytizing to Jews. The park was purchased in 2001 by Trinity Broadcasting Network, the Christian television network cofounded by (and most famously associated with) Jim and Tammy Faye Bakker. For more on the history of the park and controversies surrounding it, see Joan R. Branham, "The Temple That Won't Quit: Constructing Sacred Space in Orlando's Holy Land Experience Theme Park," *Cross Currents* 59, no. 3 (2009): 358–82.

52. Such efforts on the part of the Catholic Church were powerfully satirized in Kevin Smith's film *Dogma*, which appeared in the fall of 1999. In the opening scene of the

film, we see one Cardinal Glick (played by George Carlin) holding a press conference to announce the launch of the new "Catholicism—WOW" campaign, designed to reverse the decline in membership in his parishes. Among other things, Glick introduces a breakfast cereal (the wafer-like Hosties) and a new icon, the "Buddy-Christ," depicted as a winking, smiling Jesus giving a thumbs-up sign.

53. Howard Rosenberg, "Fox Favoritism? Catholic Jokes Toned Down on *Simpsons*," *Chicago Sun-Times*, June 7, 1999, 41.
54. Ibid.
55. Turner, *Planet Simpson*, 266.
56. An overview and specific yearly reports are available on the Feminist Majority Foundation website, online at http://www.feminist.org/rrights/clinicsurvey.html.
57. The full disclaimer reads, "Because Darwin's theory is a theory, it continues to be tested as new evidence is discovered. The theory is not a fact. Gaps in the theory exist for which there is no evidence. A theory is defined as a well-tested explanation that unifies a broad range of observations. Intelligent Design is an explanation of the origin of life that differs from Darwin's view. The reference book *Of Pandas and People* is available for students who might be interested in gaining an understanding of what Intelligent Design actually involves." Brenda Lee, "*Kitzmiller v. Dover Area School District*: Teaching Intelligent Design in Public Schools," *Harvard Civil Rights–Civil Liberties Law Review* 41 (2006): 581. For more details, see Lauri Lebo, *The Devil in Dover: An Insider's Story of Dogma v. Darwin in Small-town America* (New York: New Press, 2008).
58. Martin, *With God on Our Side*, 16.
59. Ted Gournelos, *Popular Culture and the Future of Politics: Cultural Studies and the Tao of South Park* (Lanham, MD: Lexington, 2009), 90.
60. Ibid.
61. Turner, *Planet Simpson*, 265.
62. James Rachels, *The Elements of Moral Philosophy*, 4th. ed. (New York: McGraw-Hill, 2002), 49.
63. Gerald Erion and Joseph Zeccardi, "Marge's Moral Motivation," in Irwin et al., *"The Simpsons" and Philosophy*, 46.
64. Quoted in Sharon Waxman, "*Simpsons* Animates Gay Nuptials, and a Debate," *New York Times*, February 21, 2005, B2.
65. Pinsky, *Gospel According to "The Simpsons*," 194.
66. Heit, *Springfield Reformation*, 151.
67. Pinsky, *Gospel According to "The Simpsons*," 143.
68. Quoted in ibid., 7.
69. Kevin Phillips, *American Theocracy: The Peril and Politics of Radical Religion, Oil, and Borrowed Money in the 21st Century* (New York: Viking, 2006), 100.
70. Ibid., 103.
71. Todd Gitlin, "The Renaissance of Anti-Intellectualism," *Chronicle of Higher Education*, December 8, 2000, B7.
72. Critiques of anti-intellectualism have come from the other side of the political spectrum as well, in studies such as Russell Jacoby's *The Last Intellectuals* (New York: Basic, 1987) and Alan Bloom's *The Closing of the American Mind* (New York: Simon and Schuster, 1987), both largely concerned with the status of higher education, and in Neil Postman's mildly technophobic *Amusing Ourselves to Death* (New York: Viking, 1986). Anti-intellectualism is not addressed outright in Robert Putnam's *Bowling Alone: The Collapse and Revival of American Community* (New York: Simon & Schuster, 2001), but one can infer from Putnam's prevailing thesis—i.e., in virtually every aspect of daily life, Americans have withdrawn from the public sphere

over the past half-century—that the work involved in intellectualizing has been increasingly abandoned and an antipathy toward intellectuals has steadily grown since the 1960s.

Conclusion: American Culture, Satire, and *The Simpsons*

1. From the episode "Mr. Lisa Goes to Washington," #8F01, aired September 26, 1991.
2. James D. Hunter, "The Culture War and the Sacred/Secular Divide: The Problem of Pluralism and Weak Hegemony," *Social Research* 76, no. 4 (2009): 1308.
3. Ibid., 1311.
4. Jonathan Gray, Jeffrey P. Jones, and Ethan Thompson, eds., *Satire TV: Politics and Comedy in the Post-Network Era* (New York: New York University Press, 2009), 25.
5. Paul Simpson, *On the Discourse of Satire: Towards a Stylistic Model of Satirical Humour* (Philadelphia: John Benjamins, 2003), 4.
6. Ann Johnson, Esteban del Rio, and Alicia Kemmitt, "Missing the Joke: A Reception Analysis of Satirical Texts," *Communication, Culture & Critique* 3 (2010): 397.
7. William Savage, "'So Television's Responsible!': Oppositionality and the Interpretive Logic of Satire and Censorship in *The Simpsons* and *South Park*," in *Leaving Springfield: "The Simpsons" and the Possibilities of Oppositional Television*, ed. John Alberti (Detroit: Wayne State University Press, 2004), 200.
8. *Dogma*, directed by Kevin Smith (View Askew Productions, 1999).
9. For more on Lee's film, see Ray Black, "Satire's Cruelest Cut: Exorcising Blackness in Spike Lee's *Bamboozled*," *Black Scholar* 33, no. 1 (2003): 19–24; Jamie Barlowe, "'You Must Never Be a Misrepresented People': Spike Lee's *Bamboozled*," *Canadian Review of American Studies* 33, no. 1 (2003): 1–16; Michael H. Epp, "Raising Minstrelsy: Humour, Satire, and the Stereotype in *The Birth of a Nation* and *Bamboozled*," *Canadian Review of American Studies* 33, no. 1 (2003): 17–36; and Phil Chidester et al., "'Black is Blak': *Bamboozled* and the Crisis of a Postmodern Racial Identity," *Journal of Communications* 17, no. 4 (2006): 287–306.
10. Rachel Sklar, "David Remnick on That New Yorker Cover," *Huffington Post Online*, July 13, 2008, http://www.huffingtonpost.com/2008/07/13/david-remnick-on-emnew-yo_n_112456.html.
11. Ibid.
12. Joe Gandelman, "Furor Swirls around Liberal *New Yorker*'s Caricature of Obama," *Moderate Voice*, July 22, 2008, http://themoderatevoice.com/21052/furor-swirls-around-liberal-new-yorkers-caricature-obama-cover/.
13. Rachel Weiner, "Obama's Larry King Interview," *Huffington Post Online*, July 15, 2008, http://www.huffingtonpost.com/2008/07/15/obamas-larry-king-intervi_n_112930.html.
14. See Phillip Kennicott, "It's Funny How Humor Is So Ticklish," *Washington Post*, July 15, 2008, C01; Tim Rutten, "If You Can't Take a Joke . . .," *Los Angeles Times*, July 16, 2008, A19; Scot Lehigh, "What's So Shocking about Satire?" *Boston Globe*, July 16, 2008, A15; and Lee Siegel, "We're Not Laughing at You, or With You," *New York Times*, July 20, 2008, late ed., WK5.
15. *The Daily Show* offered two separate segments dealing with the *New Yorker* cover controversy and satire in the episode that aired on July 15, 2008. Both segments can be viewed on the Comedy Central website at http://www.thedailyshow.com/watch/tue-july-15–2008/obama-cartoon.
16. Josh Ozersky, *Archie Bunker's America: TV in an Era of Change, 1968–1978* (Carbondale: Southern Illinois University Press, 2003), 70.

17. Ibid. Also see Neil Vidmar and Milton Rokeach, "Archie Bunker's Bigotry: A Study in Selective Perception and Exposure," *Journal of Communication* (Winter 1974): 36–47. The authors concluded that "many persons did not see the program as a satire on bigotry," that "these persons were more likely to be viewers who scored high on measures of prejudice," and that "high prejudiced persons were more likely to identify with Archie Bunker and to see him winning in the end." Quoted in Ozersky, *Archie Bunker's America*, 168.

18. For more on the Islamic community center in New York, see Mark Jacobson, "Muhammad Comes to Manhattan," *New York* 43, no. 27 (2010): 24–32. For more on the Dearborn Four, see Cathy Young, "Fear of a Muslim America," *Reason* 43, no. 4 (2011): 20–26.

19. All of the 2012 presidential candidates in the Republican field have worked to instill fear of Muslims and Islam generally, claiming that there is a concerted effort to impose Sharia law in the United States. In a November 2010 speech, Representative Michele Bachmann told the conservative Family Research Council that Sharia "must be resisted across the United States." In a June 2011 debate, Mitt Romney said, "We're not going to have Shariah law applied in U.S. courts. That's never going to happen." Herman Cain declared in March 2011 that he would not appoint a Muslim to a cabinet position or judgeship because "there is this creeping attempt to gradually ease sharia law and the Muslim faith into our government. It does not belong in our government." And Rick Santorum refers to Sharia as "an existential threat" to the United States. See Amy Sullivan, "Sharia Myth Sweeps America," *USA Today*, June 13, 2011, 11A.

20. Newt Gingrich, "America at Risk: Camus, National Security, and Afghanistan," Keynote Address, American Enterprise Institute conference, July 29, 2010, *American Enterprise Institute*, http://www.aei.org/events/2010/07/29/america-at-risk-camus-national-security-and-afghanistan-event/. For more on the speech, see Lisa Miller, "The Misinformants: What 'Stealth Jihad' Doesn't Mean," *Newsweek*, September 6, 2010, 16; and Scott Shane, "In Islamic Law, Gingrich Sees a Mortal Threat to U.S.," *New York Times*, December 22, 2011, A22. Gingrich and his wife, Callista, also produced and narrated a 2010 film on the threat from radical Islam that discusses the danger of both terrorism and Sharia law. See *America at Risk: The War with No Name*, directed by Kevin Knoblock (Citizens United Productions, 2010).

21. See Samuel G. Freedman, "Waging a One-Man War on American Muslims," *New York Times*, December 16, 2011, A19; and John Esposito, "The Madness over *All-American Muslim*," On Religion, *Washington Post*, December 16, 2011,http://www.washington-post.com/blogs/on-faith/post/the-madness-over-all-american-muslim/2011/12/16/gIQAquwtyO_blog.html.

22. Stuart Elliott and Brian Stelter, "Controversy Drives Advertisers from 'All-American Muslim'—Or Does It?" Media Decoder, *New York Times*, December 11, 2011, http://mediadecoder.blogs.nytimes.com/2011/12/13/.

23. Young, "Fear of a Muslim America," 20. Young further notes that 2010 witnessed an explosion of bills to ban the use of Islamic religious law in state courts, largely as a consequence of the successes of Republican and Tea Party politicians in the midterm elections. For example, in November 2010, a ballot initiative was put forth in Oklahoma to amend the state constitution to prohibit courts from considering "international law or Shariah law" in decisions. State Question 755, as it was known, passed with 70 percent of the vote during the Republican landslide that month.

24. Bill Gallagher, "*Simpsons* Episode References Dearborn," WJBK Fox 2 Detroit, myFOXdetroit.com, December 12, 2011, http://www.myfoxdetroit.com/dpp/news/local/simpsons-episode-references-dearborn-20111212-ms. The remainder of the quotes in this paragraph are taken from this source.

25. Gray et al., *Satire TV*, 15.

Bibliography

Aaron, Michele, ed. *New Queer Cinema: A Critical Reader*. New Brunswick, NJ: Rutgers University Press, 2004.

Abramowitz, Alan I., and Kyle L. Saunders. "Is Polarization a Myth?" *Journal of Politics* 70, no. 2 (2008): 542–55.

Abramson, Jill. "A New *Tanner* Joins the Race." *New York Times*, September 26, 2004, late ed., sec. 2, p. 26.

Adler, David Gray. "George Bush and the Abuse of History: The Constitution and Presidential Power in Foreign Affairs." *UCLA Journal of International Law & Foreign Affairs* 12, no. 1 (2007): 75–144.

Adorno, Theodor, and Max Horkheimer. "The Culture Industry: Enlightenment as Mass Deception." In *Media and Cultural Studies: Key Works*, edited by Meenakshi Gigi Durham and Douglas Kellner, 71–101. Malden, MA: Blackwell, 1999.

Alanen, Lilli. *Descartes's Concept of Mind*. Cambridge, MA: Harvard University Press, 2003.

Alba, Richard. *Blurring the Color Line: The New Chance for a More Integrated America*. Cambridge, MA: Harvard University Press, 2009.

Alba, Richard, and Victor Nee. *Remaking the American Mainstream: Assimilation and Contemporary Immigration*. Cambridge, MA: Harvard University Press, 2003.

Alberti, John, ed. *Leaving Springfield: "The Simpsons" and the Possibilities of Oppositional Television*. Detroit: Wayne State University Press, 2004.

———. "'War Is Not the Answer . . . Except for All of America's Problems': *The Simpsons* and the War on Terror." Unpublished manuscript, paper presented at the Cultural Studies Association conference, Tucson, AZ, April 2005.

Allen, Robert C., ed. *Channels of Discourse, Reassembled: Television and Contemporary Criticism*. Chapel Hill: University of North Carolina Press, 1992.

Allen, Theodore. *The Invention of the White Race*. New York: Verso, 1994.

Almond, Gabriel A., R. Scott Appleby, and Emmanuel Sivan. *Strong Religion: The Rise of Fundamentalisms around the World*. Chicago: University of Chicago Press, 2003.

Alterman, Eric. "The Right's Kristol Ball." *Nation*, December 23, 1996, 11–16.

———. "Steve Jobs—an America 'Disgrace.'" *Nation*, November 28, 2011, 9.

Alters, Diane. "'We Hardly Watch That Rude, Crude Show': Class and Taste in *The Simpsons*." In Stabile and Harrison, *Prime Time Animation*, 165–84.

Alvarez, Michael R., and Tara L. Butterfield. "The Resurgence of Nativism in California? The Case of Proposition 187 and Illegal Immigration." *Social Science Quarterly* 81, no. 1 (2000): 167–79.

Alwood, Edward. *Straight News: Gays, Lesbians and the News Media*. New York: Columbia University Press, 1996.

Amarasingam, Amarnath, ed. *The Stewart/Colbert Effect: Essays on the Real Impacts of Fake News*. Jefferson, NC: McFarland, 2011.

Amin, Ash, and N. J. Thrift, eds. *Cultural Economy Reader*. Oxford: Blackwell, 2003.

Appel, Alfred. *The Annotated Lolita*. New York: Vintage, 1991.

Armstrong, Karen. *The Great Transformation: The Beginning of Our Religious Traditions*. New York: Knopf, 2006.

Arnold, David L. G. "'And the Rest Writes Itself': Roland Barthes Watches *The Simpsons*." In Irwin et al., *"The Simpsons" and Philosophy*, 252–68.

———. "'Use a Pen, Sideshow Bob': *The Simpsons* and the Threat of High Culture." In Alberti, *Leaving Springfield*, 26–66.

Aronowitz, Stanley. *How Class Works: Power and Social Movement*. New Haven, CT: Yale University Press, 2003.

Arthurs, Jane. "*Sex and the City* and Consumer Culture: Remediating Postfeminist Drama." In Brunsdon et al., *Feminist Television Criticism*, 41–56.

Auster, Albert. "'Funny, You Don't Look Jewish' . . . The Image of Jews on Contemporary American Television." *Television Quarterly* 26, no. 3 (1993): 65–74.

Back, Les. "Aryans Reading Adorno: Cyber-culture and Twenty-first Century Racism." *Ethnic and Racial Studies* 25, no. 4 (2002): 628–52.

Bageant, Joe. *Deer Hunting with Jesus: Dispatches from America's Class War*. New York: Crown, 2007.

Bai, Matt. "Working for the Working-Class Vote." *New York Times Magazine*, October 15, 2008. http://www.nytimes.com/2008/10/19/magazine/19obama-t .html?pagewanted=all.

Baltzell, E. Digby. *The Protestant Establishment: Aristocracy & Caste in America*. New York: Vintage, 1964.

Barboza, David. "Deaths Shake a Titan in China." *New York Times*, May 27, 2010, B1.

Barlowe, Jamie. "'You Must Never Be a Misrepresented People': Spike Lee's *Bamboozled*." *Canadian Review of American Studies* 33, no. 1 (2003): 1–16.

Baron, Denis. *The English-Only Question: An Official Language for Americans?* New Haven, CT: Yale University Press, 1992.

Barone, Michael. *The New Americans: How the Melting Pot Can Work Again*. Washington, DC: Regnery, 2001.

Bartels, Larry M. *Unequal Democracy: The Political Economy of the New Gilded Age*. Princeton, NJ: Princeton University Press, 2010.

Barth, James R., Susanne Trimbath, and Glenn Yago, eds. *The Savings and Loan Crisis: Lessons from a Regulatory Failure*. New York: Springer, 2004.

Baxter, Judith. "Constructions of Active Womanhood and New Femininities: From a Feminist Linguistic Perspective, Is *Sex and the City* a Modernist or a Post-Modernist TV Text?" *Women & Language* 32, no. 1 (2009): 91–98.

Baym, Geoffrey. "*The Daily Show*: Discursive Integration and the Reinvention of Political Journalism," *Political Communication* 22, no. 3 (2005): 259–76.

———. *From Cronkite to Colbert: The Evolution of Broadcast News*. Boulder, CO: Paradigm, 2010.

Bartlett, Bruce. *The New American Economy: The Failure of Reaganomics and a New Way Forward*. New York: Palgrave Macmillan, 2009.

Baumgartner, Jody C., and Jonathan S. Morris. "One 'Nation' Under Stephan? The Effects of *The Colbert Report* on American Youth." *Journal of Broadcasting & Electronic Media* 52, no. 4 (2008): 622–43.

Beard, Duncan Stuart. "Local Satire with a Global Reach: Ethnic Stereotyping and Cross-Cultural Conflicts in *The Simpsons*." In Alberti, *Leaving Springfield*, 273–91.

Becker, Ron. *Gay TV and Straight America*. New Brunswick, NJ: Rutgers University Press, 2006.

Bellafante, Gina. "It's All About Me!" *Time*, June 29, 1998, 54–62.

Benshoff, Harry M., and Sean Griffin, eds. *Queer Images: A History of Gay and Lesbian Film in America*. Lanham, MD: Rowman & Littlefield, 2006.

Berkman, David. "Sitcom Reality." *Television Quarterly* 26, no. 4 (1993): 63–69.

Berlant, Lauren. "The Theory of Infantile Citizenship." *Public Culture* 5, no. 3 (1993): 395–410.

Bernstein, Matthew, ed. *Michael Moore: Filmmaker, Newsmaker, Cultural Icon*. Ann Arbor: University of Michigan Press, 2010.

Besen, Wayne R. *Anything but Straight: Unmasking the Scandals and Lies Behind the Ex-Gay Myth*. New York: Routledge, 2003.

Bettie, Julie. "Class Dismissed? *Roseanne* and the Changing Face of Working-Class Iconography." *Social Text* 45 (Winter 1995): 125–49.

Bhattacharya, Sanjiv. "Homer's Odyssey." *Sunday Herald Sun* (Melbourne), August 27, 2000, Z12.

Billen, Andrew. "Liberals? Eat My Shorts." *New Statesman*, July 9, 2007, 47.

Black, Ray. "Satire's Cruelest Cut: Exorcising Blackness in Spike Lee's *Bamboozled*." *Black Scholar* 33, no. 1 (2003): 19–24.

Blakeborough, Darren. "'Old People Are Useless': Representations of Aging on *The Simpsons*." *Canadian Journal on Aging* 27, no. 1 (2008): 57–67.

Blitzer, J. Michael. "Political Culture and Public Opinion: The American Dream on Springfield's Evergreen Terrace." In *Homer Simpson Goes to Washington: American Politics through Popular Culture*, edited by Joseph J. Foy, 41–60. Lexington: University Press of Kentucky, 2008.

Block, Alex Ben. *Outfoxed: Marvin Davis, Barry Diller, Rupert Murdoch, Joan Rivers, and the Inside Story of America's Fourth Television Network*. New York: St. Martin's Press, 1990.

Bloom, Alan. *The Closing of the American Mind*. New York: Simon and Schuster, 1987.

Blum, Richard A., and Richard D. Lindheim. *Primetime: Network Television Programming*. Boston: Focal, 1987.

Bodroghkozy, Aniko. *Sixties Television and the Youth Rebellion*. Durham, NC: Duke University Press, 2001.

———. "*The Smothers Brothers Comedy Hour* and the Youth Rebellion." In Spigel and Curtin, *Revolution Wasn't Televised*, 201–20.

Bogel, Fredric V. *The Difference Satire Makes: Rhetoric and Reading from Jonson to Byron*. Ithaca, NY: Cornell University Press, 2001.

Bogle, Donald. *Primetime Blues: African Americans on Network Television*. New York: Farrar, Straus and Giroux, 2001.

Bonilla-Silva, Eduardo. *Racism without Racists: Color-Blind Racism and the Persistence of Racial Inequality in the United States*. 2nd ed. New York: Rowman, 2006.

Bonné, Jon. "*The Simpsons*, Back from the Pit." MSNBC, November 7, 2003. http://today.msnbc.msn.com/id/3404331/ns/today-entertainment/t/simpsons-back-pit/.

———. "*The Simpsons* Has Lost Its Cool." MSNBC, October 2, 2002. http://today.msnbc.msn.com/id/3341530/ns/today-entertainment/t/simpsons-has-lost-its-cool/.

Borchard, Kurt. "*The Simpsons* as Subculture: Multiple Technologies, Group Identity and Authorship." In *The Image of Technology in Literature, the Media, and Society*, edited by Will Wright and Steve Kaplan, 314–32. Pueblo: University of Southern Colorado, 1994.

Bourdieu, Pierre. *Distinction: A Social Critique of the Judgment of Taste*. Translated by Richard Nice. 1979. Reprint, Cambridge, MA: Harvard University Press, 1984.

Boyd, Todd. *Am I Black Enough For You? Popular Culture from the 'Hood and Beyond*. Bloomington: Indiana University Press, 1997.

Boyer, Peter J. "After the Rivers Reversal, Fox is Plugging Ahead." *New York Times,* May 20, 1987, late ed., sec. C 30.

Branham, Joan R. "The Temple That Won't Quit: Constructing Sacred Space in Orlando's Holy Land Experience Theme Park." *Cross Currents* 59, no. 3 (2009): 358–82.

Brasfield, Rebecca. "Rereading *Sex and the City*: Exposing the Hegemonic Feminist Narrative." *Journal of Popular Film & Television* 34, no. 3 (Fall 2006): 130–39.

Bremmer, Jan N. "Soul: Greek and Hellenic Concepts." In *Encyclopedia of Religion,* 2nd ed., vol. 12, edited by Lindsay Jones, 8540–8544. Detroit: Macmillan, 2005.

Brewer, Mark D., and Jeffrey M. Stonecash. *Split: Class and Cultural Divides in American Politics.* Washington, DC: Congressional Quarterly Press, 2006.

Brewer, Paul R., and Emily Marquardt. "Mock News and Democracy: Analyzing *The Daily Show.*" *Atlantic Journal of Communication* 15, no. 4 (2007): 249–67.

Brodkin, Karen. *How the Jews Became White Folks . . . and What That Says about Race in America.* New Brunswick, NJ: Rutgers University Press, 1998.

"Brokeback Mountain." *Box Office Mojo,* March 10, 2008. http://www.boxofficemojo. com/movies/?id=brokebackmountain.htm.

Brook, Vincent. "Myth or Consequences: Ideological Fault Lines in *The Simpsons.*" In Alberti, *Leaving Springfield,* 250–87.

———. *Something Ain't Kosher Here: The Rise of the "Jewish" Sitcom.* New Brunswick, NJ: Rutgers University Press, 2003.

Brooker, Will, and Deborah Jermyn, eds. *The Audience Studies Reader.* New York: Routledge 2002.

Brookey, Alan, and Robert Westerfelhaus. "Pistols and Petticoats, Piety and Purity: *To Wong Foo,* the Queering of American Monomyth and the Marginalizing Discourse of Deification." *Critical Studies in Media Communication* 18, no. 2 (2001): 141–56.

Brookhiser, Richard. *The Way of the WASP: How It Made America, and How It Can Save It, So to Speak.* New York: Free Press, 1991.

Brooks, Tim, and Earle Marsh. *The Complete Directory to Prime Time Network and Cable TV Shows, 1946–Present.* 8th ed. New York: Ballantine, 2003.

Bruce, Steve. *Pray TV: Televangelism in America.* New York: Routledge, 1990.

Bruning, Jonathan. "Negotiating Complex Television: *The Simpsons* and Its Audience." PhD diss., Department of Communication Studies, University of Kansas, 2002. Ann Arbor: University of Michigan, 2002; ProQuest (AAT 3053980).

Brunsdon, Charlotte. "What Is the 'Television' in Television Studies?" In Newcomb, *Television: The Critical View,* 609–28.

Brunsdon, Charlotte, Julie D'Acci, and Lynn Spigel, eds. *Feminist Television Criticism: A Reader.* New York: Oxford University Press, 1997.

Brunsdon, Charlotte, and Lynn Spigel, eds. *Feminist Television Criticism: A Reader.* 2nd ed. 1997. Reprint, New York: McGraw-Hill, 2008.

Buchanan, Patrick. "1992 Republican National Convention Speech." *Patrick J. Buchanan Official Website.* 2011. http://buchanan.org/blog/1992-republican-national-convention -speech-148.

Buncombe, Andrew. "Doh! Murdoch's Fox News in a Spin over *The Simpsons'* Lawsuit." *Independent* (London), October 29, 2003. Lexis-Nexis Academic, November 11, 2003. http://web.lexis-nexis.com/universe.

Burfisher, Mary E., Sherman Robinson, and Karen Thierfelder. "The Impact of NAFTA on the United States." *Journal of Economic Perspectives* 15, no. 1 (2001): 125–44.

"Burger King Nabs *The Simpsons.*" *Advertising Age,* April 30, 1990, 3.

Burstein, Dan, and Arne J. de Keijzer. *Secrets of 24: The Unauthorized Guide to the Political & Moral Issues Behind TV's Most Riveting Drama.* New York: Sterling, 2008.

Bush, Alan J., et al. "The Influence of Consumer Socialization Variables on Attitude Toward Advertising: A Comparison of African-Americans and Caucasians." *Journal of Advertising* 28, no. 3 (1999): 13–25.

Butler, Judith. *Gender Trouble: Feminism and the Subversion of Identity.* 2nd ed. 1990. Reprint, New York: Routledge, 1999.

Butsch, Richard. "Ralph, Fred, Archie, and Homer: Why Television Keeps Recreating the White Male Working-Class Buffoon." In *Gender, Race, and Class in Media*, 2nd ed., edited by Gail Dines and Jean M. Humez, 575–85. Thousand Oaks, CA: Sage, 2003.

Bybee, Carl, and Ashley Overbeck. "Homer Simpson Explains Our Postmodern Identity Crisis, Whether We Like It or Not: Media Literacy After The Simpsons." *Studies in Media and Information Literacy Education* 1, no. 1 (2001): 1–12.

Byrne, Ciar. "*Simpsons* Parody Upset Fox News, Says Groening." *Guardian Unlimited*, October 29, 2003. http://media.guardian.co.uk/broadcast/story/0,7493,1073216,00 .html.

Cagle, Jess. "America Sees Shades of Gay." *Entertainment Weekly*, September 8, 1995, 20–31.

Caldwell, J. T. *Televisuality: Style, Crisis, and Authority in American Television.* New Brunswick, NJ: Rutgers University Press, 1995.

Calev, Ben-David. "Diller's Crossing." *Jerusalem Report*, October 6, 1994, 42+.

Cantor, Paul. "*The Simpsons*: Atomistic Politics and the Nuclear Family." *Political Theory* 27, no. 6 (1999): 734–50.

Capsuto, Steven. *Alternate Channels: The Uncensored Story of Gay and Lesbian Images on Radio and Television, 1930s to the Present.* New York: Ballantine, 2000.

Caputo, Richard K. "Presidents, Profits, Productivity, & Poverty: A Great Divide between the Pre- & Post-Reagan U.S. Economy?" *Journal of Sociology and Social Welfare* 31, no. 3 (2004): 5–30.

Carpenter, Joel. *Revive Us Again: The Reawakening of American Fundamentalism.* New York: Oxford University Press, 1997.

Carr, David. "Is Animation Funnier than Live Action?" *New York Times*, July 6, 2003, AR18+.

———. "White House Listens When Weekly Speaks." *New York Times*, March 11, 2003, E1.

Carr, Steven Allen. "On the Edge of Tastelessness: CBS, the Smothers Brothers and the Struggle for Control." *Cinema Journal* 31, no. 4 (1992): 3–24.

Carson, Tom. "The Gospel According to Homer." *Esquire*, July 1999, 32–35.

Carter, Bill. "Young Viewers Help Fox Turn the Corner on Profits." *New York Times*, July 17, 1989, late ed., sec. D, 9+.

Cassidy, John. "Murdoch's Game." *New Yorker*, October 16, 2006, 68–85.

Castafieda, Laura, and Shannon Campbell. *News and Sexuality: Media Portraits of Diversity.* Thousand Oaks, CA: Sage, 2006.

The Celluloid Closet. DVD. Directed by Rob Epstein and Jeffrey Friedman. Sony Pictures, 2001.

Chapman, Roger, ed. *Culture Wars: An Encyclopedia of Issues, Viewpoints, and Voices.* Armonk, NY: M. E. Sharpe, 2010.

Chasin, Alexandra. *Selling Out: The Gay and Lesbian Movement Goes to Market.* New York: Palgrave Macmillan, 2000.

Chenoweth, Neil. *Rupert Murdoch: The Untold Story of the World's Greatest Media Wizard.* New York: Crown Business, 2001.

Chester, Jeff. "A Present for Murdoch." *Nation*, December 22, 2003, 26–28.

Chidester, David. *Authentic Fakes: Religion and American Popular Culture.* Berkeley: University of California Press, 2005.

Chidester, Phil, et al. "'Black is Blak': *Bamboozled* and the Crisis of a Postmodern Racial Identity." *Journal of Communications* 17, no. 4 (2006): 287–306.

Chin, Ann. "*Simpsons* Writers Discuss Satire on TV at Stanford." *Stanford Daily*, November 10, 2003. http://archive.stanforddaily.com/?p=1013323.

Chin, Paula. "In the Eye of the Storm." *People*, October 1, 1990, 82+.

Chow, Valerie Weilunn. "Homer Erectus: Homer Simpson as Everyman . . . and Every Woman." In Alberti, *Leaving Springfield*, 107–36.

Christopher, Robert C. *Crashing the Gates: The De-WASPing of America's Power Elite*. New York: Simon and Schuster, 1989.

Clarke, John. *New Times and Old Enemies: Essays on Cultural Studies and America*. London: HarperCollins, 1991.

Clarke, Scott H. "Created in Whose Image? Religious Characters on Network Television." *Journal of Media and Religion* 4, no. 3 (2005): 137–53.

Class Dismissed: How TV Frames the Working Class. DVD. Directed by Loretta Alper. Produced by Pepi Leistyna. Northampton, MA: Media Education Foundation, 2006.

Cohen, Jonathan, and Rivka Ribek. "Sex Differences in Pleasure from Television Texts: The Case of Ally McBeal." *Women's Studies in Communication* 26, no. 1 (Spring 2003): 118–34.

Colapinto, John. "Mad Dog." *Rolling Stone*, September 2, 2004, 104–11.

Coleman, Robin R. Means. *African American Viewers and the Black Situation Comedy: Situating Racial Humor*. New York: Garland, 2000.

Colletta, Lisa. "Political Satire and Postmodern Irony in the Age of Stephen Colbert and Jon Stewart." *Journal of Popular Culture* 42, no. 5 (2009): 856–74.

Collins, Scott. *Crazy Like a FOX: The Inside Story of How Fox News Beat CNN*. New York: Portfolio (Penguin), 2004.

Connery, Brian A., and Kirk Combe. *Theorizing Satire: Essays in Literary Criticism*. New York: St. Martin's, 1995.

Considine, John. "The Simpsons: Public Choice in the Tradition of Swift and Orwell." *Journal of Economic Education* (Spring 2006): 217–28.

Cooper, Steve, Damien McLoughlin, and Andrew Keating. "Individual and Neo-tribal Consumption: Tales from the Simpsons of Springfield." *Journal of Consumer Behaviour* 4, no. 5 (2005): 330–44.

Creamer, Matthew. "Marketing's Era of Outrage." *Advertising Age*, February 12, 2007, 1–2.

Crenson, Matthew A., and Benjamin Ginsberg. "Downsizing Democracy, Upsizing the Presidency." *South Atlantic Quarterly* 105, no. 1 (Winter 2006): 207–16.

Croteau, David, William Hoynes, and Stefania Milan. *Media/Society: Industries, Images, and Audiences*. 4th ed. Los Angeles: Sage, 2012.

Crotty, Mark. "Murphy Would Probably Also Win the Election: The Effect of Television as Related to the Portrayal of the Family in Situation Comedies." *Journal of Popular Culture* 29 (Winter 1995): 1–15.

Crust, Kevin. "I Now Pronounce You Stale." Review of *I Now Pronounce You Chuck and Larry*. *Los Angeles Times*, July 20, 2007. http://articles.latimes.com/2007/jul/20/entertainment/et-pronounce20.

D'Acci, Julie. "Cultural Studies, Television Studies, and the Crisis in the Humanities." In *Television After TV: Essays on a Medium in Transition*, edited by Lynn Spigel and Jan Olsson, 418–42. Durham, NC: Duke University Press, 2004.

———. *Defining Women: Television and the Case of Cagney and Lacey*. Chapel Hill: University of North Carolina Press, 1992.

DaCosta, Kimberly McClain. "Interracial Intimacies, Barack Obama, and the Politics of Multiracialism." *Black Scholar* 39, nos. 3/4 (2009): 4–12.

Dale, Timothy M., and Joseph J. Foy, eds. *Homer Simpson Marches on Washington: Dissent through American Popular Culture*. Lexington: University Press of Kentucky, 2010.

Dalton, Lisle, Eric Michael Mazur, and Monica Siems. "Homer the Heretic and Charlie Church: Parody, Piety, and Pluralism in *The Simpsons*." In *God in the Details: American Religion in Popular Culture*, edited by Eric Michael Mazur and Kate McCarthy, 231–47. New York: Routledge, 2001.

Dalton, Mary M., and Laura R. Linder, eds. *The Sitcom Reader: America Viewed and Skewed*. Albany: SUNY Press, 2005.

Danforth, John. *Faith and Politics: How the "Moral Values" Debate Divides America and How to Move Forward Together*. New York: Viking, 2006.

Dargis, Manohla. "Dude (Nyuck-Nyuck), I Love You (as If!)." *New York Times*, July 20, 2007, 17.

Dart, John. "Simpsons Have Soul." *Christian Century*, January 31, 2001, 12–14.

Davé, Shilpa. "Apu's Brown Voice: Cultural Inflection and South Asian Accents." In *East Main Street: Asian American Popular Culture*, edited by Shilpa Davé, LeiLani Nishime, and Tasha G. Oren, 313–36. New York: New York University Press, 2005.

Davies, Tony. *Humanism*. New York: Routledge, 1997.

Davis, Nancy J., and Robert V. Robinson. "Are the Rumors of War Exaggerated? Religious Orthodoxy and Moral Progressivism." *American Journal of Sociology* 102 (1996): 756–87.

Dawkins, Richard. *The God Delusion*. New York: Houghton, 2006.

Day, Amber. *Satire and Dissent: Interventions in Contemporary Political Debate*. Bloomington: Indiana University Press, 2011.

Dean, Jodi, ed. *Cultural Studies and Political Theory*. Ithaca, NY: Cornell University Press, 2000.

de Lauretis, Teresa. "Queer Theory: Lesbian and Gay Sexualities." *differences* 3, no. 2 (1991): iii–xviii.

Delaney, Tim. *Simpsonology: There's a Little Bit of Springfield in All of Us*. Amherst, NY: Prometheus Books, 2008.

Dennett, Daniel C. *Breaking the Spell: Religion as a Natural Phenomenon*. New York: Viking, 2006.

Dennis, Jeffrey P. "'The Same Thing We Do Every Night': Signifying Same-Sex Desire in Television Cartoons." *Journal of Popular Film & Television* 31, no. 3 (2003): 132–40.

DeParle, Jason. *American Dream: Three Women, Ten Kids, and a Nation's Drive to End Welfare*. New York: Viking, 2004.

Dettmar, Kevin J. H. "Countercultural Literacy: Learning Irony with *The Simpsons*." In Alberti, *Leaving Springfield*, 137–68.

Dewey, Donald. *The Art of Ill Will: The Story of American Political Cartoons*. New York: New York University Press, 2007.

Dickinson, Tim. "The Fox News Fear Factory." *Rolling Stone*, June 9, 2011, 54–84.

Dickson-Carr, Darryl. *African American Satire: The Sacredly Profane Novel*. Columbia: University of Missouri Press, 2001.

Diffrient, David Scott. *M*A*S*H*. Detroit: Wayne State University Press, 2008.

"The Dillingham Commission Reports." Stanford University Digital Library Program. http://library.stanford.edu/catdb/e_resources/ebrary/dillingham/body.shtml.

DiMaggio, Paul, John Evans, and Bethany Bryson. "Have Americans' Social Attitudes Become More Polarized?" *American Journal of Sociology* 102 (1996): 690–755.

Dionne, E. J. Jr. *Souled Out: Reclaiming Faith and Politics after the Religious Right*. Princeton, NJ: Princeton University Press, 2008.

———. "Why the Culture War Is the Wrong War." *Atlantic Monthly*, January/February 2006, 130–35.

Dobson, Hugo. "Mister Sparkle Meets the Yakuza: Depictions of Japan in *The Simpsons*." *Journal of Popular Culture* 39, no. 1 (2006): 44–68.

Doherty, Brian. "Matt Groening." Interview. *Mother Jones* 24, no. 2 (March/April 1999): 34–38.

———. "Matt's World of Animated Satire." Interview with Matt Groening. *Ottawa Citizen*, March 27, 1999, D3+.

"Don't Have a Lawsuit, Man." *Age*, October 31, 2003. http://www.theage.com.au/articles /2003/10/31/1067233358134.html.

Doonar, Joanna. "Homer's Brand Odyssey." *Brand Strategy*, February 2004, 20–23.

Doty, Alexander. *Making Things Perfectly Queer: Interpreting Mass Culture*. Minneapolis: University of Minnesota Press, 1993.

Doty, Alexander, and Corey Creekmur, eds. *Out in Culture: Gay, Lesbian, and Queer Essays on Popular Culture*. Durham, NC: Duke University Press, 1995.

Douglas, Susan J. *Enlightened Sexism: The Seductive Message That Feminism's Work Is Done*. New York: Times Books, 2010.

———. *The Mommy Myth: The Idealization of Motherhood and How It Has Undermined All Women*. New York: Free Press, 2004.

———. *Where the Girls Are: Growing Up Female with the Mass Media*. New York: Random House, 1994.

Douglass, William. *Television Families: Is Something Wrong with Suburbia?* Mahwah, NJ: Lawrence Erlbaum, 2003.

Dow, Bonnie J. "Ally McBeal, Lifestyle Feminism, and the Politics of Personal Happiness." *Communication Review* 5, no. 4 (2002): 259–65.

———. "*Ellen*, Television, and the Politics of Gay and Lesbian Visibility." *Critical Studies in Media Communication* 18, no. 2 (2001): 123–40.

———. *Prime-Time Feminism: Television, Media Culture, and the Women's Movement Since 1970*. Philadelphia: University of Pennsylvania Press, 1996.

D'Souza, Dinesh. *The End of Racism: Principles for a Multiracial Society*. New York: Free Press, 1996.

———. *What's So Great about America*. Washington, DC: Regnery, 2002.

Du Bois, W. E. B. *The Souls of Black Folk*. 1903. Modern Library Centennial Edition, with introduction by David Levering Lewis. Reprint, New York: Random House, 2003.

Dyer, Richard. *The Matter of Images: Essays on Representation*. New York: Routledge, 1993.

———. *White*. New York: Routledge, 1997.

Dyson, Michael Eric. *Reflecting Black: African-American Cultural Criticism*. Minneapolis: University of Minnesota Press, 1993.

Egan, Timothy. "Godless" Weblog. *New York Times*, June 11, 2008. http://egan.blogs .nytimes.com/2008/06/11/godless/.

Ehrenreich, Barbara. *Fear of Falling: The Inner Life of the Middle Class*. New York: Harper, 1989.

———. *Nickel and Dimed: On (Not) Getting By in America*. New York: Metropolitan, 2001.

———. "Oh, Those Family Values." *Time*, July 18, 1994, 62.

Ehrenstein, David. "More than Friends." *Los Angeles Magazine* 41, no. 5 (1996): 60+.

Elkins, Richard. *Male Femaling: A Grounded Approach to Cross-Dressing and Sex-Changing*. New York: Routledge, 1997.

Elliott, Stuart, and Brian Stelter. "Controversy Drives Advertisers from 'All-American Muslim'—Or Does It?" Media Decoder, *New York Times*, December 11, 2011. http:// mediadecoder.blogs.nytimes.com/2011/12/13/.

Ellis, John. *Visible Fictions*. London: Routledge, 1982.

Entman, Robert M., and Andrew Rojecki. *The Black Image in the White Mind: Media and Race in America*. Chicago: University of Chicago Press, 2000.

"Episodes by Writer." *The Simpsons Archive*, May 5, 2003. http://www.snpp.com/guides /epsbywriter.html.

Epp, Michael H. "Raising Minstrelsy: Humour, Satire, and the Stereotype in *The Birth of a Nation* and *Bamboozled*." *Canadian Review of American Studies* 33, no. 1 (2003): 17–36.

Epstein, Lawrence J. *The Haunted Smile: The Story of Jewish Comedians in America*. New York: Public Affairs, 2001.

Epstein, Rob, and Jeffrey Friedman, dirs. *The Celluloid Closet*. TriStar Pictures, 1995.

Erion, Gerald, and Joseph Zeccardi. "Marge's Moral Motivation." In Irwin et al., *"The Simpsons" and Philosophy*, 46–58.

Erni, J. N. "Queer Figurations in the Media: Critical Reflections on the Michael Jackson Sex Scandal." *Critical Studies in Media Communication* 15 (1998): 158–80.

Erzen, Tanya. *Straight to Jesus: Sexual and Christian Conversions in the Ex-Gay Movement*. Berkeley: University of California Press, 2006.

Escoffier, Jeffrey. *American Homo: Community and Perversity*. Berkeley: University of California Press, 1998.

Esposito, John. "The Madness over *All-American Muslim*." On Religion, *Washington Post*, December 16, 2011. http://www.washingtonpost.com/blogs/on-faith/post/the -madness-over-all-american-muslim/2011/12/16/gIQAquwtyO_blog.html.

"Exec Shuffle." *Daily Variety*, October 13, 1994, 8.

Fabrikant, Geraldine. "Fox Broadcasting's Successful Gambles." *New York Times*, April 3, 1989, late ed., sec. D, 8+.

Faludi, Susan. *Backlash: The Undeclared War Against American Women*. New York: Crown, 1991.

———. *Stiffed: The Betrayal of the American Man*. New York: William Morrow, 1999.

Farley, Rebecca. "From Fred and Wilma to Ren and Stimpy: What Makes a Cartoon Prime-Time?" In Stabile and Harrison, *Prime Time Animation*, 147–64.

"Favorite Prime-Time Television Programs, 1997–98." In *The World Almanac Reference Database*. FACTS.com, November 30, 2002. http://0-www.2facts.com.library.dcccd .edu/WA/temp/76369tempwart01750.asp.

FeJes, Fred. "Invisibility, Homophobia, and Heterosexism." *Critical Studies in Mass Communications* 10, no. 4 (1993): 396–422.

Feldman, Noah. *Divided by God: America's Church-State Problem—and What We Should Do about It*. New York: Farrar, Straus, and Giroux, 2006.

Feldstein, Stanley, and Lawrence Costello, eds. *The Ordeal of Assimilation: A Documentary History of the White Working Class*. Garden City, NY: Anchor/Doubleday, 1974.

Ferrari, Chiara. "Dubbing *The Simpsons*: Or How Groundskeeper Willie Lost His Kilt in Sardinia." *Journal of Film and Video* 61, no. 2 (2009): 19–37.

"Final Season Ratings." *Electronic Media*, April 23, 1990, 36. Lexis-Nexis Academic, http://web.lexis-nexis.com/universe.

Finnigan, David. "Reggie Awards 2001." *Adweek*, March 13, 2001. Reprinted in *The Simpsons Archive*, http://www.snpp.com/other/articles/reggie2001.html.

Fiorina, Morris P., Samuel J. Abrams, and Jeremy C. Pope. *Culture War? The Myth of a Polarized America*. 3rd ed. New York: Longman, 2008.

Firestone, David. "While Barbie Talks Tough, G.I. Joe Goes Shopping." *New York Times*, December 31, 1993, A12.

Fiske, John. *Television Culture*. New York: Routledge, 1988.

———. *Understanding Popular Culture*. New York: Routledge, 1989.

Fiske, John, and John Hartley. *Reading Television*. London: Methuen, 1978.

Flew, Terry. "*The Simpsons*: Culture, Class and Popular TV." *Metro*, January 3, 1994. eLibrary ProQuest.

Forbes, Bruce David, and Jeffrey H. Mahan, eds. *Religion and Popular Culture in America*. Berkeley: University of California Press, 2005.

Forrest, Barbara, and Paul Gross. *Creationism's Trojan Horse: The Wedge of Intelligent Design*. New York: Oxford University Press, 2004.

"Foundation for 4th Network." *Communications Daily*, May 7, 1985, 1.

"Fox Drops Suit vs. Franken over Book." *Book Publishing Report* 28, no. 33 (September 2003): 6.

Foy, Joseph J., ed. *Homer Simpson Goes to Washington: American Politics through Popular Culture*. Lexington: University Press of Kentucky, 2008.

Frank, Lisa. "The Evolution of the Seven Deadly Sins: From God to *The Simpsons*." *Journal of Popular Culture* 35, no. 1 (Summer 2001): 95–106.

Frank, Thomas. *What's the Matter with Kansas? How Conservatives Won the Heart of America*. New York: Metropolitan, 2004.

Frankenberg, Ruth. *The Social Construction of Whiteness: White Women, Race Matters*. Minneapolis: University of Minnesota Press, 1993.

Frazer, June M., and Timothy C. Frazer. "*Father Knows Best* and *The Cosby Show*: Nostalgia and the Sitcom Tradition." *Journal of Popular Culture* 27, no. 3 (1993): 163–72.

Freedman, Samuel G. "Waging a One-Man War on American Muslims." *New York Times*, December 16, 2011, A19.

Fretts, Bruce. "The Cho Must Go On." *Entertainment Weekly*, September 16, 1994, p. 98.

Friend, Tad. "Sitcoms, Seriously." *Esquire*, March 1993, 112–24.

"Frist Backs Constitutional Ban on Gay Marriage." *USA Today*, June 29, 2003. http://www.usatoday.com/news/washington/2003-06-29-frist-gay-marriage_x.htm.

Frutkin, Alan. "Out in Prime Time." *Advocate*, May 14, 1996, 48.

Fussell, Paul. *Class: A Guide through the American Status System*. New York: Simon and Schuster, 1983.

Gabaccia, Donna R. "Race, Nation, Hyphen: Italian-Americans and American Multiculturalism in Comparative Perspective." In *Are Italians White? How Race Is Made in America*, edited by Jennifer Guglielmo and Salvatore Salerno, 44–59. New York: Routledge, 2003.

Gabler, Neal. *An Empire of Their Own: How the Jews Invented Hollywood*. New York: Random, 1990.

Gallagher, Bill. "*Simpsons* Episode References Dearborn." WJBK Fox 2 Detroit, myFOX-detroit.com, December 12, 2011. http://www.myfoxdetroit.com/dpp/news/local/simpsons-episode-references-dearborn-20111212-ms.

Gandelman, Joe. "Furor Swirls around Liberal *New Yorker*'s Caricature of Obama." *Moderate Voice*, July 22, 2008. http://themoderatevoice.com/21052/furor-swirls-around-liberal-new-yorkers-caricature-obama-cover/.

Gandy, Kim. "'Mommy Wars' Incited by Irresponsible Media." *National Organization for Women*, March 8, 2006. http://www.now.org/issues/media/mommywarsupdate.html.

Gans, Herbert. "The American Kaleidoscope, Then and Now." In Jacoby, *Reinventing the Melting Pot*, 33–45.

Garber, Marjorie. *Vested Interests: Crossdressing and Cultural Anxiety*. New York: Routledge, 1997.

Garnham, Nicolas. *Capitalism and Communications: Global Culture and the Economics of Information*. London: Sage, 1990.

———. "Political Economy and Cultural Studies: Reconciliation or Divorce?" *Critical Studies in Mass Communication* 12, no. 1 (1995): 62–72.

Gates, Henry Louis Jr. *Loose Canons: Notes on the Culture Wars.* New York: Oxford University Press, 1992.

Gaustad, Edwin, and Phillip L. Barlow. *New Historical Atlas of Religion in America.* New York: Oxford University Press, 2001.

Gaustad, Edwin, and Leigh Schmidt. *The Religious History of America.* San Francisco: Harper, 2002.

Geertz, Clifford. *The Interpretation of Cultures: Selected Essays.* New York: Basic Books, 1973.

Gerard, Jeremy. "Bad Language, Hurt Feelings and Success." *New York Times,* February 21, 1990, late ed., C18.

Gerber, Scott D. "Judging Thomas: The Politics of Assessing a Supreme Court Justice." *Journal of Black Studies* 27, no. 2 (1996): 224–259.

Gever, Martha, John Greyson, and Pratibha Parmar, eds. *Queer Looks: Perspectives on Lesbian and Gay Film and Video.* New York: Routledge, 1993.

Gibbs, Nancy. "Making Time for a Baby." *Time,* April 15, 2002, 48+.

Gibson, Katie. "*United States* v. *Virginia*: A Rhetorical Battle between Progress and Preservation." *Women's Studies in Communication* 29, no. 2 (Fall 2006): 133–64.

Gibson, Mark. *Culture and Power: A History of Cultural Studies.* Oxford: Berg, 2007.

Gilbert, Dennis L. *The American Class Structure in an Age of Growing Inequality.* Thousand Oaks, CA: Pine Forge, 2010.

Gilbert, Dennis L., and Joseph A. Kahl. *The American Class Structure: A New Synthesis.* Homewood, IL: Dorsey, 1982.

Gilbert, Jeffrey. "The Dixie Chicks: A Case Study for the Politics of Hollywood." *Texas Review of Entertainment and Sports Law* 9, no. 2 (2008): 307–34.

Gilbert, Matthew. "Satirical Yet Sweet, *Simpsons* Remains America's Favorite Nuclear Family." *Boston Globe,* February 16, 2003, N1.

Gilgoff, Dan. *The Jesus Machine: How James Dobson, Focus on the Family, and Evangelical America are Winning the Culture War.* New York: St. Martin's, 2007.

Gillis, Mark T., and Joshua Hall. "Using *The Simpsons* to Improve Economic Instruction through Policy Analysis." *American Economist* 54, no. 1 (2010): 84–92.

Giroux, Henry. *Impure Acts: The Practical Politics of Cultural Studies.* New York: Routledge, 2000.

Gitlin, Todd. "The Renaissance of Anti-Intellectualism." *Chronicle of Higher Education,* December 8, 2000, B7–B9.

———. *The Twilight of Common Dreams: Why America Is Wracked by Culture Wars.* New York: Metropolitan, 1995.

Gladwell, Malcolm. "The Tweaker." *New Yorker,* November 14, 2011, 32–35.

Glynn, Kevin. "Bartmania: The Social Reception of an Unruly Image." *Camera Obscura: A Journal of Feminism, Culture, and Media Studies* 38 (May 1996): 61–90.

Golash-Boza, Tanya. "Dropping the Hyphen? Becoming Latino(a)-American through Racialized Assimilation." *Social Forces* 85, no. 1 (2006): 27–55.

Goldberg, Jonah. "Homer Never Nods: The Importance of *The Simpsons*." *National Review,* May 1, 2000, 36–38.

Goldberg, Michelle. "A Woman's Place." *Salon,* April 23, 2002. http://www.salon.com/2002/04/23/childless_women/.

Goldstein, Kalman. "Al Capp and Walt Kelly: Pioneers of Political and Social Satire in the Comics." *Journal of Popular Culture* 25, no. 4 (1992): 81–95.

Gomes, Bruce. "Awards and Honours." *The Simpsons Archive,* November 5, 2007. http://www.snpp.com/guides/awards.html.

———. "The Complete *Simpsons* Bibliography." *The Simpsons Archive*, July 17, 2001. http://www.snpp.com/guides/bibliography01.html.

Goode, Stephen. "Tragedy Spells 'The End of Irony.'" *Insight on the News*, January 14, 2002, 24–26.

Gordon, Milton. *Assimilation in American Life: The Role of Race, Religion, and National Origins*. New York: Oxford University Press, 1964.

Gottschalk, Peter, and Gabriel Greenberg. *Islamophobia: Making Muslims the Enemy*. New York: Rowman & Littlefield, 2007.

Gournelos, Ted. *Popular Culture and the Future of Politics: Cultural Studies and the Tao of South Park*. Lanham, MD: Lexington, 2009.

Gournelos, Ted, and Viveca Greene, eds. *A Decade of Dark Humor: How Comedy, Irony, and Satire Shaped Post-9/11 America*. Jackson: University Press of Mississippi, 2011.

Graff, Gerald. *Beyond the Culture Wars: How Teaching the Conflicts Can Revitalize American Education*. New York: W. W. Norton, 1992.

Grala, Alyson. "A Salute to *The Simpsons*." *License! Global*, May 16, 2007. http://www.licensemag.com/licensemag/data/articlestandard//licensemag/192007/425752/article.pdf.

Grant, Judith. "The Cultural Turn in Marxism." In Dean, *Cultural Studies and Political Theory*, 132–46.

Gray, Herman. *Watching Race: Television and the Struggle for "Blackness."* 2nd ed. 1995. Reprint, Minneapolis: University of Minnesota Press, 2004.

Gray, Jonathan. "Imagining America: *The Simpsons* Go Global." *Popular Communication* 5, no. 2 (2007): 129–48.

———. "Television Teaching: Parody, *The Simpsons*, and Media Literacy Education." *Critical Studies in Media Communication* 22, no. 3 (2005): 223–38.

———. *Watching with "The Simpsons": Television, Parody, and Intertextuality*. New York: Routledge, 2006.

Gray, Jonathan, Jeffrey P. Jones, and Ethan Thompson, eds. *Satire TV: Politics and Comedy in the Post-Network Era*. New York: New York University Press, 2009.

Greppi, Michelle. "Ay Carumba! *The Simpsons* Bump *Cosby* in First Ratings Showdown." *New York Post*, October 13, 1990, A7.

Griffin, Dustin. *Satire: A Critical Reintroduction*. Lexington: University Press of Kentucky, 1994.

Groening, Matt. "Groening, Matt." In *Current Biography Yearbook, 1990*, edited by Charles Mortiz, 285–89. New York: H. W. Wilson Co., 1990.

———. Interview with Jon Stewart. *The Daily Show with Jon Stewart*. Comedy Central, July 18, 2007. http://www.thedailyshow.com/video/index.jhtml?videoId=90145.

———. "*Simpsons* Creator Matt Groening." Interview with Terry Gross. *Fresh Air*. National Public Radio. October 23, 2003. Streaming Audio. http://freshair.npr.org/day_fa.jhtml?display=day&todayDate=10/23/2003.

Gross, Joe. "Singer's Remarks Stir Up Country." *Austin (TX) American-Statesman*, March 15, 2003, A1.

Gross, Larry. "Out of the Mainstream: Sexual Minorities and the Mass Media." *Journal of Homosexuality* 21, nos. 1–2 (1991): 19–46.

———. *Up from Invisibility: Lesbians, Gay Men, and the Media in America*. New York: Columbia University Press, 2001.

———. "What's Wrong with This Picture? Lesbian Women and Gay Men on Television." In Ringer, *Queer Words*, 143–56.

Grossberg, Lawrence. *Bringing It All Back Home: Essays on Cultural Studies*. Durham, NC: Duke University Press, 1997.

———. "The In-Difference of Television." *Screen* 28, no. 2 (1987): 28–45.

Grossberg, Lawrence, Cary Nelson, and Paula Treichler, eds. *Cultural Studies*. New York: Routledge, 1992.

Grossman, Ben. "The First Twenty Years." *Broadcasting & Cable*, November 13, 2006, 18-21.

Grover, Ronald. "The Fourth Network." *Business Week*, September 17, 1990, 114–17.

Guinn, Jeff. "Al Franken Celebrates a Well-Timed Lawsuit with New Book." *Fort Worth Star-Telegram*, September 5, 2003, 1.

Gunster, Shane. *Capitalizing on Culture: Critical Theory for Cultural Studies*. Toronto: University of Toronto Press, 2004.

Hall, Gary, and Clare Birchall, eds. *New Cultural Studies: Adventures in Theory*. Athens: University of Georgia Press, 2006.

Hall, James. "Religious Dialogues in Prime Time." *The Simpsons Archive*, November 24, 2000. http://www.snpp.com/other/papers/jlh.paper.html.

Hall, Joshua. "Homer Economicus: Using *The Simpsons* to Teach Economics." *Journal of Private Enterprise* 20, no. 2 (2005): 165–76.

Hall, Stuart. "Encoding, Decoding." In *The Cultural Studies Reader*, edited by Simon During, 507–17. New York: Routledge, 1993.

Halperin, David. "The Normalization of Queer Theory." *Journal of Homosexuality* 45, nos. 2–4 (2003): 339–43.

Halpern, Sue. "Susan Faludi: The Mother Jones Interview." *Mother Jones*, September/October 1999. http://www.motherjones.com/media/1999/09/susan-faludi-mother-jones-interview.

Hamamoto, Darrell Y. *Nervous Laughter: Television Situation Comedy and Liberal Democratic Ideology*. New York: Praeger, 1989.

Hamilton, Trish. "Rabbit Punch." *Rolling Stone*, September 1988, 81–82, 113.

Hammers, Michelle. "Cautionary Tales of Liberation and Female Professionalism: The Case Against Ally McBeal." *Western Journal of Communication* 69, no. 2 (2005): 167–82.

Hangen, Tona J. "Evangelists/Evangelical Radio: Conservative Protestant Religious Stations and Programs." In *Museum of Broadcast Communications Encyclopedia of Radio*, vol. 1, edited by Christopher H. Sterling, 555–58. New York: Routledge, 2004.

———. *Redeeming the Dial: Radio, Religion, and Popular Culture in America*. Chapel Hill: University of North Carolina Press, 2002.

Hano, Arnold. "Can Archie Bunker Give Bigotry a Bad Name?" *New York Times*, April 12, 1972, SM32.

Hanson, Ellis, ed. *Out Takes: Essays on Queer Theory and Film*. Durham, NC: Duke University Press, 1999.

Haralovich, Mary Beth. "Sit-coms and Suburbs: Positioning the 1950s Homemaker." In *Private Screenings: Television and the Female Consumer*, edited by Lynn Spigel and Denise Mann, 111–41. Minneapolis: University of Minnesota Press, 1992.

Haralovich, Mary Beth, and Lauren Rabinovitz, eds. *Television, History, and American Culture*. Durham, NC: Duke University Press, 1999.

Harkins, Anthony. *Hillbilly: A Cultural History of an American Icon*. New York: Oxford University Press, 2004.

Harrington, Michael. *The Other America: Poverty in the United States*. New York: Macmillan, 1962.

Harrington, Richard. "The Cartoon Hell of Matt Groening." *Washington Post*, December 18, 1988, F1.

Harris, Paul. "In the Yellow Corner: Simpsons and Fox Slug It Out over 'Racism' Jibe." *Guardian*, December 1, 2010, 25.

Harris, Sam. *The End of Faith: Religion, Terror and the Future of Reason.* New York: Norton, 2005.

Hartley, John. "Housing Television: Textual Traditions in TV and Cultural Studies." In *The Television Studies Book*, edited by Christine Geragth and David Lusted, 33–50. London: Arnold, 1998.

Hartman, Ann. "Murphy Brown, Dan Quayle, and the American Family." *Social Work* 37, no. 5 (1992): 387–88.

Heit, Jamey. *The Springfield Reformation: "The Simpsons," Christianity, and American Culture.* New York: Continuum, 2008.

Heller, Dana. "Taking the Nation 'From Drab to Fab': *Queer Eye for the Straight Guy.*" *Feminist Media Studies* 4, no. 3 (2004): 347–50.

Hendershot, Heather. "God's Angriest Man: Carl McIntire, Cold War Fundamentalism, and Right-Wing Broadcasting." *American Quarterly* 59, no. 2 (June 2007): 373–96.

———. *Shaking the World for Jesus: Media and Conservative Evangelical Culture.* Chicago: University of Chicago Press, 2004.

Henry, Matthew. "'Don't Ask Me, I'm Just a Girl': Feminism, Female Identity, and *The Simpsons.*" *Journal of Popular Culture* 40, no. 2 (2007): 272–303.

———. "'Gabbin' about God': Religion, Secularity, and Satire on *The Simpsons.*" In *Homer Simpson Marches on Washington: Dissent through American Popular Culture*, edited by Joseph J. Foy and Timothy M. Dale, 141–66. Lexington: University of Kentucky Press, 2010.

———. "The Triumph of Popular Culture: Situation Comedy, Postmodernism, and *The Simpsons.*" *Studies in Popular Culture* 17, no. 1 (Fall 1994): 85–99. Reprinted in *Critiquing the Sitcom: A Reader*, edited by Joanne Morreale, 262–73. Syracuse, NY: Syracuse University Press, 2003.

———. "'The Whole World's Gone Gay!': Smithers' Sexuality, Homer's Phobia, and Gay Life on *The Simpsons.*" *Popular Culture Review* 13, no. 1 (2002): 19–33.

Herman, Didi. "'I'm Gay': Declarations, Desire, and Coming Out on Prime-Time Television." *Sexualities* 8, no. 1 (2005): 7–29.

Herron, Jerry. "Homer Simpson's Eyes and the Culture of Late Nostalgia." *Representations* 43 (1993): 1–26.

Hilton-Morrow, Wendy, and David T. McMahan. "*The Flintstones* to *Futurama*: Networks and Prime Time Animation." In Stabile and Harrison, *Prime Time Animation*, 74–88.

Himebaugh, Glenn. "Nast, Thomas." In *History of the Mass Media in the United States: An Encyclopedia*, edited by Margaret A. Blanchard, 416–17. Chicago: Fitzroy Dearborn, 2000.

Himmelfarb, Gertrude. *One Nation, Two Cultures.* New York: Knopf, 1999.

Hitchens, Christopher. *God Is Not Great: How Religion Poisons Everything.* New York: Twelve, 2007.

Hobbs, Renee. "*The Simpsons* Meet Mark Twain: Analyzing Popular Media Texts in the Classroom." *English Journal* 87, no. 1 (1998): 49–51.

Hobsbawm, Eric, and Terence Ranger, eds. *The Invention of Tradition.* Cambridge: Cambridge University Press, 1983.

Hocking, Tammy, and Matt Rose. "Section II: Series Background." L.I.S.A. (List of Inquiries and Substantive Answers). *The Simpsons Archive*, March 17, 2004. http://www.snpp.com/guides/lisa-2.html.

———. "Section III: Characters, Events and Places." L.I.S.A. (List of Inquiries and Substantive Answers). *The Simpsons Archive*, March 17, 2004. http://www.snpp.com/guides/lisa-3.html.

———. "Section IV: Cast, Staff and Production." L.I.S.A. (List of Inquiries and Substantive Answers). *The Simpsons Archive*, March 17, 2004. http://www.snpp.com/guides/lisa-4 .html.

Hodge, Barry. "King Size Homer: Ideology and Representation." *The Simpsons Archive*, 1996. http://www.snpp.com/other/papers/bh.paper.html.

Hollinger, David. "Obama, the Instability of Color Lines, and the Promise of a Postethnic Future." *Callaloo* 31, no. 4 (2008): 1033–37.

———. *Postethnic America: Beyond Multiculturalism*. New York: Basic, 1995.

Holman, Hugh. "Satire." In *A Handbook to Literature*, 10th ed., edited by Hugh Holman and William Harmon, 461–62. New York: Prentice Hall, 2005.

Holman, Hugh, and William Harmon, eds. *A Handbook to Literature*. 10th ed. New York: Prentice Hall, 2005.

Holmes, David L. *The Faiths of the Founding Fathers*. New York: Oxford, 2006.

Hontz, Jenny. "Standards Chiefs Brace for Ratings Workload." *Electronic Media*, March 11, 1996, 1+.

hooks, bell. *Feminism Is for Everybody: Passionate Politics*. Boston: South End Press, 2000.

Hoover, Stewart M. *Religion in the Media Age*. New York: Routledge, 2006.

Hoover, Stewart M., and Lynn Schofield Clarke, eds. *Practicing Religion in the Age of the Media*. New York: Columbia University Press, 2002.

Horsfield, Peter, Mary E. Hess, and Adam M. Medrano, eds. *Belief in Media: Cultural Perspectives on Media and Christianity*. Burlington, VT: Ashgate, 2004.

Horwitz, Steven, and Stewart Dompe. "From Rabbit Ears to Flat Screen: It's Getting Better All the Time!" *Social Science Research Network*, December 5, 2010. http://papers.ssrn.com/sol3/papers.cfm?abstract_id=1720060.

Hubert, Susan J. "What's Wrong with This Picture? The Politics of Ellen's Coming Out Party." *Journal of Popular Culture* 33, no. 2 (1999): 31–36.

Hughey, Michael W. "Americanism and Its Discontents: Protestantism, Nativism, and Political Heresy in America." *International Journal of Politics, Culture and Society* 5, no. 4 (1992): 533–53.

Hull, Margaret Betz. "Postmodern Philosophy Meets Pop Cartoon: Michel Foucault and Matt Groening." *Journal of Popular Culture* 34, no. 2 (Fall 2000): 57–67.

Hunter, James D. "The Culture War and the Sacred/Secular Divide: The Problem of Pluralism and Weak Hegemony." *Social Research* 76, no. 4 (2009): 1307–22.

———. *Culture Wars: The Struggle to Define America*. New York: Basic, 1991.

Hunter, James Davison, and Alan Wolfe, eds. *Is There a Culture War? A Dialogue on Values and American Public Life*. Washington, DC: Brookings Institution Press, 2006.

Hutcheon, Linda. *The Politics of Postmodernism*. New York: Routledge, 1989.

———. *A Theory of Parody: The Teachings of Twentieth-Century Art Forms*. Urbana: University of Illinois Press, 2000.

"I Now Pronounce You Chuck and Larry." *Box Office Mojo*. March 10, 2008, http://www .boxofficemojo.com/movies/?id=chuckandlarry.htm.

Impoco, Jim. "The Bundys Meet the Censors at Fox." *U.S. News & World Report*, September 11, 1995, 68.

Irons, Peter. *God on Trial: Dispatches from America's Religious Battlegrounds*. New York: Viking, 2007.

Irwin, William, Mark T. Conrad, and Aeon J. Skoble, eds. *"The Simpsons" and Philosophy: The D'oh of Homer*. Chicago: Open Court Press, 2000.

Irwin, William, and J. R. Lombardo. *"The Simpsons* and Allusion: 'Worst Essay Ever.'" In Irwin et al., *"The Simpsons" and Philosophy*, 81–92.

Isaacson, Walter. *Steve Jobs*. New York: Simon and Schuster, 2011.

Itzkoff, Dave. "Friendly Enemies on Fox: *Simpsons* and O'Reilly." *New York Times*, December 1, 2010, C3.

Itzkovitz, Daniel. "Passing Like Me." *South Atlantic Quarterly* 98, no. 1/2 (Winter/Spring 1999): 35–57.

Jacobs, A. J. "Out?" *Entertainment Weekly*, October 4, 1996, 18–25.

———. "When Gay Men Happen to Straight Women." *Entertainment Weekly*, October 23, 1998, 20–25.

Jacobson, Mark. "Muhammad Comes to Manhattan." *New York* 43, no. 27 (2010): 24–32.

Jacobson, Matthew Frye. *Whiteness of a Different Color: European Immigrants and the Alchemy of Race*. Cambridge, MA: Harvard University Press, 1998.

Jacoby, Russell. *The Last Intellectuals*. New York: Basic, 1987.

Jacoby, Susan. *Freethinkers: A History of American Secularism*. New York: Metropolitan, 2004.

Jacoby, Tamar. "Defining Assimilation for the 21st Century." In *Reinventing the Melting Pot: The New Immigrants and What It Means to Be American*, edited by Tamar Jacoby, 3–16. New York: Basic, 2004.

Jacoby, Tamar, ed. *Reinventing the Melting Pot: The New Immigrants and What It Means to Be American*. New York: Basic, 2004.

Jameson, Fredric. "Postmodernism, or, The Logic of Late Capitalism." *New Left Review* 146 (1984): 53–92.

Jansen, Eric. "Endangered Species." *Advocate*, April 4, 1995, 22–23.

Jaynes, Gerald D., ed. *Immigration and Race: New Challenges for American Democracy*. New Haven, CT: Yale University Press, 2000.

Jenkins, Henry. *Textual Poachers: Television Fans and Visual Culture*. New York: Routledge, 1992.

Jensen, Richard. "The Culture Wars, 1965–1995: A Historian's Map." *Journal of Social History* 29 (1995): 17–37.

Jermyn, Deborha. *Sex and the City*. Detroit: Wayne State University Press, 2009.

Jhally, Sut, and Justin Lewis. *Enlightened Racism: The Cosby Show, Audiences, and the Myth of the American Dream*. New York: Westview, 1992.

Johnson, Ann, Esteban del Rio, and Alicia Kemmitt. "Missing the Joke: A Reception Analysis of Satirical Texts." *Communication, Culture & Critique* 3 (2010): 396–415.

Johnson, Merri Lisa, ed. *Third Wave Feminism and Television: Jane Puts It in a Box*. New York: I. B. Tauris, 2007.

Johnson, Victoria. *Heartland TV: Prime Time Television and the Struggle for U.S. Identity*. New York: NYU Press, 2008.

Jones, Gerard. *Honey, I'm Home! Sitcoms: Selling the American Dream*. New York: St. Martin's, 1992.

Jones, Jeffrey P. *Entertaining Politics: Satiric Television and Political Engagement*. Lanham, MD: Rowman & Littlefield, 2010.

Jones, Jeffrey P., and Geoffrey Baym. "A Dialog on Satire News and the Crisis of Truth in Postmodern Political Television." *Journal of Communication Inquiry* 34, no. 3 (2010): 278–94.

Jones, William. "'People Have to Watch What They Say': What Horace, Juvenal, and 9/11 Can Tell Us about Satire and History." *Helios* 36, no. 1 (2009): 27–53.

"Journalism, Satire or Just Laughs? *The Daily Show with Jon Stewart*, Examined." Project for Excellence in Journalism, PEW Research Center, May 8, 2008. http://journalism.org/node/10953.

Kahl, Joseph A. *The American Class Structure*. New York, Rinehart, 1957.

Kalman, Richard, and Josh Belkin. "Sephardic Tradition and *The Simpsons* Connections." *The Simpsons Archive*, November 29, 2001. http://www.snpp.com/other/papers/kb.paper.html.

Kaminski, Stuart M. *American Television Genres*. Chicago: Nelson Hall, 1985.

Katz, Claire. "'The Eternal Irony of the Community': Prophecy, Patriotism, and the Dixie Chicks." *Shofar: An Interdisciplinary Journal of Jewish Studies* 26, no. 4 (2008): 139–60.

Katznelson, Ira. *When Affirmative Action Was White: An Untold History of Racial Inequality in Twentieth-Century America*. New York: W. W. Norton, 2005.

Kaufmann, Eric. "Nativist Cosmopolitans: Institutional Reflexivity and the Decline of 'Double-Consciousness' in American Nationalist Thought." *Journal of Historical Sociology* 14, no. 1 (2001): 47–78.

Keating, Ann Louise. "Interrogating 'Whiteness,' (De)Constructing 'Race.'" *College English* 57, no. 8 (1995): 901–18.

Keilwasser, Alfred P. "Mainstream Television, Adolescent Homosexuality, and Significant Silence." *Critical Studies in Mass Communications* 9, no. 4 (1992): 350–73.

Keller, Bill, et al. *Class Matters*. New York: Henry Holt, 2005.

Keller, James R., and Leslie Stratyner, eds. *The New Queer Aesthetic on Television: Essays on Recent Programming*. Jefferson, NC: McFarland, 2006.

Kelley, Robin. *Yo' Mama's Disfunktional! Fighting the Culture Wars in Urban America*. Boston: Beacon Press, 1998.

Kellner, Douglas. "Critical Theory and Cultural Studies: The Missed Articulation." In *Cultural Methodologies*, edited by Jim McGuigan, 12–41. Thousand Oaks, CA: Sage, 1997.

———. "Cultural Studies, Multiculturalism, and Media Culture." In *Gender, Race, and Class in Media*, 2nd ed., edited by Gail Dines and Jean M. Humez, 9–20. Thousand Oaks, CA: Sage, 2003.

———. "TV, Ideology, and Emancipatory Popular Culture." In *Television: The Critical View*, 4th ed., edited by Horace Newcomb, 471–503. New York: Oxford University Press, 1987.

Kendall, Diana. *Framing Class: Media Representations of Wealth and Poverty in America*. 2nd ed. Lanham, MD: Rowman and Littlefield, 2011.

Kennedy, Dana. "Can Gay Stars Shine?" *Entertainment Weekly*, September 8, 1995, 32–36.

Kennedy, Shelia. *God and Country: America in Red and Blue*. Waco, TX: Baylor University Press, 2007.

Kennicott, Phillip. "It's Funny How Humor Is So Ticklish." *Washington Post*, July 15, 2008, C01.

Kentfield, Calvin. "Far Right, Far Left and Far Out." *New York Times*, April 14, 1968, D19.

Kercher, Stephan E. *Revel with a Cause: Liberal Satire in Postwar America*. Chicago: University of Chicago Press, 2006.

Kernan, Alvin B. *Modern Satire*. New York: Harcourt, 1962.

Kerr, Peter A. "The Framing of Fundamentalist Christians: Network Television News, 1980–2000." *Journal of Media and Religion* 2, no. 4 (2003): 203–35.

Kiernan, Thomas. *Citizen Murdoch*. New York: Dodd, Mead & Co., 1986.

Kimmel, Daniel M. *The Fourth Network: How Fox Broke the Rules and Reinvented Television*. Chicago: Ivan Dee, 2004.

Kimmel, Michael S. "Saving the Males: The Sociological Implications of the Virginia Military Institute and the Citadel." *Gender & Society* 14, no. 4 (2000): 494–516.

Kincheloe, Joe L., Shirley R. Steinberg, Nelson M. Rodriguez, and Ronald E. Chennault, eds. *White Reign: Deploying Whiteness in America*. New York: St. Martin's, 1998.

King, Joyce E. "Dysconscious Racism: Ideology, Identity, and the Miseducation of Teachers." *Journal of Negro Education* 60, no. 1 (1991): 133–46.

King, Winston. "Religion." In *Encyclopedia of Religion*, 2nd ed., vol. 11, edited by Lindsay Jones, 7692–701. Detroit: Macmillan, 2005.

Kinnon, Joy Bennett. "Is Skin Color Still an Issue in Black America?" *Ebony*, April 2000, 52–55.

Kintz, Linda, and Julia Lesage, eds. *Media, Culture, and the Religious Right*. Minneapolis: University of Minnesota Press, 1998.

Kitch, Carolyn. *The Girl of the Magazine Cover: The Origins of Visual Stereotypes in American Mass Media*. Chapel Hill: University of North Carolina Press, 2001.

Kleinknecht, William. *The Man Who Sold the World: Ronald Reagan and the Betrayal of Main Street America*. New York: Nation Books, 2009.

Klinowitz, Jerome. *Literary Subversions: New American Fiction and the Practice of Criticism*. Carbondale: Southern Illinois University Press, 1985.

Knight, Deborah. "Popular Parody: *The Simpsons* Meets the Crime Film." In Irwin et al., *"The Simpsons" and Philosophy*, 93–107.

Knobel, Dale T. *America for the Americans: The Nativist Movement in the United States*. New York: Twayne, 1996.

Knowles, "The Simpsons and the Nuclear Family." *Reconstruction: Studies in Contemporary Culture* 8, no. 2 (2008): 28 para. http://reconstruction.eserver.org/082/knowles.shtml.

Knox, Simone. "Reading the Ungraspable Double-Codedness of *The Simpsons*." *Journal of Popular Film and Television* 34, no. 2 (2006): 72–81.

Kohn, Ayelet. "Prime-Time Television 'Fable Families': Political and Social Satire for Segmented Audiences." *Emergences* 10, no. 1 (2000): 105–18.

Kopelson, Karen. "Dis/Integrating the Gay/Queer Binary: 'Reconstructed Identity Politics' for a Performative Pedagogy." *College English* 65, no. 1 (September 2002): 17–35.

Kopkind, Andrew. "The Gay Moment." *Nation*, May 3, 1993, 577–602.

Korte, Dan. "*The Simpsons* as Quality Television." *The Simpsons Archive*, November 1997. http://www.snpp.com/other/papers/dk.paper.html.

Kossmann, Patricia A. "Remembering Fulton Sheen." *America*, December 6, 2004, 8–10.

Kramer, Janet. "Discourses of Sexual Morality in *Sex and the City* and *Queer as Folk*." *Journal of Popular Culture* 40, no. 3 (2007): 409–32.

Krauss, Clifford. "Gay Marriage is Extended Nationwide in Canada." *New York Times*, June 29, 2005, A4.

Krieger, Rosalin. "'Does He Actually Say the Word *Jewish*?'—Jewish Representations in *Seinfeld*." *Journal for Cultural Research* 7, no. 4 (2003): 387–95.

Kubasik, Ben. "Murphy Lays Down the Law." *Newsday*, September 22, 1992, 5+.

Kurtz, Paul. *Humanist Manifesto 2000*. Amherst, NY: Prometheus, 2000.

———. *Skepticism and Humanism: The New Paradigm*. New Brunswick, NJ: Transaction, 2001.

Lafky, Sue A., and Bonnie Brennen. "For Better or For Worse: Coming Out in the Funny Pages." *Studies in Popular Culture* 18, no. 1 (1995): 23–47.

Lakoff, George. *Moral Politics: How Liberals and Conservatives Think*. Chicago: University of Chicago Press, 2002.

Lamb, Chris. *Drawn to Extremes: The Use and Abuse of Editorial Cartoons*. New York: Columbia University Press, 2004.

Landay, Lori. "*I Love Lucy*: Television and Gender in Postwar Domestic Ideology." In Dalton and Linder, *Sitcom Reader*, 87–97.

———. *Madcaps, Screwballs & Con Women: The Female Trickster in American Culture*. Philadelphia: University of Pennsylvania Press, 1998.

Lane, Frederick S. *The Decency Wars: The Campaign to Cleanse American Culture*. Amherst, NY: Prometheus, 2006.

Lang, Berel. "Hyphenated Jew and the Anxiety of Identity." *Jewish Social Studies* 12, no. 1 (Fall 2005): 1–15.

Lardner, Jim, and David A. Smith, eds. *Inequality Matters: The Growing Economic Divide in America and Its Poisonous Consequences.* New York: New Press, 2005.

Larson, Allen. "Re-Drawing the Bottom Line." In Stabile and Harrison, *Prime Time Animation,* 55–73.

Lebo, Lauri. *The Devil in Dover: An Insider's Story of Dogma v. Darwin in Small-town America.* New York: New Press, 2008.

Lee, Brenda. "*Kitzmiller v. Dover Area School District*: Teaching Intelligent Design in Public Schools." *Harvard Civil Rights–Civil Liberties Law Review* 41 (2006): 581–90.

Lee, Janet. "Subversive Sitcoms: *Roseanne* as Inspiration for Feminist Resistance." *Women's Studies* 21, no. 1 (1992): 87–101.

Lehigh, Scot. "What's So Shocking about Satire?" *Boston Globe*, July 16, 2008, A15.

Leo, John. "The Indignation of Barbie." *U.S. News & World Report*, October 12, 1992, 25.

Leo, John R. "The Familialism of 'Man' in American Television Drama." *South Atlantic Quarterly* 88, no. 1 (1989): 31–51.

Levy, Ariel. *Female Chauvinist Pigs: Women and the Rise of Raunch Culture.* New York: Free Press, 2006.

Lewis, Lisa. *The Adoring Audience: Fan Culture and Popular Media.* New York: Routledge, 1992.

Lewis, Todd V. "Religious Rhetoric and the Comic Frame in *The Simpsons.*" *Journal of Media and Religion* 1, no. 3 (2002): 153–65.

Lichtblau, Eric, and Brian Stetler. "News Corp. Gives Republicans $1 Million." *New York Times*, August 18, 2010, A13.

Lilla, Mark. *The Stillborn God: Religion, Politics, and the Modern West.* New York: Knopf, 2007.

Lindsay, D. Michael. *Faith in the Halls of Power: How Evangelicals Joined the American Elite.* New York: Oxford University Press, 2007.

Linker, Damon. *The Theocons: Secular America Under Siege.* New York: Doubleday, 2006.

Lipsitz, George. "The Meaning of Memory: Family, Class, and Ethnicity in Early Network Television Programs." *Cultural Anthropology* 1, no. 4 (1986): 355–87.

———. *The Possessive Investment in Whiteness: How White People Profit from Identity Politics.* Philadelphia: Temple University Press, 1998.

Litman, Thomas L. "Fox Broadcasting Company: Why Now? An Economic Study of the Rise of the Fourth Network." *Journal of Broadcasting & Electronic Media* 35, no. 2 (1991): 139–58.

Lodge, David. *The Art of Fiction.* New York: Viking, 1993.

Lordan, Edward J. *Politics, Ink: How Cartoonists Skewer America's Politicians, from King George III to George Dubya.* Lanham, MD: Rowman & Littlefield, 2005.

Lorenz, Hendrik. "Ancient Theories of Soul." In *Stanford Encyclopedia of Philosophy.* The Metaphysics Research Lab. Stanford University. October 23, 2003. http://plato.stanford.edu/entries/ancient-soul/.

Lorenzo, Lourdes, Ana Pereira, and Maria Xoubanova. "*The Simpsons/Los Simpson*: Analysis of an Audiovisual Translation." *Translator* 9, no. 2 (2003): 269–91.

Lotz, Amanda, ed. *Beyond Prime Time: Television Programming in the Post-Network Era.* New York: Routledge, 2009.

———. "Postfeminist Television Criticism: Rehabilitating Critical Terms and Identifying Postfeminist Attributes." *Feminist Media Studies* 1, no. 1 (2001): 105–21.

———. *Redesigning Women: Television after the Network Era.* Urbana: University of Illinois Press, 2006.

——. "Segregated Sitcoms: Institutional Causes of Disparity among Black and White Comedy Images and Audiences." In Dalton and Linder, *Sitcom Reader*, 139–50.

——. *The Television Will Be Revolutionized*. New York: NYU Press, 2007.

——. "Textual (Im)Possibilities in the U.S. Post-Network Era: Negotiating Production and Promotion Processes on Lifetime's *Any Day Now*." *Critical Studies in Media Communication* 21, no. 1 (2004): 22–43.

Lugo, Luis, et al. "2008 U.S. Religious Landscape Survey." Pew Forum on Religion and Public Life, February 2008. http://religions.pewforum.org/.

Lynch, Gordon. *Understanding Theology and Popular Culture*. Malden, MA: Blackwell, 2005.

MacDonald, Mary. "Spirituality." In *Encyclopedia of Religion*, 2nd ed., vol. 13., edited by Lindsay Jones, 8718–8721. Detroit: Macmillan, 2005.

MacGregor, Geddes. "Soul: Christian Concepts." In *Encyclopedia of Religion*, 2nd ed., vol. 12, edited by Lindsay Jones, 8561–8566. Detroit: Macmillan, 2005.

MacGregor, Jeff. "*The Simpsons*: More Than Sight Gags and Subversive Satire." *New York Times*, June 20, 1999, late ed., sec. 2, 27.

Macionis, John. *Sociology*. 13th ed. New York: Prentice Hall, 2010.

Mahler, Jonathan. "What Rupert Wrought." *New York*, May 21, 2005. http://nymag.com/nymetro/news/people/features/11673/.

Manegold, Catherine S. *In Glory's Shadow: Shannon Faulkner, the Citadel and a Changing America*. New York: Knopf, 2000.

Maney, Gregory M., Patrick G. Coy, and Lynn M. Woehrle. "Pursuing Political Persuasion: War and Peace Frames in the United States after September 11th." *Social Movement Studies* 8, no. 4 (2009): 299–322.

Mantsios, Gregory. "Class in America—2009." In *Race, Class, and Gender in the United States: An Integrated Study*, 8th ed., edited by Paula S. Rothenberg, 177–92. New York: Worth, 2009.

"The Many Faces of Feminism." *Ms.* 5, no. 1 (July 1994): 33.

Marc, David. *Comic Visions: Television Comedy and American Culture*. 2nd ed. Malden, MA: Blackwell, 1997.

Markle, Gail. "Can Women Have Sex Like a Man? Sexual Scripts in *Sex and the City*." *Sexuality and Culture* 12, no. 1 (Winter 2008): 45–57.

Marriott, Michel. "I'm Bart, I'm Black and What About It?" *New York Times*, September 19, 1990, C1.

Marris, Paul, and Sue Thornham, eds. *Media Studies: A Reader*. Edinburgh: Edinburgh University Press, 1996.

Marschall, Richard E. "The Century in Political Cartoons." *Columbia Journalism Review*, May/June 1999, 54–58.

Marsden, George M. *Fundamentalism and American Culture*. 2nd ed. 1980. Reprint, New York: Oxford University Press, 2006.

Martin, William. *With God on Our Side: The Rise of the Religious Right in America*. New York: Broadway, 1996.

Martinez, Andres. "An All-American Family." *New York Times*, February 16, 2003, late ed., sec. 4, 10.

Martínez-Sierra, Juan José. "Using Bourdieu to Approach the Concept of Television as an Instrument of Social Reproduction in the U.S.: The Paradox of *The Simpsons*." *Applied Semiotics/Sémiotique appliquée* 18 (2006): 18–27.

Mason, M. S. "*Simpsons* Creator on Poking Fun." *Christian Science Monitor*, April 17, 1998, B7.

Matheson, Carl. "*The Simpsons*, Hyper-Irony, and the Meaning of Life." In Irwin et al., "*The Simpsons*" and Philosophy, 108–25.

Matthews, Kristin L. "A Mad Proposition in Postwar America." *Journal of American Culture* 30, no. 2 (2007): 212–21.

Mayer, Jane. "Whatever It Takes: The Politics of the Man Behind *24*." *New Yorker*, February 19, 2007, 66.

Mayerle, Judine. "*Roseanne*—How Did You Get Inside My House? A Case Study of a Hit Blue-Collar Situation Comedy." *Journal of Popular Culture* 24, no. 4 (1991): 71–88.

Mazur, Eric Michael, and Kate McCarthy, eds. *God in the Details: American Religion in Popular Culture*. New York: Routledge, 2001.

McConnell, Frank. "'Real' Cartoon Characters." *Commonweal*, June 15, 1990, 389–90.

McEnteer, James. *Shooting the Truth: The Rise of American Political Documentaries*. New York: Praeger, 2006.

McGrath, Ben. "The Radical: Why Do Editors Keep Throwing *The Boondocks* Off the Funnies Page?" *New Yorker*, April 19, 2004, 152–161.

McHale, Brian. *Postmodernist Fiction*. New York: Methuen, 1987.

McKain, Aaron. "Not Necessarily Not the News: Gatekeeping, Remediation, and *The Daily Show*." *Journal of American Culture* 28, no. 4 (2005): 415–30.

McKnight, David. "'A World Hungry for a New Philosophy': Rupert Murdoch and the Rise of Neo-liberalism." *Journalism Studies* 4, no. 3 (2003): 347–58.

McLaren, Peter. "Whiteness Is . . . The Struggle for Postcolonial Hybridity." In Kincheloe et al., *White Reign*, 63–75.

Meacham, Jon. *American Gospel: God, the Founding Fathers, and the Making of a Nation*. New York: Random House, 2006.

Medhurst, Andy. "Batman, Deviance, and Camp." In *Signs of Life in the USA*, edited by Sonia Maasik and Jack Solomon, 323–39. Boston: Bedford, 1994.

Melamed, Jodi. "The Spirit of Neoliberalism: From Racial Liberalism to Neoliberal Multiculturalism." *Social Text* 24, no. 4 (2006): 1–24.

Mellencamp, Patricia, ed. *Logics of Television: Essays in Cultural Criticism*. Bloomington: Indiana University Press, 1990.

Meyer, Birgit, and Annelies Moors, eds. *Religion, Media, and the Public Sphere*. Bloomington: Indiana University Press, 2005.

"Michael Moore Discusses His New Series, *The Awful Truth*." Interview with Scott Simon. *Weekend Edition*. National Public Radio, April 10, 1999. http://www.npr.org /templates/story/story.php?storyId=1048125.

Michaels, Walter Benn. *The Trouble with Diversity: How We Learned to Love Identity and Ignore Inequality*. Princeton, NJ: Princeton University Press, 2004.

Miller, John J. *The Unmaking of Americans: How Multiculturalism Has Undermined the Assimilation Ethic*. New York: Free Press, 1998.

Miller, Lisa. "The Misinformants: What 'Stealth Jihad' Doesn't Mean." *Newsweek*, September 6, 2010, 16.

Mills, David. "Bootleg Black Bart Simpson, the Hip-Hop T-Shirt Star." *Washington Post*, June 28, 1990, D1.

Mills, David, and Dorion Sagan. *Atheist Universe: The Thinking Person's Answer to Christian Fundamentalism*. New York: Ulysses Press, 2006.

Mink, Gwendolyn. *Welfare's End*. Ithaca, NY: Cornell University Press, 2002.

Mittell, Jason. "Cartoon Realism: Genre Mixing and the Cultural Life of *The Simpsons*." *Velvet Light Trap* 47 (2001): 15–28.

Mockabee, Stephen T. "A Question of Authority: Religion and Cultural Conflict in the 2004 Election." *Political Behavior* 29 (2007): 221–48.

Montgomery, J. "What's So Gay about the '90s?" *Pride Inside: The Newsletter of Pride Community Center of Syracuse*, August 1996, 1+.

Morey, Peter. "Terrorvision: Race, Nation and Muslimness in Fox's *24*." *Interventions: The International Journal of Postcolonial Studies* 12, no. 2 (2010): 251–64.

Morin, Richard. "America's Four Middle Classes." Pew Social & Demographic Trends, *Pew Research Center*, July 29, 2008, 1. http://www.pewsocialtrends.org/2008/07/29 /americas-four-middle-classes/2/.

Morley, David. *Television, Audiences and Cultural Studies.* New York: Routledge, 1992.

Morrison, Mark. "Year of the Fox." *Rolling Stone*, October 4, 1990, 76–77.

Morrison, Toni. *Playing in the Dark: Whiteness and the Literary Imagination.* New York: Vintage, 1992.

———, ed. *Race-ing Justice, En-gendering Power: Essays on Anita Hill, Clarence Thomas, and the Construction of Social Reality.* New York: Pantheon, 1992.

Morrow, Lance. "But Seriously, Folks . . ." *Time*, June 1, 1992, 28+.

Moseley, Rachel, and Jacinda Read. "Having It Ally: Popular Television (Post-)Feminism." *Feminist Media Studies* 2, no. 2 (2002): 231–49.

Mullen, Megan. "*The Simpsons* and Hanna-Barbera's Animation Legacy." In Alberti, *Leaving Springfield*, 108–40.

Muro, Mark. "Harvard's Laugh Track." *Boston Globe*, August 7, 1992, L25.

Murphy, Patrick D., and Marwan M. Kraidy, eds. *Global Media Studies: Ethnographic Perspectives.* New York: Routledge, 2003.

"Murphy to Dan: Read My Ratings." *Time*, October 5, 1992, 25.

Nabokov, Vladimir. *Strong Opinions.* New York: McGraw-Hill, 1973.

Nadel, Alan. *Television in Black-and-White America: Race and National Identity.* Lawrence: University of Kansas Press, 2005.

Nahshon, Edna, ed. *From the Ghetto to the Melting Pot: Israel Zangwill's Jewish Plays.* Detroit: Wayne State University Press, 2006.

Nakayama, Thomas K., and Robert L. Krizek. "Whiteness: A Strategic Rhetoric." *Quarterly Journal of Speech* 81, no. 3 (1995): 291–310.

Natoli, Joseph, and Linda Hutcheon, eds. *A Postmodern Reader.* New York: SUNY Press, 1993.

Neuhaus, Jessamyn. "Marge Simpson, Blue-Haired Housewife: Defining Domesticity on *The Simpsons*." *Journal of Popular Culture* 43, no. 4 (2010): 761–81.

New, David S. *Holy War: The Rise of Militant Christian, Jewish, and Islamic Fundamentalism.* Jefferson, NC: McFarland, 2002.

Newcomb, Horace, ed. *Television: The Critical View.* 6th ed. New York: Oxford University Press, 2000.

Nichols, John. "Huey Freeman: American Hero." *Nation*, January 10, 2001. http://www .thenation.com/doc/20020128/nichols.

Nielsen Report on Television. Nielsen Media Research. Northbrook, IL: A. C. Nielsen Company, 1998.

"Nielsens." *USA Today*, January 17, 1990, 3D. Lexis-Nexis Academic, October 2, 2003.

"Nielsens." *USA Today*, December 20, 1989, 3D. Lexis-Nexis Academic, October 2, 2003.

Noh, David. Review of *I Now Pronounce You Chuck and Larry. Film Journal International*, September 2007, 59.

"No More News Crawl on *Simpsons*." *Vancouver Province*, October 31, 2003.

Noll, Mark. *The Old Religion in a New World.* Grand Rapids, MI: Eerdmans, 2002.

Nord, David Paul. *Faith in Reading: Religious Publishing and the Birth of Mass Media in America.* New York: Oxford University Press, 2004.

Novak, Michael. *Unmeltable Ethnics: Politics and Culture in American Life.* New Brunswick, NJ: Transaction, 1995.

"NOW President to Discuss Motherhood Issues on Good Morning America." NOW.org. March 8, 2006. http://www.now.org/issues/media/mommywarsupdate.html.

Nurullah, Abu Sadat. "Portrayal of Muslims in the Media: *24* and the 'Othering' Process." *International Journal of Human Sciences* 7, no. 1 (2010): 1020–46.

Nussbaum, Martha. *Liberty of Conscience: In Defense of America's Tradition of Religious Equality*. New York: Basic, 2008.

O'Connell, Danielle. "Federal and State DOMA Language." Report to the Judiciary Committee. Report 2002-R-0957. Office of Legislative Research, Connecticut General Assembly. December 6, 2002. http://www.cga.ct.gov/2002/olrdata/jud/rpt/2002-R-0957.htm.

O'Connor, John. "The Misadventures of the Simpsons." *New York Times*, September 24, 1992, 18.

O'Donnell, Patrick, and Robert Con Davis, eds. *Intertextuality and Contemporary American Fiction*. Baltimore: Johns Hopkins University Press, 1989.

Oliver, Charles. "Box of Babel? Television and American Culture." *Current* 356 (1993): 10–14.

Ortved, John. *"The Simpsons": An Uncensored, Unauthorized History*. New York: Faber, 2009.

Orvell, Miles. "Documentary Film and the Power of Interrogation: *American Dream* & *Roger and Me*." *Film Quarterly* 48, no. 2 (1995): 10–18.

Ostrow, Joanne. "HBO Leads the Pack in Bringing Satire Back." *Denver Post*, June 8, 1997, H01.

Ott, Brian. "'I'm Bart Simpson, Who the Hell Are You?' A Study in Postmodern Identity (Re)Construction." *Journal of Popular Culture* 37, no. 1 (2003): 56–82.

Ouelette, Laurie. "Victims No More: Postfeminism, Television, and Ally McBeal." *Communication Review* 5, no. 4 (2002): 315–36.

Owen, David. "Taking Humor Seriously." *New Yorker*, March 13, 2000, 64–75.

Ozersky, Josh. *Archie Bunker's America: TV in an Era of Change, 1968–1978*. Carbondale: Southern Illinois University Press, 2003.

Page, Benjamin I., and Lawrence R. Jacobs. *Class War? What Americans Really Think about Economic Inequality*. Chicago: University of Chicago Press, 2009.

Parisi, Peter. "'Black Bart' Simpson: Appropriation and Revitalization in Commodity Culture." *Journal of Popular Culture* 27, no. 1 (1993): 125–35.

Paul, Alan. "Life in Hell." Interview with Matt Groening. *Flux Magazine*, September 30, 1995. Reprinted in *The Simpsons Archive*, November 7, 1999. http://www.snpp.com/other/interviews/groening95.html.

Pelikan, Jaroslav. "Faith." In *Encyclopedia of Religion*, 2nd ed., vol. 5, edited by Lindsay Jones, 2954–59. Detroit: Macmillan, 2005.

Penkava, Melinda. "Effects of *The Simpsons* on Television and Culture as the Show Marks Its 300th Episode." *Talk of the Nation*. National Public Radio, February 13, 2003. http://www.npr.org/templates/story/story.php?storyId=1160554.

Perea, Juan F., ed. *Immigrants Out! The New Nativism and the Anti-Immigrant Impulse in the United States*. New York: New York University Press, 1997.

Peskowitz, Miriam. *The Truth Behind the "Mommy Wars": Who Decides What Makes a Good Mother?* New York: Seal Press, 2005.

Peterson, Brian, and Bruce Gomes. "Swipes at Fox on *The Simpsons*." *The Simpsons Archive*, September 18, 2002. http://www.snpp.com/guides/foxswipe.html.

Phillips, Kevin. *American Theocracy: The Peril and Politics of Radical Religion, Oil, and Borrowed Money in the 21st Century*. New York: Viking, 2006.

Pinsky, Mark I. *The Gospel According to "The Simpsons": The Spiritual Life of the World's Most Animated Family*. Louisville, KY: Westminster John Knox Press, 2001.

———. "Saint Flanders." *Christianity Today*, February 5, 2001: 28–35.

———. "*The Simpsons*: It's Funny 'Cause It's True." *Tikkun* 22, no. 4 (July 2007): 72–75. *Humanities International Index*. EBSCO, March 10, 2008. http://search.ebscohost. com.

Pollitt, Katha. *Subject to Debate: Sense and Dissents on Women, Politics, and Culture.* New York: Modern Library, 2001.

———. "Summers of Our Discontent." *Nation*, February 21, 2005, 10.

Poniewozik. James. "What's Entertainment Now?" *Time*, October 1, 2001, 108–13.

Poplak, Richard. "Homer's Odyssey: Why *The Simpsons* Flopped in the Middle East." Canadian Broadcasting Corporation, July 25, 2007. http://www.cbc.ca/ arts/tv/dubai.html (site discontinued); reprinted, http://www.nowpublic.com/ why_simpsons_flopped_middle_east.

Postman, Neil. *Amusing Ourselves to Death.* New York: Viking, 1986.

Proffitt, Jennifer M. "Challenges to Democratic Discourse: Media Concentration and the Marginalization of Dissent." *Review of Education, Pedagogy, and Cultural Studies* 29 (2007): 65–84.

Prothero, Stephen. *American Jesus: How the Son of God Became a National Icon.* New York: Farrar, Straus and Giroux, 2003.

Pruitt, Lisa R. "The Geography of the Class Culture War." *Seattle University Law Review* 34 (2011): 767–814.

Putnam, Robert. *Bowling Alone: The Collapse and Revival of American Community.* New York: Simon & Schuster, 2001.

Rabinovitz, Lauren. "Ms.-Representation: The Politics of Feminist Sitcoms." In *Television, History, and American Culture*, edited by Mary Beth Haralovich and Lauren Rabinovitz, 144–67. Durham, NC: Duke University Press, 1999.

Rachels, James. *The Elements of Moral Philosophy.* 4th ed. New York: McGraw-Hill, 2002.

Rafter, Nicole Hahn. *White Trash: The Eugenic Family Studies 1877–1919.* Boston: Northeastern University Press, 1988.

Rebeck, Victoria A. "Recognizing Ourselves in *The Simpsons*." *Christian Century*, June 27, 1990, 622.

Reed, Jennifer. "Ellen DeGeneres: Public Lesbian Number One." *Feminist Media Studies* 5, no. 1 (2005): 23–36.

Reel Bad Arabs: How Hollywood Vilifies a People. DVD. Directed by Sut Jhally. Northampton, MA: Media Education Foundation, 2006.

Reimers, David M. *Unwelcome Strangers: American Identity and the Turn Against Immigration.* New York: Columbia University Press, 1998.

Rhodes, Joe. "Flash! 24 Simpsons Stars Reveal Themselves." *TV Guide*, October 21, 2000, 17–34. Reprinted in *The Simpsons Archive*, December 6, 2000. http://www.snpp.com/ other/articles/flash.html.

———. "The Making of *The Simpsons*: Behind the Scenes at America's Funniest Homer Video." *Entertainment Weekly*, May 18, 1990, 5+.

Rich, B. Ruby. "New Queer Cinema." *Sight & Sound*, September 1992, 30–34.

Rich, John D., and Robert W. Weisberg. "Creating *All in the Family*: A Case Study in Creative Thinking." *Creativity Research Journal* 16, nos. 2/3 (2004): 247–59.

Richardson, Kelly L. "'Simpsons Did It!': South Park and the Intertextuality of Contemporary Animation." *Studies in American Humor* 3, no. 17 (2008): 19–34.

Ringer, Jeffrey, ed. *Queer Words, Queer Images: Communication and the Construction of Homosexuality.* New York: NYU Press, 1994.

Riordan, Ellen. "Commodified Agents and Empowered Girls: Producing and Consuming Feminism." *Journal of Communication Inquiry* 25, no. 3 (2001): 279–97.

Rodriguez, Nelson M. "Emptying the Content of Whiteness: Toward an Understanding of the Relation Between Whiteness and Pedagogy." In Kincheloe et al., *White Reign*, 31–62.

Rodriguez, Richard. *Brown: The Last Discovery of America*. New York: Penguin, 2003.

Roediger, David R. *The Wages of Whiteness: Race and the Making of the American Working Class*. New York: Verso, 1991.

———. *Working Toward Whiteness: How America's Immigrants Became White*. New York: Basic, 2006.

Rogin, Michael. "Blackface, White Noise: The Jewish Jazz Singer Finds His Voice." *Critical Inquiry* 18 (1992): 417–53.

———. *Blackface, White Noise: Jewish Immigrants in the Hollywood Melting Pot*. Berkeley: University of California Press, 1996.

Rohan, Virginia. "Defining the Face of Evil." (Bergen County, NJ) *Record*, January 23, 2005, E01.

Romanowski, William. *Pop Culture Wars: Religion & the Role of Entertainment in American Life*. Downers Grove, IL: InterVarsity Press, 1996.

Romine, Damon. "Families Matter: GLAAD Examines the 2003–04 Primetime Network Lineup." GLAAD: The Gay & Lesbian Alliance Against Defamation, September 15, 2003. http://archive.glaad.org/media/release_detail.php?id=3489.

Rose, Margaret. *Parody: Ancient, Modern, and Post-Modern*. Cambridge: Cambridge University Press, 1993.

Rosen, Ruth. *The World Split Open: How the Modern Women's Movement Changed America*. Rev. ed. 2000. Reprint, New York: Penguin, 2007.

Rosenbaum, Martin. "Is *The Simpsons* Still Subversive?" *BBC News*, June 29, 2007. http://news.bbc.co.uk/1/hi/uk_politics/6252856.stm.

Rosenberg, Howard. "Fox Favoritism? Catholic Jokes Toned Down on *Simpsons*." *Chicago Sun-Times*, June 7, 1999, 41.

Rosenblatt, Richard. "The Age of Irony Comes to an End." *Time*, September 24, 2001, 79.

Ross, Michael L., and Lorraine York. "'First, They're Foreigners': *The Daily Show with Jon Stewart* and the Limits of Dissident Laughter." *Canadian Review of American Studies* 37, no. 3 (2007): 351–70.

Rossman, Gabriel. "Elites, Masses, and Media Blacklists: The Dixie Chicks Controversy." *Social Forces* 83, no. 1 (2004): 61–79.

Rothman, Stanley. "Is Dan Quayle Right?" *National Review*, October 5, 1991, 34–35.

Rowe, John Carlos. "Metavideo: Fictionality and Mass Culture in a Postmodern Economy." In O'Donnell and Davis, *Intertextuality and Contemporary American Fiction*, 214–35.

Rowe, Kathleen. "Roseanne: Unruly Woman as Domestic Goddess." *Screen* 31, no. 4 (Winter 1990): 408–19. Reprinted in *Critiquing the Sitcom: A Reader*, edited by Joanne Morreale, 251–61. Syracuse: Syracuse University Press, 2003.

Rowe-Finkbeiner, Kristin. *The F-Word: Feminism in Jeopardy—Women, Politics and the Future*. New York: Seal Press, 2004.

Rushkoff, Douglas. *Media Virus*. 1994. Reprint, New York: Ballantine, 1996.

Russo, Vito. *The Celluloid Closet: Homosexuality in the Movies*. Rev. ed. 1981. Reprint, New York: Harper & Row, 1987.

Rutten, Tim. "If You Can't Take a Joke . . ." *Los Angeles Times*, July 16, 2008, A19.

Sadownick, Doug. "Groening Against the Grain." Interview. *Advocate*, February 26, 1991, 31–35.

Said, Edward. *Orientalism*. 1978. Reprint, New York: Vintage, 2003.

Salholz, E., and T. Clifton. "The Future of Gay America." *Newsweek*, March 12, 1990, 20–25.

Salins, Peter D. *Assimilation American Style*. New York: Basic, 1997.

Saulny, Susan. "Black? White? Asian? More Young American Choose All of the Above." *New York Times*, January 29, 2011. http://www.nytimes.com/2011/01/30/us/30mixed.html?ref=us.

Savage, William. "'So Television's Responsible!': Oppositionality and the Interpretive Logic of Satire and Censorship in *The Simpsons* and *South Park*." In Alberti, *Leaving Springfield*, 197–224.

Scanlan, Stephen. "The Cartoon Society: Using *The Simpsons* to Teach and Learn Sociology." *Teaching Sociology* 28, no. 2 (2000): 127–39.

Schaller, Michael. *Right Turn: American Life in the Reagan-Bush Era, 1980–1992*. New York: Oxford University Press, 2006.

Schlesinger, Arthur M. *The Disuniting of America: Reflections of a Multicultural Society*. New York: Norton, 1992.

Schmid, Carol L. *The Politics of Language: Conflict, Identity and Cultural Pluralism in Comparative Perspective*. New York: Oxford University Press, 2001.

Schmidt, Leigh Eric. *Restless Souls: The Making of American Spirituality*. New York: Harper, 2005.

———. "Spirit Wars: American Religion in Progressive Politics." Faith Angle Conference. December 6, 2005. Transcript. Pew Forum on Religion and Public Life. http://www.pewforum.org/Politics-and-Elections/Spirit-Wars-American-Religion-in-Progressive-Politics.aspx.

Schrag, Peter. *The Decline of the Wasp*. New York: Simon and Schuster, 1970.

Schriver, Kristina. "Rhetorical Pathologies and Gender Difference: An Ideological Examination of Cultural Discourse in *Faulkner v. The Citadel*." *Women's Studies in Communication* 26, no. 1 (2003): 27–59.

Schulman, Sarah. "Gay Marketeers." *Progressive*, July 1995, 28–29.

Schultze, Quentin J. *Christianity and the Mass Media in America: Toward a Democratic Accommodation*. Lansing: Michigan State University Press, 2006.

Scott, A. O. "Homer's Odyssey." *New York Times Magazine*, November 4, 2001, 42–48.

Scott, Eugenia. *Evolution vs. Creationism: An Introduction*. Berkeley: University of California Press, 2005.

Seeto, Margot. "Caught Between Cultures: Identity, Choice, and the Hyphenated American." In *Asian American X: An Intersection of Twenty-First-Century Asian American Voices*, edited by Arar Han and John Hsu, 231–38. Ann Arbor: University of Michigan Press, 2004.

Seltzer, Robert M., and Norman J. Cohen, eds. *The Americanization of the Jews*. New York: New York University Press, 1995.

Senzani, Alessandra. "Class and Gender as a Laughing Matter? The Case of *Roseanne*." *Humor* 23, no. 2 (2010): 229–53.

Shaheen, Jack. *Guilty: Hollywood's Verdict on Arabs after 9/11*. Northampton, MA: Olive Branch Press, 2008.

———. *Reel Bad Arabs: How Hollywood Vilifies a People*. Rev. ed. 2001. Reprint, Northampton, MA: Olive Branch Press, 2009.

Shales, Tom. "America's Most Animated Family." *Washington Post*, September 24, 1992, C1.

———. "The Groening of America." *Washington Post*, May 13, 1993, C1.

———. "They're Scrapping Again—But This Time It's a Ratings Fight." *Washington Post*, October 11, 1990, C1.

Shane, Scott. "In Islamic Law, Gingrich Sees a Mortal Threat to U.S." *New York Times*, December 22, 2011, A22.

Sharlet, Jeff. "Beyond Belief." Review of *Liberty of Conscience: In Defense of America's Tradition of Religious Equality*, by Martha Nussbaum, and *Founding Faith Providence, Politics, and the Birth of Religious Freedom in America*, by Steven Waldman. *Nation*, June 9, 2008. http://www.thenation.com/doc/20080609/sharlet.

Shawcross, William. *Murdoch*. New York: Simon & Schuster, 1997.

Sheehan, Steven T. "'Pow! Right in the Kisser': Ralph Kramden, Jackie Gleason, and the Emergence of the Frustrated Working-Class Man." *Journal of Popular Culture* 43, no. 3 (2010): 564–82.

Sherman, Jennifer. *Those Who Work, Those Who Don't: Poverty, Morality, and Family in Rural America*. Minneapolis: University of Minnesota Press, 2009.

Shipler, David K. *The Working Poor: Invisible in America*. New York: Knopf, 2004.

Shorto, Russell. "Homer's Odyssey." *US Weekly*, May 22, 2000, 52–57. Reprinted in *The Simpsons Archive*. http://www.snpp.com/other/articles/homersodyssey2.html.

Shuck, Glenn W. *Marks of the Beast: The Left Behind Novels and the Struggle for Evangelical Identity*. New York: New York University Press, 2005.

Shut Up & Sing. DVD. Directed by Barbara Kopple and Cecilia Peck. New York: Weinstein Company, 2006.

Siegel, Lee. "We're Not Laughing at You, or With You." *New York Times*, July 20, 2008, late ed., WK5.

Signorile, Michelangelo. *Queer in America: Sex, the Media, and the Closets of Power*. New York: Random House, 1993.

Simpson, Bruce. "Rescuing Christ from the 'Christians.'" *Advocate*, December 23, 2003, 44–45.

Simpson, Paul. *On the Discourse of Satire: Towards a Stylistic Model of Satirical Humour*. Philadelphia: John Benjamins, 2003.

The Simpsons. Created by Matt Groening. FOX Television Network, 1989–present.

———. "Apocalypse Cow." #KABF10. April 27, 2008.

———. "Bart the General."#7G05. Aired February 4, 1990.

———. "Bart the Genius." 7G02. Aired January 14, 1990.

———. "Bart Gets an Elephant." #1F15. Aired March 31, 1994.

———. "Bart Gets Famous." #1F11. Aired February 3, 1994.

———. "Bart Has Two Mommies." #HABF07. Aired March 26, 2006.

———. "Bart Mangled Banner." #FABF17. Aired May 16, 2004.

———. "Bart Sells His Soul." #3F02. Aired October 8, 1995.

———. "Bart's Dog Gets an F." #7F14 Aired March 7, 1991.

———. "Bart's Girlfriend." #2F04. Aired November 6, 1994.

———. "Bart vs. Australia." #2F13. Aired February 19, 1995.

———. "Blood Feud." #7F22. Aired July 11, 1991.

———. "Brush with Greatness." #7F18. Aired April 11, 1991.

———. "Burns Verkaufen der Kraftwerk." #8F09. Aired December 5, 1991.

———. "Call of the Simpsons." #7G09. Aired February 18, 1990.

———. "Children of a Lesser Clod." #CABF16. Aired May 13, 2001.

———. "Colonel Homer." #8F19. Aired March 26, 1992.

———. "The Color Yellow." #MABF06. Aired February 21, 2010.

———. "The Crepes of Wrath." #7G13. Aired April 15, 1990.

———. "The Devil Wears Nada." #LABF17. November 15, 2009.

———. "Diatribe of a Mad Housewife." #FABF05. Aired January 25, 2004.

———. "Dog of Death." #8F17. Aired March 12, 1992.

———. "Donnie Fatso." #MABF19. Aired December 12, 2010.

———. "E Pluribus Wiggum." #KABF03. Aired January 6, 2008.

———. "The Father, the Son, and the Holy Guest Star." #GABF05. Aired May 15, 2005.

———. "500 Keys." #NABF14. Aired May 15, 2011.

———. "Flaming Moe." #NABF04. Aired January 16, 2011.

———. "The Fool Monty." #NABF01. Aired November 21, 2010.

———. "The Front." #9F16. Aired April 15, 1993.

———. "Girls Just Want to Have Sums." #HABF12. Aired April 30, 2006.

———. "The Great Wife Hope." #LABF16. Aired October 11, 2009.

———. "The Haw-Hawed Couple." #JABF02. Aired December 10, 2006.

———. "Holidays of Future Passed." #NABF18. Aired December 11, 2011.

———. "Home Sweet Home-Diddily-Dum-Doodily." #3F01. Aired October 1, 1995.

———. "Homer Alone." #8F14. Aired February 6, 1992.

———. "Homer's Barbershop Quartet." #9F21. Aired September 30, 1993.

———. "Homer's Night Out." #7G10. Aired March 25, 1990.

———. "Homer's Odyssey." #7G03. Aired January 21, 1990.

———. "Homer's Phobia." #4F11. Aired February 16, 1997.

———. "Homer the Heretic." #9F01. Aired October 8, 1992.

———. "Homer vs. Lisa and the 8th Commandment." #7F13. Aired February 7, 1991.

———. "Homer vs. Patty and Selma." #2F14. Aired February 26, 1995.

———. "HOMR." #BABF22. Aired January 7, 2001.

———. "Hurricane Neddy." #4F07. Aired December 29, 1996.

———. "I'm Goin' to Praiseland." #CABF15. Aired May 6, 2001.

———. "Judge Me Tender." #MABF15. Aired May 23, 2010.

———. "Last Exit to Springfield." #9F15. Aired March 11, 1993.

———. "Life on the Fast Lane." #7G11. Aired March 18, 1990.

———. "Like Father, Like Clown." #8F05. Aired October 24, 1991.

———. "Lisa on Ice." #2F05. Aired November 13, 1994.

———. "Lisa the Beauty Queen." #9F02. Aired October 15, 1992.

———. "Lisa the Skeptic." #5F05. Aired November 23, 1997.

———. "Lisa the Simpson." #4F24. Aired March 8, 1998.

———. "Lisa vs. Malibu Stacy." #1F12. Aired February 17, 1994.

———. "Lisa's Pony." #8F06. Aired November 7, 1991.

———. "Little Big Mom." #BABF04. Aired January 9, 2000.

———. "And Maggie Makes Three." #2F10. Aired January 22, 1995.

———. "Marge Be Not Proud." #3F07. Aired December 17, 1995.

———. "Marge Gets a Job" #9F05. Aired November 5, 1992.

———. "Marge vs. Singles, Seniors, Childless Couples and Teens, and Gays." #FABF03. Aired January 4, 2004.

———. "Moaning Lisa." #7G06. Aired February 11, 1990.

———. "The Monkey Suit." #HABF14. May 14, 2006.

———. "Mr. Lisa Goes to Washington." #8F01. Aired September 26, 1991.

———. "Mr. Spritz Goes to Washington." #EABF09. Aired March 9, 2003.

———. "Much Apu about Nothing." #3F20. Aired May 5, 1996.

———. "Mypods and Boomsticks." #KABF20. Aired November 30, 2008.

———. "New Kid on the Block." #9F06. Aired November 12, 1992.

———. "One Fish, Two Fish, Blowfish, Blue Fish." #7F11. Aired January 24, 1991.

———. "Rosebud." #1F01. Aired October 21, 1993.

———. "The President Wore Pearls." #EABF20. Aired November 16, 2003.

———. "Principle Charming." #7F16. Aired February 14, 1991.

——. "Radioactive Man." #2F17. Aired September 17, 1995.

——. "The Regina Monologues." #EABF22. Aired November 23, 2003.

——. "Scenes from the Class Struggle in Springfield." #3F11. Aired February 4, 1996.

——. "The Secret War of Lisa Simpson." #4F21. Aired May 18, 1997.

——. "Secrets of a Successful Marriage." #1F20. Aired May 19, 1994.

——. "Selma's Choice." #9F11. Aired January 21, 1993.

——. "She of Little Faith." #DABF02. Aired December 16, 2001.

——. "She Used to Be My Girl." #FABF22. Aired December 5, 2004.

——. "Sideshow Bob Roberts." #2F02. Aired October 9, 1994.

——. "Simpsons Bible Stories." #AABF14. Aired April 4, 1999.

——. "Simpson and Delilah." #7F02. Aired October 18, 1990.

——. "Simpsons Roasting on an Open Fire." #7G08. Aired December 17, 1989.

——. "Sleeping with the Enemy."# FABF19. Aired November 21, 2004.

——. "Smart and Smarter." #FABF09. Aired February 22, 2004.

——. "The Springfield Connection." #2F21. Aired May 7, 1995.

——. "The Springfield Files." #3G01. Aired January 12, 1997.

——. "A Star is Burns." #2F31. Aired March 5, 1995.

——. "The Strong Arms of the Ma." #EABF04. Aired February 2, 2003.

——. "Sunday, Cruddy Sunday." #AABF08. Aired January 31, 1999.

——. "A Tale of Two Springfields." #BABF20. Aired November 5, 2000.

——. "Team Homer." #3F10. Aired January 6, 1996.

——. "Thank God, It's Doomsday." #GABF14. Aired May 8, 2005.

——. "There's No Disgrace Like Home." #7G04. Aired January 28, 1990.

——. "There's Something about Marrying." #EABF12. Aired February 20, 2005.

——. "Three Gays of the Condo." #GABF04. Aired April 13, 2003.

——. "The Trouble with Trillions." #5F14. Aired April 5, 1998.

——. "Twenty Two Short Films About Springfield." #3F18. Aired April 14, 1996.

——. "Two Dozen and One Greyhounds." #2F18. Aired April 9, 1995.

——. "The Twisted World of Marge Simpson." #4F08. Aired January 19, 1997.

——. "Two Cars in Every Garage, Three Eyes on Every Fish." #7F01. Aired November 1, 1990.

——. "The Two Mrs. Nahasapeemapetilons." #5F04. Aired November 16, 1997.

——. "Yokel Chords." #JABF09. Aired March 4, 2007.

——. *The Simpsons Archive*. Edited by Gary Goldberg et al. October 15, 1998. http://www.snpp.com/.

"Simpsons Just a Cartoon to TV Academy." *USA Today*, February 21, 1992, 1D.

"The Simpsons Movie." *Box Office Mojo*. Box Office Mojo, LLC. March 10, 2008. http://www.boxofficemojo.com/movies/?id=simpsons.htm.

Singer, Marc. "'Black Skins' and White Masks: Comic Books and the Secret of Race." *African American Review* 36, no. 1 (2002): 107–19.

Singh, Robert. "Subverting American Values? *The Simpsons, South Park* and the Cartoon Culture War." In *American Politics and Society Today*, edited by Robert Singh, 206–29. Malden, MA: Blackwell, 2002.

Skill, Thomas, et al. "The Portrayal of Religion and Spirituality on Fictional Network Television." *Review of Religious Research* 35 (March 1994): 251–67.

Sklar, Rachel. "David Remnick on That *New Yorker* Cover." *Huffington Post Online*, July 13, 2008. http://www.huffingtonpost.com/2008/07/13/david-remnick-on-emnew-yo_n_112456.html.

Sloane, Robert. "Who Wants Candy? Disenchantment in *The Simpsons*." In Alberti, *Leaving Springfield*, 208–49.

Slotten, Hugh. *Radio and Television Regulation: Broadcast Technology in the United States, 1920–1960.* Baltimore: Johns Hopkins University Press, 2000.

Smith, Anna Marie. "The Politicization of Marriage in Contemporary American Public Policy: The Defense of Marriage Act and the Personal Responsibility Act." *Citizenship Studies* 5, no. 3 (2001): 303–20.

Smith, Christian. *American Evangelicalism: Embattled and Thriving.* Chicago: University of Chicago Press, 1998.

Snow, Dale E., and James J. Snow. "Simpsonian Sexual Politics." In Irwin et al., *"The Simpsons" and Philosophy,* 126–44.

Sollors, Werner. *Beyond Ethnicity: Consent and Descent in American Culture.* New York: Oxford University Press, 1986.

———, ed. *The Invention of Ethnicity.* New York: Oxford University Press, 1989.

Sontag, Susan. *Against Interpretation and Other Essays.* 1966. Reprint, New York: Picador, 2001.

Southgate, Martha. "A Funny Thing Happened on the Way to Prime Time." *New York Times Magazine,* October 30, 1994, 52–56.

Spangler, Lynn C. *Television Women from Lucy to Friends: Fifty Years of Sitcoms and Feminism.* Westport, CT: Praeger, 2003.

Spigel, Lynn. *Make Room for TV: Television and the Family Ideal in Postwar America.* Chicago: University of Chicago Press, 1992.

———, ed. *Television After TV: Essay on a Medium in Transition.* Durham, NC: Duke University Press, 2004.

Spigel, Lynn, and Denise Mann, eds., *Private Screenings: Television and the Female Consumer.* Minneapolis: University of Minnesota Press, 1992.

Spigel, Lynn, and Michael Curtin, eds. *The Revolution Wasn't Televised: Sixties Television and Social Conflict.* New York: Routledge, 1997.

Staiger, Janet. *Blockbuster TV: Must-See Sitcoms in the Network Era.* New York: New York University Press, 2000.

Stabile, Carol A., and Mark Harrison, eds. *Prime Time Animation: Television Animation and American Culture.* New York: Routledge, 2003.

Stanczak, Gregory C. *Engaged Spirituality: Social Change and American Religion.* New Brunswick, NJ: Rutgers University Press, 2006.

Stanley, Terry, and Tobi Elkin. "Intel Hires Homer to Push Pentium." *Adweek Western Edition,* November 2, 1998, 4.

Steele, Bruce. "The Gay Rights Makeover." *Advocate,* September 2, 2003, 42–43.

Steele, Shelby. "Obama's Post-Racial Promise." *Los Angeles Times,* November 5, 2008. http://www.latimes.com/news/opinion/opinionla/la-oe-steele5-2008nov05,0,6049031.story.

———. *White Guilt: How Blacks and Whites Together Destroyed the Promise of the Civil Rights Era.* New York: Harper, 2006.

Stein, Harry. "Our Times." *TV Guide,* May 23–29, 1992, 31.

Steiner, Leslie Morgan, ed. *Mommy Wars: Stay-at-Home and Career Moms Face Off on Their Choices, Their Lives, Their Families.* New York: Random House, 2007.

Stepanas, Paulilus. "*The Simpsons* Broadcast History and Ratings Information." *Simpsons Gazette,* February 7, 2002. http://simpsonsgazette.tripod.com/simprate.htm.

Sterling, Christopher H., and John Michael Kittross. *Stay Tuned: A History of American Broadcasting.* 3rd ed. London: Lawrence Erlbaum Associates, 2002.

Sterngold, James. "As Writers and Producers, Young Alumni Find They Can Make a Lot of Money Fast." *New York Times,* August 26, 1997, C11.

Stillion-Southard, Belinda. "Beyond the Backlash: *Sex and the City* and Three Feminist Struggles." *Communication Quarterly* 56, no. 2 (2008): 149–67.

Stricherz, Mark. "Who Killed Archie Bunker? Working-class Television and the Democratic Party." *Doublethink*. America's Future Foundation, October 25, 2005. http://americasfuture.org/doublethink/author/mark-stricherz/.

Stuller-Giglione, Joan. "Married with Children." *Encyclopedia of Television*, Museum of Broadcast Communications. http://www.museum.tv/eotvsection.php?entrycode = marriedw.

Sugrue, Thomas J. *Not Even Past: Barack Obama and the Burden of Race*. Princeton, NJ: Princeton University Press, 2010.

Sullivan, Amy. "Sharia Myth Sweeps America." *USA Today*, June 13, 2011, 11A.

Sullivan, Andrew. "Beware the Straight Backlash." *Time*, August 11, 2003, 35.

Sundstrom, Ronald R. *The Browning of America and the Evasion of Social Justice*. New York: SUNY Press, 2008.

Svetkey, Benjamin. "Is Your TV Set Gay?" *Entertainment Weekly*, October 6, 2000, 24–28.

Swinburne, Richard. "Soul." In *Routledge Encyclopedia of Philosophy*, vol. 9, edited by Edward Craig, 44–48. New York: Routledge, 1998.

Tasker, Yvonne, and Diane Negra, eds. *Interrogating Postfeminism: Gender and the Politics of Popular Culture*. Durham, NC: Duke University Press, 2007.

Tatalovich, Raymond. *Nativism Reborn? The Official English Language Movement and the American States*. Lexington: University Press of Kentucky, 1995.

Tatarnic, Martha Smith. "The Mass Media and Faith: The Potentialities and Problems for the Church in Our Television Culture." *Anglican Theological Review* 87, no. 3 (2005): 447–65.

Taylor, Ella. *Prime-Time Families: Television Culture in Postwar America*. Berkeley: University of California Press, 1989.

Taylor, Paul, et al. "Inside the Middle Class: Bad Times Hit the Good Life." Pew Social & Demographic Trends, *Pew Research Center*, April 9, 2008, 8. http://www.pewsocialtrends.org/2008/04/09/inside-the-middle-class-bad-times-hit-the-good-life/.

Test, George. *Satire: Spirit and Art*. Tampa: University of South Florida Press, 1991.

Thomas, Laurie, and Barry R. Litman. "Fox Broadcasting Company, Why Now? An Economic Study of the Rise of the Fourth Broadcast 'Network.'" *Journal of Broadcasting & Electronic Media* 35, no. 2 (1991): 139–48.

Thompson, Ethan. "'I Am Not Down with That': *King of the Hill* and Sitcom Satire." *Journal of Film and Video* 61, no. 2 (2009): 38–51.

Thompson, Irene Taviss. *Culture Wars and Enduring American Dilemmas*. Ann Arbor: University of Michigan Press, 2010.

Thompson, Kenneth. "Border Crossings and Diasporic Identities: Media Use and Leisure Practices of an Ethnic Minority." *Qualitative Sociology* 25, no. 3 (2002): 409–17.

Thompson, Robert J. *Television's Second Golden Age: From Hill Street Blues to ER*. New York: Continuum, 1996.

Teixeira, Ruy, and Joel Townsley Rogers. *America's Forgotten Majority: Why the White Working Class Still Matters*. New York: Basic, 2000.

Tingleff, Sam. "*The Simpsons* as Critique of Consumer Culture." *The Simpsons Archive*, 1998. http://www.snpp.com/other/papers/st.paper.html.

Tokarczyk, Michelle. "Promises to Keep: Working Class Students and Higher Education." In *What's Class Got to Do with It? American Society in the Twenty-First Century*, edited by Michael Zweig, 161–67. Ithaca, NY: Cornell University Press, 2004.

Towner, Emil B. "A <Patriotic> Apologia: The Transcendence of the Dixie Chicks." *Rhetoric Review* 29, no. 3 (2010): 293–309.

Trebay, Guy. "A Kiss Too Far?" *New York Times*, February 18, 2007, late ed., sec. 9, 1.

Tropp, Laura. "'Faking a Sonogram': Representations of Motherhood on *Sex and the City*." *Journal of Popular Culture* 39, no. 5 (2006): 861–77.

Tucker, Ken. "'Toon Terrific." *Entertainment Weekly*, March 12, 1993, 48–50.

———. "Yea, Mamas." *Entertainment Weekly*, May 13, 1994, 68–69.

Tucker, Lauren R. "Was the Revolution Televised? Professional Criticism about *The Cosby Show* and the Essentialization of Black Cultural Expression." *Journal of Broadcasting & Electronic Media* 41, no. 1 (1997): 90–109.

Tueth, Michael V. "Back to the Drawing Board: The Family in Animated Television Comedy." In Stabile and Harrison, *Prime Time Animation*, 133–46.

Tulloch, John. *Watching Television Audiences: Cultural Theories and Methods*. London: Hodder Arnold, 2000.

Turner, Chris. *Planet Simpson: How a Cartoon Masterpiece Defined a Generation*. Cambridge, MA: Da Capo, 2004.

Turner, William B. *A Genealogy of Queer Theory*. Philadelphia: Temple University Press, 2000.

Unger, Arthur. "Fox Seeking Fourth-Network Recognition." *Christian Science Monitor*, July 9, 1987, 23+.

US House Hearing Before the Subcommittee on Immigration and Claims of the Committee on the Judiciary. *Final Report of the Commission on Immigration Reform*. 105th Congress, 1st sess., November 7, 1997. Washington, DC: GPO, 1997. http://commdocs.house.gov/committees/judiciary/hju57062.000/hju57062_0.HTM.

Vidmar, Neil, and Milton Rokeach. "Archie Bunker's Bigotry: A Study in Selective Perception and Exposure." *Journal of Communication* (Winter 1974): 36–47.

Vilanch, Bruce. "Pretty In Prime Time." *Advocate*, September 16, 2003, 36.

Viner, Brian. "D'oh! I Made Murdoch a Billion Dollars." *Independent*, September 2, 2000, 8+.

Vint, Sherryl. "The New Backlash: Popular Culture's 'Marriage' with Feminism, or Love Is All You Need." *Journal of Popular Film and Television* 34, no. 4 (2007): 160–68.

Voorhees, John. "Tonight's *Simpsons* Is Guaranteed to Make You Laugh." *Seattle Times*, October 1, 1992, G8.

Waldman, Steven. *Founding Faith: Providence, Politics, and the Birth of Religious Freedom in America*. New York: Random House, 2008.

Wallace, James M. "A (Karl, Not Groucho) Marxist in Springfield." In Irwin et al., *"The Simpsons" and Philosophy*, 235–51.

Walsh, Carl. "What Caused the 1990–1991 Recession?" *Economic Review of the Federal Reserve Bank of San Francisco* 2 (1993): 34–48.

Walters, Suzanna Danuta. *All the Rage: The Story of Gay Visibility in America*. Chicago: University of Chicago Press, 2001.

Waltonen, Karma. "We're All Pigs: Representations of Masculinity in *The Simpsons*." Paper presented at the Northeast Modern Language Association Conference in Buffalo, NY, April 2000. *The Simpsons Archive*, September 16, 2001. http://www.snpp.com/other/papers/kw.paper.html.

Waltonen, Karma, and Denise Du Vernay. *"The Simpsons" in the Classroom: Embiggening the Learning Experience with the Wisdom of Springfield*. Jefferson, NC: McFarland, 2010.

Warner, Judith. *Perfect Madness: Motherhood in the Age of Anxiety*. New York: Penguin, 2005.

Warner, Michael, ed. *Fear of a Queer Planet: Queer Politics and Social Theory*. Minneapolis: University of Minnesota Press, 1993.

Waters, Harry F. "Family Feuds." *Newsweek*, April 23, 1990, 58–62.

Watson, Mary Ann. "From *My Little Margie* to *Murphy Brown*: Women's Lives on the Small Screen." *Television Quarterly* 27, no. 2 (1994): 3–24.

Waxman, Sharon. "*Simpsons* Animates Gay Nuptials, and a Debate." *New York Times*, February 21, 2005, B2.

"We Are Not Amused." Editorial. *Advocate*, March 13, 2007, 4.

Weiner, Rachel. "Obama's Larry King Interview." *Huffington Post Online*, July 15, 2008. http://www.huffingtonpost.com/2008/07/15/obamas-larry-king-intervi_n_112930.html.

Weinman, Jamie J. "Worst Episode Ever." *Salon*, January 24, 2000. http://www.salon.com/2000/01/24/simpsons_2/.

Weisenburger, Steven C. *Fables of Subversion: Satire and the American Novel*. Athens: University of Georgia Press, 1995.

Werner, Fara, and Terry Lefton. "Bart Inks Sweet New Deal." *Brandweek*, March 22, 1993, 4.

Wharton, Annabel Jane. *Selling Jerusalem: Relics, Replicas, Theme Parks*. Chicago: University of Chicago Press, 2006.

"When Life Imitates Bart." *Newsweek*, July 23, 1990, 61.

"Where We Are on TV." GLAAD: The Gay & Lesbian Alliance Against Defamation, August 24, 2006. http://archive.glaad.org/eye/ontv/past.php.

"Where We Are on TV: 1996–1997 Season." GLAAD: The Gay & Lesbian Alliance Against Defamation, March 12, 2008. http://archive.glaad.org/eye/ontv/past/1996_1997.php.

"Where We Are on TV: 1997–1998 Season." GLAAD: The Gay & Lesbian Alliance Against Defamation, March 12, 2008. http://archive.glaad.org/eye/ontv/past/1997_1998.php.

"Where We Are on TV Report, 2007–2008." GLAAD: The Gay & Lesbian Alliance Against Defamation, March 12, 2008. http://archive.glaad.org/eye/ontv/index2007.php.

"Where We Are on TV Report, 2010–2011." GLAAD: The Gay & Lesbian Alliance Against Defamation, September 2008, http://www.glaad.org/publications/whereweareontv11.

Whitman, David, and Dorian Friedman. "The War over 'Family Values.'" *U.S. News & World Report*, June 8, 1992, 35–36.

Wickberg, Daniel. "Homophobia: On the Cultural History of an Idea." *Critical Inquiry* 27 (Autumn 2000): 42–57.

Williams, Fiona. "Reiss to Tell Animated Story of *Simpsons* Success." *Encore Magazine* (Australia), August 1, 2005. Lexis-Nexis Academic. http://web.lexis-nexis.com/universe.

Williams, Joan C. *Reshaping the Work-Family Debate: Why Men and Class Matter*. Cambridge, MA: Harvard University Press, 2010.

Williams, Steve, and Ian Jones. "Cartoons Have Writers?" *Off the Telly*, May 2002. http://www.offthetelly.co.uk/?page_id=371.

Willis, Ellen. "Giving Feminism Life." Review of *Creating a Life: Professional Women and the Quest for Children*, by Sylvia Hewlett. *Dissent* 49, no. 4 (Fall 2002): 95–100.

Wilson, James Q. "How Divided Are We?" *Commentary*, February 2006, 15–21.

Winston, Diane. "Back to the Future: Religion, Politics, and the Media." *American Quarterly* 59, no. 3 (September 2007): 969–89.

Wise, Tim. *Between Barack and a Hard Place: Racism and White Denial in the Age of Obama*. San Francisco: City Lights Books, 2009.

———. *Colorblind: The Rise of Post-Racial Politics and the Retreat from Racial Equity*. San Francisco: City Lights Books, 2010.

Wittebols, James H. *Watching M*A*S*H, Watching America: A Social History of the 1972–1983 Television Series*. Jefferson, NC: McFarland, 1998.

Wolf, Mark. "Rude Dude Bart Crosses Cultural Line." *Rocky Mountain News* (Denver, CO), June 21, 1990, F1.

Wolf, Naomi. *The Beauty Myth: How Images of Beauty Are Used Against Women.* New York: Morrow, 1991.

Wolf, Reva. "Homer Simpson as Outsider Artist, or How I Learned to Accept Ambivalence (Maybe)." *Art Journal* (Fall 2006): 100–111.

Wolfe, Alan. *One Nation, After All: What Middle-Class Americans Really Think about God, Country, Family, Racism, Welfare, Immigration, Homosexuality, the Right, the Left, and Each Other.* New York: Viking, 1998.

Wolterstorff, Nicholas P. "Faith." In *Routledge Encyclopedia of Philosophy*, vol. 3, edited by Edward Craig, 538–44. New York: Routledge, 1998.

Womack, Craig. *Red on Red: Native American Literary Separatism.* Minneapolis: University of Minnesota Press, 1999.

Wray, Matt. *Not Quite White: White Trash and the Boundaries of Whiteness.* Durham, NC: Duke University Press, 2006.

Wray, Matt, and Annalee Newitz, eds. *White Trash: Race and Class in America.* New York: Routledge, 1997.

Wu, Frank H. *Yellow: Race in America Beyond Black and White.* New York: Basic, 2003.

Wuthnow, Robert. *After Heaven: Spirituality in America since the 1950s.* Berkeley: University of California Press, 1998.

Wyley, Annemarie. "*The Simpsons*' Creator Groening Grows Up." *Reuters*, September 3, 1999. Reprinted in *The Simpsons Archive*, September 4, 1999. http://www.snpp.com/other/interviews/groening99b.html.

Wynter, Leon E. "*All-American Girl* Puts Asians on the Dial." *Wall Street Journal*, June 15, 1994, B1.

———. *American Skin: Pop Culture, Big Business & the End of White America.* New York: Crown, 2002.

Yin, Tung. "Through a Screen Darkly: Hollywood as a Measure of Discrimination Against Arabs and Muslims." *Duke Forum for Law & Social Change* 2, no. 1 (2010): 103–23.

Yang, J. E. "Quayle: 'Hollywood Doesn't Get It.'" *Washington Post*, May 21, 1992, A1+.

Yates, Michael D., ed. *More Unequal: Aspects of Class in the United States.* New York: Monthly Review Press, 2007.

Young, Cathy. "Fear of a Muslim America." *Reason* 43, no. 4 (2011): 20–26.

Zehme, Bill. "The Only Real People on TV," *Rolling Stone*, June 28, 1990, 40–43.

Zimmerman, Jonathan. *Whose America? Culture Wars in the Public Schools.* Cambridge, MA: Harvard University Press, 2005.

Zoglin, Richard. "The Fox Trots Faster." *Time*, August 27, 1990, 64–67.

———. "Where Fathers and Mothers Know Best." *Time*, June 1, 1992, 33.

Zook, Kristal Brent. *Color by Fox: The Fox Network and the Revolution in Black Television.* New York: Oxford University Press, 1999.

Zurawik, David. *The Jews of Prime Time.* Hanover, NH: Brandeis University Press, 2003.

Zweig, Michael, ed. *What's Class Got to Do with It? American Society in the Twenty-First Century.* Ithaca, NY: Cornell University Press, 2004.

———. *The Working Class Majority: America's Best Kept Secret.* 2nd ed. 2000. Reprint, Ithaca, NY: Cornell University Press, 2012. Kindle edition.

Index

63639781R00177

Made in the USA
Middletown, DE
27 August 2019